Working with children and young people who ... se ...eld

University of
Chester

D1347597

Russell House Publishing

Published in 2007 by
Russell House Publishing Limited
4 St George's House
Uplyme Road
Lyme Regis
Dorset
DT7 3LS

Tel: 01297 443948
Fax: 01297 442722
e-mail: help@russellhouse.co.uk

British Library Cataloguing-in-Publication Data:

A catalogue record of this book is available from the British Library

ISBN: 978-1-905541-01-0

Typeset by: TW Typesetting, Plymouth, Devon
Front cover artwork by Emma Calder
Printed by: Biddles Ltd, King's Lynn

Russell House Publishing

RHP is a group of social work, probation, education and youth and community
work practitioners and academics working in collaboration with a professional
publishing team.

Our aim is to work closely with the field to produce innovative and valuable
materials to help managers, trainers, practitioners and students.

We are keen to receive feedback on publications and new ideas for
future projects.

For details of our other publications please visit our website or ask us for a
catalogue. Contact details are on this page.

Contents

Dedication

To Janet, Stacey and Emma: three gems who encourage
and support my multi-tasking behaviours and
believe that there is always a light at the end of the tunnel.

Acknowledgements

I would like to thank:

Leigh Library for their endless patience and pursuit of hidden articles and books.

Debbie Hulme for her computer skills and dedication beyond the call of duty.

All the contributors for chapters of a high standard with challenging content.

About the Contributors

The Editor

Martin C. Calder is Director of Calder Training and Consultancy having recently left his Child Protection Operational Manager post with Salford City Council to work with managers and workers to produce evidence-based assessment materials in a range of areas. He is contactable through his website at www.caldertrainingandconsultancy.co.uk

The Contributors

Lesley Ayland is a clinical psychologist and has worked for WellStop, a community-based treatment programme for people with sexually abusive behaviour, for the past 10 years. She is the Clinical Manager of the four WellStop (formerly Wellington STOP) Youth Programmes, which are located in Wellington, Palmerston North, Napier and Gisborne in New Zealand. Lesley has an interest in working with people with intellectual disability, working with families affected by abuse, and the impact on professionals working in this field.

Arnon Bentovim is a Child and Adolescent Psychiatrist who has been involved in the Child Protection field and the development of thinking and practice in all aspects of family violence which impacts on children's development. He founded the Child Sexual Abuse Team at Great Ormond Street Children's Hospital, which was the first of a comprehensive therapeutic approach in the UK, and working with young people who have both been abused and are responding with an abusive orientation is a particular interest that has emerged from that work. He has worked with the Team at SWAAY for some years to help develop the therapeutic approach described in the chapter.

Brigette Bulanda, MSSA is a Licensed Independent Social Worker currently providing Outpatient Counselling for children, adolescents and their families at Applewood Centers, Inc. in Cleveland, Ohio. She has over eleven years experience in the treatment of youth offenders in both residential and outpatient settings and has made multiple professional presentations on this topic. You may contact her at 2525 East 22nd Street, Cleveland, OH USA 44115-3266 or on the web at www.forensicare.org.

Dr Kurt Bumby received his doctoral degree from the Law/Psychology and Clinical Psychology Training Program at the University of Nebraska-Lincoln. He has had a diverse career in the juvenile justice and adult criminal justice fields in the United

States, maintaining roles as an administrator, clinician, consultant, court expert and researcher. Currently, he is a Senior Manager with the Center for Effective Public Policy, a private, non-profit criminal justice consulting firm based in the Washington, DC area. Dr. Bumby has published on a variety of forensic topics such as youth violence, child maltreatment, prisoner re-entry, judicial education, alternative sentencing for adults and juveniles, and sex offender management, in several professional journals and books.

Rosalind Catchpole, MA is a PhD Candidate at Simon Fraser University in British Columbia, Canada, and a Psychology Intern at British Columbia's Children's Hospital. Her primary research focus is on the nature and course of youth psychopathy. Her PhD research investigates the attachment patterns of adolescents who present with psychopathic features. Her research is supported by a Canada Graduate Scholarship Doctoral Scholarship from the Social Sciences and Humanities Research Council and by a Senior Graduate Trainee award from the Michael Smith Foundation for Health Research. The research presented in her chapter was conducted while Ms Catchpole was a research assistant at Youth Forensic Psychiatric Services in Burnaby, British Columbia.

Robert J.W. Clift, MA is a PhD Candidate in Forensic Psychology at the University of British Columbia, and a Psychology Assistant at Youth Forensic Psychiatric Services (YFPS) in British Columbia, Canada. His research interests include perpetrators and victims of sexual harassment, intimate partner abuse, and violent and sexual offences.

Rachael M. Collie, MA, DipClinPsyc. is a clinical psychologist who has worked in the clinical forensic field since 1996. She currently teaches at Victoria University in clinical and forensic psychology. She is completing her PhD on personality processes in violent offenders.

Kevin S. Douglas, LLB, PhD, is an assistant professor in the Department of Psychology at Simon Fraser University and a guest professor of applied criminology at Mid-Sweden University, Sundsvall, Sweden. His work generally focuses on forensic assessment and more specifically on violence risk assessment and psychopathy. In 2005, he received the Saleem Shah Award for Early Career Contributions to Law and Psychology. He is supported by the Michael Smith Foundation for Health Research as a Career Scholar.

Julian Dunn CQSW qualified as a social worker in 1989. He worked for a ten year period as a probation officer in the Thames Valley with a generic caseload, gaining experience in working with mentally disordered offenders; young offenders as well as specialising in work with adult sexual offenders. He worked for the NSPCC as a Child Protection Officer and was part of an Offender Management Team where he undertook the assessment and treatment of adult and adolescent sexual offender and has been a social work practice teacher since 1995. He has been associated with the

SWAAY organisation for 14 years where he currently works as Manager of Behavioural Therapies. He has designed and implemented comprehensive, effective treatment programmes (both offence related and offence specific) based on sound research that is theoretically underpinned.

Rachel Edwards BA (Hons) Psychology, MSc Criminological Psychology is a forensic psychologist and is hoping to achieve chartership status this year. She has ten years experience of working directly with adolescents who have sexually abused, primarily in the context of SWAAY, a specialist therapeutic residential treatment resource for adolescents with complex needs. She is an experienced group worker developing, and delivering programmes that include social and emotional competency, offence-specific, and relapse prevention work. She also delivers individual cognitive behavioural therapy, individual interventions and undertakes psychometric assessments. Rachel has given training in these areas of work as well as presenting her own published research on evaluation of treatment programmes at national and international conferences.

Dr Rachel Fyson is currently a lecturer in Social Work at the University of Nottingham. She has previously worked as a Research Fellow for both the Ann Craft Trust, University of Nottingham, and the Norah Fry Research Centre, University of Bristol. Her research interests include issues around sexual abuse, learning disability, interagency working and policy implementation. She recently undertook the first UK study into the response of statutory education and social services to young people with learning disabilities who display sexually inappropriate or abusive behaviours.

Heather M. Gretton, PhD is Program Director of Program Evaluation and Research at Youth Forensic Psychiatric Services (YFPS) in British Columbia, Canada. In this position, Dr Gretton has conducted large scale studies examining characteristics and outcomes of sexual and violent offending adolescents referred by the courts to YFPS for psychological and psychiatric evaluation and treatment.

Simon Hackett is Reader in the School of Applied Social Sciences at Durham University. His work in relation to sexual abuse and sexual aggression by children and young people is internationally known. With Helen Masson, he has recently completed a two-year research project into the state of policy, theoretical approaches, service responses and user perspectives in relation to young people who have sexually abused others across the UK and Republic of Ireland. Simon's practice base with children and young people with sexually abusive behaviours extends back to the early 1990s. He was involved in the first UK groupwork programme for young men who have sexually abused. With Bobbie Print and Dave O'Callaghan, he was co-founder and a Programme Director of G-MAP, a leading community based specialist service for young people who have sexually abused. Simon has published widely in relation to children and young people with sexually abusive behaviours, including *What Works for Children and Young People with Harmful Sexual Behaviours?*

(2004, Barkingside, Barnardos). Simon is also Editor of the *Journal of Sexual Aggression*.

Julie Henniker is the manager of the AIM project, which has provided policies, procedures, assessment models and a range of interventions in respect of children and young people who sexually harm on a multi-agency basis across the 10 local authorities in Greater Manchester. The work of the project has been successfully adopted and adapted in a significant number of other local authorities across Great Britain. Her background is in local authority child protection social work, moving on to specific work at the NSPCC with adults who sexually offend and children and adolescents who sexually harm, on both a groupwork and individual basis. She has worked with the AIM project since its creation in January 2000. She has undertaken research for the Youth Justice Board, mapping responses and services to young people who sexually offend. She has contributed to the Youth Justice Board's Effective Practice Paper in relation to this group and has co-authored a number of chapters on the subject. She has a special interest in the development of potential restorative approaches to the work, in cases of sibling and wider family abuse.

Tess Johnson is a qualified social worker with a background in statutory children and families work. She has been a Childrens' Services Practitioner at the NSPCC Kaleidoscope service since 2003. During this time she has developed knowledge and experience in working with children and young people with sexually harmful behaviour, and with their families.

Jennifer LaCortiglia, MSW, LISW is currently the Foster Care Supervisor for the Cleveland Christian Home in Cleveland, Ohio. She was instrumental in developing the Socially Healthy Education and Development (SHED) Program which was the first Social Responsibility Therapy programme for preteens in Forensic Foster Care. Ms LaCortiglia has over eight years experience in the treatment of youth offenders in residential and outpatient settings including serving as an Abuse Treatment Specialist in the Treatment for Appropriate Social Control (TASC) Program and later serving as the Director of the SHED Program. Ms LaCortiglia has conducted a number of workshops along with professional presentations on working with multiple abuser youth. You may contact her via email at SHEDJGL@cox.net.

Tom Leversee is a clinical social worker who has 25 years of experience working with juveniles who have committed sexual offenses. He is currently the coordinator of sex offense specific services for the Colorado Division of Youth Corrections. Tom's private practice includes consultation, training, and the administration of sex offense specific evaluations. His other publications include *Moving Beyond Sexually Abusive Behavior: A Relapse Prevention Curriculum* and the accompanying *Moving Beyond* client workbook, available through the NEARI Press.

Vince Mercer worked for 10 years as team leader in a Youth Justice Team covering all of South Manchester. During this time he developed an interest in, and commitment to, restorative justice as an innovative approach to work with young offenders, bringing the perspectives of victims into the operation of the local criminal justice system. For the past six years he has managed a Restorative Family Group Meetings Project working with serious and persistent offenders, their families and the victims of their offences. More recently that project established a national reputation for its pioneering work, undertaken with the AIM Project, in working in the field of adolescent sexually harmful behaviour. Vince now works with the AIM Project in establishing an integrated approach, including restorative justice, in the field of adolescent sexually harmful behaviour.

Dr L.C. Miccio-Fonseca has over 25 years of forensic and clinical experience with children, adolescent and adults who have unconventional sexual practices and interests. Her background is extensive and highly specialised in the area of sex disorders, the paraphilias. She maintains a practice in her field of specialisation in Southern California, and has both researched and published in the area of sex offenders and victims of sexual abuse. She is a forensic expert in California and Washington, a Diplomat, and on the American Board of Sexology. Her ongoing research on sex offenders has been selected on separate occasions by the International Congress on the Treatment of Sex Offenders (Minneapolis, Minnesota; 1993: Caracas, Venezuela; 1998: Toronto, Canada; May 2000). Dr. Miccio-Fonseca has also published a first of its kind inventory used in exploring erotic development, The Personal Sentence Completion Inventory (PSCI). The PSCI is used in psychological evaluations by other notable clinicians across the country and is on its second printing.

Baseer Mir is employed by the NSPCC as a Children's Services Manager at the SHIELD Project in Huddersfield working with children and young people with sexually harmful behaviour. He has worked for the NSPCC for the last 11 years in a variety of settings and roles including the Black Youth Counselling and Advocacy Service, the Stockport Child Protection Team and more recently managing the Family Support Team in Leeds. Baseer is currently developing the AIM assessment manual, focusing on working with black and Asian young people with sexually harmful behaviour and has been delivering training on this subject for several years.

Elleen Okotie has recently moved to G-Map having worked for the NSPCC for seven years. Elleen has many years experience of working both with young people and adults who sexually harm and has worked with young people in both individual and group work settings. Elleen and Baseer Mir have published a piece of research on black and Asian young people who sexually harm and have been training on the subject for the last four years. They are currently developing the AIM assessment model focusing on black and Asian young people.

Gregory Parks, PhD is the Clinical Director for the Oklahoma Juvenile Re-entry Initiative and an Adjunct Clinical Instructor at the University of Oklahoma Health

Sciences Center, Center on Child Abuse and Neglect. He has been a psychologist for the Texas Youth Commission and the Oklahoma Office of Juvenile Affairs, and was on staff with the US Department of Justice, Office of Juvenile Justice and Delinquency Prevention.

David Prescott has worked in and around inpatient settings since 1984, and specifically with individuals who have sexually abused, since 1987. He has a strong interest in sharing resources, networking, and training to increase knowledge in these fields. He currently serves as the Treatment Assessment Director at the Sand Ridge Secure Treatment Center in Mauston, Wisconsin. In this position, he oversees the progress of patients and groups of patients and coordinates an early stage of the conventional treatment track. Mr Prescott has published articles on risk assessment, interviewing, and providing residential treatment to youth, and is the editor of recent books on youth who have sexually abused. He has presented on these topics around North America and in Europe. He is President Elect of the Association for the Treatment of Sexual Abusers (ATSA) and former editor of that organisation's newsletter, *The Forum*. He is a charter member of the International Association for the Treatment of Sex Offenders and also serves on the Board of Directors of *Stop it Now!* an organisation dedicated to the prevention of sexual abuse. Mr Prescott is also a member of the Motivational Interviewing Network of Trainers (MINT) an international organisation devoted to a client-centered, directive method for enhancing intrinsic motivation to change by exploring and resolving ambivalence.

Ethel Quayle is a lecturer with the Department of Applied Psychology and a researcher with the COPINE Project. This research examines the ways in which children are made vulnerable through the new technologies, with particular reference to abusive images. Her recent collaborative research with Barnardo's and NSPCC has taken as its focus children and young people who engage in sexually problematic behaviour in relation to the Internet. She has published widely in this area.

Gordana Rajlic has been a Research Assistant at Youth Forensic Psychiatric Services, British Columbia since 1999. She completed the Psychology Programme at the Department of Psychology, University of Belgrade.

Lucinda A. Rasmussen, PhD, LCSW is an Associate Professor at San Diego State University School of Social Work. She has over 25 years of clinical and research experience (15 years clinical experience treating sexually abused children, children and adolescents who sexually abuse, and adult sexual offenders, and 10 years experience as a social work educator and researcher). She completed two years of post-doctoral training as a clinician at SHARPER FUTURE, San Diego, which is an intensive outpatient programme treating adult sexual offenders on probation or recently discharged from parole. She is currently licensed as a clinical social worker in California and in Utah. Dr. Rasmussen's research interests are in the areas of sexually abusive youth and family violence. She has developed a conceptual model for assessing the impact of traumatic experiences (Trauma Outcome Process Assessment or *TOPA model*) and has presented on this model at numerous national and international conferences, including invited presentations in Israel and Mexico.

Katherine V. Regan, MA is a doctoral student in social psychology at Simon Fraser University in British Columbia, Canada. Ms Regan was an assistant in the Program Evaluation and Research Department at Youth Forensic Psychiatric Services in British Columbia, Canada at the time of the study. Her research interests include the study of violence in intimate relationships.

Phil Rich holds a doctorate in behavioural and organisational studies and a master's degree in social work. He is the Clinical Director of Stetson School, a residential programme for sexually abusive children and adolescents in Massachusetts. Phil is the author of 12 books, including *Understanding Juvenile Sexual Offenders: Assessment, Treatment, and Rehabilitation*, and *Attachment and Sexual Offending: Understanding and Applying Attachment Theory to the Treatment of Juvenile Sexual Offenders*.

Graeme Richardson has worked in the field of conduct-disordered children, juvenile delinquency, serious young offenders, and mentally disordered young offenders since 1985. The practice settings have included social services residential care, secure residential care, young offender prisons, an NHS outpatient clinic, and a medium secure NHS hospital. He has worked in the field of sexually abusive adolescents since 1989. In 1991 he was a part of a team that opened the first residential treatment programme for sexually abusive adolescents in the UK. In 1993 he was part of a team that opened an NHS outpatient service for sexually abusive adolescents. Since 1996 he has worked with mentally disordered sexually abusive adolescents in a secure hospital setting, including adolescents with emerging personality disorder. He has published in the areas of adolescent sexual offenders, adolescent interrogative suggestibility and false confessions, and risk assessment and risk management. He currently manages a psychology team of both clinical and forensic psychology staff within an NHS forensic mental health service for young people.

Gail Ryan is a Program Director at the Kempe Center for Prevention and Treatment of Child Abuse and Neglect, and recently retired from the University of Colorado School of Medicine. She continues part-time as a Clinical Assistant Professor and is focusing on dissemination training in all 50 states. She has worked at the Kempe Center since 1975, has worked with abusive parents and abused children, and provided offense specific treatment for 11–17-year-old males who have molested children since 1986. Her primary interests have been in the correlation between early life experience and dysfunctional behaviour with an emphasis on prevention of the development of sexually abusive behaviour in 'at-risk' groups. She is Director of the Kempe Perpetration Prevention Program; Facilitator, National Adolescent Perpetration Network; Facilitated the National Task Force on Juvenile Sexual

Offending (1987–1993), and is a Clinical Specialist for the Kempe Center's national resource center. She is an experienced trainer and has published widely in the field, co-editing the textbook *Juvenile Sexual Offending: Causes, Consequences and Correction* (1991, 1997), a booklet on *Childhood Sexuality* for parents, and *Web of Meaning: A Developmental-contextual Approach in Sexual Abuse Treatment*. She is currently training trainers to use the Kempe curriculum: *Primary, Secondary and Tertiary Perpetration Prevention in Childhood and Adolescence* to train others in their own communities.

Jane Scott is a children's services practitioner at Kaleidoscope (NSPCC) providing direct services to children and young people who display sexually harmful behaviour and to their carers. Jane has worked at the service for six years and before that worked in statutory child protection with a local authority for nine years.

Alicia Spidel is a PhD student at the University of British Columbia. Her research interests include psychopathy, domestic violence, and violence and mental illness. Her research is currently funded by the Vancouver Foundation, the Michael Smith Foundation for Health Research, the Mind Foundation of British Columbia, the American Psychology and Law Society and CIHR.

Thomas Talbot holds a Bachelor of Arts Degree from Bowdoin College in Brunswick, Maine where he graduated Summa Cum Laude and was inducted into the Phi Beta Kappa honor society. He has worked as a practitioner in diverse criminal and juvenile justice settings in several States, and is currently a Senior Manager with the Center for Effective Public Policy. Mr Talbot's responsibilities include overseeing national training initiatives for justice system professionals on sex offender management, providing technical assistance to jurisdictions that are working to enhance their approaches to working with this specialised offender population, and managing a project designed to promote and improve multi-disciplinary collaboration among criminal and juvenile justice system actors.

Paula Telford has been a social worker for over 30 years, working in both statutory and the third (voluntary) sectors, both as a practitioner and a manager. For the last twelve years she has worked exclusively with children and young people who display sexually harmful behaviour (and their families). Since 2000 she has managed the Kaleidoscope (NSPCC) team. She has co-written previous chapters on *Similarities and Differences in Working with Boys and Girls with Sexually Harmful Behaviour* and on *Working with Groups of Parents of Children with Sexually Harmful Behaviour*.

Tony Ward, PhD, DipClinPsyc. has worked in the clinical forensic field since 1987 and was formerly Director of Kia Marama Sexual Offenders' Unit at Rolleston Prison in New Zealand. Currently the Director of Clinical Training at Victoria University of Wellington, New Zealand, his major research interests are: offenders' cognition, rehabilitation and problem behaviour processes; the implications of naturalism for theory construction and clinical practice; assessment and case formulation in clinical psychology.

Bill West was born in York and spent time teaching in England and Ireland before moving to Zambia in 1970 where he lived and taught for 6 years. After studying at the Nottingham University School of Education, he moved to New Zealand where he trained in counselling and social work at Victoria University of Wellington. Having worked with offenders for 26 years as a probation officer and therapist, he is currently a Senior Therapist working with both the youth and adult teams at WellStop, New Zealand, a community-based sex offender programme, with a particular focus on working with people with an intellectual disability. He is also a jazz musician, and is married with two teenage children.

James Yokley, PhD is a Clinical Psychologist on the medical staff in the Department of Psychiatry at MetroHealth Medical Center in Cleveland, Ohio, with Assistant Professor appointments at Case Western Reserve University School of Medicine and Department of Psychology. Dr Yokley has expertise in the treatment of multiple forms of harmful, abusive behaviour, has authored over 50 research publications, book chapters, professional presentations and is a regular conference speaker on Social Responsibility Therapy for harmful behaviour. He has almost 20 years of experience in training, teaching and supervising in the area of managing harmful, abusive behaviour. You may contact him at PO Box 538, Hudson, Ohio USA 44236 or on the web at www.forensicare.org.

Chapter 1

Introduction

Martin C. Calder

This volume is my fourth edited book in the area of young people who sexually abuse since 1999 (Calder, 1999, 2002, 2005, current volume). The very fact that there is a need to produce so many texts in a relatively short period of time reflects the importance of the subject matter and the pace of change in our thinking, research and practice, but it does raise some questions about a need to perhaps digest the enormous amount of materials and package them in a more accessible way to try and respond to the pressure on workers and agencies (see Calder, 1997, 2001). It is for this reason that this may represent the last edited volume as a search for more streamlined and accessible avenues for dissemination are explored. The four edited volumes are very much to be seen as a jigsaw puzzle. In the first edited text (Calder, 1999) I argued that:

> All puzzles have clues, and each chapter offers us either a new piece of the jigsaw or some clues as to how it may be constructed. We must try to complete the jigsaw as best we can in order to provide the most informed and tested interventions in the best possible way. This can be done even if some bits are missing, although the risk of a distorted overall view is higher.

The same thinking applies across the subsequent three volumes. The most productive way of thinking about the four volumes is to see them as providing more clarity to the jigsaw picture as it expands. The early materials are not necessarily redundant simply because new materials have appeared. They are an important part of the evolution of our evidence-based practice approach and they represent an important foundation upon which the jigsaw puzzle has since been constructed. The contents of the four books appear at the end of this chapter to illustrate the links that can and should be made. Other issues are relevant within the timeframe of the work. Firstly, there has been a broadening of the authorship in terms of professional disciplines and countries represented as well as consideration of research and theoretical issues; intervention, assessment and treatment issues; professional considerations; engagement issues

and management issues. Secondly, this has illustrated a very broad use of similar but different terms relating to this group and this remains unresolved and once again in this volume is evident to the reader. Thirdly, there has been a significant change in the professional guidance, statute and public expectation and involvement in the debate and the context of the learning has to be actively embraced rather than marginalised and/or seen as peripheral. Public protection arrangements to deal with a whole range of people who commit sexual and violent offences is emerging and impacts directly and indirectly on the professional task and the amount of professional discretion allowed. The criminal justice field is adopting an actuarial 'what works' approach that strips professionals of their professional judgement in contrast to the emergence of the perpetrator-friendly assessment framework in social care that leaves professionals with the task of generating their own assessment materials. There is a zero tolerance environment for abuse as well as no margin for error in the assessment and management by professionals. We have seen the breadth of the types of harm grow to encapsulate internet offending and chat room activities, and we have seen the demise of sexual abuse across all major professional monitoring systems. The debate continues about whether this is due to a failure to recognise, an inability to accommodate the true volume within the struggling professional response systems diverted to implement multiple (often competing or contradictory) initiatives or a more informed and informal response as we become more comfortable with the issues raised. There has also been recognition that the approach to females, those presenting with a learning disability or from different ethnic backgrounds as well as families, require consideration of different causal factors as well as assessment and intervention materials.

A great many of these issues have been addressed in the four volumes and should provide either some suggested solutions or stimuli to add to professional debates. I now turn to the current volume after contextualising it in the other Russell House publications in this area.

The choice of chapters is partly a product of a search for authors and projects in emerging areas of practice as well as coming across them on my travels, web searching moments and conference attendances. Once again I have attempted to balance the contributions so that we address a wide range of themes: research and theory; assessment; intervention; treatment; engagement; management and outcomes; as well as trying to draw on a range of professional disciplines who may see issues in slightly different ways, potentially extending the available options for workers. There remains a continuing tension and debate surrounding a common language surrounding this subject area and once again I have been permissive in allowing the authors to use their preferred terminology as long as it is explained.

In **Chapter 2**, Simon Hackett argues that the field has much to gain from careful attention to issues of diversity. He believes that we should shift from viewing diversity issues negatively as if it is a problem or a burden, to seeing the notion of difference positively and optimistically. Instead of merely *dealing* with diversity we should be *embracing* it enthusiastically as a key organising theme for our work with young people who present with abusive sexual behaviours. In this sense, diversity is not only a critical consideration in relation to young people from minority groups, such as Black or disabled young people, though the needs of these groups are vital, but more generally the notion of difference and diversity can help support effective approaches to all children and young people who present with problematic or abusive sexual behaviours. The chapter addresses a number of associations raised by the notion of difference and in so doing establishes some pointers from research which indicate something of the importance of the concept of diversity across a range of considerations.

In **Chapter 3**, Mir and Okotie study the experiences of Black and Asian young people whose behaviour is sexually harmful and examine whether current models of practice in working with adolescent sexual offenders are adequately meeting the needs of offenders from Black and Asian cultures. Through their research they examine current practice as well as making recommendations about future developments and refinements.

In **Chapter 4**, Tom Leversee summarises some of the significant typology research and delineates four subtypes of sexually abusive youth according to clinical characteristics and then examines the implications for ongoing assessment and differentiating subtype specific supervision and treatment needs. He examines the subtype specific treatment with an emphasis on individualised areas of focus and skill development.

In **Chapter 5**, Rachael Collie and colleagues describe the Good Lives Model (GLM) of rehabilitation: a strengths-based approach with a *dual focus* on risk management and psychological wellbeing. The GLM proposes rehabilitation will be most effective when offenders learn to manage their risk of re-offending within the broader goal of learning to lead a better kind of life. A better kind of life is one in which an individual meets their basic human needs in socially acceptable and personally satisfying ways. From a GLM perspective, it is not sufficient to simply teach skills to reduce or manage risk factors. Instead the task of achieving and maintaining behaviour change needs to be *meaningfully* embedded within the notions of personal wellbeing, personal identity, and a positive lifestyle. Attention to individuals' internal capacity (e.g., knowledge, skills, attitudes, and values) and ecological contexts (e.g., social supports and opportunities) are critical for understanding the development of sexual offending and the interventions necessary to achieve psychological wellbeing and desistance from offending. This chapter builds on the holistic approach to working with young people who sexually abuse articulated by Rob Longo in Calder (2001).

In **Chapter 6** Graeme Richardson studies the relationship between offending behaviour and maladaptive/dysfunctional personality characteristics and then goes on to consider the general relevance of this research in the identification of sub-groups of sexual offenders who can be differentiated on the basis of their personality characteristics or personality difficulties. The consideration of five personality types is useful when mapping it over to the issue of typologies discussed in Chapter 3.

In **Chapter 7**, Clift and colleagues move on to consider the relationship between deviant arousal and sexual recidivism. They examined the relationship between both pre-treatment and post-treatment deviant arousal and sexual recidivism in a sample of 116 adolescent sex offenders. The group was followed for a mean of approximately four years post-treatment. Finding that over one-third of the sample had a new offence during the four-year follow-up period compared to a high presence of non-sexual crimes (83.3 per cent), it would appear that sexual offending is part of a generally criminal lifestyle for some adolescent offenders. Reasons for the low level of sexual recidivism are explored.

Chapter 8 sees the examination of the issues for working with the families as well as the young person with a descriptive consideration of the process and outcomes being considered through the eyes of the Kaleidoscope project.

Chapters 9 and 10 see us turn to the issue of special needs. Rachel Fyson starts by providing an overview of current knowledge about young people with learning disabilities who sexually abuse within UK studies before going on to report key findings from her recent study (Fyson et al., 2003; Fyson, 2005) which examined how special schools and statutory child protection and youth offending services in four English local authorities responded to sexually inappropriate or abusive behaviours exhibited by young people with learning disabilities. It concludes by highlighting areas of current practice which give cause for concern, and suggest some pointers for future best practice. In Chapter 10, Katherine Regan and her colleagues report on an important study which examined and characterised a group of 60 clinician-determined special needs (SN) adolescent sex offenders attending a modified sex offender treatment programme (SOTP) by comparing them to a group of 58 non-special needs (Non-SN) adolescent sex offenders who completed a regular SOTP. Recidivism rates following treatment were obtained for an average of eight years and the implications of this considered.

There is then a series of chapters examining risk assessment in this area.

In **Chapter 11**, David Prescott invites professionals to look closely at the language they use before moving on to review many of the challenges inherent in risk assessment, before concluding with frameworks for moving through an assessment. Greg Parks then moves on to consider the joint utility of the development of offender subtypes (explored by Leversee also in Chapter 4) and risk prediction and how they inform treatment options and outcomes. He strongly argues that all professional judgement should be informed by the available empirical

data. In making such a recommendation he acknowledges the limitations of some research and the fact that several authors and chapters partially overlapping their materials have selected different studies and drawn their arguments from the same papers in slightly different ways is a reflection of this. Gail Ryan then takes us through a review of the literature surrounding static, stable and dynamic risks and assets and models the fact that we need to look towards a holistic conceptualisation of risk. This chapter reviews research and study of risk factors thought to be relevant to the development of abusive behaviours and suggests hypotheses for primary, secondary and tertiary prevention, assessment and treatment to reduce the risk of children becoming abusive adults. Drawing on recent advances in research specific to sexual offending, as well as other fields, a comprehensive model is provided to aid clinicians and researchers in thinking about both risks and assets. Of particular importance is the distinction between changeable and unchangeable factors. Risk assessment and treatment models based solely on unchangeable risk factors in the past are likely to over-estimate risk, as well as missing important opportunities in treatment to change what is changeable. By balancing offence specific interventions with preventive interventions to increase healthy functioning, outcomes may improve, and iatrogenic risks may be reduced. This will undoubtedly influence the development or refinement of most existing or prospective risk assessment tools in this area of work.

In **Chapter 14**, Lucinda Rasmussen and Dr Miccio-Fonseca present the *Multiplex Empirically Guided Inventory of Ecological Aggregates for Assessing Sexually Abusive Children and Adolescents (Ages 19 and Under) – MEGA*, an empirically guided risk assessment tool for assessing sexually abusive youth. This tool addresses limitations of previous risk assessment tools and can be applied to *all* youth under the age of 19, male or female, child or adolescent, and youths with developmental disabilities. Grounded within an ecological framework that is consistent with the assessment framework in England and Wales, it also encourages an examination of causes as well as symptoms of risk though reviewing the available literature on definitions and risk assessment of children and adolescents who are engaging in sexually abusive behaviours. *MEGA* is developmentally sensitive; all of the elements within the seven aggregates of the tool are anchored on the empirical research for risk or recidivism related to sexually abusive youth, not adults. It is a time sensitive risk assessment tool that can be utilised to monitor the youth over time, and evidence changes and improvement as compared to baseline assessment.

Hot on the back of his seminal book around attachment theory and young people who sexually abuse (Rich, 2005) Phil Rich in **Chapter 15** describes ideas about the relevance of the theory (and attachment itself) in understanding sexually abusive behaviour, and implications for its use in an attachment-informed model of treatment. Ethel Quayle then considers the additional assessment issues in relation to young people who engage in sexually abusive behaviours through new technologies. The chapter tries to situate assessment in the context of how young people use the new technologies and how they might function in their lives. She argues that thinking about function might help us work fairly with young people, and also enable us to formulate their problems in ways that increases the likelihood of a working hypothesis that enables us to proceed, evaluate and monitor progress. It also allows us to think about behaviours as being topographically similar, but which may function in different ways. What this chapter has not been able to do is to give any easy answers about risk. The chapter offers an excellent overview of the available research in this area and concludes with some practical suggestions for assessors.

Having referred to the AIM model (Print et al., 2001) in the previous chapter, Julie Henniker and Vince Mercer (AIM Project Coordinators) address the issue of restorative justice and whether it is a useful and viable concept applied to the population of young people who sexually abuse. They review the origins and principles of the approach and then examine the pros and cons of its use in this field. They draw on their operational experiences and offer a case study to explore the points made.

In **Chapter 18**, Bumby and Talbot review the expansion of important research and professional literature involving this special population of youthful offenders that can be useful for informing intervention strategies. The aim of their chapter is to highlight some of this literature within the context of contemporary approaches, with an eye toward the future of promising practices for the treatment of juvenile sex

offenders, concluding with an analysis of where the field currently stands.

Jim Yokley and his colleagues in **Chapter 19** examine Preteen SRT: an innovative new cognitive-behavioural treatment designed to help develop social responsibility in children whose multiple forms of abusive behaviour impacts the future quality of living in our society. In the final chapter, Rachel Edwards and her colleagues from SWAAY* introduce us to their Pathway Social and Emotional Competency Group Work Programme. This inclusive programme aims to engage young people of all abilities, ages, degrees of sexually problematic behaviour, and all types of behavioural issues. The group provides for functions such as building attachments, managing emotional issues, and gaining a sense of self confidence in relationships. In addition it can provide a useful insight into an individual's ability to function in groups and assists in both the timing and decisions around the type of moves onto other group work programmes.

Finally, I hope that this collection of chapters adds further stimulus to the debates surrounding how best to understand and intervene with young people who sexually abuse and their families.

References

Calder, M.C. (1997) *Juveniles and Children who Sexually Abuse: A Guide to Risk Assessment.* Lyme Regis: Russell House Publishing.

Calder, M.C. (Ed.) (1999) *Working with Young People who Sexually Abuse: New Pieces of the Jigsaw Puzzle.* Lyme Regis: Russell House Publishing.

Calder, M.C. (2001) *Juveniles and Children who Sexually Abuse: Frameworks for Assessment.* 2nd edn. Lyme Regis: Russell House Publishing.

Calder, M.C. (Ed.) (2002) *Young People who Sexually Abuse: Building the Evidence Base for your Practice.* Lyme Regis: Russell House Publishing.

Calder, M.C. (Ed.) (2005) *Children and Young People who Sexually Abuse: New Theory, Research and Practice Developments.* Lyme Regis: Russell House Publishing.

---

*SWAAY is a multi-component treatment facility which seeks to maximise the range of resources and services available to young people, while allowing for the highest level of continuity and coordination amongst these services.

Longo, R. (2002) A Holistic Approach to Working with Young People who Sexually Abuse. In Calder, M.C. (Ed.) (2002) *Young People who Sexually Abuse: Building the Evidence Base for your Practice.* Lyme Regis: Russell House Publishing.

Print, B., Morrison, T. and Henniker, J. (2001) An Inter-agency Assessment Framework for Young People who Sexually Abuse: Principles, Processes and Practicalities. In Calder, M.C. (2001) *Juveniles and Children who Sexually Abuse: Frameworks for Assessment.* Lyme Regis: Russell House Publishing.

Previous edited volumes

Working with Young People who Sexually Abuse: New Pieces of the Jigsaw Puzzle (1999)

Introduction: How to Begin the Assembly Process.
Martin C Calder, Child Protection Co-ordinator, City of Salford Community and Social Services Directorate

Chapter One: Causal Explanations: Filling the Theoretical Reservoir.
Kevin J Epps, Forensic Clinical Psychologist, Glenthorne Youth Treatment Centre, Birmingham

Chapter Two: The Case for Paraphilic Personality Disorder: Detection, Diagnosis and Treatment.
Frank J MacHovec PhD, Christopher Newport University, Newport News, VA

Chapter Three: CASPARS: Clinical Assessment Instruments That Measure Strengths and Risks in Children and Families.
Jane F Gilgun PhD, Professor of Social Work at the University of Minnesota

Chapter Four: Recovery Assessments With Young People Who Sexually Abuse.
Mark S Carich PhD, Big Muddy Correctional Center, State of Illinois Department of Corrections
Matt Lampley BS, Intern at Big Muddy River Correction Center and Graduate student at Southern Illinois University at Carbondale

Chapter Five: Attachment and Intimacy in Young People Who Sexually Abuse.
Spencer Santry, The Tizard Centre, The University of Kent at Canterbury
Gerard McCarthy, Principal Clinical Child Psychologist, North Somerset

Chapter Six: A Framework for a Multi-Agency Approach to Working With Young Abusers: A Management Perspective.
Jacqui McGarvey, Team Manager Craigavon NSPCC
Lynne Peyton, Regional Director, NSPCC, Northern Ireland

Chapter Seven: A Conceptual Framework for Managing Young People Who Sexually Abuse: Towards a Consortium Approach.
Martin C Calder, Child Protection Co-ordinator, City of Salford Community and Social Services Directorate

Chapter Eight: Juveniles Who Sexually Abuse: The Relationship Between Fathers and Their Sons: A Psychoanalytical View.
Michael Murray, Barnardo's, Belfast

Chapter Nine: A description of a Community-Based Project to Work With Young People Who Sexually Abuse.
Dr Rachael Leheup, Child and Adolescent Psychiatrist, Thorneywood Unit, Nottingham NHS Health Care Trust
Steve Myers Senior Lecturer, The Manchester Metropolitan University

Chapter Ten: A Psycho-educational Support Group for a Neglected Clinical Population: Parents/Carers of Young People Who Sexually Abuse Children and Others.
Loretto McKeown, Family Therapist, Private Practice, Newry
Jacqui McGarvey, Team Manager, Craigavon NSPCC

Chapter Eleven: Developing Groupwork With Young People Who Sexually Abuse.
Kate O'Boyle and Kevin Lenehan, Child Protection Officers, and Jacqui McGarvey, Team Manager, Craigavon NSPCC

Chapter Twelve: Young Abusers With Learning Disabilities: Towards Better Understanding and Positive Interventions.
Dave O' Callaghan, Programme Director, G-MAP, Manchester

Chapter Thirteen: The Young Person With an Autistic Spectrum Disorder and Sexually Abusive Behaviour: Themes Around Asperger's Syndrome and a Case Study.
Graham Birtwell, and Andy Bowly, Barnardos North-West

Chapter Fourteen: The Significance of Trauma in Problematic Sexual Behaviour.
Stuart Mulholland, The Halt Project, Glasgow
Jeannie McIntee, Consultant Clinical and Forensic Psychologist, Chester Therapy Centre

Chapter Fifteen: Dilemmas and Potential Work With Sexually Abusive Young People in Residential Settings.
Meg Lindsay OBE, Director, The Centre for Residential Child Care, Glasgow

Chapter Sixteen: Adolescent Sex Offenders: Characteristics and Treatment Effectiveness in the Republic of Ireland.
Audrey Sheridan, Senior Clinical Psychologist, Dublin
Kieran McGrath, Senior Social Worker, St Clare's sexual abuse unit, Dublin

Young People who Sexually Abuse: Building the Evidence Base for your Practice (2002)

Introduction: Martin C Calder

Research and theoretical developments

Providing a Research-Informed Service for Young People Who Sexually Abuse.
Dave O' Callaghan, Director, G-MAP

Childhood Maltreatment Histories of Male Adolescents With Sexual Offending Behaviours: A Review of the Literature.
Ineke Way, Assistant Professor, School of Social Work, Western Michigan University

Impact issues

I'm sorry I Haven't a Clue: Unconscious Processes in Practitioners Who Work With Young People Who Sexually Abuse.
Nick Bankes, ACT, Surrey Social Services

Negotiating Difficult Terrain. The Personal Context to Work With Young People Who Sexually Abuse Others.
Simon Hackett, Centre for Applied Social Studies, University of Durham

'No One's Prepared for Anything Like This': Learning From Adults Who Care for Children Who Sexually Offend: A Narrative Study.
Sue Maskell, Child Protection Coordinator, Flintshire Social Services

Broad practice issues

Therapeutic Communities: A Model for Effective Intervention With Teenagers Known to Have Perpetrated Sexual Abuse.

Peter Clarke, Glebe House Children's Home, Cambridgeshire

Developing Focused Care: A Residential Unit for Sexually Aggressive Young Men.
Dr Andrew Kendrick, Department of Social Work, University of Dundee
Ranald Mair, Head, Geilsland School, Beith, Ayrshire

Accreditation of Work and Workers Involved in Providing a Service to Children and Young People Who Sexually Abuse.
Colin Hawkes, Young Abusers Project, London

Residential Standards of Care for Adolescent Sexual Abusers.
Robert Freeman-Longo, Director of Special Programming and Clinical Training, New Hope Treatment Centers, Summerville, SC

Groupwork With Parents of Children Who Have Sexually Harmed Others.
Simon Hackett, Centre for Applied Social Studies, University of Durham
Paula Telford and Keeley Slack, Kaleidoscope Project

Assessment issues

An Integrated Systemic Approach to Intervention With Children With Sexually Abusive Behaviour Problems.
Lucinda Rasmussen, Assistant Professor, San Diego State University

The Assessment of Young Sexual Abusers.
Dr Eileen Vizard, Consultant Child and Adolescent Psychiatrist, Young Abusers Project, London

South Asian Adolescent Sex Offenders: Effective Assessment and Intervention Work.
Kamran Abassi and Shabana Jamal, Probation Officers, Pakistani resource Centre, Manchester

Abused and Abusing: Work With Young People Who Have a Dual Sexual Abuse Experience.
Simon Hackett, Centre for Applied Social Studies, University of Durham

Treatment issues

A Holistic Approach to Treating Young People Who Sexually Abuse.
Robert E Longo, Director of Special Programming and Clinical Training, New Hope Treatment Center, Summerville, SC

Knocking on Shame's Door: Facing Shame Without Shaming Disadvantaged Young People Who Have Abused.
Alan Jenkins, NADA Counselling, Consulting and Training, Hindmarsh, South Australia

You Can Get An Adolescent to Grunt But You Can't Make Them Talk: Interviewing Strategies With Young People Who Sexually Abuse.
Ian Lambie PhD, University of Auckland

Assessment issues

Assessment and Treatment Strategies for Children With Sexually Abusive Behaviours: A Review of the Cognitive, Developmental and Outcome Considerations.
Dr Lesley French, Forensic Clinical Psychologist, Young Abusers Project, London

Empathy, Emotional Intelligence and Alexithymia: Implications for Research and Practice With Young People With Sexually Abusive Behaviours.
Ineke Way, Western Michigan University

Considerations for the Assessment of Female Sexually Abusive Youth.
Susan Robinson, Progressive Therapy Systems, Denver

Treatment issues

Integrating Trauma and Attachment Research Into the Treatment of Sexually Abusive Youth.
Kevin Creeden MA, Whitney Academy, East Freetown, MA

Experiential Therapy: Interactive Interventions for Young People Who Sexually Abuse.
Cindy Tyo MSW, New Hope Treatment Centers, SC

Cognitive Behavioural Treatment Under the Relapse Prevention Umbrella.
Charlene Steen PhD, Napa Valley Sex Offender Treatment Program, Napa, CA

Emotion-focused Therapy and Children With Problematic Sexual Behaviours.
Professor Jane Gilgun PhD, University of Minnesota, Kay Rice and Danette Jones, St. Paul, MN

Sexual Offending and Sexual Behaviour Problems: Treatment With Multisystemic Therapy.

Elizabeth J Letourneau and Dr Cynthia Cupit Swenson, Family Services Research Center, Medical University of SC

Mode Deactivation Therapy: Cognitive-Behavioural Therapy for Young People With Reactive Conduct Disorders or Personality Disorders or Traits Who Sexually Abuse.
Jack A Apsche, The Pines Behavioural Studies Treatment Program, VA
Serene R Ward Bailey MA, Private Practice, lake View Psychotherapy

Management issues

The Extra Dimension: Developing a Risk Management Framework.
Christine McCarlie and Ann Brady, The Halt Project, Glasgow

The Use of Sex Offender Registration With Young People Who Sexually Abuse.
Robert E Longo and Martin C Calder

Outcomes

Family Reunification in Cases of Sibling Incest.
Jerry Thomas and C Wilson Viar III, Consulting and Training Services, Memphis

Sex Offender Treatment in a Juvenile Correctional Setting: Program Description and Nine-Year Outcome Study.
Edward Wieckowski, Dennis Waite, Relana Pinkerton, Elizabeth McGarvey and Gerald L Brown, Virginia Department of Juvenile Justice, Hanover

Just How Different are They? Diversity and the Treatment of Young People with Harmful Sexual Behaviours

Simon Hackett

Introduction: Diversity as a central concept in work with young people who have sexually abused

Increasing attention has been given in recent years to policy and practice responses to children and young people who present with harmful or abusive sexual behaviours. This has led to claims that something of a treatment orthodoxy has developed in the UK in respect of this issue (Hird and Morrison, 1996). The results of recent research bear this out. In our survey of intervention providers in the UK and Republic of Ireland (see Masson and Hackett, 2003) we found that 92 per cent of programmes cited either cognitive behavioural or relapse prevention models as one of the primary approaches underpinning their work. This is consistent with findings from a review of programmes in North America, for example in the work of Burton and colleagues (2000) who reported that 79 of 118 (67 per cent) North American adolescent treatment programmes identified their primary theory selection as a combination of cognitive behavioural and relapse prevention. In our study, we also found high levels of consensus amongst a group of 78 specialist practitioners from across the UK and Republic of Ireland in relation to the goals, components and approaches to interventions (Hackett et al., 2006 in press).

If claims of increased sophistication in the adolescent field are accurate, this is due to the considerable effort practitioners and researchers alike have made in pooling knowledge and, over time, recognising and describing the similar presentation of young people, their commonalities in terms of their offence patterns (Wolf, 1984; Ryan at al., 1987) experiences and backgrounds, etc. (Ryan et al., 1996). Whilst these are not insignificant developments in a relatively newly developed field, one of the problems is that some policy and practice responses to children and young people have been predicated on the assertion that 'juvenile sex offenders' are one homogeneous group, as this example, an extract from one area child protection committee's guidance, suggests:

It is now widely accepted that sexually aggressive behaviour in children and young people are unlike other anti-social behaviours in that they do not cease as the participants get older. On the contrary, research indicates sexual behaviour problems will escalate in terms of seriousness and incidences if left untreated.

It is my contention in this chapter that this process of homogenisation is unhelpful and out of step with current research findings. As such, I believe that the field has much to gain from careful attention to issues of diversity. Although discussion of diversity issues is sometimes framed negatively as if it is a problem or a burden, it is my view that we should and can use the notion of difference positively and optimistically. Instead of merely *dealing* with diversity (this is the title of a position paper published by the National Organisation for the Treatment of Abusers exploring these issues) we should be *embracing* it enthusiastically as a key organising theme for our work with young people who present with abusive sexual behaviours. In this sense, diversity is not only a critical consideration in relation to young people from minority groups, such as Black or disabled young people, though the needs of these groups are vital, but more generally the notion of difference and diversity can help support effective approaches to all children and young people who present with problematic or abusive sexual behaviours. In a sense then, a child or young person's position as a *child* in itself means that they are part of a marginalised and vulnerable group in our society. Moreover, attention to this marginalisation and vulnerability is often a key element of any professional intervention with that child.

Therefore, this chapter seeks to explore how the concept of 'difference' can help guide professional interventions in this area. I begin by exploring why the adolescent sexual aggression field may have been relatively slow to consider issues of diversity. Then, I aim to consider several important questions, all of which are linked by the theme of 'difference', about young people who present with abusive sexual behaviours, specifically:

- How different are young people with harmful sexual behaviours from each other – to what extent do they constitute a homogeneous or heterogeneous group?
- How different are young people who sexually abuse from other young people, especially those with difficulties or significant adversities in their lives?
- What differentiates young people from adult sex offenders? And, as a result, how different should approaches be different for young people as opposed to those used with adult sex offenders?
- And finally, how can we diversify in order to better meet the needs of young people from minority groups who present with these behaviours?

Barriers to the recognition of diversity in sexual aggression work

Has the adolescent sexual aggression field really been slow to recognise and consider the implications of issues of diversity? What evidence is there for these claims? A brief examination of existing British studies describing clinical samples of young people who have sexually abused may provide some indicators to support this claim. These important demographic studies have been highly influential in raising professional awareness about who these young people are, what characteristics their families possess, what behaviours they have exhibited, etc. However, many fail to identify or even mention the ethnic background or racial origin of the young people in their sample. Are we to assume that they are all white? Or should we conclude that any differences in racial origin are irrelevant next to abuse specific variables being identified? This omission would be unthinkable in other parallel areas of child welfare research.

Gender is another factor at the forefront of work with sex offenders. One of the most strikingly consistent findings across studies of young people demonstrating harmful sexual behaviours is, of course, the gender bias towards boys and young men. However, an analysis of some of the standard and classic texts from the UK literature suggests that there is rarely any level of critical analysis of gender as a key factor. Indeed, most texts simply take the gendered nature of sexual abuse and adolescent sexual abusers 'as read'. For example, the index of the well-respected book edited by Hoghughi and colleagues (1997) has only three passing references to gender, one reference to 'males as abusers' and no reference to 'masculinity'. Although it's not my intention to stereotype a diverse field where there are many examples of good practice with regard to young people from minority groups, it is important to pause to think about what might have contributed to the under-emphasis of these issues. This needs to happen at a number of levels, from a macro agency and system context, to a more micro individual practitioner level.

Why might it be the case that the development of work with young people who are sexually aggressive has, as yet, failed to adequately recognise diversity issues? First, these can be difficult and potentially threatening issues and can involve practitioners, researchers and organisations in an uncomfortable level of self-scrutiny. But I suspect that this under-emphasis on issues of diversity runs much deeper. It may strike at the heart of our work and the context in which it occurs. Sex offender intervention has been influenced by a socio-political context that could scarcely be more hostile to abusers as a group (Gocke, 1995; Fisher and Beech, 1999; Featherstone and Lancaster, 1997). There are many contemporary examples of how this hostility towards sex offenders is exhibited. This kind of socio-political context clearly has an impact on the way in which we operate our programmes and offer our services. Have we, as a result, been forced to stress the more punitive and controlling aspects of our work at the cost of recognising diversity?

More specifically relating to adolescents, young people who sexually abuse share one powerful and readily identifiable aspect of commonality: their status as 'abusers'. For practitioners, this is the fundamental concern and the core reason for our attempts to work with them. Next to this crucial aspect of their commonality, young people's differences, and the implications of these differences for intervention, it seems to me, have at times become subsumed (Featherstone and

Lancaster, 1997). Consequently, their identification as 'sex offenders' has been seen to override their status or needs as children, adolescents, black or white, male or female, heterosexual or gay young people.

There may be two distinct processes which have happened as a result. Firstly, it has been very difficult to contemplate in our field how we might use models and frameworks – such as those of anti-oppressive practice, empowerment and cultural competence – that have been proposed in other areas of child welfare provision to help with issues of diversity (Featherstone and Lancaster, 1997; Lewis, 1999). Secondly, the tendency to lump all young people who present with harmful sexual behaviours together as one group (Featherstone and Lancaster, 1997) may at times have led to dull and defensive practice; e.g. uncritical use of theoretical models such as the cycle of sexual assault to suggest that all young people have the same kind of repetitive patterns of abusive behaviours underpinned by the same cognitive distortions and driven by the same kind of sexual fantasies, or that one standardised programme can meet the needs of all young people presenting with sexually abusive behaviours.

How different are young people with harmful sexual behaviours from each other – to what extent do they constitute a homogeneous or heterogeneous group?

It is now increasingly recognised across studies that a substantial degree of heterogeneity exists within the overall adolescent sexual abuser population. For example, in their large sample Ryan and colleagues (1996) found significant diversity within their sample according to key demographic variables, such as ethnicity, religion and social class. Similarly, although social isolation is frequently seen as a feature of the 'typical adolescent sexual abuser', Vizard and colleagues (1995) suggest that this is not supported strongly by the empirical evidence. Likewise, although factors such as low self-esteem, dysfunctional families, poor academic achievement, and previous victimisation are often suggested as key features in young people who have sexually abused, according to Vizard and colleagues, the empirical

support for these factors is also inconclusive. Of course some young people with sexually abusive behaviours have all of these factors and for these young people, they may be highly significant in the development and the expression of their sexual behaviours, but for other young people they are not a feature at all.

The issue of heterogeneity is more important, however, insofar as the clues it gives us in terms of identifying evidence-based sub groups of young people which can assist us to better target and focus our interventions. Several attempts have been made to describe typologies or sub groups of young sexual abusers. Most researchers have, as Worling (2001) has noted, taken their lead from the adult field and have compared adolescents who offend against children with those who target peers or adults – the classic 'child abuser' versus 'rapist' distinction. So, a common picture is that of the adolescent child abuser who has poor social skills and low self esteem, is frequently rejected by peers and has problems with intimacy, which mean that he seeks sexual gratification through younger children. By contrast, adolescent 'rapists' have been seen to have higher levels of non sexual criminality, higher levels of conduct disorder and display higher levels of aggression and violence. The key elements of this distinction are demonstrated in Table 2.1, proposed by the Center for Sex Offender Management (1999). Whilst this may be appealing, it is somewhat crude. Worling (2001) has also suggested that it is problematic as the distinction is formulated wholly on the basis of victim age. With young people as opposed to adults, it may well be that victim age (and indeed victim gender) are much less of a marker of sexual abuse preference, as adolescents are much more fluid in terms of their sexual development. Worling (2001) suggests that a more meaningful distinction with young people may have little to do with the age of victims they select. Alternatively, he proposes a personality based typology of adolescent sexual abusers and used data on 112 young men with sexually abusive behaviours aged between 12 and 19 to describe four personality based sub groups, as depicted in Table 2.2.

In Worling's study, the largest group (representing almost a half of the young people in the sample) was the Antisocial/Impulsive group and these young people were seen to have high levels of delinquency and impulsivity. There were no significant differences between the four

Table 2.1 Comparing two sub-groups of sexually abusive youth (Centre for Sex Offender Management)

Characteristics	Offends against peers or adults	Offends against children
Victims	• Victims are mainly female • Assaults mainly strangers or acquaintances	• Females victimised at slightly higher rates • Nearly half assault one male • Up to 40% of victims are siblings or relatives
Offence patterns	• More likely to commit in conjunction with other criminal activity • More likely to commit offences in public areas	• Reliant on opportunity and guile • Tricks child using bribes or threatening loss of relationship
Social and criminal history	• More likely to have histories of non-sexual criminal offences • Generally delinquent and conduct-disordered	• Deficits in self-esteem and social competency are common • Often lacks skills and attributes necessary for forming and maintaining healthy relationships
Behaviour pattern	• Displays higher levels of aggression and violence • More likely to use weapons and cause injuries to victims	• Frequently displays signs of depression • Youths with severe personality and or psychosexual disturbance may display high levels of aggression and violence

Table 2.2 Worling's (2001) personality based typology of adolescent sexual abusers

Group	Personality descriptors
Antisocial/impulsive	Antisocial, impulsive, anxious, unhappy, rebellious
Unusual/isolated	Unusual, undependable, isolated, confused Trusting, spontaneous
Overcontrolled/reserved	Emotionally overcontrolled, responsible, reserved, reliable Suspicious of others, rigid
Confident/aggressive	Confident, self-centred, outgoing, aggressive, sociable Dependable, organised, optimistic

groups in terms of victim age, gender, or relationship. Frequencies of sexual abuse victimisation were also comparable across the groups. However, there were several significant group differences. For example, young people from the Antisocial/Impulsive group were significantly more likely to have experienced physical abuse from their parents and also to have received criminal charges for their sexual behaviours.

Worling's findings demonstrate well that young people (even those whose overt behaviours and victim characteristics are similar) may have taken very different developmental pathways into the abuse and, in terms of the need to diversify our responses, they may have very distinct profiles and treatment needs. For example, as Worling says, as young men in the Antisocial/Impulsive group have an overall tendency to rule breaking, their sexually abusive behaviours may (at least initially) be more a

result of this general rule breaking behaviour than connected to, for example, deviant sexual arousal. As a result, orthodox sex offender specific relapse prevention interventions may not be all that successful unless other factors seen as important in the treatment of general delinquency – such as fostering prosocial attitudes, anger management and alternatives to aggression – are emphasised.

By contrast, young people in the Over-controlled/Reserved sub group were not seen to share the same delinquent attitudes or behaviours as those in the Antisocial/Impulsive group. Specifically, these young people, according to Worling, endorse pro-social attitudes, are cautious to interact with others, and tend to keep their feelings to themselves. The sexually abusive behaviours are often, therefore, developed within the context of an overall shy and rigid interpersonal style, which may make it difficult for these young people to access more normative intimate relationships with peers. In contrast to the Antisocial/Impulsive group, these young people are not likely to require an emphasis within treatment on general delinquency issues such as impulsivity or attitudes supportive of criminality, rather, they need to develop ways of emotional expression and appropriate social relationships; including themes such as 'expressing yourself', 'standing up for yourself' or 'joining in the group'.

So, overall then, there is substantial evidence to suggest we can clearly answer the question about differences between young people presenting with abusive and problematic sexual behaviours. They are clearly not all one homogeneous group and indeed, differences in personality and offence variables can help us to better diversify and target intervention responses between young people.

How different are young people who have sexually abused to other young people?

In some ways a related second question about diversity is that concerning differences between young people who have sexually abused and other young people. In many senses, young people with harmful sexual behaviours have been traditionally envisaged or marked out as fundamentally different from both non-offending peers and other non-sexual offenders. For example, in what is by and large (in my view) a helpful book by Lundrigan (2001: 29) (note that this is a relatively recent publication) the author suggests that:

> The adolescent who commits sexual offences tends to be different from other young delinquents . . . and the types of treatment that work best with this population must likewise be different . . . to do offence-specific therapy, one must break with traditional therapy.

This idea of a fundamental difference between young people who sexually abuse and other young offenders was brought home to me in a training event recently which I was facilitating when a worker said she felt that young people who had sexually abused were different as they have crossed over a 'certain line'. Interestingly, when I asked why she felt this was the case, the only response she could give was that it is because 'what they do is about sex'. I have

wondered about her response ever since. Was her view because these young people's particular behaviours of concern are sexual in nature? We know that sexual behaviour is a key aspect of adolescent development, for example the findings of a fairly unique and valuable study into young adolescents' heterosexual activity in Scotland by Henderson and colleagues (2002) suggests that 18 per cent of boys and 15 per cent of girls aged 14 reported having had sexual intercourse. Or was this worker of the view that these young people are different as they had used coercion in the course of their sexual behaviours? In Henderson and colleagues' study, 20 per cent of these 14-year-olds who had experienced sexual intercourse indicated that there had been some level of coercion, either from them or the other young person. I certainly do not wish to suggest that what was occurring for these young teenagers in this study was in any way similar, either qualitatively or quantitatively, to an adolescent sexually abusing a younger child, but it does highlight the importance of placing the behaviours of young sexual abusers very carefully in the context of what we know about normative adolescent development including the high frequency of risk related sexual behaviours.

I am not suggesting that there are no differences between young people with harmful sexual behaviours and other groups. It may be for example that, as a group, young people with sexually abusive behaviours demonstrate greater problems in perspective taking and higher levels of impulsivity than their non-offending counterparts (O'Halloran et al., 2002). However, the clear message is that we need to be careful not just to fall into the trap of demonising any young person, or even more so a pre-adolescent, with sexual behaviour problems as having fundamentally different needs from other children. One of the consistent things I have felt when meeting young people referred to me with harmful sexual behaviours over the course of the years is in most cases how similar they are to other young people around them. Sometimes I have felt a great degree of relief that the offender demonised in reports or referral information is first and foremost a child in distress and in need with the same kinds of interests, anxieties, problems, fears and hopes, as other children, even though the sexual context for their difficulties may be causing specific concern. My clinical impression has a growing level of empirical support. For example, O'Halloran and colleagues (2002) compared a community sample of Irish young people with a history of sexual abusive behaviour with a clinical control group who had significant behavioural difficulties but no history of sexual offending, and a 'normal' control group of adolescents without significant behavioural, interpersonal or psychological problems. They found that the group of young people with sexually abusive behaviours had fewer behaviour problems overall than the clinical control group and more closely resembled normal controls. Taking into account measures on anger, self-esteem, general conduct issues and family problems, they conclude from their study that:

> . . . the psychological adjustment of adolescents with a history of sexual abusing is more problematic than that of normal controls but less problematic than that of youngsters who have significant behavioural problems but no history of sexual offending. (2002: 36)

This is clearly good news from the point of view of diversifying intervention practice. If young people with sexually abusive behaviours are not fundamentally different from other young people in trouble and with problems, this means that we could, and indeed should, be able to take what we know constitutes 'good practice' from work with other groups of children and young people and apply them to this population too. This opens up a whole range of possible interventions, for example:

- Fostering young people's talents and supporting them in achieving educational success at whatever level (Jackson and Martin, 1998).
- Providing young people with interpersonal and social supports, such as through mentoring schemes (Utting and Vennard, 2000).
- Offering family interventions to improve the quality of parenting responses and relationships within the home (Farrington and Welsh, 1999).

These are all interventions which have demonstrable success in relation to other groups of vulnerable young people. Such interventions, whilst not traditionally part of orthodox 'adolescent sexual offender treatment' are likely to show positive outcomes, alongside more focused 'sexual abuse specific work'. In this way, the clear message is that we can think more

broadly than just the *sex offending literature* when working with this group and allow ourselves to be informed by the richness of the literature from other areas of child welfare practice.

Differentiating approaches to young people from adult sex offenders

I'd like to turn now to the third of the specific questions I set at the beginning of the chapter; that is, what it is about approaches to children and young people with harmful sexual behaviours that should be different from models used with adult sex offenders?

There has been a longstanding acknowledgement in the adolescent field that the original reference point for responses to young people came very much from models used with adults. Longo (2003) has called this the 'trickle down effect' and suggests that this process, which has been going on for the last two decades, has been highly destructive to the work with children and young people and has resulted in children being viewed simply as mini versions of adult sex offenders. This particular theme was raised very strongly in our recent study of experienced practitioners in the UK and ROI (Hackett et al., 2006). This group of 78 practitioners persistently talked about the need to differentiate approaches to adolescents from adult sex offender work. Thus, for example, two of the statements which gained almost universal strong support (99 per cent of the participants strongly agreed with both) were:

> Children who display sexually harmful behaviours are first and foremost children and should not be regarded as mini adult sex offenders.

and

> Work with children and young people should be developmentally appropriate. We cannot assume that research, models and methods designed for adults can be applied to adolescents.

At the same time, when we went on to ask participants to list which *models* and *methods* they actually used in their work with young people, many of the items that were identified and were emphasised as central to their approach (such as cognitive behavioural therapy, relapse prevention, the cycle of sexual assault and development of empathy) have certainly come to adolescent work through this 'trickle down' process from adult sex offender work.

Although this finding might seem somewhat paradoxical and contradictory, it is not necessarily the case. It is not that practitioners working with children and young people with harmful sexual behaviours have dismissed out of hand the models which have empirical validity from adult sex offender work, but the shift has been more to do with a concern about the implications of developmental differences in childhood and through adolescence which have placed a different emphasis on how these models are used with young people. To illustrate, it is possible to chart a shift of focus in the literature towards more developmental and holistic interventions which take into account these important developmental differences. For example, an early paper by Ryan and colleagues in 1990 addressing the assessment and treatment of young people advocated the following approach, directly drawn from the style and philosophy of adult sex offender work:

The denial systems of these offenders must be penetrated during the early phases of treatment or no real progress can be made. The levels of confrontation necessary to accomplish this are greater than any used by most traditional therapists.

(Ryan et al., 1990: 269)

In contrast, by 1999, Ryan was able to articulately identify that a major point of change in the intervening decade had been the realisation of the need to introduce a more developmental and contextual understanding of young people. In place of confrontational and adult focused methods had emerged a strong call for the notion of child-focused and holistic intervention, targeting both abuse specific and more generalised areas of unmet need. As Ryan (1999: 426) summarises:

Although the need to specifically address the sexual offence characteristics was still called for, a new emphasis was placed on the need to . . . treat the whole youth, not solely the issues specific to the offending behaviour.

Along with this has come a realisation that it is *as important* to address issues within the young person's broader social existence, including family relationships and context, as it is to work individually with the young person (Ryan, 1999, Hackett, 2001; Masson and Hackett, 2003).

So what does this idea of developmentally sensitive practice mean?

First, a developmentally sensitive approach to young people with harmful sexual behaviours is underpinned by a clear awareness that developmental competence – in this case living a non-sexually abusive lifestyle in adolescence and into adulthood – is composed of a complex interplay between the young person's ecology or context and the developing individual.

Second is the need to ensure that the concepts, norms and resources we use with children and young people are sensitive to their developmental understandings. It is clear that we need to base our approach within the parameters of child and adolescent development. As Rich puts it, we know that adolescents: 'have not attained adult levels of moral development, cognitive ability, personality integration, emotional stability, socialisation and so forth' (1998: 109). She goes on to highlight how this means that young people shift through different stages through adolescence as they begin to learn about concepts such as intimacy, power, gender relations, sexuality, etc. integrating into each of these the learning they have from family members and peers. Rich suggests that this means that we have to be open to the fact that some of these developing understandings, whilst they would be considered abusive in adulthood, are in fact reflections in adolescence of developmental immaturity. She cites the example of the cycle of sexual assault as a good example of a model that is of limited use with children and young people, saying that many of the adolescents she works with struggle to fit their own sexually abusive behaviour within the highly structured sequence of behaviours, feelings and cognitions associated with each step of the model.

So, developmentally sensitive practice for Rich includes the following elements:

- It is firstly flexible enough to adapt to the individual needs of the young person and family.
- It looks not just at the sexual abuse behaviour in isolation but examines other patterns of behaviour and helps the young person to make links between these elements of his life.
- It is comprehensive – addressing not just the sexual abuse but also other aspects of the young person's needs. This might include, for example, the young person's own victimisation

experiences alongside, and as a necessary part of addressing the abuse.

- And fourth, it is integrated, mobilising all aspects of the young person's ecology and system in an effort to support the behavioural change being sought.

(Rich, 1998)

What are the particular needs of young people from minority groups with harmful sexual behaviour?

The fourth and final question I set myself earlier in the chapter concerned the particular needs of young people from minority groups with HSB. These are important to consider on a number of different levels. First, we know that outcomes for young people in our systems vary significantly across groups. To take just one current example about general adolescent offenders, Feilzer and Hood (2004) examined how ethnic minority young people are dealt with at all stages of the youth justice process. The authors examined information on 17,054 case decisions relating to young people aged between 12 and 17 years. They found that young Black people are particularly at risk for disproportionately punitive responses in the criminal justice system. Thus, it was nearly three times as likely for a young person of mixed parentage to be prosecuted than a young white offender with similar case characteristics (both male and females). Higher proportions of cases involving Black and mixed parentage young men were remanded in secure conditions and all cases involving young men from minority ethnic groups were sentenced to more restrictive community penalties than would have been expected. The chances of a young Black male's custodial sentence at crown court being 12 months or longer were nearly 7 times those of a white male offender. These are familiar, and depressing findings, and it is likely that young sexual offenders from ethnic minority groups are subject to these same discriminatory processes as are their non-sexual offending counterparts in the criminal justice system.

Second, and perhaps more positively, if we are to aspire to the overall aim of developmentally sensitive and holistic intervention as I have tried to advocate above, it is clear that this includes attention to the *additional* difficulties in terms of adolescent development often placed onto young

people by society by virtue of their minority status. To cite just a few examples:

- Research on the developmental implications of disability in adolescence has found that disabled young people often have few friends of their same age, are often excluded from peer group settings and seldom involved spontaneously in peer group activities, especially in sport-related events. It has been established that adolescents with disabilities frequently experience social isolation. In a recent small scale study of disabled teenagers, Skär (2003) found that the young people in her sample had serious additional difficulties and obstacles to overcome in their attempts to form relationships with peers and adults. The barriers were twofold: the inaccessibility to many physical and social environments and the tendency of adults (both parents and professionals) to plan, control and restrain their lives (Skär, 2003).
- Similarly, previous research has documented very vividly the particular difficulties faced by gay, lesbian and bisexual adolescents and the developmental costs of social stigma, victimisation and the influence of living in homophobic environments. Indeed, in research using in-depth interviews with 164 gay, lesbian and bisexual young adults aged 17–25 years, recruited through multiple sites, Savin-Williams and Diamond (2000) found an average of 10 years gap for gay and lesbian young people between first same-sex attractions to first disclosure of their sexual orientation. This suggests that many young people from sexual minority groups with whom we come into contact will be having to address their sexually abusive behaviours at the same time as coming to terms with their own sexual identification in the face of all-pervasive homophobia within our society.
- Finally, in terms of young Black people, it is the case that ethnic identity has been consistently found to be positively related to self-esteem in minority ethnic adolescents (Herman, 2004).

All of these factors underline the importance of putting issues of diversity and minority status centrally in our interventions as a key feature of addressing risk and preventing relapse. For example, no matter how oppressive a Black offender is in his/her sexually aggressive behaviour, this clearly does not invalidate that

The anti-oppressive fulcrum

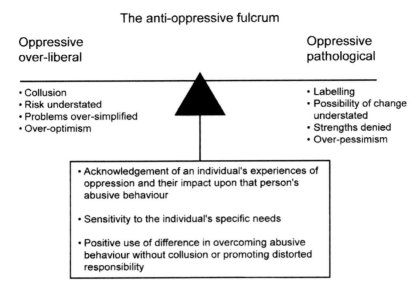

**Oppressive
over-liberal**

- Collusion
- Risk understated
- Problems over-simplified
- Over-optimism

**Oppressive
pathological**

- Labelling
- Possibility of change
  understated
- Strengths denied
- Over-pessimism

- Acknowledgement of an individual's experiences of oppression and their impact upon that person's abusive behaviour

- Sensitivity to the individual's specific needs

- Positive use of difference in overcoming abusive behaviour without collusion or promoting distorted responsibility

Figure 2.1 Fulcrum model of anti-oppressive practice with sexual abusers (Hackett, 2000)

person's own experiences of racism. Addressing a young person's position as a member of a minority group is not just a luxury secondary item to the real business of offence focused work, but is integral to the process of challenging risk and preventing relapse.

As such, it is my belief that the concepts of empowerment and anti-oppressive practice have much to offer here. But they are not without challenges. How do we achieve anti-oppressive practice with someone who has so overtly oppressed others? How should we empower someone who has misused their power? These are difficult questions, but ones that we need to address on both a macro theory level as well as on a micro level with individual young people. I have previously suggested a model which seeks to articulate how we might use such concepts in our work (Hackett, 2000). The model is based on, and developed from, the work of Ahmad who warned against the dangers of white practitioners' responses to Black service users at two ends of a continuum; on the one hand *overly liberal and ineffectual* and on the other *overly prejudiced and harsh* (Ahmad, 1992). This is a distinction which I have found to be useful in scrutinising my own approaches and responses to young people who have sexually abused from a range of minority groups. I have tried to use this notion therefore to depict the relative relationship, as I see it, between pathological,

over-liberal and anti-oppressive approaches in responses to young people with harmful sexual behaviours.

Essentially, the oppressive pathological approach is one where the worker's stereotypical assumptions regarding the abuser's minority status mean that the sexually abusive behaviour is perceived as 'doubly deviant'. Correspondingly, the young person is pathologised and higher risk is attributed to the abusive behaviours not by virtue of the behaviours themselves but due to the oppressive stereotypes associated with the person's diversity and difference. Individuals and their families can be easily marginalised through assessment and intervention based on this approach. Individual's strengths are denied and people are defined primarily in terms of deviance or deficit. The following case example illustrates an oppressive pathological approach:

Alan, a young white man of fifteen years who had abused an eight-year-old boy, identified himself in treatment as gay. His heterosexual workers viewed this as evidence of heightened risk to male children, drawing on a pathological and oppressive view that all gay men were promiscuous, dangerous to male children and unable to control their sexual desires. They insisted that Alan make a contract with them to avoid any contact with not only younger children, but also with several peer-aged gay friends he had made at school and to stay away from the gay village in the city where he lived as this was a 'risk'. This increased Alan's sense of rejection, isolation and low self-esteem, all core factors identified by the workers concerned as having motivated Alan to abuse in the first instance.

By contrast, on the other end of a continuum, the idea in an overly-liberal oppressive approach is where, in an attempt to acknowledge the abuser's experiences of structural inequality, the practitioner fails adequately to address the abuse behaviour. In this way, the oppressive over-liberal approach can fail to challenge risk factors and can leave others vulnerable. This is also oppressive to the young person concerned as it can deny the young person the interventions required to deal with the behaviours. This approach was demonstrated through the following case illustration:

Bernadette was a sixteen year old white young woman, who had sexually abused two girls, aged three and four, whilst baby-sitting. As the social worker in the case concerned did not readily accept that females sexually abused, and given Bernadette's own experience of being sexually abused as a child, the worker saw little or no risk that the abusive behaviour would persist or develop, instead interpreting the abusive behaviour solely as a symptom of Bernadette's own abuse, and thus a 'cry for help'. As a result, few measures were taken to restrict Bernadette's contact with other young children and the worker offered a limited series of only six low key individual sessions which focused exclusively on her own experiences as a victim of sexual abuse. Whilst this work was ongoing, Bernadette continued to baby-sit for other children and went on to abuse again.

I should say that in considering responses to young people from minority groups, it is my experience that most inadequate practice falls towards the end of the pathological approach, but I have also seen approaches to individual children that veer wildly from one approach to the other. Instead of responses at either end of this continuum, I have argued that what we need is a balanced approach which is sensitive to the particular cultural meanings of the person's experience without using these meanings as an excuse to explain away the abuse; a balanced position that I have called the *critical fulcrum* of intervention. The notion of anti-oppressive assessment as a 'fulcrum' reflects the need, given the dual status of an abuser from a minority oppressed group as both 'oppressor' and

'oppressed', to maintain a balance between empowerment and control. It acknowledges the nature of the person's experiences of structural oppression in the development of abusive behaviours and seeks to challenge these experiences as a fundamental element in helping the young person to move on, as in the case of Shahid below:

Shahid was a seventeen-year-old young Black Asian man with moderate learning disabilities, who had lived for ten months in a large children's home for adolescents, following his sexual abuse of his sister. In the residential unit, which was staffed exclusively by white workers, Shahid was the only Black resident and the only Muslim. Although contact with his mother, a lone parent, had been anticipated, the unit was distant from Shahid's family home and little effort had been put into maintaining family contacts, or to helping his family deal with the impact of Shahid's abuse. The unit staff had also problematised Shahid's mother as they could not speak to her in her first language and therefore failed to update her of her son's progress. After 10 months of inaction, an independent assessment of Shahid was sought from a specialist adolescent sex offender programme only when his general behaviour in the unit was seen to deteriorate.

As part of the assessment process the workers spent time exploring with Shahid what it had been like as a young Black man living in a white society and latterly in a white residential environment, trying to communicate knowledge of, commitment to, and respect of his cultural background. Shahid spoke of his experience of being bullied, scorned and ridiculed by his peers as a Black young person in the unit. Workers identified that residential unit staff had covertly added to Shahid's sense of low self-esteem by suggesting to him that he should 'not draw attention to himself' i.e. that he should give up the practices associated with his family background and cultural heritage so as not to highlight his difference. They were also concerned that Shahid's social life had been restricted as, given his learning disabilities, he was not adjudged to be capable of having the level of external freedom and privilege given to his non-learning disabled peers. Most notable in workers' conversations was Shahid's degree of personal isolation and sexual frustration he had felt in the unit, and the intense anger that the racism which he experienced promoted in him. Significant time was also spent with Shahid's mother, seeking her views and opinions of Shahid's behaviour and development. Her strength in raising her four children alone in a hostile and racist society was acknowledged and built upon. Weight was also given to her views as to the potential role in relapse prevention of reinforcing Shahid's Muslim values and identity.

In completing their assessment, the assessors drew specific attention to how the residential unit had failed to meet Shahid's needs as a young Black man with learning disabilities and commented upon how these issues were linked to ongoing risk. At the same time, they commented upon the lack of an effective risk management and monitoring strategy in the unit. In order to support a programme of intervention work, they identified practical tasks for the residential unit and suggested strategies for reinstating and appropriately maintaining work involving his family. They drew up a detailed management plan for Shahid which involved safely monitored external social activities. They recommended an intervention programme which was congruent with his level of cognitive ability, but also reflected and valued cultural diversity in its imagery and material.

Conclusion: Is it time to diversify and to what?

This chapter has sought to address a number of associations raised by the notion of difference. I have attempted to establish some pointers from research which indicate something of the importance of the concept of diversity across a range of considerations. I have argued that the research supports the idea that children and young people with harmful sexual behaviours are a very diverse group and that they share many of the same characteristics of other young people in trouble and with difficulties. I have also suggested that this means that we can diversify our approaches to them to include those which constitute good practice with other groups of children and young people. Additionally, I have suggested that we need to develop specific practices and empowering and appropriate interventions to young people from minority groups who present with harmful sexual behaviours.

Does this mean that we should move away from some of the more orthodox cognitive behavioural interventions in this field? We need to be careful not to ignore the evidence that we have from the child maltreatment field in general which supports the efficacy of these kinds of interventions. For example, in their review of treatment models for child physical and sexual abuse, Saunders, Berliner and Hanson (2003) suggest that the interventions which are best

supported empirically are those which are based on behavioural or cognitive behavioural approaches and which are multisystemic in nature, intervening at both the level of the child and the child's wider family. Saunders and colleagues further identify a range of factors which appear to be common to these empirically supported approaches. First, such interventions are generally *goal-oriented* and 'designed to address specific, measurable problems identified through systematic assessment of children and their families' (2003: 104). Second, such approaches are *structured* and geared around a sequential range of intervention stages, using specific techniques in order to achieve a reduction in the level of assessed problems and to meet overall intervention goals. Third, such interventions tend to emphasise the teaching of *specific skills* which can be used by children to manage their thinking, emotions and behaviours. Such skills are rehearsed repeatedly in therapy with the hope that the child will, over time, be able to generalise and apply them in their broader environment and life context. A similar process is also used with parents and carers, with an emphasis on the development of skills to assist in the appropriate management of their child. It would seem that the best available evidence to date suggests that we should not deviate from these core elements. But maybe the vital point is to ask not 'what is effective' but 'why it's effective'. It may be that the key to real success in responding in these cases is concerned with the therapeutic engagement of both carers and children. In other words, taking an interest in the children and carers and their situations and difficulties, helping them to express difficult emotions and involving them in an interpersonal exchange with others which is supportive and positive may make the difference over and above therapeutic modality.

This leads me to a final framework that has significantly enhanced my own practice and beliefs about this area of work; that is, research into children's resilience in situations of adversity (see also Hackett, 2006). Resilience researchers have consistently argued that we should shift our focus away from the long-standing tradition of emphasising users' deficits towards explicit attention to the strengths of individuals in situations of adversity, so that we can better understand the factors and processes which support the achievement of positive adaptation despite exposure to risk (Luthar et al., 2000).

This is a clear diversification from traditional interventions methodologies. A resilience based approach in this sense is based on the notion that building young people's competences and adding resources at individual, familial and environmental levels can help them negotiate challenges and difficulties associated with addressing sexual abusive behaviours. Theoretically, a resilience based approach to young people who have sexually abused seeks to mobilise two distinct processes. The first is to attempt to increase the presence or power of the people who are themselves assets to young people – for example parents and teachers. Parent education programmes or mentoring schemes are two good examples. The second process is to mobilise or enhance the most powerful adaptational systems for young people, including their ability to use key relationships, intellectual functioning, self efficacy and motivation.

It is not that we drop the offence specific or psycho educative elements of intervention but we add to it interventions in the young person's wider social context which feed these resilience needs. For example, what can we do to provide young people with opportunities to develop their talents, learn new skills, develop cultural traditions and identity, succeed in whatever ways possible, particularly success in relationships? These are the vital building blocks of a resilience approach but they do not flow automatically from a more rigid, offence focused programme or from the traditional ways in which our professional systems have dealt with young people. For example, a tendency to exert planning in relation to life decisions has been shown to constitute a significant protective factor and in research with young people in care (Jackson and Martin, 1998) whereas the belief of many young people that they were simply the victims of fate and could do little to influence the trajectories of their lives brought about vicious circles of negative experiences and destructive behaviours. This reminds me very strongly of the very passive and seemingly hopeless situations that many young people with harmful sexual behaviours find themselves in following the discovery of their abuse.

Furthermore, Herrenkohl et al. (1994) identified four ways through which protective processes work to promote positive outcomes:

- By generating positive self esteem.
- By enhancing an internal locus of control.
- By increasing goal setting abilities.
- By increasing planning behaviours.

These four protective processes have, in my view, tremendous relevance for intervention with young people who have sexually abused others, who are often managed and controlled in such a way as to further limit their life opportunities and undermine their capacities to set their own goals and determine their own futures. The implication is that we should work directly to develop young people's self-esteem and social competence, let them set their own goals and targets and allow them to exercise safe levels of decision-making over decisions affecting them. While we focus on the ' big issue' of the abusive behaviours, it is all too easy to forget the small, but nonetheless significant, contributions we can make towards enhancing young people's own capacities to move forward from abuse. As Gilligan (2000: 45) concludes:

[Professionals] should remember that the detail of what they do with children counts. The rituals, the smiles, the interest in little things, the daily routines, the talents they nurture, the interests they stimulate, the hobbies they encourage, the friendships they support, the sibling ties they preserve make a difference. All of these little things may foster in a child the vital senses of belonging, or mattering, of counting . . . All of these little details may prove decisive turning points in a young person's developmental pathway. It is important not to be distracted or seduced only by the big questions. While, for example, professionals agonise or stall over whether or when to place a child in a permanent family, they may have lost sight of crucial details of what can sustain the positive development of this child today.

References

Ahmad, B. (1992) *Black Perspectives in Social Work.* Birmingham: Venture Press.

Burton, D. and Smith-Darden, J. (2000) *North American Survey of Sexual Abuser Treatment and Models. Summary Data.* Brandon VT: Safer Society Press.

Center for Sex Offender Management (1999) *Understanding Juvenile Sexual Offending Behavior: Emerging Research, Treatment Approaches and Management Practices,* Center for Sex Offender Management available at: http://www.csom.org/pubs/juvbrf10.html (accessed 15.02.06).

Farrington, D.P. and Welsh, B.C. (1999) Delinquency Prevention Using Family-based Interventions, *Children and Society,* 13, 287–303.

Featherstone, B. and Lancaster, E. (1997) Contemplating the Unthinkable: Men who Sexually Abuse Children. *Critical Social Policy*, 17: 4, 51–71.

Feilzer, M. and Hood, R. (2004) *Differences or Discrimination? The Summary of the Report on Minority Ethnic Young People in the Youth Justice System*. London: Youth Justice Board.

Fisher, D. and Beech, A. (1999) Current Practice in Britain with Sexual Offenders. *Journal of Interpersonal Violence*, 14: 3, 240–57.

Gilligan, R. (2000) Adversity, Resilience and Young People: The Protective Value of Positive School and Spare Time Experiences. *Children and Society*, 14, 37–47.

Gocke, B. (1995) Working with People who have Committed Sexual Offences: What Values Underpin the Behaviour and What Value Base are we Using in Attempting to Address It? In Williams, B. (Ed.) *Probation Values*. Birmingham: Venture Press.

Hackett, S. (2000c) Sexual Aggression, Diversity and the Challenge of Anti-oppressive Practice. *The Journal of Sexual Aggression*, 5: 1, 4–20.

Hackett, S. (2001) *Facing the Future. A Guide for Parents of Young People who have Sexually Abused*. Lyme Regis: Russell House Publishing.

Hackett, S., Masson, H. and Phillips, S. (2006) Exploring Consensus in Practice with Youth who are Sexually Abusive: Findings from a Delphi Study of Practitioner Views in the United Kingdom and the Republic of Ireland. *Child Maltreatment*, 11: 2, 146–56.

Hackett, S. (2006, in press) Towards a resilience-based intervention model for young people with harmful sexual behaviours. In Erooga, M. and Masson, H. (Eds.) *Children and Young People who Sexually Abuse Others: Challenges and Responses* (2nd Edition). London: Brunner Routledge.

Henderson, M. et al. (2002) Heterosexual Risk Behaviour among Young Teenagers in Scotland. *Journal of Adolescence*, 25, 483–94.

Herman, M. (2004) Forced to Choose: Some Determinants of Racial Identification in Multiracial Adolescents, *Child Development*, 75: 3, 730–48.

Herrenkohl, E.C., Herrenkohl, R.C. and Egolf, B. (1994) Resilient Early School-age Children from Maltreating Homes: Outcomes in Late Adolescence. *American Journal of Orthopsychiatry*, 64, 301–9.

Hird, J. and Morrison, T. (1996) Six Groupwork Interventions with Adolescent Sexual Abusers. *Journal of Sexual Aggression*, 2(1): 49–63.

Hoghughi, M., Bhate, S. and Graham, F. (1997) *Working with Sexually Abusive Adolescents*. London, Sage.

Jackson, S. and Martin, P. (1998) Surviving the Care System: Education and Resilience. *Journal of Adolescence*, 21: 569–83.

Longo, R. (2003). Emerging Issues, Policy Changes, and the Future of Treating Children with Sexual Behaviour Problems. *Annals of the New York Academy of Sciences*, 989, 502–14.

Lewis, A.D. (ed) (1999) *Cultural Diversity in Sexual Abuser Treatment: Issues and Approaches*. Brandon VT: The Safer Society Press.

Lundrigan, S. (2001) *Treating Youth who Sexually Abuse: An Integrated Multi-Component Approach*. New York: Haworth Press.

Luthar, S., Cicchetti, D. and Becker, B. (2000) The Construct of Resilience: A Critical Evaluation and Guidelines for Future Work. *Child Development*, 71: 3, 543–62.

Masson, H. and Hackett, S. (2003) A Decade on from the NCH Report (1992): Adolescent Sexual Aggression Policy, Practice and Service Delivery across the UK and Republic of Ireland. *Journal of Sexual Aggression* 9: 2, 109–24.

O'Halloran, M. et al. (2002) Psychological Profiles of Sexually Abusive Adolescents in Ireland. *Child Abuse and Neglect*, 26, 349–70.

Rich, S. (1998) A Developmental Approach to the Treatment of Adolescent Sexual Offenders, *Irish Journal of Psychology*, 17: 1, 102–18.

Ryan, G., Lane, S., Davies, J. and Isaac, C. (1987) Juvenile Sex Offenders: Development and Correction, *Child Abuse and Neglect*, 11, 385–95.

Ryan, G., Metzner, J.L. and Krugman, R.D. (1990) When the Abuser is a Child. The Assessment and Treatment of the Juvenile Sex Offender. In Oates, R.K. (ed.) *Understanding and Managing Child Sexual Abuse*. Marrickville: Harcourt, Brace and Jovanovich.

Ryan, G. et al. (1996) Trends in a National Sample of Sexually Abusive Youths. *Journal of the American Academy of Child and Adolescent Psychiatry*, 33, 17–25.

Ryan, G. (1999) Treatment of Sexually Abusive Youth: The Evolving Consensus. *Journal of Interpersonal Violence*, 14: 4: 422–36.

Saunders, B.E., Berliner, L. and Hanson, R.F. (Eds.) (2003) *Child Physical and Sexual Abuse:*

Guidelines for Treatment. (Final Report: January 15, 2003). Charleston: National Crime Victims Research and Treatment Center.

Savin-Williams, R.C. and Diamond, L.M. (2000) Sexual Identity Trajectories among Sexual-Minority Youths: Gender Comparisons. *Archives of Sexual Behavior*, 29: 6, 607–27.

Skär, R.N. (2003). Peer and Adult Relationships of Adolescents with Disabilities. *Journal of Adolescence*, 26: 6, 635–49.

Utting, D. and Vennard, J. (2000) *What Works with Young Offenders in the Community?* Barnardo's, Barkingside.

Vizard, E., Monck, E. and Misch, P. (1995) Child and Adolescent Sex Abuse Perpetrators: A Review of the Research Literature. *Journal of Child Psychology and. Psychiatry*, 36: 5, 731–56.

Wolf, S. (1984) A Multi-factor Model of Deviant Sexuality. Third International Conference on Victimology. Lisbon, Portugal, November 1984.

Worling, J. (2001) Personality Based Typology of Adolescent Male Sexual Offenders: Differences in Recidivism Rates, Victim-selection Characteristics, and Personal Victimisation Histories. *Sexual Abuse: A Journal of Research and Treatment*, 13: 3, 149–66.

Chapter 3

A Study of the Experiences of Black and Asian Young People Whose Behaviour is Sexually Harmful

Baseer Mir and Elleen Okotie

Introduction

In this chapter we will be focusing on a study we undertook to examine whether current models of practice in working with adolescent sexual offenders are adequately meeting the needs of offenders from Black and Asian cultures. The study was undertaken in partnership with the AIM Project based at the Youth Justice Trust in the North West.

The term Black is used to refer to those of African-Caribbean, African and dual heritage. It has been the experience of the authors who work in this field, that few Black and Asian offenders are referred for treatment services. Current literature in relation to adolescents who sexually abuse makes little reference, if at all, to the impact of ethnicity and culture on the work process.

Historically, approaches to the treatment of sex offenders have been one-dimensional, tending to view all sex offenders as a homogeneous group. Whilst more recently there appears to be some awareness of the impact of cultural diversity on treatment approaches, there remains a dearth of research which actually addresses this issue. This has far-reaching implications for the effectiveness of treatment for non-white offenders whose first language is not English.

Traditionally professionals have primarily applied a cognitive-behavioural model to working with adult abusers. This model has also been employed in the treatment of adolescent abusers. Whilst there have tended to have been and are merits in this approach, it has tended to have been applied in a Eurocentric way, giving little consideration to the cultural differences abusers bring to treatment. The abusers' experiences as non-white people living in a racist society and their differing experiences of family and culture cannot be separated out in the treatment process. To ignore the impact and influences they play denies who they are and can serve to reinforce their experiences of powerlessness.

As well as the models not reflecting cultural diversity, many of the practitioners in this area of work are white European and their perspectives are likely to differ greatly from those from minority cultural backgrounds. Whether or not considerations are made around ethnically sensitive practice is therefore very much dependent on the practitioner's level of awareness of how cultural issues influence the abuser's experiences and also their awareness of the need to integrate cultural diversity into treatment. Simon Hackett's (2000) paper goes some way to discussing this point within the context of anti-oppressive practice and a broader consideration appears in Chapter two of this volume.

> ... notions of 'anti-oppressive practice' and cultural competence remain underdeveloped in interventions with abusers.
>
> (Lewis, 1999 in Hackett, 2000: 5)

Further, Gahir and Garrett (1999) in looking at treatment provision specifically to Asian sex offenders whose language is not English, identifies that little is known about culturally appropriate treatment for sex offenders from minority groups. Also, they identify that little is known about the differences that exist within minority groups. This is an important point as what may be relevant for one minority group may not be applicable to others. Other issues raised by Gahir and Garrett (1999) were around intervention by professionals. They found that professionals were often lacking in confidence in how best to intervene when sexual abuse was identified in Asian families and also lacked confidence in working effectively with these families.

In examining the experiences of treatment for minority adult sex offenders on Sex Offender Treatment Programmes (SOTP) Patel and Lord (2001) found that the majority felt the programme met their treatment needs and that race and culture were not issues in relation to this. However, the material used and the cultural awareness of those that facilitated the programme was criticised. They concluded that there was value in some statistical analysis to examine these variables and the impact they might have on the response to treatment of ethnic minority offenders. An earlier paper by Cowburn (1996) makes reference to similar issues raised by Patel and Lord (2001).

An important factor in working with all adolescent sexual offenders is for practitioners to have an awareness of the power imbalance that exists in the client professional relationship. Where the abuser is from a minority group, this power differential is heightened (Sciarra 1999), particularly where the professional is white, which is invariably going to be the case. Sciarra (1999) also makes the point that whilst it is right to acknowledge the oppression experienced by minority offenders, professionals must also seek to empower clients to move them towards taking responsibility for their behaviour. Unless professionals begin to have some dialogue around the issues raised by cultural diversity in treatment, achieving best practice in this field will remain ad hoc.

Certainly it is encouraging to see that awareness of the need to provide a culturally sensitive service to sexual offenders is evolving. However, the research is limited and much of it is focused on adult ethnic minority sexual offenders. There is still much to explore and the need to identify the issues specific to adolescent sexual offenders from minority groups and their families is a clear example.

Method

The study involved three elements; interviews of young Black and Asian people; interviews with the parents or carers of those young people and interviews with professionals who have worked with Black and Asian young people whose sexual behaviour was abusive. The interviews of each group identified issues around culture and ethnicity as being of significance to differing degrees. The implications of this for practice will be discussed and possible reasons given for responses from young people who did not identify ethnically sensitive practice as an issue.

Very little is known about the experiences of treatment for adolescents from ethnic minorities who sexually abuse. The aim of the study was to identify ways in which service provision to this client group can be improved.

The intention of the study was to derive the sample from within the ten local authorities of the Greater Manchester area. It was expected that the number of young people fitting our criteria might be low as it was our experience that few are referred for treatment. However, the numbers generated were even lower than our initial expectations. This may be attributed, at least in part, to the very low response from the initial questionnaires sent out to professionals within Greater Manchester. In all, approximately 2,000 initial questionnaires were sent out across Greater Manchester, fewer than 50 were returned. In light of this the geographical boundary of the study was extended to include Bradford in West Yorkshire. This area had been previously identified as having had a number of convictions amongst Asian adolescents. In addition, contact was also made with other agencies in Greater Manchester known to provide a service to adolescent abusers. The overall poor response from agencies resulted in the study being of a much smaller scale than anticipated.

In order to get a picture of convictions of Black and Asian abusers, statistical data was gathered of convicted adolescent abusers from the Greater Manchester Police. It was the intention to gather this data spanning a five year period. Unfortunately this presented some problems because of the way in which data was collated. In addition, inconsistencies in how ethnic monitoring is recorded made the accuracy of the data questionable. Whilst some police statistics were obtained, for the reasons given, it was not felt that they would provide an accurate picture of the number of convicted sexual offenders of Black and Asian origin.

In an effort to identify numbers of cases outside the criminal justice system, contact was made with the child protection units in Greater Manchester. This however failed to identify any relevant cases.

The sample of young people

The sample was identified by sending out an initial brief questionnaire to all agencies within Greater Manchester known to provide a service to adolescent abusers. Prior to this some information had been sent out to these agencies informing them of the proposed study and requesting responses regarding their involvement with the specific client group we were focusing on. As stated, the low response prompted us to involve the Change Partnership in Bradford, West Yorkshire which identified a number of suitable candidates. It was expected that professionals who responded would identify relevant cases.

The total sample included eight young people, one of mixed race, the rest were of British Asian origin, between the ages of 13–17 years who had all been convicted and undertaken varying levels of work as part of their conviction. All were male.

Whilst a number of other cases were identified, some young people did not wish to participate in the study. In the main this was due to their involvement in services having ended, and a desire not to revisit their offences. Those who participated in the study were currently involved with professionals.

It was disappointing that the sample did not include any adolescents from African-Caribbean or African heritage. Although some similarities may exist between this group of young people and the experiences of Asian young people, there is still felt to be a gap left by not accessing this group.

Contact with the young people and their family was initially made by the professionals to gain their consent. Prior to interviews with the young person, an agreement was completed with them in line with NSPCC procedures.

The interviews lasted between 30 and 60 minutes and were semi-structured to enable responses to be quantified as well as allowing for other issues to be raised. The interviews were arranged at a mutually convenient venue but away from the young person's home.

The sample of parents and carers

This sample included four parents from the sample of young people interviewed and the older sister of one of the boys. In the latter case neither parent spoke much English so the sister played a significant role in the process regarding her brother.

The parents of the others in the sample did not wish to participate and in one case the young person lived away from home and did not wish his parents to be involved.

The sample of professionals

This included eleven professionals, five of whom were from the Youth Offending Teams within

Greater Manchester, four social workers which included one worker employed by Bradford SSD, and two NSPCC workers.

Prior to interviewing, the professionals completed a pre-interview questionnaire. This provided an opportunity to consider some of the core areas of the cases that would be discussed in interview.

The interviews were conducted using a semi-structured process and lasted between 1–4 hours. Some interviews took place over two meetings.

Findings

Young people

Six of the young people were charged with indecent assault whilst two had been charged with attempted rape.

The study focused on young people of a variety of ages and from different ethnic groups. All young people interviewed were male whose first language was English. The young people's ages ranged from 12–15 years. A breakdown of the ethnicity of the sample can be seen in the table below:

Table 3.1 Ethnic origin

Ethnicity	Number
Dual Heritage	1
Pakistani	5
Bangladeshi	2

Ethnicity of the worker

Half of the young people felt that if they had a worker from the same ethnic background as themselves they would have benefited. The young people identified that they would benefit in the following ways:

- They would not have to explain certain information to a worker of the same ethnic background relating to cultural and religious practices.

One young person stated '. . . with an Asian worker it would have been easier because he could understand what it is like for me as a young Asian man'.

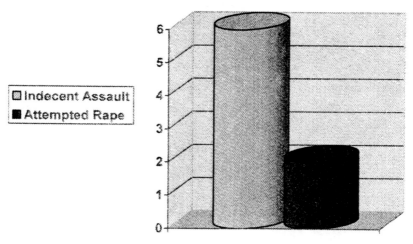

Figure 3.2   Nature of offence

Terminology – a worker of the same ethnicity would use language they could more easily understand e.g. less use of jargon and use of less complex words. For those young people who did not identify the need to have a worker of the same ethnicity the issues were:

- That a worker from the same ethnic background would not have made any difference.
- That it would have been more difficult to discuss sexual matters with someone of the same ethnic/faith background.

Impact of behaviour on family

In all the cases there were varying levels of shame identified. This related to:

- The impact on the immediate family of the extended family becoming aware of the offence.
- Shame felt by the young person at his father hearing what he'd done at the police enquiry stage.
- Shame was experienced by having professionals involved in the family. In one particular case the young person identified his sister's feeling of shame and embarrassment at having to accompany him to the police station.

The young person reported that his sister 'got a lot of hassle' for doing this.

In 50 per cent of the cases, there were imposed restrictions on the young person's movements. Also in all but one of the cases there was identified some emotional withdrawal for a period of time. Significantly one young person identified that some discussion with the family by professionals to help them understand his behaviour would have helped the family to respond more appropriately. In one case the incident resulted in a complete breakdown in the relationship between the young person's mother and her brother who is the father of the victim.

Choice of victim

In all but one of the cases the victim was white British. The victim who was non-white was the sibling of the perpetrator. Fifty per cent of the sample stated that choice of victim had nothing to do with ethnicity but was more about opportunity, accessibility to the victim as well as finding the victim attractive.

Twenty-five per cent of the sample identified that their choice of victim was influenced by stereotypical beliefs held about white girls being more readily available for sex. The remaining 25 per cent of the sample did not identify that there was a victim i.e. It was their view that no offence had been committed.

View of the quality of service received

Twenty-five per cent of the sample felt that they had received a good service and that some consideration had been given to their culture and ethnicity. The example given of this was that there were questions asked about their faith and the workers seemed to have some knowledge of their religion.

In only one case did the young person feel that no consideration was given to his culture or ethnicity in the course of the work. It was his view that he would not necessarily have found this beneficial. However, this young person did go on to state that he felt he had a lack of knowledge to be able to comment on how this issue would have made a difference.

The remaining young people identified that although they were happy with the service they received no consideration was made with regard to their ethnicity and culture and they would have found this helpful. Two stated that they felt they would have benefited from having a worker of the same ethnicity.

Parents and carers

The sample in this group totalled five. We focused on five specific areas in our interviews, the findings of which are discussed below.

1. Parents or carers awareness of the role of professionals involved and the process of the work.

Sixty per cent of parents or carers felt that they were aware of the role that professionals played and the process of intervention. The remaining 40 per cent felt that information was either not given or not shared in a way that was accessible to them.

2. Parents or carers level of participation

Eighty per cent of parents or carers were able to participate on some level. However, all reported that there were language difficulties for one or both parents. Also participation related more to attending initial interviews and ensuring that the young person attended appointments rather than undertaking any direct work themselves. One parent stated that '. . . it would have been helpful to have someone explain what would happen at court and what was being discussed, because they use long words don't they?'

Sixty per cent of parents or carers said that they would have welcomed support and input in respect of knowledge and information around what underpinned their child's behaviour.

3. Parents or carers view of their child's behaviour

Eighty per cent of parents or carers condemned their child's inappropriate behaviour. Responses included the expected reactions of anger and shame, and added to this were strong feelings in respect of religious/cultural teachings, which strongly condemn such behaviour.

The view of the remaining 20 per cent was that their child had not committed the offence.

4. Impact upon family following disclosure

As expected all families experienced a negative impact following disclosure. The degree of the impact was dependant upon who knew about the behaviour. Some parents/carers chose not to share information with family members due to concerns of being ostracised by both family and the local community.

5. Change in child's behaviour following professional intervention

Eighty per cent of the parents or carers interviewed identified some positive change in behaviour as a result of professional intervention. Examples of positive change include:

- Improvement in parent/child communication.
- Development of victim empathy.
- Actively participating in intervention.

In one case where change had been identified the parent/carer was unable to be specific as to the nature of that change. In relation to the remaining 20 per cent, although there was change in levels of aggression in the young person, the parent or carer did not attribute this to intervention.

Professionals

These results stem from interviews with 11 professionals. They were identified from a number of agencies, including youth offending team, social services department and NSPCC.

Note: A number of the young people referred to by the professionals in this section were not willing to participate in the study. This accounts for the disparity in the numbers of young people recorded in this section and that in the sample of young people interviewed.

Ethnicity of the professionals

The total number of professionals was 11, of which eight were white British females and the remaining three were Black and Asian.

Experience of working with young abusers and ethnicity

Only three professionals from the sample of 11 identified themselves as having a significant level of experience in working with young abusers. The majority of the sample identified themselves as having a low level of experience. In two cases workers reported having no prior experience. With regards to experience of working with ethnic groups 50 per cent of the sample reported having a high level of experience in working with ethnic groups, the remainder reported having had some experience, only one professional identified having no experience at all.

The significance of the value of having experience in working with different ethnic groups was illustrated in comments made by the professionals as follows:

I had no knowledge of the young person's cultural heritage therefore my Asian co-worker's role was crucial ... It helped the young person to engage actively and build up a good working relationship with us.

... the young person said having an Asian worker made him feel more comfortable and found the work genuinely useful ... I thought the work progressed and developed quicker due to having an Asian co-worker.

Engaging the family as part of the work programme

'... families benefit from having professionals working with them that they can relate to ...'

The majority of professionals reported that they were able to engage the family. However, the extent to which this was achieved was dependant upon the parents' ability to communicate and understand English. Some workers talked about their colleagues experiencing 'professional paralysis' when it came to working with black families in general. This was based on the fear of getting it wrong.

... Asian families tend to be suspicious of agencies ... sometimes this is justified based on their prior negative experiences.

... it was difficult to engage the family and to help them develop some understanding of his behaviour when working through an interpreter ... this affected how the family were able to support their child.

Families' response to intervention

Professionals reported a high level of response from the majority of families. Of those that were reported as having a low response to intervention, the reason cited for this was primarily language difficulties.

... the family have been very involved and very concerned for him and for the victim, they have been appalled and very upset at his behaviour.

... although the interpreter was from an interpreting service, he had no training around the issues and terminology of sexually abusive behaviour.

Differences identified when working with Black and Asian adolescent offenders

A number of differences were identified by the professionals interviewed which are detailed below:

- Issues around language:
  – The use of interpreters.
  – The need for simple English.
  – Young person able to use colloquialisms and terminology without explanation where worker of the same ethnic background.
    ... although the Asian young people were from third generation immigrant families, use of written and spoken English appeared to present some barriers.
- Discussions around sex, sexuality and sexual health were more difficult to discuss with Asian young people. There is a need to assess the appropriateness and context of this.
    ... Some of the young people I worked with preferred to have two male workers rather than a male and a female worker. They stated they found it difficult to discuss sexual matters in front of women.
- Black young people treated more harshly by the system and may have been subject to racial abuse, which needs to be taken into account.
- Family of young person likely to be more responsive if the worker is from same ethnic background.

. . . found the experience of working alongside an Asian worker very useful in terms of how they were able to engage the family.

- Black and Asian young people may have additional stereotyping around white young women.
- Where one worker is from the same ethnic background as the young person the burden is put upon them to educate their white co-worker in relation to racial and cultural issues.

Cultural and religious considerations made

Professionals identified a number of considerations made which included:

- The use of an interpreter when working with the family.
- Ensuring appointment times did not clash with times of worship and or festivals.
- Having a co-worker from the same ethnic background as a young person.
  . . . it was clear to me that the young person could relate to the Asian worker which had a positive impact on his level of participation.
- Having an awareness of the additional power imbalance that exists for Black and Asian young people.
- A longer period of engagement to establish a trusting working relationship.

Difficulties encountered in the course of the work

These included:
- Lack of cultural and religious awareness.
- Difficulty in discussing sexual matters with young person and family.
- Where interpreters were used the worker was not always confident that sexual terms were translated accurately. This was of particular difficulty where the interpreter was female.
  . . . sometimes felt that the interpreter struggled to share with the family some of the more sensitive issues around the young person's sexual behaviour.
- Added fears around the community finding out and implications for the family of this.
  . . . the family did not want me to bring an interpreter . . . preferring to use a family member instead.

Consultation

All of the professionals identified that some form of consultation would have been helpful. However, the majority reported that they did not have access to this. Professionals identified that consultation would have been useful on issues relating to culture, religion, family dynamics as well as specifics around working with adolescent sex offenders.

Did ethnicity play a role in the choice of victim?

In 50 per cent of the cases ethnicity was felt to have been a factor in the choice of victim. This figure however, could be greater than this as in 25 per cent of the cases the worker and young person were unable to identify whether it played a role or not.

Completion rate

In over 50 per cent of the cases the work was completed, in the remaining cases the work was not completed due to a variety of reasons which included; order expiring, young person had moved area, or the work was still ongoing. In the cases where the work was completed professionals felt that there was a reduction in the level of risk.

Professional learning

Professionals identified that they would have made a number of changes and considerations in future work, and these included the following;

- More planning in respect of making the work culturally sensitive.
- Ensured a co-worker was in place.
- Would seek to have in place a co-worker of the same ethnicity as the young person.
- Consultation from a specialist Black service i.e. Pakistani resource centre.
- Undertake identity work with young person prior to abuse-focused work.
- Learn to speak and understand Asian languages and dialects.
- Where groupwork was part of the programme of work, to consider more carefully the appropriateness of having only one Black or Asian group member.

Discussion

In discussing service delivery to Black and Asian young people it is impossible to do this without reference to the impact of institutionalised racism. The insidious nature of institutionalised racism within organisational structures was clearly highlighted in the Macpherson Report (1999). What this form of racism does if not recognised and challenged is continue to perpetrate the marginalisation of minority groups by the dominant culture (Lewis, 1999). In terms of how this presents itself in practice, standards and principles of practice are very much guided by the dominant culture that holds the balance of power. Where institutionalised racism exists in organisations, what is often seen is a eurocentric approach to practice. Brislin (1990, in Lewis, 1999, p5) provides a useful definition of ethnocentrism, '. . . the process of using standards from one's own cultural background to judge and draw conclusions about people from other cultures'. The assumption that Western theoretical models and psychometric tools are equally applicable to those from other cultures reflects at worst arrogance and at the very least short-sightedness, and has a massive consequence in terms of offenders' ability to fully benefit from treatment (Gahir and Garrett, 1999). It also has implications for the conclusions drawn from assessment and treatment tools used. An example of this is the exclusion of adult sexual offenders from Sex Offender Treatment Programmes (SOTP) because IQ was assessed to be below the 'normal range'. Groth-Marnat (1990, in Patel and Lord, 2001) argues that those from ethnic minorities who have come out with lower scores have been disadvantaged because of the cultural bias in the test instruments.

Other considerations for professionals include how religion and spirituality are addressed. None of the existing models address these areas and yet they are significant for many Black and Asian families. These areas play a role in the practical sense in terms of ensuring appointments and other meetings not being at significant times i.e. times of worship. Also, the young person's beliefs and/or those of their family will influence their ability to be open about particular issues.

Given what is known about the impact of racism (Vincenti, 1999) treatment of non-white offenders may need to incorporate work on identity. Whilst identity is of importance for all young people, it has particular significance for ethnic minorities, particularly those of dual heritage, because of the impact racism can have on their identity formation (DoH, 2000; Lewis 1999 and Hopkinson (undated). As professionals, we need to try and move towards a real understanding of the experience of minority groups to be able to empathise with them whilst also helping them to take responsibility for their behaviour and empowering them to make change.

A number of distinct themes have emerged from the results of the three groups interviewed. These are as follows:

1. The experience of the professionals
2. Ethnicity of the worker
3. Impact on the family
4. Language
5. Choice of victim
6. Sex and sexuality
7. Consultation

These themes will be discussed below.

Whilst we cannot comment as fully as we would have liked to about the experiences of Black African-Caribbean and African young people some inferences can be drawn from the data gathered. In the main, the findings will relate to Asian young abusers.

1. The experience of professionals

The study highlighted the importance for professionals not only to have key training with regard to issues around sexually abusive behaviour, but equally important is training with regard to working with clients from diverse communities. It has been established that Black clients do have different needs from White clients when entering the therapeutic process (Hampton, 1987). This could be argued to be no less the case in relation to treatment services for sexual abusers from minority groups, thus in order for treatment to be most effective, this must be a consideration in the treatment process.

The study found that many of the professionals embarked upon work with adolescent abusers with very little and sometimes no formal training in both the area of working with perpetrators of sexual abuse and diversity. Coupled with this, some of these professionals also found that they were supervised by managers who themselves had little or no experience in these areas.

With regard to how cases were allocated, this tended to be on the basis of the interest of the worker or a perception of 'expertise' because the worker may have had one prior experience of doing the work. Where a young person was allocated a worker who was experienced in the field of sexually abusive behaviour and either knowledgeable about cultural issues relating to non-white clients or themselves were of the same ethnicity as the young person, this appeared in many cases to be due more to luck rather than design.

Appropriate and quality training in the area of sexually abusive behaviour and ethnically sensitive practice are key to providing effective treatment programmes to minority groups. Training in regards to anti-oppressive practice and working with minority clients and their families should not be a 'one-off' exercise but part of a continuous process of the practitioner's development. It is important to note that such training should be prioritised for all practitioners, black and white, as it is presumptuous to assume that black practitioners have all the answers.

Training on issues around race and culture remains an issue that many white workers continue to shy away from addressing in any real sense. 'Although many professionals are aware that it is essential to take account of race and culture and in particular to be culturally sensitive in their practice, they are often at a loss to translate this into practical terms' (Assessment Framework, 2001: p38). There is no doubt that it is a subject that raises uncomfortable feelings and strong emotion on both sides, for Black and White workers. The way forward on this is for senior managers across agencies to prioritise relevant training which will support the work of practitioners in the field.

. . . cultural competence thus requires systemic initiatives that not only promote and nurture change at all levels within a given setting but also measure its impact and effectiveness.

(Lewis, 1999: 23)

The experiences of the Black professionals interviewed who felt that they were sometimes perceived as the expert on issues around culture and also felt the burden of having to 'educate' their White colleagues, further illustrates the importance of 'cultural competence' being prioritised within agencies.

Minority professionals may be concerned that they are expected unconditionally to have a breadth and depth of cultural knowledge.

(Lewis, 1999: 11)

2. Ethnicity of the worker

On initial discussion with the sample of young people interviewed about the ethnicity of their workers, 50 per cent of them identified that it had not made a difference. However, that said they were clearly able to identify benefits to having a worker of the same ethnicity.

There could be a number of reasons for the responses of the 50 per cent who did not feel the ethnicity of the worker was significant. We considered that the age and life experiences of the young people interviewed could have an impact on their ability to make an analysis of this issue. Whilst they may have experienced racism and inequality in different areas of their life, they may not be at a stage of awareness where they are conscious of the impact this has upon them. Cross (1971) suggests that the development of Black identity formation is characterised by the progression through five stages; pre-encounter, encounter, immersion-emersion, internalisation and internalisation-commitment. Each stage identifies the process through which a Black individual will progress from denial of the existence of racism at the pre-encounter stage, to the individual coming to accept their Black identity and feeling more comfortable with this. Depending upon where the Black and Asian young people interviewed are on this continuum will impact upon their ability to recognise the relevance of the ethnicity of the professional.

Identity formation and the role it can play in the treatment process is also relevant for white professionals. Helms (1990) provides a useful model of white racial awareness development. The white person may either get stuck at a certain stage or progress through the stages towards the White individual attaining an appreciation of cultural differences.

The stage which the professional is at will influence their ability to recognise the impact of racism and could therefore impinge upon their ability to value and work with difference.

In discussions with the young people who felt the ethnicity of the professional was important, the issue of understanding of language and having a common understanding of cultural and religious practices seemed to be significant. Issues which came into play here seemed to be an affinity held by minority groups which may be linked to their common experience of racism and oppression. Also due to this common understanding, the ability to openly discuss those aspects of their culture or religion that are significantly different to that of the dominant culture, without fear of ridicule or misinterpretation. Added to this, not having to explain aspects relating to culture and religion may better facilitate the engagement process.

Similarly, the experiences of the young people, professionals and parent/carers highlighted the positives and advantages of having a worker from the same ethnicity as the service users.

Black and Asian professionals interviewed also cited the benefits of the above. However, some felt that the experience for themselves could sometimes be negative due to them being perceived as the expert in all aspects of the work i.e. language, culture and religion.

We do not seek to suggest that minority clients should in all cases only have a worker of the same ethnicity. In some cases, as was the case with some of the sample group of young people, minority clients may prefer a worker not from the same cultural background because of perceptions they might have about how their behaviour may be viewed.

They may also perceive that their confidentiality will be compromised. Clearly, White professionals with knowledge around sexual abuse and cultural diversity in treatment would be able to provide an effective service to this client group.

3. Impact on the Family

The benefits of including the family in the work with the perpetrators are well documented in respect of the overall effectiveness of the work programme. In the past it has been suggested that Black and Asian families do not take seriously the issue of sexual abuse. Lachman (1996, in Gahir and Garrett, 1999) makes the point that cultural attitudes towards child sexual abuse vary a great deal. It is our experience that sexual abuse is condemned by Black communities as is illustrated in our findings.

All families will experience some adverse impact from sexual abuse, particularly where the perpetrator is a family member. One of the major

concerns reported by family members in the sample was that of shame, which falls into two categories. The first category is with regard to reducing the family's standing in the community, which in itself has far-reaching implications for the family. These implications are discussed below. The second category is the shame of having people from outside of the community involved in 'family matters' linked together with historical mistrust of white 'helping' agencies. Pierce and Pierce (1984, in Gahir and Garrett, 1999: 97) suggest that 'blacks in need of help do not easily trust outsiders'. Also contributing to this is the response of the professional particularly as noted in the 'Results' section.

Given that the family unit is an integral part of many Black people's lives which in turn carries the ability to influence those within the family, the importance and relevance of considering the impact upon the family becomes clear.

The implications of the community finding out about their child's sexualised behaviour can be devastating to the family, although it can be argued that this would be the same for any family regardless of ethnicity. There are, however, clear additional factors that arise. These factors include:

- Being ostracised by the local community. If one of the main sources of support is the community within which you live, then experiences of marginalisation and isolation will be increased.
- The potential in particular for daughters to become unmarriageable following a disclosure of abuse regardless of sexual abuse occurring within or outside of the family. The same would apply to male members of the family but perhaps to a lesser extent.
- The extra responsibility placed upon the family of bringing shame on the whole community due to their child's behaviour.

4. Language

All three groups who participated in the study reported that language played an important role in the facilitation of the work. In relation to the accessibility of information, some parents reported that information was presented in a form not accessible to them, in that they were unable to either understand spoken English or read written English. Although some professionals did report that they did use the services of interpreters, or family members, the effectiveness of them seemed to be limited.

The solution to the problem of language may at first glance seem simple, i.e. always use interpreters when the family's first language is not English and have all written material translated into the mother-tongue. However, in a limited-resource environment the use of translators and interpreters seldom occurs and this may not always be appropriate in all cases. We should strive to make information accessible to all service users but the question arises as to the best way to do this.

Written material on the subject of sexual abuse is actually very difficult to translate accurately into Asian languages as some of the terminologies do not have direct translations, often requiring a series of words to get somewhere near the original meaning. For example, Gahir and Garrett (1999, 100) found that 'no word exists for "rape" in Punjabi although the act obviously exists. Rape therefore had to be translated as . . . forced sex . . . but obviously "forced sex" and 'rape' are not really synonymous'.

Producing translations that are accurate and contextual is expensive and time-consuming. Given the many tens of dialects that exist within the same language, one has to question not only the appropriateness of this but also the meaningfulness of this to the target audience.

In respect of interpreters, there are a number of important factors to consider, perhaps one of the most important being identifying an appropriate one. Within the Asian communities, many different languages are spoken. Therefore employing an Asian interpreter for an Asian family does not necessarily mean that they will speak the same language. This may seem an obvious point to some yet it is our experience that professionals have made these errors. The study found that some professionals did not trust that what they were saying was being interpreted accurately. This may have been for a number of reasons such as the interpreter not being familiar with the terminology, words, or phrases about sexualised behaviour, the interpreter feeling that the sexual language needs to be softened either due to their own feelings or in consideration for those present, particularly females or because the interpreter was not pre-briefed about the sensitive and sometimes harrowing nature of the work.

Connected to this is the issue of gender of the interpreter. The use of female interpreters can lead to the difficulties mentioned above, particularly if they are relaying the information to a male. Cowburn and Modi (1995, in Gahir and Garrett, 1999: 100) noted that 'sexual matters are taboo for discussion outside of marriage, since the language is either academic or viewed as obscene'. The authors also recommend that only male workers should become involved in discussion of sexual material with Asian males. This could equally apply to interpreters. Some professionals reported using family members as interpreters. The potential for this to fail, apart from the factors already mentioned, increases as family members are unlikely to be able to relay accurately information about a family member's sexually abusive behaviour to other family members due to a sense of respect and embarrassment towards their family.

When a professional is of the same ethnic origin as the perpetrator, there are obvious benefits, however as Gahir and Garrett (1999, p100) found: 'the Punjabi speaking therapist was forced to adopt a dual role of interpreter and therapist and breaks for translation tended to interrupt the flow of the session and to be time-consuming'. Further, it should be remembered that professionals who are of the same ethnicity as the perpetrators are not trained interpreters therefore where necessary, support in this area should be made available.

Finally, in respect of interpreters, the question as to whether or not a family wants an interpreter to be involved arises. Some families prefer interpreters not to be used, even though there may be a need for one because of fears that confidentiality may be compromised. This anxiety is related to the close-knit nature of Asian communities which means it may be more likely that an interpreter would know the family or someone connected to the family. Due to this real fear, the use of interpreters from a source other than the local community should be considered.

5. Choice of victim

In the majority of cases in the sample of young people interviewed and also identified in the interviews with professionals, the victims were white females not previously known to the perpetrator.

Given that admitting to ethnicity playing a part in the choice of victim can be extremely difficult to do, for the young people who were unable to do this it may be the case, that they were unwilling rather than unable to identify this.

There are a number of reasons why this may be, including:

- **Ethnicity of the worker** Disclosing whether ethnicity played a part or not to a white worker if the victim was white would be difficult and more difficult again if the worker was of the same gender as the victim.
- **Stereotypes and distorted thinking** Black and Asian people, like any other peoples, have stereotypes, however many would not admit to them. Some may not recognise these stereotypes and the associating distorted thinking. We have deliberately distinguished between stereotypes and distorted thinking which is discussed further on.
- **Implications for others** Obviously all Black and Asian people do not choose white victims but there may be a fear about this becoming the common perception should one disclose that ethnicity played a part in their choice of victim.

Returning to the subject of stereotypes and distorted thinking, clearly generally held stereotypes about groups of people, in this case white British, form the foundation of distorted thinking. Professionals may need to consider how factors such as race, culture and religion influence the development of distorted thinking. Below are listed two areas which, either separately or combined, may serve to aid distorted thinking.

Stereotypes about White British people in general, these include:

- White British people have sex before marriage.
- White British people do not adhere to a strict moral code.
- White British people like showing parts of their body off.
- Young White British people do not have any restrictions placed upon their movements or who they mix with.
- When White British people drink, they always get drunk and lose their sexual inhibitions.
- White British people are sexually promiscuous.

Religious and cultural teachings

Broadly speaking there are distinct differences and practices between Asian and white communities. Intentionally, we have chosen not to detail all of these differences; however, what follows are the relevant differences, which, when linked with the above-mentioned stereotypes may aid distorted thinking:

- *Dress code* – Muslims in particular tend to follow a distinct dress code, the difference particularly in females is that most parts of the body are covered i.e. legs, arms, stomach and cleavage tend not to be exposed.
- *Contact between males and females* – again referring to Muslim communities, there would be limited acceptable physical contact between male and females. We are not here referring to contact between direct family members such as mothers, sisters or aunts, rather, the emphasis here is on contact between males and females who could potentially engage in an intimate relationship.
- *Sex before marriage* – as is the case in many religions, is not permitted. Generally speaking, within the Asian community this would still be condemned, therefore any intimate relationship, whether sexual or not would be covert.

6. Sex and sexuality

In any discussion around sex, a good starting point is to have an understanding of what the normative sexual behaviour is within the culture of the individual (Lewis, 1999).

We know that for all young people who sexually abuse one of the difficult aspects of treatment is discussing the sexual element of their behaviour. As professionals we understand this and take pains to be sensitive as to how this is discussed with the young person. It was anticipated that this subject would present additional difficulties for Black and Asian young people. This is supported in the study and in existing literature. There are a number of differences that present themselves when addressing the subject of sex and sexuality with those from minority groups. For instance, there is considerable variance across cultures about the degree to which sexual activity is permitted or which issues about sex are discussed within families (Miller and Dreger, 1973, in Lewis, 1999). Lewis (1999) found that in Native American families, to discuss sexual issues was considered a cultural taboo. Our research found that this is very similar in many Asian families though to a lesser extent with African-Caribbean families, particularly those that hold strong religious beliefs. The added element of one's religious beliefs can act as a further inhibitor to discussing sexual matters in treatment. Many African-Caribbean families with religious backgrounds will promote sexual behaviour only in marriage. This is very much the same for Asian families. For an Asian young man to admit to sexual activity outside of marriage is in serious contravention of their religious teaching. This, along with the shame their behaviour would bring upon the family, can make it extremely difficult for them to admit their behaviour.

Historically, the approach to working with sexual abusers has been that it should be male/female co-worked. Whilst this approach has its merits it is not always relevant in all cases, for both White and non-White clients. An assessment should be made as to the appropriateness of co-working and also the gender of the worker or workers. Cowburn and Modi (1995: 100) identified that 'Asian males may find it particularly difficult and distressing to discuss sexual matters in the presence of a woman' (from Gahir and Garrett, 1999: 100).

Again, we do not wish to suggest that female professionals should not work with Asian offenders just as one would not suggest that men should not work with female victims of abuse. The issue is raised so that professionals are mindful of the impact of additional dynamics that may exist in the treatment process where one or both workers are female.

An issue which is particularly pertinent to those from African-Caribbean cultures is that of sexuality which is considered to be outside of the norm. There is still considerable taboo attached to same sex encounters within Black communities (Lewis, 1999: Hopkinson (undated)). This stigma which has its roots, at least in part, from religious beliefs and homophobia can present difficulties for young abusers from African-Caribbean backgrounds admitting their behaviour to themselves and their family. For Black young men who may already feel like outsiders in the wider society because of their experiences of racism, to admit to something which they perceive may alienate them from their own

community presents a very high risk and perhaps in the minds of some, one not worth taking.

7. Consultation

All of the professionals interviewed identified that the availability of consultation would have been an invaluable resource. Consultation can be useful for a myriad of issues, specifically in relation to working with Black and Asian young people. It is helpful to be able to tap into expertise about cultural-specific issues around family dynamics, the relationship between sex and faith, the wider impact of sexual abuse within Black and Asian families, as well as issues around theory and practice in the treatment of sexual abusers. Resources are limited and as is identified in the study, workers and sometimes their managers are not always confident about the issues which come into play when working with this client group.

Seeking consultation should not be seen as a failure on the part of managers but a step towards seeking to achieve best practice and effective services to all groups.

Conclusions

In undertaking this study, we set out firstly to examine how far current practice meets the needs of adolescent sexual abusers of Black and Asian ethnicity. We also wanted to begin to identify how practice could begin to incorporate a diverse perspective.

The initial part of the study whereby we sought to identify our sample groups proved to be more difficult than we had anticipated. Consequently, the sample of young people is lower than desired. We were hoping to interview at least twenty young people. Also the sample was not as diverse as we would have preferred. The same can also be said for the sample of parents and carers. It had also been intended to interview a number of Black adolescents, that is those of African-Caribbean or African heritage, recognising that some of the issues may be different for this group. It is unfortunate that we were unable to access any young people from this ethnic group although we are aware some have received convictions for sexual offences. This remains an area that needs exploration.

In recent years we have seen a number of changes in approaches to working with adolescent sexual abusers. There is recognition that the treatment of adolescents should not be approached in the same way as that with adults. Also, significantly, there is an understanding that adolescents' inappropriate sexual behaviour should not be dealt with in isolation to other issues which may relate to the behaviour. It is the generally held view that adolescent sexual abusers benefit much more from a holistic approach to treatment which also involves the family in the treatment process. Whilst there is an acknowledgement of the pressures some professionals may experience with heavy caseloads and limited resources, there is a need in this area of work particularly to provide a service that can effect change and thereby reduce risk.

The diversity of client group goes beyond Black and Asian young people, indeed in some areas it has begun to include refugees from parts of Europe, not to mention the impact of gender and disability. It is clearly identified in the study that professionals must at least have a basic foundation of knowledge and training before embarking upon work with adolescent sexual offenders. Alongside this, professionals should also seek through training and accessing relevant resources, to develop an understanding of what they need to consider in working with young people and their families from minority groups. This should also involve some self-examination. We do not expect that professionals become experts (McGoldrick et al., 1982: in Lewis, 1999) but are at least mindful of and strategic about how they may need to approach a piece of work differently where the young person is of a different ethnicity. It was apparent in our interviews with professionals, that some used their own initiative to 'educate' themselves on issues around culture and were sensitive to how they could best empower the young person and their family. Until senior managers see the need for strategic approaches in working with adolescent sexual offenders from minority groups, best practice will continue in an ad hoc way.

One of the ways of effecting real change in service provision is to canvas the views of those that use the service. One of the key issues identified by both the young people and their families is in relation to language and its impact on the accessibility of information to parents and on the young people's ability to fully participate in the treatment process. It may be that in some cases an interpreter is needed but this can present its own difficulties as discussed.

Professionals should be particularly mindful of how they use language and also use of language in their recording so that what is shared is user-friendly. Another issue for consideration is in relation to the possible impact on the family of the young person's sexual behaviour. Whilst it is acknowledged that all families will experience some adverse consequences, it is important to have an awareness of how this can be compounded for Black and Asian young abusers and their families. This can make all the difference during the initial period of engagement between concluding that a young person does not want intervention and being prepared to extend the period of engagement to work with the young person and their family on their fears and anxieties. This also includes endeavouring to identify appropriate support networks.

Issues in relation to the choice of victim exist at a number of different levels. The relevance of this should be individually assessed. We do not seek to suggest that victims of Black and Asian adolescent abusers are targeted for the same reason. Areas like this would benefit from specialist consultation to explore how best to address it with the young person where it is identified as an issue.

Having identified some of the issues in relation to working with diversity, it is useful to have some strategies for addressing them. Alvin (1999, 65) provides a good starting point:

1. Be an explorer; be willing to form hypotheses and test them.
2. Be open to consulting with colleagues who are familiar with an offender's culture.
3. Understand that the offender and their family will need to teach the therapist about some aspects of their culture.
4. Ask about the obvious if you do not understand it (e.g. why do Muslim women cover their bodies?).
5. Use an interpreter, if necessary, to help with the language and as an expert on the culture.
6. Remain aware that some communication styles and therapeutic techniques will be more effective than others in cross-cultural work.
7. Be aware of subjects that are taboo and bring them up only when the client seems ready to discuss them.
8. Learn to appreciate and work with the offender's natural helping system and indigenous healers when appropriate.

9. Honour and respect cultural diversity and differences.
10. Increase awareness and understanding of the contributions of various cultures.

Although this is a small scale study, it is the only piece of research to our knowledge that looks specifically at the experiences and issues for Black and Asian adolescent sexual abusers. Clearly the findings cannot be generalised for all Black and Asian young abusers and caution should be exercised in drawing out too many conclusions. We are also mindful that the points raised within the themes identified could apply to white perpetrators of sexual abuse. It is our view that for Black and Asian perpetrators there are added dynamics which compound the impact of sexually abusive behaviour. It is hoped that this study will raise some of the pertinent issues for this client group and create a starting point for dialogue amongst practitioners.

References

Camp, B. et al. (1993) Treatment of Adolescent Sex Offenders: A Review of Empirical Research. *The Journal of Applied Social Sciences*, 17, 2.

Charles, G. and McDonald, M. (1997) Adolescent Sexual Offenders. *The Journal of Child and Youth Care*, 11: 1, 15–25.

Cowburn, M. (1996) The Black Male Sex Offender in Prison: Images and Issues. *The Journal of Sexual Aggression* 2: 2, 122–42.

Cowburn, M. and Modi, P. (1995) Justice in an Unjust Context: Implications for Working with Adult Male Sex Offenders. In Ward, D. and Lacey, M. (Eds.) *Probation: Working for Justice.* London: Whiting and Birch.

Cross, W.E. (1971) The Negro to Black Conversion Experience: Towards a Psychology of Black Liberation. *Black World.* 20: 9, 13–27.

DoH et al. (2000) *Framework for the Assessment of Children in Need and Their Families.* London: The Stationery Office.

Gahir, M. and Garrett, T. (1999) Issues in the Treatment of Asian Sexual Offenders. *The Journal of Sexual Aggression*, 4: 2, 94–104.

Hackett, S. (2000) Sexual Aggression, Diversity and the Challenge of Anti-oppressive Practice. *The Journal of Sexual Aggression* 5: 1, 4–20.

Hampton, R.L. (1987) *Violence in the Black Family: Correlates and Consequences.* Lexington, MA: Lexington Books.

Helms, J. (1990) (Ed) *Black and Ethnic Racial Identity.* London: Greenwood Press.

Hopkinson, J. (undated) Some Thoughts on Working with Sex Offenders and Racial Difference. *NOTA News*, 13, 18–22.

Lewis, A. (1999) *Cultural Diversity in Sexual Abuser's Treatment.* New York: Safer Society Press.

Macpherson, W. Sir (1999) *Stephen Lawrence Enquiry.* London: Home Office.

Patel, K. and Lord, A. (2001) Ethnic Minority Sex Offenders, Experiences of Treatment. *The Journal of Sexual Aggression* 7: 1, 40–50.

Postlethwaite, J. (1998) A Critical Approach to Working with Young Abusers. *NOTA News*, 28.

Sciarra, D.T. (1999) Assessment and Treatment of Adolescent Sex Offenders: A Review from a Cross-cultural Perspective. *The Journal of Offender Rehabilitation*, 28: 3–4, 103–18.

Vincenti, D. (1999) *NSPCC Services to Ethnic Minority Children and their Families.* London: NSPCC.

Chapter 4

Using Typologies to Individualise the Assessment, Treatment, and Supervision of Sexually Abusive Youth

Tom Leversee

Introduction

In my approximately 25 years of experience working with juveniles who have committed sexual offences, the field has evolved a great deal. Recidivism research with juveniles has contradicted the old assumption that 'once a sex offender, always a sex offender'. There is a research-based consensus that sexually abusive youth are more amenable to treatment than adults and that successful completion of treatment can significantly reduce recidivism among young offenders (ATSA, 2000). We have learned that juveniles who commit sexual offences are a heterogeneous population who differ on a wide range of characteristics including types of offending behaviours, history of child maltreatment, social and interpersonal skills and relationships, sexual knowledge and experiences, academic and cognitive functioning, and mental health issues (Righthand and Welch, 2002). Significant progress has been made in the identification of typologies and the formulation of empirically guided risk assessment instruments.

The heterogeneity of this population has informed us as to the need for treatment and supervision to be tailored to individual offenders. A 'one-size fits all' approach is neither appropriate nor effective. Our challenge is to protect community safety by identifying, treating, and effectively managing those youth at highest risk to re-offend while at the same time facilitating low to moderate risk youth in returning to a more normative path of development. Typology research offers an essential conceptual and empirical foundation for understanding the diversity that exists among juveniles who commit sexual offences. To the degree that we are able to understand subtype specific risks, treatment needs, and outcomes, clinical practice and policy formulation can be further refined. This would provide increasing empirical support for determining amenability to treatment, the appropriate focus for intervention, and the required level and intensity of

supervision and clinical intervention (Hunter, 2001a).

This chapter will summarise some of the significant typology research and delineate four subtypes of sexually abusive youth according to clinical characteristics. Evaluation and ongoing assessment is addressed with a focus on identifying evaluation methods that can aid in differentiating subtype specific supervision and treatment needs. Subtype specific treatment is discussed with an emphasis on individualised areas of focus and skill development.

Delineating subtypes of sexually abusive adolescents

O'Brien and Bera (1986) developed one of the most utilised early typologies of adolescent offenders, consisting of seven categories. Each category describes the youth's behaviour and considers motivational, psychological, and situational factors that contribute to the sexual offending behaviour. The categories range from the younger adolescent attempting to explore and experiment with developing sexual feelings to the adolescent who displays an acute disturbance of reality testing and has a history of psychological, family and substance abuse problems, which contribute to more aggressive sexual behaviour.

More recent typology research has resulted in similar findings that allow for grouping sexually abusive youth according to clinical characteristics. The following summarises this research and presents four major subtypes of sexually abusive youth.

Social and interpersonal deficits

Becker (1988) described the youth whose impaired social and interpersonal skills result in his turning to younger children for sexual gratification and social interaction. Hunter et al. (2003) delineated differences between sexually abusive youth who offend against prepubescent children and those who target pubescent females, with those who offended against children being characterised by deficits in psychosocial functioning. In comparison to offenders of pubescent females, these youth were found to be less aggressive in their sexual offending, more likely to offend against victims to whom they were related, less likely to be under the influence of drugs or alcohol at the time of the sexual offence, and less likely to use a weapon.

The greater deficits in psychosocial functioning supported findings that suggested a lack of social confidence and associated depression and anxiety (Hunter et al., 2003). Many of these youth tend to perceive themselves as socially inadequate and expect to be ridiculed and rejected by their peers. This sense of social alienation is associated with feelings of sadness and loneliness, a dependency on adults, and a preference for the company of young children. These may be youth who lack the self-confidence and social skills to successfully attract and interpersonally engage same age females. Hunter et al. (2003: 42) states that, 'this is consistent with the clinical interpretation that the sexual offending of many of these youth reflects compensatory social behaviour and an attempt to satisfy unmet intimacy needs'.

In contrast to Hunter's findings, Worling (2001) found that subtype membership was unrelated to the victim's age or gender. He delineated two subtypes that are characterised by issues related to social and interpersonal difficulties. The Overcontrolled/Reserved youth endorse pro-social attitudes, are cautious to interact with others, and tend to keep their feelings to themselves. They may initiate offending behaviours, in part, as a result of their shy and rigid interpersonal orientation, which may result in limited access to intimate interpersonal relationships. Worling described the Unusual/Isolated youth as emotionally disturbed and insecure. These youth are characterised by a peculiar presentation and social isolation. The development and maintenance of a healthy and intimate sexual relationship with a consenting peer may be particularly problematic for these offenders given their awkward personality features.

One youth with whom this author worked described experiencing a difficult time fitting in and didn't always feel accepted by youth his age. He expressed considerable feelings of rejection, issues around self-esteem and self-concept, and

what he described as a 'deep and unmet need for love and acceptance'. As he became sexually mature and interested in females, he reported that he did not feel adequate to pursue same age relationships for fear of being rejected. He engaged in sexually abusive behaviour with his siblings who he perceived to be 'safe'. He also reported that accessing pornography and exposing himself was 'safer' and kept 'relationships at a distance'.

Youth characterised by social and interpersonal deficits may identify core beliefs such as: nobody likes me; I'm a reject; no girl my own age will go out with me; I will never have any friends; and I am afraid of not being accepted. One youth addressed one of the motivations underlying his sexually abusive behaviour as, 'I had no friends . . . I think it kept me depressed and made me want to feel better about myself'. When asked to identify risky feelings as part of relapse prevention planning, these youth have endorsed feelings such as rejected, unloved, insecure, inadequate, lonely, and sad.

Antisocial

Becker (1988) described the anti-social youth whose sexual offending behaviour is one aspect of a more generalised pattern of exploiting others. Hunter et al. (2003) found that offenders of peers and adults appear to be more violent and generally criminal in behaviour. These youth's offences are less influenced by psychosocial deficits. In comparison to offenders against children, these youth were more likely to:

- Sexually offend against females.
- Use force, and a higher level of force than offenders of children.
- Offend against victim with whom they are not related.
- Be under the influence of drugs or alcohol at the time of the sexual offence.
- Use a weapon.

Worling (2001) described the Antisocial/ Impulsive youth as likely to have a propensity for rule violations and their sexual offending may, at least initially, be more a result of this factor than deviant sexual arousal. In addition to anti-social and impulsive, these youths' personality descriptors include anxious, unhappy, and rebellious.

In this author's experience, youth whose sexual offending was one aspect of a more generalised pattern of delinquent behaviour tended to manifest a higher degree of anger. One youth identified a primary core belief motivating his sexually and physically assaultive behaviour as, 'I would hurt other people because I wanted them to feel my pain . . . it made me feel better'. These youth were more likely to identify power struggles, fighting, and using drugs and alcohol as additional aspects of their general pattern of delinquency.

Those anti-social youth who meet the criteria for being highly psychopathic are one of the subtypes of adolescents that Hunter et al. (2003) identified as being at high risk to offend into adulthood.

Early onset paraphilia

Becker (1988) identified the youth with a well-established deviant pattern of sexual arousal. Hunter et al. (2003) delineates that a small subset of juveniles who engage in sexually abusive behaviour against children may represent early onset paedophilia. Research cited by Hunter (1999) found that:

- A minority of sexually abusive youth manifest established deviant sexual arousal and interest patterns.
- Deviant sexual arousal is more clearly established as a factor in adult sexual offending, particularly as it relates to paedophilia.
- The highest levels of deviant sexual arousal in adolescents have been found in those who target young male children exclusively, specifically when penetration is involved.
- In general, it has been found that the deviant sexual arousal and interest patterns of sexually abusive adolescents appear more changeable than those of adult sex offenders and relate less directly to their patterns of sexually abusive behaviour. Related to this, Prentky (2001) notes that the fluidity of sexual preference in adolescence raises the question as to whether we can capture a stable snapshot.

One youth with whom this author worked had engaged in sexually abusive behaviour toward male and female children. An Abel assessment found an extremely high degree of sexual interest in young males between the ages of two to four and eight to ten. This youth reported that approximately 80 per cent of his masturbation fantasies involved males between the ages of 9–13. He had been sexually abused at the age of seven by a 12-year-old male with the sexual contact involving anal intercourse. The early onset paedophilia is one of the subtypes of youth that was identified by Hunter et al. (2003) as being at high risk to re-offend.

Co-occurring mental disorders

Becker (1988) describes the adolescent compromised by a psychiatric condition, which interferes with his ability to regulate and inhibit his aggressive and sexual impulses. Studies addressing the prevalence of co-occurring mental disorders in juveniles who have committed sexual offences have found that 35–50 per cent have some type of mood disorder, 30–50 per cent have anxiety disorders, 10–20 per cent have Attention-Deficit Hyperactivity Disorder, and 20–30 per cent have engaged in substance abuse (Becker et al., 1986, 1991; Kavoussi et al., 1988; Shaw et al., 1993).

In some cases, the symptom profile of these disorders may contribute to increasing risk in a relatively significant manner. The sexually abusive behaviour may reflect compensatory behaviour secondary to depression and associated low self-esteem and hopelessness (Ryan and Lane, 1997). This author has evaluated youth in whom the hyper-sexuality and impulsivity associated with mania appeared to have been an important contributing factor to his sexually abusive behaviour. For those sexual offending youth who have been sexually abused, Finkelhor (1987) identifies the behavioural manifestations of traumatic sexualisation as including sexual preoccupations and compulsive sexual behaviours, precocious sexual activity, and aggressive sexual behaviours. Dailey (1996) also identifies youth whose obsessive-compulsive disorders appear to drive paraphilic behaviours.

Ongoing research

John Hunter is currently administering research that was initiated in 2001(a) based on a grant from the US Department of Research to the Virginia Department of Criminal Justice Services.

Hunter's hypothesised subtypes are relatively consistent with and offer further support to the findings above. It is hypothesised that subtype specification and prospective tracking will reveal the following:

'Adolescent-onset', non-paraphilic youth are believed to engage in sexual offending as a form of adolescent experimentation and in compensation for psychosocial deficits that impair the development of healthy relationships. These youth will:

- Have the greater percentage of victims to whom they are biologically or familially related.
- Manifest the highest level of investment in treatment.
- Demonstrate the most improvement in psychosocial/psychosexual functioning.
- Have the lowest level of continued engagement in sexual and non-sexual aggression and delinquency.

'Life course persistent' youth are characterised by psychopathic traits, including superficial attachments to peers and family. They are thought to distrust others, aggressively seek dominance interpersonally, and manifest hostility toward females. These youth will:

- Have a greater percentage of pubescent or post-pubescent female victims.
- Have more sexual assault victims that are strangers or acquaintances.
- Manifest the highest level of violent offending.
- Demonstrate the highest level of resistance to treatment.
- Show the least improvement in psychosocial and psychosexual functioning.
- Have the highest level of continued engagement in non-sexual aggression and delinquency.

'Early adolescent onset', paraphilic youth are believed to represent cases of early onset paedophilia. As such, they are motivated by deviant sexual arousal and interests. These youth will:

- Have more prepubescent male victims.
- Demonstrate the most enduring interest in deviant sexuality.
- Have the highest rate of sexual recidivism.

Aetiology

Researchers have reported the following findings related to aetiology:

- Developmental exposure to violence toward females was associated with deficits in self-efficacy and psychosocial functioning in juveniles who commit sexual offences, and higher levels of non-sexual violence and delinquency (Hunter et al., 2003).
- Developmental exposure to anti-social males was associated with more pronounced non-sexual delinquent attitudes and behaviour and negative masculinity in these youths (Hunter et al., 2003). Related to the more generally anti-social youth, Burton and Meezan (2004: 51) hypothesise that, 'sexual offending and rule breaking is a logical progression when they become developmentally focused on their sexuality – they see no reason not to break the rules, and have been taught that rule breaking is a way to fulfil their desires'.
- A history of physical abuse by fathers and step-fathers in juveniles who commit sexual offences was associated with depression and anxiety (Hunter et al., 2003). Worling (2001) found that the anti-social-impulsive youth were more likely to have been physically abused by their parents.
- A history of non-coercive sexual abuse by non-relative males was associated with sexual perpetration against a male child (Hunter et al., 2003). Worling (2004) cited research that found that in some cases, deviant arousal may have been shaped by long-term abuse that has involved fear, violence, and physiological arousal. More broadly speaking, research has found significant relationships between youth's sexual victimisation experiences and the sexually abusive behaviour perpetrated by the youth as it relates to dimensions including type of sexual contact, gender, relationship, modus operandi, and severity of acts (Veneziano et al., 2000; Burton, 2003).
- A history of child abuse, exposure to abuse of women, and exposure to anti-social males often occurred together in the lives of juveniles who commit sexual offences (Hunter et al., 2003).
- Prentky et al. (1989) found that a history of caregiver inconstancy and sexual deviation and abuse independently and additively predicted future sexually abusive behaviour.
- Burton and Meezan (2004) cited a relatively significant body of research that found early

exposure to and frequent use of pornography, including exposure to violent pornography, in adults and juveniles who have committed sexual offences. Burton and Meezan suggest that pornography is another means of learning sexually abusive behaviour.

Evaluation and ongoing assessment

Purpose and goals

The comprehensive sex offence specific evaluation is an essential prerequisite to the formulation of an individualised and thorough treatment plan. Sex offence specific evaluations provide the following potential values (Bonner et al., 1998; Epperson et al., 2005; CSOMB, 2002):

- Provision of information regarding whether the youth can be safely treated in the community.
- Segregation of low risk juveniles from high risk.
- More efficient use of limited resources.
- Assessment of youth's strengths and deficits and determination of specific treatment needs.
- To identify individual differences, potential barriers to treatment, and static and dynamic risk factors.
- Determination of youths' and families' amenability to treatment.
- Increased ability to provide differential levels of treatment intensity.

Evaluation areas and methodology

A comprehensive evaluation protocol is necessary in order to develop an appropriate treatment and supervision plan. This discussion will be limited in scope to focus on specific evaluation areas and methodology that will aid in differentiating subtypes of sexually abusive youth.

Social/developmental history, developmental competency, delinquency and conduct/behavioural issues, and amenability to treatment are all important areas to address in the clinical and family interviews in order to gather information relevant to delineating subtypes of sexually abusive youth (CSOMB, 2002). The sexual history interview can address typology related issues including sexual development, consensual sexual experiences, sexual apprehension/confidence, exposure to/use of pornography, sexual victimisation, masturbation fantasies, involvement in other paraphilias, victim profile, and the youth's intent and motivation (Lane, 1997).

It is important to be cognisant that there are no empirically validated risk assessment instruments designed for juveniles who commit sexual offences. Prentky (2001) cautions that, 'instruments that are still in the incubator are being used to make profoundly important decisions that impact people's liberty'. One of the more promising risk assessment instruments is the Juvenile Sexual Offender Assessment Protocol II (J-SOAP II) (Prentky and Righthand, 2002). The J-SOAP II is an empirically guided risk assessment instrument that can be utilised as part of a comprehensive sex offence specific evaluation in assessing risk for re-offence. The J-SOAP II contains 28 items representing four scales that include static (historical) domains and dynamic factors. The Sexual Drive/Preoccupation and the Impulsive/Antisocial are the static scales. The Intervention (treatment progress) and the Community Stability and Adjustment are the dynamic scales.

The static scales both inform and can be used in conjunction with the typology research as far as helping to differentiate between those youth who have exclusively committed sex offences and those who commit sex offences as one part of a larger pattern of both sexual and non-sexual delinquent behaviour. As such, the individual scale scores can be useful in informing and guiding treatment and risk management decisions. Prentky and Righthand propose that youth who have a relatively high score on the Sexual Drive/Preoccupation scale but a relatively low score on the Impulsive/Antisocial scale may require more sex offence specific treatment interventions and less of a focus on delinquency interventions. They contend that mixing such a youth with more hard-core delinquents may do more harm than good.

In contrast, a youth who has a relatively high score on the Impulsive/Antisocial scale but a relatively low score on Sexual Drive/Preoccupation scale may have sexually offended as part of a more general pattern of antisocial behaviour. In cases such as this, the sexual offence may not reflect serious issues with the management of sexually deviant or sexually coercive behaviour. This type of youth may require delinquency focused treatment interventions.

The Minnesota Multiphasic Personality Inventory – Adolescent (MMPI-A) (1992) is the most widely utilised psychological test designed to broadly assess clinical symptomatology and personality characteristics in adolescents. The Multiphasic Sex Inventory II Juvenile (MSI IIJ) (Nichols and Molinder, 2003) can provide useful information for determining a youth's subtype. The 'Heterosexual Inadequacies' and 'Emotional Neediness' scales can be particularly useful in identifying those youth whose social and interpersonal deficits are a motivational factor to their engaging in sexually abusive behaviour. These scales help to identify those youth who feel apprehensive about making social/sexual contact with same age females. Reflecting the compensatory aspect of this subtype's sexually abusive behaviour, these scales distinguish youth who are 'affection starved' and 'emotionally needy' and who are likely to associate deep feelings of the need for affection and feelings of loneliness with sexual desires. The responses on the 'Body Image' and 'Asocial (Loner) Type' can also be useful in providing diagnostic information for this subtype. The 'Conduct Disorder' scale and the 'Sex Deviance' scale and indices can provide important information for differentiating the anti-social and the early onset paraphilic youth.

Placement and supervision

The Center for Sex Offender Management (2004) cites the core correctional principles of risk, need, and responsivity as providing a useful framework to facilitate evaluation and treatment planning within juvenile justice systems. These principles ensure that assessment processes effectively and appropriately drive treatment and supervision interventions. Risk prediction facilitates the ability to match the levels of treatment/service to the risk level of the offender. This allows us to focus limited resources on youth who need the most intensive treatment and supervision interventions. The need principle focuses on identifying the specific targets of treatment and supervision that will have the greatest impact on reducing risk and matching youth to programmes that meet their needs. Responsivity focuses on delivering treatment and supervision interventions in a style and mode that is consistent with the ability and learning style of the youth (Andrews et al., 1990).

The heterogeneity of the juvenile sexual offender population calls for the availability of a continuum of care that provides the appropriate level of care based on the risk, amenability to treatment, and treatment and supervision needs of youth. The ability to continue to refine our classification of offender typologies will provide more precise guidance for placements, interventions, and case management planning. The ability to offer a range of interventions and placement options makes it possible to provide cost-effective, individualised interventions while at the same time addressing community safety. The lack of a comprehensive continuum of care has implications for community safety as well as the effective and efficient use of resources. A youth in a more restrictive level of care than is required is not only a poor use of limited resources but may also create the potential of a lower risk youth being aggregated with and influenced by more anti-social youth (Dishion et al., 1999). Conversely, placing youth into a lower level of care than is appropriate may pose an increased risk to the community. John Hunter (2002) has developed case management protocols for the Virginia Department of Juvenile Justice that address the effective management of sexually abusive youth in the community by delineating risk profiles and corresponding levels of supervision.

It is my experience that we talk a lot better game than we deliver when it comes to individualising the treatment and supervision of these youth. There are a number of factors that contribute to regressing into a 'one size fits all' approach in spite of what we are learning about the heterogeneity of this population. Leversee and Pearson (2001) and others have asserted that the socio-political context of fear and anger that exists toward individuals who commit sexual offences impacts our ability and willingness to provide truly individualised treatment and supervision. In spite of the research based consensus that most sexually abusive youth can be safely and effectively managed in the community (ATSA, 2000) it could be argued that public policy and what we know about sexually abusive youth is moving in opposite directions at times, resulting in an increasingly punitive approach to juveniles who commit sexual offences. Research with adult offenders has been used to convince the public and the courts that sexual offenders cannot be cured and that both juvenile and adults sex offenders are in need of lifetime treatment and management strategies. These old assumptions as well as reactivity to high profile adult cases seem to be the driving forces behind many of the laws and policies enacted to address the problem of sexually abusive youth. It would be naïve to believe that this socio-political environment doesn't also impact on our clinical decision making at times. These types of external factors can create pressure on individual providers to adopt a self-protective philosophy. Research cited by Bonner et al. (1998) suggest, that treatment providers tend to over-predict sexual recidivism rather than risk the dire consequences associated with failing to predict recidivism that comes to pass. In this climate, an empirically guided ethical practice takes a certain degree of courage and perseverance.

General treatment framework and outcomes

Conceptual framework

The diversity that exists among the juvenile sexual offending population would support a comprehensive, holistic approach to treatment that targets both decreasing abusive behaviour and improving overall health. This conceptual framework for treatment encompassed within a comprehensive, holistic approach should include:

- Cognitive-behavioural theory hypotheses that an individual's feelings and behaviour are influenced by their thoughts and perceptions of their environment.
- Developmental theories help us to understand the contribution that inadequate or dysfunctional growth has on developmental competence and abusive behaviour. This is related to the victim to victimiser model. The cause or origin of offending may be in the offender's attempt to master his own helplessness and powerlessness by taking on the aggressor's role (Ryan, 1997).
- Contextual theories provide a foundation for understanding the interaction between individual experiences and the environment as it relates to basic beliefs about self and others in our environment (Ryan, 1997).
- Social-ecological model treatment is viewed as multi-systemic with interventions provided in, and directed at, all relevant systems and environments – school, home, peer, and other environmental factors – using the identified strengths in these domains to promote positive change (Hunter, 2001b).
- Teaching of new skills is necessary so that youth are able to respond in an adaptive manner when they become aware of high risk factors (Pithers, 1990).

Treatment outcomes

Sex offence specific treatment should be designed to maximise measurable outcomes relevant to the dynamic functioning of the juvenile by decreasing the risk of sexual and non-sexual deviance, dysfunction, and offending and improving overall health, strengths, skills and resources relevant to successful functioning (CSOMB, 2002). Treatment programmes are relatively consistent in regard to the focus on acceptance of responsibility for abusive behaviour, the ability to identify and verbalise skills and coping responses necessary to interrupt thoughts, feelings, and behaviours associated with the abuse cycle, victim awareness and empathy, and the ability to manage behaviour in a structured setting. Just as important, however, is the second half of the equation associated with improving overall health, strengths, skills, and resources. This consists of focusing on outcomes including:

- Demonstration of pro-social relationship skills that facilitate the ability to establish closeness and trust.
- Improved self-image in order to become independent and competent.
- Demonstration of conflict resolution and decision-making skills.
- Ability to relax, play and celebrate positive experiences.
- Seeking out and maintaining pro-social peers.
- Ability to plan for and participate in structured pro-social activities.
- Identification of family and/or community support systems.
- Willingness to work to achieve delayed gratification.
- Persisting in the pursuit of goals.
- Respecting reasonable authority and limits.
- Ability to think and communicate effectively.
- The demonstration of rational cognitive processing, adequate verbal skills. (CSOMB, 2002).

Treatment methods

The Center for Sex Offender Management (CSOM, 2004) summarised literature supporting group therapy as the preferred method of treatment for juveniles who commit sexual offences. Youth may be more accepting of feedback from their peers than authority figures, particularly during the 'early phases' treatment. The opportunity to observe advanced offenders who have progressed in treatment can enhance self-efficacy and instil hope in offenders who have just begun the treatment process. Advanced clients can model positive behaviour such as acceptance of personal responsibility and empathy. Exposure to others' viewpoints provides natural opportunities for perspective taking and self-examination. Peers can help to identify and challenge denial, cognitive distortions, high-risk behaviours, and manipulation. Group facilitation and interactions provide the opportunity to teach, model, evaluate, and target social skills and relationship skills.

Hunter (2001c) stresses that research does not support that all sexually abusive youth are in need of or will benefit from group therapy. Group therapy may be contraindicated for those adolescents who experience difficulty curbing their sexual arousal during disclosures of sexually abusive behaviour (Worling, 2004). Research has not been done to establish the effect of exposure to deviant sexual information or stimuli on the arousal patterns of juveniles. For this reason, treatment providers should control and minimise the exposure of youth to deviant sexual stimuli. Such work may need to be done outside of a group setting in some cases in order to minimise risk to other group members (National Task Force, 2004, in draft). Additionally, the efficacy of group therapy needs to be evaluated for youth with serious expressive and receptive language disabilities. Individual therapy may be more appropriate and efficacious for youth with serious co-occurring mental disorders, particularly in cases in which the youth needs to be stabilised before he is able to benefit from treatment. The placement of developmentally delayed youth in groups with more cognitively capable youth may be contraindicated (CSOM, 2004). It is also important to be cognisant of how youth are grouped. As discussed above, exposure of young adolescents with histories of delinquency to older antisocial youth may escalate engagement in antisocial behaviour (Dishion et al., 1999).

Subtype specific treatment

To reiterate, the need principle focuses on identifying the specific targets of treatment and supervision that will have the greatest impact on reducing risk and on matching youth to programmes that meet their needs. As stated above, typology research offers an essential conceptual and empirical foundation for understanding the diversity that exists among juveniles who commit sexual offences. The increased understanding of the differential etiological pathways and treatment needs facilitates our ability to further refine clinical practice (Hunter, 2001a). Subtype specific treatment will be discussed, with particular emphasis on Worling's (2001) utilisation of *Skillstreaming the Adolescent* (Goldstein and McGinnis, 1997) to delineate specific skills for each subtype of offender.

Social and interpersonal deficits

The treatment needs of the youth characterised by social and interpersonal deficits would call for a focus on sex offence specific/skills based treatment interventions. The degree and intensity of the sex offence specific treatment interventions with this subtype can be guided by the score on the Sexual Drive and Preoccupation Scale on the J-SOAP II. Because the sexual offending of many of these youth reflects compensatory social behaviour and an attempt to satisfy unmet intimacy needs, Hunter et al. (2003) place emphasis on the importance of addressing deficits in self-esteem, self-efficacy, and social competency. Worling (2001) identifies the treatment needs of the Unusual/Isolated youth as traditional sex offence specific treatment and treatment aimed at their unusual interpersonal orientation and resulting social isolation. Worling recommends behavioural instruction in a number of 'Beginning Social Skills' including (Goldstein and McGinnis, 1997): 'listening'; 'starting a conversation'; 'having a conversation'; 'asking a question'; 'saying thank you'; 'introducing yourself'; 'introducing other people'; and 'giving a compliment'.

Worling (2001) identifies the treatment needs of the Overcontrolled/Reserved youth as the outward expression of affect and the need to take risks to form social relationships. Worling recommends instruction in skills including (Goldstein and McGinnis, 1997): 'joining in'; 'expressing your feelings'; and 'standing up for your rights'.

Antisocial

The anti-social subtype may have sexually offended as part of a more general pattern of anti-social behaviour and, as such, the sexual offence may not reflect serious issues with the management of sexually deviant or sexually coercive behaviour. This type of youth may require delinquency focused treatment interventions (Prentky and Righthand, 2002). Worling (2001) identifies the treatment needs of the anti-social youth as sexual offence specific relapse prevention treatment that includes concomitant work on the major set of risk/need factors associated with general juvenile delinquency.

Edward Latessa (2005) identifies the major set of risk/need factors for juvenile delinquents as follows:

1. Anti-social/pro-criminal attitudes, values, beliefs, and cognitive-emotional states.
2. Pro-criminal associates and isolation from anti-criminal others.
3. Temperamental and personality factors conducive to criminal activity including:
   - psychopathy
   - weak socialisation
   - impulsivity
   - restless aggressive energy
   - egocentrism
   - below average verbal intelligence
   - a taste for risk
   - weak problem-solving/self-regulation skills
4. A history of anti-social behaviour
5. Familial factors that include criminality and a variety of psychological problems in the family of origin including:
   - low levels of affection, caring, and cohesiveness
   - poor parental supervision and discipline practices
   - outright neglect and abuse
6. Low levels of personal educational, vocational or financial achievement.

Worling (2001) recommends instruction on the following set of nine social skills categorised as 'Alternatives to Aggression' (Goldstein and McGinnis, 1997): 'asking permission'; 'sharing something'; 'helping others'; 'negotiating'; 'using self-control'; 'standing up for your rights'; 'responding to teasing'; 'avoiding trouble with others'; and 'keeping out of fights'. In addition, Prentky and Righthand (2002) recommend some limited psycho-educational interventions that address appropriate sexual boundaries, non-abusive sexual behaviour, and healthy masculinity. Burton and Meezan (2004) cite research to support Multisystemic Therapy as an effective treatment method with the delinquent population and in a pilot study with juveniles who have committed sexual offences.

Early onset paedophilia

There are a number of cognitive-behavioural techniques that have been utilised with juveniles in order to manage deviant sexual arousal. Thought stopping and covert sensitisation stress increased cognitive control. Covert sensitisation is a self-conducted technique that develops uncomfortable association with fantasy and behaviour that has occurred immediately antecedent to the youth's sexually abusive behaviour. The process is designed to interrupt the pleasurable association and anticipation that the youth has previously experienced. The youth is taught to pair antecedent fantasy and behaviours with mentally aversive stimuli through a structured sequence. The youth may be expected to record the sessions on audiotape or to complete the assignments in the treatment setting (Ryan and Lane, 1997). Ryan and Lane caution that because fantasies of sexually abusive behaviours are very reinforcing, journal work describing sexual interactions should be limited to defining the abusive aspects of the sexually abusive thoughts rather than the sexually explicit descriptions of arousal and orgasm.

Satiation therapy, arousal conditioning, and vicarious sensitisation are among the more controversial techniques designed to reduce deviant arousal or to increase sexual interest. These techniques have been used sparingly due to the inconsistent empirical data on their efficacy as well as questions as to the appropriateness of techniques that expose youth to physically or emotionally aversive stimuli or that involve masturbation (Hunter and Goodwin, 1992; National Task Force, 1993). Behavioural conditioning with noxious stimuli such as ammonia is similarly controversial. The National Task Force on Juvenile Sexual Offending (1993) recommends that this type of aversive conditioning only be used if self-administered by the juvenile and with appropriate consent from the juvenile, parent, and referring authority.

Hunter and Lexier (1998) cite reports on the use of Selective Serotonin Reuptake Inhibitors (SSRI) in the treatment of paraphilias. These medications are typically prescribed as anti-depressant and anti-obsessional agents but have been utilised with juveniles who commit sexual offences due to side effects that include suppression of sexual desire and delayed ejaculation. Similar to the above, there is not enough known about the effectiveness of SSRIs or about the types of juveniles with whom they may be effective.

The higher risk to re-offend that this subtype represents in combination with the questionable efficacy of interventions designed to address deviant arousal necessitates an enhanced external supervision component.

Co-occurring mental disorders

The Revised Report from the National Task Force on Juvenile Sexual Offending (1993: 69–70) articulates the following important assumptions in regard to the treatment of youth with co-occurring mental disorders:

- Some co-occurring disorders may impede the juvenile's ability to successfully participate and progress in offence specific treatment.
- Some co-occurring disorders may require stabilisation prior to acceptance into offence specific treatment programmes. Examples include psychotic symptoms, substance abuse, suicidal ideation, affective disorders, PTSD, etc.).
- Specialised inpatient, outpatient, and aftercare treatment programmes for youth with multiple diagnoses should be included in the continuum of services for sexually abusive youth. Such programmes must integrate management of chronic psychiatric disorders and specialised, offence specific treatment either within the psychiatric programme or in a congruent fashion with other programmes that are available.

- Management and treatment of co-occurring disorders must always be congruent with the goals of offence specific treatment.
- In some cases, psychiatric consultation may suggest pharmacological interventions that can be helpful in managing symptoms which are impeding the client's ability to succeed in the offence specific treatment process.

Dialectical Behavioural Therapy (DBT) (Linehan, 1993) is a promising mental health treatment designed to treat severe and chronic multi-diagnostic, difficult-to-treat patients. DBT targets behaviours in a descending hierarchy as follows: decreasing high-risk suicidal behaviours; decreasing responses or behaviours that interfere with therapy; decreasing behaviours that interfere with/reduce quality of life; decreasing and dealing with post-traumatic stress responses; enhancing self-respect; acquisition of skills taught in group; and additional goals set by the youth. The four primary components of the skills training portion of DBT are core mindfulness, interpersonal effectiveness, emotional regulation, and distress tolerance. The use of DBT resulted in significant reductions with the symptoms of suicidal teens including anxiety, depression, interpersonal sensitivity, and obsessive-compulsive symptom patterns. Additional reductions were found in the problem areas of confusion about self, impulsivity, emotion dysregulation, and interpersonal difficulties (Miller et al., 1996). Research on an adult male forensic population found significant decreases in depressed and hostile mood, paranoia, and psychotic behaviours, as well as a significant decrease in several maladaptive interpersonal coping styles and an increase in adaptive coping (McCann et al., 1996). The cognitive behavioural chain utilised in DBT as well as the skills based focus is very congruent with the goals of offence specific treatment.

The predominance of childhood maltreatment and trauma in the etiological pathways of sexually abusive youth would support the importance of trauma resolution being a key component in treatment. Van der Kolk et al. (1996) identified the primary treatment issues in the resolution of trauma as establishing safety and predictability, de-conditioning and decreasing anxiety and arousal levels, and altering the way victims view themselves and their world. The treatment approach should incorporate cognitive-behavioural components, including exposure strategies, stress management/relaxation, cognitive/narrative restructuring, and a parental treatment component (Cohen et al., 2000). Sex offence specific treatment can then be utilised in order to identify the cognitive and emotional outcomes of childhood maltreatment that may be contributing factors in the youth subsequently engaging in sexually abusive behaviour. The focus then shifts to cognitive restructuring and the learning of new skills that the youth can utilise in order to change thinking and beliefs that support and justify abusive behaviour and manage painful emotions that may trigger the sexual abuse cycle (Ryan, 1989).

Additional treatment issues and methods

Enhancing healthy sexuality

While the field has improved in our ability to target the factors related to sexually abusive behaviour, we have too often placed a low priority on the importance of enhancing healthy sexuality. Perhaps it is difficult for us to fathom or accept that a segment of the population of juveniles who have committed sexually abusive behaviour may be able to move toward a more normative path in regard to intimate relationships and sexuality. Intentional or not, the treatment of sexually abusive youth may result in the youth being confused about how to evaluate and respond to healthy sexual thoughts, fantasies, and urges. Brown (2000) describes the overall goal as challenging the youth's abusive sexuality without making them feel that they need to renounce their sexuality altogether.

Brown (2000) recommends that sexuality education groups for sexually abusive youth include a range of topics including reproductive and sexual anatomy, sexual feelings, sexual decision-making, puberty, teen pregnancy, HIV/AIDS, safer sex, sexual orientation, sexual values, healthy relationships, and courtship and dating skills.

In addition, agencies working with juveniles who commit sexual offences should address and establish protocols where appropriate in regard to issues including differentiating between acceptable and prohibited erotica/pornography, sexual fantasies and masturbation, and

differentiating between sexual contact that constitutes a rule infraction versus sexually abusive and/or illegal sexual behaviour. One of the additional challenges inherent in the supervision of juveniles who commit sexual offences has to do with the issue of grooming. Brown (2000: 43) describes an all-to-common approach, stating that, 'it is easier for treatment staff to treat all sexualised behaviour as grooming rather than engage in the difficult and often anxiety producing task of distinguishing between sexualised behaviours that are meant to set up victims and those that have another, more benign meaning'. When we are dealing with youth who manifest psychosocial deficits, it is important to differentiate grooming from awkward attempts to demonstrate social skills and establish interpersonal relationships. Unless we accept this challenge, we may inadvertently discourage these youth from taking the social risks and practicing the new social skills necessary in order for them to increase their social competence.

Learning new skills

All too frequently, there is a 'disconnect' between what occurs in the clinical arena and what occurs in the youth's milieu as far as reinforcing and strengthening the development of new skills. Whether it is a residential milieu or the youth's community, it is important for services to be delivered in a manner that facilitates the learning and the successful assimilation of new pro-social skills (CSOM, 2004).

In residential settings, the therapeutic milieu is 'used to promote growth, development and relationship skills; to practice pro-social life skills; and to supervise, observe, and intervene in the daily functioning of the juvenile' (CSOMB, 2002: 39–40).

The milieu is characterised by physical safety, nurturance, and psychological safety, with therapists being challenging but supportive, and in control versus overly directive or aggressively confrontational (Ryan, 1997; CSOM, 2004). CSOM (2004) cites literature to support the need for all staff to be educated about sex offence specific treatment and to be interested in the success of these youth. Milieu staff involvement as part of treatment teams enhances the chances of success by improving the integrity, generalisability, and sustainability of the services. Milieu staff can provide the following (CSOM, 2004):

- Information to the treatment staff related to observing the youth in multiple settings outside of treatment groups.
- Mitigate some of the negative influences, including negative peer associations.
- Assist the youth with practicing skills that are learned in treatment.

Latessa (2005) identifies the milieu factors that facilitate the learning of new skills as the modelling and demonstration of the behaviour by staff and caregivers, specifying the rewards for behaving this way, and providing reinforcement every time that the youth demonstrates the new skill. Boys Town (1998) emphasises a positive teaching atmosphere and a high ratio of corrective teaching interactions with each youth.

Latessa (2005) further identifies the three factors necessary for a new behaviour to occur as:

- Having a strong positive intention to perform the behaviour.
- Having the skills necessary to carry out the behaviour.
- Being in an environment that is free of constraints so that the behaviour can occur.

Skill acquisition requires demonstration, rehearsal, and practice.

Programmes that are effective have clearly defined risk factors for each youth that all staff are able to confront. This includes the use of a common language in confronting risk factors and a common skills-based curriculum that all staff can utilise (Underwood, 1997). Individualised teaching on target behaviours from a common skills based curriculum is congruent with Worling's use of *Skillstreaming the Adolescent* to identify needed skill development areas for the different subtypes of sexually abusive youth. *Thinking for a Change* (Bush, Glick, and Taymans, 1997) is a another cognitive self-change skills based curriculum available through the National Institute of Corrections that has been adapted for use with juveniles.

Goldstein and McGinnis (1997) offer the following steps for learning new skills that can be used in a collaborative fashion by clinical and residential milieu staff or community supervision and support teams in assuring the transfer of new skills:

1. **Modelling** – having someone show you the skill;

2. **Role-playing** – trying out the skill yourself;
3. **Feedback** – having someone tell you how well you did;
4. **Transfer** – trying the skill when, where, and with whom you really need the skill. Transferring the skill outside of the group involves a 'homework assignment' and a 'homework report' that includes the following:
- What skill will you use?
- What are the steps for the skill?
- Where will you try the skill?
- With whom will you try the skill?
- When will you try the skill?
- What happened when you did the homework?
- Which skill steps did you really follow through?
- How good a job did you do in using the skill?
- What do you think should be your next homework assignment?

Transition/aftercare

Aftercare services are needed to support juveniles who have committed sexual offences in managing ongoing risks. Strategies related to transition/aftercare should ensure continuity of care to bridge institutional and community based services (CSOM, 2004). Relapse prevention planning may be utilised throughout treatment, but it is emphasised more during the final stages of treatment, during aftercare, and as a long-term support following treatment. Relapse prevention planning stresses a high level of accountability for thinking and personal choices, recognising high risk factors, internal and external, and averting the dysfunctional cycle' (Ryan and Lane, 1997: 316).

The relapse prevention model is a collaborative effort between the treatment provider and the youth that makes extensive use of both internal self-monitoring by the youth and external supervision by the treatment provider, family members, probation and parole officers, and others who can observe changes in behaviour which might precede relapse (Pithers, 1990). The degree of structure and services contained in the external supervision component should be related to the level of risk and ongoing treatment needs of the youth. As stated above, the highly anti-social youth and the early onset paedophilic youth represent those at highest risk to re-offend.

Many of the strategies outlined in regard to milieu staff can be applied to the community supervision and support team as it relates to the monitoring risk factors and supporting the learning and the successful assimilation of new pro-social skills. For example, supporting the youth's involvement in structured and supervised activities in the community allows for more opportunities to practice and generalise social skills, provide opportunities for social interaction and friendship, and assist the youth in forming new recreational interests (Worling, 2004).

Conclusion

It is incumbent on juvenile justice and treatment systems to protect the community, respect the rights and welfare of all youth, and support low to moderate-risk youth to return to a more healthy and non-abusive developmental path (Chaffin and Bonner, 1998; Leversee and Pearson, 2001). The research to date on the delineation of different subtypes of sexually abusive youth has provided invaluable information as we strive to individualise the treatment and supervision of this population. The ability to apply this information in a systematic manner to guide our placement and treatment planning decisions begins with clinically competent evaluators who utilise protocols that integrate empirically guided risk assessment instruments and knowledge of typologies. The capacity to offer a range of interventions and placement options in the context of a comprehensive continuum of care makes it possible to provide cost-effective, individualised interventions while at the same time addressing community safety. A multi-disciplinary team with clearly defined roles is essential in assuming responsibility for the treatment, care, and supervision of sexually abusive youth, including the ongoing process of assessing risk and treatment needs. Treatment providers and supervising officers must have the experience, training, and supervision necessary to meet the individualised treatment and supervision needs of this heterogeneous population. To the degree possible, treatment interventions should utilise evidence-based curricula.

Finally, the primary caregivers and milieu staff need to be educated and trained in order to provide the informed supervision and therapeutic care necessary for a safe environment while at the same time enhancing the learning and growth of sexually abusive youth (CSOMB, 2002).

References

Andrews, D.A., Bonta, J. and Hoge, R.D. (1990) Classification for Effective Rehabilitation: Rediscovering Psychology. *Criminal Justice and Behavior*, 17, 19–52.

The Association for the Treatment of Sexual Abusers (2000) *The Effective Legal Management of Juvenile Sexual Offenders*. Adopted by the ATSA Executive Board of Directors on March 11.

Becker, J.V. (1988) Adolescent Sex Offenders. *Behavior Therapy*, 11, 185–87.

Becker, J.V., Kaplan, M.S., Cunningham-Rather, J. and Kavoussi, R.J. (1986) Characteristics of Adolescent Incest Sexual Perpetrators: Preliminary Findings. *Journal of Family Violence*, 1, 85–97.

Bonner, B.L., Marx, B.P., Thompson, J.M. and Michaelson, P. (1998) Assessment of Adolescent Sexual Offenders. *Child Maltreatment: Journal of the American Professional Society on the Abuse of Children*, 3: 4, 374–83.

Boys Town USA. (1998) *Boys Town's Staff-Secure Detention Program for Female Juvenile Offenders*.

Brown, S.M. (2000) Healthy Sexuality and the Treatment of Sexually Abusive Youth. *Siecus Report*, 29: 1, 40–46.

Burton, D.L. (2003) The Relationship between the Sexual Victimization of and the Subsequent Sexual Abuse of Male Adolescents. *Child and Adolescent Social Work Journal*, 20: 4, 277–96.

Burton, D.L. and Meezan, W. (2004) Revisiting Recent Research on Social Learning Theory as an Etiological Proposition for Sexually Abusive Male Adolescents. *Journal of Evidenced Based Social Work*, 1, 41–80.

Bush, J., Glick, B. and Taymans, J. (1997) *Thinking for a Change*. Washington, DC/Longmont, Col: National Institute of Corrections.

Butcher, J.N. et al. (1992) *Minnesota Multiphasic Personality Inventory – Adolescent (MMPI-A): Manual for Administration, Scoring, and Interpretation*. Minneapolis: University of Minnesota Press.

Center for Sex Offender Management (2004) *Comprehensive Assessment Protocol of Sex Offender Management Practices: Pilot Test Version*. US Department of Justice, Office of Justice Programs, Bureau of Justice Assistance.

Chaffin, M. and Bonner, B. (1998) 'Don't Shoot, We're Your Children': Have we Gone too Far in our Response to Adolescent Sexual Abusers with Sexual Behavior Problems. *Child*

Maltreatment: *Journal of the American Professional Society on the Abuse of Children.* 3: 4, 314–16.

Cohen, J.A., Berliner, L. and March, J.S. (2000) Treatment of Children and Adolescents. In Foa, E.B., Keane, T.M. and Friedman, M.J. (Eds.) *Effective Treatments for PTSD.* New York: The Guilford Press.

Colorado Sex Offender Management Board (2002) *Standards and Guidelines for the Evaluation, Assessment, Treatment, and Supervision of Juveniles who have Committed Sexual Offenses.* Colorado Department of Public Safety, Division of Criminal Justice.

Dailey, L. (1996) *Adjunctive Biological Treatments with Sexually Abusive Youth.* Paper presented at the Twelfth Annual Conference of the National Adolescent Perpetration Network, Minneapolis.

Dishion, T.J., McCord, J. and Pouli, F. (1999) When Interventions Harm. Peer Groups and Problem Behavior. *American Psychologist*, 54: 9, 755–64.

Epperson, D.L., Ralston, C.A., Fowers, D. and DeWitt, J. (2005) *Optimal Predictors of Juvenile Sexual Recidivism in a Large Scale Study of Utah Adolescents who have Offended Sexually.* Denver, CO: National Adolescent Perpetration Network Conference.

Finkelhor, D. (1987) The Trauma of Sexual Abuse. *Journal of Interpersonal Violence*, 2: 4, 348–66.

Goldstein, A.P. and McGinnis, B. (1997) *Skillstreaming the Adolescent (Revised Edition): New Strategies and Perspectives for Teaching Pro-social Skills.* Champaign, IL, Research Press.

Hunter, J.A. (1999) *Understanding Juvenile Sexual Offending Behavior: Emerging Research, Treatment Approaches and Management Practices.* Center for Sex Offender Management.

Hunter, J.A. (2001a) *Research Plan.* Corrections Program Office of the US Department of Justice grant to the Virginia Department of Criminal Justice Services.

Hunter, J.A. (2001b) *Juvenile Sex Offender Standards Training Series.* Lakewood: Colorado Sex Offender Management Board.

Hunter, J.A. (2001c) *What Research tells us about this Population.* Kansas City: National Adolescent Perpetration Network Conference.

Hunter, J.A., Figueredo, A.J., Malamuth, N.M. and Becker, J.V. (2003) Juvenile Sex Offenders: Toward the Development of a Typology. *Sexual Abuse: A Journal of Research and Treatment.* 15, 1.

Hunter, J.A. (2002) *Risk Profiles and Corresponding Levels of Supervision following Adjudication.* Virginia Department of Juvenile Justice.

Hunter, J.A. and Goodwin, D.W. (1992) The Utility of Satiation Therapy in the Treatment of Juvenile Sexual Offenders: Variations and Efficacy. *Annals of Sex Research*, 5, 71–80.

Hunter, J.A. and Lexier, L.J. (1998) Ethical and Legal Issues in the Assessment and Treatment of Juvenile Sex Offenders. *Child Maltreatment: Journal of the American Professional Society on the Abuse of Children*, 3: 4, 339–48.

Kavoussi, R.J., Kaplan, M. and Becker, J.V. (1988) Psychiatric Diagnoses in Adolescent Sexual Offenders. *Journal of the American Child Adolescent Psychiatry.* 27, 241–43.

Lane, S. (1997) Assessment of Sexually Abusive Youth. In Ryan, G. and Lane, S. (Eds.) *Juvenile Sexual Offending: Causes, Consequences, and Corrections.* San Francisco, Jossey-Bass Publishers.

Latessa, E.J. (2005) *What Works and What Doesn't in Reducing Recidivism: The Principles of Effective Intervention.* Colorado Division of Youth Corrections Provider Council Conference, Vail.

Leversee, T. and Pearson, C. (2001) Eliminating the Pendulum Effect: A Balanced Approach to the Assessment, Treatment, and Management of Sexually Abusive Youth. *Journal of the Center for Families, Children, and the Courts.* 3, 45–57.

Linehan, M. (1993) *Skills Training Manual for Treating Borderline Personality Disorder.* New York: Guilford Press.

McCann, R. and Ball, E.M. (1996) *Using Dialectical Behavior Therapy with an Inpatient Forensic Population.* Workshop presented at the First annual meeting of the International Society for the Improvement and Teaching of Dialectical Behavior Therapy, New York.

Miller, A.L., Rathus, J.H., Leigh, E. and Landsman, M. (1996) *A Pilot Study: Dialectical Behavior Therapy Adapted for Suicidal Adolescents.* Paper presented at the First annual meeting of the International Society for the Improvement and Teaching of Dialectical Behavior Therapy, New York.

National Task Force on Juvenile Sexual Offending, National Adolescent Perpetration Network. (1993) The Revised Report from the National Task Force on Juvenile Sexual Offending. *Juvenile and Family Court Journal.* 44: 4, 69–70.

National Task Force on Juvenile Sexual Offending, National Adolescent Perpetration Network. (2004, In draft). Revision of *The Revised Report from the National Task Force on Juvenile Sexual Offending, 1993.*

Nichols, H.R. and Molinder, I. (2003) *The Multiphasic Sex Inventory II.* Tacoma, WA.

O'Brien, M. and Bera, W. (1986) Adolescent Sexual Offenders: A Descriptive Typology. *Preventing Sexual Abuse*, 1, 3.

Pithers, W.D. (1990) *Handbook of Sexual Assault.* New York: Plenum Press.

Prentky, R.A. et al. (1989) Developmental Antecedents of Sexual Aggression. *Development and Psychopathology*, 153–69.

Prentky, R. (2001) *Assessing Actuarial and Dynamic Risk with Sexually Abusive Youth.* National Adolescent Perpetration Network Conference, Kansas City.

Prentky, R. and Righthand, S. (2001) *Juvenile Sex Offender Assessment Protocol – II (J-SOAP-11).* Colorado: Office of Juvenile Justice and Delinquency Prevention.

Righthand, S. and Welch, C. (2002) Juveniles who have Sexually Offended: An Introduction. *The Prevention Researcher*, 9: 4, 1–4.

Ryan, G. (1997) Phenomenology: A Developmental-Contextual View. In Ryan, G. and Lane, S. (Eds.) *Juvenile Sexual Offending: Causes, Consequences, and Corrections.* San Francisco: Jossey-Bass.

Ryan, G. and Lane, S. (1997) Integrating Theory and Method. In Ryan, G. and Lane, S. (Eds.) *Juvenile Sexual Offending: Causes, Consequences, and Corrections.* San Francisco: Jossey-Bass.

Ryan, G. (1997) Creating an 'Abuse-Specific Milieu'. In Ryan, G. and Lane, S. (Eds.) *Juvenile Sexual Offending: Causes, Consequences, and Corrections.* San Francisco: Jossey-Bass.

Ryan, G. (1989) Victim to Victimizer: Rethinking Victim Treatment. *Journal of Interpersonal Violence*, 4: 3, 325–41.

Shaw, J.A., Campo-Bowen, A.E. and Applegate, B. (1993) Young Boys who Commit Sexual Offenses: Demographics, Psychometrics, and Phenomenology. *Bulletin of American Psychiatry and Law*, 21, 399–408.

Underwood, L. (1997) *Treatment of the Juvenile Offender with Co-occurring Disorders.* Technical Assistance: Co-Occurring Disorders.

Van der Kolk, B., McFarlane, A. and Weisaith, L. (1996) *Traumatic Stress.* New York: Guilford Press.

Veniziano, C., Veniziano, L. and LeGrand, S. (2000) The Relationship between Adolescent Sex Offender Behaviors and Victim Characteristics with Prior Victimization. *Journal of Interpersonal Violence*, 15: 4, 363–74.

Worling, J.R. (2001) Personality-Based Typology of Adolescent Male Sexual Offenders: Differences in Recidivism Rates, Victim Selection Characteristics, and Personal Victimization Histories. *Sexual Abuse: A Journal of Research and Treatment*, 13; 3, 149–66.

Worling, J.R. (2004) Essentials of a Good Intervention Programme for Sexually Abusive Juveniles: Offence Related Treatment Tasks. In O'Reilly, G., Marshall, W.L., Carr, A. and Beckett, R.C. (Eds.) *The Handbook of Clinical Intervention with Youth People who Sexually Abuse.* Hove: Taylor and Francis.

Wylie, M.S. (2004) Mindsight. *Psychotherapy Networker*, September/October, 29–39.

Chapter 5

The Good Lives Model of Rehabilitation: Reducing Risks and Promoting Strengths with Adolescent Sexual Offenders

Rachael Collie, Tony Ward, Lesley Ayland and Bill West

Introduction

Sexual offending is a socially significant and complex problem that attracts great concern from researchers, practitioners, and the community alike. Recent figures suggest a substantial amount of sexual offending is committed by young people (Barbaree, Hudson, and Seto, 1993; Weinrott, 1996) and many adult and lifetime sexual offenders begin their offending as juveniles (Hanson and Bussière, 1998; Rich, 2003). Although intensive efforts have shed light on the causes of sexually abusive behaviour and shown rehabilitation efforts can substantially reduce future sexual offending rates (Hanson et al., 2002), much of what is known comes from research and practice with adult sexual offenders (Print and O'Callahan, 2004; Rich, 2003). In the adult area the dominant approach to rehabilitation is *risk management* and *relapse prevention*. From a risk management perspective treatment aims to identify deficits or problems with offenders' psychological and behavioural functioning that are associated with sexual offending (e.g. offence-supportive beliefs, deviant sexual arousal). Treatment is designed to eliminate, reduce, or manage the extent of these problems (risk factors) so the likelihood of future sexual offending is lessened. The ultimate goal of treatment is to increase public safety by reducing future sexual offences in those offenders who remain living, or return to live, in the community.

Does a risk management and relapse prevention approach to rehabilitation meet the needs of adolescent sexual offenders? Although the risk management and attendant relapse prevention models have been adopted with some success in adolescent sexual offender treatment (Worling and Curwen, 2000), researchers and practitioners in the adolescent area have identified limitations in this approach (Print and O'Callahan, 2004; Rich, 2003). Of most concern is that risk management rehabilitation fails to provide a holistic theory of sexual offending and rehabilitation that is sensitive to the developmental and contextual needs of young people. An alternate theory of rehabilitation gaining attention in the adult area is the Good Lives Model (GLM) of sexual offender rehabilitation (Ward and Stewart, 2003a; Ward and Marshall, 2004). The GLM of rehabilitation is a strengths-based approach (Rapp, 1998) with a *dual focus* on risk management and psychological wellbeing. The GLM proposes rehabilitation will be most effective when offenders learn to manage their risk of re-offending within the broader goal of learning to lead a better kind of life. A better kind of life is one in which an individual meets his or her basic human needs in socially acceptable and personally satisfying ways.

From a GLM perspective, it is not sufficient to simply teach skills to reduce or manage risk factors. Instead, the task of achieving and maintaining behaviour change needs to be *meaningfully* embedded within the notions of personal wellbeing, personal identity, and a positive lifestyle. Attention to individuals' internal capacity (e.g. knowledge, skills, attitudes, and values) and ecological contexts (e.g. social supports and opportunities) are critical for understanding the development of sexual offending and the interventions necessary to achieve psychological wellbeing and desistance from offending. Hence, we believe the GLM provides a theory of rehabilitation that is applicable to adolescent offenders also. In particular, we think the GLM can inform emerging strengths-based innovations in adolescent sexual offender rehabilitation and anchor these within a sophisticated understanding of human behaviour that includes attention to developmental and contextual issues.

In this chapter we describe the GLM approach to sex offender rehabilitation and illustrate how it informs and compliments an emerging innovation in adolescent sex offender rehabilitation here in New Zealand. First, we outline the fundamental tenets of the GLM and discuss how the model improves upon the problems of the risk management approach. We show how the GLM integrates aetiological assumptions about the causes of sexual offending and incorporates risk management principles into a much more holistic, strengths-based approach to sex offender rehabilitation. Second, we introduce an innovative approach to treatment with adolescent sex offenders developed in New Zealand that demonstrates some of the principles of the GLM perspective with a challenging young population. Third, we highlight how developmental and contextual issues present with adolescent sexual offenders are easily and automatically addressed within the GLM framework. We conclude with comments on the future application of this new approach with adolescent sexual offenders.

Good Lives Model (GLM): A strengths-based rehabilitation theory

A good *theory of rehabilitation* should explicitly identify the goals of treatment, justify these goals according to the aetiology of the problem and the values underpinning treatment, specify the clinical targets to be addressed in treatment, and describe how treatment will proceed in light of the goals, problem aetiology, and values (Ward and Marshall, 2004). As previously mentioned, the approach dominating current adult sex offender rehabilitation is risk management and relapse prevention. The primary goal of the risk management approach is to *enhance public safety* by reducing the risk that apprehended offenders will engage in future sexually abusive behaviour (Andrews and Bonta, 2003; Gendreau, 1996). Risk management theory is based on the premise that by identifying and reducing risk factors predictive of sexual offending, offending rates will be reduced. While historical (static) risk factors are unchangeable and have their value in helping predict the likelihood of recidivism over time, dynamic risk factors (i.e. criminogenic needs) are potentially modifiable and become the clinical problems to target in treatment. In essence, dynamic risk factors are treated as the cause of future offending and hence the appropriate clinical targets for intervention.

The risk management approach to rehabilitation is enunciated by a core set of Risk-Need principles (Andrews and Bonta, 2003). The *risk principle* states the assessed risk level should determine the need for treatment (i.e.

higher risk offenders should receive more intensive and longer-term treatment). The *need principle* states treatment should aim to modify dynamic risk factors (i.e. criminogenic needs). Non-criminogenic needs (i.e. those presenting problems that are not dynamic risk factors) can become the legitimate focus of intervention if they interfere with individuals' ability to engage in a risk reduction programme. Otherwise such problems are not appropriate treatment targets; their amelioration will not contribute to reduced risk of recidivism and therefore will not contribute to the overarching goal of enhancing public safety. The *responsivity principle* states interventions should be matched to individuals' learning styles. In general cognitive-behavioural programmes are recommended because they are highly structured, directive, and skills-oriented and meta-analyses have shown more favourable outcomes for such programmes (Hanson et al., 2002). The major form that risk management rehabilitation takes is *relapse prevention programmes*. Relapse prevention is a form of cognitive-behaviour treatment that teaches offenders to (a) recognise the psychological and situational dynamic risk factors associated with past sexual offending and (b) how best to avoid or respond to these risk factors in the future to support desistance from sexual offending (Ward and Hudson, 2000).

Thus, risk management rehabilitation theory connects assumptions about the causes of sexual offending, the type of interventions that should be used, and the way these interventions should be implemented (Ward and Marshall, 2004). In risk management rehabilitation the aim is to enhance public safety by targeting dynamic risk factors from a cognitive-behavioural and relapse prevention perspective. Additional humanistic therapeutic virtues such as creating a safe and supportive therapeutic atmosphere and improving psychological wellbeing are of interest only to the extent that they are instrumental to increasing community safety. The focus is on eliminating risk factors, rather than enhancing individuals' capacity to live more fulfilling lives (Ward and Marshall, 2004).

In contrast, the GLM of rehabilitation has the overarching goal of *enhancing* individuals' capacity to live meaningful, constructive, and ultimately satisfying lives so they can desist from further offending (Ward, Polaschek, and Beech, 2005). The central premise is that rehabilitation should seek to equip individuals with the necessary psychological (internal) and social (external) conditions to meet their *inherent human needs* in socially acceptable and personally satisfying ways. The GLM is a comprehensive rehabilitation theory that provides (a) a set of overarching principles, assumptions, and values that underpins rehabilitation and guides clinicians' decision-making (b) a set of aetiological assumptions that explain the causes of sexual offending, and (c) treatment guidelines that anchor existing therapeutic practices with sexual offenders in a more meaningful structure (Ward and Gannon, 2006). We outline the core features of each component in the following sections and highlight important differences between the GLM and the risk management approach. For more detailed analysis readers are referred to Ward and Gannon (2006), Ward and Marshall (2004, 2005), and Ward and Stewart (2003a).

GLM: Overarching principles and values

The GLM views humans (including sexual offenders!) as active, goal-seeking beings whose actions reflect attempts to meet inherent human needs or *primary human goods* (Emmons, 1999; Ward, 2002). Primary human goods are states of affairs, states of mind, activities or experiences that are inherently beneficial to humans and are sought for their own sake rather than as a means to some other end (Arnhart, 1998; Deci and Ryan, 2000; Emmons, 1999; Schmuck and Sheldon, 2001). Examples of primary human goods are autonomy, relatedness, and competence (Deci and Ryan, 2000). To secure primary human goods individuals engage in a range of activities, strategies, relationships, and experiences (referred to as secondary goods). For example, the primary human good of intimacy (a subclass of relatedness) can be sought through a romantic relationship or friendship (i.e. types of secondary goods).

Findings from a number of disciplines (e.g. anthropology, evolutionary theory, philosophy, practical ethics, and psychology) converge on a set of primary human goods that are necessary for a fulfilling life (see Arnhart, 1998; Aspinwall and Staudinger, 2003; Cummins, 1996; Emmons, 1999; Linley and Joseph, 2004; Murphy, 2001; Nussbaum, 2000; Rescher, 1990). The main categories of primary human goods sought are:

- *Life* (i.e. healthy living, optimal physical functioning, sexual satisfaction).
- *Knowledge* (i.e. wisdom and information).
- *Excellence in work and play* (i.e. mastery experiences).
- *Excellence in agency* (i.e. autonomy, self-directedness).
- *Inner peace* (i.e. freedom from emotional turmoil and stress).
- *Friendship* (i.e. intimate, family, romantic).
- *Spirituality* (i.e. finding meaning and purpose to life).
- *Community*.
- *Happiness*.
- *Creativity*.

As a comprehensive list, these ten primary human goods are multi-faceted and may be broken down into related sub-clusters of goods. For example, the primary good of agency may be further subdivided into the goods of autonomy and self-directedness.

The pursuit and achievement of primary human goods is integral to individuals' sense of meaning and purpose in life and, in turn, psychological wellbeing. No one primary human good is 'better' to attain than others. Instead, when individuals secure the full range of primary human goods (i.e. meet their inherent human needs) psychological functioning and wellbeing flourishes. In contrast, inability to secure a number of primary human goods frustrates and compromises the ability to construct meaningful and purposeful lives and achieve optimal psychological wellbeing (Ward, 2002; Ward and Stewart 2003a, 2003b). To attain the full range of goods in socially acceptable and personally satisfying ways individuals require both the *internal capacity* (e.g. knowledge, skills, attitudes and values) and *external conditions* (e.g. social support and opportunities) to do so.

Although the full range of primary human goods are required for psychological wellbeing, the unique priorities and weightings given to different types of goods and the strategies chosen to achieve these goods differs between individuals as a result of personal preferences, strengths, cultural contexts, and opportunities. Thus all individuals have unique *Good Lives Plans* that reflect their unique differences and personal identity (Bruner, 1990; Cavareo, 2000; DeGrazia, 2005).

From a GLM perspective individuals offend due to problems in one or more dimensions of their good lives plans: individuals may use inappropriate *means* to secure goods (e.g. seeking intimacy through child sexual abuse); lack *scope* in the goods sought (e.g. devaluing relatedness resulting in a lack of socially acceptable means to achieve sexual satisfaction); have *conflict* amongst the goods sought (e.g. wanting both autonomy of sexual freedom and intimacy within the same relationship); lack the skills or internal capacity to achieve goods (e.g. poor self-regulation skills and impulsive decision making); or lack the opportunity, support or *ecological context* to achieve the goods sought (e.g. being geographically and socially isolated or dislocated). The presence of dynamic risk factors, such as social skills deficits and emotional congruence with children, simply alerts clinicians to problems in the way offenders are seeking to achieve primary human goods (Ward and Stewart, 2003a, 2003b). For example, hostile and anti-social attitudes are understood as an internal obstacle to establishing the trust necessary to meet the basic human need of intimacy in relationships.

The principles and values informing the GLM have a number of important implications for how rehabilitation of sexual offenders should proceed. First, the GLM explains offending as a socially unacceptable (and often personally frustrating) attempt to pursue primary human goods. Rather than viewing individuals as the disembodied bearers of risk, individuals are seen as integrated agents for whom offending is meeting primary human needs (albeit through a destructive means). When a person sexually offends, the GLM proposes that there is a problem in the person's *Good Lives Plan*. Dynamic risk factors simply inform the therapist that problems exist and steer the therapist toward an understanding of the nature of these problems; either a healthy good lives plan was never present or it was compromised in some way. The aim of treatment therefore is not to remove risk factors per se but to equip individuals with the necessary psychological (internal) and social (external) conditions to meet their *inherent human needs* through socially acceptable and personally satisfying means.

Second, individuals are understood to be goal-directed beings whose personal identity arises out of pursuit and achievement of primary human goods. Thus it is not *sufficient* in treatment to equip offenders with skills to control or manage risk factors. Treatment also needs to provide offenders with the opportunity and

support to build a more adaptive personal (or narrative) identity that provides a sense of meaning and fulfilment and is realisable in daily activities and experiences (see Ward and Marshall, 2005).

Third, individuals have unique good lives plans but it is important that the full range of goods is achieved in these plans. Treatment planning therefore needs to incorporate some means of attaining all the various primary goods in a manner that is congruent with individuals' personal identity and inconsistent with offending. Treatment interventions need to target developing individuals' internal skills and capacity, and external opportunities and supports, to secure the full range of goods. While the promotion of specific goods in the treatment of offenders is likely to automatically eliminate (or reduce) commonly targeted dynamic risk factors, focusing *only* on the reduction of risk factors in treatment (as in the risk management approach) is unlikely to promote the full range of goods necessary for longer term desistence from offending (Ward and Marshall, 2004).

Fourth, individuals exist within distinct environments or ecological contexts. Tailoring the development of internal resources (e.g. skills, attitudes) and external resources (e.g. social supports, work opportunities) to each offender's distinct social contexts is central to the GLM and is likely to improve treatment relevance and effectiveness. In contrast, the risk management approach does not explicitly address the crucial role of context or ecological variables in the process of rehabilitation.

In summary, when using a GLM conceptualisation of rehabilitation a *Good Lives Plan* becomes a central organising tool for understanding offending and implementing treatment. The Good Lives Plan should take account of individuals' personal preferences and strengths, relevant environments, and the competencies and resources required to achieve the full range of primary goods. Risk factors and appropriate self-management are not ignored, instead they are explicitly contextualised as part of achieving good lives plans for each individual.

GLM: Aetiological assumptions about sexual offending

Research and theory indicate a core cluster of problems are evident in adult (and often adolescent) sexual offenders that lead to sexual offending: these are emotion regulation difficulties, interpersonal and social difficulties, cognitive distortions, and deviant sexual arousal (Beech and Ward, 2004; Hanson and Harris, 2000; Marshall, 1989; Ward, Keenan, and Hudson, 2000). Empathy deficits are subsumed under cognitive distortions and emotion regulation difficulties (Ward and Beech, 2006). Ward and Beech formulated the Integrated Theory of Sexual Offending (ITSO) to show how specific genetic predispositions and social learning (ecological) experiences (i.e. distal risk factors) interact to influence the development of vulnerabilities in three inter-related psychological systems that underpin this cluster of problems; these are the motivation/emotion, action selection and control, and perception and memory systems (Pennington, 2002; Ward and Beech, 2006). In combination with situational (i.e. proximal) risk factors these vulnerabilities can result in commission of a sexual offence.

Failure to meet individuals' inherent human needs (i.e. primary human goods) during development is likely to cause some harm to the psychological systems underpinning human action (Deci and Ryan, 2000; Emmons, 1999; Kekes, 1989) and result in problems in individuals' good lives plans. Problems in the *scope* of goals and the *planning* necessary to achieve them are located in the motivation/emotion and action selection and control psychological systems, respectively. For example, high levels of stress hormones can compromise the function of the action selection and control systems and result in impulsive behaviour (Sapolsky, 1997). Such individuals are likely to have insufficient capacity to implement a *Good Lives Plan* or regulate behaviour sufficiently to resolve conflict among the goods sought. Alternatively, high levels of sex hormones can influence the calibration of the motivation/emotion system by increasing the salience and availability of sexual goals and strengthening the influence of these goals on a person's life. Problems in the *choice* of goals and the *means* to achieve goals arise from distorted knowledge in the perception and memory system. For example, experiences of sexual abuse during childhood can lead to distorted beliefs about sex with children being normal or acceptable under certain conditions. Such individuals are likely to choose inappropriate secondary goods (i.e. a sexual relationship with a child) to achieve other valued primary goods (e.g. sexual satisfaction or intimacy).

As previously mentioned, the way people secure primary human goods depends crucially on: (a) the resources or opportunities available in their social and cultural environment (i.e. the external conditions), and (b) the skills and competencies acquired through socialisation in these environments (i.e. the internal conditions). For some individuals, early exposure to severe adverse ecological factors will compromise their basic internal resources, and underlying psychological systems, to such an extent that offending is the *direct route* (i.e. secondary good) to secure primary human goods (e.g. sexual satisfaction, intimacy, autonomy) (Ward and Gannon, 2006). For others, initiation of offending will arise when the pursuit of primary human goods through appropriate means (i.e. secondary goods) becomes frustrated in some way. For example, a relationship break-up results in loneliness and emotional distress and, in turn, strong feelings of connection with a child that are acted upon sexually. In this situation offending provides an *indirect route* to obtain the primary human goods that were otherwise obtained through socially appropriate routes.

In summary, approaching the aetiology of sexual offending from a GLM perspective enables us to appreciate the role of human goods in offending behaviour. According to the GLM the cluster of problems evident in sexual offenders indicates problems in their good lives plan. However, the GLM encourages clinicians to go beyond only understanding offenders' deficits or problems and instead encourages clinicians to think clearly about just what it is the person is *seeking* when committing an offence and where problems reside in the good lives plan.

GLM: Grounding current relapse prevention treatment

The GLM theory of sexual offender rehabilitation provides a resource to ground contemporary relapse prevention practice within a more holistic and meaningful structure that attends to risk management within an understanding of psychological wellbeing. Most contemporary relapse prevention programmes utilise a multi-pathway Self-Regulation Model (SRM) of the relapse or offence process to guide treatment formulation and planning. In essence, the SRM describes the relapse process as a series of pathways characterised by offenders' offence-related goals (i.e. offence avoidance or approach goals), distinct self-regulation styles (i.e. under-regulation, misregulation, or effective regulation), and level of awareness (see Ward and Hudson, 2000, for further details). The GLM enhances the current SRM relapse conceptualisation at least in two ways. First, whereas the SRM focuses exclusively on offenders' sexual goals, in the GLM sexual offending is a secondary good through which primary human goods are attained. Thus the GLM provides a clearer and more comprehensive understanding of the broad range of offenders' motivations for sexual offending (Ward and Gannon, 2006). Second, whereas the SRM describes the various self-regulatory styles implicated in sexual offending it doesn't explain the causal factors underlying these regulatory styles. The GLM provides an account of the causal mechanisms underlying the various self-regulation strategies that informs treatment planning (Ward and Gannon, 2006).

From a GLM perspective treatment is seen as an activity that adds to a sexual offender's repertoire of personal functioning, rather than being an activity that removes or manages a problem. The aims of GLM treatment are always specified as approach goals (Emmons, 1996; Mann, 2000; Mann, Webster, Schofield, and Marshall, 2004). Approach goals involve defining what individuals will achieve and gain, in contrast to avoidance goals that specify what will be avoided or ceased. Specifying the aims of treatment as life-enhancing goals rather than problem-avoiding goals creates intrinsic reasons for change rather than almost entirely relying on extrinsic influences (i.e. to avoid trouble with the law). Notably, research shows use of approach (versus avoidance) treatment goals can lead to enhanced motivation (Mann et al., 2004) and fewer lapses (Cox, Klinger, and Blount, 1991). Hence, incorporating offenders' goals as well as society's goals into treatment is more likely to tap into offenders' intrinsic motivation for change and enhance engagement in the rehabilitation process.

In summary, the GLM provides a way of anchoring current relapse prevention based treatments within a more comprehensive and meaningful framework. The GLM improves upon the SRM of relapse by accounting for the broad range of motivations that underlie sexual offending (e.g. sexual, intimacy, competency,

agency) and providing an aetiological explanation for each of the self-regulatory styles evident in offenders. The end result is a more comprehensive and internally coherent theory of rehabilitation to guide treatment with sexual offenders. The strengths-based focus ensures treatment adds to offenders' internal and external resources and facilitates constructing treatment goals in approach rather than avoidance terms; something which is intrinsically more motivating and a more effective learning strategy. The values, assumptions, and notions inherent in the GLM provide clinicians and clients with a meaningful and holistic way of making sense of past offending and a future *good life* without offending. Ultimately treatment aims to assist offenders to (1) think of themselves as someone who can secure all the important primary human goods in socially acceptable and personally satisfying ways and (2) develop the scope, strategies, coherence, and capacities necessary for living a healthy personal good lives plan.

Wellington STOP Adolescent Sexual Offender Programme

Two of the authors (LA and BW) have been involved in the development of a strengths-based programme to meet the specific needs of adolescent sexual offenders who are intellectually disabled/developmentally delayed in Wellington New Zealand. The client group is primarily young males aged 11–20 with intelligence levels in the lower range (IQ 45–80). Many are considered at 'high risk' of sexual re-offending and are characterised by co-occurring mental health diagnoses, histories of neglect and abuse, and insecure attachment styles. Most live with family or caregivers in the community, although some are in specialist group homes where extra monitoring and support is provided. After early attempts to implement a modified version of standard adult relapse prevention (Steen, 1993), Haaven, Little and Petre-Miller's (1990) Old Me/New Me treatment model for adult offenders with an intellectual disability was modified for use with adolescent clients. Instead of using Haven et al.'s concepts of Old Me (past behaviour) and New Me (new behaviour) the programme adopted the terminology *Good Side* and *Good Way*, and *Bad Side* and *Bad Way*, as the young people frequently used these terms in their own descriptions and essentially found these terms less abstract and easier to work with. The model that evolved was named the *Good Way* model.

The Good Way model is consistent with many of the GLM principles and values. Most notably, it incorporates a risk management and relapse prevention approach (Andrews and Bonta, 2003; Gendreau, 1996) within a strengths-based approach. Although developed independently from the GLM, the Good Way programme primarily aims for young people to attain psychological wellbeing and desist from offending through living a *good life*. A combination of therapeutic and educational modalities are used to build the young peoples' internal capacity (e.g. skills, knowledge, competence) and the external conditions (e.g. social support, opportunity) to achieve a good life including individual therapy, family-based therapy, psycho-educational and therapeutic group sessions, and work with a community of interest for each client. Although structured, the programme also retains the ability to tailor interventions to clients' specific needs and capacity. For example, for clients who are more severely disabled greater use of behavioural interventions helps focus attention on creating the external conditions necessary for desistance and living a good life. For more able clients greater use of individual cognitive interventions focuses on enhancing the internal resources necessary for implementing a good lives plan.

The Good Way model has two streams as shown in Figure 1. The first stream is named the *Good Way/Bad Way* and focuses on helping the young person to identify and develop a positive lifestyle. The second stream is named the *Good House/Bad House* and deals with clients' own loss and trauma, and the impact of their abusive behaviour on others. The two streams are drawn together by the ultimate goal of keeping safe and having a *Good Life*. Typical programme assignments are shown in the middle section of the diagram and are the Milestones (i.e. key pieces of work) that mark young peoples' progress through the programme. Although for reasons of clarity the two streams are presented here as separate and in a fixed order, in practice therapists individually sequence interventions in response to clients' needs.

The Good Way/Bad Way stream

Externalising conversations (White, 2001; White and Epston, 1990; Monk, Winslade, Crockett and Epston, 1997) are used to provide separation between the person and their positive (i.e. Good Side) and negative (i.e. Bad Side) impulses, cognitions, and behaviour. A new and more therapeutically useful way of seeing the problem is proposed: that is, the young person's behaviour has been under the influence of their Bad Side (i.e. their problematic good lives plan). Young people are then assisted to link the Good Side and Bad Side to their behaviour, so they realise that the Good Way (i.e. behaviour or what we do) occurs when we act on the advice of our Good Side (i.e. thoughts, feelings, and impulses). Listening to our Bad Side and following its direction leads us the Bad Way. The consequences of choosing the Good or Bad Way are made explicit, as clients are usually unable to link behaviour in the present with consequences in the future. Through repetition the young people make the connection that if they learn to go the Good Way this will lead to rewards and ultimately to their Good Life. This process continues throughout the programme with various identified problem behaviours and is consistent with the GLM's dual focus on risk management and capacity building.

The *Decision* step entails the young person making a choice about their future intentions and taps directly into components of personal identity: What sort of person do I want to be? Will I live my life the Good Way or the Bad Way? Once commitment to the Good Way (i.e. pro-social behaviour and personal identity) is achieved, a simple Good Way plan is developed whereby clients identify safety rules and strategies for dealing with suggestions of the Bad Side. Thereafter clients continue to increase their capacity to understand and strengthen their Good Side and go the Good Way through creating opportunities and reinforcement for pro-social values (e.g. honesty, respect) and learning problem solving and social skills (Ross and Fabiano, 1986, T3 Associates, 1997; Stallard, 2002).

For more able young people (i.e. those in the mild mental retardation range; American Psychiatric Association, 2000), subsequent work on traditional offence-related areas (e.g. offending patterns, sexual fantasy, and relapse prevention) involves a more detailed examination of the thinking, feeling and behaviour that characterises both the Good Side and the Bad Side. For this work, the programme creates another externalisation: the Gang of Three and the Three Wise Men. The *Gang* consists of three principal

The Good Way Model

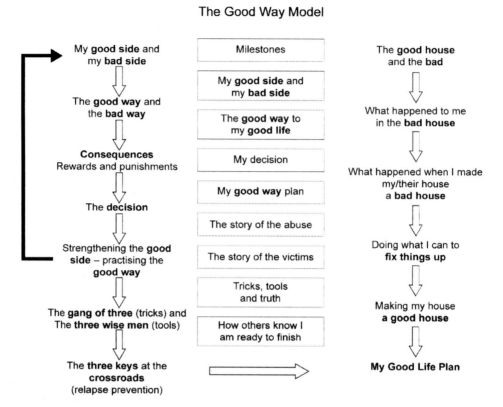

Figure 5.1   The Good Way Model

players on the Bad Side: Mr. Sneaky, Mr. Bully and Mr. Just Do It. These characters were developed after being consistently identified by clients as key personifications of their Bad Side. Familiarity with the *Gang* makes abusive behaviour easier to talk about and provides heightened recognition of the psychological processes that impact on safety. In contrast, the *Three Wise Men* encapsulate key qualities of the young person's Good Side and are the *tools* that will help them avoid relapse and continue to go the Good Way. The Three Wise Men offer the opportunity for the Good Side to counteract the activities of the Bad Side with more precision. The identification and development of each Wise Man also focuses clients on more positive aspects of their personality and builds on their experience of themselves as a capable pro-social person.

The *Three Keys at the Crossroads* is a simple relapse prevention component rendered more concrete and accessible to youth and adapted to fit with the *Good Way* model. The crossroads

refers to any decision point that involves a choice between the Good Way and the Bad Way, especially one leading to re-offending. The three keys are the *Tricks*, *Tools*, and the *Truth*. The term *Trick* is used to draw attention to that internal state in which the young person's desire to stay safe conflicts with urges to act on opportunities to offend. *Tools* are the specific strategies that a particular young person will use to avoid being tricked by the Gang of Three, thereby staying safe and not re-offending. The *Truth* is not only a powerful tool ('what is the Truth?') but also triggers reflection on abuse generally and the relapse prevention process in particular.

The Good House/Bad House stream

The second stream of the model begins by addressing the client's own victimisation and issues such as neglect, separation, insecure attachment, grief and loss, through the medium of the *Good House* and the *Bad House* (inspired by John Briere, 2001). These terms are extended to include other places such as schools, camps, care programmes, parks, community halls, and churches as needed. Through identifying times when their house, or other place, was a Good House or a Bad House, or through questions about the behaviour of others (e.g. Do you know anyone who acts like Mr. Sneaky?) the young person may begin to discuss their experiences of abuse, loss or rejection. This is the main emotionally opening, and potentially healing part of the work, and may deal with issues either from when they were young or as a consequence of their offending.

Later the emphasis shifts to reflect on how others have experienced the young peoples' abusive behaviours, thereby assisting them to gain some understanding of the negative impact. The young people can then begin to strategise how they could make amends for their past behaviour and the impact it has had on the victims and the families. This step differs for each client depending on his circumstances but may involve writing letters of apology, attending *face-up* meetings with victims, and having discussions with family or others who were affected by the abuse. Family reconstruction work may also be started for those young people who were removed from, and who may be returning to live with family.

The step of *making my house a good house* involves practising the skills of being part of a good house. This includes such things as learning social skills, dealing with conflict, and learning to apologise for mistakes, all understood as part of *Going the Good Way*. It also involves helping the young person to clarify the goals and values of their Good Life: How do I want to live? What sort of person will I be when I move back home? This step often involves working with the client, family and/or involved agencies to plan for their future living situation. The final piece of formal work involves developing a *Good Life Plan*. It may be prepared in both a written and pictorial form, the latter being a poster that young people feel comfortable having on their wall at home.

The Good Way programme has run over the last four years and to date none of the young people who have completed the Good Way programme are known to have sexually re-offended. For those individuals who are lower risk and/or higher functioning, completing the Good Way programme is sufficient to ameliorate further offending and result in successful community living with the usual support someone with an intellectual disability might receive. For those who are higher risk and/or significantly more intellectually disabled, completion of the Good Way programme is regarded as a step in an ongoing process of being supported to stay safe through ongoing attention to maintenance, refresher sessions, and regular training of support people. Positive outcomes for these clients include increased compliance with supervision and monitoring and placement in lower levels of secure care. In addition, the young people who participate in the programme report that the Good Way model is accessible to them and readily apply the language to describe their behaviour, difficulties and successes. Increasingly the Good Way model is being applied to children and young people without an intellectual disability and they too respond extremely well to it. It is also being introduced to programmes for adults with an intellectual disability.

The GLM and adolescents: Thinking holistically, developmentally and contextually

The GLM provides a valuable and much-needed alternate rehabilitation theory to inform and anchor emerging innovations in adolescent sex offender treatment such as the Wellington STOP programme. Although the Wellington STOP programme for adolescent sex offenders with intellectual disabilities developed largely independently (and in parallel time) to the GLM it is apparent that the programme illustrates some of the principles of the GLM. To some extent, the GLM can provide a theoretical rationale for the success of this 'out of the field' innovation. The GLM also provides a comprehensive set of resources to further inform and guide future developments in the programme and clinicians' routine decision-making. In particular, the GLM, and resulting *Good Lives Plan*, provides a stronger focus on understanding what primary human goods were being *sought* through offending and how the Good Lives Plan that is built with clients needs to ensure the full range of goods are met. The GLM also provides a theoretical rationale to inform how the various aspects of the programme and therapeutic modalities are tailored to individuals' needs and capacity.

The GLM provides an overarching rehabilitation framework that integrates capability enhancement and relapse prevention in an internally coherent and clinically useable manner. Through understanding individuals' offending as a socially unacceptable (and often personally frustrating) attempt to pursue primary human goods, psychological wellbeing and offence-related problems are intricately linked. From a GLM perspective, interventions to enhance the internal and external resources available to individuals are not delivered haphazardly but are clearly linked to offence-related problems and problems in the good lives plan. The GLM does not ignore risk factors, instead risk and relapse prevention are contextualised and understood within a holistic understanding of human behaviour and rehabilitation. In contrast, the risk management and relapse prevention rehabilitation approach only attends to one side of the coin (i.e. risk not goods) and thus provides no theoretical or practical guidance about how programmes should proceed to meet the psychological needs of offenders. Such a rehabilitation approach encourages programmes to either ignore individuals' psychological wellbeing altogether or to develop risk and wellbeing interventions in a piecemeal, unintegrated manner.

In addition to its holistic approach, we believe the GLM has several developmental and contextual strengths that further lend its application to adolescent rehabilitation. First, we argue the full range of primary human goods is equally relevant for adolescents but the *manner* (i.e. secondary goods) used to secure those goods will be developmentally dependent. For example, the types of activities and experiences that bring happiness to a 14-year-old are likely to be different to those used to secure happiness by a 35-year-old. Similarly the types of decisions and activities that provide the experience of autonomy and relatedness will be dependent on developmental maturity (i.e. knowledge, skills and attitudes) and contextual opportunities and support (e.g. parental competence, access to social activities). Thus the GLM does not simply transfer knowledge about sexual offending and rehabilitation from the adult area to the adolescent area but instead encourages a developmentally informed understanding of offending.

Second, the GLM places significant importance on the role of context in both the development of problems in individuals' *Good Lives Plans* as well as in effective rehabilitation. Hence, attention to

adolescents' ecological contexts would be integrated throughout GLM assessment and treatment. For example, adolescents' developmental needs (e.g. greater dependency on others to meet their needs and less control over the contexts of their lives) require that particular attention is paid to the external conditions necessary to construct and achieve a healthy *Good Lives Plan*. Both the interventions that aim to increase the social systems' capacity (e.g. opportunities for appropriate intimate relationships) and increase adolescents' internal capacity (e.g. impulse control, mood regulation) would coherently derive from the Good Lives Plan and be tailored to adolescents' distinct social contexts.

Third, the fact that adolescents' good lives plans are developing (rather than developed) points to the critical role of personal identity development in adolescence. From a GLM perspective all human beings seek certain goods and construct their identity through realising these goods in different activities and lifestyles (Becker, 1997; Emmons, 1999; Nussbaum, 2001). A GLM rehabilitation perspective gives explicit attention to personal identity and the use of goal setting, skills enhancement, and opportunities to fashion a more pro-social identity. The language and concepts of the GLM provide a coherent and respectful narrative through which individuals can structure an understanding of past offending and evolve a more pro-social identity and lifestyle.

Conclusions

The GLM is a newly emerging theory of sexual offender rehabilitation that has the major aim of equipping offenders with the necessary internal and external resources to live better lives. We believe the GLM provides an alternate and much-needed holistic theory of rehabilitation to the strictly risk management and relapse-prevention approach that can inform and anchor some of the innovations emerging in adolescent sex offender rehabilitation. In particular, the GLM provides clinicians and programmes with the necessary resources to coherently integrate psychological and social interventions that attend to both risk management and overall wellbeing and function. The developmental and contextual considerations so important to working with adolescents are also inherent within the GLM rather than being additions. Hence, we are confident the GLM addresses researchers and practitioners concerns about basing adolescent sex offender rehabilitation solely on the risk management and relapse prevention approach. We anticipate that many aspects of existing programmes can be reformulated within a GLM but further developed to provide comprehensive GLM rehabilitation. It is our hope that researchers' and practitioners' will seize upon this opportunity to understand and use the GLM in their work with adolescent sexual offenders.

References

American Psychiatric Association (2000) *Diagnostic and Statistical Manual of Mental Disorders*. 4th Edn. Text Revision. Washington DC: American Psychiatric Association.

Andrews, D.A. and Bonta, J. (2003) *The Psychology of Criminal Conduct*. 3rd Edn. Cincinnati: Anderson Press.

Arnhart, L. (1998) *Darwinian Natural Right: The Biological Ethics of Human Nature*. Albany: State University of New York Press.

Aspinwall, L. and Staudinger, U.M. (Eds.) (2003) *A Psychology of Human Strengths: Fundamental Questions and Future Directions for a Positive Psychology*. Washington DC: American Psychological Association.

Barbaree, H.E., Hudson, S.M. and Seto, M.C. (1993) Sexual Assault in Society: The Role of the Juvenile Sexual Offender. In Barbaree, H.E., Marshall, W.L. and Hudson, S.M. (Eds.) *The Juvenile Sex Offender*, New York: Guilford Press.

Becker, G. (1997) *Disrupted Lives: How People Create Meaning in a Chaotic World*. Los Angeles: University of California Press.

Beech, A.R. and Ward, T. (2004) The Integration of Etiology and Risk in Sexual Offenders: A Theoretical Framework. *Aggression and Violent Behavior*, 10, 31–63.

Briere, J. (2001) *Recent Developments in the Treatment of Complex Psychological Trauma*. Seminar 5th November 2001, Wellington.

Bruner, J. (1990) *Acts of Meaning*. Cambridge: Harvard University Press.

Cavarero, A. (2000) *Relating Narratives: Storytelling and Selfhood*. London: Routledge.

Cox, M., Klinger, E. and Blount, J.P. (1991) Alcohol Use and Goal Hierarchies: Systematic Motivational Counselling for Alcoholics. In

Miller, W.R. and Rollnick, S. (Eds.) *Motivational Interviewing: Preparing People to Change Addictive Behavior*. New York: Guilford Press.

Cummins, R.A. (1996) The Domains of Life Satisfaction: An Attempt to Order Chaos. *Social Indicators Research*, 38, 303–28.

Deci, E.L. and Ryan, R.M. (2000) The 'What' and 'Why' of Goal Pursuits: Human Needs and the Self-determination of Behavior. *Psychological Inquiry*, 11, 227–68.

DeGrazia, D. (2005) *Human Identity and Bioethics*. New York: Cambridge University Press.

Emmons, R.A. (1999) *The Psychology of Ultimate Concerns*. New York: Guilford Press.

Gendreau, P. (1996) Offender Rehabilitation: What we Know and What needs to be Done. *Criminal Justice and Behavior*, 23, 144–61.

Haaven, J., Little, R. and Petre-Miller, D. (1990) *Treating Intellectually Disabled Sex Offenders: Model Residential Programme*. Orwell, VT: Safer Society.

Hanson, R.K. and Bussière, M.T. (1998) Predicting Relapse: A Meta-analysis of Sexual Offender Recidivism Studies. *Journal of Consulting and Clinical Psychology*, 66, 348–62.

Hanson, R.K. and Harris, A.J.R. (2000) Where Should we Intervene? Dynamic Predictors of Sex Offense Recidivism. *Criminal Justice and Behaviour*, 27, 6–35.

Hanson, R.K. et al. (2002) First Report of the Collaborative Outcome Data Project on the Effectiveness of Psychological Treatment for Sex Offenders. *Sexual Abuse: A Journal of Research and Treatment*, 14, 169–94.

Kekes, J. (1989) *Moral Tradition and Individuality*. Princeton, New Jersey, Princeton University Press.

Linley, P.A. and Joseph, S. (Eds.) (2004) *Positive Psychology in Practice*. New York: John Wiley and Sons.

Mann, R.E. (2000) Managing Resistance and Rebellion in Relapse Prevention. In Laws, D.R., Hudson, S.M and Ward, T. (Eds.) *Remaking Relapse Prevention with Sex Offenders*. Thousand Oaks, CA: Sage.

Mann, R.E., Webster, S.D., Schofield, C. and Marshall, W.L. (2004) Approach versus Avoidance Goals in Relapse Prevention with Sexual Offenders. *Sexual Abuse: A Journal of Research and Treatment*, 16, 65–75.

Marshall, W.L. (1989) Intimacy, Loneliness, and Sexual Offenders. *Behaviour Research and Therapy*, 27, 491–503.

Monk, G., Winslade, J., Crockett, K. and Epston, D. (Eds.) (1997) *Narrative Therapy in Practice:*

The Archaeology of Hope. San Francisco: Jossey-Bass.

Murphy, M.C. (2001) *Natural Law and Practical Rationality*. New York: Cambridge University Press.

Nussbaum, M.C. (2000) *Women and Human Development: The Capabilities Approach*. New York: Cambridge University Press.

Pennington, B.F. (2002) *The Development of Psychopathology: Nature and Nurture*. New York: Guilford Press.

Print, B. and O'Callaghan, D. (2004) Essentials of an Effective Treatment Programme for Sexually Abusive Adolescents: Offence Specific Treatment Tasks. In O'Reilly, G., Marshall, W.L., Carr, A. and Beckett, R.C. (Eds.) *The Handbook of Clinical Intervention with Young People who Sexually Abuse*. East Sussex: Brunner-Routledge.

Rapp, C.A. (1998) *The Strengths Model: Case Management with People Suffering from Severe and Persistent Mental Illness*. New York: Oxford University Press.

Rescher, N. (1990) *Human Interests: Reflections on Philosophical Anthropology*. Stanford, CA: Stanford University Press.

Rich, P. (2003) *Understanding, Assessing and Rehabilitating Juvenile Sexual Offenders*. New York: John Wiley and Sons.

Ross, R. and Fabiano, E. (1986) *Reasoning and Rehabilitation: A Handbook for Teaching Cognitive Skills*. Ottawa: T3 Training and Consulting Inc.

Sapolsky, R. (1997) *The Trouble with Testosterone and other Essays on the Biology of the Human Predicament*. New York, Scribner.

Schmuck, P. and Sheldon, K.M. (2001) (Eds.) *Life Goals and Well-being*. Toronto: Hogrefe and Huber.

Stallard, P. (2002) *Think Good – Feel Good: A Cognitive Behaviour Therapy Workbook for Children and Young People*. Chichester: John Wiley and Sons.

Steen, C. (1993) *The Relapse Prevention Workbook for Youth in Treatment*. Brandon, VT: Safer Society Press.

T3 Associates (1997) *R and R for Adolescents: Reasoning and Re-'Acting'. A Handbook for Teaching Cognitive Skills*. Ottawa: T3 Associates Training and Consulting.

Ward, T. (2002) Good Lives and the Rehabilitation of Offenders: Promises and Problems. *Aggression and Violent Behavior*, 7, 513–28.

Ward, T. and Beech, A.R. (2006) An Integrated Theory of Sexual Offending. *Aggression and Violent Behavior*, 11, 44–63.

Ward, T. and Gannon, T.A. (2006) Rehabilitation, Etiology, and Self-regulation: The Comprehensive Good Lives Model of Treatment for Sexual Offenders. *Aggression and Violent Behavior*, 11, 77–94.

Ward, T. and Hudson, S.M. (2000) A Self-regulation Model of Relapse Prevention. In Laws, D.R., Hudson, S.M. and Ward, T. (Eds.) *Remaking Relapse Prevention with Sex Offenders: A Sourcebook*. Thousand Oaks, CA: Sage.

Ward, T., Keenan, T. and Hudson, S.M. (2000) Understanding Cognitive, Affective, and Intimacy Deficits in Sexual Offenders: A Developmental Perspective. *Aggression and Violent Behavior*, 5, 41–62.

Ward, T. and Mann, R. (2004) Good Lives and the Rehabilitation of Offenders: A Positive Approach to Sex Offender Treatment. In Linley, P.A. and Joseph, S. (Eds.) *Positive Psychology in Practice*. New York: John Wiley and Sons.

Ward, T., Mann, R. and Gannon, T. (2005) *The Comprehensive Model of Good Lives Treatment for Sex Offenders: Clinical Implications*. Manuscript submitted for publication.

Ward, T. and Marshall, W.L. (2004) Good Lives, Etiology and Rehabilitation of Sexual Offenders: A Bridging Theory. *Journal of Sexual Aggression*. 10, 153–69.

Ward, T. and Marshall, W.L. (2005) *Narrative Identity and Offender Rehabilitation*. Manuscript submitted for publication.

Ward, T., Polaschek, D. L. and Beech, A.R. (2005). *Theories of Sexual Offending*. Chichester: John Wiley and Sons.

Ward, T. and Stewart, C.A. (2003a) The Treatment of Sex Offenders: Risk Management and Good Lives. *Professional Psychology: Research and Practice*, 34, 1–8.

Ward, T. and Stewart, C.A. (2003b) Criminogenic Needs or Human Needs: A Theoretical Critique. *Psychological, Crime and Law*, 9, 125–43.

Weinrott, M.R. (1996) *Juvenile Sexual Aggression: A Critical Review* (Center Paper 005). Boulder, Colorado: University of Colorado Center for the Study and Prevention of Violence.

White, M. (2001) Narrative Practice and the Unpacking of Identity Conclusions. *Gecko 2001*, 2. Adelaide: Dulwich Centre Publications.

White, M. and Epston, D. (1990) *Narrative Means to Therapeutic Ends*. New York: Norton.

Worling, J.R. and Curwen, R. (2000) Adolescent Sexual Offender Recidivism: Success of Specialized Treatment and Implications for Risk Prediction. *Child Abuse and Neglect*, 24, 965–82.

Chapter 6

Emerging Personality Disorders in Sexually Harmful Young People

Graeme Richardson

Introduction

People are different by virtue of their personalities. These differences are not infinite and can be grouped or typed. The ability to identify another person's personality type enables us to understand the type of person we are interacting or dealing with. Personality helps make the person identifiable and distinguishable. An understanding of their personality informs the ways we might approach, interact with, and respond to that person. Personality is a complex mix of various and different characteristics or traits. So is personality akin to IQ (intelligence)? Is more better? The answer is dependent upon identifying which traits are present, as some personality traits are more functional than others in terms of adaptability and achievement in relationships and society. Equally, some traits are dysfunctional in that they impede adaptability and achievement. Some traits, or combinations of traits, may be so dysfunctional that they reflect a disorder. In their case, less is better. Consider the person characterised by the following traits: extrovert, affable, empathetic, and trusting, and compare that person with another person characterised by these traits: introvert, belligerent, callous, and suspicious. Who is most likely to adapt to and be successful in terms of their family, interpersonal, social, and economic functioning? So personality may be divided in terms of being adaptive and functional or maladaptive and dysfunctional, and there is variation in degree within both. A widely accepted conceptualisation of functional personalities is the Five Factor Model (Widiger and Costa, 1994). A widely accepted conceptualisation of dysfunctional personalities is the Biosocial Learning Model (Millon, 1996).

Forensic research, that is, the empirical investigation into criminal behaviour, including sexual offending, has studied the relationships between offending behaviour and maladaptive or dysfunctional personality characteristics. This is the focus of this chapter. The general relevance of this research is the identification of sub-groups of sexual offenders who can be differentiated on the basis of their personality characteristics or personality difficulties. This contributes to the body of knowledge that attests to the heterogeneity (diversity) of sexual offenders. This is in keeping with the essence of research into personality, which is to explain individual differences. Critical questions pertain to how much sexual offenders differ from other offender groups, such as, non-sexual violent offenders, and how much sex offenders differ from each other. This is said to lead to a better understanding of sexual offenders and of their different deficits and difficulties, in order that their forensic and clinical needs might be better understood. The more particular relevance of this research has to do with personality dysfunction itself. The research and clinical consensus is that *Interpersonal difficulties*, that is, chronic and global dysfunctional interpersonal relationships, are a central defining feature of personality dysfunction or personality disorders. This is consistent across different approaches to assessment, formulation and categorisation of personality dysfunction. Both the psychiatrically diagnosed personality disorders, such as, schizoid, avoidant, dependent, paranoid, borderline, and antisocial types, and the dimensional model of personality pathology, which psychometrically measures core personality traits, equally emphasise life-long interpersonal and social relationship difficulties. The corollary of this approach is the clinical utility of the identification of a sub-group of sexual offenders who have 'special needs" in relation to chronic and severe interpersonal and social adjustment difficulties. Then these 'special needs' ought to be addressed through a range of co-ordinated and targeted interventions.

Temperament

Let's start at the beginning and put our cards on the table. The genetic shuffle is influential in the determination of individual differences. Temperament is said to predate and influence personality development, and have a strong biological basis. Personality emerges later in development and is shaped by our interpersonal and social experiences, including significant life events. However, the professional consensus is that both temperament and personality are influenced by environmental experiences in childhood and both reflect individual differences (Emde and Hewitt, 2001; Rothbart and Bates, 1998). Temperament refers to stable individual differences discernable from birth and infancy, which have their basis in the genetic and neurobiological make up of the infant. These differences are in terms of: (1) emotionality; (2) activity levels; and (3) attention (Rothbart and Bates, 1998; Chess and Thomas, 1996). There are several descriptive models of temperament (see Buss and Plomin, 1975, 1984; Derryberry and Rothbart, 1997). Mervielde and Asendorph (2000) have formulated an amalgam of several different models of temperament that incorporates four dimensions: (1) emotionality; (2) extraversion; (3) activity; and (4) persistence. The research and clinical literatures accepts the reality of something akin to a problematic temperament, described as a 'difficult' temperament. This has been used to differentiate the 'easy' child from the 'difficult' child, with the difficult child being more difficult to parent and manage (Maziade et al., 1990; Thomas et al., 1963). Also, 'shyness' has been conceptualised as a temperamental disposition and has been associated with temperamental difficulties (Kagan, 1994). Recent research has attempted to make links between models of temperament and personality, and personality dysfunction or disorder (Mervielde et al., 2005).

Personality

Personality refers to a person's individual psychological characteristics, and their established patterns of cognitions, emotions, and behaviours. Personality is relational in that it develops and takes shape within the context of our interpersonal and social relationships. Features of our personality are especially prominent in our interactions with other people, as it shapes the way we relate and respond to other people. There are several models of personality differences such as: (1) Factorial (Cattell, 1965); (2) Circumplex (Pincus and

Wiggins, 1990); and (3) Five-Factor (Costa and McCrae, 1992a). The most supported model is the Five-Factor model, which describes five higher-order traits, known as the 'Big Five' (McCrae and Costa, 1990). It represents a model of individual differences in adults. A simple but critical point relates to the relationship between adult personality and child/adolescent personality. Do children exhibit the same personality traits as adults? The Big Five model of personality has recently been found to be relevant to children and adolescents (Mervielde et al., 2005; Putnam et al., 2001). De Clercq et al. (2004) have described the childhood version of the Big-Five personality dimensions, which they have termed the 'Little Five'. A comprehensive classification of personality differences in childhood and adolescence is provided by Shiner and Caspi (2003) and Caspi, Roberts, and Shiner (2005). This classification system is consistent with and informed by the Big Five model of personality (Widiger et al., 2002). This work has produced a typology of personality traits in children and adolescents: (1) Extroversion; (2) Neuroticism; (3) Conscientiousness; (4) Agreeableness; and (5) Openness-to-experience (Shiner, 2005).

Personality pathology and personality disorders

The clinical and personality research literatures describe personality gone wrong. That is, dysfunctional or maladaptive personality functioning. It is variously referred to as 'personality pathology' or 'personality disorder'. Both imply an abnormality. Our understanding of personality dysfunction requires the integration of knowledge of 'normal' and 'pathological' personality development and functioning. Personality dysfunction may be described in terms of a combination of adaptive and maladaptive personality traits and their associated behaviours (Widiger and Simonsen, 2005). In the relevant literature, adult personality disorders are associated with: (1) genetic; (2) temperamental; and (3) developmental factors. Currently there is no widely accepted model of the severity of personality disorder or dysfunction (Tyrer, 2005). Rather, the debilitating impact of the disorder on the general functioning of the individual, conceived of as 'maladaptiveness', is emphasised (Svanborg et al., 1999).

Categorical psychopathology models

The medical or clinical approach to defining dysfunctional personality refers to 'disordered' personality and different personality 'disorders'. Each 'Personality Disorder' is distinguishable in terms of its own diagnostic criteria. Personality dysfunction then becomes a psychiatric condition, which may be diagnosed using specific diagnostic criteria. Although 'Personality Disorder' is an 'Adult' disorder the psychiatric literature acknowledges that it reflects an 'enduring pattern' that may be traced back to adolescence or even childhood. This refers the historical precursors to a psychiatric illness, which manifests itself much later in life, typically early adulthood.

A personality disorder is a psychiatric diagnosis and requires a mental health assessment, typically involving the professions of psychiatry, psychology, and psychiatric nursing. A diagnosis will be based upon a detailed history of the person's life and functioning, clinical interviews, and self-report questionnaires. It is technically an adult (18 years and over) disorder, and is not included, nor has it an equivalent, in the psychiatric classification of childhood and adolescent disorders. The psychiatric classification of personality disorders has identified multiple types, so it is feasible for a person to be diagnosed with more than one personality disorder. Each separate personality disorder has a set of diagnostic criteria that include both personality traits and behaviours. There are two psychiatric diagnostic classification systems that define and describe a range of different personality disorders: (1) DSM-IV (North American system: American Psychiatric Association, 1994); and (2) ICD-10 (European system: WHO, 1992). DSM-IV distinguishes ten personality disorders, and ICD-10 eight. Despite their inclusion in psychiatric classifications, personality disorders are not the same as mental illnesses. Essentially they reflect inflexible and maladaptive personality traits, which cause the individual psychological distress and seriously impair their interpersonal and social functioning. These impairments are chronic, enduring rather than transitory, and pervasive, adversely affect all aspects of the person's life. The person's thinking, emotions, and behaviours are all affected by the presence of dysfunctional personality traits. Classically, such individuals' experience significant, recurrent, and long-standing difficulties in relating to other people and in their relationships. They are more likely to be emotionally labile and impulsive, and less likely to be able to adequately cope with the vagaries of everyday life and associated stresses. In terms of the aetiology (cause) of personality disorders, they do not fall out of the sky when the person becomes 18 years of age. To use a medical analogy, they are not an acute illness that suddenly infects the person, rather they are akin to an insidious illness, which takes a long time to manifest itself as detectable symptoms.

Several criticisms have been raised in relation to the psychiatric model of personality disorders. Young and Gluhoski (1996) have cited: (1) shared diagnostic criteria across different personality disorders, which suggests that they are not discrete disorders; (2) a patient may be diagnosed with several different personality disorders; and (3) weak diagnostic reliability and validity, that is, too much variation and disagreement in diagnosis between clinicians. Similarly, Widiger and Frances (1985) contended that a categorical approach is inadequate due to overlapping diagnostic boundaries, and so proposed a dimensional model, a continuum between normal and pathological behaviour.

Dimensional psychopathology models

The essence of this non-psychiatric approach is that some personality traits are pathological because they are extreme versions of functional personality traits (Widiger and Costa, 1994). The Circumplex and Five-Factor models of personality explicitly address pathology, and view personality disorders as developing in a social context. Pincus and Wiggins (1990) argue that maladaptive interpersonal behaviour is the defining characteristic of personality disorders, that is, inflexible and ineffective patterns of interacting with other people. The Circumplex model defines pathological personalities as extremes of naturally occurring personality traits. Individuals with dysfunctional personalities use certain behaviours to an extreme degree, and possess a limited repertoire of interpersonal behaviours. Consequently, their behaviour elicits a limited range, and usually negative, responses from other people. Similarly in the Five Factor model personality dysfunction reflects an extreme variation of the dimensions of normal personality (Costa and McCrae, 1990, 1992a). These dimensional models are descriptive of personality types, but are limited in terms of explaining the development of personality pathology, that is, the aetiology of personality disturbance. In the Social Learning Theory model of personality dysfunction (Millon, 1981) temperament and social learning combine to produce eight maladaptive personality types. These are based on how the person goes about gaining rewarding experiences from their social environment and how they interact with that environment. In this model maladaptive personality functioning is characterised by: (1) the rigid use of particular unsuccessful coping behaviours; (2) repeated self-defeating cycles of behaviour; and (3) emotional and behavioural instability in stressful situations. There have been some recent studies into the relationships between the Five Factor model of personality and personality disorders, both in adults (Saulsman and Page, 2004) and adolescents (De Clercq and De Fruyt, 2003; De Clercq, De Fruyt, and Van Leeuwen, 2004). These represent investigations into which personality traits correspond to adult personality disorders as they are defined in the psychiatric literature. Preliminary findings have indicated that the dimension of *neuroticism* is most strongly and consistently associated with several of the psychiatrically defined personality disorders. Preliminary conclusions are that the personality disorders may be defined in terms of the Big-Five basic dimensions of personality (O'Connor and Dyee, 2002) although clear differentiation between the various different psychiatric categories of personality disorders has proved difficult using these Big-Five personality dimensions (Morey et al., 2002). This approach is also beginning to be applied to adolescents (De Clercq and De Fruyt, 2003).

Aetiology of personality disorders

The psychiatric literature accepts that personality disorders are not an illness. So if they cannot be contracted, then where do personality disorders come from? There has been only relatively recent research into the developmental antecedents of personality disorders (Bernstein et al., 1996; Kasen et al., 1999, 2001; Ramklint et al., 2003). Consequently there is limited empirical knowledge regarding the different aetiologies for the various personality disorders, as they have

been categorised in the psychiatric literature. The main problem has been the relative distinctiveness of the personality disorders as they are defined in the psychiatric literature, as well as the overlapping diagnostic criteria across these different disorders. This is an inherent and intractable weakness of the psychiatric classification of personality disorder.

The professional consensus in the field of personality research is that disordered personalities are extreme versions of normal dimensions of personality (e.g., Costa and McCrae, 1990, 1992a; Pincus and Wiggins, 1990). Formation of these extreme manifestations occurs when innate temperaments interact with social learning experiences (Millon, 1981). A vulnerable temperament (largely genetically determined) and adverse childhood experiences (typically multiple adversities and/or of relatively long duration) combine to seriously compromise the personality development of the child. This manifests itself as severe emotional and behavioural difficulties, which, if they persist unabated into adolescence, consolidate as an emerging personality disorder or combination of discrete disorders. Temperamental difficulties and early adverse life experiences, such as, childhood physical and sexual abuse, have been shown to predict personality dysfunction (Bryer et al., 1987; Carter et al., 1999; Paris and Frank, 1989; Svrakic et al., 1993). The work of Johnson and colleagues has consistently found that victims of early childhood abuse, emotional, physical, and sexual are much more likely to be diagnosed with a personality disorder in their early adulthood (Johnson et al., 1999, 2001, 2000). Similarly, Carter et al. (2001) reported that lack of parental care, emotional and psychological abuse, and physical abuse were predictive of high rates of personality disorder in adults. Interestingly, Battle et al. (2004) reported that childhood maladjustment, which is acknowledged to be associated with neglect and abuse, was associated with later personality disorder in adulthood. This finding was based on retrospective reports by adults about their experiences of abuse and neglect, and also of early loss and prolonged separations from parents. This association was strongest for adults diagnosed with Borderline Personality Disorder and Antisocial Personality Disorder. Two broad conclusions may be drawn from this body of research into the possible causes of adult personality disorders. Firstly, personality dysfunction originates in childhood and adolescence, and secondly, it is possible to identify risk factors for the development of personality dysfunction (Carter et al. 2001; Mervielde et al. 2005).

Stability of personality and personality disorders

Research into 'normal' personality documents the stability of temperament and personality across the life span (Roberts and Del Vecchino, 2000). There is a growing research evidence base for the stability of temperament and personality across the life span, whereby personality traits remain moderately stable throughout childhood and adolescence, with stronger stability from late adolescence through adult years (Caspi et al., 2003, 2005; Roberts, Caspi, and Moffitt, 2001; Roberts and Del Vecchio, 2000). The corollary is that: (1) disordered personality is also likely to remain stable over these years; and (2) disordered personality in adulthood will have its equivalent in, at least, adolescence, if not childhood. Some studies have reported the stability of disordered personality (Johnson et al., 2000a). The stability of normal personality might be disappointing to some who would wish to be 'a bit more like' someone else who they admire. However, the stability of a dysfunctional or disordered personality is likely to have much more serious consequences for the individual. For instance, a dysfunctional personality may confine them to the margins of society and even lead to their confinement in a hospital or a prison.

Personality disorders in childhood and adolescence

The clinical application of 'personality disorders' to children and adolescents is problematic, both conceptually and empirically. This is because of: (1) the very limited research into childhood and adolescent antecedents of personality disorders; and (2) the psychiatric classification of disorders in childhood and adolescence does not include an equivalent to the adult personality disorders. Nevertheless, there are some critical questions to be answered when personality disorder is considered in relation to children and young people:

1. Do children and young people exhibit the same dysfunctional personality traits as adults?

2. What is the impact of dysfunctional personality traits on the child's or young person's general development?
3. Are particular childhood traits precursors to later personality disorders?
4. Do personality disorders manifest themselves during childhood or adolescence?
5. Do adult personality disorders have their origins in childhood or adolescence?
6. Is a diagnosis of personality disorder appropriate?

Research in this area seeks to identify a developmental pathway from childhood, through adolescence and on to adulthood. The critical clinical task is to identify what the disorder looks like during childhood and adolescence. The American psychiatric literature defines personality disorders as 'stable and of long duration' and states that their onset 'can be traced back at least to adolescence or early adulthood' (American Psychiatric Association, 1994: 630). The emerging dominant position based on research in this field is that personality disorder does manifest itself during adolescence, and adult personality disorder does have its origins in childhood (Geiger and Crick, 2001; Kernberg, Weiner, and Bardenstein, 2000; Shiner, 2005). Internalising (emotional) and externalising (behavioural) dimensions of childhood and adolescent disorders, have been proposed as two counterparts in terms of broad personality dimensions, which may be used to understand and describe childhood and adolescent personality dysfunction (Krueger, 1999; Krueger et al., 1998; Krueger, McGue, and Iacono, 2001; Tackett et al., 2003). Accepting this conceptualisation, it may be inferred that internalising difficulties are the precursors to particular personality disorders, while externalising difficulties are precursors to a different set of personality disorders. Bernstein et al. (1993) identified adolescence as a high-risk developmental period for the onset of personality disorder, and Bernstein et al. (1996) concluded that childhood conduct disorder was the strongest predictor of personality disorder in adolescence.

Freeman and Rigby (2003) have argued that the existence of 'personality disorders' in children and young people is a clinical reality. They contend that in their clinical experience they have been able to identify maladaptive personality traits, and inflexible and persistent dysfunctional behaviours in clinically referred children and adolescents. They also report children and young people suffering functional impairment or subjective distress because of their 'personality disorders'. They advocate for an early identification-early intervention clinical model, which is dependent on acceptance of the concept and label of 'personality disorder'. Their rationale is that early diagnosis leads to early and appropriate interventions at a time when the person is more 'treatable' and the condition is less entrenched. Intervention at this stage is more likely to ameliorate presenting problems and alter the developmental course of the disorder. Interestingly, this rationale mimics the rationale for early intervention in young people who sexually harm, which was used to lobby for treatment services during the 1980s (see Knopp, 1985). A developmental perspective in combination with a family systems perspective informs Freeman and Rigby's formulation of 'personality disorder'. In this formulation family relations and the family environment are critically important factors in the development of personality dysfunction in children and young people. More specifically, disrupted and or dysfunctional child-parent attachments lie at the heart of the development of personality dysfunction. They also draw upon the schema therapy model of Young (1990). They argue that adverse developmental experiences, such as neglect, rejection, abuse, witnessing domestic or spousal violence, lead to the formation of early maladaptive schemas that persist throughout the course of child and adolescent development. They advocate a combination of family and cognitive therapies, and caution against ignoring the exact nature of the problem:

> *Choosing to ignore the reality of personality disorders among children and adolescents, to downplay the problem, or to search for euphemistic terms all downplay the severity and impact of these disorders. The sooner we accept their reality, the sooner we will focus our efforts on treatment and relieve the suffering of these children.*
>
> (p. 462)

Assessment and classification

Personality

Measurement of personality characteristics is primarily based on completion of self-report questionnaires. Some include 'rater' versions,

whereby another person, such as a parent, provides ratings of observed behaviours that are related to the various personality dimensions. Such measures are based upon a conceptual model of what constitutes personality. For example, the NEO Personality Inventory (Costa and McCrea, 1992b) is based on the Five-Factor model of personality (Digman, 1990; John, 1990). It is a measure of normal personality traits, and measures five dimensions of personality:

1. neuroticism
2. extraversion
3. openness
4. agreeableness
5. conscientiousness

Scores on this measures of the Five-Factor model of personality have been associated with maladaptive personality functioning (Coker, Samuel, and Widiger, 2002). A range of other related measures have been produced and validated. For instance, the Hierarchical Personality Inventory for Children (HiPIC: Mervielde and De Fruyt, 1999) is a measure of adaptive personality differences, and the Dimensional Personality Symptom Item (DIPSI) (Mervielde et al., 2005) which is still under development, is a measure of childhood personality symptoms or dysfunction.

Personality disorder

In relation to 'personality disorder' psychiatric diagnosis is the order of the day. Psychiatric classification and diagnostic systems are utilised, such as, the Diagnostic and Statistical Manual of Mental Disorders, 4th edn. (DSM-IV: American Psychiatric Association, 1994) and the International Statistical Classification of Diseases and Health Related Problems (ICD-10: WHO, 1993). Accompanying diagnostic semi-structured interviews are available (Loranger, 1999; Widiger et al., 1995).

A different methodology uses psychometric measures of psychopathology and personality disorder. The two that have been used most widely are the Minnesota Multiphasic Personality Inventory (MMPI; Graham, 1987), which also has an adolescent version, the MMPI-A (Butcher et al., 1992), and the Millon Multiaxial Clinical Inventory (MMCI) (Millon, 1987) which also has an adolescent version, the Millon Adolescent

Clinical Inventory (MACI) (Millon et al., 1993). However, a psychiatric diagnosis cannot be reliably determined on the basis of either a clinical interview or a self-report questionnaire, as information about the behaviour and functioning of the individual over the course of their life is required for accurate diagnosis.

Cognitive model

The cognitive model adopts a different methodology again. Self-report questionnaires are used to identify cognitive schemas or core dysfunctional beliefs that are associated with specific personality disorders. Examples of this approach are the Schema Questionnaire (Young and Brown, 1994) and Personality Belief Questionnaire (Beck and Beck, 1991).

Clinical assessment of young people

When determining the presence of a disordered personality in young people, the evaluation of personality 'symptoms' or maladaptive personality traits is critical. This requires some form of assessment of dysfunctional personality characteristics. Notwithstanding this, a comprehensive and reliable assessment also needs to identify patterns of behaviour and evaluate adaptive functioning. This requires a broad assessment, which takes into account several domains, such as, behaviour, affect, cognition, styles of interaction and levels of social adjustment and integration. This needs to be informed by multiple sources of information across a range of situations, and include a detailed family and developmental history, and school reports.

The cognitive model of personality disorder

The cognitive model represents an alternative approach to the psychiatric classification of personality disorders. The cognitive model incorporates both theoretical conceptualisations and therapeutic practices (Beck et al., 1990; Young, 1990). Schemas or core beliefs about the self (self-schemas) are central to the cognitive conceptualisation of personality disorder. Questionnaires are used in conjunction with clinical interview techniques to elicit

dysfunctional beliefs (Young, 1990; Beck, 1995). Beck et al. (1990) conceptualised each of the psychiatric personality disorder as having its own set of core beliefs and behavioural patterns of coping responses. Individuals with a disordered personality are characterised by intense emotional feelings to situations leading to disproportionate emotional reactions. Their emotions are driven by their negative core beliefs about themselves and other people. Personality disordered individuals typically have experienced traumatic childhoods and view themselves, other people and their relationships in excessively negative ways. Trauma may be physical or sexual abuse, or the child may have suffered chronic negative experiences such as neglect, critical parents, or demeaning and rejecting peers. Some children may be genetically predisposed to develop personality dysfunction, as they may possess no or few resilient or protective factors. Also they may have had no or few positive experiences to compensate for their negative life experiences. In addition, these core beliefs become immune to the potentially remedial influences of positive experiences, which then have no beneficial impact on the child's or young person's development. Beck et al. (1990) and Young (1990) hypothesise how adverse life experiences impact on the cognitive development of children, resulting in the formation of overly negative and stable perceptions and beliefs about themselves, other people and their relationships. This distorted belief system (schemas or core beliefs) leads to the formation of maladaptive ways of behaving and interacting with other people, which are self-defeating and damage relationships. Typically, individuals with a disordered personality possess a very restricted repertoire of ways of behaving and interacting. They are not responsive to new and different situations, whereas, normal or healthy personalities are adaptive and responsive.

Criminal personality disorder

The concept of a 'criminal personality', as described by its most famous protagonist, H. J. Eysenck (1964) was used to explain persistent criminal behaviour and individual differences in relation to criminality. Eysenck's theory was based on his personality constructs of Extroversion, Neuroticism, and Psychoticism and measured by the Eysenck Personality

Questionnaire (Eysenck and Eysenck, 1975). Criminality was linked with high psychoticism and high extroversion scores. His theory has been around for several decades, however, fashions change and the concept was never adequately supported by empirical evidence. For example, Kelly and Richardson (unpublished) investigated Eysenck's (1964) theory of criminality in a British sample of 390 young offenders. The general pattern that emerged was one of high scores on Neuroticism and low scores on Extroversion, which did not support Eysenck's theory. Nevertheless, the concept of a criminal personality lives on and is embodied in the much more fashionable concept of 'psychopathy', which does have empirical support in relation to its associations with serious, violent, and persistent criminality (Hart, 1998; Hemphill et al., 1998). The major difference between a notion of a criminal personality and psychopathy, in terms of their scientific acceptability, is that between arguing that criminals share a common profile of personality traits versus arguing that there is a sub-group of criminals who are predisposed to criminality because of their personality profile. The later being more valid. The concept of psychopathy is not a recognised psychiatric disorder and cannot be diagnosed. The most pertinent personality disorder is Antisocial Personality Disorder in the American diagnostic system, and Dissocial Personality Disorder in the European diagnostic system. In many respects these diagnoses are tautologies as they are heavily dependent upon an established pattern of antisocial and criminal behaviour, and essentially describe such behaviour as critical features of the disorder. The critical questions then become: (1) When does persistent behaviour become a personality disorder? and (2) Is a personality disorder more than an established pattern of behaviour?

Antisocial personality disorder

Antisocial personality disorder is strongly associated with increased risk for criminal behaviours. Johnson et al. (2000) found that adolescent antisocial personality disorder was associated with violence and criminal behaviour during adolescence and early adulthood. The disorder is characterised by a pervasive pattern of disregard for, and violation of, the rights of others occurring since age 15 years. The following features are characteristic of the disorder:

- Inability to tolerate boredom.
- Low frustration tolerance.
- Lack of empathy.
- Callousness.
- Indifferent to others suffering, loss or plight.
- Disregard of others welfare and rights.
- Irresponsible and exploitative in their acquaintances, relationships, and interactions with others.
- History of many sexual partners or impersonal sex.
- Substance misuse.
- Early onset Conduct Disorder (before age 10 years).

In the research literatures pertaining to Conduct Disorder (a childhood behavioural disorder) and young offenders, attempts have been made to identify a developmental pathway to severe and persistent antisocial behaviour. This research had identified precursors to this extreme pattern of antisocial behaviour, which are used to identify children at high risk, but who may still be amenable to interventions to ameliorate their antisocial behaviours. For instance, the combination of childhood hyperactivity and aggression has been found to be a strong predictor of antisocial and aggressive behaviour in adolescence, continuing into adulthood (Dolan, 1994). Within these research and related clinical literatures, a developmental pathway from conduct problems in childhood leading to antisocial personality disorder in adolescence and/or young adulthood is beginning to emerge (Dolan, 1994). For example, Eppright et al. (1993) have reported the prevalence of antisocial personality disorder in a population of juvenile offenders. Conduct Disorder has been found to be the strongest predictor of Antisocial Personality Disorder (Harrington et al., 1991). Consequently, in the clinical specialism of forensic mental health in young people, the concept of an emerging antisocial personality disorder (DSM-IV) (or emerging dissocial personality disorder: ICD-10) has been largely accepted (Harrington and Bailey, 2003). Dolan and Millington (2004) reported the evidence for the associations between impulsivity and aggression and an emerging antisocial personality disorder. They termed this the 'impulsivity-aggression dimension', which is characterised by difficulty in inhibitory control, acting-out behaviours, a lack of tolerance for frustration, sensation seeking, and a tendency towards criminality. Research has shown this dimension to be associated with EEG abnormalities, reduced serotonergic functioning, and fronto-temporal deficits on neuropsychological testing (Siever and Davis, 1991). Harrington and Bailey (2003) have summarised the known precursors (or risk factors) associated with the development of antisocial personality disorder. These are:

- Callous temperament or personality (Loeber et al., 2002).
- Depression (Kasen et al., 2001).
- Oppositional disorder (Loeber et al., 2002).
- Conduct disorder (Harrington et al., 1991).
- Substance abuse (Loeber et al., 2002).

Psychopathy

In a similar way to the growing acceptance of the validity of a diagnosis of Antisocial Personality Disorder in young people, there has been an emerging acceptance of the application of the concept of 'psychopathy' to young people (Forth and Burke, 1998). In the pursuit of an understanding of the developmental course taken by extreme and persistent antisocial behaviour, the concept of 'psychopathic traits', which are the precursors to the emergence of 'psychopathy', have been proposed and researched (Frick, 1998; Frick and Ellis, 2000). This has had the effect of raising the issue of psychopathy in relation to not just adolescents, but also children. Related assessment instruments are now available: the Hare Psychopathy Checklist Youth Version (Forth, Kosson, and Hare, 2003) and the Antisocial Process Screening Device (Frick and Hare, 2001). The Hare Psychopathy Checklist Youth Version essentially measures the same constructs as the adult version. The constructs measured by the Antisocial Process Screening Device (Frick and Hare, 2001) are: (1) Callous/Unemotional traits; (2) Narcissism; and (3) Impulsivity. The rationale for these conceptual and assessment developments is to:

1. Identify a particularly severe group of antisocial and aggressive children and young people.
2. Identify the early manifestations of the traits associated with psychopathy.
3. Predict a severe sub-group of pre-adolescent conduct disordered children.

The corollary of early identification of 'juvenile psychopathy' and/or 'psychopathic traits in children' is the provision of early and intense relevant interventions. Gretton et al. (2001) administered the PCL: YV to a sample of young offenders and was able to identify a high psychopathy subgroup based on PCL: YV scores. This sub-group was found to be three to four times more likely to reoffend when compared with a low psychopathy group. Recent research has found that the Antisocial Process Screening Device dimension that reflects a callous and unemotional interpersonal style is most strongly associated with a sub-group of children and young people who exhibit extreme and persistent antisocial behaviour. This psychopathic style is characterised by:

- Poverty of emotional experience.
- Lack of guilt over wrongdoing.
- Lack of empathy.
- Impulsivity.
- Egocentricity.
- Callous use of others for their own gain.

This sub-group has been found to have a temperament defined by 'low behavioural inhibition'. This is defined as: (1) physiological underactivity in the autonomic nervous system (lack of emotional response to distress of others); (2) behaviourally low fearlessness to novel or threatening situations (reckless risk taking behaviours); and (3) poor responsiveness to cues to punishment (insensitive to rules, sanctions and consequences). Frick, Barry, and Bodin (2000) have reported that children and young people who score higher on this callous/unemotional dimension exhibit the following when compared with other conduct disordered children or antisocial young people:

- More thrill seeking and adventure seeking tendencies.
- Less sensitivity to cues to punishments when a reward-oriented response set is primed.
- Less reactive to emotional words.
- Less reactive to threatening stimuli.
- Less distressed by the negative effects of their behaviour on others.
- More impaired in their moral reasoning.
- More impaired in their empathic concern towards others.
- Expect more instrumental gain from their aggressive actions.

Several conclusions may be drawn from the emerging research and clinical literatures in these two related areas:

1. Emerging antisocial personality disorder can be traced to childhood emotional and behavioural disorders.
2. Children and adolescents who function on the extreme pole of the impulsivity-aggression dimension may warrant a diagnosis of emerging antisocial personality disorder.
3. Psychopathy is different to antisocial personality disorder as it is conceptualised as two dimensions: (1) Factor 1 that reflects personality functioning, and (2) Factor 2 that reflects a chronic antisocial lifestyle. Psychopathy emphasises deficits in affective and interpersonal functioning and not simply antisocial behaviours.
4. The concept of psychopathy is being applied to young people in the same way it is applied to adults.
5. The concept of psychopathy is being applied to children and is conceived as consisting of an Interpersonal dimension (callous-unemotional traits) and an antisocial behaviours dimension (impulsive-conduct problems).
6. Psychopathic traits may be potentially useful for identifying a sub-group of high-risk children or antisocial young people who are likely to have a poor prognosis and be intervention resistant.
7. 'Psychopathy' and psychopathic traits are typically associated with the highest risk for antisocial behaviours.

Antisocial personality disorder, psychopathy and sexual offending

As measures of psychopathy and psychopathic traits have become available, so these concepts have been studied in relation to their associations with sexual offending and sexual recidivism.

Adult studies

The commission of sexual offences has been associated with an antisocial orientation and lifestyle instability, which has been termed a *crime-prone personality*. These people are found to engage in a range of impulsive, and reckless behaviours, and present with a hostile and resentful attitude (Andrews and Bonta, 2003;

Caspi et al., 1995). A crime-prone personality type has been found to be more prevalent in rapists when compared to child molesters (Firestone et al., 2000). Antisocial orientation and lifestyle instability are associated with sexual recidivism in rapists and child molesters (Hanson and Bussiere, 1998; Quinsey et al., 1995; Roberts, Doren and Thornton, 2002; Prentky et al., 1995; Rice, Quinsey and Harris, 1991). Hanson and Morton-Bourgon (2004) in their meta-analytic review found that antisocial orientation was strongly associated with sexual recidivism. This included all of the studied indicators of antisocial orientation: antisocial personality, antisocial traits, and a history of rule violation.

The prevalence of psychopathy in adult sexual offenders has been reported to be between 10 per cent and 15 per cent in known child molesters and between 40 per cent and 50 per cent in rapist and 'mixed' (both rapists and child molesters) groups. Quinsey et al. (1995) and Seto and Barbaree (1999) found that total PCL-R (Hare, 1991) scores predicted both sexual and violent recidivism among adult sexual offenders. Hanson and Morton-Bourgon (2004) found that PCL-R scores and other measures of antisocial personality, such as, psychiatric diagnoses, and responses to self-report questionnaires predicted sexual recidivism. Antisocial traits and general self-regulation problems (measures of lifestyle instability, impulsivity, and Factor 2 of the PCL-R) were most strongly associated with sexual recidivism.

Adolescent studies

Caputo, Frick, and Brodsky (1999) utilised the Antisocial Process Screening Device (Frick and Hare, 2001) to compare juvenile sex offenders to a group of juvenile non-sexual offenders. They found that the sexual offender group had significantly higher scores on the callous-unemotional factor (which corresponds to Factor 1 of the PCL-YV (Forth et al., 2003)). This group were characterised by less guilt, less empathy, and were more emotionally restricted. Gretton et al. (2001) in their study of adolescent sexual offenders found that for a sub-group of young psychopathic sexual offenders, their sexual recidivism was greater and they were more criminally versatile, in that they committed general and violent offences in addition to sexual offences. Parks (2004) found that high scores on the PCL: YV Interpersonal factor (Factor 1) was significantly associated with sexual recidivism with risk for sexual recidivism increasing by 47.9 per cent with each 1-point increase in the scale score.

Disordered personality and sexually harmful behaviour

The sex offender literature has predominantly investigated the presence of dysfunctional or pathological personality characteristics in populations of sexual offenders. The research has utilised psychometric personality and psychopathology assessment instruments on the one hand, and psychiatric diagnosis on the other hand. There is very little published research on 'normal' personality characteristics and sexual offenders.

Adult literature

Studies of adult sexual offenders have reported the presence of disordered personality characteristics (Berner et al., 1992; Seghorn, Prentky, and Boucher, 1987; Kalichman, 1991; Knight, 1988; Schlank, 1995). The presence or absence of personality pathology has been utilised in the classification of sexual offenders to produce offender types (Groth 1979; Knight, 1988; Prentky, Cohen, and Seghorn, 1985; Knight and Prentky, 1990). Also, models of the aetiology of sexual offending have included disordered personality (Hall and Hirschman, 1991; Malamuth, Heavey, and Linz, 1993; Prentky and Knight, 1991). Psychometric measures of personality dysfunction and psychopathology have underpinned this approach for example, the Minnesota Multiphasic Personality Inventory (MMPI; Graham, 1987) and the Millon Multiaxial Clinical Inventory (MMCI) (Millon, 1987). The available literature indicates that there is no single MMPI profile unique to sexual offending, which supports the heterogeneity of MMPI profiles both within and across sex offence types (Erickson et al., 1987; Hall, 1990; Herkov et al., 1996; Kalichman, 1990; Marshall and Hall, 1995; Okami and Goldberg, 1992). Millon (1977, 1987, 1997) has developed an alternative psychometric approach to the measurement of dysfunctional personality functioning and psychopathology in adults. This measure is the Millon Clinical

Multiaxial Inventory (MCMI) which generally corresponds to Axis II Personality Disorders as described in the American Psychiatric Association Diagnostic and Statistical Manual of Mental Disorders (APA, 1994). Bard and Knight (1987) were unable to identify a single personality profile for adult sex offenders using the MCMI. Rather, several subtypes were differentiated. The Detached Type had elevations on three of the Personality scales – Schizoid, Avoidant, and Dependent. These offenders were socially inadequate and isolated. The Criminal Type had elevations on four of the Personality scales – Histrionic, Narcissistic, Antisocial and Aggressive/Sadistic. These offenders were socially skilled, aggressive, and wanted to control other people. The Negativistic/Angry Type had elevations on three of the Personality scales – Antisocial, Aggressive/Sadistic, and Passive-Aggressive. These offenders were characterised by chronic resentment and anger in relation to perceived maltreatment or unfair treatment, and experienced difficulties forming positive relationships with others. The Healthy Type obtained scores within normal limits or had minor elevations on the Compulsive, Histrionic, and Narcissistic scales. Langevin et al. (1988) also utilised the Millon Inventory when they compared adult child molesters with rapists. They did not find any significant differences between these two groups on any of the personality disorder scales. Both groups were found to have higher scores than a non-offender control group on the Schizoid, Avoidant, Dependent and Negativistic (Passive-Aggressive) scales. Lehne (1994) investigated personality differences in a mixed offence group of adult offenders, using two personality measures, the Millon Clinical Multiaxial Inventory (MCMI) and the NEO Personality Inventory (NEO-PI) (Costa and McCrae, 1992). It was found that the Schizoid personality disorder scale was related to Neuroticism as measured by the (NEO-PI). Adult sexual offenders were found to be high on Neuroticism (anxiety, hostility, depression, self-consciousness, impulsiveness, and vulnerability) when compared with other offender types. Chantry and Craig (1994) investigated adult child molesters and rapists and compared them to non-violent offenders on the MCMI. The sexual offenders in general were found to be higher on the Avoidant scale compared to non-sex offenders, and the child molester group, in particular, was higher than the non-sexual offender group on the Schizoid, Dependent, and Borderline personality scales. The child molester group was also the most neurotic.

Findings reported in the latest manual for the Millon Inventory MCMI-III (Millon, 1994, 1997), have shown that sex offenders in general score higher on Schizoid, Avoidant, Dependent, and Schizotypal personality scales, which are indictors of social inadequacies and social isolation as well as dysfunctional interpersonal relationships. There is some evidence for differences between child molesters and rapists, where child molesters' obtain higher scores on the Avoidant and Dependent personality scales. Lussier, Proulx, and McKibben (2001) derived two personality profiles from the Millon Inventory (MCMI-I): (1) the 'Dramatic' profile; and (2) the 'Anxious' profile. The Dramatic profile had high elevations on the Histrionic, Narcissistic, and Compulsive scales, and was characterised by being more socially skilled and more assertive. Whereas, the Anxious profile had high elevations on the Avoidant, Schizoid, and Passive-Aggressive, Schizotypal, and Borderline scales. This profile was characterised by social skill deficits, more anxiety, more difficulties relating to other people, lower self-esteem, and greater use of avoidant coping strategies. However, no scale or profile differences were found in relation to the type of sexual offending. Bogaerts, Vervaeke, and Goethals (2004) adopted a clinical diagnostic approach in their investigation of personality disorder in a group of adult child molesters, who were then compared with a matched control group. The assessment of the DSM-IV Personality Disorders utilised a semi-structured interview (ADP-IV: Schotte and De Doncker, 2000). The Schizoid, Antisocial and Narcissistic personality disorders were found to be associated with sexual offending. Similarly, Chantry and Craig (1994) and Chesire (2001) reported the prevalence of diagnosed Dependent and Narcissistic Personality Disorder in adult sexual offenders. Langstrom, Sjostedt and Grann (2004) investigated the presence of a broad range of psychiatric disorders in a group of imprisoned adult sexual offenders. The most commonly found psychiatric disorders included Antisocial Personality Disorder. They further investigated the relationship between the presence of psychiatric disorder and recidivism for a sexual offence. They found that the presence of any category of personality disorder was associated

with sexual recidivism, and increased the odds of reconviction tenfold. Similarly, Hanson and Bussiere's (1998, 2003) meta-analysis of sexual recidivism in adult sexual offenders found that the presence of any personality disorder significantly predicted sexual recidivism.

Adolescent literature

Some of the early literature reported clinical opinion rather than the results of psychometric assessments. Groth (1979) differentiated a sample of adolescent child molesters from a sample who sexually assaulted peer or adult aged females in terms of personality traits, such as, dependency and impulsivity. Richardson, Loss, and Ross (1988) found that adolescent child abusers were characteristically shy, immature, socially unskilled, and had significant social difficulties in relation to their peers. In contrast, adolescents who had sexually assaulted peer-aged or adult females had an aggressive and intimidating interpersonal style when interacting with other people.

MMPI profiles have been reported for samples of adolescent sexual offenders (Cooper, Murphey and Haynes, 1996; Herkov et al., 1996; Jacobs, Kennedy, and Meyer, 1997; Oliver, Nagayama-Hall, and Neuhaus, 1993; Smith, Monastersky, and Deisher, 1987). Smith, Monastersky, and Deisher (1987) delineated a MMPI derived typology for an outpatient sample of sex offenders aged between 13 and 17 years old. Four groups were derived from cluster analytic procedures and were described in terms of their respective mean profiles. Groups I and III obtained normal range profiles, Group IV had an abnormal range profile, and Group II had the most disturbed profile. Group I ('immature') members were shy, over controlled, worried about having few friends, and they attempted to portray themselves as morally righteous. Group II ('personality disordered') members were emotionally disturbed, they were demanding and narcissistic, used illness to gain attention, were argumentative, insecure, and used fantasy to solve problems. Group III ('socialised delinquents') members were socially outgoing and well adjusted, with normal affect and no impairment in judgement; they were emotionally over controlled and prone to temper outbursts. Group IV ('conduct disordered') members were characterised by schizoid and under socialised personality disturbance, with poor self-control and poor judgement; they were distrustful, vulnerable to perceived threat, impulsive and prone to violence. Studies have compared the MMPI scores and profiles of juvenile sexual offenders with other juvenile offender groups. Truscott (1993) compared the MMPI scores of juvenile sex offenders with other groups of juvenile offenders, and reported no significant differences between the groups. Valliant and Bergeron (1997) compared juvenile sex offenders with general offenders and non-offenders on their MMPI scores and, again, found no differences between juvenile sex offenders and other young offenders. Freeman et al. (2005) compared juvenile sex offenders with non-sex offending delinquent peers and also failed to find significant differences between these groups.

The methodological weakness of using the MMPI to described personality dysfunction in adolescent sexual offenders is that this instrument measures psychopathology, rather than personality characteristics (see Butcher and Tellegen, 1978). Consequently, other psychometric measures have been used in some other studies. Carpenter, Peed and Eastman (1995) administered the Millon Clinical Multiaxial Inventory (MCMI) to determine the personality characteristics of a sample of adolescent sexual offenders with a mean age of 18.25 years. The following Personality scales were clinically elevated – Antisocial, Narcissistic, Dependent and Avoidant. The authors found that adolescents who abused children scored significantly higher on the Schizoid, Avoidant, and Dependent Scales when compared with adolescents who had assaulted peer-aged or adult females. The child abuser sub-group was characterised by submissive dependency and avoidance of personal autonomy. They were self-effacing, for example, they perceived themselves as ineffectual, and they were socially isolated from their peers. The group who had assaulted peer-aged and adult women had a clinically significant score on the Narcissistic scale that was taken to suggest that they had an inflated self-image, and were arrogant and exploitative of others. Carpenter, Peed, and Eastman (1995) found that the scores on the Antisocial personality scale were in the clinical range and were not significantly different for both adolescent rapist and adolescent child molester groups.

Worling (2001) described a personality based typology for adolescent sexual offenders aged between 12 and 19 years utilising the California Psychological Inventory (Gough, 1987). The four groups were Antisocial/Impulsive described as essentially antisocial and impulsive; Unusual/Isolated described as emotionally disturbed and insecure; Over controlled/Reserved, described as emotionally over controlled and socially reserved; and Confident/Aggressive described as socially outgoing and prone to interpersonal aggression. The Antisocial/Impulsive (44 per cent of the sample) and the Unusual/Isolated groups were regarded as the most pathological. Worling (2001) concluded that there were similarities between personality based sub-groups delineated in his study and those described by Smith et al. (1987). The Over controlled/Reserved group resembled Group I; the Unusual/Isolated group resembled Group II; the Confident/Aggressive group resembled Group III; and the Antisocial/Impulsive group resembled Group IV.

Overall, the findings derived from these studies provide supportive evidence for heterogeneity rather than homogeneity in terms of the presence and nature of disordered personality characteristics. There is no evidence to support a personality type or profile or personality characteristics that are unique to adolescent sexual offenders.

Conclusions

Several conclusions may be made based on the preceding review and discussion:

1. Both the adult and adolescent literatures on sexual offender populations indicate that there is a sub-group that is characterised by the presence of personality dysfunction as either clinically diagnosed or measured by psychometric testing. This sub-group is itself heterogeneous in terms of the nature or type of personality dysfunction. Two distinct groups are discernable across a range of studies. Firstly, there is an anti-social group, who share characteristics associated with Antisocial Personality Disorder and Psychopathy. Secondly, there is an a-social group, who are characterised by neurotic traits, interpersonal inadequacies, and social anxiety and avoidance.
2. There is a growing professional consensus that supports the appropriateness and clinical

utility of applying the diagnostic category of 'personality disorder' to young people (the developmental stage of adolescence). It is prudent, from a developmentally sensitive perspective, to talk about an *'emerging'* personality disorder in young people.

3. There is emerging evidence that supports a developmental pathway for disordered personality, which seems to begin in childhood, consolidate in adolescence, and be fully recognisable as a disorder in adulthood.

4. Research into the aetiology (causes) of disordered personality suggests that it is associated with the pathogenic (disorder causing) combination of: (1) genetic predisposition (or inherent vulnerability); and (2) early adverse life experiences (environmental and interpersonal stressors).

5. Professionals working with young people may be alerted to the potential for a presenting disordered personality by the presence of the following factors: (1) evidence of at least one highly dysfunctional biological parent; (2) evidence of a 'difficult' temperament as an infant; (3) severe childhood onset emotional and behavioural difficulties; and (4) the persistence and exacerbation of emotional and behavioural difficulties during adolescence.

6. There are valid and reliable methods and instruments to assist in the identification of dysfunctional or disordered personality development.

7. A combination of psychiatric and psychological assessments and mutually agreed diagnosis is likely to prove to be prudent (valid) and more clinically reliable.

8. Early identification (diagnosis) and early interventions (management and treatment) are likely to be more clinically effective.

9. Therapeutic interventions have been developed for the therapeutic management of people with personality disorders.

10. The concepts of 'maladaptiveness' and 'functional impairment' are likely to be clinical priorities because the presence of a personality disorder has a significantly adverse impact on the young person's emotional, interpersonal and social functioning across all areas of their lives (family, school, peer relations, social and recreational activities).

11. A diagnosis of an emerging Antisocial Personality Disorder is relevant and

applicable to some young people who sexually harm. Similarly, the related clinical concepts of psychopathic traits and emerging psychopathy are relevant and applicable to some young people who sexually harm, although in all likelihood to a smaller number.

12. There will be a group of sexually harmful young people whose personality will be dominated by neuroticism, and as a consequence they will experience chronic interpersonal and social relationship difficulties. These difficulties will be underpinned by anxiety associated with peer relationships, friendships, heterosocial relationships, and dating relationships.

Studies with British young people

The vast majority of published studies report findings for North American populations. The author and colleagues at the Northern Forensic Mental Health Service for Young People, which is based in Newcastle upon Tyne, have investigated personality and personality dysfunction in British young people who have exhibited sexually harmful behaviours. The findings from three studies and their implications for treatment are reported below.

EPQ study

Adult sexual offenders against children have been found to score higher on the Neuroticism scale of the Eysenck Personality Questionnaire (Eysenck and Eysenck, 1975) when compared to non-sexual offender groups (Denniston, Stough, and Birgden, 2001; Wilson and Cox, 1983).

Richardson (unpublished) compared 47 sexually abusive adolescents with 45 other young offenders (characterised by mixed violent and property offending) on scores on the Eysenck Personality Questionnaire – Junior (Eysenck and Eysenck, 1975). These sexually abusive adolescents were taken from the larger sample described by Richardson et al. (1995). No significant differences between the two groups were found on any of the scales. Within the sexually abusive group, those who had abused younger children (28 young people) were compared with those who had sexually assaulted peer aged or adult females (19 young people). A

significant difference was found for the
Neuroticism (N) scale scores, with the child
abuser sub-group having much higher scores.
This sub-group score was elevated relative to the
normative data provided in the test manual. This
study indicated that young people who sexually
harm younger children are characterised by
personality traits defined by Eysenck's
'Neuroticism'. Essentially, this personality
dimension describes individuals of a nervous
disposition, who may be prone to 'nervous
disorders', such as anxiety or depression. They
are predisposed to exaggerated and debilitating
worry. They may well suffer from extreme
shyness and or social anxiety. La Greca and
Lopez (1998) have reported the adverse affect of
social anxiety on peer relationships in a
population of non-offending adolescents. It may
be hypothesised that young people with a
nervous temperament and debilitating worry
may be vulnerable to peer relationship
difficulties. They may deliberately avoid peer
interactions. They may over-react emotionally
leading to social rejection and isolation. This may
be heightened in relation to opposite sex
relations, where anxiety and worry seem to be
more common in adolescents generally,
especially in relation to dating relationships
(Grover and Nangle, 2003; Zimmer-Gembeck,
2002). In these cases, their social and dating
isolation may be precursors to the onset of their
sexually abusive behaviour. They may
compensate for their social isolation from peers
by befriending and socialising with younger
children. Then they may compensate for their
isolation from dating and sexual exploration
experiences by sexually exploiting younger
children.

Relevant childhood psychiatric disorders in
relation to Neuroticism are those characterised by
anxiety. For example, Social Sensitivity Disorder
of Childhood as described in ICD-10, or
Overanxious Disorder of Childhood described in
DSM-IV. The critical treatment targets associated
with neuroticism are worry, anxiety, and social
avoidance. A combination of cognitive
behavioural therapy and prescribed medication is
indicated when neuroticism manifests itself as a
childhood anxiety disorder. Cognitive therapy
approaches have been developed to address
anxiety, excessive and exaggerated worry, and
social avoidance (Wells, 1997).

Millon Adolescent Clinical Inventory (MACI) study

Richardson et al. (2004) described a
personality-based taxonomy (typology), which
grouped a British sample of sexually abusive
adolescents into five personality types based on
their scores on the Millon Adolescent Clinical
Inventory (MACI) (Millon et al., 1993). The MACI
is not a measure of 'normal' personality types;
rather it is a clinical instrument that purports to
identify emerging personality difficulties. A brief
description of these five types is provided below.
It is important to note that when these
adolescents were divided into two groups on the
basis of their sexually abusive behaviour: (1)
those that had abused younger children; and (2)
those that had assaulted peer-aged or adult
females, no differences were found in terms of the
distribution of the five personality types.
Consequently, their personality type did not
predict the nature of their sexual offending.

Normal type

This sub-group represented 25 per cent of the
total sample and did not obtain a clinically
relevant score on any of the personality scales.
This type of adolescent abuser presents with very
minor personality difficulties relative to the other
groups. He may be characterised by being under
assertive and eager to please other people.

Antisocial type

This sub-group was relatively small and
represented only 11 per cent of the total sample.
The Forceful personality scale was most elevated
and there was a relatively high score on the
Unruly scale. This describes an adolescent abuser
who seeks to control, dominate and intimidate
other people, and who derives a sense of
satisfaction from humiliating them or violating
their rights. He is characterised by antisocial
attitudes and behaviours, and adopts a hostile
and belligerent interpersonal style when
interacting with other people. He is likely to use
physical power to meet his needs and he will seek
retribution for perceived injustices or
maltreatment. This group is more likely to be
diagnosed with an emerging Antisocial
Personality Disorder, and is more likely to score
highly on both the Antisocial Process Screening

Device (Frick and Hare, 2001) and the Hare Psychopathy Checklist Youth Version (Forth, Kosson, and Hare, 2003).

Submissive type

This was the smallest sub-group making up only 10 per cent of the total sample. The Submissive personality scale was the most elevated with lesser elevations on related scales: Inhibited, Conforming and Introversive. This describes an adolescent abuser who is passively dependent on others, is excessively compliant with rules, defers to authority, and defers his needs to the wishes of others. He is likely to feel inadequate compared with his peers, and avoids interactions with them because of peer-related worries and anxiety.

Dysthymic/inhibited type

This was the largest sub-group, constituting 35 per cent of the total population. The Inhibited Personality scale was the most elevated with related elevations of the Introversive, Doleful, Submissive, Self-Demeaning and Oppositional scales. This describes an adolescent abuser who experiences very little or no personal satisfaction in interpersonal and social interactions. He is likely to be socially anxious and socially withdrawn. He may experience depressed mood and angry resentment due to his social isolation and his submissiveness. This young person is most likely to be high in Neuroticism.

Dysthymic/negativistic type

This sub-group represented 20 per cent of the total sample, and had the greatest number of elevated personality scales. The most elevated scales were the Unruly and Oppositional scales. The Self-Demeaning, Borderline and Forceful scales were also elevated. This profile describes an adolescent abuser who is experiencing a more severe degree and broader range of personality dysfunction. This adolescent presents with antisocial personality characteristics and he will intimidate others in order to get what he wants. He experiences strong feelings of resentment about limitations that are placed on his behaviour.

Four of these adolescent subtypes resembled the four adult subtypes differentiated by Bard and

Knight (1987) on Millon Clinical Multiaxial Inventory (MCMI) scores. The Submissive type shares three elevated personality pattern scales with Bard and Knight's Detached Type: Introversive, Inhibited and Submissive on the MACI, and Schizoid, Avoidant, and Dependent on the MCMI. The Normal type was comparable with Bard and Knight's Healthy Type. The Dysthymic/Negativistic type shared three equivalent scales with the Negativistic/Angry type described by Bard and Knight. These were the Unruly, Oppositional, and Forceful scales on the MACI and the Antisocial, Passive-Aggressive, and Aggressive/Sadistic scales on the MCMI. Finally, the Antisocial type shared two equivalent scales with Bard and Knight's Criminal Type. These were the Forceful and Unruly scales on the MACI and the Aggressive/Sadistic and Antisocial scales on the MCMI. In addition, several of the adolescent subtypes resemble groups described by Smith et al. (1987) and Worling (2001). The Submissive type is similar to the Immature group described by Smith et al. (1987) and the Overcontrolled/Reserved group described by Worling (2001). Similarly, the Dysthymic/Inhibited type resembles Smith et al's Conduct Disordered group and Worling's Unusual/Isolated group; the Dysthymic/ Negativistic type resembles Worling's Antisocial/Impulsive group, and the Antisocial type resembles Smith et al's Socialized Delinquent group and Worling's Confident/Aggressive group. These similarities across studies provide additional support for these sub-types.

There were several treatment implications in terms of the personality subtypes identified by Richardson et al. (2004). The group with the poorest treatability was the Antisocial group. This was because of their entrenched antisocial attitudes, their hostility towards and rejection of adult and institutional authority, and their generalised lack of empathy or sensitivity for other people. Treatment will need to incorporate general criminogenic needs as well as those specific to their sexual offending. A dual approach would therefore be required. This was not, however, complicated by additional mental health needs. The group with the best treatability was the Submissive group. These young people were essentially compliant and responded to guidance. This group required support in becoming more self-confident and more assertive. The Normal group was the simplest in terms of their treatment needs. They required a combination of a family therapy approach and a straightforward offense specific approach, as there was an absence of complicating psychopathology. The Dysthymic/Inhibited group had additional mental health needs in relation to low mood, anxiety, and low self-esteem. The Dysthymic/Negativistic group were the most complex as they presented with the highest severity and broadest range of psychopathology. This group was closest to a personality-disordered sub-group, and were most likely to require mental health oversight and psychological and/or psychiatric interventions.

Early Maladaptive Schema study

Richardson (2005) described the presence of Early Maladaptive Schemas (EMS's), as conceptualised by Young (1990), in a British sample of sexually abusive adolescents. It was found that abusive adolescents could be differentiated on the basis of the presence of maladaptive schemas, the most significant of which were: (1) *Emotional Inhibition*; (2) *Social Isolation/Alienation*; and (3) *Mistrust/Abuse*. **Emotional Inhibition** refers to the excessive inhibition of spontaneous action, feeling, or communication to ensure a sense of security and predictability, or to avoid making mistakes or disapproval by others, or to avoid losing control of one's impulses, especially anger and aggression. **Social Isolation/Alienation** refers to feeling one is isolated from the rest of the social world, different from other people, and not part of any social group. **Mistrust/Abuse** refers to the expectation that others are sources of pain, humiliation, manipulation, or abuse, which includes a perception that others seek to inflict intentional harm.

It was found that the presence of specific maladaptive schemas differentiated those adolescents who had sexually abused children from those who had sexually assaulted peer-aged or adult females, termed the *Peer/Adult* group. Three maladaptive schemas differentiated the *Peer/Adult* offence group: (1) *Entitlement/Self-Centredness*; (2) *Insufficient Self-Control/Self-Discipline*; and (3) *Emotional Inhibition* described above. **Entitlement or Self-Centredness** refers to the belief that one is superior to others and entitled to special rights and privileges, or entitled to special dispensations, and not bound by normative social rules and conventions. This can involve the domination of others and an

absence of empathy for others. **Insufficient Self-Control or Self-Discipline** refers to the difficulty or refusal to tolerate frustration of immediate desires, or exercise sufficient self-control in order to achieve personal goals, or restrain the excessive expression of one's impulses and emotions. **Emotional Inhibition** refers to the excessive inhibition of spontaneous action, feeling, or communication to ensure a sense of security and predictability, or to avoid making mistakes or disapproval by others, or to avoid losing control of one's impulses, especially anger and aggression. Interestingly, the group of adolescents who abused younger children scored higher on the *Emotional Deprivation* schema, which refers to the entrenched belief that their needs for affection, emotional closeness, empathetic understanding, and guidance have not and will not be met by significant people in their lives. This is closely associated with attachment difficulties.

The relative presence of schemas also distinguished those adolescents with a prior history of sexual victimisation from those without a history of sexual victimisation. Two maladaptive schemas differentiated the *victim* group: (1) *Abandonment/Instability*; and (2) *Defectiveness/Shame*. **Abandonment/Instability** refers to the perceived instability or unreliability of those significant others available to provide practical nurturance and emotional support, and the belief that one will be abandoned by significant others. **Defectiveness/Shame** refers to feeling one is bad, inferior, and unwanted, or believing one would be unlovable if these inherent defects become apparent to others. The *non-victim* group was differentiated by the presence of (1) *Emotional Inhibition*; and (2) *Entitlement/Self-Centredness*.

A sub-group of seven sexually harmful young people with a clinically diagnosed personality disorder was identified. Young (1990) hypothesised five schema domains that are higher-order factors, made up of specific clusters of the 16 early maladaptive schemas. The most pertinent in this subgroup was the **Disconnection and Rejection** domain. This refers to expectations that one's needs for security, nurturance, understanding, acceptance and respect will not be met in a predictable and consistent manner. Like *Emotional Deprivation* schema, this schema domain is closely associated with attachment. The hypothesised family of origin is detached, cold, rejecting, withholding, lonely, explosive, unpredictable or abusive. Interestingly, the majority (five out of the seven) reported the following negative life events: (1) being chronically rejected by peers; (2) being persistently bullied by peers; (3) feeling socially isolated; and (4) attempting suicide. This provides tentative support for the characterisation of personality disordered individuals as experiencing, firstly, significant difficulties in their interpersonal and social relationships, in these cases beginning in childhood/early adolescence, and secondly, emotional and psychological distress.

Overall, the results of this study provided an additional way of classifying sexually harmful young people by identifying dysfunctional cognitive factors. They provided evidence for heterogeneity in terms of the presence of maladaptive schemas. Also the study found further heterogeneity across different sub-groups of young people. That is, those who sexually abused children reported different maladaptive schemas from those who assaulted peer-aged or adult females, and those with a childhood history of sexual victimisation reported different maladaptive schemas from those who had not been sexually abused as children. In terms of psychological assessment and treatment planning, the schema-focused approach appears to provide a means of developing a cognitive conceptualisation of deficits in emotional and interpersonal functioning and social competency. The results indicate that these deficits are underpinned by a sense of social exclusion, pervasive mistrust, low self-esteem, and emotional dysphoria and dysregulation.

In terms of the provision of schema-relevant treatment, the finding that the two critical maladaptive schemas in the sample were *Emotional Inhibition* and *Social Isolation/Alienation* supports these being regarded as core treatment targets. However, the results of this study, in conjunction with the conceptual model of cognitive psychotherapy, suggest that the application of psychoeducational and skills training approaches to anger management and social competency skills training interventions, are unlikely to produce any meaningful or lasting improvement in those young people whose schema profile incorporates these two schemas. This is because the educational/skills training approach leaves intact those dysfunctional schemata which, when activated by contingencies in the social

environment, are likely to precipitate maladaptive behaviours, which are the antithesis of the skills learned during the course of treatment. Regarding the remediation of social competency deficits, this ought to be not simply about training the young person in the overt behaviours that comprise social competency, because the deficit is not exclusively behavioural in nature. Rather, the problem lies at the deeper level of those core beliefs about self, relative to others in the social environment, as well as the negative emotions they produce. The therapeutic task is to utilise cognitive therapy interventions to modify those cognitive processes that underpin interpersonal and social deficiencies. Similarly, treatment for emotional dysphoria and dysregulation is not about controlling anger, but rather it is about the psychological process of one seamless source of anger derived from activated maladaptive schemas. It is also about the young person's suppression of their anger for specific psychological reasons that may be the consequence of other activated schemas. The therapeutic task is not a simple matter of remediation through skills training as the problem lies at a deeper level and requires a concomitant deeper level of intervention, namely cognitive psychotherapy. This ought to address the symptoms of anger problems by targeting the schemata and dysfunctional assumptions that underpin and activate those affective symptoms. Also the young person's suppression of their angry feelings may be termed anger therapy as opposed to anger management. In addition, the results pertaining to the various sub-groups indicates that other critical therapeutic targets for particular sub-groups of adolescents are chronic low self esteem, feelings of shame associated with sexual victimisation, pervasive mistrust, and a perception of self as physically and sexually unattractive.

It was concluded in this study that some sexually harmful adolescents have therapeutic needs that would only be met through the provision of cognitive therapy (Beck et al., 1990, Beck, 1995) or schema therapy (Young, Klosko, and Weishaar, 2003) to address these dysfunctional beliefs or maladaptive schemas. The corollary is that cognitive psychotherapy would become a central component of sex offender treatment, but only alongside established cognitive behavioural offence-specific treatment interventions, which incorporated a relapse prevention component (Marshall, Anderson and Fernandez, 1999).

Emerging Severe Personality Disorder Study

Hickey, Vizard, McCrory, and French (2006) identified a sub-group of British juvenile sexual abusers, with a mean age of 14 years, who were distinguishable by the presence of marked conduct disorder and psychopathic personality traits as measured by the Psychopathy Checklist Youth Version (PCL-YV). They termed this the 'emerging severe personality disorder' group. When this sub-group was compared with a non-emerging severe personality disorder group they were found to have higher rates of parents with mental health difficulties; difficult temperaments in infancy; exposure to inconsistent parenting; higher levels of insecure attachment, and greater residential placement disruptions.

Indicators of sexually harmful behaviour motivated by a disordered personality

What ever happened to motive? Criminal behaviour has been classified in terms of not just the nature of the offence but also the motive driving the offence: what it sets out to achieve or gain for the offender. This is exemplified in the Federal Bureau of Investigation (FBI's) crime classification manual (Ressler et al., 1993). Our current classification systems in relation to sexually harmful young people tend to focus on the type of offending based on victim characteristics and to a lesser extent of offender characteristics. There has been insufficient investigation into the motives that drive sexually harmful behaviour.

An important practical question in relation to providing diverse and relevant services to different groups of sexually harmful young people is: Is the sexually harmful behaviour of personality disordered young people discernibly and qualitatively different? Unless the behaviour was obviously sadistic in nature, it is likely to prove difficult to distinguish the sexually harmful behaviour perpetrated by a personality disordered young person on the basis of the sexual behaviour itself. So where does that leave us? Well it leaves us with motive. It is proposed that the telltale indicator is likely to be the motive driving the sexually harmful behaviour in conjunction with the nature of the gratification

derived from the behaviour. That is, the needs met by the behaviour. Based entirely on clinical experience, it has been helpful to differentiate 'normal' needs from 'abnormal' needs, where 'normal' includes sexual and intimate interpersonal needs, and 'abnormal' includes non-sexual and antisocial needs. Then it is possible to view the presence of 'abnormal' needs to be associated with the presence of serious personality difficulties or an emerging personality disorder.

Groth's (1979) typology of adult rapists was based on the nature of their non-sexual needs met by their sexual offending, and is relevant here. Three types were distinguished: (1) anger rapists; (2) power rapists; and (3) sadistic rapists. Their sexual offending behaviour was motivated respectively by the expression of anger and hostility, the need to dominate and subjugate, and the need to degrade and hurt. All were characterised by interpersonal intimacy deficits and interpersonal inadequacies, and their non-sexual needs (motives) were driven by their disordered personalities. Millon's (1996) Biosocial Learning model of personality disorder conceptualises dysfunctional personalities in terms of impaired interpersonal and psychosocial functioning, which are underpinned by different styles of self-regulation. For example, on the one hand, a person may be passive or active in interactions with other people, and on the other hand, they may be reliant on others or self-reliant. Drawing on the theories of Groth and Millon, Chesire (2004) conceived the function of sexual offending in terms of: (1) to control the absence of interpersonal intimacy; and (2) to control the experience of interpersonal inadequacy.

A pragmatic way of conceptualising *personality-disorder-driven* sexually harmful behaviour in young people is to view it in terms of: (1) it is motivated by antisocial non-sexual needs (e.g., negative emotions, revenge, domination, humiliation, inflicting pain); (2) it functions to regulate (counter and sooth) dysfunctional beliefs and emotions experienced by the young person; and (3) it compensates for impaired interpersonal functioning (a lack of interpersonal intimacy and personal adequacy), which was the very source of the dysfunctional beliefs and emotions, and which is associated with the underlying personality disorder. Allied to this conceptualisation is the added indicator of personality-disorder-driven sexual offence as well as other non-sexually harmful behaviour, that is, the interpersonal or interactional style adopted by the young person, and other non-sexual behaviours that occurred, during the commission of the sexual offence as well as other non-sexual behaviours that occured at the time. This conceptualisation has not been researched and is in its infancy.

Practice implications

Emerging personality disorder

What is the relevance and importance of an emerging personality disorder to sexually harmful behaviour?

For practitioners, the critical questions are:

1. How do we know if a young person has an emerging personality disorder?
2. How is the disorder related to the nature and degree of the sexually harmful behaviour?
3. How does the disorder increase the risk for re-offending?
4. What, if any, interventions are necessary to treat the disorder?
5. Where do I access these specialist services?

A crucial question relates to the relationship between an emerging personality disorder and sexually harmful behaviour. In terms of possible relationships to sexually harmful behaviour, the presence of a personality disorder or disorders may be:

1. An aetiological factor, which plays a significant role in the onset of the behaviour.
2. A sustaining factor, which plays a significant role in maintaining the behaviour due to severe and chronic interpersonal and social deficits.
3. An independent complicating factor, which has no direct or indirect influence on the behaviour, but does have an impact on the health and interpersonal and social functioning of the individual.

Prevalence

How prevalent are emerging personality disorders in populations of sexually harmful young people?

Unfortunately this is not well researched and consequently no confident answer may be given.

We simply do not know what the prevalence rates are in sexually harmful adolescents. This may be a consequence of the limited contact that this population of young people have with mental health services, and especially forensic mental health services, which tend to be more experienced in the assessment of emerging personality disorders in young people. Notwithstanding this, based on the Richardson et al. (2004) study, 55 per cent of the young people were assessed as having significant personality difficulties, excluding antisocial characteristics, which are commonly found in offending populations. Based on the Richardson (2005) study, 74 per cent of the young people were found to report maladaptive schemas, which indicated significant personality disturbance. From clinical experience, pertinent clinical disorders in childhood and adolescence seem to be:

- Attachment disorder
- Conduct disorder
- Mixed disorder of emotion and conduct
- Social anxiety or phobia
- Aspergers Syndrome

All of these share symptoms with several personality disorders.

Aetiology

What causes an emerging personality disorder?

Given the findings of research into the aetiologies of personality dysfunction, and the significant detrimental impact that a dysfunctional personality has on interpersonal relationships, it may be concluded that a disordered personality is most likely forged in the fire of neglectful, abusive or dysfunctional early relationships, and is responsible for the burn out or destruction of subsequent relationships over the life of the individual. A genetic predisposition is also likely to be necessary for the development of the disorder.

Assessment

What additional assessments are required in the case of sexually harmful young people suspected of exhibiting an emerging personality disorder?

The assessment of an emerging personality disorder in a sexually harmful young person is important, in order to identify their condition and related therapeutic needs. There are several assessment instruments available. In the experience of the author, The Millon Adolescent Clinical Inventory (MACI) is particularly informative. In addition to psychometric personality assessment, a comprehensive assessment of any functional impairments across all the 'systems' in the young person's life is critically important. This ought to include interpersonal behaviour and quality of relationships in the family, or residential placement, in the school setting, recreational activities, and peer relations.

To inform a cognitive-behavioural conceptualisation of the young person's personality functioning, it is important to identify cognitive schemas or core beliefs that underpin maladaptive behaviours, relationships, and impaired functioning. The presence of early acquired maladaptive schemas is critical in this process (Freeman and Rigby, 2003). It is recommended that the Schema Questionnaire (Young and Brown, 1994) and the Personality Belief Questionnaire (Beck and Beck, 1991) are used to facilitate this assessment.

Special needs

What additional needs do sexually harmful young people presenting with an emerging personality disorder have?

Just as sexually harmful young people with a learning disability have special needs, so do those with an emerging personality disorder. It may even be more appropriate to talk about a *personality disability*? In general, childhood and adolescent psychiatric disorders have some degree of adverse impact on the child's or young person's development and their adaptive functioning. Shiner and Caspi (2003) have found that personality dysfunction has a negative impact on a young person's adaptive functioning in relation to being successful at school and subsequent employment. Given that personality dysfunction has a critically adverse impact on interpersonal functioning and adaptation it is likely to be of significant importance in relation to sexually harmful young people in terms of impairing their adaptive functioning in relation to being successful at forming friendships and dating relationships. The functional implications of the presence of serious personality difficulties

or emerging personality disorders are (1) impaired interpersonal and social functioning and adjustment, and (2) impaired social integration. The essential risk associated with these serious impediments to the young person's development is marginalisation in its widest sense from mainstream society.

Functional impediments associated with personality dysfunction are likely to have a critical and detrimental impact on the young person's social development and peer relations. Given that sexual behaviour is relational in nature, and is normally dependent upon at least an interpersonal, if not intimate, relationship, it is critically allied to interpersonal functioning (ability to establish a one to one relationship). Also, given that the relational context is normally that of peer relations, sexual behaviour is equally critically allied to social functioning (peer acceptance and integration) which provides opportunities for closer one to one relationships and dating relationships.

One way of conceptualising the impact of a personality disorder on the young person's sexually harmful behaviour is to conceive of it as a constellation of vulnerabilities, made up of deficits and excesses across cognitive, emotional, and behavioural functioning that render the young person prone to sexually harmful behaviour. This is not the same as saying that the young person so affected is predisposed to sexually harmful behaviour. This constellation of vulnerabilities still needs the essential added ingredients of life experiences, life circumstances, life stressors and opportunity, prior to the onset of sexually harmful behaviour.

The accepted variation in the type or nature of personality disorders implies that each has its own constellation of associated vulnerabilities (deficits and excesses). Consequently, in terms of legitimising the application of personality disorder to young people under the age of 18 years, the potential benefit lies in: (1) identifying and remediating their specific vulnerabilities; and (2) accessing specialist services knowledgeable and experienced in the management and treatment of personality disordered offenders.

A pertinent issue for practice concerns the associations between different personality disorders and particular vulnerabilities relevant to the onset or maintenance of sexually harmful behaviour. For example, clinical experience shows that an asocial type personality disorder leaves the young person vulnerable to social isolation and emotional loneliness, which reflect impaired social-affective functioning. This in turn leaves the young person vulnerable to the sexual abuse of younger children or sexual assault on a peer-aged female. An avoidant type personality disorder is likely to be associated with social anxiety and social avoidance, which are likely to result in social isolation and emotional loneliness. This type of disorder may render the young person unable to form intimate attachments with other young people. This in turn may leave the young person vulnerable to seeking sexual gratification through impersonal sexual experiences, mediated by manipulative or aggressive behaviours. An antisocial type personality disorder may leave the young person vulnerable to the callous exploitation of another child or young person, in the egocentric pursuit of their own needs.

Risk

Are sexually harmful young people who present with an emerging personality disorder more at risk of sexual recidivism?

Personality characteristics are associated with a person's ability to effectively cope with negative life events and life stressors (Costa, Somerfield, and McCrea, 1996). The highly regarded relapse process model of sexual offending (Laws, 1989; Pithers, 1990) has identified negative moods, such as depression and anxiety, interpersonal conflicts, relationship difficulties, and an inability to effectively cope with life stresses as precipitators in the relapse (re-offending) process. This suggests that sexually harmful young people with an emerging personality disorder are at greater risk of sexual recidivism. In the adult field, it has been proposed that personality disorder represents an *enduring* risk factor for sexual recidivism (Craig, Browne and Stringer, 2003; Hanson and Harris, 1998; Hanson and Morton-Bourgon, 2004; Rice, Harris and Quinsey, 1990; Serin, Mailoux and Malcolm, 2001).

What are the implications for risk assessment? Risk assessment ought to incorporate the potential impact of personality disorder on risk status and risk stability. A personality diagnosis indicates significant and serious difficulties in interpersonal and social functioning. The corollary is that these impairments are likely to sustain and retain risk for sexually harmful behaviour over a considerable period of time. Prolonged risk will be associated

with the enduring nature of dysfunctional personality traits that fuel emotional disturbance and interpersonal and social impairments. Emotional lability, impulsivity and/or risk taking behaviours may heighten risk and make that risk imminent. A pervasive antisocial disposition may heighten risk and make that risk severe in terms of harm done to the victim. It is noted that empirically derived risk assessment guides for adult sexual offenders include personality disorder or psychopathy as a risk factor (e.g., SVR–20 Boer et al., 1997; SVRP Hart, Kropp and Laws, 2003).

Case management

How should sexually harmful young people who present with an emerging personality disorder be managed?

These are likely to be the more clinically complex and higher risk cases. Once an emerging personality disorder is identified there is a need to plan and muster a rapid containing response. This may later be followed by a valid therapeutic response to ameliorate the disorder. A multi-agency and multi-profession co-ordinated response to case management is required. Mental health professionals, more appropriately within a forensic specialism, will need to be part of this multi-agency case management, and adopt a central role.

Personality disordered individuals are at risk of criminal behaviour. This is especially true for Antisocial Personality Disorder (DSM-IV) or Dissocial Personality Disorder (ICD-10) (see Dolan and Millington, 2004; Harrington and Bailey, 2003). In England and Wales, the person diagnosed with a personality disorder in combination with antisocial behaviour, may be classified as suffering from 'psychopathic disorder', which is a catchall legal category, under the Mental Health Act (1983) (Jones, 1996). If this person is judged to be treatable (in terms of the diagnosis of personality disorder) and is judged to pose a significant risk to the public, then they may be detained involuntarily in hospital or treated in the community by means of a compulsory treatment order. Future legislation is likely to remove the treatability clause, allowing detention on the basis of risk containment (DoH/Home Office, 1999, 2000).

Based on clinical experience, with the emergence and development of specialist forensic mental health services for young people, it has been found that more often serious young offenders, including sexual offenders, are diagnosed with serious personality difficulties or an emerging personality disorder. Similarly, with the establishment of medium secure hospitals for young people, there are now five such NHS facilities based in England, more of these serious and disturbed young offenders are detained in a secure hospital using the Mental Health Act (1983) legislation, under the category of 'psychopathic disorder'. It should be noted that under existing legislation, a young person is not detainable in a psychiatric hospital for sexually harmful behaviour or risk for future sexually harmful behaviour per se. They may only be detained on the basis of a psychiatric diagnosis of mental illness, mental impairment, or psychopathic disorder.

Treatment

What additional treatments are required in the case of sexually harmful young people suspected of exhibiting an emerging personality disorder?

Practitioners ought not simply spectate on significant personality difficulties once they have been identified. In part, treatment is about the identification and provision of valid and appropriate treatment components (the what). The treatment of sexually harmful behaviour in young people presenting with an emerging personality disorder will be more complex given their 'special needs' status. In addition to the focused treatment for the sexually harmful behaviour itself, relevant and appropriate psychological and psychosocial treatments will be required to address the young person's personality dysfunction. Therefore, the treatment of sexually harmful young people with an emerging personality disorder will need to incorporate additional treatment components to meet their specialist needs. As we have seen, the treatment of choice is cognitive behavioural therapies for personality disorders (Beck et al., 1990; Freeman et al., 2003; Young et al., 2003). The critical component is the identification and modification of dysfunctional core beliefs or maladaptive schemas, which are associated with underlying interpersonal and social dysfunction, and affective disturbance. In addition to cognitive therapy, cognitive behavioural interventions will be required to help the young person learn new cognitive and behavioural skills to improve their

interpersonal and social functioning, and learn adaptive coping skills to more effectively deal with negative life events and stressors. In the adult field, Buschman and Van Beek (2003) proposed a treatment model for personality disordered sexual offenders, which was based on Ward and Hudson's (1998) self-regulation model of sexual offending. This approach proposed that deficits associated with core affective, cognitive and behavioural processes played a significant role in the offence pathway or offence chain. It incorporates a cognitive model of personality disorder, which emphasises dysfunctional cognitions (Beck et al., 1990).

Cognitive therapy requires the practitioner to establish a working alliance with the young person and to work collaboratively. Coercive cognitive therapy will never work! The practitioner must also engender a sense of optimism both in the young person and other professionals, to avoid professionalised rejection and exclusion of personality disordered young people on the basis of poor prognosis and un-treatability. The reality however, is that some of the most disturbed personality disordered young people will be treatment resistant, and deemed untreatable.

Treatment responsivity

Do practitioners have to adopt different approaches and interactional styles when working with sexually harmful young people suspected of exhibiting an emerging personality disorder?

In part, treatment is about the delivery process (the how). The principle of individual differences that is inherent in the personality literature may be usefully emphasised to inform an appreciation of the individual differences that distinguish one sexually harmful adolescent from another. The presence of significant personality difficulties will undoubtedly complicate treatment in terms of this delivery process. This approach emphasises the responsivity principle in offender treatment (Andrews and Bonta, 2003), from which it may be deduced that dysfunctional personality traits will need to be taken into account when seeking to motivate and engage the young person in offence-specific interventions. In tune with the responsivity principle the delivery of treatment ought to be consistent with the young person's particular personality characteristics and difficulties. For instance, how do we approach and engage an extremely shy (socially anxious/phobic) young person?

An additional delivery issue concerns the treatability of the young person. Based on our knowledge of the features and sequlae of an emerging personality disorder, these young people are likely to be more difficult to engage and sustain in treatment because of significant interpersonal difficulties, they experience more frequent and more debilitating crises in their everyday lives because of emotional dysregulation and poor coping abilities (that will require a rapid interventionist response, that is likely to interfere with planned treatment interventions) and be more difficult to manage in the community due to their dysfunctional life styles. Treatment responsivity and treatability are very significant issues in young people with an emerging Antisocial Personality Disorder or emerging Psychopathic Disorder. These young people tend to be habitually dishonest and manipulative in their interpersonal style and interactions with other people, including therapists. These characteristics are likely to complicate and potentially sabotage the therapeutic process and endeavour, and significantly reduce the potential effectiveness of therapeutic interventions.

An emerging sub-specialism

If we accept the clinical reality of an *emerging personality disorder* in some sexually harmful young people, then we need to propose the recognition and development of an *emerging sub-specialism* in the field. There is a need to develop multi-agency and multi-profession case management arrangements. There is a need to identify appropriate professional resources and service providers. There is a need to develop specialised treatment interventions that address personality disability and associated special needs, and to evaluate best practice for this sub-group of sexually harmful young people.

This demands that we support and resource a new emerging sub-specialism, within the current specialist field of service provision delivered to sexually harmful young people. There already exists the conceptual, theoretical, and clinical beginnings of such a sub-specialism in the UK as evidenced by recent publications (Dolan and Millington, 2004; Harrington and Bailey, 2003;

Hickey, Vizard, McCrory and French, 2006; Richardson, 2005; Richardson et al., 2004).

References

American Psychiatric Association. (1994) *Diagnostic and Statistical Manual of Mental Disorders.* 4th Edn. Washington, DC: Author.

Andrews, D.A. and Bonta, J. (2003) *The Psychology of Criminal Conduct.* 3rd Edn. Cincinnati, OH: Anderson.

Bard, L.A. and Knight, R.A. (1987) Sex Offender Subtyping and the MCMI. In Green, C. (Ed.) *Proceedings of the First Conference on the Millon Clinical Inventories.* Minneapolis: National Computer Systems.

Battle, C.L., Shea, M.T., Johnson, D.M., Yen, S., Zlotnick, C. and Zanarini, M.C. (2004) Childhood Maltreatment Associated with Adult Personality Disorders: Findings from the Collaborative Longitudinal Personality Disorders Study. *Journal of Personality Disorders,* 18, 193–211.

Beck, J.S. (1995) *Cognitive Therapy: Basics and Beyond.* New York: Guilford Press.

Beck, A.T. and Beck, J.S. (1991) *The Personality Belief Questionnaire.* Bala Cynwyd, PA: The Beck Institute for Cognitive Therapy and Research.

Beck, A.T., Freeman, A. and Associates. (1990) *Cognitive Therapy of Personality Disorders.* New York: Guilford Press.

Berner, W., Berger, P., Gutierez, K., Jordan, B. and Berger, J. (1992) The Role of Personality Disorder in the Treatment of Sexual Offenders. *Journal of Offender Rehabilitation,* 18, 25–37.

Bernstein, D.P., Cohen, P., Skodol, A., Bezirganian, S. and Brook, J.S. (1996) Childhood Antecedents of Adolescent Personality Disorders. *American Journal of Psychiatry,* 153, 907–13.

Bernstein, D.P., Cohen, P., Velez, C.N., Schawb-Stone, M., Siever, L.J. and Shinsato, L. (1993) Prevalence and Stability of the DSM-III-R Personality Disorders in A Community-Based Survey of Adolescents. *American Journal of Psychiatry,* 150, 1237–43.

Boer, D.P., Hart, S.D., Kropp, P.R. and Webster, C.D. (1997) *Manual for the Sexual Violence Risk – 20: Professional Guidelines for Assessing Risk of Sexual Violence.* Vancouver, BC, Canada: Institute Against Family Violence.

Bogaerts, S., Vervaeke, G. and Goethals, J. (2004) A Comparison of Relational Attitude and

Personality Disorders in the Explanation of Child Molestation. *Sexual Abuse: A Journal of Research and Treatment*, 16: 1, 37–47.

Bryer, J., Nelson, B., Miller, J. and Krol, P. (1987) Childhood Sexual and Physical Abuse as Factors in Psychiatric Illness. *American Journal of Psychiatry*, 144, 1426–30.

Buschman, J. and Van Beek, D.J. (2003) A Clinical Model for the Treatment of Personality Disordered Sexual Offenders: An Example of Theory Knitting. *Sexual Abuse: A Journal of Research and Treatment*, 5: 3, 183–99.

Buss, A.H. and Plomin, R. (1975) *A Temperament Theory of Personality Development*. New York: Wiley.

Buss, A.H. and Plomin, R. (1984) *Temperament: Early Developing Personality Traits*. Hillsdale, NJ: Erlbaum.

Butcher, J.N. and Tellegen, A. (1978) Common Methodological Problems in MMPI Research. *Journal of Consulting and Clinical Psychology*, 46, 620–8.

Butcher, J.N., Williams, C.L., Graham, J.R. et al. (1992) *MMPI-A (Minnesota Multiphasic Personality Inventory – Adolescent): Manual for Administration, Scoring and Interpretation*. Minnespolis: University of Minnesota Press.

Carpenter, D.R., Peed, S.F. and Eastman, B. (1995) Personality Characteristics of Adolescent Sexual Offenders: A Pilot Study. *Sexual Abuse: A Journal of Research and Treatment*, 7: 3, 195–203.

Carter, J.D., Joyce, P.R., Mulder, R.T. and Luty, S.E. (2001) The Contribution of Temperament, Childhood Neglect and Abuse to the Development of Personality Dysfunction: A Comparison of Three Models. *Journal of Personality Disorders*, 15: 2, 123–35.

Carter, J.D., Joyce, P.R., Mulder, R.T., Luty, S.E. and Sullivan, P. (1999) Early Deficient Parenting in Depressed Outpatients is Associated with Personality Dysfunction and not with Depression Subtypes. *Journal of Affective Disorders*, 54, 29–37.

Cattell, R.B. (965) *The Scientific Analysis of Personality*. Baltimore, MD: Penguin Books.

Caputo, A.A., Frick, P.J. and Brodsky, S.L. (1999) Family Violence and Juvenile Sex Offending: Potential Mediating Roles of Psychopathic Traits and Negative Attitudes toward Women. *Criminal Justice and Behaviour*, 26, 338–56.

Caspi, A., Roberts, B.W. and Shiner, R.L. (2005) Personality Development: Stability and Change. *Annual Review of Psychology*, 56, 453–85.

Caspi, A., Henry, B., Mcgee, R.O., Moffitt, T.E. and Silva, P.A. (1995) Temperamental Origins of Child and Adolescent Behaviour Problems: From Age 3 to Age 15. *Child Development*, 66, 55–68.

Caspi, A., Harrington, H., Milne, B., Amell, J.W., Theodore, R.F. and Moffitt, T.E. (2003) Children's Behavioural Styles at Age 3 are Linked to Their Adult Personality Traits at Age 26. *Journal of Personality*, 71, 495–513.

Chantry, K. and Craig, R.J. (1994) Psychological Screening of Sexually Violent Offenders with the MCMI. *Journal of Clinical Psychology*, 50: 3, 430–5.

Chesire, J.D. (2001) *Personality, Power and Sexual Assault: Exploration of the Relationship Between Behaviour in Sexual Assault and Offender Personality Regulation*. Published Doctoral Dissertation. Cleveland, OH: Case Western Reserve University.

Chesire, J.D. (2004) Review, Critique and Synthesis of Personality Theory in Motivation to Sexually Assault. *Aggression and Violent Behavior*, 9, 633–44.

Chess, S. and Thomas, A. (1996) *Temperament: Theory and Practice*. New York: Brunner/Mazel.

Coker, L.A., Samuel, D.B. and Widiger, T.A. (2002) Maladaptive Personality Functioning within the Big Five and the Five-Factor Model. *Journal of Personality Disorders*, 16, 385–401.

Cooper, C.L., Murphy, W.D. and Haynes, M.R. (1996) Characteristics of Abused and Non-abused Adolescent Sexual Offenders. *Sexual Abuse: A Journal of Research and Treatment*, 8: 2, 105–19.

Costa, P.T. and McCrae, R.R. (1990) Personality Disorders and the Five Factor Model. *Journal of Personality Disorders*, 4, 362–71.

Costa, P.T. and McCrae, R.R. (1992a) The Five Factor Model of Personality and Its Relevance to Personality Disorders. *Journal of Personality Disorders*, 6, 343–59.

Costa, P.T. and McCrae, R.R. (1992b) *The NEO Personality Inventory – Revised (NEO PI-R)*. Lutz, FL: Psychological Assessment Resources.

Costa, P.T., Somerfield, M.R. and Mccrae, R.R. (1996) Personality and Coping: A Reconceptualization. In Zeidner, M. and Endler, N.S. (Eds.) *Handbook of Coping: Theory, Research, Applications*. New York: John Wiley.

Craig, L.A., Browne, K.D. and Stringer, I. (2003) Risk Scales and Factors Predictive of Sexual Offence Recidivism. *Trauma, Violence and Abuse: A Review Journal*, 4, 45–69.

De Clercq, B. and De Fruyt, F. (2003) Personality Disorder Symptoms in Adolescence: A Five-Factor Model Perspective. *Journal of Personality Disorders*, 17, 269–92.

De Clercq, B., De Fruyt, F. and Van Leeuwen, K. (2004) A Little Five Lexically-Based Perspective on Personality Disorder Symptoms in Adolescence. *Journal of Personality Disorders*, 18, 477–96.

De Clercq, B., De Fruyt, F., Van Leeuwen, K., Mervielde, I. and De Medts, L. (2004) *A Hierarchical Representation of Personality Pathology in Childhood and Adolescence.* Unpublished Manuscript.

Denniston, S.M., Stough, C. and Birgden, A. (2001) A Dimensional Personality Approach to Understanding Sex Offenders. *Psychology, Crime and Law*, 7, 243–62.

Derryberry, D. and Rothbart, M,K. (1997) Reactive and Effortful Processes in the Organisation of Temperament. *Development and Psychopathology*, 9, 633–52.

Digman, J.M. (1990) Personality Structure: Emergence of The 5-Factor Model. *Annual Review of Psychology*, 41, 417–40.

Dolan, M. (1994) Psychopathy: A Neurological Perspective. *British Journal of Psychiatry*, 165, 151–9.

Dolan, M. and Millington, J. (2004) Personality Dysfunction and Disorders in Childhood and Adolescents. In Bailey, S. and Dolan, M. (Eds.) *Adolescent Forensic Psychiatry*. London: Arnold.

DoH/Home Office. (1999) *Managing Dangerous People with Severe Personality Disorder: Proposals for Policy Development*. London: DoH.

DoH/Home Office. (2000) *Reforming The Mental Health Act: Part I: The New Legal Framework and Part II: High Risk Patients*. London: The Stationery Office.

Emde, R.N. and Hewitt, J. (2001) *Infancy to Early Childhood: Genetic and Environmental Influences on Developmental Change*. New York: Oxford University Press.

Eppright, T.D., Kashani, J.H. and Robinson, B.D. (1993) Co-Morbidity of Conduct Disorder and Personality Disorder in an Incarcerated Juvenile Population. *American Journal of Psychiatry*, 150, 1233–6.

Erickson, W.D., Luxenberg, M.G., Walbeck, N.H. and Seely, R.K. (1987) Frequency of MMPI Two-Point Code Types among Sex Offenders. *Journal of Consulting and Clinical Psychology*, 55, 566–70.

Eysenck, H.J. (1964) *Crime and Personality*. London: Routledge and Kegan Paul.

Eysenck, H.J. and Eysenck, S.B. (1975) *Manual of the Eysenck Personality Questionnaire (Adult and Junior)*. London: Hodder and Stoughton.

Firestone, P., Bradford, J., Greenberg, D. and Serran, G. (2000) The Relationship of Deviant Sexual Arousal and Psychopathology in Incest Offenders, Extrafamilial Child Molesters and Rapists. *Journal of The American Academy of Psychiatry and The Law*, 28: 3, 303–8.

Forth, A.E. and Burke, H.C. (1998) Psychopathy in Adolescence: Assessment, Violence and Developmental Precursors. In Cooke, D.J., Forth, A.E. and Hare, R.D. (Eds.) *Psychopathy: Theory, Research and Implications for Society*. Dordrecht, NL: Kluwer.

Forth, A., Kossen, D and Hare, R.D. (2003) *The Hare Psychopathy Checklist-Youth Version (PCL: YV)*. New York: Multi-Health Systems.

Freeman, A.M. and Rigby, A. (2003) Personality Disorders among Children and Adolescents. In Reinecke, M.A., Dattilio, F.M. and Freeman, A.M. (Eds.) *Cognitive Therapy with Children and Adolescents: A Casebook for Clinical Practice*. New York: Guilford Press.

Freeman, A.M., Pretzer, J., Fleming, B. and Simon, K.M. (2003) *Clinical Applications of Cognitive Therapy*. 2nd Edn. New York: Kluwer Academic.

Freeman, K.A., Dexter-Mazza, E.T. and Hoffman, K.C. (2005) Comparing Personality Characteristics of Juvenile Sex Offenders and Non-sex Offending Delinquent Peers: A Preliminary Investigation. *Sexual Abuse: A Journal of Research and Treatment*, 17: 1, 3–12.

Frick, P.J. (1998) Callous-Unemotional Traits and Conduct Problems: Applying the Two-Factor Model of Psychopathy to Children. In Cooke, D.J., Forth, A.E. and Hare, R.D. (Eds.) *Psychopathy: Theory, Research and Implications for Society*. Boston, MA: Kluwer Academic.

Frick, P.J. and Ellis, M.L. (2000) Callous-Unemotional Traits and Subtypes of Conduct Disorder. *Clinical Child and Family Psychology Review*

Frick, P.J. and Hare, R.D. (2001) *The Antisocial Process Screening Device*. Toronto: Multi-Health Systems.

Frick, P.J., Barry, C.T. and Bodin, S.D. (2000) Applying the Concept of Psychopathy to Children: Implications for the Assessment of Antisocial Youth. In Gacono, C.B. (Ed.) *The Clinical and Forensic Assessment of Psychopathy*. Mahwah, NJ: Lawrence Erlbaum Associates.

Geiger, T.C. and Crick, N.R. (2001) A Developmental Psychopathology Perspective on Vulnerability to Personality Disorders. In Ingram, R.E. and Price, J.M. (Eds.) *Vulnerability to Psychopathology*. New York: Guilford Press.

Gough, H.G. (1987) *California Psychological Inventory: Administrator's Guide*. Palo Alto, CA: Consulting Psychologists Press.

Graham, J.R. (1987) *The MMPI: A Practical Guide*. 2nd Edn. New York: Oxford University Press.

Gretton, H.M., Mcbride, M., Hare, R.D., O'Shaughnessy, R. and Kumka, G. (2001) Psychopathy and Recidivism in Adolescent Sex Offenders. *Criminal Justice and Behavior*, 28, 427–99.

Groth, A. (1979) *Men Who Rape: The Psychology of the Offender*. New York: Plenum Press.

Grover, R.L. and Nangle, D.W. (2003) Adolescent Perceptions of Problematic Heterosocial Situations: A Focus Group Study. *Journal of Youth and Adolescence*, 32, 129–39.

Hall, G.C. (1990) Prediction of Sexual Aggression. *Clinical Psychology Review*, 10, 229–45.

Hall, G.C. and Hirschman, R. (1991) Toward a Theory of Sexual Aggression: A Quadripartite Model. *Journal of Consulting and Clinical Psychology*, 59, 662–9.

Hanson, R.K. and Bussiere, M.T. (1998) Predictors of Relapse: A Meta-Analysis of Sexual Offender Recidivism Studies. *Journal of Consulting and Clinical Psychology*, 66, 348–62.

Hanson, R.K. and Harris, A.J. (1998) *Dynamic Predictors of Sexual Recidivism. (User Report No. 1998-01)*. Ottawa: Department of The Solicitor General of Canada.

Hanson, R.K. and Morton-Bourgon, K.E. (2004) Predictors of Sexual Recidivism: An Updated Meta-Analysis. Available At: Http:// Www.Psepc.Gc.Ca/Publications/Corrections/Pdf/200402–E.Pdf

Hare, R.D. (1991) *The Hare Psychopathy Checklist – Revised*. Toronto: Multi-Health Systems.

Harrington, R. and Bailey, S. (2003) *The Scope for Preventing Antisocial Personality Disorder by Intervening in Adolescence*. Report from the National Programme on Forensic Mental Health R and D Seminar Preventing Personality Disorder by Intervening in Adolescence. Manchester. March.

Harrington, R.C., Fudge, H., Rutter, M., Pickles, A. and Hill, J. (1991) Adult Outcomes of Childhood and Adolescent Depression: II. Risk for Antisocial Disorders. *Journal of The American Academy of Child and Adolescent Psychiatry*, 30, 434–9.

Hart, S.D. (1998) The Role of Psychopathy in Assessing Risk for Violence: Conceptual and Methodological Issues. *Legal and Criminological Psychology*, 3, 123–40.

Hart, S.D., Kropp, P.R. and Laws, D.R. (2003) *The Risk for Sexual Violence Protocol (RSVP)*. Pacific Psychological Assessment Corporation.

Hemphill, J.F., Hare, R.D. and Wong, S. (1998) Psychopathy and Recidivism: A Review. *Legal and Criminological Psychology*, 3, 139–70.

Herkov, M.J, Gynther, M.D, Thomas, S. and Myers, W.C. (1996) MMPI Differences Among Adolescent Inpatients, Rapists, Sodomists and Sexual Abusers. *Journal of Personality Assessment*, 66, 81–90.

Hickey, N., Vizard, E., McCrory, E. and French, L. (2006) Links Between Juvenile Sexually Abusive Behaviour and Emerging Severe Personality Disorder Traits in Childhood. DoH/Home Office. Available at: Www.Dspdprogramme.Gov.Uk

Jacobs, W.L., Kennedy, W.A. and Meyer, J.B. (1997) Juvenile Delinquents: A Between-Group Comparison Study of Sexual and Nonsexual Offenders. *Sexual Abuse: A Journal of Research and Treatment*, 9, 201–17.

John, O.P. (1990) The 'Big Five' Factor Taxonomy: Dimensions of Personality in the Natural Language and in Questionnaires. In Pervin, L.A. (Ed.) *Handbook of Personality: Theory and Research*. New York: Guilford.

Johnson, J.G., Cohen, P., Brown, J., Smailes, E.M. and Bernstein, D.P. (1999) Childhood Maltreatment Increases Risk of Personality Disorders during Early Adulthood. *Archives of General Psychiatry*, 56, 600–6.

Johnson, J.G., Smailes, E.M., Cohen, P., Brown, J. and Bernstein, D.P. (2000) Associations between Four Types of Childhood Neglect and Personality Disorder Symptoms during Adolescence and Early Adulthood: Findings of Community-Based Longitudinal Study. *Journal of Personality Disorders*, 14, 171–87.

Johnson, J.G., Cohen, P., Smailes, E., Kasen, S., Oldham, J.M. and Skodol, A. (2000) Adolescent Personality Disorders Associated with Violence and Criminal Behaviour during Adolescence and Early Adulthood. *The American Journal of Psychiatry*, 157: 9, 1406–12.

Johnson, J.G., Cohen, P., Smailes, E.M., Skodol, A.E., Brown, J. and Oldham, J.M. (2001) Childhood Verbal Abuse and Risk for Personality Disorders during Adolescence and Early Adulthood. *Comprehensive Psychiatry*, 42, 16–23.

Jones, R.M. (1996) *Mental Health Act Manual*. 5th Edn. London: Sweet and Maxwell.

Kagan, J. (1994) *Galen's Prophecy*. New York: Basic Books.

Kalichman, S.C. (1990) Affective and Personality Characteristics of Replicated MMPI Profile Subgroups of Incarcerated Adult Rapist. *Archives of Sexual Behaviour*, 19, 443–59.

Kalichman, S.C. (1991) Psychopathology and Personality Characteristics of Criminal Sexual Offenders as a Function of Victim Age. *Archives of Sexual Behavior*, 20, 187–97.

Kasen, S., Cohen, P., Skodol, A.E., Johnson, J.G. and Brook, J.S. (1999) Influence of Child and Adolescent Psychiatric Disorders on Young Adult Personality Disorder. *American Journal of Psychiatry*, 156, 1529–35.

Kasen S., Cohen, P., Skodol, A.E., Johnson, J.G., Smailes, E. and Brook, J.S. (2001) Childhood Depression and Adult Personality Disorder: Alternative Pathways of Continuity. *Archives of General Psychiatry*, 58, 231–6.

Kelly, T.P. and Richardson, G. (Unpublished) Eysenck Personality Questionnaire – Junior: Data on A British Sample of Juvenile Delinquents.

Kernberg, P.F., Weiner, A.S. and Bardenstein, K.K. (2000) *Personality Disorders in Children and Adolescents*. New York: Basic Books.

Knight, R.A. (1988) A Taxonomic Analysis of Child Molesters. *Annals of The New York Academy of Sciences*, 528, 2–20.

Knight, R.A and Prentky, R.A. (1990) Classifying Sexual Offenders: The Development and Corroboration of Taxonomic Models. In Marshall, W.L., Laws, D.R. and Barbaree, H.E. (Eds.) *Handbook of Sexual Assault: Issues, Theories and Treatment of the Offender*. New York: Plenum Press.

Knopp, F.H. (1985) *The Youthful Sex Offender: The Rationale and Goals of Early Intervention and Treatment*. The Safer Society Press: Orwell, VT.

Krueger, R.F. (1999) The Structure of Common Mental Disorders. *Archives of General Psychiatry*, 56, 921–6.

Krueger, R.F., Mcgue, M. and Iacono, W.G. (2001) The Higher-Order Structure of Common DSM Mental Disorders: Internalisation, Externalisation and their Connections to Personality. *Personality and Individual Differences*, 30, 1245–59.

Krueger, R.F., Caspi, A., Moffitt, T.E. and Silva, P.A. (1998) The Structure and Stability of Common Mental Disorders (DSM-III-R): A Longitudinal-Epidemiological Study. *Journal of Abnormal Psychology*, 107, 216–27.

La Greca, A,M. and Lopez, N. (1998) Social Anxiety among Adolescents: Linkages with Peer Relations and Friendships. *Journal of Abnormal Child Psychology*, 26, 83–94.

Langevin, R., Wright, P. and Handy, L. (1988) Empathy, Assertiveness, Aggressiveness and Defensiveness among Sex Offenders. *Annals of Sex Research*, 1, 533–47.

Langstrom, N., Sjostedt, G. and Grann, M. (2004) Psychiatric Disorders and Recidivism in Sexual Offenders. *Sexual Abuse: A Journal of Research and Treatment*, 16: 2, 139–50.

Laws, R.D. (Ed.) (1989) *Relapse Prevention with Sex Offenders*. New York: Guilford.

Lehne, G.K. (1994) The NEO-PI and the MCMI in the Forensic Evaluation of Sex Offenders. In Costa, P.T. and Widiger, T.A. (Eds.) *Personality Disorders and The Five-Factor Model*. Washington, DC: American Psychological Association.

Loeber, R., Burke, J.D. and Lahey, B.B. (2002) What are Adolescent Antecedents to Antisocial Personality Disorder? *Criminal Behaviour and Mental Health*, 12, 24–36.

Loranger, A.W. (1999) *International Personality Disorder Examination: DSM-IV and ICD-10 Interviews*. Lutz, FL: Psychological Assessment Resources.

Lussier, P., Proulx, J. and Mckibben, A. (2001) Personality Characteristics and Adaptive Strategies to Cope with Negative Emotional States and Deviant Sexual Fantasies in Sexual Aggressors. *International Journal of Offender Therapy and Comparative Criminology*, 45: 2, 159–70.

Malamuth, N.M., Heavey, C.L. and Linz, D. (1993) Predicting Men's Antisocial Behavior against Women: The Interaction Model of Sexual Aggression. In Hall, G.C., Hirschman, R., Graham, J.R. and Zaragoza, M.S. (Eds) *Sexual Aggression: Issues in Etiology, Assessment and Treatment*. Washington, DC: Taylor and Francis.

Marshall, W.L. and Hall, G.C. (1995) The Value of the MMPI in Deciding Forensic Issues in Accused Sexual Offenders. *Sexual Abuse: A Journal of Research and Treatment*, 7, 205–19.

Marshall, W.L., Anderson, D. and Fernandez, Y. (1999) *Cognitive Behavioural Treatment of Sexual Offenders*. New York: John Wiley and Sons.

Maziade, M., Caron, C., Cote, R., Merette, C., Bernier, H., Laplante, B., Boutin, P. and Thivierge, J. (1990) Psychiatric Status of Adolescents who had Extreme Temperaments at Age 7. *American Journal of Psychiatry*, 147, 1531–6.

McCrae, R. and Costa, P. (1990) *Personality in Adulthood*. New York: Guilford.

Mervielde, I. and Asendorpf, J.B. (2000) Variable-Centered and Person-Centered Approaches to Childhood Personality. In Hampton, S.E. (Ed.) *Advances in Personality Psychology*. Philadelphia: Taylor and Francis.

Mervielde, I. and De Fruyt, F. (1999) Construction of the Hierarchical Personality Inventory for Children (Hipic) in Mervielde, I. Deary, I. De Fruyt, F. and Ostendorf, F. (Eds.) *Personality Psychology in Europe*. Tilburg, NL: Tilburg University Press.

Mervielde, I., De Clercq, B., De Fruyt, F. and Van Leeuwen, K. (2005) Temperament, Personality and Developmental Psychopathology as Childhood Antecedents of Personality Disorders. *Journal of Personality Disorders*, 19: 2, 171–201.

Millon, T. (1981) *Disorders of Personality: DSM-III: Axis II*. New York: Wiley.

Millon, T. (1987) *Manual for The Millon Clinical Multiaxial Inventory–II*. Minneapolis, MN: National Computer Systems.

Millon, T. (1994) *Manual for The Millon Clinical Multiaxial Inventory – III*. Minneapolis, MN: National Computer Systems.

Millon, T. (1996) *Disorders of Personality: DSM-IV and Beyond*. New York: John Wiley.

Millon, T., Davis, R. and Millon, C. (1977) *Millon Clinical Multiaxial Inventory Manual*. Minneapolis, MN: National Computer Systems.

Millon, T., Davis, R. and Millon, C. (1997) *The Millon Clinical Multiaxial Inventory – III Manual*. 2nd Edn. Minneapolis, MN: National Computer Systems.

Millon, T., Millon, C. and Davis, R. (1993) *Millon Adolescent Clinical Inventory Manual*. Minneapolis, MN: National Computer Systems.

Morey, L.C., Gunderson, J.G., Quigley, B.D., Shea, M.T., Skodol, A.E., McGlashan, T.H. and Stout, I. (2002) A Representation of Borderline, Avoidant, Obsessive-Compulsive and Schizotypal Personality Model. *Journal of Personality Disorders*, 16, 215–34.

O'Connor, B.P. and Dyee, J.A. (2002) Tests of General and Specific Models of Personality Disorder Configuration. In Costa, P.T. Jr. and Widiger, T.A. (Eds.) *Personality Disorders and The Five-Factor Model of Personality*. 2nd Edn. Washington DC: American Psychological Association.

Okami, P. and Goldberg, A. (1992) Personality Correlates of Pedophilia: Are They Reliable Indicators? *Journal of Sex Research*, 29: 3, 297–328.

Oliver, L.L., Nagayama-Hall, G.C. and Neuhaus, S.M. (1993) A Comparison of the Personality and Background Characteristics of Adolescent Sex Offenders and Other Adolescent Offenders. *Criminal Justice and Behaviour*, 20, 359–70.

Paris, J. and Frank, H. (1989) Perceptions of Parental Bonding in Borderline Patients. *American Journal of Psychiatry*, 146, 1498–9.

Parks, G.A. (2004) *Juvenile Sex Offender Recidivism: Typological Differences in Risk Assessment*. Unpublished Doctoral Dissertation. Walden University.

Pincus, A.L. and Wiggins, J.S. (1990) Interpersonal Problems and Conceptions of Personality Disorders. *Journal of Personality Disorders*, 4, 342–52.

Pithers, W.D. (1990) Relapse Prevention with Sexual Aggressors: A Method for Maintaining Therapeutic Gain and Enhancing External Supervision. In Marshall, W.L. Laws, D.R. and Barbaree, H.E. (Eds.) *Handbook of Sexual Assault: Issues, Theories and Treatment of the Offender*. New York: Guilford.

Prentky, R.A. and Knight, R.A. (1991) Identifying Critical Dimensions for Discriminating among Rapists. *Journal of Consulting and Clinical Psychology*, 59, 643–61.

Prentky, R.A., Cohen, M. and Seghorn, T. (1985) Development of a Rational Taxonomy for the Classification of Rapists: The Massachusetts Treatment Center System. *Bulletin of The American Academy of Psychiatry and The Law*, 13, 39–70.

Prentky, R.A., Knight, R.A., Lee, A.F. and Cerce, D.D. (1995) Predictive Validity of Lifestyle Impulsivity for Rapists. *Criminal Justice and Behaviour*, 22: 2, 106–28.

Putnam, S.P., Ellis, L.K. and Rothbart, M.K. (2001) The Structure of Temperament from Infancy through Adolescence. In Eliasz, A. and Angleneiter, A. (Eds.) *Advances in Research on Temperament*. Miami, FL: Pabst Science Publishers.

Quinsey, V., Lalumiere, M., Rice, M. and Harris, G. (1995) Predicting Sexual Offenses. In Campbell, J.C. (Ed.) *Assessing Dangerous: Violence by Sexual Offenders, Batterers and Child Abusers*. Thousand Oaks, CA: Sage.

Quinsey, V.L., Rice, M.E. and Harris, G.T. (1995) Actuarial Prediction of Sexual Recidivism. *Journal of Interpersonal Violence*, 10, 85–105.

Ramklint, M., Von Knorring, A.L., Von Knorring, L. and Ekselius, L. (2003) Child and Adolescent Psychiatric Disorders Predicting Adult Personality Disorder: A Follow-Up Study. *Nordic Journal of Psychiatry*, 57, 23–8.

Ressler, R.K., Douglas, J.E., Burgess, A.W. and Burgess, A.G. (1993) *Crime Classification Manual: The Standard System for Investigating and Classifying Violent Crimes.* London: Simon and Schuster.

Rice, M.E., Harris, G.T. and Quinsey, V.L. (1990) A Follow-Up of Rapists Assessed in a Maximum-Security Psychiatric Facility. *Journal of Interpersonal Violence*, 5, 435–48.

Rice, M.E., Quinsey, V.L. and Harris, G.T. (1991) Sexual Recidivism among Child Molesters Released from Maximum Security Psychiatric Institution. *Journal of Consulting and Clinical Psychology*, 59, 381–6.

Richardson, J., Loss, P. and Ross, J.E. (1988) *Psychoeducational Curriculum for Adolescent Sex Offenders.* New London, CT: Loss Press.

Richardson, G. (2005) Early Maladaptive Schemas in a Sample of British Adolescent Sexual Abusers: Implications for Therapy. *Journal of Sexual Aggression*, 11: 3, 259–76.

Richardson, G. (Unpublished A) In-Patient Risk Status Assessment. Northern Forensic Mental Health Service for Young People, Roycroft Clinic, St Nicholas Hospital, Newcastle Upon Tyne.

Richardson, G. (Unpublished B) Personality Differences in a British Sample of Sexually Abusive Adolescents: as Measured by The Eysenck Personality Questionnaire. Northern Forensic Mental Health Service for Young People, St Nicholas Hospital, Newcastle Upon Tyne.

Richardson, G., Graham, F., Bhate, S.R. and Kelly, T.P. (1995) A British Sample of Sexually Abusive Adolescents: Abuser and Abuse Characteristics. *Criminal Behaviour and Mental Health*, 5, 187–208.

Richardson, G., Kelly, T.P., Graham, F. and Bhate, S.R. (2004) A Personality-Based Taxonomy of Sexually Abusive Adolescents derived from The Millon Adolescent Clinical Inventory (MACI) *British Journal of Clinical Psychology*, 43, 285–98.

Roberts, B.W. and Del Vecchino, W.F. (2000) The Rank-Order Consistency of Personality Traits from Childhood to Old Age: A Quantitative Review of Longitudinal Studies. *Psychological Bulletin*, 126, 3–25.

Roberts, B.W., Caspi, A. and Moffitt, T. E. (2001) The Kids are Alright: Growth and Stability in Personality Development from Adolescence to Adulthood. *Journal of Personality and Social Psychology*, 81, 670–83.

Roberts, C.F., Doren, D.M. and Thornton, D. (2002) Dimensions Associated with Assessments of Sex Offender Recidivism Risk. *Criminal Justice and Behaviour*, 29: 5, 569–89.

Rothbart, M.K. and Bates, J.E. (1998) Temperament. In Damon, W. and Eisenberg, N. (Eds.) *Handbook of Child Psychology: Social, Emotional and Personality Development.* 5th Edn. New York: Wiley.

Saulsman, L.M. and Page, A.C. (2004) The Five-Factor Model and Personality Disorder Empirical Literature: A Meta-Analytic Review. *Clinical Psychology Review*, 23, 1055–85.

Schlank, A.M. (1995) The Utility of The MMPI and The MSI for Identifying a Sexual Offender Typology. *Sexual Abuse: A Journal of Research and Treatment*, 7: 3, 185–94.

Seghorn, T.K., Prentky, R.A. and Boucher, R.J. (1987) Childhood Sexual Abuse in the Lives of Sexually Aggressive Offenders. *Journal of American Child and Adolescent Psychiatry*, 26, 262–7.

Serin, R.C., Mailloux, D.L. and Malcolm, P.B. (2001) Psychopathy, Sexual Arousal and Recidivism. *Journal of Interpersonal Violence*, 16, 234–46.

Seto, M.C. and Barbaree, H.E. (1999) Psychopathy, Treatment Behaviour and Sex Offender Recidivism. *Journal of Interpersonal Violence*, 14, 1235–48.

Shiner, R.L. (2005) A Developmental Perspective on Personality Disorders: Lessons from Research on Normal Personality Development in Childhood Adolescence. *Journal of Personality Disorders*, 19: 2, 202–10.

Shiner, R.L. and Caspi, A. (2003) Personality Differences in Childhood and Adolescence: Measurement, Development and Consequences. *Journal of Child Psychology and Psychiatry*, 44, 2–32.

Siever, L.J., and Davis, K.L. (1991) A Psychobiological Perspective on Personality Disorders. *American Journal of Psychiatry*, 148, 1647–58.

Smith, W.R, Monastersky, C and Deisher, R.M. (1987) MMPI-Based Personality Types among Juvenile Sex Offenders. *Journal of Clinical Psychology*, 43, 422–30.

Svanborg, P., Gustavsson, P.J., Mattila-Evenden, M. and Asberg, M. (1999) Assessment of

Maladaptiveness: A Core Issue in the Diagnosing of Personality Disorders. *Journal of Personality Disorders*, 13: 3, 241–56.

Svrakic, D.M., Whitehead, C., Przybeck, T. and Cloninger, R. (1993) Differential Diagnosis of Personality Disorders and The Seven-Factor Model of Temperament and Character. *Archives of General Psychiatry*, 50, 991–9.

Tackett, J.L., Krueger, R.F., Sawyer, M.G. and Graetz, B.W. (2003) Subfactors of DSM-IV Conduct Disorder: Evidence and Connections with Syndromes from the Child Behaviour Checklist. *Journal of Abnormal Child Psychology*, 31, 647–54.

Thomas, A., Chess, S., Birch, H.G., Herzig, M.E. and Korn, S. (1963) *Behavioural Individuality in Early Childhood*. New York: University Press.

Truscott, D. (1993) Adolescent Offenders: Comparison of Sexual, Violent and Property Offences. *Psychological Reports*, 73, 657–8.

Tyrer, P. (2005) The Problem of Severity in the Classification of Personality Disorder. *Journal of Personality Disorders*, 19: 3, 309–14.

Valliant, P.M. and Bergeron, T. (1997) Personality and Criminal Profile of Adolescent Sexual Offenders, General Offenders in Comparison to Non-offenders. *Psychological Reports*, 81, 483–9.

Ward, T. and Hudson, S.M. (1998) A Model of The Relapse Process in Sexual Offenders. *Journal of Interpersonal Violence*, 13, 700–25.

Wells, A. (1997) *Cognitive Therapy of Anxiety Disorders: A Practice Manual and Conceptual Guide*. Chichester: John Wiley and Sons.

Widiger, T.A. and Costa, P.T. (1994) Personality and Personality Disorders. *Journal of Abnormal Psychology*, 103, 78–91.

Widiger, T.A. and Frances, A. (1985) The DSM-III Personality Disorders: Perspectives from Psychology. *Archives of General Psychiatry*, 42, 615–23.

Widiger, T.A. and Simonsen, E. (2005) Alternative Dimensional Models of Personality Disorder. *Journal of Personality Disorder*, 19, 110–30.

Widiger, T.A., Mangine, S., Corbitt, E.M., Ellis, C.G. and Thomas, G.V. (1995) *Personality Disorder Interview – IV: A Semistructured Interview for the Assessment of Personality Disorders*. Lutz, FL: Psychological Assessment Resources.

Widiger, T.A., Trull, T.J., Clarkin, J.F., Sanderson, C.J. and Costa, P.T. (2002) A Description of the DSM-IV Personality Disorders with The Five-Factor Model of Personality. In Costa, P.T. Jr. and Widiger, T.A. (Eds.) *Personality Disorders and The Five-Factor Model of Personality*. Washington, DC: American Psychological Association.

Wilson, G.D. and Cox, D.N. (1983) Personality of Paedophile Club Members. *Personality and Individual Differences*, 4: 3, 323–9.

WHO (1992) *The ICD-10 Classification of Mental and Behavioural Disorders: Clinical Descriptions and Diagnostic Guidelines*. Geneva: Author.

Worling, J.R. (2001) Personality-Based Typology of Adolescent Male Sexual Offenders: Differences in Recidivism Rates, Victim-Selection Characteristics and Personal Victimization Histories. *Sexual Abuse: A Journal of Research and Treatment*, 13, 149–66.

Young, J.E. (1990) *Cognitive Therapy for Personality Disorders: A Schema-Focused Approach*. Sarasota, FL: Professional Resource Exchange.

Young, J.E. and Brown, G. (1994) Young Schema Questionnaire. 2nd Edn. In Young, J.E. *Cognitive Therapy for Personality Disorders: A Schema-Focused Approach*. Sarasota, FL: Professional Resource Press.

Young, J.E. and Gluhoski, V.L. (1996) Schema-Focused Diagnosis for Personality Disorders. In Kaslow, F.W. (Ed.) *Handbook of Relational Diagnosis and Dysfunctional Family Patterns*. New York: Wiley.

Young, J.E., Klosko, J.S. and Weishaar, M.E. (2003) *Schema Therapy: A Practitioner's Guide*. New York: Guilford Publications.

Zanarini, M.C., Frankenburg, F.R., Sickel, A.E. and Yong, L. (1996) *The Diagnostic Interview for DSM-IV Personality Disorders (DIPD-IV)*. Belmont, MA: Mclean Hospital.

Zimmer-Gembeck, M.J. (2002) The Development of Romantic Relationships and Adaptations in the System of Peer Relations. *Journal of Adolescent Health*, 31, 216–25.

Chapter 7

The Relationship Between Deviant Arousal and Sexual Recidivism in Adolescent Sex Offenders

Robert J.W. Clift, Heather M. Gretton and Gordana Rajlic

Introduction

Sex offenders' risk for recidivism is of great concern to the public and the criminal justice system alike (Hanson, 2000). Hanson, Morton and Harris (2003) recently addressed this risk in a sample of nearly 5000 sex offenders drawn from North America, England and Wales. They found the five-year sexual recidivism rate to be 14 per cent. Recidivism rates had risen to 20 per cent after 10 years, 24 per cent after 15 years, and 27 per cent after 20 years. However, these rates were based on new charges or convictions. Given that many sex offences are not reported, the true rate of sexual recidivism is considerably higher. Some authors estimate that it is as high as 40 per cent (Hanson, 2000).

Researchers and clinicians are challenged with the task of identifying factors associated with increased risk for re-offending. In a meta-analysis of 61 studies and over 20,000 sex offenders Hanson and Bussière (1998) found that the strongest predictor of sex-offence recidivism was deviant sexual arousal to children. Other predictors of sexual recidivism included early onset of sex offending, history of prior sex offences, choosing strangers as victims, choosing males as victims, and committing diverse sexual crimes.

Clinical assessment of sexual deviancy may include examination of verbal reports or attitudinal measures (Becker et al., 1992a). However, self-report methods are weakened by offenders' propensity to distort information, falsely deny crimes, or claim amnesia for events (Hunter and Becker, 1994). Due to the weaknesses of self-report in the assessment of sexual deviance, researchers and clinicians have sought an objective psychophysiological measure of offenders' sexual preferences (Launay, 1994). One such measure is the penile plethysmograph (PPG). The PPG is used to measure penile tumescence while males are presented with sexual scenarios (Seto, Lalumiere and Blanchard, 2000). Relative increases in penile blood volume

are interpreted as an index of the male's interest in that type of scenario. Relatively little research has been conducted with the PPG using the adolescent population (Hunter and Becker, 1994). One finding that seems to be consistent is that adolescent sex offenders with male child victims have higher levels of deviant arousal (Becker et al., 1989; Hunter, Goodwin, and Becker, 1994; Murphy et al., 2001; Seto et al., 2000).

Current study

Gretton and colleagues have assessed the relationship between pre-treatment deviant PPG responses and sexual recidivism in an adolescent sample (Gretton et al., 2001). They found no relationship between a general measure of pre-treatment deviant arousal and recidivism. The current study examines the relationship between both pre-treatment and post-treatment deviant arousal and sexual recidivism in a sample of 116 adolescent sex offenders. The group was followed for a mean of approximately four years post-treatment.

Given that the strongest findings to date relate to sexual arousal to male child stimuli we hypothesised that this indicator of deviant arousal would have the strongest relationship with sexual recidivism. We further hypothesised that post-treatment PPG responses would have a stronger relationship with sexual recidivism than pre-treatment responses. This hypothesis follows from findings that younger adolescents respond to more types of stimuli (Kaemingk et al., 1995) and suggestions that juveniles may not have developed a fixed pattern of sexual arousal (Hunter et al., 1994). At the time of the post-treatment PPG assessments the subjects were older, and having been exposed to treatment, they would have been highly cognisant of appropriate versus inappropriate arousal patterns. Presumably, because of maturation and the influence of treatment, post-treatment PPG assessments are more contemporary estimates of the subjects' sexual preferences, and therefore more likely to be related to sexual outcomes.

Method

Subjects

The subjects were 116 male adolescents who were admitted to the Sex Offender Treatment Program (SOTP) at Youth Forensic Psychiatric Services (YFPS) Burnaby, British Columbia (BC) between 1996 and 2000. Most subjects had been formally charged or convicted of a sexual offence (88.7 per cent). The others had a history of sexual offending that did not result in a formal charge (11.2 per cent). Twenty-one per cent of the subjects had been formally charged with multiple sexual offences. For 111 of the subjects the gender of their victims was known. Of those, 37.8 per cent had at least one male victim and 62.2 per cent did not have a male victim.

The majority of subjects were Caucasian (64.7 per cent) or First Nations (23.3 per cent). The remaining 12 per cent were mostly of Asian or South Asian origin. Their mean age was 16.4 years ($SD=1.6$) at the beginning of treatment, 17.7 years ($SD=1.5$) at discharge from treatment, and 21.6 years ($SD=1.8$) at the end of the follow up period.

Penile plethysmograph data

Adolescents admitted to the SOTP at YFPS in Burnaby, BC undergo PPG assessment both pre- and post-treatment. In the current study we have both pre- and post-treatment PPG data for 70 of the 116 subjects (60.3 per cent). Of the remaining 46 we have only pre-treatment data for 37 (31.8 per cent) and only post-treatment data for 9 (7.8 per cent). The typical reason for having only pre-treatment data is that the subject did not complete the programme. In cases where we only have post-treatment data the subjects had generally undergone a pre-treatment PPG; however, the pre-treatment PPG was performed before 1996 using a different methodology.

Some PPG data were not used in the study because either the subject was noncompliant with the PPG testing procedure or they showed minimal response to all of the stimuli (i.e. maximum change in penile circumference during the exam was less than 5 mm). After these exclusions there was data for 98 pre-treatment PPG tests and 70 post-treatment PPG tests. There was both pre- and post-treatment data for 56 of the subjects. The excluded subjects did not differ significantly from the included subjects in terms of age. They also did not differ significantly in the number of pre-treatment general, violent, or sexual offences on their record.

Procedure

Prior to each PPG the procedure was discussed with the subject. All PPG assessments were conducted in a laboratory setting, in a sound-attenuated room. Subjects were tested using a RS3010 Medical Monitoring System with stretchistor mercury strain gauges. The technologist's room, which contained the recording equipment, was separated from the subject's area by a wall that contained a one way mirror. Communication was maintained using an intercom system.

Once the subject understood the procedure he was asked to sit in a chair with a sheet covering his lap. He was instructed to take a circumference measurement of his flaccid penis using a strip of paper. This measurement was used to calibrate the recording equipment. The subject was then asked to place the mercury strain gauge midway down his penis. Once the technician was confident that the gauge was fitted properly a video clip from a sex education tape was presented. This was intended to stimulate full erection. If full erection was not obtained the subject was instructed to imagine an erotic scenario that would aid him in achieving a full erection. After that, a neutral stimulus was presented, and the subject was given time to detumesce below 20 per cent erection.

Subjects were then presented with 10 test stimuli, being allowed to detumesce below 20 per cent erection after each one. They were instructed to let themselves become aroused without trying to inhibit their responses. The stimuli were presented in video format, composed of still photographs of children in naturalistic settings, accompanied by verbal descriptions of sexual situations. Each stimulus was two minutes, ten seconds in length. In order to ensure that the subject attended to the videos yellow stars were embedded within them. When a star appeared the client was required to give a verbal signal.

Additionally, after each stimulus the client was required to report a subjective estimate of his arousal using a light bar with a vertical light display. After each assessment the strain gauge was sterilised using Cidex-plus disinfectant solution. The ten stimuli used were:

1. male infant;
2. sexual activity with a male aged 2 to 5 years;
3. sexual activity with a male aged 6 to 11 years;
4. coercive sexual activity with a male aged 6 to 11 years;
5. female infant;
6. sexual activity with a female aged 2 to 5 years;
7. sexual activity with a female aged 6 to 11 years;
8. coercive sexual activity with a female aged 6 to 11 years;
9. consensual sexual activity with a female aged 12 to 17 years; and
10. coercive sexual activity with a female aged 12 to 17 years.

The stimuli set was specifically designed for use with adolescents. The stimulus depicting consensual sexual activity with a female aged 12 to 17 years was considered to be non-deviant.

Changes in penile circumference were initially recorded as a percentage of maximum erection achieved during the session. That is, peak arousal to any given stimulus was expressed as a percentage of the maximum erection achieved over the entire assessment. Percentage scores where then transformed into z-scores – a distribution with a mean of 0 and a standard deviation of 1. The advantage of z-scores is that they allow direct comparison across subjects (Launay, 1994). Earls, Quinsey, and Castonguay (1987) have compared the effectiveness of using raw scores, percentage of full erection, and z-scores. They found that z-scores were able to account for a higher percentage of variance than the other two methods. It should be noted, however, that z-scores do not provide a measure of the magnitude of the responses. That is, subjects who display low arousal to all stimuli and subjects who display high arousal to all stimuli could have similar z-scores. A positive z-score represents greater than average arousal for that individual across the stimuli that were presented, and a negative z-score represents less than average arousal for that individual across stimuli.

The z-scores were then used to form mean measures of sexual deviance and deviance indices. The 9 mean measures of sexual deviance were: 1. All Deviant Stimuli; 2. Deviant Male Stimuli; 3. Deviant Female Stimuli; 4. Child Stimuli; 5. Deviant Teen Stimuli; 6. Force Stimuli; 7. Male Force Stimuli; 8. Female Force Stimuli; and 9. Deviant Non-Force Stimuli. Table 1 describes which stimuli were included in each mean.

The deviance indices were calculated by subtracting the subject's z-score for appropriate stimuli from his z-score for each mean measure of sexual deviance. For example, the Generally Deviant Index was created by subtracting the subject's z-score for a female aged 12–17 without force from his mean z-score for All Deviant Stimuli. Therefore, positive values represent deviant arousal; a value of zero indicates a lack of differentiation between the deviant and appropriate stimuli; and negative values indicate that the subject was less aroused by that category of deviant stimuli than by appropriate stimuli. In line with the mean measures of sexual deviance the indices created were: the 1. Generally Deviant Index; 2. Deviant Male Index; 3. Deviant Female Index; 4. Child Index; 5. Teen Force Index; 6. Force Index; 7. Male Force Index; 8. Female Force Index; and 9. Deviant Non-Force Index.

We then assessed the relationship between the mean measures of sexual deviance, the sexual deviance indices and recidivism. Recidivism was defined as a formal charge and/or conviction during the follow-up period, and was divided into three categories: violent offences, sexual offences, and offences that were neither violent or sexual in nature. Violent offences included: robbery; assault (including threats, intimidation, and criminal harassment); homicide (including attempted homicide); weapons offences; kidnapping; and arson with intent to injure. Sexual offences included both contact and non-contact offences. All other offences we coded as non-violent and non-sexual. New charges and convictions were coded from British Columbia Corrections records. The follow-up period began when the subject was discharged from treatment. The length of the follow-up period ranged from 10 to 73 months, with a mean of 3.9 years ($SD = 1.2$). Actual time free in the community ranged from 10 to 73 months, with a mean of 3.7 years ($SD = 1.1$).

Sex Offender Treatment Program (SOTP)

The SOTP at YFPS, Burnaby, BC, is an outpatient programme designed for adolescents who have been charged with, or convicted of a sexual offence, or have a history of sexual offending. The programme follows a primarily cognitive-behavioural approach to treatment, consisting of both group and individual components. The group component consists of two-hour sessions twice a week and lasts approximately six to eight months. The length of the individual component depends on the needs of the individual. The average length of all the components of SOTP is about one to two years. The effectiveness of the SOTP is not evaluated in the current study.

Results

Recidivism rates

During the follow up period 42 of the 116 adolescents were charged or convicted with a new crime (36.2 per cent). The mean number of new offences among recidivists was 7.95 ($SD = 10.1$). However, many recidivists were not charged with or convicted of any new violent or sexual crimes (47.6 per cent). In total, 40 subjects (34.5 per cent) were charged with a non-violent crime; 18 (15.5 per cent) were charged with a violent crime; and seven (6.0 per cent) were charged with a sexual crime. Recidivists were charged or convicted with a mean of 1.1 violent offences ($SD = 2.0$), 0.26 sexual offences ($SD = 0.7$), and 6.45 offences that were neither violent nor sexual ($SD = 9.1$).

As a group, the sexual recidivists were charged or convicted with 11 new sex offences. One subject had four new sexual offences; one had two; and five had one. Nine of the offences were sexual assaults; one was sexual interference; and one was committing an indecent act in public. All seven subjects who recidivated sexually had other offences as well during the follow up. Four of them (57 per cent) had recorded non-violent crimes; two had violent crimes (29 per cent); and one recidivated with both non-violent and violent crimes in addition to his sex offence (14 per cent).

Sex offenders with male child victims have been found to have higher levels of deviant arousal than sex offenders without male child victims (Becker et al., 1989; Hunter et al., 1994; Murphy et al., 2001; Seto et al., 2000).

Additionally, deviant arousal has been found to be a strong predictor of sexual offence recidivism (Hanson and Bussière, 1998). Therefore, we compared sexual recidivism rates of those adolescents who had male victims to those who did not. Of those subjects who were known to have at least one male victim 4.8 per cent ($N = 2$) had a subsequent sexual offence. Comparatively, 7.2 per cent ($N = 5$) of the subjects who did not have a male victim recidivated sexually within the follow-up period. These proportions are not significantly different, χ^2 (1, $N = 111$) $= 0.01$, $p > .9$ (Yates' correction for continuity was applied due to the small expected frequencies).

Deviant arousal and sexual recidivism

None of the pre-treatment mean measures of sexual deviance correlated significantly with sexual recidivism (Table 2). Similarly, none of the pre-treatment indices correlated significantly with sexual recidivism (Table 3). However, the post-treatment measures of mean deviant arousal to Child Stimuli and Deviant Non-Force stimuli were both significantly correlated with sexual recidivism ($rs = 0.262$ and 0.236, respectively; $ps < 0.05$; Table 2). Additionally, four of the post-treatment indices correlated significantly with sexual offence recidivism (all $ps < 0.05$; Table 3). These included the Deviant Male Index ($r = 0.241$); Male Force Index ($r = 0.238$); Child Index ($r = 0.241$); and Deviant Non-Force Index ($r = 0.251$).

Discussion

Over one-third of the sample (36.2 per cent) had a new offence during the four-year follow-up period. However, the vast majority of recidivists only committed non-sexual crimes (83.3 per cent). Only 6.0 per cent of the sample were charged or convicted with a new sexual crime. It would appear that sexual offending is part of a generally criminal lifestyle for some adolescent offenders. This argument is bolstered by the large number of crimes recorded for the typical recidivist ($M = 7.95$).

There are several possible explanations for this sample's low rate of sexual recidivism. It could be that the sexual recidivism rate among treated youths is low over a four-year follow-up period. However, it is also possible that some subjects

Table 7.1 Stimulus categories included in mean measures of deviance

Deviance measure	Stimulus categories included in mean
All Deviant Stimuli	male infant male age 2–5 non-force male age 6–11 non-force male age 6–11 with force female infant female age 2–5 non-force female age 6–11 non-force female age 6–11 with force female age 12–17 with force
Deviant Male Stimuli	male infant male age 2–5 non-force male age 6–11 non-force male age 6–11 with force
Deviant Female Stimuli	female infant female age 2–5 non-force female age 6–11 non-force female age 6–11 with force female age 12–17 with force
Child Stimuli	male infant male age 2–5 non-force male age 6–11 non-force male age 6–11 with force female infant female age 2–5 non-force female age 6–11 non-force female age 6–11 with force
Deviant Teen Stimuli	female age 12–17 with force
Force Stimuli	male age 6–11 with force female age 6–11 with force female age 12–17 with force
Female Force Stimuli	female age 6–11 with force female age 12–17 with force
Male Force Stimuli	male age 6–11 with force
Deviant Non-Force Stimuli	male infant male age 2–5 non-force male age 6–11 non-force female infant female age 2–5 non-force female age 6–11 non-force

committed offences that went undetected by the system; British Columbia Corrections records are not an absolute measure of recidivism. Many sex offences go unreported (Hanson, 2000). Other subjects may no longer have sexually deviant urges due to therapy or other reasons, or they may have found a way to resist their urges. Another possibility is that some never had deviant sexual preferences. It has been suggested

that some adolescents molest children due to curiosity, low self-esteem, and a lack of social skills (Ryan, Lane, Davis and Isaac, 1987; Fehrenbach, Smith, Monastersky, and Deisher, 1986). In other words, their true preference is consensual sex with age-appropriate peers, but they are unable to develop relationships. This may be particularly true for adolescents with only female victims. Studies have found that

Table 7.2 Correlations between mean measures of deviant arousal and sexual recidivism pre- and post-treatment

Measure of Deviant Arousal	Pre-treatment r (p-value)	Post-treatment r (p-value)
All Deviant Stimuli	0.030 (0.770)	0.223 (0.063)
Deviant Male Stimuli	0.090 (0.379)	0.184 (0.127)
Deviant Female Stimuli	−0.079 (0.439)	−0.073 (0.546)
Child Stimuli	0.125 (0.221)	0.262 (0.028)*
Deviant Teen Stimuli	−0.156 (0.125)	−0.183 (0.130)
Force Stimuli	−0.057 (0.575)	−0.118 (0.331)
Male Force Stimuli	0.118 (0.248)	0.156 (0.198)
Female Force Stimuli	−0.122 (0.233)	−0.185 (0.125)
Deviant Non-Force Stimuli	0.071 (0.488)	0.236 (0.049)*

Note. $* = p < .05$; pre-treatment $n = 98$; post-treatment $n = 70$.

Table 7.3 Correlations between deviance indices and sexual recidivism pre-and post-treatment

Measure of Deviant Arousal	Pre-treatment r (p-value)	Post-treatment r (p-value)
Generally Deviant Index	0.030 (0.770)	0.223 (0.063)
Deviant Male Index	0.053 (0.602)	0.241 (0.044)*
Deviant Female Index	0.006 (0.949)	0.184 (0.128)
Child Index	0.047 (0.664)	0.241 (0.044)*
Teen Force Index	−0.102 (0.319)	−0.006 (0.960)
Force Index	0.004 (0.970)	0.137 (0.258)
Male Force Index	0.084 (0.412)	0.238 (0.047)*
Female Force Index	−0.041 (0.690)	0.058 (0.632)
Deviant Non-Force Index	0.042 (0.684)	0.251 (0.036)*

Note. $* = p < 0.05$; pre-treatment $n = 98$; post-treatment $n = 70$.

adolescent child molesters with only female victims display far less deviant arousal on the PPG (e.g., Becker, Kaplan, and Tenke, 1992b; Hunter et al., 1994). In fact, Seto et al. (2000) found that they showed no more deviant arousal than non-offenders. However, it should be noted that in the current study there was no significant difference in recidivism rates between those subjects who had at least one male victim and those who did not.

In the current study, sexual recidivism was not significantly correlated with any of the pre-treatment measures of sexual deviance. This is consistent with previous findings (Gretton et al., 2001). It is thought that many adolescents have not yet developed a fixed pattern of sexual arousal (Hunter et al. 1994). Therefore, post-treatment PPGs may be a more accurate reflection of the subjects' sexual interests. At that time the subjects were older and may have developed a more fixed pattern of arousal. Additionally, they had completed a treatment programme and would have been highly cognisant of appropriate versus inappropriate

sexual cues. Consistent with this hypothesis, post-treatment PPG scores were related to sexual re-offending. Four of the deviance indices were significantly correlated with sexual recidivism. These included the Deviant Male Index, Male Force Index, Child Index, and Deviant Non-Force Index (Table 1; Table 3). That is, the indices that correlated with sexual recidivism represent deviant arousal to forced and non-forced sexual situations involving male and female children.

Summary

The present data suggest that some adolescent sex offenders have a low rate of sexual recidivism over a four-year period. It is not clear if this is due to changing sexual interests, treatment, or other factors. Furthermore, results from the current study suggest that pre-treatment deviant arousal, as measured by the PPG, has no relationship with sexual recidivism in adolescents. Conversely, in the current study, post-treatment deviant arousal to sexual situations involving male and female children, as measured by the PPG, was related to sexual recidivism. The current study provides some much needed data on the predictive validity of adolescent PPG assessments over a four year follow-up period. Results suggest that there is a link between post-treatment PPG indices of deviant arousal and risk for sexual re-offence. These findings are consistent with Hanson and Bussière's (1998) meta-analysis, which found that sexually deviant arousal to children is the most effective predictor of sexual offence recidivism. Further research in this area is warranted.

References

Becker, J.V. Hunter, J.A., Stein, R.M. and Kaplan, M.S. (1989) Factors Associated with Erection in Adolescent Sex Offenders. *Journal of Psychopathology and Behavioral Assessment*, 114, 353–62.

Becker, J., Kaplan, M.S. and Tenke, C.E. (1992b) The Relationship of Abuse History, Denial and Erectile Response Profiles of Adolescent Sexual Perpetrators. *Behavior Therapy*, 23, 87–97.

Becker, J.V., Stein, R.M., Kaplan, M.S. and Cunningham-Rathner, J. (1992a) Erection Response Characteristics of Adolescent Sex Offenders. *Annals of Sex Research*, 5: 2, 81–6.

Earls, C.M., Quinsey, V.L. and Castonguay, L.G. (1987) A Comparison of Three Methods of Scoring Penile Circumference Changes. *Archives of Sexual Behavior*, 16, 493–500.

Fehrenbach, P.A., Smith, W., Monastersky, C. and Deisher, R.W. (1986) Adolescent Sexual Offenders: Offender and Offence Characteristics. *American Journal of Orthopsychiatry*, 56: 2, 225–33.

Gretton, H.M., McBride, M., Hare, R.D., O'Shaughnessy, R. and Kumka, G. (2001) Psychopathy and Recidivism in Adolescent Sex Offenders. *Criminal Justice and Behavior*, 28: 4, 427–49.

Hanson, K. (2000) Will they do it Again? Predicting Sex-offence Recidivism. *Current Directions in Psychological Science*, 9: 3, 106–9.

Hanson, R.K. and Bussière, M.T. (1998) Predicting Relapse: A Meta-analysis of Sexual Offender Recidivism Studies. *Journal of Consulting and Clinical Psychology*, 66: 2, 348–62.

Hanson, R.K., Morton, K.E. and Harris, A.J.R. (2003) Sex Offender Recidivism Risk: What we Know and What we need to Know. In Prentky, R., Janus, E., Seto, M. and Burgess, A.W. (Eds.) *Annals of the New York Academy of Sciences: Vol. 989. Sexually Coercive Behavior: Understanding and Management* (pp. 154–66). New York: New York Academy of Sciences.

Hunter, J.A. and Becker, J.V. (1994) The Role of Deviant Sexual Arousal in Juvenile Sexual Offending. Etiology, Evaluation and Treatment. *Criminal Justice and Behavior*, 21: 1, 132–49.

Hunter, J.A., Goodwin, D. W. and Becker, J.V. (1994) The Relationship between Phallometrically Measured Deviant Sexual Arousal and Clinical Characteristics in Juvenile Sexual Offenders. *Behavior Research and Therapy*, 32: 5, 533–38.

Kaemingk, K.L., Koselka, M., Becker, J.V. and Kaplan, M.S. (1995) Age and Adolescent Sexual Offender Arousal. *Sexual Abuse: A Journal of Research and Treatment*, 7: 4, 249–57.

Launay, G. (1994) The Phallometric Assessment of Sex Offenders: Some Professional and Research Issues. *Criminal Behavior and Mental Health*, 4, 48–70.

Murphy, W.D., DiLillo, D., Haynes, M.R. and Steere, E. (2001) An Exploration of Factors Related to Deviant Sexual Arousal among Juvenile Sex Offenders. *Journal of Research and Treatment*, 13: 2, 91–103.

Ryan, G., Lane, S., Davis, J. and Isaac, C. (1987) Juvenile Sex Offenders: Development and Correction. *Child Abuse and Neglect*, 11, 385–95.

Seto, M.C., Lalumiere, M.L. and Blanchard, R. (2000) The Discriminative Validity of a Phallometric Test for Paedophilic Interests among Adolescent Sex Offenders against Children. *Psychological Assessment*, 12: 3, 319–27.

Working with the Families of Children and Young People Who Sexually Harm: It Shouldn't be an Optional Extra

Tess Johnson, Jane Scott and Paula Telford

Introduction

The Kaleidoscope (NSPCC) team in the Northeast of England has been working with children and young people who sexually harm, and with their families, for almost twelve years. It has always been one of their principles that the children and young people cannot undertake such work in a vacuum. They need trusted adults at the very least to support them and give them appropriate messages. Over the intervening years we have increasingly seen the importance of parents and carers being involved not only in the assessment of risk and the needs of young people, but also in the control and change work which almost inevitably follows. Unless parents have directly sexually abused their children we do not hold them responsible but as Hackett (2001) states:

The responsibility for the sexual abuse needs to be given to your child, but this should not stop you from making positive and necessary changes to your family.

(p68)

This chapter will consider the rationale for involving appropriate adults in the young person's work, highlighting the process at Kaleidoscope for involving parents and carers from the first introductions through to the abuse prevention plan, Helping Team and the post-intervention call back. In doing so it will call on the experience of work with three children and young people and their parents or carers. We trust that readers will acknowledge and applaud the courage shown by these service users in engaging in the work regardless of the reasons that made it necessary. Finally we will explore, albeit from a relatively subjective point of view, the outcomes of the work and the contribution of all involved to those outcomes.

We should say something about the language used in the chapter. For the most part we will refer to children and young people who sexually harm. Kaleidoscope works with children, some as young as four years old, and young people up to the age of 18 years. For that reason we use the term sexually harmful behaviour. This is neither to minimise the seriousness or impact of the behaviour nor to dismiss the fact that many of our service users are 'sexual offenders'. In the interests of economy we will use the term children and young people and parents and carers interchangeably, unless specifying otherwise.

Involving families from the outset

Kaleidoscope aims to work in partnership with parents and families of their service users from the earliest opportunity. Once a referral is received and accepted one of the allocated Kaleidoscope workers will make a joint visit with the referrer to the parents or carers (if parents and carers are happy with this). The point is to try to 'level the playing field', as well as to begin to hear from parents their view of the child/young person we might work with.

The young person or child is invited to visit Kaleidoscope, to meet the person they will work with and familiarise themselves with the Kaleidoscope building. It is important that they are supported in this visit by trusted adults, whether they are parents or carers.

The next point at which the young person, parents/carers, Kaleidoscope and other agencies come together is the 'starting meeting'. Only here, after hearing the concerns, and everyone's hopes and fears for the work, is it decided whether they will 'buy in' to the work. It is at this meeting that risk management plans for the work are confirmed.

When work commences, the parents and carers of the young person are made aware that they will be invited to engage in the assessment process and will be part of reviewing the work from assessment to control and change work. As this chapter will show there are often changes that parents need to make in meeting their child's need and safely supporting them in the work. By the end of the work each young person will have made their abuse prevention plan, to be shared with parents, themselves part of the Helping Team, who then identify their role in supporting that 'keep safe' plan.

To exemplify how this has worked in practice we have drawn together three case studies where parents have been particularly intensively involved in the work. It should be noted, however, that the timing of this joint work follows the young person having undertaken a significant period of individual work and having taken responsibility for their behaviour, within the context of their own experiences.

Holistic approaches

Amongst many others the Bridge Child Care Development Service's report *Childhood Lost* (2001) re-focused the need for young people with sexually harmful behaviour to be worked with holistically, taking account of their developmental needs as well as the sometimes not inconsiderable risks from their behaviour. Parents and caregivers have extensive knowledge and information to share about their child's experiences and behaviour. Without their input, it is likely that there will be significant gaps in any developing understanding of the child or young person and the presenting behaviour.

In addition to the information that parents and caregivers can provide, they often play a key role in supporting their child and ensuring appropriate supervision. Alongside this, they experience a range of emotions that result from the impact of learning of their child's sexually harmful behaviour.

Hackett (2001) identifies a range of feelings described by parents, which include: failure as a parent; shock and denial; guilt, shame and blame; isolation and stigma; and loss or grief.

> ... *it was like my child had died. Another child had been put in his place and I had to get to know the new one. I've grown to like the new one now, but the old one, my child, has gone forever.* (Mother of a 15-year-old boy who had abused his brother)
>
> (Hackett, 2001, p32)

Recognising the potential impacts for parents and involving them in the work is essential in enabling them to successfully support their child through the process of interventions relating to the sexually harmful behaviour. Maskell (in Calder, 2002) cites the experiences of parents in her study:

> *Parents expressed despair that children were not receiving adequate help and thus anxiety about re-offending was high. This anxiety may have been reduced had they been more involved in what was being done with their child.*
>
> (p99)

Therefore, there appears to be growing recognition of the benefits of family involvement in this work with children and young people. Not only are families a source of vital information about the child's history and experiences, they also play a key role in supporting a child or young person through the work. If they are struggling with the impact of their child's behaviour or feel isolated from agencies, they may not be as able to provide the appropriate support. A key finding from Hackett et al's (2003) research into what works in interventions with children and young people with sexually harmful behaviour, was that engaging with families and wider systems was not a luxury or simply a useful addition to the work, but an absolute necessity. Thus, by adopting this approach, it is likely to have positive effects on the outcomes for children and young people.

We described earlier in the chapter the level of involvement we invite all parents and caregivers to have. However, in some cases, we have identified a need for more focused work with parents and their children.

The children and young people Kaleidoscope work with have consistently suffered trauma and abuse in varying degrees and in different settings. For the vast majority, their sexualised and other harmful adaptive behaviours are strategies in which to regain some power and control over the effects of these experiences. Later in this chapter we will describe case examples that further illustrate this.

Over the last three years we have become increasingly aware of the particular relevance and impact of attachment experiences for many of our service users and their parents and caregivers. Often such experiences have led them to develop a negative internal working model, in which they view themselves as inherently *bad*. They have also contributed to a situation where these service users are unable to regulate their emotions, achieve containment or to enjoy closeness. In a number of situations, therefore, we have undertaken joint work which has sought, if not to 'repair' those attachments, at least to help children and parents revisit their shared history and revise their internal working model or mental representation of their attachment. Howe (2005) asserts that interventions which aim to improve the quality of the parent and child relationship, including the promotion of open communication, can have the result of changing a disorganised attachment style to a more organised or even secure attachment. The issue of encouraging open and coherent communication, which may have been absent in past relationships, appears to be a key theme for many of the young people and their carers that we have worked with. Therefore, a focus of joint work has been to develop meaningful communication about past experiences and difficulties and to explore a possible shared vision of a different future.

We would like to be able to say that this was a planned redirection of the work borne out of lengthy research. Rather it evolved from our clinical judgments in a range of situations: knowledge of a child and parent's shared trauma early in the child's life; the impact of the parental and attachment relationship on the work; the development of a significant worry about a particular child or the parent's efficacy in supporting the work and the key role they would have in the child's future.

We want to acknowledge here the gendered issues in the joint work. We have only worked in this way with mothers and sons. Why mothers? In each of the cases the boys' birth fathers were no longer in the family due to their domestic violence. Therefore, it was neither possible nor appropriate to engage with their fathers. Also, although Kaleidoscope has worked with relatively high numbers of girls their referrals to the service have tended to be long after their behaviour began and so many of them are children who are looked after and who often have had disrupted connections with their families.

Case examples

In this section are three case studies that detail the nature of the joint work and some of the resulting outcomes. The cases have been anonymised and some details changed to protect the families' confidentiality.

Case study 1 – Craig

One such piece of work was with Craig and his mother, Laura. Craig and his mother had had a very fragile attachment, which was, in all likelihood, contributed to by Laura having experienced extreme domestic abuse from Craig's father when Craig was an infant. When she finally ended that relationship she had another baby, Alan, with whom she had a very different relationship. Craig experienced Alan as the favoured child and, through a pathway of complex contributing factors, sexually abused his brother.

Once Craig had been assessed and undertaken a period of individual therapeutic work, work took place jointly with him and Laura to strive for a shared understanding of their histories. Together they recalled, in detail, the time line of their lives, filling in the gaps for each other of how life had been experienced. Laura was able to recall Craig as a child who cried all the time and, as he grew up, as someone who lacked confidence and who clung to her. She also shared her own experiences as a woman experiencing domestic violence, of feeling emotionally numb and not able to respond to Craig other than to meet his physical needs. Craig disclosed vivid memories of hiding from his father's violence and of the shame he had felt. It became increasingly apparent that what had happened in the years that followed was an increasing separation between this mother and her son. Laura had been managing her acrimonious separation from Craig's father and the practical difficulties that went with this and Craig had felt increasingly isolated and unprotected by his mother.

Laura had since met and married a new partner but she was aware that life was still not good for Craig. In the joint work Craig was able to share his experiences at school of feeling bullied by other children and, at home, of being the focus of name calling. Together they considered how to manage this differently.

With a greater sense of their shared history, Craig and his mother looked at existing and desired Parent Messages (Fahlberg, 1991) and Laura was able to say how she wished things could have been different for Craig. This was an emotional and powerful stage in the work, which demonstrated the potential for repair of their relationship, based on the commitment on both their parts to change. With a greater shared understanding they were more able to discuss and make sense of Craig's sexually harmful behaviour towards his brother and to consider a way forward as a family.

Shortly after the joint work concluded, Craig disclosed that he had been and continued to be sexually abused by his birth father. Whilst this was devastating news for Laura she was in a stronger position to support Craig and their strengthened attachment was evident as they worked together to face up to the painful time that followed.

Case study 2 – Mark

Mark was referred to Kaleidoscope when he was 10-years-old as his school had increasing concerns about his sexually inappropriate behaviour, which dated back to when he was five or six years old. It was felt that his behaviour was escalating and included the use of sexually explicit language and drawings, and rubbing himself against girls and inappropriately touching targeted adults. There were also considerable concerns about Mark displaying other harmful behaviours which were aggressive.

Mark had always lived with his mother, Karen. From an early age, he witnessed domestic violence perpetrated by his birth father towards his mother. At the time of our involvement she had a partner who Mark regarded as his step father. There appeared to be difficulties in the adults' relationship which led to occasional separations but there was regular contact with Mark throughout. Professionals involved with the family had concerns that there was ongoing domestic violence.

An assessment was completed and Mark engaged in further Change and Control work. He explored many themes and issues in this work, focusing on his feelings about his behaviour and his victim experiences. He identified considerable anger, fear and sadness through his play, but struggled to talk directly about his experiences. He was able to identify a sense of never feeling safe, leaving workers concerned about current levels of safety. His preoccupation and fantasy about violence seemed to be strongly connected to this. A great deal of Mark's anger was directed towards his mother, and she struggled to manage his behaviour.

From discussions with Karen she identified her fears for Mark in the longer term and had been proactive in accessing services for him. She, too,

could recognise that Mark's anger was directed towards her and was keen to understand this more in order to support him. In individual sessions she was able to look back at the impact of her own childhood experiences of domestic violence and begin to consider how it had continued to impact on her life. From this she began to consider how Mark was experiencing life. Karen denied that there was any physical violence in her current relationship but acknowledged that her partner could be controlling and regularly undermined her. She started to recognise patterns of behaviour from her current and previous partners but also in her relationship with Mark. The option of joint work was considered in acknowledgment of the need to rebuild attachments and to prevent negative patterns becoming more established.

Workers looked individually at hopes and fears for this work and were struck by the similarities. Both Karen and Mark were clear that they would want to be properly heard and to have a real opportunity to tell the other how they experienced family life. They both described wanting to re-establish themselves in their appropriate roles of mother and son. They worried about things becoming out of control and were clear of their need for support from workers in sessions. Both were clear that they saw joint work as an appropriate way forward.

The aims of the joint work were to develop a shared understanding of their histories, promote improved communication and rebuild their relationship for the future.

The first part of the work involved Karen and Mark talking through their memories of Mark's life. This provided the opportunity for Karen to give positive messages about her early experiences of motherhood but also to acknowledge their world within a violent household and the fears that this left her with. Mark was able to hear some fundamental messages about being a much loved and wanted baby albeit in a situation that was less than stable. Karen provided photographs of them as a family and was able to say that despite his father's violent behaviour at times, he had also shown the capacity to be a loving father to Mark. This was a significant message to Mark who in individual work had said that his father was evil and all bad, and that he saw himself as the same.

The next period of Mark's life was for both of them an extremely difficult time with the most significant memories of domestic violence. In sessions Karen and Mark were able to create their memories through artwork in a way that allowed them to share individual experiences but also acknowledge those which they had shared. Workers' prior knowledge of both Mark and Karen's artistic and creative skills prompted the idea for using art. This medium enabled them to explore these times in a way that appeared to be more comfortable and less daunting than using words. They were able to express their experiences very powerfully in their drawings.

In an activity using parenting messages from *A Child's Journey Through Placement* (Vera Fahlberg, 1991) they considered the messages that they had received from each other during this period with interesting results. Mark believed that his mother had experienced him as a 'problem child' and who thought that 'if something goes wrong it must be his fault'. Karen, however, described Mark as her 'beautiful boy' saying that she was 'glad he was her child'. She was concerned, however, that he had received the message that she 'didn't have time for him' as she had been a working parent. Mark saw his negative messages as being cancelled out by his mothers' positive ones with great delight. He also talked about his experiences of day care very positively, recalling happy memories which allowed Karen to let go of some of her own feelings of guilt.

Further work around their life together, particularly when looking at specific events, highlighted a significant communication issue. Messages and needs, which seemed apparently clear, when retold had somehow been lost in the translation at the time. One of the workers described this as a scrambling machine between them. Whilst this seemed clear to both Karen and Mark, what had built up was a pattern where neither felt listened to nor heard. This resulted in Karen feeling deskilled and without any parental control, and Mark being left without boundaries. Paradoxically, Mark had too much control but simultaneously felt out of control and uncontained.

Within sessions Karen and Mark used activities that allowed them to practice positive communication and to begin to establish, in very small chunks, their new roles. Mark struggled to let go of the control he had in the relationship and it was openly acknowledged that this had been built up over several years and was therefore, in itself, anxiety provoking to change. Karen described feeling overwhelmed at times by the enormity of the task, and was fearful that whilst

in the boundaries of our building she could perhaps make progress, the reality in the community may be very different. With this in mind and to redress the imbalance, towards the end of the work, we increased our time with Karen, individually looking at videotapes and hearing about her experiences at home. Over time her confidence grew and she was able to regularly bring to the sessions examples of success.

At the end of the work Karen and Mark looked back at the goals and yhe hopes they had set and acknowledged shared progress. Mark could recognise that he had used power taking behaviours, including sexual behaviours, at times when he felt unsafe and that he was more comfortable now in his role as 12-year-old boy. Whilst workers still saw some attempts to undermine his mother these were far less serious and, more importantly, well managed by his mother. Karen had used the work to reflect on her own experiences and shared some of this appropriately with Mark, again giving a clear message that it was his experiences and not his innate 'badness' that had led to these behaviours. She also reinforced the message that he now had choices of his own to make about behaviour and that she would be there to guide him in this.

Case study 3 – Daniel

Daniel was referred to Kaleidoscope when he was 15 years old. A chronology compiled by the social worker outlined an early onset of sexual behaviours and prolific concerns regarding sexual comments made by Daniel. He also presented with an unhealthy interest and possible fixation with much younger and more vulnerable children. At this stage there was no evidence to suggest that Daniel had directly assaulted a child, but given the length of time that there had been concerning behaviours, it was felt that it was appropriate to offer a direct service.

Throughout his involvement with Kaleidoscope, Daniel demonstrated a clear understanding of and a significant motivation to work on issues relating to his sexually harmful behaviour. He has taken responsibility for this behaviour and over time has acknowledged distortions in his thinking. Prior to beginning work at Kaleidoscope, Daniel had disclosed that he had been sexually abused by his father and he also subsequently disclosed abuse by his sister. In sessions he was able to explore these experiences further and consider the meanings they had for him.

Daniel had experienced particular difficulties in his relationship with his mother, Wendy. However, she was involved throughout the work at Kaleidoscope and was hugely supportive of him, which was essential in progressing the work. She was keen to understand and make sense of the concerns around Daniel's behaviour. She and Daniel have both identified the personal impact that his behaviour has had on them, both individually and as a family.

Joint sessions were undertaken with Daniel and Wendy. Primarily sessions were planned to consider how Wendy could safely support and supervise Daniel whilst he managed his behaviour. Another aim was to improve communication between them. These joint sessions enabled Daniel and Wendy to share memories and information, which filled in gaps and developed a sense of a shared history. They were able to see each other's perspective on how they have experienced life and to discuss their knowledge, understanding and feelings around Daniel's experiences of abuse. Daniel was able to understand his mother's victim experiences and the impact that these have had upon her mental health and subsequently their relationship. For a long time he believed his mother had been aware of his abuse and had blamed her for what had happened. By engaging in joint work, Wendy made it clear that she was unaware of the sexual abuse that had taken place. Further, she disclosed that both Daniel and she had been victims of his father's behaviour.

During this work, Wendy demonstrated her understanding of the concerns about Daniel's behaviour and the need to manage this and the importance of her support for him, both at the time and in the future. Wendy and Daniel were able to share their feelings for one another and she provided positive messages to him, which were accepting and of extreme significance to him, particularly around his sexuality. These messages were vital in progressing Daniel's work. The joint sessions provided an opportunity for Daniel and Wendy to reconnect in a different way and assisted them in developing communication and their relationship further.

As stated earlier, Kaleidoscope has worked with a number of boys and their mothers. The length and depth of these pieces of work has varied, depending on the individual issues and needs of those involved. However, there have been many similarities in the themes that have emerged. Developing a shared history has been a central part of each piece of work. It has given the child information about their early life that they may not previously have known, and allowed for both parent and child to hear how the other experienced important events. This has provided opportunities for parents to share happy memories as well as acknowledging mistakes. Children have been able to have their experiences heard by these most significant adults. This process, which has included responsibility taking by adults, has enabled some young people to access feelings that they had previously been unable to access. As a result of this, they have been able to move into a different phase of individual work where they have explored their experiences and developed a new understanding of their sexually harmful behaviour.

In addition to having a shared history, another common theme is the identification of a shared vision for the future. This has enabled them to consider how life could be different and to think about what that would involve. Children and their parents are encouraged to draw on their own strengths and consider what is already working, to promote a sense that their vision of the future is a possibility rather than a pipe dream. This also gives children a message that, whilst they are responsible for their harmful behaviour, they do not have the full responsibility of sorting everything out.

Finally, one of the most fundamental themes that has come out of the joint work has been the overall message that children have received from their parents in the act of joining sessions. They learn that the parent is committed to them and committed to helping them change and control their behaviour in the future. Parents have expressed understandable anxiety about participating directly in the work, but have still engaged in the work. It has involved considerable honesty and courage to explore painful issues, but they have all talked of feeling that it was worthwhile and an important process to go through.

In a piece that Karen wrote for other parents and for publication she described the process as follows:

Like being lifted out of a stormy sea and given a resting place for a while, and being able to go back to the stormy sea with a bit more courage and a bit more strength to cope with it. The work we did has done much to improve our quality of life together. Although we will still have problems and it will be a slow process, we have a solid base on which to build our future.

Conclusions

Children and young people who display sexually harmful behaviours are a highly heterogeneous group and, as such, approaches to their work have to be tailored to their individual needs, environments and experiences, as well as to the level of risk their behaviour poses. That said, this chapter has come about as a result of the Kaleidoscope team identifying some recurring contributing factors, such as trauma, whether it be physical and including experiences of domestic violence or abuse, sexual or emotional, or themes, such as children who have histories of attachment difficulties.

As stated earlier, the joint work always followed an assessment which identified the levels and nature of risk, and specific individual interventions to address the sexually harmful behaviour. However, having identified such outstanding unmet needs in terms of ongoing relationships, communication and attachments, we believed they warranted intervention in order that they should not undermine the individual work already completed or indeed the young people's relapse prevention/safety plans.

In each case where this work took place there was evidence of better understandings of their shared history and of the emotional, social and behavioural impact of those histories. In turn that improved understanding led to more open communication, strategies for resolving conflict and therefore, we believe, to reduced feelings of isolation and disempowerment so routinely experienced in our service users' lives.

While it is too soon to make a correlation between these positive outcomes, the fact that unresolved conflict, isolation and feelings of disempowerment contributed to the original behaviour, suggests to us some reason to be optimistic.

References

The Bridge Child Care Development Service (2001) *Childhood Lost: Part 8 Case Review Overview Report.* The Bridge Publishing House Ltd.

Hackett, S. (2001) *Facing the Future: A Guide for Parents of Young People who have Sexually Abused.* Lyme Regis: Russell House Publishing.

Hackett, S., Masson, H.C. and Phillips, S. (2003) *Mapping and Exploring Services for Children and Young People who have Sexually Abused: Final Report.* Durham/Huddersfield: University of Durham and University of Huddersfield, available on Youth Justice Board website at http://www.youth-justice-board.gov.uk/Publications/Scripts/prodView.asp?idproduct=267&ep=

Howe, D. (2005) *Child Abuse and Neglect: Attachment, Development and Intervention.* Aldershot: Palgrave Macmillan.

Maskell, S. (2002) In Calder, M.C. (ed) *Young People who Sexually Abuse: Building the Evidence Base for your Practice.* Lyme Regis: Russell House Publishing.

Chapter 9

Young People with Learning Disabilities Who Sexually Abuse: Understanding, Identifying and Responding from Within Generic Education and Welfare Services

Rachel Fyson

Introduction

This chapter will start by providing an overview of current knowledge about young people with learning disabilities who sexually abuse. Research cited will, unless otherwise indicated, be limited to UK studies since international variations in the definitions of both learning disability and sexual abuse make the use of a wider literature base problematic – particularly that relating to prevalence and incidence. It will then go on to report key findings from a recent study (Fyson et al., 2003; Fyson, 2005) which examined how special schools and statutory child protection and youth offending services in four English local authorities responded to sexually inappropriate or abusive behaviours exhibited by young people with learning disabilities. It will conclude by highlighting areas of current practice which give cause for concern, and suggest some pointers for future best practice.

For the purposes of this chapter, the term 'learning disability' will be used in accordance with the current UK Government definition:

*Learning disability includes the presence of a significantly reduced ability to understand new or complex information, to learn new skills (**impaired intelligence**), with a reduced ability to cope independently (**impaired social functioning**), which started before adulthood, with a lasting effect on development.*

(DoH, 2001)

Current understandings of the association between learning disability and juvenile sexual abuse

In attempting to explore and explain the phenomena of young people who sexually abuse others, many UK studies have noted the apparent over-representation of young people with learning disabilities. As long ago as 1995 Vizard et al., in their review of the research literature on

young people who sexually abuse, stated that 'learning difficulties and poor school achievement are commonly noted'. As evidence for this assertion they cite a study by Epps (1991, cited in Vizard et al., 1995) which found that 44 per cent of referrals to a specialist clinic for young people who sexually abuse others had some degree of learning disability, with half of these having attended a special school.

Other, more recent, UK studies have consistently found that a high proportion of young people who sexually abuse have some degree of learning disability. For example, James and Neil (1996) found that 58.1 per cent of the cases identified in their prevalence survey of juvenile sexual offending were individuals of 'below average ability'. In the same year, Dolan et al. (1996) undertook a retrospective analysis of case study notes on 121 young people referred to an adolescent forensic unit because of their sexually abusive behaviour. They found that:

Just over half, 68 (56.2 per cent) required special schooling. A total of 55 (45 per cent) had learning difficulties with 46 (38 per cent) classified as mildly impaired, 7 (5.8 per cent) moderate and 2 (1.6 per cent) severely impaired.

(ibid: 344)

In 1998 O'Callaghan, writing about a service for young abusers, commented that:

While the project has continued to work with young people from across the ability spectrum, young people assessed as having some form of learning disability now constitute approximately half of all referrals to the service.

(ibid: 437)

Similarly, Manocha and Mezey (1998) analysed the background characteristics of 51 young people referred to a specialist assessment and treatment facility for young sexual abusers and found that:

There were 17 (33.3 per cent) who were described as poor academic achievers with 10 (19.6 per cent) formally diagnosed as learning disabled (mild 8, moderate 2). Of the subjects, 16 (31.4 per cent) had been formally 'statemented'.

(ibid: 592)

More recently, in 2002, Boswell and Wedge reported, in their evaluation of a residential therapeutic community for sexually abusive adolescent males, that eight out of ten of those who completed the therapeutic programme and participated in their study 'had been assessed as having mild, moderate or serious learning difficulties' (ibid: 18).

Yet, despite these findings, few researchers have chosen to focus their work directly on young people with learning disabilities who sexually abuse. The limited evidence which is available about this sub-set of abusers tends to be drawn from research based on clinical samples, studies which by their very nature are skewed (O'Callaghan, 1999; Balogh et al., 2001). However, despite their limitations, such studies have identified a number of characteristics which appear to differentiate learning disabled juvenile sexual abusers from those of average or above average ability.

The seminal work – undertaken in Canada – of Gilbey, Wolf and Goldberg (1989) involved comparisons between learning disabled and non-learning disabled adolescents who had been referred to a specialist psychiatric service. They found that adolescents with a learning disability were no more or less likely than others to have perpetrated sexual assaults, but they *were* more likely to have engaged in 'nuisance' behaviours, including flashing, public masturbation and voyeurism. It was also noted that the adolescents with a learning disability appeared to be less discriminating in their choice of victim, offending equally against males and females, and in 30 per cent of cases offending against victims of both gender. This finding is in line with findings from studies of men with learning disabilities who sexually abuse (Thompson and Brown, 1997), and has been interpreted as suggesting that people with learning disabilities who sexually abuse may often do so in a less planned, more impulsive, manner.

In the years since the study by Gilbey et al., a number of further studies have been undertaken in the UK and elsewhere based on clinical samples of young people with learning disabilities who sexually abuse. None of these has contradicted the key findings of Gilbey et al., and

several have added further to our understandings. Work published by Tudiver and Griffin in the United States (1992) and Balogh et al. in the UK (2001) both confirm the hypothesis that young people with learning disabilities who sexually abuse are less gender specific than other young people with regard to their choice of victim. The findings of Balogh et al. (2001) and Firth et al. (2001) suggest that there are further gender differences in the patterns of previous victimisation experienced by these young people. A number of authors, from both sides of the Atlantic, confirm the tendency of some young people with learning disabilities to abuse on impulse and the fact that they may have poor social skills (Tudiver and Griffin, 1992; Sternac and Sheridan, 1993; O'Callaghan, 1998; Timms and Goreczny, 2002; Hackett, 2004) both of which are characteristics which have elsewhere been associated with an increased risk of sexual offending.

Despite these findings, it remains true that there are more commonalities than differences between young people with and without learning disabilities who sexually abuse. In particular, findings from both the United States and the UK indicate that these two groups of young people are likely to share similar histories of family dysfunction, abuse and neglect (Sternac and Sheridan, 1993; O'Callaghan, 1998; McCurrey et al., 1998).

Identification and treatment of young people with learning disabilities who sexually abuse others

A number of UK studies have provided evidence that young people with learning disabilities who sexually abuse others can benefit from therapeutic interventions (Lindsay et al., 1999; O'Callaghan, 1999; Boswell and Wedge, 2002). However, it remains the case that there are insufficient therapeutic services willing and able to offer support to this group of young people (O'Callaghan, 1998; Vail, 2002; Masson and Hackett, 2003).

In relation to *all* young people who sexual abuse others, Hoghughi (1997) estimated that only 10–15 per cent of cases where adolescents are known to have behaved in a sexually harmful or abusive manner ever become 'cases' in statutory services of any kind, let alone are referred for specialist assessment or treatment. More recently, Hackett (2004) has asserted that:

One of the key changes in the response to adolescent sexual aggression over the past decade is a rapid increase in the number of young people with learning disabilities being identified and referred for intervention.

(ibid: 44)

However, care must be taken in determining the reasons for this, which may have little to do with any changes in the behaviour of young people with learning disabilities and much to do with changes in patterns of referral (Balogh et al., 2001).

Reasons for the over-representation of learning disabilities amongst clinical populations of young people who sexually abuse are undoubtedly complex and should certainly not be taken as evidence of any greater propensity for abuse on the part of young people with learning disabilities (Hackett, 2004). Indeed, studies of men with learning disabilities who sexually abuse which have been undertaken in both Australia (Hayes, 1991) and the UK (Thompson and Brown, 1997) demonstrate that these men are no more or less likely than others to engage in acts of sexual abuse.

In addition to the individual characteristics noted earlier, such as impulsivity and social skills deficits, there are a number of wider factors which may impact upon both the (sexual) behaviour of young people with learning disabilities and the likelihood of such behaviour resulting in a referral to specialist services:

- Young people with disabilities, including learning disabilities, are more likely than non-disabled young people to have experienced abuse of all kinds (Kelly, 1992; NSPCC, 2003; Sullivan and Knutson, 1998 and 2000) and disability is also associated with longer durations of abuse (Westcott and Jones, 1999). Whilst there is no direct or linear relationship between experiencing childhood abuse and going on to perpetrate acts of sexual abuse (Freidrich, 1998) high levels of abuse are noted in almost all samples of sexual abusers.
- The sex education available to young people with learning disabilities may be limited and insufficient (O'Callaghan, 1998: 1999; Hackett, 2004). Even when high quality sex education is provided by schools, the nature of a learning disability may mean that it is difficult for such young people to translate concepts which they have been taught in a classroom situation into their everyday behaviours – particularly in situations where they may be sexually aroused.

- People with learning disabilities have, in the recent past, commonly been regarded by others in society as somehow 'asexual' (Craft, 1987). Some parents and carers may still find it difficult to accept sexual expression as a natural part of the expressive behaviour of a young person with a learning disability (O'Callaghan, 1998). This may lead not only to a denial of the sexuality of young people with learning disabilities, but also to a failure on the part of parents and care givers to socialise young people with learning disabilities in the same way that they would other children, thus making it even harder for this group of young people to learn the unspoken social norms of sexual behaviour.
- Young people with learning disabilities who sexually abuse may be less adept than others at hiding or denying what they have done and, in some cases, less aware that what they have done is socially unacceptable (Timms and Goreczny, 2002). Those with moderate to severe learning disabilities may also be subject to higher levels of supervision than young people of average ability, thus making their acts of abuse disproportionately likely to come to the attention of adults.
- There is a tendency for criminal justice systems in both the UK and elsewhere to favour diverting juvenile sexual abusers, especially those who have a learning disability, away from criminal proceedings and towards alternative clinical services (Gilbey et al., 1989; O'Callaghan, 1999).

To summarise: factors such as those outlined above have led to a number of commentators noting the apparent overlap between populations of young people who sexually abuse and populations of young people with learning disabilities (Vizard, 1995; O'Callaghan, 1998: 1999; Hackett, 2004) but our understanding of the dynamics of this relationship remain at best sketchy. More importantly, it is not yet clear what the implications of this knowledge are for those who work with young people who sexually abuse, although Masson and Erooga (1999) suggest that:

Clearly management and treatment of these young people have to be planned in the light of careful assessment of their cognitive and social functioning so that, for example, treatment delivery attends to issues such as shortened attention spans, more experiential styles of learning and the need for careful use of language and repetition of messages.

(ibid: 8)

The present study

Although the various studies cited above all reveal facts of interest, they shed very little light – individually or collectively – on why and how the behaviours of some young people with learning disabilities who sexually abuse others come to the attention of statutory social work and/or criminal justice agencies, whilst others do not. They also fail to address the role of non-specialist statutory services in identifying sexually inappropriate behaviours and responding to these in a timely fashion, such that they do not lead on to acts of more serious sexual abuse. Several of the studies cited have demonstrated the efficacy of specialist therapeutic interventions, but it is clear that such services are only ever made available to a small minority of young people with learning disabilities who sexually abuse. The more immediate interventions of professionals who work directly with children and young people with learning disabilities under a wider educational or social welfare remit are therefore likely to be of importance.

The Ann Craft Trust (http://www.anncrafttrust.org/) is a national charitable organisation, based in Nottingham, which works to protect people with learning disabilities from abuse through providing training to professionals, producing publications and undertaking original research. It first became aware of the problem of young people with learning disabilities who sexually abuse others when its then Director, Pam Cooke, undertook a study of disabled children and abuse. In it, she compared the outcomes for a matched sample of disabled and non-disabled children who were identified by statutory social services as having been abused (Cooke, 2000; Cooke and Standen, 2002). An unexpected finding of this study was that a significant minority of the abused children had been sexually abused by young people with learning disabilities. Further investigation revealed that not only was legal action pending against some of these young people with learning disabilities – in particular those who had offended against non-disabled children – but that all of the young people with learning disabilities

who had abused others had previously suffered abuse themselves and *no* action had been taken against any of their abusers. It appeared that, for these young people, their plight as victims of abuse was ignored whilst any perpetration of abuse was liable to be punished. In no cases had these young learning disabled victim-abusers been offered help in the form of therapeutic interventions.

From these findings, it was hypothesised that sexual abuse perpetrated by young people with a learning disability may be one of the many factors which puts children with disabilities at increased overall risk of abuse in comparison to non-disabled children. The Ann Craft Trust therefore wanted to find out more about the phenomenon of young people with learning disabilities who sexually abuse, in order to both explore how statutory services might develop strategies which could offer more supportive interventions to these troubled and troubling young people and to support the Trust's wider aim of helping to protect (disabled) children from potential abuse.

Methodological overview

The research consisted of two separate, but linked, elements – both of which were undertaken simultaneously in four English local authorities. The first element involved a survey of all special schools to determine their experiences of, and responses to, any sexually inappropriate and/or abusive behaviours displayed by pupils. A total of 40 special schools whose intake was wholly or primarily composed of children with learning disabilities were identified within the research areas. Each school was asked to complete a brief questionnaire which asked about the frequency with which they identified sexually inappropriate or abusive behaviour between pupils; the nature of the behaviours noted; the extent to which schools had sought assistance from statutory social services and/or other welfare agencies; and details of school policies which might inform staff responses to incidents arising. Permission was also sought to undertake follow-up interviews with staff in order to gather more in-depth information about school policy and practice in relation to incidents of potential or actual sexual abuse.

At the same time, work was undertaken in conjunction with statutory child protection and youth offending services to identify all cases of young people with learning disabilities who sexually abused others which came to light over a twelve month period.

Whenever such a case was identified, the author undertook a structured interview with a key worker. By this means information was gathered about the young person's family and educational background; any known history of abuse; details of the abuse which was alleged to have been perpetrated, including information on victims; details of any involvement with the criminal justice system; and evidence of any therapeutic interventions. In all, 15 cases were identified during the twelve months of data collection. The findings from these case studies are presented alongside wider commentaries on issues arising, from the viewpoints of the various professions involved. It is important to note, however, that there were undoubtedly other cases held by statutory child protection and youth offending teams during this period which, due to failures of communication, were not identified for inclusion in this study. The author was personally made aware of three other cases during the research period where it was not possible to identify a key worker willing to be interviewed; other cases also undoubtedly existed which simply never came to light.

The difficulties experienced in identifying all relevant cases highlights the problems inherent in using a prospective survey methodology when working across four large and complex organisations. However, despite the drawbacks, this approach benefited from the fact that the professionals who participated were all currently and actively engaged with the young people concerned. This therefore ensured that a more detailed and holistic understanding of each young person was gathered than would have been possible from an analysis of historical case notes.

Key findings: special schools

Of the 40 special schools initially contacted, 26 returned a completed questionnaire. This gave a response rate of 65 per cent. In addition, staff from ten of the schools agreed to be interviewed about their policies and practices in this area. The individuals interviewed were all either the school's designated child protection co-ordinator (often the head teacher or deputy head teacher)

or the member of staff with particular responsibility for sex education.

Prevalence of sexually inappropriate or abusive behaviour

It was clear that sexually inappropriate behaviour was, to a greater or lesser extent, a problem which arose in most special schools. In total, 88 per cent of schools indicated that they had experienced sexually inappropriate or abusive incidents between pupils, with (cumulatively) 19 per cent reporting that such incidents occurred at least once a week; 46 per cent reporting incidents at least once a month and 65 per cent at least once a term. Only 12 per cent of schools stated that they had never experienced any incidents of sexually inappropriate or abusive behaviour between pupils. This represented three individual schools, one of which was at pains to explain that the reason for this seemingly unlikely scenario was that all of their pupils had profound and multiple disabilities, which precluded them from independently initiating any physical engagement with others.

The nature of the sexual behaviours observed

The sexually inappropriate and abusive behaviours between pupils which were identified within special schools ranged from the relatively minor to the extremely serious: 54 per cent of schools reported incidents of genital exposure (flashing); 58 per cent reported public masturbation; 88 per cent unwanted sexual touching; and 15 per cent reported that actual or attempted vaginal or anal penetration had occurred. Although the first of these four categories might be dismissed by some as likely to include instances of behaviour which were neither intentionally abusive nor necessarily always harmful, the final category undoubtedly demonstrates that serious acts of sexual abuse can and do occasionally occur – even in the highly structured and well-supervised setting of special schools. The four schools which reported the most serious acts described them in the following ways: 'anal rape'; 'vaginal rape'; 'digital penetration of vagina'; and 'alleged rape – not proven'.

School policies

Despite evidence of the extent of sexually inappropriate and/or abusive behaviours between pupils in these schools, only a small minority (19 per cent) had in place specific policies to govern staff responses to, and recording of, such incidents. Interviews revealed that the minority of schools which had policies in place also regularly updated them. However, it was more common to find that schools relied on standard child protection guidance issued by local Area Child Protection Committees, which inevitably focused on how staff should respond when they suspected that a child was being abused at home, rather than advising how to proceed if a pupil acted in a sexually abusive manner. One interviewee commented that their school's policies were 'generic documents that are suitably bland and not necessarily written for our setting'; another admitted that at their school 'a lot of people, if I'm honest, have probably never read it'.

In practice, what typically appeared to happen was that sexually inappropriate or abusive behaviours – particularly those which could be classified as 'nuisance' rather than abuse – were dealt with under the broader remit of school behavioural guidelines. This usually meant imposing simple behaviour modification programmes, designed to prevent unwanted behaviours without necessarily exploring any of the underlying reasons why such behaviours might have developed in the first place. Given that so many apparently sexual behaviours amongst this group of young people were described by school staff as lacking in intent such an approach would appear to be both pragmatic and largely effective. However, for more serious acts this approach may run the risk of minimising the impact of abusive behaviours and disregarding early indicators of an emerging problem – a scenario which O'Callaghan (1998) has argued is detrimental to longer term outcomes for young people with learning disabilities who sexually abuse.

Key triggers for intervention

Despite often lacking relevant policies, interviewees unanimously identified four factors which they said were used to determine whether any given incident was simply a case of inappropriate behaviour or might more properly be viewed as indicative of abuse. These factors were:

1. **The act itself** – unwanted sexual contact of any kind between two pupils was of greater concern than 'nuisance' behaviours such as exposure or public masturbation (although, importantly and depending on their age and other factors, interviewees also noted that in some cases such nuisance behaviours could indicate that a pupil had been the victim of abuse).
2. **Imbalances of power** between the two pupils involved. This included any significant differences in age, physical size and cognitive ability.
3. **Attempts at secrecy** were also thought to be potentially indicative of abuse, since seeking secrecy implied that a pupil knew that what they were doing was wrong.
4. **Repetition** of sexually inappropriate acts was likewise viewed with concern, on the basis that behaviours which could not be ameliorated by behavioural interventions could be either another sign that a pupil might themselves have been abused, or an indicator that the behaviour was in danger of escalating into something more serious.

Taken at face value, these four factors would seem to represent a reasonable approach to assessing the seriousness of any given incident. However, further questioning revealed that putting these principles into practice was neither straightforward nor consistent. Of particular concern was the indication from a majority of interviewees that their schools lacked a consistent approach to the recording of incidents – a situation which immediately made a mockery of the idea that repetition of sexual behaviours would give rise to concern, for there was no obvious way of knowing whether such repetition had occurred.

The involvement of other services

Where an incident was serious enough to be regarded as being of immediate concern teachers typically informed the school's designated child protection co-ordinator or the school nurse. It was stressed that any decision to intervene would be based initially on the school's knowledge of the particular pupils concerned, but if simple behavioural techniques failed to improve the situation then a variety of other strategies might be adopted.

However, schools varied widely in their willingness to engage the support of statutory social services or other relevant social welfare agencies. The reason for this appeared to be that a significant number of schools had previously experienced negative outcomes following requests for help from social services. The survey results indicated that although over half (54 per cent) of special schools had previously sought help from local authority child protection services because of concerns about sexually inappropriate or abusive behaviour between pupils, in 43 per cent of these cases the schools were dissatisfied with the response they received. No other potential sources of external support received such a high dissatisfaction rate. For example, only one quarter of schools expressed dissatisfaction with the assistance offered by educational psychologists, and this was largely on the basis that there was insufficient availability of such services.

Although almost every interviewee was keen to express their support for hard-pressed social workers, they nevertheless remained frustrated that when issues of sexually inappropriate or abusive behaviour arose between pupils, statutory child protection services typically failed to provide effective input. There were a number of specific issues which were repeatedly brought up, relating to both the organisational structure of children's social services and the lack of knowledge amongst many social workers about disabled children.

On an organisational level, staff in special schools reported that they could largely expect supportive advice if the pupil with a difficulty already had a named social worker. However, despite the fact that – under the Children Act 1989 – *all* disabled children are automatically classified as 'children in need', most disabled children do not in fact have a designated social worker. In light of this, when problems arose schools were frequently obliged to make contact with social services through the 'duty team' system, which meant speaking to someone with no prior knowledge of the child concerned.

Complaints about duty teams took various forms: that they were unable to offer advice, and would act only to initiate a full-blown child protection investigation:

If you just go cold to somebody quite often it triggers a 'We must investigate it' because they don't know us and they don't know the school.

Or that they were unwilling to get involved in allegations involving children with disabilities:

I would like social workers to respond as if I wasn't working in a special school, because the minute you say the name of the school then you can hear the silence.It does mean more work, but I'm sorry, that's just the way it is.

Part of the difficulty was presented by another interviewee as stemming from resource constraints:

In this area at the moment we've just been told they can't do anything other than child protection. So there's no preventative stuff. And sometimes we can see what's going on. We can see that a bit of help in the home – just to explain that perhaps if the boys slept in one room and the girls slept in another – that might help.

Whatever the precise nature of the difficulties experienced by particular schools, communication with social services always worked best when based on individual relationships between teachers and social workers and often fell apart when staff turnover or reduced resources meant relying on accessing support through official channels. Schools were aware that social workers could not offer a panacea for all ills, but were also aware that social services were the gatekeeper for further resources, in particular some of the more specialist therapeutic services offered by voluntary and independent sector organisations. Schools therefore had an obvious vested interest in maintaining harmonious relations with social services. Despite this, many remained vocal in their criticisms: calling for all social workers to enhance both their awareness of disability and their skills in communicating with young people with learning disabilities.

Key findings: case histories

Over the course of twelve months, case study interviews were undertaken with professionals in respect of fifteen young people with learning disabilities who were identified by child protection and/or youth offending services as having sexually abused others. The findings confirmed some of the outcomes from other studies of young people (with learning disabilities) who sexually abuse, but also highlight a number of issues which have not previously been addressed.

Demographic, family and educational backgrounds

The young people whose histories were captured as case studies ranged in age from 11 to 17 at the time their sexually abusive behaviour came to the attention of statutory child protection or criminal justice agencies. Fourteen of the young people were male and one was female. Thirteen were of white British origin, one was of African-Caribbean origin and one was of dual British and African-Caribbean heritage.

Only four of the fifteen (26 per cent) came from intact family backgrounds. The others lived in a variety of family configurations and many had experienced numerous disruptions to their home life; three were in foster care. Two of the young people had mothers whom social services had identified as themselves having a learning disability.

In relation to education, five (33 per cent) of the young people attended (or had attended) a special school for children with learning disabilities. Of the ten who attended mainstream school half (33 per cent of the total) had statements of special educational need and half (the remaining 33 per cent) did not. The fact that one third of the sample had neither attended special school nor been statemented should *not* be regarded as suggestive that they were not learning disabled. The policy of some of the education authorities where this research was undertaken explicitly rejects the idea that statementing is a necessary or helpful process. This has inevitably led to statementing becoming something of a postcode lottery: for example, one of the five young people who had *not* been statemented by his local educational authority was later assessed (at the request of his crown court defence team) and found to have 'moderate to severe learning disabilities'.

Histories of abuse

In all but two of the fifteen cases the young people were either known to have been neglected; emotionally, physically or sexually abused; to have witnessed domestic violence; or social workers strongly suspected that abuse had taken place. The category of 'strongly suspected' abuse was not based on the young person's behaviour, but on what social services knew about their family background, for example:

There has been no disclosure, but in that house – while he was living there – we have got an allegation that birth dad was sexually abusing his sister; mum has been implicated in an assault on a child; this guy who was Schedule one was living with mother.I think it is quite possible he was sexually abused by any or all of them and I think it was almost impossible that he wasn't sexually abused, or at least witnessed his sister's abuse.

The abusive acts and victim information

The acts of sexual abuse which these young people were alleged to have perpetrated were almost always extremely serious. Five individuals were alleged or proven to have committed vaginal rape; two to have committed anal rape and one to have committed oral rape. In several cases the young person had been charged with raping more than one other person: one young man was charged in court with six counts of rape. Two others were alleged to have attempted to rape, with the remainder alleged or proven to have committed a variety of serious sexual assaults including – for example – breast biting and digital penetration.

There were only two cases where the alleged acts of sexual abuse were less immediately serious. In both of these cases the young person concerned was in foster care and had behaved in an inappropriately sexualised manner towards foster siblings.

The victims of these sexual assaults ranged from children as young as five or six through to (in one case) adult women. Most of the young people had abused exclusively female victims; two had abused only males, whilst a further two cases involved male and female victims. There were two cases of sibling incest. In three cases one or more of the victims had a disability of some kind.

In 7 out of 15 cases either the young person's school or a social services child protection team was aware of previous incidents of alleged sexual abuse which had not been acted upon in any formal capacity.

Criminal justice

The majority of these young people (12 out of 15) had been involved with the criminal justice system as a result of their sexually abusive behaviour. In fact, it was most often the case that social services only became aware of the young person when a victim complained to the police. The only exceptions to this were the young people who were already known to social services because they were the subject of care orders and/or were placed in foster care.

Six of the young people had been convicted on charges ranging from rape to indecent assault, and a further two had avoided court appearances by accepting a final police warning. This meant that over half of these young people (8 out of 15) were registered sex offenders. Interviewees doubted whether any of the young people had much idea what this meant.

Social work, youth offending and therapeutic interventions

The input which each young person received from statutory child protection services and/or youth offending services varied considerably in both structure and content. None of the four local authorities adhered in the strictest sense to current Government guidance, which suggests that the needs of young people who sexually abuse should be assessed and met through children in need procedures (Department of Health et al., 1999). However, the same guidance also says that:

> A young abuser shall be the subject of a child protection conference if he or she is considered personally to be at risk of continuing significant harm.
>
> (ibid, para. 6.37)

Two of the local authorities had chosen to use this proviso to bring *all* such cases forward as child protection procedures, with initial child protection conferences – when necessary – resulting in the young person being registered on their YPSA (Young People who Sexually Abuse) register. This meant that case reviews occurred every six months and the young people continued to benefit from the more substantial level of input and review provided by child protection teams, as compared to children in need teams. In cases where the police had brought charges, this was handled separately – and would

result in the additional involvement of the youth offending team.

The two other social service departments had devised rather different procedures, involving all young people who were alleged to have sexually abused appearing before multidisciplinary 'assessment and early intervention panels'. These panels included representatives from child protection teams, youth offending teams, and the local police. Panels considered all relevant available information before recommending a particular course of action; they sought to divert away from the criminal justice system whenever possible, passing cases on to child protection; children in need or YOT teams as deemed appropriate.

In all authorities the involvement of youth offending services was dependent upon charges being laid. As previously noted, this had the immediate effect of requiring the young person to register as a sex offender. However, it also had an impact upon the nature of the support which the young people could expect to receive. Put simply, support from child protection social workers was individual but largely unstructured; support from youth offending teams could be provided on a one-to-one or group basis, but normally followed a predetermined, carefully structured programme.

Each approach had its advantages and its drawbacks. Child protection social workers expressed concern that:

> It seems that once young people are on the YPSA register it is impossible to get them off. And yet, when they reach eighteen, they come off just like that.

Whilst some youth offending team workers were concerned that young people with learning disabilities were unable to keep up with the pace of programmes which had been designed with young abusers of average or above average ability in mind.

However, both sets of workers were acutely aware that what many – if not all – of these young people needed was long-term therapy from professionals specialising in working with young people who sexually abuse. Unfortunately, such services were not readily available. At the time interviews took place only three out of the 15 young people were receiving therapeutic support. Of the others, one had been sent to a residential school for children with learning disabilities; two were detained in young offender institutes and nine were receiving no input other than that offered by generic child protection and youth offending services.

Interviewees described a number of barriers to accessing the limited therapeutic services which were available, including funding issues and – worryingly – the reluctance of some services to work with young people with learning disabilities. None of the interviewees were confident that, given the right (or perhaps wrong) circumstances the young person with whom they were working would not sexually abuse again. In 9 out of 15 cases it was thought that the young person would 'almost certainly' abuse again. This made the lack of appropriate therapy all the more alarming; as one interviewee put it:

I think he is a worrying teenager who is going to turn into an incredibly worrying young man. I worry that I am going to see him on Crimewatch in a few years time if something isn't done now.

Other issues

Over and above their concerns over the lack of appropriate specialist provision for young people who sexually abuse, interviewees were also acutely aware of their own lack of knowledge and skills in relation to learning disability. In several cases the interviewee had never previously worked with a young person with a learning disability and many expressed uncertainty as to whether their approach was the right one.

Discussion

Perhaps the most immediately striking fact about this study was the almost complete lack of crossover between the young people with learning disabilities who were the focus of each of the two elements of research. In contrast to the difficulties experienced within special schools, which most often constituted 'nuisance' behaviours, young people who became 'cases' within child protection or youth offending teams had committed far more serious acts of abuse – in most cases constituting sexual offences. However, the preponderance of known histories of earlier, less serious, acts of sexual abuse amongst the individual case histories makes a compelling argument in favour of the proposition that concerns expressed by staff in special schools should be taken more seriously by social services' duty teams.

In practice, the apparent reluctance of overstretched child protection teams to involve themselves in 'nuisance' cases, and perhaps also the (understandable) reluctance of special schools to identify their pupils as sexual abusers, enabled a small but dangerous minority to progress from nuisance behaviours to serious acts of sexual offending. These young people were typically being failed twice by the system – once when it failed to protect them from abuse and again when it failed to prevent their nuisance behaviours from escalating. The result of this failure was evident in the number of young people known to statutory child protection and youth offending services (8 out of 15) that ended up on the sex offender register. The social consequences (both immediate and long term) of being 'legally' labelled as a sexual abuser in this way are extremely damaging to young people in general (Longo and Calder, 2005) – and arguably even more damaging for those whose life chances are already circumscribed by learning disability.

Frontline professionals from both child protection and youth offending teams were evidently doing their utmost to offer effective support to young people with learning disabilities who had sexually abused. At an organisational level, managers of child protection services had also put time and effort into devising policies and procedures intended to enable their staff to take on these cases. However, there remained a dearth of therapeutic services, or indeed any professionals with specialist knowledge of both learning disability and young people who sexually abuse. Most worryingly, a number of the specialist services which did exist for young people who sexually abused had refused (after an initial assessment period) to work with young people with learning disabilities, on the basis that they were not able to progress fast enough. This might appear unfair, but in fact is probably a case of service providers having to put organisational survival above the needs of any individual – these services were typically funded on the basis of a prescribed minimum throughput of clients and so could not afford to become 'clogged up' with young people with learning disabilities.

Conclusion

The findings from this study highlight a number of issues, some of which may help to explain the apparent over-representation of young people with learning disabilities in clinical samples of young people who sexually abuse. In particular, the lack of confidence expressed by staff from child protection and youth offending teams in working with this group of young people may explain their eagerness to refer on to specialist facilities whenever possible. The fact that low-level or nuisance behaviours are often left to develop into more serious (and, in all likelihood, more intransigent) sexually abusive behaviours may be another reason why specialist interventions become necessary.

It is evident that educational and welfare services could work more closely together, but perhaps unsurprising that such co-operation is only easily forthcoming when based on individual relationships: just as special school staff complained about social services' duty teams, so child protection and youth offending teams complained that these young people were frequently excluded from schools and – once this happened – it was often extremely difficult to find an alternative educational placement.

Our original hypothesis, that the abuse perpetrated by young people with learning disabilities was one of the factors which contributes to the elevated rates of abuse amongst children with disabilities was given some credence by the research findings. The rates of sexually inappropriate and abusive behaviour reported in special schools demonstrated that many disabled children experience low levels of abuse or harassment from their fellow pupils, and a few fall victim to serious sexual acts. Equally, the fact that three of the individual case studies involved disabled victims suggests that disabled children may be disproportionately targeted by young people with learning disabilities who sexually abuse. This may be due to the proximity of other children and young people with disabilities to impulsive young people with learning disabilities who are potential abusers, but the arguable lack of intent is of scant consolation to victims.

Better sharing of both information and expertise between education, child protection and youth offending services is required in order to minimise the likelihood that young people with learning disabilities sexually abuse others. Systems need to be developed which both identify, and respond to, problematic sexual behaviours at an early stage. Alongside their continuing battle to minimise the social exclusion

experienced by many young people with learning disabilities, educational and welfare services must seek a more effective way of meeting the *specific* needs of young people with learning disabilities who sexually abuse. In doing so, they will need to weigh their reluctance to label nuisance behaviours as sexually abusive against the consequences (for a minority) of later being labelled through the sex offender registration process.

The needs of young people with learning disabilities who sexually abuse are complex, rooted in both their cognitive impairment and their often difficult home circumstances. In responding to these needs, statutory services will need to take into consideration not only the act of sexual abuse that has arisen, but also the circumstances in which it occurred. All professionals need to be fully aware of the way in which these young people are frequently (if not continually) disempowered by their social and cognitive impairments and of how they may struggle to grasp and replicate the intricate rules of social interaction, including those of a sexual nature, which most other people understand implicitly.

It is certain that many (and probable that most) young people with learning disabilities who sexually abuse will never come into contact with specialist services. It is therefore important that, despite the difficulties inherent in identifying and studying non-clinical samples of these young people, research is not limited to clinical and/or therapeutic settings. Generic education, child protection and youth offending workers are in many instances attempting to work with these young people without the benefit of expert training or other forms of guidance. It is true that more specialist services need to be provided, but it is doubtful that such provision will ever meet demand: long-term therapeutic services are expensive to run and, outside of the major cities, population demand for such provision is unlikely to be deemed cost-effective. It therefore appears to be imperative that information and simple programmes outlining effective intervention strategies are developed for use by non-specialist staff, for it is they who continue to bear the brunt of this heavy caseload.

The research upon which this chapter is based was funded by the *Diana, Princess of Wales Memorial Fund* and was undertaken by the author whilst she was working as Research Fellow for the Ann Craft Trust.

References

Balogh, R. et al. (2001) Sexual Abuse in Children and Adolescents with Intellectual Disability. *Journal of Intellectual Disability Research*, 45: 194–201.

Boswell, G. and Wedge, P. (2002) *Sexually Abusive Adolescent Males: An Evaluation of a Residential Therapeutic Facility.* Community and Criminal Justice Monograph 3. Leicester: De Montfort University.

Cooke, P. (2000) *Disabled Children and Abuse.* Nottingham: Ann Craft Trust.

Cooke, P. and Standen, P. (2002) Abuse and Disabled Children: Hidden Needs? *Child Abuse Review* 11, 1–18.

Craft, A. (1987) *Mental Handicap and Sexuality: Issues and Perspectives.* Tunbridge Wells: Costello.

Department of Health (2001) *Valuing People: A New Strategy for Learning Disability for the 21st Century.* London: The Stationery Office.

Department of Health, Home Office, Department for Education and Employment (1999) *Working Together to Safeguard Children.* London: The Stationery Office.

Dolan, M., Holloway, J., Bailey, S. and Kroll, L. (1996) The Psychosocial Characteristics of Juvenile Sexual Offenders Referred to an Adolescent Forensic Service in the UK. *Medical Science Law* 36, 343–52.

Firth, H. et al. (2001) Psychopathology of Sexual Abuse in Young People with Intellectual Disability. *Journal of Intellectual Disability Research*, 45, 244–52.

Freidrich, W. (1998) Behavioural Manifestations of Child Sexual Abuse. *Child Abuse and Neglect*, 22 523–31.

Fyson, R., Eadie, T. and Cooke, P. (2003) Adolescents with Learning Disabilities who show Sexually Inappropriate or Abusive Behaviours. *Child Abuse Review*, 12, 305–14.

Fyson, R. (2005) *Young People with Learning Disabilities who show Sexually Inappropriate or Abusive Behaviours.* Nottingham: The Ann Craft Trust.

Gilbey, R., Wolf, L. and Goldberg, B. (1989) Mentally Retarded Adolescent Sex Offenders: A Survey and Pilot Study. *Canadian Journal of Psychiatry*, 34: 542–8.

Hackett, S. (2004) *What Works for Children and Young People with Harmful Sexual Behaviours?* Ilford: Barnardo's.

Hayes, S. (1991) Sex Offenders. *Australia and New Zealand Journal of Developmental Disabilities*, 17, 220–7.

Hoghughi, M. (1997) Sexual Abuse by Adolescents. In Hoghughi, M., Bhate, S. and Graham, S. (Eds.) *Working with Sexually Abusive Adolescents.* London: Sage.

James, A. and Neil, P. (1996) Juvenile Sexual Offending: One-Year Period Prevalence Study within Oxfordshire. *Child Abuse and Neglect*, 20, 477–85.

Kelly, L. (1992) The Connections Between Disability and Child Abuse: A Review of the Research Evidence. *Child Abuse Review*, 1, 157–67.

Lindsay, W., Olley, S., Baillie, N. and Smith, A. (1999) Treatment of Adolescent Sex Offenders with Intellectual Disabilities. *Mental Retardation*, 37, 201–11.

Longo, R. and Calder, M. (2005) The Use of Sex Offender Registration with Young People who Sexually Abuse. In Calder, M.C. (Ed.) *Children and Young People who Sexually Abuse: New Theory, Research and Practice Developments.* Lyme Regis: Russell House Publishing.

McCurrey, C. et al. (1998) Sexual Behaviour Associated with Low Verbal IQ in Youth who have Severe Mental Illness. *Mental Retardation*, 36, 23–30.

Manocha, K. and Mezey, G. (1998) British Adolescents who Sexually Abuse: A Descriptive Study. *The Journal of Forensic Psychiatry*, 3, 588–608.

Masson, H. and Erooga, M. (1999) Children and Young People who Sexually Abuse Others: Incidence, Characteristics and Causation. In Erooga, M. and Masson, H. (Eds.) *Children and Young People who Sexually Abuse Others: Challenges and Responses.* London: Routledge.

Masson, H. and Hackett, S. (2003) A Decade on from the NCH Report (1992): Adolescent Sexual Aggression, Policy and Service Delivery across the UK and Republic of Ireland. *Journal of Sexual Aggression*, 9, 1–22.

NSPCC (2003) *'It Doesn't Happen to Disabled Children': Child Protection and Disabled Children.* Report of the National Working Group on Child Protection and Disability. London: NSPCC.

O'Callaghan, D. (1998) Practice Issues in Working with Young Abusers who have Learning Disabilities. *Child Abuse Review*, 7, 435–48.

O'Callaghan, D. (1999) Young Abusers with Learning Disabilities: Towards Better

Understanding and Positive Interventions. In Calder, M.C. (Ed.) *Working with Young People who Sexually Abuse: New Pieces of the Jigsaw Puzzle.* Lyme Regis: Russell House Publishing.

Sternac, L. and Sheridan, P. (1993) The Developmentally Disabled Adolescent Sex Offender. In Barbaree, H.E., Marshall, W.L. and Hudson, S.M. *The Juvenile Sex Offender.* New York: The Guilford Press.

Sullivan, P. and Knutson, J. (1998) The Association between Child Maltreatment and Disabilities in a Hospital-based Epidemiological Study. *Child Abuse and Neglect,* 22, 271–88.

Sullivan, P. and Knutson, J. (2000) Maltreatment and Disabilities: A Population-based Epidemiological Study. *Child Abuse and Neglect,* 24, 1257–74.

Timms, S. and Goreczny, A. (2002) Adolescent Sex Offenders with Mental Retardation. *Aggression and Violent Behaviour,* 7, 1–19.

Thompson, D. and Brown, H. (1997) Men with Learning Disabilities who Abuse: A Review of the Literature. *Journal of Applied Research in Intellectual Disabilities,* 10, 125–39.

Tudiver, J. and Griffin, J. (1992) Treating Developmentally Disabled Adolescents who have Committed Sexual Abuse. *SIECCAN Newsletter,* 27, 2.

Vail, B. (2002) An Exploration of the Issue of Sexuality and Abusive Behaviour amongst Adolescents who have a Learning Disability. *Child Care in Practice,* 8, 201–15.

Vizard, E., Monck, E. and Misch, P. (1995) Child and Adolescent Sex Abuse Perpetrators: A Review of the Research Literature. *Journal of Child Psychology and Psychiatry,* 36, 731–56.

Westcott, H. and Jones, P. (1999) Annotation: The Abuse of Disabled Children. *Journal of Child Psychology and Psychiatry,* 40, 497–506.

Chapter 10

Special Needs Adolescent Sex Offenders: Characteristics and Treatment Outcome

Katherine V. Regan, Alicia Spidel, Heather M. Gretton, Rosalind E.H. Catchpole and Kevin S. Douglas

Introduction

Sexual violence is a serious public concern and assessing the treatment needs of sexual offenders presents a challenge for professionals working in this field. Adolescents are responsible for a significant proportion of sexual offences (Gal and Hoge, 1999; Worling and Curwen, 2000) compelling the need for ongoing development of clinical interventions for sex offending youths. To date, the development of clinical services has vastly outpaced empirical research aimed at understanding characteristics of adolescent sex offenders (Becker, 1998).

The literature examining characteristics of adolescent sex offenders indicates that they are a heterogeneous group (Becker, 1998; Becker, Harris and Sales, 1993; Shaw et al., 1993) with a wide range of problems and needs. Some problems identified among adolescent sex offenders include a history of serious learning or behavioural difficulties in school (Awad and Saunders, 1989; Becker, Cunningham-Rathner and Kaplan, 1986; Davis and Leitenberg, 1987) immaturity, social isolation and poor peer relationships (Gal and Hoge, 1999; Graves et al., 1996) impulse control problems and conduct disorder (CD) (Awad and Saunders, 1989; Gal and Hoge, 1999; James and Neil, 1996; Smith, Monastersky and Deisher, 1987) and high rates of depression, attention deficit hyperactivity disorder (ADHD) and other mental health issues (Becker et al., 1991; Kavoussi, Kaplan and Becker, 1988). Researchers have also found a relatively high prevalence of alcohol and substance abuse among both adolescent sex offenders and their parents (Newcombe, Measham and Parker, 1995). Moreover, their environments are more likely to be characterised by family instability, disorganisation, and violence (Awad and Saunders, 1989; Gal and Hoge, 1999; Graves et al., 1996).

Although some co-morbidity is present among most adolescent sexual offenders, some adolescent sex offenders present with a pattern of co-morbid problems characterised as 'special needs' (SN) (Gilby, Wolf and Goldberg, 1989; Schilling and Schinke, 1989) and require a remedial approach to sex offender treatment. These SN can be reflected in intellectual or interpersonal deficits that impact a youth's ability to benefit from treatment. Although definitions vary, estimates of the prevalence of SN among sex-offending adolescents range from 21 to 50 per cent (Day, 1989; Hayes, 1991; Schilling and Schinke, 1989). When considered in the context of SN, social contextual histories, diagnostic patterns, and offence types are also factors that may potentially interfere with the youths' abilities to comprehend and succeed in a regular treatment programme.

At this time, there is little literature to guide clinicians in the assessment and treatment of SN sex offenders. Some Sex Offender Treatment Programs (SOTPs) simply exclude youths who do not have the intellectual capacity to participate in a standard programme (Scavo and Buchannan, 1989). Other programmes do admit youths with 'wide-ranging needs' (Bremer, 1992: 331) to group sex offender treatment, and acknowledge that although these youths may not get the individual attention they need, they are at least addressing their sex offending issues. Finally, other programmes develop in-house strategies for assessing and implementing remedial programmes for SN adolescent sex offenders.

Youth Forensic Psychiatric Services (YFPS) in Burnaby, British Columbia is a forensic assessment and treatment facility that has developed an in-house programme for SN adolescent sex offenders. In the course of providing sex offender treatment, clinicians at YFPS began to identify certain youths that required extra attention and support beyond that offered in the regular treatment programme. Consequently, in 1990, a modified SOTP was initiated to meet the needs of these clinician-identified youths. Despite the implementation of a modified programme, to date there has been no consistent, empirically determined assessment strategy for making decisions about whether or not a youth is considered as having SN and thus requiring a remedial approach to treatment. A review of the literature provided no assistance in developing guidelines for determining whether a youth has SN. Furthermore, research on the efficacy of SN SOTP programmes is lacking, leaving the question open as to whether this modified SOTP is effective in reducing re-offending. As an initial step towards addressing some of these basic questions, we undertook a review of the SN SOTP at YFPS.

The present study examined 60 SN adolescent sexual offenders that attended a modified adolescent SOTP at YFPS and compared them to 58 randomly chosen non-special needs (Non-SN) adolescent sex offenders that attended a regular SOTP during the same time period. The goals of the present study were twofold. The primary goal was to describe relevant characteristics (intellectual functioning, diagnostic patterns, social-contextual factors and offence history) of SN sex offending youths that could assist clinicians and others in planning intervention and risk management strategies. Given the high prevalence of SN among youth involved in the clinical justice system (Gilby et al., 1989) the lack of studies in this area is in need of redressing. A secondary goal of the present study was to examine criminal recidivism for these SN youths following intervention and compare this with the Non-SN youths. Given the additional challenges faced by SN youths, we raised the question about a possible increased risk for criminal recidivism following treatment. We present criminal record outcome data for both the SN and Non-SN youths at an average of eight years following participation in the programs. The present study represents a preliminary step towards the development of a systematic, empirically driven assessment strategy for SN youths that is linked specifically to their treatment needs.

Method

Participants

Participants were 118 adolescent males who had confessed to or were convicted of one or more violations of sections in the Criminal Code of Canada relating to sexual offending. These

youths were directed by the courts or by their probation officers to attend the SOTP at YFPS, an outpatient treatment facility in British Columbia, between October 1990 and June 1999.

SN participants included 60 adolescent males, aged 12 to 19 at the time of assessment ($M = 15.7$ years, $SD = 1.4$). Comparison group participants were 58 Non-SN adolescent males, aged 13 to 18 at the time of assessment ($M = 15.7$ years, $SD = 1.5$). The 58 youths in the Non-SN group were randomly selected from all youths who attended the non-modified SOTP.

The ethnic composition of the SN and Non-SN groups (valid percentages) was as follows: White, 56.9 per cent and 71.1 per cent respectively; Aboriginal, 33.3 per cent and 19.1 per cent respectively; Asian 0 per cent and 6.5 per cent respectively; and East Indian, 7.8 per cent and 2.2 per cent respectively. The treatment groups did not differ significantly in terms of ethnic composition.

Referral criteria

The SOTP co-ordinator, in consultation with a psychologist or psychiatrist and a social worker, assessed all youths prior to their attendance in the SOTP to determine whether they would participate in the regular or modified SOTP. A youth's designation as SN, and subsequent referral to the modified SOTP, was based on the clinicians' global sense of the youth, and incorporated factors such as cognitive level, adaptive functioning, and social skills. There were no specific criteria for referral to the SN treatment group; however, prior to admission to the SOTP the youths underwent a battery of psychological tests and interviews. Some youths were referred to the SN group based on clinical assessments and psychological testing, whereas others were assigned to the SN group after an interview with the SOTP co-ordinator.

Sex Offender Treatment Programme (SOTP)

The SOTP at YFPS employs a cognitive-behavioural approach to treatment, and includes both group and individual components. Topics covered during group sessions included: sex education; victim empathy; social skills; dating and dating violence; 'problem cycles' (routes to offending, or individual areas of difficulty associated with youths' sexual offending) and relapse prevention techniques. SOTP groups met twice weekly for one and one-half hours at a time for approximately eight months. Youths also attended individual appointments with one of the group leaders during the course of the group. In some cases the individual treatment began before the group and in some cases it started after the group had finished. During individual appointments, youths reviewed group material, addressed personal issues, and underwent covert sensitisation treatment that involved pairing deviant fantasy with aversive consequences.

SN youths attended a remedial version of the SOTP group. There was a maximum of six SN youths in each treatment group, compared to approximately eight youths in the regular SOTP. Although the material covered in the SN group sessions was very similar to that covered in the regular SOTP, SN group leaders used additional methods of presenting and reviewing material. For example, newspaper articles, role-playing, videos, cartoons, homework exercises, and quizzes were used to reinforce learning. In addition, more time was spent reviewing previous material than in the regular SOTP. There were no specific differences between SN and Non-SN individual meetings. Both the SN and non-SN group components of treatment have manuals that detailed treatment protocols.

Procedures

We recorded intellectual, diagnostic, background and offence data from extensive file history information. This file information included psychiatric and psychological evaluations (including psychological test data and reports) social histories, police and victim statements, predisposition reports, interview notes, and progress summaries documented for the duration of each participant's attendance in treatment. Individual information and identifying features were kept confidential through a data coding system.

Intellectual

Data from the Wechsler Intelligence Scale for Children – Third Edition (WISC-III; Wechsler, 1991) or Wechsler Adult Intelligence Scale – Third

Edition (WAIS-III; Wechsler, 1997) were obtained from file records. The WISC-III and WAIS-III are individually administered clinical instruments for assessing intellectual functioning. The WISC-III is used with children aged 6 to 16 years; while the WAIS-III is used with adults aged 16 through to 89. In the present study, we used three composite scores: the Full Scale IQ (FSIQ) derived from both the Verbal and Performance subtests; the Verbal IQ (VIQ), derived from the Verbal subtests; and the Performance IQ (PIQ), derived from the Performance subtests. IQ scores are normally distributed with a mean of 100 and a standard deviation of 15 (Wechsler, 1991, 1997). Reliability data show that the Wechsler Intelligence Scales are reliable and valid measures of cognitive functioning (Allen and Thorndike, 1995a, 1995b; Siegel and Piotrowski, 1994). Several youths in both groups completed either the WISC-R or the WAIS-R, previous and comparable versions of the WISC-III and WAIS-III, as a result of the time of their assessment.

Diagnostic variables

CD and ADHD symptoms were coded according to DSM-IV (American Psychiatric Association, 1994) criteria from clinical notes in the file, which were based on observed behaviour, as well as on information obtained from collateral sources, parents and probation officers.

Presence or absence of foetal alcohol syndrome or foetal alcohol effects (FAS/FAE) was determined from clinical notes in the file, which were based on information obtained during the psychiatric/psychological evaluations and from collateral sources. Substance use information was obtained from clinical notes in the files based on self-report or collateral information. After reviewing the information on substance abuse, coders were instructed to rate the severity of substance abuse as 'none' (no substance abuse) 'mild' (occasional recreational use that has little impact on the youth's functioning) 'moderate' (use more frequent, causes some impairment in functioning) or 'severe' (frequent use, causes significant impairment in functioning).

Background and offence history

Educational background (average education attained, number of alternate schools attended and reasons for attending alternate schools), family background (primary caregivers, time in foster care and number of foster homes lived in) referral offence information (index offence and victim characteristics), and suicide history were coded from clinical notes in the file. These were based on observed behaviour as well as information obtained from collateral sources.

Outcome variables

We obtained criminal record information from BC Cornet, a provincial data source, on December 10, 2003, corresponding to an 8-year follow-up. Offence-related data were recorded from this source. The follow-up period was defined as the number of months from discharge from the SOTP to December 10, 2003. The mean follow-up time was 98 months ($SD=35.7$ months) or slightly over eight years, for both groups. The mean age at follow-up was 28.7 years ($SD=49.2$ years) for both SN and Non-SN youths.

General (i.e. any) offences were defined as any charges or convictions that occurred during the follow-up period. Non-violent offences included theft, break and enter, possession of stolen property, arson, fraud, escaping custody, breaches, resisting arrest, obstructing a police officer, mischief, driving offences, and drug offences. Violent offences included murder, assault, assault causing bodily harm or with a weapon, aggravated assault, robbery, intimidation, harassment or stalking, and possession or use of a weapon or firearm. Sexual offences included sexual assault, sexual interference, and sexual assault with a weapon.

Results

SN and non-SN group characteristics
A. Intellectual functioning

The mean intellectual scores for youths in both groups are shown in Table 1. Measures of intellectual functioning (WAIS-III/WISC-III) were available for 83 per cent of SN and 78 per cent of Non-SN youths. SN youths exhibited lower overall intellectual functioning, as exhibited by lower average FSIQ scores (Low Average Range) when compared to the Non-SN group (Average Range), $t(88) = -5.52$, $p < .001$. FSIQ scores for the SN group were, on average, 15 points below that of the Non-SN group. SN youths also had lower verbal IQs than did Non-SN youths. There was a 15-point difference between the two groups in average VIQ. On average, the SN youths had VIQs in the Borderline Range, compared to Average Range functioning in the Non-SN group, $t(88) = -5.76$, $p < .001$. There was a 10-point difference in PIQ between the SN and Non-SN groups. The SN group had a PIQ in the Low Average Range whereas the Non-SN group had a PIQ in the Average Range, $t(88) = -3.46$, $p = 0.001$.

B. Diagnostic information

Diagnostic information, as well as information about suicide, self-injurious behaviour, and alcohol and drug use, is presented in Table 2. A higher proportion of SN youths compared to Non-SN youths were diagnosed with a learning disability (χ^2 (1, $N=94$) $= 18.43$, $p < .001$), ADHD (χ^2 (1, $N=95$) $= 5.61$, $p = 0.018$), and FAS/FAE (χ^2

Table 10.1   Intellectual functioning and educational background of SN and non-SN groups

	SN Group		Non-SN Group	
	Mean (SD)	% Under 70	Mean (SD)	% Under 70
Full scale IQ**	80.2 (12.4)	13.3	94.9 (12.7)	0.0
Verbal IQ**	78.5 (11.3)	16.7	93.5 (13.4)	3.4
Performance IQ**	87.2 (13.7)	5.0	97.3 (14.0)	1.7
Mean grade achieved	8.5 (1.5)		8.8 (1.3)	
Attended alternate school (%)	41.7		32.8	
Learning difficulties[a]	20.0		5.3	
Behavioural problems[a]	32.0		52.6	
Behavioural and learning difficulties[a]	24.0		42.1	

[a]These are percentages of those youths in each group who attended alternate school.
**$p < .01$.

Table 10.2 Psychological characteristics of SN and non-SN groups

	SN Group	Non-SN Group
Learning disability diagnosis (%)**	63.3	22.4
ADHD diagnosis (%)*	55.0	36.2
FAS/FAE diagnosis (%)**	13.3	0.0
Conduct disorder diagnosis (%)	45.0	46.6
Suicide/Self-injurious behaviour (%)		
Considered suicide	25.0	32.8
Attempted suicide	18.3	8.6
Engaged in self-injurious behaviour	35.0	19.0
Daily or weekly alcohol and/or drug use (%)[a]	18.3	19.0

[a]Data available for 63% of SN youths and 67% of Non-SN youths *$p<.05$. **$p<.01$.

$(1, N=93)=7.53, p=0.019)$. The SN and Non-SN groups did not differ with respect to the proportion of youths diagnosed with CD. The SN and Non-SN groups also had similar rates of drug and alcohol use.

C. Family background

SN youths were less likely than were Non-SN youths to have had both biological parents as primary caregivers throughout childhood until age 12 (2 per cent versus 21 per cent, respectively), $\chi^2 (1, N=115)=11.62, p=0.001$. More youths in the SN group had their biological mother as their sole caregiver (77 per cent) as compared to Non-SN youths (43 per cent), $\chi^2 (1, N=115)=11.83, p=0.001$, who were more likely to have other family members or foster parents as their caregivers. A similar proportion of youths in both the SN and Non-SN groups had spent time in foster homes during childhood (67 per cent and 53 per cent, respectively). The average number of foster homes youths in both groups had lived in (2.4 and 3.1, respectively) was also similar.

D. Offenders' background and offence history

Educational background. Table 1 shows that youths in both the SN and Non-SN groups had obtained, on average, a grade 8 education. A similar percentage of youths in each group had attended an alternate school at some point in their lives. Although not statistically significant, the relative percentages suggest a greater tendency for SN youths to attend alternate school due to learning difficulties, and a tendency for Non-SN youths to attend alternate school because of behavioural problems, or due to a combination of behavioural and learning difficulties.

Offence history. The SN and Non-SN groups had similar offence histories prior to treatment (see Table 3). Most youths in both groups had been charged with or convicted of a sexual offence prior to treatment. Fifteen percent of the SN group and 9 per cent of the Non-SN group, however, were referred to treatment without being specifically charged or convicted of a sexual offence because they had a history of engaging in deviant sexual activity. This type of referral for treatment without a charge or

Table 10.3 Pre-treatment offences in the SN and Non-SN groups

	SN Group		Non-SN Group	
	Percent offending	Average number of offences (SD)	Percent offending	Average number of offences (SD)
Any offence[a]	95.0	6.31 (6.8)	98.3	6.00 (6.9)
Non-violent offence	60.0	4.08 (5.5)	48.3	3.70 (6.3)
Violent offence	38.3	0.95 (1.5)	29.3	0.79 (1.8)
Sexual offence	85.0	1.27 (0.9)	91.4	1.30 (0.7)

[a]The average number of offences is not significantly different between groups.

Table 10.4   Characteristics of index offending for the SN and Non-SN groups

	SN Group	Non-SN Group
Mean age at index offence (*SD*)	14.9 (*1.5*)	15.1 (*1.7*)
Age of index offence victim (%)*		
≤5 years	40.0	27.6
6–11 years	43.3	44.8
12–18 years*	5.0	19.0
19–60 years	18.3	6.9
Over 60 years	1.7	0.0
Relationship to index offence victim (%)		
Family member	40.0	41.4
Friend	5.0	12.1
Acquaintance	33.3	22.4
Stranger	20.0	12.1
Index offence occurred baby-sitting (%)*	18.3	31.0
Gender of index offence victim (%)		
Female only	60.0	69.0
Male only	20.0	17.2
Both	13.3	8.6
Threats used in index offence (%)	28.3	31.0
Location of index offence (%)		
Private home	76.0	70.7
Public	20.0	18.9
Intoxication during index offence (%)ᵃ	8.3	10.3

ᵃData available for 82% of SN and 52% of Non-SN youths.
*$p < .05$.

conviction for a sexual offence may represent the tendency of the Youth Courts to in some circumstances convict on a lesser but related charge and may in some cases be the result of plea bargaining. For example, a youth could commit an offence of a sexual nature but due to insufficient evidence be charged with a simple assault.

Characteristics of index offence

Table 4 shows the index offence and victim characteristics for both the SN and Non-SN group. Youths in both groups were similar in age at the time of the index offence. The age of the index offence victim differed significantly between the SN and Non-SN groups, χ^2 (3, $N = 108) = 10.19$, $p = 0.017$. Specifically, Non-SN youths were more likely to victimise peer-aged youths (ages 12–18 years) than were SN youths, χ^2 (1, $N = 108) = 8.97$, $p = 0.003$. However, for both groups, the majority of victims were still children aged 11 years and younger (83 per cent of SN youths and 72 per cent of Non-SN youths).

SN and Non-SN youths had similar relationships to their victims. About 40 per cent of index offences in both groups involved a family member, and about 35 per cent involved a friend or acquaintance (i.e., a known non-family member or babysitting relationship). One fifth (20 per cent) of index offences in the SN group and 12 per cent of index offences in the Non-SN group involved a stranger. More index offences in the Non-SN (31 per cent) group than in the SN group (18 per cent) occurred while baby-sitting, χ^2 (1, $N = 104) = 4.10$, $p = 0.043$.

There were no differences between SN and Non-SN youths in the gender of the victim. In both groups, the majority of index offences involved only female victims. In both groups slightly less than a third of the index offences involved threats. The majority of index offences for both groups took place in a private home, but about one fifth took place in a public setting (e.g., school, park, etc.). A relatively small proportion of youths in both groups were intoxicated during the commission of the index offence.

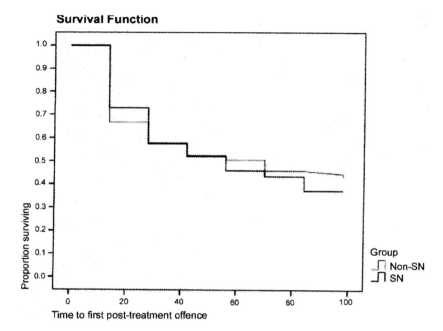

Figure 10.1   Recidivism rates for SN and Non-SN adolescent sex offenders during the 98-month follow-up period.

Criminal outcome following discharge from treatment

Recidivism rates for both groups at follow up (i.e. the 98-month follow-up period) are shown in Figure 10.1. A similar proportion of youths in the SN (57.6 per cent) and non-SN (55.2 per cent) groups re-offended during the eight-year follow-up period. The number of offences, on average, that SN and Non-SN youths committed after release from treatment was not significantly different. Overall, the combined recidivism rates across SN and Non-SN youths eight years following discharge were, on average, 14 per cent for sexual offences, 32 per cent for violent offences, 54 per cent for non-violent offences, and 57 per cent for general (any) offences. There were no significant differences across any of these offence types between SN and non-SN youths.

Survival analyses for each group were performed for offences committed during the follow-up period. This is an important analysis when examining recidivism data as it examines the time it takes for a youth to re-offend, rather than simply the occurrence of re-offending. The survival function or survival curve represents the cumulative proportion of youths who have *not* re-offended by a fixed point in time. Over time, as participants re-offend, the survival curve

decreases (Greenhouse, Stangl, and Bromberg, 1989). The average number of months to first offence was 55.5 months for non-violent offences, 75.3 months for violent offences, and 86.6 months for sexual offences. The survival functions between the SN and Non-SN groups were not significantly different for any of the offence types.

Discussion

Although the development of clinical services for adolescent sex offenders has exploded in recent years (McGrath, Hoke and Vojtisek, 1998; Worling and Curwen, 2000) theoretical understanding and characterisation of the functioning of these individuals has not kept pace. In particular, the identification and characterisation of adolescent sex offenders that present with special needs that impact their ability to benefit from treatment is an important, yet under-researched area of study (Timms and Goreczny, 2002). The present study represents a first step in examining this significant topic.

The first goal of the present study was to compare the intellectual, diagnostic, background and offence histories of SN and Non-SN treated adolescent sex offenders in order to determine the ways in which SN youths present with unique challenges that may influence treatment amenability. Overall, the characteristics of youths in both groups are consistent with those described in the literature on adolescent sex offenders in general. Similar to what has been found in past research (Awad and Saunders, 1989; Becker et al., 1991; Gal and Hoge, 1999) SN youths were characterised by lower overall intellectual functioning than their Non-SN counterparts. Of particular relevance, their verbal intellectual scores were on average fifteen points lower than those of Non-SN youths, and in the Borderline range. This indicates a significant impairment in verbal functioning. SN youths also had substantially higher rates of learning disabilities. Intellectual weaknesses and learning deficits among SN adolescent sex offenders have implications for understanding routes to offending and intervention needs of these youths. Weak verbal skills may limit the ability of SN youths to verbally modulate their behaviour (Hayes, 1991). In addition, learning deficits are likely to affect the integration and application of materials presented in a psycho-educational or cognitive behavioural treatment setting. These intellectual deficits highlight the need for specialised programming that takes into account individual needs and cognitive deficits (Schoen and Hoover, 1990).

Diagnostically, SN youths had higher rates of FAS/FAE and ADHD than did Non-SN youths. Higher rates of these disorders suggest attentional and impulse-related behavioural problems amongst SN sex offending youths that should be addressed. Weak intellectual skills and learning deficits, along with attention and impulsive behavioural problems, may contribute to limited internal resources to reason and to inhibit sexually intrusive or aggressive behaviour (Schilling and Schinke, 1989; Schoen and Hoover, 1990). The high rates of FAS/E and ADHD in this sample of SN youths, when viewed in combination with intellectual deficits, indicate the importance of incorporating impulse-control modules into an intervention programme for SN youths.

Some clinicians and researchers have recommended that programmes for youths with relatively weak verbal intellectual skills, along with attentional and impulsive behavioural problems, are behaviourally based, structured, and have consistent behavioural expectations (Cantwell, 1996; Short and Hess, 1995). Those working specifically with SN youths suggest that

programmes designed for them incorporate continuity of tasks from week to week, a progression from simpler to more complex tasks, and short-term tasks and goals where completion and success are attainable (Marriage, Gordon, and Brand, 1995; Short and Hess, 1995). Moreover, researchers and educators advocate an individualised approach to treatment that includes identifying and bolstering the individuals' particular strengths (Short and Hess, 1995; Szatmari, 1991). Overall, as suggested by the current study and previous research, intellectual functioning, learning deficits, attention deficits and impulsivity are important areas to evaluate and focus on when planning sex offending interventions, follow-up in the community, and risk management strategies.

Other factors that have been shown in the literature to have a relationship to sex offending are social-contextual factors such as family support and strong bonds with caregivers and other adults. Family dysfunction, including childhood separation from the primary caregiver, is a risk factor for adolescent sex offending and delinquency (Davis and Leitenberg, 1987; Kandel, 1996). In line with this research, the SN youths in our sample were less likely to have both biological parents as primary caregivers throughout childhood compared with the Non-SN youths, although both SN and Non-SN youths had family backgrounds characterised by marked instability. A stable home environment and a family's ability to provide secure attachment relationships and consistency are other factors associated with adaptive psychological development in children (Rey et al., 1997). Further, research suggests that youths that exhibit behavioural or psychological problems are more likely to benefit from and complete treatment if they come from a stable home environment (Morrissey-Kane and Prinz, 1999). This suggests that an examination of the family functioning of sex-offending youths is an important area of study when planning sex offender treatment. In the present study, SN youths were less likely than were Non-SN youths to have had both biological parents as primary caregivers throughout childhood until age 12. Clinically, one can hypothesise that, given SN youths' cognitive and psychosocial vulnerabilities, family instability may be an especially important consideration for the development of a comprehensive treatment strategy. Interestingly, the majority of SN sex offending youths had only their biological mother as the most consistent caregiver throughout childhood. Furthermore, almost two-thirds of SN sex offending youths had been in foster care at some point, suggesting instability of caregiving in these youths' upbringing. This suggests that future research into treatment for sex offending youths may benefit from an examination of how attachment and other child-caregiver factors may be incorporated into these intervention programmes (Moore, Moretti and Holland, 1998).

The second goal of the current investigation was to examine and compare criminal record outcome for SN and non-SN youths at the eight-year follow-up time. At the end of the follow-up period, the general (60 per cent) and sexual (14 per cent) rates for youths who have committed another offence fell within the range of outcomes reported in the literature for treated adolescent sex offenders (Becker, 1990; Gretton et al., 2001). The few controlled outcome studies examining the effectiveness of treatment for adolescent sex offenders generally find sexual re-offence rates ranging from 6 to 15 per cent, depending on the follow up length (Becker, 1990; Bremer, 1992; Gretton et al., 2001; Smith and Monastersky, 1986). Recidivism rates are higher for general re-offending, at around 50 per cent (Kahn and Chambers, 1991). In spite of their cognitive and behavioural deficits and presumed need for greater intervention, SN outcomes following a remedial treatment programme were consistent with those found in the general literature on treated adolescent sex offenders, and were similar to the rates of re-offending among non-SN youths in this study. These findings are promising in that they indicate that a modified SOTP is associated with similar recidivism rates as a standard SOTP, despite the general consensus that SN individuals are more treatment resistant and have more issues that need to be addressed in treatment (Gilby et al., 1989; Schilling and Schinke, 1989). The finding that SN youths in our study re-offended at rates similar to their treated Non-SN counterparts provides some preliminary evidence that sex offender treatment strategies may be effectively modified for use with SN adolescent sex offenders, although clearly more work is needed in this under researched area.

Current trends in youth justice include treatment programmes in which criminogenic factors are specifically targeted for treatment (Andrews, Bonta and Hoge, 1990; Dowden and

Andrews, 2000; MacKenzie, Wilson, Armstrong and Gover, 2001). This risk-needs approach allows for the tailoring of treatment to particular youth needs, rather than the 'one size fits all,' offence-based treatment approaches, which have been the norm to date. Establishing differential risk factors among SN sex offending youths is an important step in understanding the course of sex offending behaviour from adolescence into adulthood, and will allow clinicians and others to plan and modify risk management strategies accordingly (Worling, 2001). The present study found important differences in the intellectual, diagnostic, and family history profiles of adolescent sex offenders presenting with SN. Treatment programmes for SN youths would benefit from intervention strategies that specifically target some of the co-morbid difficulties faced by these youths.

Some limitations of the current investigation need to be acknowledged. First, the data collected was based exclusively on retrospective file information. This resulted in a lack of information in some cases, and did not allow for an exhaustive review of the clinical characteristics of SN youths. Second, the present study did not directly address the question of whether the modified SOTP was associated with specific improvements in treatment outcome, above and beyond what would occur when SN youths attended a regular SOTP. In order to address these issues, a prospective randomised design whereby SN youths attend either a regular or modified programme, where the variables of interest are decided prior to the treatment beginning, is needed, and an important goal for future research.

Despite these limitations, the present investigation demonstrated that although SN individuals presented with characteristics that may contribute to treatment resistance (e.g., impulsive behavioural disorders and learning deficits) modification of a standard sex offender programme was associated with recidivism rates comparable to those of non-SN sexual offenders. These findings are of particular interest to those working with special needs sex offenders. The current study proposes that even at a follow-up time of eight years, a modified SOTP may be worthwhile with SN populations. Perhaps most importantly, the present study represents an initial step in investigating this extremely important, and previously neglected, area of research. It raises important questions for further study regarding the characteristics and treatment prognosis of adolescent sexual offenders presenting with SN.

References

Allen, S.R. and Thorndike, R.M. (1995a) Stability of the WAIS-R and WISC-III Factor Structure Using Cross-Validation of Covariance Structures. *Journal of Clinical Psychology*. 51, 648–57.

Allen, S.R. and Thorndike, R.M. (1995b) Stability of the WPPSI--R and WISC-III Factor Structure Using Cross-Validation of Covariance Structure Models. *Journal of Psychoeducational Assessment*. 13, 3–20.

Andrews, D.A., Bonta, J. and Hoge, B.D. (1990) Classification for Effective Rehabilitation: Rediscovering Psychology. *Criminal Justice and Behaviour*, 17, 19–52.

American Psychiatric Association (1994) *Diagnostic and Statistical Manual of Mental Disorders*. 4th edn. Washington, DC: Author [DSM-IV].

Awad, G.A. and Saunders, E.B. (1989) Adolescent Child Molesters: Clinical Observations. *Child Psychiatry and Human Development*, 19, 195–206.

Becker, J.V. (1990) Treating Adolescent Sexual Offenders, *Professional Psychology: Research and Practice*. 21, 362–5.

Becker, J.V. (1998) The Assessment of Adolescent Perpetrators of Childhood Sexual Abuse. *The Irish Journal of Psychology*. 19, 68–81.

Becker, J.V., Cunningham-Rathner, J. and Kaplan, M.S. (1986) Adolescent Sexual Offenders: Demographics, Criminal and Sexual Histories, and Recommendations for Reducing Future Offences. *Journal of Interpersonal Violence*. 1, 431–45.

Becker, J.V., Harris, C.D. and Sales, B.D. (1993) Juveniles Who Commit Sex Offenses: A Critical Review of Research. In Hall, G.C.N. et al. (Eds.) *Sexual Aggression: Issues in Etiology, Assessment and Treatment*. Washington, DC: Taylor and Francis.

Becker, J.V., Kaplan, M.S., Tenke, D.E. and Tartaglini, A. (1991) The Incidence of Depressive Symptomatology in Juvenile Sex Offenders with a History of Abuse. *Child Abuse and Neglect*. 15, 531–36.

Bremer, J.F. (1992) Serious Juvenile Sex Offenders: Treatment and Long-Term Follow-up. *Psychiatric Annals*. 22, 326–32.

Cantwell, D.P. (1996) Attention Deficit Disorder: A Review of the Past 10 years. *Journal of the American Academy of Child and Adolescent Psychiatry*. 35, 978–87.

Davis, G.E. and Leitenberg, H. (1987) Adolescent Sex Offenders. *Psychological Bulletin*. 101, 417–27.

Day, K. (1994.) Male Mentally Handicapped Sex Offenders. *British Journal of Psychiatry*. 165, 630–9.

Dowden, C. and Andrews, D.A. (2000) Effective Correctional Treatment and Violent Reoffending: A Meta-analysis. *Canadian Journal of Criminology*. 42, 449–69.

Gal, M. and Hoge, R.D. (1999) A Profile of the Adolescent Sex Offender. *Forum on Corrections Research*. 11, 7–11.

Gilby, R., Wolf, L. and Goldberg, B. (1989) Mentally Retarded Adolescent Sex Offenders: A Survey and Pilot Study. *Canadian Journal of Psychiatry*. 24, 542–8.

Graves, R.B. et al. (1996) Demographic and Parental Characteristics and Youthful Sexual Offenders. *International Journal of Offender Therapy and Comparative Criminology*. 40, 300–17.

Greenhouse, J.B., Stangl, D. and Bromberg, J. (1989) An Introduction to Survival Analysis: Statistical Methods for Analysis of Clinical Trial Data. *Journal of Consulting and Clinical Psychology*. 57, 536–44.

Gretton, H.M. et al. (2001) Psychopathy and Recidivism in Adolescent Sex Offenders. *Criminal Justice and Behaviour*. 28, 427–49.

Hayes, L.L. (1991) Sex Differences in Demands and Support of Social Networks. *Dissertation Abstracts International*. 52, 32–94.

James, A.C. and Neil, P. (1996) Juvenile Sexual Offending: One-Year Period Prevalence Study within Oxfordshire. *Child Abuse and Neglect*. 20, 477–85.

Kahn, T.J., and Chambers, H. (1991) Assessing Re-offense Risk with Juvenile Sex Offenders. *Child Welfare*. 70, 333–45.

Kandel, D.B. (1996) The Parental and Peer Contexts of Adolescent Deviance: An Algebra of Interpersonal Influences. *Journal of Drug Issues*. 26, 289–315.

Kavoussi, R., Kaplan, M. and Becker, J.V. (1988) Psychiatric Diagnoses in Adolescent Sex Offenders. *Journal of the American Academy of Child and Adolescent Psychiatry*. 27, 241–3.

MacKenzie, D.L. et al. (2001) The Impact of Boot Camps and Traditional Institutions on Juvenile

Residents: Perceptions, Adjustment, and Change. *Journal of Research in Crime and Delinquency.* 38, 279–313.

Marriage, K.J., Gordon, V. and Brand, L. (1995) A Social Skills Group for Boys with Asperger's Syndrome. *Australian and New Zealand Journal of Psychiatry.* 29, 58–62.

McGrath, R.J., Hoke, S.E. and Vojtisek, J.E. (1998) Cognitive-behavioural Treatment of Sex Offenders: A Treatment Comparison and Long-Term Follow-up Study. *Criminal Justice and Behaviour.* 25, 203–25.

Moore, K., Moretti, M.M. and Holland, R. (1998) A New Perspective on Youth Care Programs: Using Attachment Theory to Guide Interventions for Troubled Youth. *Residential Treatment for Children and Youth.* 15, 1–24.

Morrissey-Kane, E. and Prinz, R.J. (1999) Engagement in Child and Adolescent Treatment: The Role of Parental Cognitions and Attributions. *Clinical Child and Family Psychology Review.* 2, 183–98.

Newcombe, R., Measham, F. and Parker, H. (1995) A Survey of Drinking and Deviant Behaviour among 14/15 Year Olds in North West England. *Addiction Research.* 2, 319–41.

Rey, J.M. et al. (1997) A Global Scale to Measure the Quality of the Family Environment. *Archives of General Psychiatry.* 54, 817–22.

Scavo, R. and Buchanan, B.D. (1989) Group Therapy for Male Adolescent Sex Offenders: A Model for Residential Treatment. *Residential Treatment for Children and Youth.* 7, 59–74.

Schilling, R.F. and Schinke, S.P. (1989) Mentally Retarded Sex Offenders: Fact, Fiction and Treatment. *Journal of Social Work and Human Sexuality.* 7, 33–48.

Schoen, J. and Hoover, J.H. (1990) Mentally Retarded Sex Offenders. *Journal of Offender Rehabilitation.* 16, 81–91.

Shaw, J.A. et al. (1993) Young Boys who Commit Serious Sexual Offenses: Demographics, Psychometrics, and Phenomenology. *Bulletin of the American Academy of Psychiatry and Law.* 21, 399–408.

Short, R.H. and Hess, G.C. (1995) Foetal Alcohol Syndrome: Characteristics and Remedial Implications. *Developmental Disabilities Bulletin.* 23, 12–29.

Siegel, D.J. and Piotrowski, R.J. (1994) Reliability of WISC-III Subtest Composites. *Assessment.* 1, 249–53.

Smith, W.R. and Monastersky, C. (1986) Assessing Juvenile Sexual Offenders' Risk for Reoffending. *Criminal Justice and Behaviour.* 13, 115–40.

Smith, W.R., Monastersky, C. and Deisher, R.M. (1987) MMPI-based Personality Types among Juvenile Sex Offenders. *Journal of Clinical Psychology.* 43, 422–30.

Szatmari, P. (1991) Asperger's Syndrome: Diagnosis, Treatment, and Outcome. *Psychiatric Clinics of North America,* 14, 81–93.

Timms, S. and Goreczny, A.J. (2002) Adolescent Sex Offenders with Mental Retardation Literature Review and Assessment Considerations. *Aggression and Violent Behaviour.* 7, 1–19.

Wechsler, D. (1991) *Wechsler Intelligence Scale for Children, Manual.* 3rd edn. Orlando, FL: Harcourt Brace Jovanovich.

Wechsler, D. (1997) *Wechsler Adult Intelligence Scale, Administration and Scoring Manual.* 3rd edn. Orlando, FL: Harcourt Brace Jovanovich.

Worling, J.A. (2001) Personality-based Typology of Adolescent Male Sexual Offenders: Differences in Recidivism Rates, Victim-Selection Characteristics, and Personal Victimisation Histories. *Sexual Abuse: Journal of Research and Treatment.* 13, 149–66.

Worling, J.R. and Curwen, T. (2000) Adolescent Sexual Offender Recidivism: Success of Specialised Treatment and Implications for Risk Prediction. *Child Abuse and Neglect.* 24, 965–82.

Chapter 11

Adolescent Risk Assessment: Practice, Policy, Language, and Ourselves

David S. Prescott

Introduction

Events of the past few years have changed the way professionals think about youth who have sexually abused. In America, public policy and the legal system have turned to increasingly harsh punishments for sexual abuse in the form of tougher dispositions, community notification, and registration. Waiving youth to adult courts has become commonplace, and efforts to enforce lifetime registration for youthful sexual abusers are occurring at the state and national level. Coffey (2006) observes that the sealing of young peoples' criminal records upon their entry into adulthood is no longer a core philosophy of the legal system. These changes have accompanied dramatic shifts in perspective for the public. Where so-called juvenile delinquents of all types, were once thought to be in need of education about accountability, public outcry increasingly demands that they be held accountable. Ironically, this has occurred in tandem with research demonstrating that base rates for sexual recidivism are lower than once believed (Alexander, 1999; Epperson et al., 2006), and that general criminality is often limited to adolescence (Moffitt, 1993).

The policies accompanying increased media coverage and public furore often prove the adage that 'bad cases make bad law.' Trivits and Repucci (2002) report that over half the states in the US required juveniles adjudicated for sex crimes to register despite the lack of evidence of either enhanced public safety or any reduction in recidivism. In a recent review, Coffey (2006: 82) notes that:

> Wisconsin is just one state that recently established a juvenile sexual offender registration law that significantly limits the confidentiality of this juvenile information (Assembly Bill 99, Wisconsin State Legislature, May 2005). While juveniles have already been required to register, this new law allows the community to be notified about the juvenile's sexual offence history. Law enforcement officials are the designated individuals to decide if the risk requires community notification. Unfortunately, law enforcement officials are not typically trained in making these types of assessments. Judges still have the option not to place a juvenile on the register in the disposition process, but this process has passed for the majority of the offenders on the list. The goal behind these laws is to provide information to the community with the hope that this will help protect the public from dangerous sexual offenders. Unfortunately, there is reason to be concerned that this public exposure for juvenile behaviour may make it more difficult for the juvenile to establish a non-offending adult lifestyle.

Wherever one stands on issues related to how punitive society should be towards young people who sexually abuse, it is clear that the pressure on professionals for accurate assessment risk has never been greater. Communities want safety in the short term, but it is not certain how current policy helps youth to refrain from misconduct in the long term. Further, there are no empirically validated methods for determining the risk of young people to re-offend sexually. Professionals working with youth who have sexually abused face increasing challenges to understand emerging research and changing policies in order to be most helpful to youth, communities, and those adults who supervise, educate, and treat young people.

This chapter invites professionals to look closely at the language they use. In doing so, new aspects of this work can become apparent. The chapter then moves on to review many of the challenges inherent in risk assessment, and concludes with frameworks for moving through an assessment. It does not review the current tools, which have received considerable attention elsewhere, but provides references for further information. Given the remarkable accumulation of information regarding youth who have sexually abused, risk assessment, and the active ingredients of change, professionals have an obligation to familiarise themselves with the emerging research, and to educate others.

Returning to the basics

Against the backdrop of advancing research and social attention to sex crimes, professionals may wish to reconsider some basic terms and tools in order to best strike a balance between the long-term needs of communities and youth.

Language

The meaning of words can change dramatically over time, and our use of language can often contribute to thoughts and actions. The term *juvenile sex offender* has come into criticism in many quarters (Longo and Prescott, 2006). In the US, the organisers of the National Adolescent Perpetration Network's annual conference actively reject the term. Criticisms range from the idea that professionals should label behaviour and not the youth to the idea that the term's origins in the law belie the complexities underlying the action. Given that youth who have sexually abused are more likely to re-offend non-sexually (Langstrom and Grann, 2000; Worling and Curwen, 2000), and emerging evidence that sexually abusive youth have more in common with other delinquent youth than with paedophiles (Chaffin, 2006) *juvenile sex offender* may subtly mislead lay people into further believing that these young people are destined to a lifetime of sex-related crime. With the increased media attention paid to the most egregious offences by adults, the term sex offender has (in the US) come to carry so many undesirable connotations that its effectiveness for describing youth is severely limited.

Some professionals feel that using the term *juvenile sex offender* can capture the attention of those youth and families that are minimising the harm of their actions. Given the changing climate of the public's understanding of sexual abusers, however, this term may have any number of undesired effects. For example, it could serve to convince young people that adults will never understand them due to their different perceptions of the term. It could also introduce new distorted thoughts about a young person's identity, and it may convince them and others that they are monsters rather than individuals who have engaged in hurtful behaviour, but have a future. It may be more useful to capture a youth's attention with more accurate language, such as 'you hurt someone'. Wherever one stands

on the issue of language, professionals will want to choose terminology that protects the long-term wellbeing of both youth and their environment.

The term *risk assessment* has gained currency among professionals working with youth, perhaps due to the recent validation of actuarial scales for adult sex offenders, and professionals' understandable desire to have information about an individual's dangerousness. These terms also deserve consideration. Hart, Kropp, and Laws (2004: 2) define *risk* as 'a hazard that is incompletely understood and whose occurrence therefore can only be forecast with uncertainty. The concept is multi-faceted, referring to the nature of the hazard, the likelihood that the hazard will occur, the frequency or duration of the hazard, the seriousness of the hazard's consequences, and imminence of the hazard; also, the concept of risk is inherently contextual, as hazards arise and exist in specific circumstances'.

The word *assessment* is also important. Hart, Kropp, and Laws (2004) define assessment in the mental health field as 'the process of gathering information for use in making decisions'. This differentiates the task from appraisal and evaluation, each of which often imply the use of testing and numerical values, but not necessarily the contribution of the process to decision-making or risk reduction strategies. Assessment, in this context, suggests that the examiner is interested in aspects beyond a simple probabilistic statement. This could include information about the seriousness, frequency, or context of future sexual abuse. It could also address specific contexts in which risk might increase or decrease. Thus, the phrase 'risk assessment' becomes the gathering of information specific to making decisions about a multi-faceted hazard, a hazard made more complicated by the developmental and contextual issues of youth (Ryan and Lane, 1997; Prentky and Righthand, 2003).

Taken together, professionals may wish to reconsider aspects of their language to avoid unknowingly handicapping their assessments. After all, the term *risk* does not necessarily lend itself to a comprehensive assessment of the individual's resilience or protective factors (Bremer, 2001, 2006). Nor does it account for an understanding of how family-based interventions can mitigate risk (Schladale, 2006; Thomas and Viar, 2006; Thomas, 1991). Likewise, the term risk assessment does not necessarily mean an assessment of those therapeutic or supervisory aspects that will mitigate risk. Professionals may wish to decide for themselves whether they are assessing a *juvenile sex offender* (with the inaccuracies and connotations that the term implies) or a *youth who has sexually abused* (which may be more statistically accurate). Given that youth are more likely to come into conflict with the law for non-sexual crimes than sexual ones, examiners may be more helpful to the youth, their family, and community by assessing a number of possible outcomes (Worling and Curwen, 2000; Langstrom and Grann, 2000; Nisbet, Wilson and Smallbone, 2004). These include sexual re-offence, violent re-offence, general re-offence, suicide, readiness for treatment, and ability to benefit from available treatment services.

In the end, however, the importance of attention to the varying shades of language is most apparent in professionals' determining what the specific referral question is. Some professionals asking for a risk assessment may simply be asking for a vague assessment of dangerousness, while others may be asking what specific steps will mitigate risk in the short and long terms. Some may ask for recommendations regarding placement, while others are not sure what they are asking. Without clarifying the nature of the language in the request, professionals may have no other way of knowing.

Tools

The field of assessing sexual abusers has experienced welcome growth in recent years. However, it is unfortunate that many outmoded tools such as those found in Gray and Wallace's (1992) *Adolescent Sexual Abuser Packet* are still in frequent use today. Many are self-report forms (e.g., the PHASE assessment of sexual interests), while others are checklists for clinicians (e.g., the Ross and Loss assessment tool, 1991) or other resources (e.g. the O'Brien and Bera Typology, 1986). Each of these tools made important contributions at a time when there were no alternatives; none has empirical validation. Although many of these tools remain in print and unrevised, professionals will wish to reconsider their use and, hopefully, discard them entirely in favour of newer scales that take better account of the literature from the years since the first tools became available.

In a recent review, Chaffin (2006) has summarised the history of evidence-based

assessment and treatment of youths who have sexually abused (which for purposes of his chapter he abbreviates as ASOs).

Finally, we might advance our treatment evidence knowledge base by changing how we define ourselves as a field and how we define our clients. The field of ASO treatment exists as a demarcated speciality area because a generation ago we defined the ASO population as special and different. Certainly, we did not discover the problem of adolescent sexual offending. The population has long existed, in approximately the same proportions as today. It was simply never defined as special or different. Prior to defining these youth as special, they were simply known as 'delinquents', and treated using the approaches of the larger delinquency field. The juvenile justice system and the delinquency treatment world have accepted the definition of these youth as different and special, and largely ceded them to the specialised field of adolescent sex offender treatment (Zimring, 2004). There is no controlled scientific evidence to suggest whether this has helped, hurt or made no difference. One thing, however, is certain. The general delinquency intervention field has moved rapidly forward in terms of Evidence-Based Practice, and the specialised ASO treatment field has not. The general delinquency intervention field has generated a range of empirically well-supported, evidence-based practices (Mihalic et al., 2001). In fact, identifying effective practices for delinquents is no longer the primary task. The primary task is to disseminate and implement known effective practices on a large-scale (Elliott and Mihalic, 2004; Washington State Institute for Public Policy, 2004). Perhaps we might ask what our field could gain from shifting back to viewing our ASO clients (or at least some of them) as generalists rather than a unique subpopulation with completely different and unique problems. Arguably, most ASOs have more in common with other delinquents or other behaviour-problem youth than they do with paedophiles. Perhaps what we define as specialised sex offender treatment should be reserved for the small subpopulation of ASOs with demonstrable paraphilias. If the non-paraphilic majority of ASOs were given back to the general delinquency field, would they ultimately be better served? Would we better be able to develop effective evidence-based treatments if we focused on a single problem?

A proper review of more recent and helpful instruments such as the JSOAP–II (Prentky and

Righthand, 2003) ERASOR (Worling, 2005) JSORRAT – II (Epperson, 2006) or Abel Assessment of Sexual Interest (see www.abelscreen.com; Letourneau and Prescott, 2005) is beyond the scope of this chapter. However, a review of each will guide professionals away from older methods and towards a careful examination not only of these newer tools, but also the state of our knowledge. Some of these tools are examined in the next two chapters.

Other problems

Beyond the recent advances and areas for further inquiry, fundamental problems with risk assessment remain. First, youth can change quickly, dramatically, and unpredictably. Epperson (2006) has observed that the JSORRAT-II appears to be more predictive of adolescent offending than adult offending. Caldwell (2005) has suggested that early and later-aged populations of adolescents who have sexually abused possess different characteristics. If *heterotypic continuity* (Kernberg, Weiner and Bardenstein, 2000) refers to the changing expression of personality across childhood and adolescence (e.g. an early proneness to boredom may manifest itself later as thrill-seeking behaviour), youthful sexual abuse may be a behavioural expression of elements in flux. While there is no doubt that some forms of sexual disorder and life-persistent anti-sociality have their origins in adolescence, some sexual abuse by adolescents might occur because of the sexual interest and willingness to break rules that can define the teenage years. Adding to this confusion, Vitacco et al. (in press) have found evidence that some affective aspects of psychopathy can result from behaviour. For example, youth engaging in callous and harmful behaviour may display shallower affect later in their development. Professionals examining risk may therefore wish to consider whether an adolescent's sexual misconduct signals a trajectory of antisocial conduct, sexual disorder, or a willingness to engage in indiscriminate activities.

Although it is tempting to take pride in one's assessment abilities, there is ample literature demonstrating that the use of unguided clinical judgment is ineffective for assessing risk (Hanson, 2000). In a well-known meta-analysis,

Hanson and Bussiere (1998) found that typical clinical judgment yielded an average correlation not much better than chance ($r = 0.10$), while prior convictions on their own correlated at 0.20. Others have observed that considering large amounts of information can result in reduced accuracy of assessments (Monahan, 1981: 88; Quinsey, 2000). Worse et al. (1998: 56) observe that, 'More importantly, the amount of information available to the clinician was unrelated to accuracy but was highly related to the degree of confidence in the judgment', and that humans 'are, in fact, most confident when making extreme judgments'. Certainly, the issue of confidence in assessment is different from the issue of accuracy (Doren, 2006). Finally, there is evidence that risk assessments by treatment providers can become less effective the longer a professional is in contact with the subject (Williams, 1975; also see De Vogel and De Ruiter, 2004). Perhaps this is a result of professionals over-relying on their clinical impressions and not reviewing file information adequately. Many (Doren, 2005) argue against treatment providers engaging in risk assessment. Whatever the case, treatment providers should consider the ethics and nature of their therapeutic relationships before making statements about risk in most situations. In the end, professionals should consider whether it is better to use their unproven judgment, unproven scales, or some combination that includes knowledge of the existing research and history of investigation into assessing dangerousness.

Another problem for those entering the world of risk assessment is that many of the elements once thought to be important have turned out not to be predictive in themselves. For example, aspects of the youth's most recent offence (sometimes known as the 'instant' or 'index' offence) have not proved to be predictive (Marczyk et al., 2003; Hanson and Thornton, 1999). However, the persistence of behaviour despite detection, sanction, and treatment is. Denying one's offence was for many years thought to be predictive of future harm, but this has also turned out to be contradicted by the literature (Worling, 2005; Hanson and Bussiere, 1998; Hanson and Morton-Bourgon, 2004). This has been the source of considerable debate (Lund, 2000), but it is possible that its role is simply contributory. For example, it may be that denial of one's offence (or of harm) may simply indicate an unwillingness to take the necessary steps to reduce existing risk. It may also simply indicate that a young person is not yet ready to engage in meaningful conversations with a given adult. Finally, neither empathy nor remorse have empirical support as risk factors for re-offence (Worling, 2005. Hanson and Bussiere, 1998; Hanson and Morton-Bourgon, 2004).

Finally, another significant problem for risk examiners is in understanding and identifying emerging sexual disorders in those cases where they exist. Although many American programmes for adolescents provide behavioural treatment to reduce 'deviant' sexual arousal (McGrath, Cumming and Burchard, 2003), the available evidence indicates that sexual arousal in youth is more dynamic than once believed, that its changing nature prevents it from being an effective predictor, and that it is therefore less of a treatment target for youthful sexual abusers than their adult counterparts (Johnson, 2005; Rich, 2003). Nisbet, Wilson and Smallbone (2004: 231) observe:

> *Hanson and Bussiere (1998) noted that the strongest predictors of sexual offense recidivism among adults were indices of sexual deviance, particularly phallometrically assessed sexual interest in children, especially male children. The extent to which this may also be true of adolescents remains unclear. Not only does the use of plethysmography remain controversial (Murphy, DiLillo, Haynes and Steere, 2001) but a recent recidivism study failed to find any significant relationship between phallometrically assessed deviant sexual arousal and clinical characteristics may be weaker in adolescent than adult sex offenders (Hunter, Goodwin and Becker, 1994) perhaps due to the greater fluidity of sexual arousal patterns among adolescents as compared to adults (Hunter and Lexier, 1998).*

Professionals working with youth must therefore ask fundamental questions: Is the current instance of sexual aggression the result of sexual interest or a willingness to engage in harmful behaviour? Should professionals be more concerned about sexual deviance, anti-sociality, or some combination of both? More importantly, how can professionals best understand sexual arousal and anti-sociality in the broader context of adolescence? Given the developmental demands of adolescence, might professionals understand sexual arousal more effectively in the broader context of other arousal states and the capacity for self-management?

Taken together, the above considerations provide more questions than answers. To summarise to this point, however, prudent risk examiners may wish to ask themselves questions such as the following:

- What are the adults in this young person's life asking for? Is it how best to help keep them on track? Are they asking how much of an underlying willingness the youth possesses to re-offend? Is it to provide assistance with determining treatment targets?
- What is the most unacceptable element of this case? Is it of concern because of the young person's willingness to break rules or because it may signal an emerging offence-related sexual disorder?
- Of all the elements of concerns, which ones could drive or contribute to a re-offence process, and how?

To summarise, there is no proven method to determine an individual's willingness to engage in future problem behaviour. No psychological test can predict how an individual will make decisions, particularly in the long term. Given the dimensions of harmful sexual behaviour (e.g. emanating from anti-sociality, emerging sexual deviance, or within specific or general contexts), it likely makes the most sense for professionals to have a plan for breaking down the various elements they are assessing.

Frameworks

There is evidence that risk assessment is most effective when it occurs early in an assessment/treatment sequence and outside of a therapeutic relationship (Williams, 1975; Quinsey et al., 1998). Professionals will therefore wish to follow a protocol that can help ground them not only in risk assessment research, but also in how human observers can best remain free of bias. These next sections describe perspectives that can help professionals as they enter an assessment situation. In many cases, this will be a formal risk assessment, but in other circumstances, this can be treatment team meetings, incident report reviews, and similar situations. The guiding value is for professionals to have a scheme for breaking down the complexities of sexual misconduct and, in residential settings, related behaviour.

Andrews and Bonta (2003) describe three principles in understanding criminal offenders:

risk, need, and *responsivity*. The *risk principle* states that professionals should match interventions to the risk the offender poses. The authors cite problems coming to terms with this principle as contributing to the failure of such programmes as DARE and Scared Straight. Separate from the *need* and *responsivity* principles described below, examiners may therefore best conceptualise *risk* as an underlying predisposition in a specific direction, akin to a psychological trait, related to the willingness to abuse others despite factors that would deter others. This willingness is nearly impossible to view directly, except in occasional statements and threats (e.g. 'I'll do it again'). Even the actuarial scales in existence only employ 'markers' or 'proxies' for risk, such as number of prior convictions and other historical factors fixed in an individual's history.

It is important to differentiate this notion of risk from those contextual aspects that can elevate or mitigate risk. Parents who actively apprentice their children into sexual aggression or consistently ignore warning signs, or overtly anti-social peer groups can certainly contribute to risk, but may have more to do with imminence than long-term risk. Cautious professionals will wish to consider these elements separately from an underlying predisposition or long-term willingness.

Many authors (Hanson, 2000; Rich, 2003) have differentiated between static (i.e. fixed in an individual's history) and dynamic (i.e. changeable) risk factors. Exploring dynamic risk factors, Hanson and Harris (2001) differentiate between those dynamic factors that are relatively stable across time (e.g., marital status, personality traits) and those that are *acute* (e.g., escalating negative mood). Distinguishing between static and dynamic risk factors is important, as dynamic factors can lend themselves to treatment, and contribute to refinement of risk classification and assessment (Thornton, 2002; Ward and Beech, 2004). In some cases where an individual's static factors appear to indicate low risk, careful assessment of dynamic factors may confirm or cast doubt on this classification. Perhaps more importantly, however, an understanding of dynamic risk can inform the establishment of treatment targets. Gail Ryan addresses this particular issue in Chapter 13.

The research to date is all too often inconclusive with respect to static risk factors. Generally, early onset (when coupled with persistence; often measured as prior to the age of

thirteen) and persistence (despite consequences) appear to be robust indicators (Epperson et al., 2006; Caldwell, 2005; Quinsey et al. 1998).

The *need principle* states that interventions should specifically target areas related to criminal behaviour (also known as 'criminogenic needs'). Depending upon the circumstances, this might mean identifying needs around criminal behaviour that otherwise have not yet emerged as problematic. For example, a youth who has sexually abused and who has a small history of substance abuse may possess factors indicating a higher risk for substance abuse, and therefore benefit from interventions in this area. However, these same interventions may be ineffective or counterproductive with individuals when not properly matched to their propensity to engage in substance abuse. For these reasons, it is not useful to regard the need principle as necessarily the same thing as treatment needs.

However, it is not difficult to see that there is a significant overlap of dynamic risk, treatment need, and the need principle. The latter reminds us to attend to all aspects of a potential re-offence process. When looking at the harmful aspects of sexual abuse, and in the community's rush to hold a young person accountable, it can be easy to miss how some aspects of the youth's relationships with others, as well as the youth's experience of themselves within those relationships, can contribute to risk. However, it is equally important to distinguish these affective ties from simple social skills. For some individuals, social skills may simply be the treatment target that facilitates the relationships that in turn reduce the risk over time. For others, the relationships themselves can be the direct treatment target, criminogenic need, and dynamic risk factor.

With respect to sexual re-offence, it may be useful to think in terms of the following domains (based on Ageton, 1983; Prentky and Righthand, 2003; Thornton, 2000; Thornton, 2002; Thornton, 2004; Ward and Beech, 2004):

- Offence-related sexual deviance.
- Contributory/distorted attitudes (i.e. permission-giving self-statements that support sexual aggression).
- Interpersonal/socio-affective functioning (e.g. Dysfunctional evaluation of self-worth or self-efficacy).
- Self-management (e.g. problem-solving, impulsivity).

- Significant others (i.e. that support sexual aggression, whether implicitly or explicitly).

The *responsivity principle* states that interventions should match the characteristics of the offender. Developmentally delayed individuals require treatment that accommodates their particular learning styles (Blasingame, 2005), while traumatised individuals may need less obvious treatment considerations (Creeden, 2006; Bengis and Cunninggim, 2006; Stien and Kendall, 2004). More importantly, perhaps, what can appear as a risk factor may simply relate more to responsivity. Denial, empathy deficits, the apparent absence of remorse, and clinical presentation may all relate more to responsivity than risk. Each can interfere with progress in the treatment that can help reduce risk, but none necessarily drives a re-offence process.

These distinctions are critical to assessment and communication. Novices can easily equate treatment needs with level of risk, or mistake risk indicators for responsivity factors. A low-risk youth who does not respond to poorly designed treatment can worry those around him, and therefore appear at higher risk than he is. For example, a low-functioning incest abuser who is non-compliant with treatment targeting sexual deviance may appear more problematic than he is. Assuming that he is truly low risk (e.g. no prior history of sexual aggression, no attitudes supportive of sexual abuse, etc.), these interventions may be less effective than education and restorative treatment tailored to his abilities and targeting interpersonal deficits. In this case, an assessment of *risk*, *need*, and *responsivity* would be more helpful to others than simply making a statement about 'high risk' or 'low risk'.

Andrews and Bonta's (2003) principles may not effectively capture one aspect of adolescent development that can both mitigate risk and facilitate treatment. *Protective Factors*, the building blocks of resilience (Bremer, 2006), are often overlooked in risk assessment. This may be because past literature on assessing dangerousness and risk among adults has often ignored it, and it could be that when professionals' central questions are in the direction of dangerousness it is easy to look past indicators of safety. Bremer (2001, 2006) has developed the *Protective Factors Scale*, a system of examining three areas that can attenuate risk: *Personal development, sexuality, and environmental support*. Professionals have successfully used this scale to aid in placement decisions (ibid).

Finally, Ward et al. (2004: 646) argue for adding readiness to the risk, need, and responsivity principles. They write:

> We argue that there has been little attempt in the literature to distinguish between three distinct, although related, constructs: treatment motivation, responsivity, and readiness. Motivation involves assessing whether or not someone really wants to enter treatment and therefore is willing to change his or her behaviour in some respect (e.g. cease to behave aggressively). Typical clinical criteria for deciding that offenders are motivated to enter treatment include expressions of regret for their offences, a desire to change, and sounding enthusiastic about the treatments available. In one important respect, the judgement that an offender is motivated for therapy is essentially a prediction that he or she will engage in, and complete, therapy. In current practice, it is widely accepted that offender motivation constitutes an important requirement for selection into rehabilitation programs, and therapists are expected to have the skills to initiate, enhance, and sustain motivation in reluctant individuals. Ironically, despite a plethora of literature on motivational interviewing and related interventions, there has been comparatively little attention paid to clarifying the relevant underlying mechanisms or consideration of the relationship between motivational states and other aspects of treatment preparedness.

The authors go on to distinguish between internal and external readiness, and provide simple ideas for motivating the 'low-readiness' client. The concept of readiness is valuable, as it reminds us that youth who are unready for treatment can still be low-risk, and that just because a young person categorically denies their harmful sexual behaviour in one context does not mean they cannot become ready to change under circumstances that are more favourable.

To summarise, having a framework of risk, need, responsivity, resilience, and readiness can guide professionals away from trying to consider too much information (which research shows can reduce accuracy). Useful questions for the professional to ask at this point include:

- With the information available, was the behaviour that brought this youth into assessment the result of some kind of anti-sociality (e.g. using sexual behaviour to meet non-sexual needs, being willing to break rules generally, including sexual boundaries) or the result of some emerging problematic sexual interest or script?
- Given the available data, what aspects of this young person's life relate to risk, need, responsivity, readiness, and resilience?

To clarify these elements, a system for looking at dynamic risk is useful.

Dynamic Risk

Much of what follows is adapted from Thornton (2000, 2004) and Thornton and Prescott (2001) and appears in Prescott (2006):

Sexual deviance

In this instance, deviance refers to the range and intensity of factors driving an adolescent's harmful sexual behaviour. This can include elements of the youth's functioning that are markedly unusual when compared to non-abusive adolescents, that contribute to harmful behaviours, or that will bring them into conflict with themselves, others, society, and the law. As noted earlier, precise language is important, and professionals will want to use this term only in the context of the cautions outlined in this chapter.

Professionals should consider this domain only with great care. The sexual arousal patterns of adolescents are more fluid and dynamic than those of adults (Hunter and Becker, 1994; Hunter, 1999). Further, given that adolescence is a time when sex and sexuality are salient themes for all adolescents, adults can overestimate their role in the long term. What may appear sexually deviant may simply be a willingness to break rules, expressed through harmful sexual behaviour. This is not intended to downplay the impact of sexual abuse on its victims, but to underscore the importance of differentiating the elements that contribute to sexual abuse. Finally, while true sexual pre-occupation is clearly important to understand, it is easy to overestimate in youth, for whom a level of pre-occupation is normative.

Key questions to ask are:

- What is the direction of the young person's sexual interest?
- How narrowly is that interest defined?
- What is the intensity of that interest?

Professionals can consider three forms of sexual deviance:

- *Sexual preference* for children refers to the youth's having a stronger response to those significantly younger (by four or five years).
- *Sexualised violence* refers to either a preference for coerced sex or a strong sexual response to the victim's pain, suffering, or fear.
- *Sexual preoccupation* refers to the intensity of the youth's sexual interest. How much time do they spend thinking about sex? Do they think about sex to such an extent that it becomes uncomfortable or has caused them concern? Do they engage in frequent indiscriminate and diverse sexual behaviours? Do they regularly masturbate several times a day? Do they regularly use or collect pornography over and above what is normal for a teenager? How difficult is it to let go of a sexual idea once it has occurred? While none of these in themselves defines preoccupation, the guiding principle is that it is over and above what one would expect to find in an adolescent.

Distorted attitudes/contributory attitudes

This refers to the permission-giving self-statements that precede sexual aggression. It is important to note that this includes the attitudes before the incidents of sexual aggression, and not the defensive statements made afterwards ('I didn't think I'd get caught'). This is a precarious area of assessment because, although these attitudes can be easy to treat, they can also be easy to hide. Examples include:

- *Sexual entitlement.* The belief that having a sexual desire entitles one to gratify it can be common in sexually abusive youth, as is the belief that their sex drive is stronger than others (e.g. 'You don't understand: I'm a very sexual person'). Central to entitlement is the belief that one has a right to satisfy their sexual urges.
- *Child sexual abuse supportive beliefs.* This involves seeing much younger children as peers, and the belief that children can consent to sex. In some cases, the youth may believe that his actions are of benefit to the child or that the child is interested in sex.
- *Rape minimisation.* This includes the idea that victims enjoy or desire rape.
- *Rape justification.* This includes the belief that others deserve rape, especially when they behave badly. This belief is sometimes seemingly absent in normal functioning but activated when the young person is upset, angry, or anxious.

- *Seeing others as deceitful* can correspond with a worldview that others are deceitful or manipulative, and that the youth has to fight back to gain the respect and safety they deserve. It can also correspond to a worldview that the world is cold, hostile, or out of control.

Interpersonal/Socio-Affective functioning

The relationship of the young person to the world around him, himself, and his future. It includes both relationships to others and perceptions of one's self within the context of these relationships:

- *Dysfunctional evaluation of self worth* includes an emotionally painful or negative view of one's identity and ongoing functioning. Conversely, it can be an ongoing sense of pride based on anti-social characteristics. It can also include a narcissistic self-image that combines an explicit, conscious evaluation of one's self that is arrogant or grandiose but fragile, unstable, and vulnerable to injury. When threatened, negative self-appraisal can occur quickly.
- *Dysfunctional evaluation of self-efficacy* includes inaccurate perceptions that the youth has no control over his current or future behaviour, and that other individuals and situations are responsible for his actions. The youth may engage in passive behaviours and view himself as helpless.
- *Lack of emotionally intimate relationships* includes youth who, for a variety of reasons, are neither able to establish healthy and stable peer relationships nor dating relationships.
- *Emotional congruence with younger children* involves an adolescent feeling that it is easier to engage in relationships with much younger others.
- *Callousness/shallow emotions* includes a combination of callous and ruthless behaviours towards others in the absence of any strong emotions. While many youth do not appear to demonstrate guilt, remorse, or empathy in clinical interviews, a key feature of this is its duration across time and situation. Youths for whom this factor is prominent often fail to accept responsibility for their actions and demonstrate a lack of concern for the rights and welfare of others to an extent that is unusual even among other sexually abusive youth. This is the equivalent of the affective facet in Hare's (2003) four-facet model of psychopathy.

- *Grievance thinking* involves both an active belief that one is a victim of others and a persistent scanning of one's environment in search of potential threats. It can provide a sense of justification for harming others. It can often motivate behaviour that leads to high-risk situations.

Self-management refers to the youth's ability to manage their behaviour in a way that reflects long-term goals rather than short-term gratification:

- *Lifestyle impulsivity* includes behaviour patterns that do not reflect healthy self-regulation. Impulsivity can range from failure to manage impulses (e.g. blurting out the answers in class) to an ongoing pervasive failure to consider the effects of one's actions on others and one's self. It also refers to reckless and irresponsible behaviour as described in factor two of the *Psychopathy Checklist: Youth Version* (Forth, Kosson and Hare, 2003).
- *Dysfunctional coping* refers to recurrent difficulties dealing with stress or other problems. It might include over-reliance on only a handful of coping skills that become ineffective over time. It can include over-reliance on sexual behaviour as a coping mechanism. Dysfunctional coping can include the following:
- Poor cognitive problem solving.
- Poor problem anticipation.
- Continued engagement in problem behaviour despite obvious consequences.
- Affective dysregulation, including irritability or other easily triggered negative affect.
- Emotional rumination, where the youth copes with stress by persistently ruminating upon it in a negative way.
- Avoidant coping, where the youth attempts to manage stress by avoiding it.
- Poor executive functioning. In some cases, prefrontal cortex disturbances or deficits can contribute to poor self-management.

Influential others

Key questions are whether peers or family members actively support sexual aggression, or whether they might tacitly support sexual abuse by ignoring risk situations or treatment recommendations.

Upon assessment through file review and clinical interview, professionals can discuss these dynamic factors in the body of the report, along with information on how they interact. A list of treatment targets can then be generated that may help concerned adults provide services. Professionals can also assemble a list of behaviours and situations that signal imminence or escalating risk, and provide these to other concerned adults who supervise youth.

This framework should not replace the existing tools, but supplement them and aid the professional attempting to understand complex behaviour and/or situations. The author has experienced this framework as particularly helpful in reviewing incidents in residential situations and in other situations where one has to rely on one's own wits. In situations requiring quick decisions, it can be more effective to rely on this easily recalled framework than on gut reactions.

Conclusion

Despite the remarkable gains in understanding youth across the past decade, many questions haunt the conscientious professional. Knowing that the existing tools are not exact, and may provide more information via their subscales than their total score, how should the professional best interpret them? How can the professional best balance static and dynamic factors? How can the professional best remain rooted in empirical knowledge while taking into account diverse family, cultural, and ecological circumstances? Knowing that even professional observers are subject to bias when considering too much information, what safeguards might the field develop to prevent unnecessary bias? How can we rise above our environments and ourselves to make accurate assessments?

This chapter has sought to outline inherent problems in risk assessment and our limitations as professionals and human beings. There remains no empirically validated means for accurate risk classification, but the existing tools and frameworks described above can be helpful both as anchor points and as systems for coping with professionals' own limitations. In many cases, professionals continue to use language and methods that may no longer be appropriate in the increasingly high-stakes arena of sexual abuse assessment and treatment. Faced with the enormity of the task of risk assessment, professionals are not only obligated to remain familiar with the research and re-think their practice, they possess wonderful opportunities to educate others concerned by the scope of sexual abuse.

References

Ageton, S.S. (1983) *Sexual Assault among Adolescents.* Lexington, MA: Lexington Books.

Alexander, M. (1999) Sexual Offender Treatment Efficacy Revisited. *Sexual Abuse: A Journal of Research and Treatment,* 11, 101–16.

Andrews, D.A. and Bonta, J.L. (2003) *The Psychology of Criminal Conduct.* 3rd edn. Cincinnati: Anderson Publishing.

Bengis, S.M. and Cunninggim, P. (2006) Brain-based Approaches that Impact Behaviour, Learning, and Treatment. In Longo, R.E. and Prescott, D.S. (Eds.) *Current Perspectives: Working with Sexually Aggressive Youth and Youth with Sexual Behaviour Problems.* Holyoke, MA: New England Adolescent Research Institute Press.

Blasingame, G.D. (2005) *Developmentally Disabled Persons with Sexual Behaviour Problems: Treatment, Management, Supervision.* 2nd edn. Oklahoma City: Wood'N'Barnes.

Bremer, J.F. (2001) *The Protective Factors Scale: Assessing Youth with Sexual Concerns.* Plenary address at the annual conference of the National Adolescent Perpetration Network, Kansas City, May 7.

Bremer, J. (2006) Building Resilience: An Ally in Assessment and Treatment. In Prescott, D.S. (Ed.) *Risk Assessment of Youth who have Sexually Abused: Theory, Controversy, and Emerging Strategies.* Oklahoma City, OK: Wood'N'Barnes.

Caldwell, M. (2005, May) *What we do and do not Know About Juvenile Sex Offenders.* Presentation at a conference of the Wisconsin Association for the Treatment of Sexual Abusers, Madison, Wisconsin.

Chaffin, M. (2006) Can We Develop Evidence-Based Practice with Adolescent Sex Offenders? In Longo, R.E. and Prescott, D.S. (Eds.) *Current Perspectives: Working with Sexually Aggressive Youth and Youth with Sexual Behaviour Problems.* Holyoke, MA: New England Adolescent Research Institute.

Coffey, P. (2006) Forensic Issues in Evaluating Juvenile Sexual Offenders. In Prescott, D.S.

(Ed.) *Risk Assessment of Youth who have Sexually Abused: Theory, Controversy, and Emerging Strategies*. Oklahoma City, OK: Wood'N'Barnes.

Creeden, K. (2006) Neurological Impact of Trauma and Implications. In Longo, R.E. and Prescott, D.S. (Eds.) *Current Perspectives: Working with Sexually Aggressive Youth and Youth with Sexual Behaviour Problems*. Holyoke, MA: New England Adolescent Research Institute.

Curwen, T. (2000) *Utility of the Interpersonal Reactivity Index (IRI) as a Measure of Empathy in Male Adolescent Sex Offenders*. Paper presented at the International Conference on the Treatment of Sexual Offenders, Toronto, May 29.

De Vogel, V., and Ruiter, C. de (2004) Differences between Clinicians and Researchers in Assessing Risk of Violence in Forensic Psychiatric Patients. *The Journal of Forensic Psychiatry and Psychology*, 15, 145–64.

Doren, D.M. (2005) What Weight Should Courts give to Treaters' Testimony Concerning Recidivism Risk. *Sex Offender Law Report*.

Doren, D.M. (2006) Assessing Juveniles' Risk within the Civil Commitment Context. In Prescott, D.S. (Ed.) *Risk Assessment of Youth who have Sexually Abused: Theory, Controversy, and Emerging Strategies*. Oklahoma City, OK: Wood'N'Barnes.

Edmunds, S.B. (1999) *Impact: Working with Sexual Abusers*. Brandon, VT: Safer Society Press.

Elliot, D.S. and Mihalic, S. (2004) Issues in Disseminating and Replicating Effective Prevention Programs. *Prevention Science*, 5, 47–52.

Epperson, D.L. et al. (2006) Actuarial Risk Assessment with Juveniles who Offend Sexually: Development of the Juvenile Sexual Offense Recidivism Risk Assessment Tool – II. In Prescott, D.S. (Ed.) *Risk Assessment of Youth who have Sexually Abused: Theory, Controversy, and Emerging Strategies*. Oklahoma City, OK: Wood'N'Barnes.

Fernandez, Y. (2002) *In Their Shoes: Examining the Role of Empathy and its Place in the Treatment of Offenders*. Oklahoma City: Wood'N'Barnes.

Forth, A.E., Kosson, D.S. and Hare, R.D. (2003) *The Psychopathy Checklist: Youth Version (PCL:YV)*. Toronto, Ontario: Multi-Health Systems.

Gray, A.S., and Wallace, R. (1992) *Adolescent Sex Offender Packet*. Brandon, VT: Safer Society Press.

Grady, J. and Reynolds, S. (2003, October) *Holistic Assessment and Treatment of Sexually Abusive Youth*. Presentation at the Annual Meeting of the Association for the Treatment of Sexual Abusers, Montreal, Canada.

Greenland, C. (1985) Dangerousness, Mental Disorder, and Politics. In Webster, C.D., Ben-Aron, M.H. and Hucker, S.J. (Eds.) *Dangerousness: Probability and Prediction, Psychiatry and Public Policy*. Cambridge: Cambridge University Press.

Gretton, H.M. et al. (2001. Psychopathy and Recidivism in Adolescent Sexual Offenders. *Criminal Justice and Behaviour*, 28, 427–49.

Grove, W.M. et al. (2001) Clinical Versus Mechanical Prediction. *Psychological Assessment*, 12: 1, 19–30.

Hanson, R.K. (2000) *Risk Assessment*. Beaverton, OR: Association for the Treatment of Sexual Abusers.

Hanson, R.K. (2003) Empathy Deficits of Sexual Offenders: A Conceptual Model. *Journal of Sexual Aggression*, 9, 13–23.

Hanson, R.K., and Bussiere, M.T. (1998) Predicting Relapse: A Meta-analysis of Sexual Offender Recidivism Studies. *Journal of Consulting and Clinical Psychology*, 66: 2, 348–62. Also available at http://www.psepc-sppcc.gc.ca/.

Hanson, R.K., and Morton-Bourgon, K.E. (2004) Predictors of Sexual Recidivism: An Updated Meta-analysis. Available at: http://www.psepc.gc.ca/publications/corrections/pdf/200402_e.pdf.

Hanson, R.K., and Harris, A.J.R. (2001) A Structured Approach to Evaluating Change among Sexual Offenders. *Sexual Abuse: A Journal of Research and Treatment*, 13: 2, 105–22.

Hanson, R.K. and Thornton, D. (1999) *Static 99: Improving Actuarial Risk Assessments for Sex Offenders* (User Report 1999-02) Ottawa: Department of the Solicitor General of Canada. Available at www.sgc.gc.ca.

Hare, R.D. (2003) *The Hare Psychopathy Checklist – Revised* (2nd Edn). Toronto, Ontario: Multi-Health Systems.

Hart, S.D., Kropp, P.R. and Laws, R.L. (2004) *The Risk for Sexual Violence Protocol* (RSVP) Burnaby, BC: Mental Health, Law, and Policy Institute, Simon Fraser University.

Hecker, J., Scoular, J., Righthand, S. and Nangle, D. (2002, October) *Predictive Validity of the J-SOAP over 10-plus Years: Implications for Risk Assessment*. Paper presented at the Annual

Meeting of the Association for the Treatment of Sexual Abusers, Montreal, Quebec, Canada.

Henggeler, S.W. et al. (1998) *Multisystemic Treatment of Antisocial Behaviour in Children and Adolescents*. New York: Guilford Press.

Hunter, J. (1999) *Understanding Juvenile Sexual Offending Behaviour: Emerging Research, Treatment Approaches, and Management Practices*. Center for Sex Offender Management. Available at www.csom.org.

Hunter, J. (2005) Understanding Diversity in Juvenile Sexual Offenders: Implications for Assessment, Treatment, and Legal Management. In Longo, R.E. and Prescott, D.S. (Eds.) *Current Perspectives: Working with Sexually Aggressive Youth and Youth with Sexual Behaviour Problems*. Holyoke, MA: NEARI Press.

Hunter, J.A. and Becker, J.V. (1994) The Role of Deviant Sexual Arousal in Juvenile Sexual Offending: Etiology, Evaluation, and Treatment. *Criminal Justice and Behaviour*, 21, 132–49.

Hunter, J.A., Goodwin, D.W. and Becker, J.V. (1994) The Relationship between Phallometrically Measured Deviant Sexual Arousal and Clinical Characteristics in Juvenile Sexual Offenders. *Behaviour Research and Therapy*, 32: 5, 533–8.

Hunter, J.A. and Lexier, L.J. (1998) Ethical and Legal Issues in the Assessment and Treatment of Juvenile Sex Offenders. *Child Maltreatment*, 3, 339–48.

Johnson, B.R. (2005) Comorbid Diagnosis of Sexually Abusive Youth. In Longo, R.E. and Prescott D.S. (Eds.) *Current Perspectives: Working with Sexually Aggressive Youth and Youth with Sexual Behaviour Problems*. Holyoke, MA: NEARI Press.

Kernberg, P.F., Weiner, A.S. and Bardenstein, K.K. (2000) *Personality Disorders in Children and Adolescents*. New York: Basic Books.

Langstrom, N. and Grann, M. (2000) Risk for Criminal Recidivism among Young Sex Offenders. *Journal of Interpersonal Violence*, 15, 855–71.

Letourneau, E.J. and Prescott, D.S. (2005) Ethical Issues in Sex Offender Assessments. In Cooper, S.W., Giardano, A.P., Vieth, V.I. and Kellogg, N.D. (Eds.) *Medical and Legal Aspects of Child Sexual Exploitation: A Comprehensive Review of Child Pornography, Child Prostitution, and Internet Crimes against Children*. St. Louis, MO: G.W. Medical Publishing.

Litwack, T.R. (2001) Actuarial Versus Clinical Assessments of Dangerousness. *Psychology, Public Policy, and Law*, 7: 2, 409–43.

Longo, R.E. and Prescott, D.S. (2006) *Current Perspectives: Working with Sexually Aggressive Youth and Youth with Sexual Behaviour Problems*. Holyoke, MA: New England Adolescent Research Institute.

Lund, C.A. (2000) Predictors of Sexual Recidivism: Did Meta-analysis Clarify the Role and Relevance of Denial? *Sexual Abuse: A Journal of Research and Treatment*, 12, 275–88.

Marczyk, G.R., Heilbrun, K., Lander, T. and DeMatteo, D. (2003) Predicting Juvenile Recidivism with the PCL: YV, MAYSI, and YLS/CMI. *International Journal of Forensic Mental Health*, 2, 7–18. Available at http://www.iafmhs.org/files/Marczyk.pdf.

McGrath, R.J., Cumming, G.F. and Burchard, B.L. (2003) *Current Practices and Trends in Sexual Abuser Management*: The Safer Society 2002 Nationwide Survey. Brandon, VT: Safer Society.

Mihalic, W. et al. (2001) Blueprints for Violence Prevention. *Juvenile Justice Bulletin*, July 2001. US Department of Justice: Office of Juvenile Justice and Delinquency Prevention.

Moffitt, T.E. (1993) Adolescence-limited and Life-course-persistent Anti-social Behaviour: A Developmental Taxonomy. *Psychological Bulletin*, 100, 674–701.

Monahan, J. (1981/1995) *The Clinical Prediction of Violent Behaviour*. Northvale, NJ: Jason Aronson Inc.

Monahan, J. et al. (2001) *Rethinking Risk Assessment: The Macarthur Study of Violence and Mental Disorder*. New York: Oxford University Press.

Murphy, W.D., DiLillo, W., Haynes, M.R. and Steere, E. (2001) An Exploration of Factors Related to Deviant Sexual Arousal among Juvenile Sexual Offenders. *Sexual Abuse: A Journal of Research and Treatment*, 13, 91–103.

Nisbet, I.A., Wilson, P.H. and Smallbone, S.W. (2004) A Prospective Longitudinal Study of Sexual Recidivism among Adolescent Sex Offenders. *Sexual Abuse: A Journal of Research and Treatment*, 16, 223–234.

O'Brien, M.J. and Bera, W. (1986) Adolescent Sexual Offenders: A Descriptive Typology. *Preventing Sexual Abuse*, 1: 3, 1–4.

Poole, D., Liedecke, D. and Marbibi, M. (2001) *Risk Assessment and Recidivism in Juvenile Sex Offenders: A Validation Study of the Static 99*. Austin, TX: Texas Youth Commission.

Prentky, R., Harris, B., Frizzell, K. and Righthand, S. (2000) An Actuarial Procedure for Assessing Risk with Juvenile Sex Offenders. *Sexual Abuse: A Journal of Research and Treatment*, 12, 71–94.

Prentky, R. and Righthand, S. (2003) *Juvenile Sex Offender Assessment Protocol – II (JSOAP – II)*. Available from Center for Sex Offender Management at www.csom.org.

Prescott, D.S. (2006) *Risk Assessment of Youth who have Sexually Abused: Theory, Controversy, and Emerging Strategies*. Oklahoma City, OK: Wood'N'Barnes.

Quinsey, V.L. (2000) *The Violence Risk Appraisal Guide (VRAG)*. Presentation at Sinclair Seminars' Sex Offender Re-Offense Risk Prediction Symposium, Madison, Wisconsin, March 2000. Available at www.sinclairseminars.com.

Quinsey, V.L., Skilling, T.A., Lalumiere, M.L. and Craig, W.M. (2004) *Juvenile Delinquency: Understanding the Origins of Individual Differences*. Washington, DC: American Psychological Association.

Quinsey, V.L., Harris, G.T., Rice, M.E. and Cormier, C.A. (1998) *Violent Offenders: Managing and Appraising Risk*. Washington DC: American Psychological Association.

Rich, P. (2000) *Juvenile Risk Assessment Tool*. Barre, MA: Stetson School.

Rich, P. (2003) *Understanding, Assessing and Rehabilitating Juvenile Sex Offenders*. Hoboken, NJ: John Wiley and Sons.

Righthand, S., Knight, R. and Prentky, R. (2002) *A Path Analytic Investigation of Proximal Antecedents of J-SOAP Risk Domains*. Paper presented at the Annual Meeting of the Association for the Treatment of Sexual Abusers, Montreal, Quebec, Canada.

Ross, J. and Loss, P. (1991) Assessment of the Juvenile Sexual Offender. In Ryan, G.D. and Lane, S.L. (Eds.) *Juvenile Sexual Offending: Causes, Consequences, and Correction*. Lexington, MA: Lexington Books.

Ryan, G. and Lane, S. (1997) *Juvenile Sexual Offending: Causes, Consequences, and Correction*. San Francisco: Jossey-Bass.

Salter, A.C. (1988) *Treating Child Sex Offenders and Victims*. Newbury Park, CA: Sage.

Schladale, J. (2002) *The TOP. (Trauma Outcome Process) Workbook for Taming Violence and Sexual Aggression*. Freeport, ME: Self-published. Available at www.resourcesforresolvingviolence.com.

Schladale, J. (2005) Family Matters: The Importance of Engaging Families in Treatment with Sexually Aggressive Youth. In Longo, R.E. and Prescott, D.S. (Eds.) *Current Perspectives: Working with Sexually Aggressive Youth and Youth with Sexual Behaviour Problems*. Holyoke, MA: New England Adolescent Research Institute Press.

Schwartz, B., Cavanaugh, D., Prentky, R. and Pimental, A. (2006) Family Violence and Severe Maltreatment in Families of Sexually Reactive Children and Adolescents. In Longo, R.E. and Prescott, D.S. (Eds.) *Current Perspectives: Working with Sexually Aggressive Youth and Youth with Sexual Behaviour Problems*. Holyoke, MA: New England Adolescent Research Institute Press.

Serin, R.C. and Brown, S.L. (2000) The Clinical use of the Hare Psychopathy Checklist – Revised in Contemporary Risk Assessment. In Gacono, C.G. (Ed.) *The Clinical and Forensic Assessment of Psychopathy*. Mahwah, NJ: Lawrence Erlbaum Associates.

Stien, P.T. and Kendall, J. (2004) *Psychological Trauma and the Developing Brain: Neurologically Based Interventions for Troubled Children*. Binghamton, NY: Haworth Press.

Stone, A.A. (1985) The New Legal Standard of Dangerousness. In Webster, C.D., Ben-Aron, M.H. and Hucker, S.J. (Eds.) *Dangerousness: Probability and Prediction, Psychiatry and Public Policy*. Cambridge, UK: Cambridge University Press.

Thomas, J. (1991) The Adolescent Sex Offender's Family in Treatment. In Ryan, G.D. and Lane, S.L. (Eds.) *Juvenile Sexual Offending: Causes, Consequences and Corrections*. San Fransisco: Jossey-Bass.

Thomas, J. and Viar, W. (2006) From Family Research to Practice. In Longo, R.E. and Prescott, D.S. (Eds.) *Current Perspectives: Working with Sexually Aggressive Youth and Youth with Sexual Behaviour Problems*. Holyoke, MA: New England Adolescent Research Institute Press.

Thornton, D. (2000) *Structured Risk Assessment*. Presentation at Sinclair Seminars' Sex Offender Re-Offense Risk Prediction Symposium, Madison, WI: March. Available at www.sinclairseminars.com.

Thornton, D. (2002) Constructing and Testing a Framework for Dynamic Risk Assessment. *Sexual Abuse: A Journal of Research and Treatment*, 14, 139–154.

Thornton, D. (2004) *Psychological Factors Underlying Offending*. Workshop at Sand Ridge

Secure Treatment Center, Mauston, WI: April 27, 2004.

Thornton, D. and Prescott, D.S. (2001) *Structured Risk Assessment: Youth Version*. Unpublished manuscript.

Trivits, L.C. and Repucci, N.D. (2002) Application of Megan's Law to Juveniles. *American Psychologist*, 57, 690–704.

Vitacco, M.J. et al. (2005, in press) A Comparison of Factor Models on the PCL-R with Mentally Disordered Offenders: The Development of a Four-factor Model. *Criminal Justice and Behaviour*.

Ward, T. and Beech, A.R. (2004) The Etiology of Risk: A Preliminary Model. *Sexual Abuse: A Journal of Research and Treatment*, 16, 271–84.

Washington State Institute for Public Policy (2004) *Outcome Evaluation of Washington State's Research-based Programs for Juvenile Offenders*. Olympia, WA: Washington State Institute for Public Policy.

Webster, C.D., Hucker, S.J. and Bloom, H. (2002) Transcending the Actuarial versus Clinical Polemic in Assessing Risk for Violence. *Criminal Justice and Behaviour*, 29: 5, 659–65.

Williams, M. (1975) Aspects of the Psychology of Imprisonment. In McConville, S. (Ed.) *The Use of Imprisonment: Essays in the Changing State of English Penal Policy*. London: Routledge and Kegan Paul.

Worling, J.R. (2001) *Estimate of Risk of Adolescent Sex Offender Recidivism*. Plenary address at the 16th annual conference of the National Adolescent Perpetration Network, Kansas City, Mo. May 7, 2001.

Worling, J.R. (2005) Assessing Sexual Offense Risk for Adolescents who have Sexually Offended. In Schwartz, B. K. (Ed.) *The Sex Offender: Issues in Assessment, Treatment, and Supervision of Adult and Juvenile Populations*. Kingston, NJ: Civic Research Institute.

Worling, J.R. and Curwen, T. (2000) Adolescent Sexual Offender Recidivism: Success of Specialized Treatment and Implications for Risk Prediction. *Child Abuse and Neglect*, 24, 965–82.

Zimring, F.E. (2004) *An American Travesty: Legal Responses to Adolescent Sex Offending*. Chicago: University of Chicago Press.

Zolondek, S.C., Abel, G.G., Northey, W.F. and Jordan, A.D. (2001) The Self-reported Behaviours of Juvenile Sex Offenders. *Journal of Interpersonal Violence*, 16.

Chapter 12

Emerging Data for Risk Prediction and Identification of Offender Sub-groups: Implications for Specialised Treatment and Risk Management

Gregory Parks

Introduction

As a relatively young area of specialised treatment with limited empirical research, clinical intervention and assessment with adolescent sex offenders has been largely guided by clinical assumptions, beginning with recommendations published by the National Adolescent Perpetrator Network in 1988, and later revised in 1993. While the general field of sex offender treatment has had limited empirical data to guide practice, those working with adolescents have encountered an even greater vacuum, often resulting in the inappropriate application of adult treatment assumptions to adolescents.

Two emerging research areas with potential for enhancing clinical practice with adolescents who have sexually offended include the identification of offender subtypes and the assessment of risk. Hunter and colleagues (Hunter, 2006; Hunter et al., 2000; Hunter et al., 2003) have made great strides in the identification of adolescent subtypes, and there is a growing body of preliminary research in the area of risk prediction. In addition, there is preliminary data indicating differences in risk factors among offender sub-groups (Parks and Bard, 2006). This chapter will address developments in the knowledge of adolescent subtypes and risk prediction, as well as the treatment implications of integrating these two important areas of research.

Risk prediction

The identification of factors that reliably predict recidivism has been an ongoing challenge for researchers (Bonner et al., 1998; Caldwell, 2002; Hunter and Lexier, 1998). Attempts to validate a risk assessment instrument for adolescent sexual offenders have been met with the repeated obstacle of low recidivism base rates (Parks and

Bard, 2006; Prentky et al., 2000). Studies of recidivism among adolescent sexual offenders have consistently found relatively low rates of re-offence with most studies resulting in recidivism rates below 15 per cent among US samples (Parks and Bard, 2006). For unidentified reasons, samples outside the United States often find higher rates of re-offence (Langstrom, 2002; Langstrom and Grann, 2000; Nisbet et al., 2004), possibly due to the use of different criteria in labelling adolescents as sexual offenders or longer mean follow-up periods in some cases (Langstrom, 2002).

Risk factors

While a number of factors have been identified in the literature to be significantly associated with sexual recidivism among adolescents, there has been little consistency among studies in how recidivism is defined, or what types of sexual offences are included (Parks and Bard, 2006). Earlier studies tended to be less consistent in their use of risk factors as predictive variables. However, more recent studies have used structured risk assessments or other standardised instruments (Auslander, 1998; Gretton et al., 2001; Hecker et al., 2002; Parks and Bard, 2006; Prentky et al., 2000; Waite et al., 2005; Worling and Curwen, 2000).

Sexual interest in children has been identified as a significant predictor in two studies (Boyd, 1994; Worling and Curwen, 2000) using differing recidivism criteria, and was supported with a marginal relationship in a third study (Smith and Monastersky, 1986). Total number of victims (or multiple victims) was reported as a significant predictor in two studies (Langstrom and Grann, 2000; Rasmussen, 1999). Prior sexual offending was identified as a significant predictor in two studies that used an overlapping sample (Langstrom, 2002; Langstrom and Grann, 2000), contradicting a previous finding (Sipe et al., 1998). Two other significant predictors, presence of a male victim and having a stranger victim (Langstrom, 2002; Langstrom and Grann, 2000) were supported with marginal relationships by Smith and Monastersky (1986).

Other significant predictors have been supported by single studies, including multiple female victims (Rasmussen, 1999), social skills deficits (Langstrom and Grann, 2000), verbal threats (Kahn and Chambers, 1991), blaming the victim (Kahn and Chambers, 1991), history of intrafamily violence (Boyd, 1994), higher socioeconomic status (Boyd, 1994), and sexual drive/preoccupation, as measured by Scale 1 of the Juvenile Sex Offender Assessment Protocol (JSOAP) (Hecker et al., 2002). Using the revised version of the same instrument (JSOAP-II), Impulsive/Antisocial Behaviour (Scale 2) was found to be a significant predictor (Parks and Bard, 2006). Prior non-sexual delinquent history was identified as a significant predictor by Boyd (1994), although the opposite finding was later reported by Worling and Curwen (2000).

Structured risk assessment

A history of poor predictive accuracy by mental health professionals using only clinical judgment in the assessment of risk for future violence resulted in the development of statistically based actuarial methods and other structured clinical assessments (Borum, 1996, 2000; Borum et al., 1993; Faust and Ziskin, 1988; Grove and Meehl, 1996; Quinsey et al., 1998). Actuarial scales differ from structured clinical assessments in that they are based upon statistical formulas with different assignment of weight to variables based upon their strength of statistical association with recidivism (Borum, 1996, 2000; Hanson, 1998; Quinsey et al., 1998). Structured clinical assessments provide lists of risk factors that have been empirically associated with recidivism and may include scoring criteria to produce a total score that is subject to the interpretation of the evaluator, but within the context of other clinical information (Borum, 2000; Hanson, 1998). Although it lacks statistical probability data, the structured approach guides the assessment process based upon the most current research literature and has been shown to be superior to clinical judgment alone (Borum, 2000; Hanson, 1998). Because pure actuarial scales are based

upon a limited number of factors and do not take context into consideration, Hanson (1998) recommends a compromise in the adjusted actuarial method, which begins with a statistically derived risk score, but allows for adjustment based upon other relevant clinical or contextual factors.

Following the example of actuarial scales and structured clinical assessments for general and violent risk prediction with adult offenders, similar instruments have been developed that are specific to risk prediction for sexual recidivism. Specifically, the Sex Offender Risk Appraisal Guide (SORAG) (Quinsey et al., 1998), Rapid Risk Assessment of Sexual Offence Recidivism (RRASOR) (Hanson, 1997), and Static-99 (Hanson and Thornton, 1999) have demonstrated significant predictive accuracy for adult sexual recidivism, general recidivism, and violent non-sexual recidivism among adults (Barbaree et al., 2001). The Minnesota Sex Offender Screening Tool-Revised (MnSOST-R) (Epperson et al., 1999) has demonstrated significant predictive accuracy for adult sexual recidivism.

The SORAG (Quinsey et al., 1998) was derived from the Violence Risk Appraisal Guide (VRAG) (Harris et al., 1993) with modifications that added items specific to sexual offending. Its 14 items consist of static historical variables, offence characteristics, mental disorder diagnostic criteria, and deviant sexual interest. Additionally, one item is based upon a total score for the PCL-R, which requires the coding of the 20 PCL-R items prior to coding the SORAG. The SORAG is an actuarial scale and items are weighted based upon empirically based predictive relationships with recidivism.

The RRASOR (Hanson, 1997) is a brief four item actuarial scale derived from a meta-analysis of 61 sex offender recidivism studies (Hanson and Bussiere, 1998). The strongest combination of sexual recidivism predictors, consisting of offence history and victim selection factors, were included in the scale. The Static-99 (Hanson and Thornton, 1999) was developed as an improvement upon the RRASOR with the addition of six additional items to the four original RRASOR items. Added items include factors related to non-sexual offence history and victim characteristics.

The MnSOST-R (Epperson et al., 1999) consists of 16 items that include both static and dynamic factors. This instrument includes a more thorough assessment of offence related factors and victim characteristics. It is unique in its inclusion of dynamic treatment related factors that measure participation in sex offender treatment and substance abuse treatment while incarcerated, as well as quality of behaviour in prison.

While the development of such instruments has been successful with application to adult sex offender populations (Barbaree et al., 2001; Hanson, 1997; Hanson and Thornton, 1999, 2000; Quinsey et al., 1998), similar attempts at standardised risk assessment among juvenile sex offenders have yet to reach the same level of predictive accuracy (Prentky et al., 2000; Prentky and Righthand, 1998, 2003; Worling and Curwen, 2001). The Estimate of Risk of Adolescent Sexual Reoffence Recidivism (ERASOR) (Worling and Curwen, 2001), the Juvenile Sex Offender Assessment Protocol-II (JSOAP-II) (Prentky and Righthand, 2003) and the Juvenile Sexual Offence Recidivism Risk Assessment Tool (JSORRAT) (Epperson et al., 2004) have been the most recently developed risk assessment instruments for juvenile sex offenders and the only known attempts to replicate empirically derived scales modelled with adult sex offenders. The JSORRAT has not been widely disseminated and differs somewhat from the ERASOR and JSOAP by excluding dynamic risk factors. It shares most of the static risk factors assessed by the ERASOR and JSOAP, with slightly different evaluation criteria. Preliminary validity research appears promising, having the benefit of a larger sample and higher recidivism base rate than prior risk assessment validation studies (Epperson et al., 2004).

The ERASOR is a structured clinical assessment modelled after the Sexual Violence Risk-20 (SVR-20) (Boer et al., 1997) for adult sex offenders. While there have been no published reports of predictive validity for the ERASOR, it has been shown to discriminate between first time sexual offenders and re-offenders (Worling, 2004). Unlike the JSOAP, the ERASOR does not provide numerical scale values, but is organised as a structured checklist, resulting in a categorical rating of low, moderate, or high risk. Although organised differently, the ERASOR and JSOAP measure common risk factors.

The Juvenile Sex Offender Assessment Protocol (JSOAP) (Prentky and Righthand, 1998) was the first published attempt to develop an actuarial risk assessment for juvenile sex offenders and has subsequently been modified in the JSOAP-II (Prentky and Righthand, 2003). Risk factors included in the JSOAP and the JSOAP-II were chosen based upon a review of both adult and juvenile sex offender literature as well as general juvenile delinquency literature. The JSOAP-II includes both historical static variables and dynamic variables. There are two static scales, the sexual drive/preoccupation scale and impulsive/antisocial behaviour scale, as well as two dynamic scales, an intervention scale for treatment related factors and a community stability scale for youth not in residential placement. While modelled after adult actuarial scales, research has not yet produced sufficient data to provide item weighting and estimates of probability. Thus far, predictive validity studies of the JSOAP have not had sufficient sample sizes or base rates of recidivism to develop actuarial data (Hecker et al., 2002; Parks and Bard, 2006; Prentky et al., 2000; Waite et al., 2005). The authors emphasise that the JSOAP-II is an experimental scale that cannot provide reliable cut-off scores (Prentky and Righthand, 2003). While continuing research contributes to its predictive validity, the JSOAP-II is recommended for use as an empirically based structured clinical assessment (Prentky and Righthand, 2003).

Psychopathy and risk prediction

Psychopathy has been summarised as a 'constellation of affective, interpersonal, and behavioural characteristics, including egocentricity; impulsivity; irresponsibility; shallow emotions; lack of empathy, guilt, or remorse; pathological lying; manipulativeness; and the persistent violation of social norms and expectations' (Hare, 1996: 25). The Hare Psychopathy Checklist (PCL) (Hare, 1985) and Psychopathy Checklist-Revised (PCL-R) (Hare, 1991) utilise a two-factor model. Factor 1 measures the personality characteristics derived from affective and interpersonal traits and Factor 2 measures behavioural characteristics associated with DSM-IV Antisocial Personality Disorder. Factor 1 and Factor 2 scores are combined to produce a Total PCL score. The PCL-R 2nd edition (Hare, 2003) divides Factor 1 items into Interpersonal and Affective factors, and Factor 2 items into Behavioural and Anti-social factors, resulting in a revised four-factor model.

The Psychopathy Checklist:Youth Version (PCL:YV) (Forth et al., 2003) is an adaptation of the PCL-R 2nd edition for offenders between the ages of 12 and 18 and is designed to measure traits that may contribute to the development of adult psychopathy. The assessment of psychopathy in juveniles is controversial due to the transitional nature of adolescence and uncertainty regarding the stability of measured traits from adolescence into adulthood (Seagrave and Grisso, 2002).

PCL scores have been repeatedly associated with general and violent recidivism among adult offenders (Harris et al., 1991, 1993; Hart et al., 1988; Salekin et al., 1996; Serin, 1996; Serin and Amos, 1995) and juvenile offenders (Auslander, 1998; Forth et al., 1990; Gretton et al., 2001; Langstrom and Grann, 2000). The relationship between psychopathy and sexual recidvism, however, remains less certain. Quinsey, Rice, and Harris (1995) found total PCL-R scores to predict both sexual and violent recidivism among adults. While the PCL-R alone predicted only violent recidivism, Rice and Harris (1997) found sexual recidivism to be predicted by the combination of a high total PCL-R score and evidence of deviant sexual arousal in their adult sample. Serin et al. (2001) found that the combination of a high total PCL-R score and deviant sexual arousal was associated with higher general recidivism, and that PCL-R Factor 2 score alone was associated with general recidivism among adult sex offenders. However, no significant associations were found between PCL-R scores and sexual recidivism. Barbaree et al. (2001) also found that the total PCL-R score predicted general and violent recidivism among adult sex offenders, but failed to predict sexual recidivism. In the same study, however, the Sex Offender Risk Appraisal Guide (SORAG) (Quinsey et al., 1998) which includes the PCL-R total score as a heavily weighted item, predicted sexual recidivism in addition to general and violent recidivism.

Studies using the PCL-R or similar instruments with juvenile sex offender samples have also produced mixed results. Auslander (1998) found the Factor 1 score on the PCL-R to be significantly associated with lower sexual recidivism among juvenile sex offenders, while the total score was predictive of violent non-sexual recidivism. Langstrom and Grann (2000) found the total PCL-R score to be significantly associated with general recidivism but not with sexual recidivism. Using a research version of the PCL:YV, Gretton et al. (2001) found those in a high psychopathy group three to four times more likely to re-offend than those in a low psychopathy group. In a subsequent study, the

Interpersonal and Anti-social factors of the PCL:YV were found to be significant predictors of sexual recidivism (Parks and Bard, 2006).

Typology

It is apparent that adolescent sex offenders are a heterogeneous group with varying victim characteristics, levels of violence, developmental paths, and underlying motivations for offending (Becker, 1998; Boyd et al., 2000; Davis and Leitenberg, 1987; Fehrenbach et al., 1986; Graves et al., 1996; Hunter et al., 2000; Hunter et al., 2003; Vizard et al., 1995; Zolondek et al., 2001). This heterogeneity has resulted in the investigation of typologies based upon the assumption that distinct subtypes of adolescent sex offenders may represent differing treatment needs and developmental risk factors (Hunter et al., 2003).

The exploration of distinct subtypes of adolescent sex offenders has emerged in various ways in the research literature. O'Brien and Bera (1986) proposed a seven group typology that consisted of Naïve Experimenters, Undersocialised Child Exploiters, Pseudosocialised Child Exploiters, Sexual Aggressives, Sexual Compulsives, Disturbed Impulsives, and Group Influenced Offenders. While this classification system was based upon extensive clinical experience by the authors, it is yet to be empirically validated and there have been no subsequent published investigations identified to support the typology. Others have attempted to validate offender subtypes based upon personality assessment (Carpenter et al., 1995; Smith et al., 1987; Worling, 2001), victim selection characteristics (Kaufman et al., 1998; Richardson et al., 1997; Worling, 1995a, 1995b, 1995c), or the analysis of multiple clinical and historical factors (Langstrom, Grann and Linblad, 2000). Some have combined the later two designs and compared groups determined by victim selection for differences on various personality, developmental, clinical, and historical factors (Awad and Saunders, 1991; Carpenter et al., 1995; Hsu and Starzynski, 1990; Hunter et al., 2000; Hunter et al., 2003; Richardson et al., 1997; Saunders et al., 1986).

The victim age dichotomy

The most parsimonious classification found in the exploration of subtypes is based upon victim selection, with a simple dichotomy between those who victimise children and those who victimise peers or adults, a distinction commonly labelled as child molesters versus rapists (Awad and Saunders, 1991; Carpenter et al., 1995; Ford and Linney, 1995; Groth, 1977; Hsu and Starzynski, 1990; Hunter et al., 2000; Hunter et al., 2003; Richardson et al., 1997; Saunders et al., 1986; Worling, 1995a). The investigation of this dichotomy among juveniles follows a number of comparisons between those who commit rape and those who molest children in the adult sex offender literature. Among adults who commit rape, anger and aggression have been identified as primary motivational factors (Barbaree et al., 1994; Serin et al., 1994), whereas those who molest children may tend to be more motivated by deviant sexual arousal (Malcolm et al., 1993). Those who molest children, furthermore, have been found to be unassertive and lacking in social skills (Miner and Dwyer, 1997; Prentky and Knight, 1991; Segal and Marshall, 1985a, 1985b, 1986). Adults who rape have been reported to have higher rates of general recidivism compared to adults who molest children, in addition to more remarkable histories of anti-social behaviour that mostly consist of non-sexual offences (Hall and Proctor, 1987; Prentky et al. 1997; Quinsey et al., 1995). Personality measures have also been indicative of more antisocial traits among those who rape as compared to those who molest children (Valliant and Antonowicz, 1992; Valliant et al., 2000). Similarly, adults who rape tend to score higher than those who molest children on measures of psychopathy (Firestone et al., 2000; Porter et al., 2000).

Among juvenile studies, there is variation in the operational definitions for these dichotomous categories. While some studies define child victims as those four or more years younger than the offender (Awad and Saunders, 1991; Richardson et al., 1997; Saunders et al., 1986; Smith et al., 1987), others require a five year age difference (Ford and Linney, 1995; Groth, 1977; Hunter et al., 2000). Hsu and Starzynski (1990) and Hunter et al. (2003) defined child victims as those under the age of 12. Carpenter et al. (1995) required victims to be age 12 or younger and at least three years younger than the offender. Similarly, Worling (1995a) defined child victims as under the age of 12 and at least four years younger than the offender. Prentky and Righthand (2003) identify a child victim as age 10 or younger and at least four years younger than

the offender in operationalising one of the items of the JSOAP-II.

Differences on personality measures

Smith et al. (1987) identified four sub-groups utilising cluster analysis of personality profiles utilising the Minnesota Multiphasic Personality Inventory (MMPI) with adolescent sex offenders. While not statistically significant, it was noted that offenders against children were more likely to obtain profiles characterised by social introversion, depression, and insecurity, while those who victimised peers or adults were more likely to display typical anti-social traits and profiles characterised by narcissism, anger, hostility, and superficial relationships. The four group clusters identified by multivariate analysis, however, were not directly related to victim age selection.

Worling (2001) replicated the research of Smith et al. (1987) using the California Psychological Inventory (CPI) in place of the MMPI. Cluster analysis produced four groups that were consistent with those revealed by the prior study, although no relationship was identified between victim age selection and any of the cluster groups.

Langstrom et al. (2000) proposed a five-group typology from a cluster analysis of offence related variables. The typology is consistent with the victim age dichotomy, while presenting additional sub-groups based upon other offence characteristics, such as victim-offender relationship and level of violence. The five clusters consist of two child victim clusters and three peer/adult victim clusters, one of which contains non-contact exhibitionist offenders. The combination of the two child victim clusters and the two contact peer adult victim clusters provides a dichotomous contrast in offender characteristics that is consistent with prior research.

Carpenter et al. (1995) found offenders against children to exhibit significantly greater dependent, avoidant, and schizoid characteristics, as measured by the Millon Clinical Multiaxial Inventory (MCMI), compared to offenders against peers. Although not reaching the level of statistical significance, peer offenders produced a notably higher degree of narcissistic traits, with scores in the range of clinical significance. No group differences were reported on the anti-social scale.

Descriptive group comparisons

The comparison of adolescent sex offender subtypes using the victim age dichotomy began with a descriptive analysis of adolescents who sexually assaulted peer or adult victims and adolescents who sexually victimised children (Groth, 1977). The peer/adult offenders appeared to be more likely to use weapons, assault strangers, and abuse drugs or alcohol than those who victimised children. While Groth's (1977) analysis was limited to the evaluation of descriptive trends, subsequent studies have identified significant differences between victim age subtypes with the use of inferential statistical analyses.

Saunders et al. (1986) reported statistically significant differences in a comparison of those who victimised children, peers or adults, and non-contact offenders. Those who victimised children were reported to be significantly more socially isolated compared to those who victimised peers or adults, and to have experienced more intrafamily violence. Offenders against peers/adults were characterised by more caregiver disruption, greater use of violence in their sexual offences, and lower intellectual functioning. In a subsequent comparison with an expanded sample, Awad and Saunders (1991) found consistent results with regard to social isolation, differences in intellectual functioning, and the use of violence. Additionally, those who victimised peers or adults were significantly more likely to have multiple victims and exclusively victimised females, while offenders against children victimised both males and females. There was a significantly greater occurrence of repeat victimisation of the same victim by victimisers of children, who also exhibited a significantly earlier age of onset of sexually deviant behaviour.

Hsu and Starzynski (1990) found a number of statistically significant differences in their comparisons of adolescents who victimised peers or adults with adolescents who victimised children. Offenders against peers or adults were significantly older than the offenders against children and exclusively victimised females, while offenders against children victimised both males and females. Peer/adult offenders were also more likely to have victims of different races and to commit their assaults indoors. Child offenders were most likely to commit offences outdoors. The tendency for peer/adult offenders to use weapons in their offences and to victimise strangers approached statistical significance.

Ford and Linney (1995) found no statistically significant difference between groups on a measure of self-concept, although there was a notable trend toward lower self-concept among offenders against children as compared to offenders against peers or adults, and non-sexual offenders. Significant differences among groups were reported on measures of intrafamily violence and abuse, with those who victimised children reporting more experiences of physical and sexual abuse, parental violence, and total family violence compared to non-sexual offenders and those who victimised peers or adults.

Worling (1995a) compared groups based upon the victim age dichotomy, but only included those with female victims. Excluding offenders against male victims was an effort to eliminate the confounding variable of victim gender, due to the tendency for peer/adult offenders to primarily victimise females, while child offenders tend to have both male and female victims (Worling, 1995a). No significant differences were found between the two groups on measures of self-concept, interpersonal skills, sexual abuse, or sexual attitudes. In contrast to that reported by Ford and Linney (1995), Worling (1995a) found peer/adult offenders to be recipients of significantly more physical punishment from parents as compared to child offenders.

Hunter et al. (2000) found results consistent with prior research in their comparison. Peer/adult offenders exhibited significantly more violence and aggression in their offences compared to offenders against children, primarily victimised females, and had significantly more stranger victims. Peer/adult offenders were also more likely to participate in group offences with co-perpetrators and to commit sexual offences in combination with other non-sexual crimes.

In a subsequent study comparing offenders against children with offenders against peer/adult females, Hunter et al. (2003) confirmed the previous findings that peer/adult offenders were significantly more likely to use violence in their offences and to victimise strangers. Additionally, peer/adult offenders in this sample were significantly more likely to use a weapon and to be under the influence of alcohol or drugs during the offence. Offenders against children exhibited significant psychosocial deficits and a tendency to victimise relatives.

Offenders against children were more likely to have a prior arrest for non-sexual offending.

Richardson et al. (1997) made distinctions among victimisers of children by separating incest offenders and extrafamilial offenders. Their comparison of four sub-groups consisted of incest offenders, extrafamilial child offenders, peer/adult offenders, and mixed group offenders. The mixed group offenders, which included offences against victims in at least two of the other three categories, began offending at a significantly younger age and exhibited a longer duration of offending behaviour. The mixed offenders and peer/adult offenders had significantly more victims. Those in the peer/adult group exclusively victimised females and were significantly more likely to victimise strangers. The peer/adult offenders were significantly less likely to have been sexually victimised themselves as compared to other groups. The mixed group offenders were most likely to have experienced sexual abuse, followed by extrafamilial child offenders and incest offenders. Mixed offenders and child offenders were significantly more likely to have had social services intervention for abuse or neglect. Peer/adult offenders were significantly more likely to have a history of non-sexual delinquency and other anti-social behaviour. Peer/adult offenders and mixed group offenders were most likely to exhibit school behaviour problems.

Graves et al. (1996) proposed three categories of juvenile sex offenders to include paedophilic offenders, sexual assault offenders, and mixed type offenders. These three subtypes were identified from a descriptive meta-analysis of demographic data collected over a twenty-year period. Paedophilic offenders are characterised by social isolation, poor social skills, and a comparatively higher rate of foster-care placement histories, and they victimise children significantly younger than themselves. Sexual assaulters tend to be older than paedophilic offenders and have a pattern of victimising a variety of age groups. Mixed offenders commit a wider variety of offences, including both contact and non-contact offences, and are characterised by more psychopathology.

Summary of typology literature

In summary, the literature presents mixed results when comparing groups of juvenile sex offenders

based upon victim age selection. The assumption that offenders against children are characterised by social skills deficits has been supported empirically by at least three studies (Awad and Saunders, 1991; Carpenter et al., 1995; Hunter et al., 2003; Saunders et al., 1986) and with descriptive trends in two additional studies (Graves et al., 1996; Smith et al., 1987). Worling (1995a, 2001) emphasised a lack of statistical significance between groups on several factors, including interpersonal skills and self-concept. While Ford and Linney (1995) found no statistical significance between groups on a measure of self-concept, they reported a notable trend toward lower self-concept among offenders against children. Intrafamily violence, including significantly more incidence of physical abuse, sexual abuse, and child neglect, was more often identified with offenders against children (Ford and Linney, 1995; Richardson et al., 1997; Saunders et al., 1986), although Worling (1995a) found that offenders against peers or adults were significantly more likely to be the recipients of physical discipline from parents. Other factors found to be significantly associated with offenders against children as compared to offenders against peers or adults include earlier onset of offending (Awad and Saunders, 1991; Richardson et al., 1997), relative victims (Hunter et al., 2003), and repeat victimisation of the same victim (Awad and Saunders, 1991).

The assumption of more aggression and violence among juvenile offenders against peers or adults has been consistently supported (Awad and Saunders, 1991; Hunter et al., 2000; Hunter et al., 2003; Saunders et al., 1986) and, more specifically, greater incidence of the use of weapons in their sexual offences (Hsu and Starzynski, 1990; Hunter et al., 2003). Similarly, Richardson et al. (1997) found significantly more anti-social behaviour among offenders against peers or adults, while Hunter et al. (2000) found the sexual offences of offenders against peers or adults to be perpetrated more often in combination with other non-sexual crimes. Smith et al. (1987) identified a trend toward more anti-social and narcissistic personality traits among offenders against peers or adults, while Carpenter et al. (1995) identified a trend toward more narcissistic traits, but noted no differences between groups for anti-social traits. In contrast to the association of general delinquency with offenders against peers or adults, Hunter et al. (2000) found offenders against children to have a significantly greater history of non-sexual delinquency compared to offenders against peers or adults. Offenders against peers or adults were also found to victimise females either primarily (Hunter et al., 2000) or exclusively (Awad and Saunders, 1991; Hsu and Starzynski, 1990; Richardson et al., 1997), to have significantly more total victims (Awad and Saunders, 1991; Richardson et al., 1997), and significantly more stranger victims (Hsu and Starzynski, 1990; Hunter et al., 2000; Hunter et al., 2003; Richardson et al., 1997). Two studies derived from the same sample found intellectual functioning among offenders against peers or adults to be significantly lower than offenders against children (Awad and Saunders, 1991; Saunders et al., 1986), while others have found no significant differences in intellectual functioning between groups (Ford and Linney, 1995; Hsu and Starzynski, 1990). Hunter et al. (2003) found offenders against peers or adults to be significantly more likely to be under the influence of alcohol or drugs during their offence, consistent with Groth's (1977) descriptive analysis. Hunter et al. (2000) found offenders against peers or adults to be significantly more likely to commit their offences with a group of other offenders. Saunders et al. (1986) found that offenders against peers or adults were significantly more likely to have a history of caregiver disruption, while Graves et al.'s (1996) descriptive analysis reported more incidence of foster care placement among offenders against children.

While most research has been limited to the two group comparison of offenders against children and offenders against peers or adults, others have acknowledged the existence of those who cannot be placed exclusively into either category, resulting in a third category of mixed type offenders (Graves et al., 1996; Parks, 2005; Richardson et al., 1997).

Integration of risk assessment and typology

In a comparison of offenders against children, offenders against peers/adults, and mixed type offenders on potential risk factors for recidivism, as measured by the JSOAP-II and the PCL:YV, mixed type offenders produced consistently higher risk scores (Parks and Bard, 2006). Mixed type offenders (those with at least one child

victim and at least one peer or adult victim) demonstrated higher risk on the total scores and all scale scores of these two instruments. With the exception of two PCL:YV scale scores (Interpersonal and Antisocial), all differences were statistically significant. Those offenders with only one known victim type (child or peer/adult) produced no significant differences on most comparisons. Those with child victims did demonstrate significantly more sexual drive/preoccupation, as measured by the JSOAP-II, than those with peer or adult victims.

While this was the first study to compare the three subtypes using structured risk assessment instruments, findings were generally consistent with previous assumptions about the three offender groups (Parks and Bard, 2006). The lower level of sexual preoccupation exhibited by those with only peer or adult victims is consistent with literature indicating that such offenders often commit sexual offences in the context of more general non-sexual delinquency, and that they have a higher percentage of female victims. Findings are also consistent with the assumption of more deviant arousal among those who victimise children. Sexual drive and preoccupation may be a greater risk factor for adolescents with child victims (Prentky et al., 2000), particularly in the absence of more general delinquent behaviour. The particularly high level of sexual drive and preoccupation among the mixed type group is not surprising, since these offenders, by definition, have a greater diversity and number of victims and do not appear to discriminate in their victim selection.

With no pre-treatment risk scores available, it is unknown whether dynamic treatment related factors, as measured by the JSOAP-II Intervention scale were significantly different among the three sub-groups prior to treatment (Parks and Bard, 2006). However, post-treatment scores clearly indicate poor treatment outcome for mixed type offenders. In addition to higher risk scores, mixed type offenders were also less likely to be successfully discharged from treatment and more likely to age out of the juvenile system or be transferred to the adult system. Based upon characteristics measured by the PCL:YV, mixed type offenders exhibit significantly higher levels of affective deficits that may contribute to higher risk on items measured by the JSOAP-II Intervention scale, such as empathy and remorse.

Future directions

As noted, Hunter and colleagues (Hunter, 2006; Hunter et al., 2000, 2003) have expanded upon the victim age dichotomy to identify a three-group typology, which classifies offenders against children into two distinct types, paraphilic and non-paraphilic. The third subtype is characterised by general delinquent behaviour, including sexual offences primarily against peer or adult female victims. Future research comparing risk factors among subtypes should consider this distinction among offenders against children. Paraphilic offenders would be expected to display higher risk scores on sexual drive and preoccupation, as measured by JSOAP-II Scale 1, while the early onset delinquent subtype would be expected to score higher on a measure of anti-social behaviour, such as those factors measured by JSOAP-II Scale 2. The adolescent onset non-paraphilic subtype would be expected to exhibit the lowest overall risk scores. It is unknown how those identified in other studies as mixed type offenders (Graves et al., 1996; Parks and Bard, 2006; Richardson et al., 1997) fit into this classification scheme.

Evaluation of different treatment approaches, based upon the most relevant risk factors for each identified subtype, is the logical next step for the heterogeneous population of adolescents who commit sexual offences. Based upon variation in risk factors among different subtypes, specialised treatment approaches targeting the most powerful risk factors for each group has the potential to increase treatment effectiveness. Preserving the most intensive and restrictive treatment options for those at highest risk also allows for more efficient use of limited treatment resources.

As knowledge of both recidivism risk factors and offender subtypes continue to develop, the field seems to be moving away from the prevailing 'one size fits all' approach to adolescent sex offender treatment. There appears to be growing recognition of the limitations of the traditional relapse prevention model for sex offender treatment in general, and for adolescents in particular. While some of the traditional treatment concepts may be appropriate for those few adolescents with emerging paraphilic or paedophilic traits, most appear to be candidates for treatment approaches targeting risk factors for general delinquency, or more limited psycho-educational treatment for lower risk, non-delinquent adolescents.

Emerging research in the areas of risk assessment and identification of offender subtypes has positioned the field of adolescent sex offender treatment to move beyond practice guided by clinical assumptions to more empirically guided practice. Given the potential life-altering consequences for clients, it would be irresponsible for clinicians to rely upon purely subjective clinical impressions when assessing risk or making treatment recommendations. Responsible clinical judgment should be informed by available empirical data. However, it is also important to recognise the limitations of the available research while remaining current as data increases. In the absence of a validated actuarial instrument, empirically guided risk assessments here emerged as the current best practice for incorporating research data into risk management decisions.

References

Auslander, B.A. (1998) *An Exploratory Study Investigating Variables in Relation to Juvenile Sexual Reoffending*. Unpublished Doctoral Dissertation. Florida State University, Tallahassee.

Awad, G.A. and Saunders, E.B. (1991) Male Sexual Assaulters: Clinical Observations. *Journal of Interpersonal Violence*. 6, 446–60.

Barbaree, H.E., Seto, M.C., Langton, C.M. and Peacock, E.J. (2001) Evaluating the Predictive Accuracy of Six Risk Assessment Instruments for Adult Sex Offenders. *Criminal Justice and Behavior*, 28, 490–521.

Barbaree, H., Seto, M., Serin, R., Amos, N. and Preston, D. (1994) Comparisons between Sexual and Non-sexual Rapist Subtypes. *Criminal Justice and Behavior*, 21, 95–114.

Becker, J.V. (1998) What we know about the Characteristics and Treatment of Adolescents who have Committed Sexual Offenses. *Child Maltreatment*, 3, 317–29.

Boer, D.P., Hart, S.D., Kropp, P.R. and Webster, C.D. (1997) *Manual for the Sexual Violence Risk-20*, Burnaby, British Columbia: The Mental Health, Law, and Policy Institute, Simon Fraser University.

Bonner, B.L., Marx, B.P., Thompson, J.M. and Michaelson, P. (1998) Assessment of Adolescent Sexual Offenders. *Child Maltreatment*, 3, 374–83.

Borum, R. (1996) Improving the Clinical Practice of Violence Risk Assessment: Technology,

Guidelines, and Training. *American Psychologist*, 51, 945–56.

Borum, R. (2000) Assessing Violence Risk among Youth. *Journal of Clinical Psychology*, 56, 1263–88.

Borum, R., Otto, R. and Golding, S. (1993) Improving Clinical Judgment and Decision Making in Forensic Evaluation. *Journal of Psychiatry and Law*. 21, 35–76.

Boyd, N.J. (1994) *Predictors of Recidivism in an Adolescent Sexual Offenders' Population*. Unpublished doctoral dissertation, University of Wisconsin-Madison.

Boyd, N.J., Hagan, M. and Cho, M.E. (2000) Characteristics of Adolescent Sex Offenders: A Review of the Research. *Aggression and Violent Behavior*, 5, 137–46.

Caldwell, M.F. (2002) What we do not Know about Juvenile Sexual Reoffense Risk. *Child Maltreatment*. 7, 291–302.

Carpenter, D.R., Peed, S.F. and Eastman, B. (1995) Personality Characteristics of Adolescent Sexual Offenders: A Pilot Study. *Sexual Abuse: A Journal of Research and Treatment*, 7, 195–203.

Davis, G.E. and Leitenberg, H. (1987) Adolescent Sex Offenders. *Psychological Bulletin*, 101, 417–27.

Epperson, D., Kaul, J. and Hesselton, D. (1999) *Minnesota Sex Offender Screening Tool-Revised (MnSOST-R): Development, Performance, and Recommended Risk Level Scores*. St. Paul: Minnesota Department of Corrections.

Epperson, D., Ralston, C. and Fowers, D. (2004) *Juvenile Sex Offender Recidivism into Adulthood: A Long-Term Study of Characteristics and Predictors*. Paper presented at the Annual Conference of the Association for Treatment of Sexual Abusers, Albuquerque, New Mexico.

Faust, D. and Ziskin, J. (1988) The Expert Witness in Psychology and Psychiatry. *Science*, 241, 31–5.

Fehrenbach, P.A., Smith, W., Monastersky, C. and Deisher, R.W. (1986) Adolescent Sexual Offenders: Offender and Offense Characteristics. *American Journal of Orthopsychiatry*, 56, 225–33.

Firestone, P., Bradford, J.M., Greenberg, D.M. and Serran, G.A. (2000) The Relationship of Deviant Sexual Arousal and Psychopathy in Incest Offenders, Extrafamilial Child Molesters, and Rapists. *Journal of the American Academy of Psychiatry and the Law*, 28, 303–8.

Ford, M.E. and Linney, J.A. (1995) Comparative Analysis of Juvenile Sexual Offenders, Violent Non-sexual Offenders, and Status Offenders. *Journal of Interpersonal Violence*, 10, 56–70.

Forth, A.E., Hart, S.D. and Hare, R.D. (1990) Assessment of Psychopathy in Male Young Offenders. *Psychological Assessment: A Journal of Consulting and Clinical Psychology*, 2, 342–44.

Forth, A.E., Kosson, D.S. and Hare, R.D. (2003) *The Psychopathy Checklist: Youth Version*. Toronto: Multi-Health Systems.

Graves, R.B., Openshaw, D.K., Ascione, F.R. and Ericksen, S.L. (1996) Demographic and Parental Characteristics of Youthful Sexual Offenders. *International Journal of Offender Therapy and Comparative Criminology*, 40, 300–17.

Gretton, H.M., McBride, M., Hare, R.D., O'Shaughnessy, R. and Kumka, G. (2001) Psychopathy and Recidivism in Adolescent Sex Offenders. *Criminal Justice and Behavior*, 28, 427–49.

Groth, A.N. (1977) The Adolescent Sexual Offender and his Prey. *International Journal of Offender Therapy and Comparative Criminology*, 21, 249–54.

Grove, W.M., and Meehl, P.E. (1996) Comparative Efficiency of Informal (Subjective, Impressionistic) and Formal (Mechanical, Algorithmic) Prediction Procedures: The Clinical-Statistical Controversy. *Psychology, Public Policy, and Law*, 2, 293–323.

Hall, G.N. and Proctor, W.C. (1987) Criminological Predictors of Recidivism in a Sexual Offender. *Journal of Consulting and Clinical Psychology*, 55, 111–12.

Hanson, R.K. (1997) *The Development of a Brief Actuarial Risk Scale for Sexual Offense Recidivism*. Ottawa: Department of the Solicitor General of Canada.

Hanson, R.K. (1998) What do we Know about Sex Offender Risk Assessment? *Psychology, Public Policy, and Law*, 4, 50–72.

Hanson, R.K. and Bussiere, M.T. (1998) Predicting Relapse: A Meta-Analysis of Sexual Offender Recidivism Studies. *Journal of Consulting and Clinical Psychology*, 66, 348–62.

Hanson, R.K. and Thornton, D. (1999) *Static 99: Improving Actuarial Risk Assessments for Sex Offenders*. Ottawa: Department of the Solicitor General of Canada.

Hanson, R.K. and Thornton, D. (2000) Improving Risk Assessments for Sex Offenders: A Comparison of Three Actuarial Scales. *Law and Human Behavior*, 24, 119–36.

Hare, R.D. (1985) *The Hare Psychopathy Checklist*. Toronto: Multi-Health Systems.

Hare, R.D. (1991) *The Hare Psychopathy Checklist-Revised*. Toronto: Multi-Health Systems.

Hare, R.D. (1996) Psychopathy: A Clinical Construct whose Time has Come. *Criminal Justice and Behaviour*, 23, 25–54.

Hare, R.D. (2003) *The Hare Psychopathy Checklist-Revised*. 2nd edn. Toronto: Multi-Health Systems.

Harris, G.T., Rice, M.E. and Cormier, C.A. (1991) Psychopathy and Violent Recidivism. *Law and Human Behavior*, 15, 223–36.

Harris, G.T., Rice, M.E. and Quinsey, V.L. (1993) Violent Recidivism of Mentally Disordered Offenders: The Development of a Statistical Prediction Instrument. *Criminal Justice and Behavior*, 20, 315–35.

Hart, S.D., Kropp, P.R. and Hare, R.D. (1988) Performance of Male Psychopaths following Conditional Release from Prison. *Journal of Consulting and Clinical Psychology*, 56, 227–32.

Hecker, J., Scoular, J., Righthand, S. and Nangle, D. (2002) Predictive Validity of the J-SOAP over 10-plus Years: Implications for Risk and Assessment. Paper Presented at the Annual Conference of the Association for Treatment of Sexual Abusers, Montreal.

Hsu, L.K.G. and Starzynski, J. (1990) Adolescent Rapists and Adolescent Child Sexual Assaulters. *International Journal of Offender Therapy and Comparative Criminology*, 34, 23–30.

Hunter, J.A. (2006) Understanding Diversity in Juvenile Sexual Offenders. In Longo, R. and Prescott, D. (Eds.) *Current Perspectives: Working with Aggressive Youth and Youth with Sexual Behavior Problems*. Holyoke, MA: NEARI Press.

Hunter, J.A., Figueredo, A.J., Malamuth, N.M. and Becker, J.V. (2003) Juvenile Sex Offenders: Toward the Development of a Typology. *Sexual Abuse: A Journal of Research and Treatment*, 15, 27–48.

Hunter, J.A., Hazelwood, R.R. and Slesinger, D. (2000) Juvenile-Perpetrated Sex Crimes: Patterns of Offending and Predictors of Violence. *Journal of Family Violence*, 15, 81–93.

Hunter, J.A. and Lexier, L.J. (1998) Ethical and Legal Issues in the Assessment and Treatment of Juvenile Sex Offenders. *Child Maltreatment*, 3, 339–48.

Kahn, T.J. and Chambers, H.J. (1991) Assessing Reoffense Risk with Juvenile Sexual Offenders. *Child Welfare*, LXX: 333–45.

Kaufman, K.L. et al. (1998) Factors Influencing Sexual Offenders' Modus Operandi: An Examination of Victim-Offender Relatedness and Age. *Child Maltreatment*, 3, 349–61.

Langstrom, N. (2002) Long-Term Follow-Up of Criminal Recidivism in Young Sex Offenders: Temporal Patterns and Risk factors. *Psychology, Crime and Law*, 8, 41–58.

Langstrom, N. and Grann, M. (2000) Risk for Criminal Recidivism among Young Sex Offenders. *Journal of Interpersonal Violence*, 15, 855–71.

Langstrom, N., Grann, M. and Linblad, F. (2000) A Preliminary Typology of Young Sex Offenders. *Journal of Adolescence*, 23, 319–29.

Malcolm, P.B., Andrews, D.A. and Quinsey, V.L. (1993) Discriminant and Predictive Validity on Phallometrically Measured Sexual Age and Gender Preferences. *Journal of Interpersonal Violence*, 8, 486–501.

Miner, M.H. and Dwyer, S.M. (1997) The Psychosocial Development of Sex Offenders: Differences between Exhibitionist Child Molesters and Incest Offenders. *International Journal of Offender Therapy and Comparative Criminology*, 41, 36–44.

National Adolescent Perpetrator Network (1988) Preliminary Report from the National Task Force on Juvenile Sexual Offending. *Juvenile and Family Court Journal*, 39, 1–67.

National Adolescent Perpetrator Network (1993) Revised Report from the National Task Force on Juvenile Sexual Offending. *Juvenile and Family Court Journal*, 44, 1–120.

Nisbet, I.A., Wilson, P.H. and Smallbone, S.W. (2004) A Prospective Longitudinal Study of Sexual Recidivism among Adolescent Sex Offenders. *Sexual Abuse: A Journal of Research and Treatment*, 16, 223–34.

O'Brien, M.J., and Bera, W.H. (1986) Adolescent Sexual Offenders: A Descriptive Typology. *Preventing Sexual Abuse*, 1, 1–4.

Parks, G.A. and Bard, D.E. (2006) Risk Factors for Adolescent Sex Offender Recidivism: Evaluation of Predictive Factors and Comparison of Three Groups Based upon Victim Type. *Sexual Abuse: A Journal of Research and Treatment*. 18: 319–42.

Porter, S. et al. (2000) Profiles of Psychopathy in Incarcerated Sexual Offenders. *Criminal Justice and Behavior*, 27, 216–33.

Prentky, R.A. and Knight, R.A. (1991) Identifying Critical Dimensions for Discriminating among Rapists. *Journal of Consulting and Clinical Psychology*, 59, 643–61.

Prentky, R., Harris, B., Frizzell, K. and Righthand, S. (2000) An Actuarial Procedure for Assessing

Risk with Juvenile Sex Offenders. *Sexual Abuse: A Journal of Research and Treatment*, 12, 71–93.

Prentky, R.A., Lee, R.F.S., Knight, R.A. and Cerce, D. (1997) Recidivism Rates among Child Molesters and Rapists: A Methodological Analysis. *Law and Human Behavior*, 21, 635–59.

Prentky, R. and Righthand, S. (1998) *Juvenile Sex Offender Assessment Protocol Manual.* Bridgewater, MA: Justice Resource Institute.

Prentky, R. and Righthand, S. (2003) *Juvenile Sex Offender Assessment Protocol-II Manual.* Bridgewater, MA: Justice Resource Institute.

Quinsey, V.L., Harris, G.T., Rice, M.E. and Cormier, C.A. (1998) *Violent Offenders: Appraising and Managing Risk.* Washington, DC: American Psychological Association.

Quinsey, V.L., Rice, M.E. and Harris, G.T. (1995) Actuarial Prediction of Sexual Recidivism. *Journal of Interpersonal Violence*, 10, 85–105.

Rasmussen, L.A. (1999) Factors Related to Recidivism among Juvenile Sexual Offenders. *Sexual Abuse: A Journal of Research and Treatment*, 11, 69–85.

Rice, M.E. and Harris, G.T. (1997) Cross Validation and Extension of the Violence Risk Appraisal Guide for Child Molesters and Rapists. *Law and Human Behavior*, 21, 231–41.

Richardson, G., Kelly, T.P., Bhate, S.R. and Graham, F. (1997) Group Differences in Abuser and Abuse Characteristics in a British Sample of Sexually Abusive Adolescents. *Sexual Abuse: A Journal of Research and Treatment*, 9, 239–57.

Salekin, R.T., Rogers, R. and Sewell, K.W. (1996) A Review and Meta-Analysis of the Psychopathy Checklist and Psychopathy Checklist-Revised: Predictive Validity of Dangerousness. *Clinical Psychology: Science and Practice*, 3, 203–15.

Saunders, E., Awad, G. and White, G. (1986) Male Adolescent Sexual Offenders: The Offender and the Offense. *Canadian Journal of Psychiatry*, 31, 542–49.

Seagrave, D. and Grisso, T. (2002) Adolescent Development and the Measurement of Juvenile Psychopathy. *Law and Human Behavior*, 26, 219–39.

Segal, Z.V. and Marshall, W.L. (1985a) Heterosexual Social Skills in a Population of Rapists and Child Molesters. *Journal of Consulting and Clinical Psychology*, 53, 55–63.

Segal, Z.V. and Marshall, W.L. (1985b) Self-Report and Behavioral Assertion in Two Groups of Sex Offenders. *Journal of Behavior Therapy and Experimental Psychiatry*, 16, 223–29.

Segal, Z.V. and Marshall, W.L. (1986) Discrepancies between Self-Efficacy Predictions and Actual Performance in a Population of Rapists and Child Molesters. *Cognitive Therapy and Research*, 10, 363–76.

Serin, R.C. (1996) Violent Recidivism in Criminal Psychopaths. *Law and Human Behavior*, 20, 207–17.

Serin, R.C. and Amos, N.L. (1995) The Role of Psychopathy in the Assessment of Dangerousness. *International Journal of Law and Psychiatry*, 18, 231–38.

Serin, R.C., Mailloux, D.L. and Malcolm, P.B. (2001) Psychopathy, Deviant Sexual Arousal, and Recidivism among Sexual Offenders. *Journal of Interpersonal Violence*, 16, 234–46.

Serin, R.C., Malcolm, P.B., Khanna, A. and Barbaree, H.E. (1994) Psychopathy and Deviant Sexual Arousal in Incarcerated Sexual Offenders. *Journal of Interpersonal Violence*, 9, 3–11.

Sipe, R., Jensen, E. L. and Everett, R.S. (1998) Adolescent Sexual Offenders Grown Up. *Criminal Justice and Behavior*, 25, 109–24.

Smith, W.R. and Monastersky, C. (1986) Assessing Juvenile Sexual Offenders' Risk for Reoffending. *Criminal Justice and Behavior*, 13, 115–40.

Smith, W.R., Monastersky, C. and Deisher, R.M. (1987) MMPI-Based Personality Types among Juvenile Sexual Offenders. *Journal of Clinical Psychology*, 43, 422–30.

Valliant, P.M. and Antonowicz, D.H. (1992) Rapists, Incest Offenders, and Child Molesters in Treatment: Cognitive and Social Skills Training. *International Journal of Offender Therapy and Comparative Criminology*, 36, 222–30.

Valliant, P.M., Gauthier, T., Pottier, D. and Kosmyna, R. (2000) Moral Reasoning, Interpersonal Skills, and Cognition of Rapists, Child Molesters, and Incest Offenders. *Psychological Reports*, 86, 67–75.

Vizard, E., Monck, E. and Misch, P. (1995) Child and Adolescent Sexual Abuse Perpetrators: A Review of the Research Literature. *Journal of Child Psychology and Psychiatry*, 36, 731–56.

Waite, D. et al. (2005) Juvenile Sex Offender Re-Arrest Rates for Sexual, Violent Non-sexual and Property Crimes: A 10-year Follow-up. *Sexual Abuse: A Journal of Research and Treatment*, 17, 313–31.

Worling, J.R. (1995a) Adolescent Sex Offenders against Females: Differences Based on the Age of their Victims. *International Journal of Offender Therapy and Comparative Criminology*, 39, 276–93.

Worling, J.R. (1995b) Adolescent Sibling-Incest Offenders: Differences in Family and Individual Functioning when Compared to Non-sibling Sex Offenders. *Child Abuse and Neglect*, 19, 633–43.

Worling, J.R. (1995c) Sexual Abuse Histories of Adolescent Male Sex Offenders: Differences Based on the Age and Gender of their Victims. *Journal of Abnormal Psychology*, 104, 610–13.

Worling, J.R. (2001) Personality-Based Typology of Adolescent Male Sexual Offenders: Differences in Recidivism Rates, Victim-Selection Characteristics, and Personal Victimization Histories. *Sexual Abuse: A Journal of Research and Treatment*, 13, 149–66.

Worling, J.R. (2004) The Estimate of Risk of Adolescent Sexual Offense Recidivism (ERASOR): Preliminary Psychometric Data. *Sexual Abuse: A Journal of Research and Treatment*, 16, 235–54.

Worling, J.R. and Curwen, T. (2000) Adolescent Sexual Offender Recidivism: Success of Specialized Treatment and Implications for Risk Prediction. *Child Abuse and Neglect*, 24, 965–82.

Worling, J.R. and Curwen, T. (2001) *Estimate of Adolescent Sexual Offense Recidivism (The ERASOR) (Version 2.0)*. Toronto, Canada: Ontario Ministry of Community and Social Services.

Zolondek, S.C., Abel, G.G., Northey, W.F. and Jordan, A.D. (2001) The Self-Reported Behaviors of Juvenile Sexual Offenders. *Journal of Interpersonal Violence*, 16, 73–85.

Chapter 13

Static, Stable and Dynamic Risks and Assets Relevant to the Prevention and Treatment of Abusive Behaviour

Gail Ryan

Introduction

People exhibit a wide range of abusive behaviours. Such behaviours are not always defined as abuse but share the common characteristics of causing harm, in a variety of ways, to self, others, or property. Children are not always held accountable for abusive behaviours. The child who throws the doll against the wall; the playground bully; or the siblings who hit or denigrate each other. Yet these behaviours are abusive, and when chronic and resistant to change may eventually result in referrals for clinical services and/or in legal charges as the child is held culpable for behaviours which violate the law or cause harm to self, others, or property. The sexually abusive behaviour of children and adolescents has been the focus of intense scrutiny in the community, the courts, human services, and the mental health field for nearly 20 years. More recently, extreme aggression and violence of juveniles have attracted public concern. Due to the sexual aspect, sexually abusive behaviour has been viewed as different from other abusive behaviours, and has been studied in terms of development and the risk of reinforcement of arousal patterns and sexual interest/identity (Ryan et al., 1988; Ryan, 2000). However, as more and more clinical work and research illuminate the development and correction of sexually abusive behaviour in childhood and adolescence, it has become apparent that there is tremendous crossover in the etiological risk factors, as well as the dynamics and treatment, relevant to a wide spectrum of abusive behaviours (Ryan, 1998: 1999). This chapter focuses on the abusive aspects of behaviour.

Retrospective and prospective studies have identified many factors which appear related to the risk of children developing dysfunctional patterns of behaviour which may be abusive to themselves, others, and/or property. Some factors may be associated with heritable characteristics, some with prenatal insults which affect foetal development and the condition at birth, others may occur as a product of failures in early caregiving and developmental differences and some result from exposure and events in the child's early life experience. It is apparent that risk factors do not operate in isolation, but interact in ways that may be moderated or exacerbated by other variables including both risks and assets. Correlations are not directly causal, for better and worse.

Awareness of the range and interaction of various types of risk factors can inform our ability to predict that some children are at greater risk than others. Such knowledge provides opportunities for primary and secondary prevention, as well as the identification of early manifestations that may benefit from tertiary interventions. This chapter will review recent research relevant to our understanding of factors which may increase the risk of children developing or maintaining abusive behaviours, with some emphasis on sexually abusive behaviours, and suggests identification and preventive intervention strategies. Public health and community mental health models inform the discussion of primary, secondary and tertiary prevention.

Background

Beginning in 1987, a multi-disciplinary, multi-agency study group began to meet monthly to review research into 'victim-to-victimiser' hypotheses which had been posed in relation to sexual abuse perpetration (Ryan, 1989). Studying new publications and exploring their relevance to prevention and treatment, the group of clinical researchers began with the knowledge that:

1. A history of childhood sexual victimisation is over-represented in both juveniles and adults who commit sexual offences.
2. Adults abused as children may experience sexual dysfunctions, non-sexual dysfunctions, or no dysfunction later in life.

3. Dysfunctional behaviours seem to occur in repetitive patterns representative of a common defensive strategy (Ryan, 1989).

This knowledge has continued to be reaffirmed by numerous studies reviewed by the group (Ryan et al., 1999).

The group has hypothesised, as did many researchers at that time, that some combination of variables were descriptive of:

1. The child's own experience of sexual abuse.
2. The process of discovery/disclosure.
3. Subsequent reactions/interventions would be explanatory and thus predictive of an outcome of sexual offending.

Careful review of the research which became available over the next decade revealed that, although sexual victimisation is over-represented in both clinical and criminal justice populations, it is not explanatory of dysfunction or offending. There is some support for the power of validating, protective, and supportive responses (following the disclosure of child sexual abuse) in moderating subsequent symptoms, but there is little evidence linking long-term outcomes to treatment of child victims, for better or worse (Rind, Tromovitch and Bauserman (1998).

Emerging research has demonstrated that:

1. Childhood neglect, physical abuse, and witnessing family violence may precede sexual offending even more often than sexual abuse (Widom and Williams, 1996).
2. Many child victims recover without long-term damage or dysfunction, even without treatment (Rind, Tromovitch and Bauserman, 1998).
3. Sexually abusive youths are less at risk of sexual offence recidivism than non-sexual re-offence, and juveniles re-offend less often than adult sex offenders, especially after treatment (Bourdin et al., 1990; Alexander, 1999; Worling, 2000).
4. Only a small portion of juveniles who sexually abuse have deviant sexual arousal patterns (Hunter and Becker, 1994; Hunter, 1996: 1999).

Combining offence-specific theories with developmental contextual, and ecological theories (Strayhorn, 1998; Donovan and McIntyre, 1990; Scales and Leffert, 1998) a new set of hypotheses

developed and were described by Ryan et al. (1999).

One of the hypotheses generated was that the developmental status (relative competency) and prior life experience of the child (context) were likely to be more predictive of outcomes than any combination of variables descriptive of the sexual abuse events (Ryan et al., 1999). That is, the most powerful variables might be related to who the child was at the time of the abuse experience, and what beliefs, skills, strategies and/or resources were available to them to cope with the experience (Steele, 1987). A developmental, contextual, ecological model encompasses the complexity of variables (see Figure 1).

Identifying specific risks and deficits in each area may be an endless task, but the model underscores the need for comprehensive, individualised assessment and differential treatment plans. Still, despite the complexity, Ryan (1998, 1999) has suggested that the three most common deficits found in all abusive persons may be:

1. Poor communication.
2. Lack of empathy for self and others.
3. Lack of an internal sense of responsibility.

It was suggested that developmental, contextual, and ecological assessments require an ongoing process of discovery which is guided by observations of daily functioning (Yager et al., 1999).

Recent Research

Most recently, research on prediction of sexual recidivism has focused on the development of *actuarial* risk assessment (Quinsey, 1995; Quinsey et al., 1998; Hanson, 2000; Prentky et al., 2000). Hanson (2000) typifies the findings of research on adults who sexually offend in isolating factors most predictive of sexual recidivism over time by adults (regardless of treatment status). Prentky et al. (2000) similarly describe a tentative model of predictors of recidivism for sexually abusive youths. However, as was pointed out by Quinsey in early presentations of actuarial research (1995) actuarial models can be discouraging for treatment providers, parole boards, and clients because retrospective factors found to predict greater risk of recidivism cannot be changed. In 1995, Quinsey called for similar work to identify

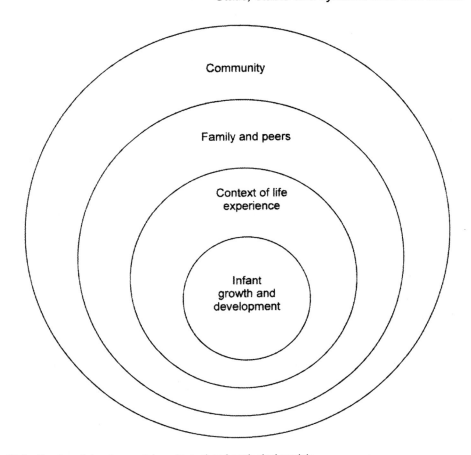

Figure 13.1 Overlay of developmental, contextual and ecological models

dynamic predictors which might be more changeable in treatment.

The inclusion of developmental assessment and differential diagnosis in evaluating sexually abusive youth had been suggested by the National Task Force on Juvenile Sexual Offending (1993). In many areas, clinical work on risk management for juvenile behaviour problems has begun incorporating both risks and assets in models for assessment, prediction, and prevention (see for example, Scales and Leffert, 1998). Whittaker (1990) had incorporated developmental competencies into programming for violent and sexually aggressive youth. Bremer (1998) had introduced a risk assessment model for sexually abusive adolescents that included protective factors. Rasmussen et al. (1992: 2000) and Rich (2000) have also considered protective factors in the design of programme models. Most recently, Gilgun (1996: 1998) has published

models specifically relevant to sexually abusive prepubescent children that describe risk and protective factors. Gilgun's model emphasises the balance of risks and assets in assessment and treatment, pointing out that the youth with high risks but also high assets may be less at risk to re-offend than the low risk youth who is also low in assets (Figure 2).

The recent research detailing actuarial and dynamic risk factors further advances our ability to build relevant, empirically based models for clinical assessment and treatment. For example, Prentky et al. describes unchangeable historical variables which indicate higher risk for juveniles to relapse. These include a history of: Prior charges for sexual offences; Predatory behaviour; Sexual preoccupation; Duration of sexually abusive history; Caregiver instability, Arrest before age 16; School behaviour problems; Suspension or expulsion from school; Diagnosis

A	B
Low risk	Low risk
Low asset	High asset
C	D
High risk	High risk
Low asset	High asset

Figure 13.2   Balance of risks and assets (Gilgun, 1996: 1998)

of conduct disorder; Multiple types of sexual offences; Impulsivity; and Alcohol or drug use by either the youth or parent (Prentky et al., 2000). While it is assumed that the cessation of offending predatory behaviour, disordered conduct, school behaviour problems and drug/alcohol use are obvious and immediate treatment goals, the cessation of such behaviours will still not erase their presence in the history of the youth. At the same time, the history of sexual preoccupation, impulsivity and caregiver instability may be more stable factors, likely to continue to be characteristic of this youth and his relationships across the lifespan, and so will be ongoing goals to be addressed in the treatment and relapse prevention plans for the particular youth.

Similarly, the factors described by Hanson (2000) as unchangeable risk factors in the history of adult offenders suggest some immediate goals in treating juveniles to prevent the development and/or maintenance of those factors by the time they become adults. For example, Hanson describes sexual deviance, range of victims, persistence of offending and anti-social personality as high risk factors for the adult who offends, but the developmental trajectory and reinforcement of these factors might be changed by successful treatment of juveniles. Fortunately, Hunter (2000) assures us that the plethysmographic research indicates that the sexually abusive behaviour of juveniles is not always associated with deviant arousal. It is usually much more about being abusive than about being sexually deviant. Nonetheless, for the minority of sexually abusive youth who do have deviant arousal, a range of victims, persistent offending after early intervention, or have

conduct disorder traits thought to be associated with the development of anti-social personality, these are likely to continue to predict higher risk. For such youth, intensive targeted interventions to assess the weight of deviant arousal and, when indicated, to undertake arousal reconditioning, and cognitive work to address irresponsible and criminal thinking patterns in general (Yochelson and Samenow, 1977), and beliefs and attitudes supportive of sexually exploitive and abusive behaviours specifically (Malamuth, 1986) would clearly be indicated.

However, the most changeable factors are apparent in the area of dynamic risk assessment. Prentky et al. (2000) describes the reduction of dynamic risks in terms of what might be observable in the treatment process: accepting responsibility, internal motivation to change, understanding the cycle, showing empathy and remorse, no cognitive distortions, anger management, stability in home and school, support systems, and quality peer relationships. Gilgun (1998) describes markers of protective factors related to emotional expressiveness, family relationships, peer relationships, sexuality and family embeddedness in the community. In a very detailed treatment model for adolescents, Rich (2000) charts factors related to responsibility, relationships, cognitive functioning, social skills, co-morbid psychiatric disorders and substance abuse, anti-social behaviours, family, environment and work on past experiences.

Dynamic factors are markers of functioning which reflect important aspects of the youths' developmental competence, their perceptual experience of the world, relationships, and self, and the characteristics of the family, peer group, community and culture in which they have lived

Table 13.1 Factors relevant to human functioning. (For better or worse)

Static (Historical/unchangeable)	*Stable* (Life spanning/less changeable)	*Dynamic* (Change/manage/moderate)
• Condition at birth • Permanent disability • Family of origin/culture • Early life experience	• Temperament • Intellectual potential • Physical attributes • Heritable neurological characteristics	• Situations • Thoughts • Feelings • Behaviours

and will continue to live. In treatment, interventions to change the dynamic risk factors, while moderating and managing the effects of static and stable factors, is likely to have the best effect. Both Gilgun (1998) and Rich (2000) detail specific elements of each domain, which can be observed in the daily circumstances and functioning of the individual, in order to rate progress in acquiring dynamic assets which may offset the unchangeable risks.

Static, stable and dynamic factors

By thinking first about the factors which relate to all human functioning (see Table 1), and then as they might specifically relate to more or less risk for abusive behaviour, a framework for conceptualising static, stable and dynamic risks and assets emerges.

Defining static factors as those which are retrospective/historical variables, we know that these factors cannot be changed because we cannot change history. Such factors might include:

1. The condition at birth.
2. Permanent disabilities.
3. Family of origin.
4. Early life experience.

Stable factors might be defined as life spanning (that is, likely to remain somewhat stable over time), but might include characteristics which can be either moderated or exacerbated in the effect they have on one's functioning. Such factors might include such variables as:

1. Temperament.
2. Intellectual potential.
3. Physical attributes.
4. Heritable neurological characteristics.

Finally, dynamic factors might be defined as those factors that are constantly changing, or at

least are changeable. Specifically, dynamic factors would include situational, cognitive, emotional, and behavioural factors which may change (for better or worse) and may be managed or coped with (for better or worse) throughout the individual's life, and on a daily basis. All will affect and be affected by developmental, contextual, and ecological factors.

Risks and assets relevant to the likelihood of sexually abusive behaviour

Based on the aforementioned course of study, Tables 2, 3 and 4 depict factors which seem most relevant to the risk of abusive behaviours or sexual deviance or dysfunction.

Risk factors that affect the condition at birth might include genetic abnormalities, foetal exposure to drugs or alcohol or disease, inborn disabilities and premature or traumatic birth. The condition at birth describes all that the infant brings with them, which will profoundly affect their experience of the world, relationships, and self. Risk factors may cause the infant to be chronically distressed and hard to care for, increasing the risk of breakdown in their ability to communicate their needs and emotions and interfering in the process of attachment and bonding between the child and caregiver. The distress of sick, premature or low birth weight babies has been a dilemma described in neonatology (Goldson et al., 1978), as well as the effects of prenatal exposure to drugs and alcohol (Baumbach, 2000).

Upon arrival, the infant is dependent upon caregivers in the family of origin to read their cues and provide care and nurturance to meet their needs. If the caregiver is not consistently empathic (that is, providing for the infant's needs either sporadically or consistently but without regard for the infant's cues), the infant may learn to disregard their internal cues and become

Table 13.2 Static factors

Risks	Assets
• Prenatal insults	• Prenatal care
• Premature/traumatic birth	• Normative birth
• Unempathic care	• Empathic care
• Caregiver loss/disruption	• Consistent caregivers
• Trust failure	• Trustworthy relationship
• Disordered attachment	• Secure attachment
• Dysfunctional modelling	• Normal growth/development
• Witness domestic violence	• Functional modelling
• Abuse, neglect, FTT, trauma	• Nurturance and protection

helpless to identify and communicate their needs and emotions effectively. The lack of empathic care precludes the infant's natural acquisition of empathic recognition for self and others (Landry and Peters, 1992). Disruption of the caregiver relationship (whether through omission or commission of the caregiver) further jeopardise the infant's emerging interpersonal skills and sense of self (Steele, 1987). The infant fails to achieve basic trust and internalises a negative internal model for future relationships (Ainsworth, 1985; Bowlby, 1985).

The family into which the child is born is not only the source of many factors affecting the condition at birth and early caregiving, but also provides the child's first experience of the world. For better or worse, every factor affecting the family has an effect on the child: Control/helplessness; competence/failure; functional/dysfunctional; safety/vulnerability; protect/harm; support/deprivation; embeddedness/isolation in the community, etc. The stresses on the family and their strategies for coping become the model for the child's earliest beliefs. The family of origin creates the ecological 'pond' within which the child grows and as the child matures, the pond widens to include peer, community and cultural influences. This ecological pond may be the source of both risks and assets.

The physiological effects of early care can also be profound. Recent research on early brain development (Karr-Morse and Wiley, 1997) has demonstrated that the infant's brain is growing in 'use dependent' ways; that is, the functions that are most active increase growth in some areas while under used areas fail to grow. The infant using his/her brain to hold and process knowledge about the world may be developing hyper-sensitivities to some cues and fail to

develop at all in other areas. Severe neglect can be seen in the absence of brain growth in some areas (Karr-Morse and Wiley, 1997), while fear responses to abuse or trauma can overdevelop defensive brain functions (Van der Kolk, 1987; Knopp and Benson, 1996). When experiences occur in an organised and predictable manner, the brain grows in an organised way, but chaotic and unpredictable experiences create chaos in the brain.

Factors arising from both positive and negative early life experiences include both risks and assets for all children. Children who lack the internal and/or external assets necessary to successfully cope with adverse experiences may become deviant or dysfunctional as a result of developmental failures that allow and shape accommodation and assimilation. When children are victims of abuse, neglect, or trauma they may either accept or reject all or parts of the experience as congruent or incongruent in the context of their view of themselves, the world and relationships. Very often, in the face of helplessness, the child takes on a sense of responsibility for the behaviour of others and imagines that they have caused (or failed to prevent) their own victimisation, or that they are unworthy of the care and attention they need. This misattribution of responsibility distorts the locus of control. Believing oneself responsible for the behaviour of others, lessens one's sense of personal responsibility and contributes to a dysfunctional coping style in which the child seeks:

1. To regain a sense of control by controlling others.
2. To compensate for unmet needs with whatever self-gratifying substitutions are available to them (Ryan, 1989).

Table 13.3   Stable factors

Risks	Assets
• Difficult temperament traits • Low functioning/DD/learning disability • Negative internal working model (self and others) • Heritable psychiatric disorders; attention deficit disorder • Chronic PTSD reactivity	• Easy/adaptive temperament • Average – high intelligence (IQ) • Positive internal working model (self and others) • Normative physical and neurological functioning

Stable risk factors, which may be relevant to the risk of dysfunctional behaviours, may include such things as difficult temperament, low intellect or learning difficulties, negative internal working model, heritable psychiatric disorders, and chronic PTSD reactivity (Table 3)

Temperament traits are usually described as either easy or difficult. 'Difficultness' is often defined in terms of how difficult certain characteristics may be for other people to deal with (Thomas and Chess, 1977). Therefore, temperament traits may be viewed as either risks or assets, depending upon the particular family, community, or culture a child arrives in. A lack of fit, when the child's temperament does not meet the expectations of the family or community, can contribute to chronic conflicts and negative interactions which affect the child's self esteem and relationships (Turecki, 1985). However, the person most affected by temperament is the person him/herself. Some traits contribute to irritability and discontent to such a degree that the child is at risk of chronic stress, and thus, dysfunctional coping. It is thought that temperament traits remain somewhat stable across the lifespan, although their effects can be moderated or exacerbated by many factors (Thomas and Chess, 1977; Turecki, 1985). Physical attributes (such as gender, appearance or stature) can similarly affect the child in terms of a lack of fit, when the child does not meet the expectations of the parents or is not viewed positively by others. Discontent with one's physical attributes can also affect self-esteem and contribute to the child's risk of dysfunctional coping in general, and specifically affect sexual risk taking and self-destructive behaviour (Taussig, 2000).

Intellectual potential (IQ) is also thought to remain somewhat stable across the lifespan, although brain growth, stimulation, and learning disabilities can severely affect intellectual functioning. As previously stated, the influence of environment and care on brain growth is now known to be profound (Karr-Morse and Wiley,

1997) and it is likely that further research will contribute additional insight regarding brain functioning and the propensity for problems with both sexuality and aggression. It is apparent, however, that one's ability to learn, process information, and cognitively and verbally articulate their needs, emotions and thoughts is very relevant to successful human functioning. Intellectual functioning can be further affected by some psychiatric disorders which can cause confusion, delusions, rapid or sluggish thought processing, attention deficits or intrusive images.

Some psychiatric disorders are frequently found to be over-represented in samples of sexually abusive youth. Becker et al. (1991) Dailey (1996) Cavazos (2000) and Kavoussi et al. (1998) have described the co-occurrence of mood disorders, attention disorders, obsessive-compulsive disorders, and post-traumatic stress disorder in work with sexually abusive youth. The relationship between co-occurring disorders and the risk of abusive behaviours and/or sexual deviance is not always clear and is not thought to be causal, but it is clear that both psychological and neurological functioning may provide fuel for dysfunctional patterns associated with sexual and aggressive behaviours. We also know that brain functioning can be altered by traumatic events, causing either acute or chronic reactivity. When brain functioning has been permanently altered by trauma (Van der Kolk, 1987) or in the case of neurologically based disorders which are inherited, these disorders are likely to remain somewhat constant across the lifespan. Co-occurring psychiatric disorders may contribute to the risk of dysfunctional or abusive behaviours in two ways. One is to contribute to the symptoms that precede the behaviour (fuel for the cycle) and the other is to benefit from and be reinforced by the neurochemical reactions generated by some behaviours ('self-medicating' effects). The risks associated with the most prevalent psychiatric disorders can be

Table 13.4 Dynamic risk factors

Global Foreseeable in life span	Circumstantial Specific/fluctuating daily
• Constant/expected stressors • Unresolved emotional issues • Unsafe environment/persons • Injury/illness • Temporary disabilities • Lack of opportunity/support • Change/loss • Failed relationships • Access to vulnerable persons	• Current/unexpected stressors or (conflict or emotional trigger) • Perceived threat/vulnerability • Lowered self esteem/efficacy • Negative expectations • Isolation/lack of support • Mood dysregulation: anger, depression, anxiety • Projection/externalising • Limited options/skill deficit • Abusive memory/fantasy • Lowered inhibitions • Access to vulnerable persons • Rationalisation, justification

significantly moderated by effective treatment or may exacerbate risk when untreated.

Dynamic risks and assets are those which fluctuate from day to day and over time and are, therefore, more changeable and/or manageable. By observing daily functioning, it is possible to see the characteristics of situations, thoughts, feelings, and behaviours which precede and follow abusive behaviours. Recognition of a common pattern (cycle) has been used to target interventions which will interrupt this pattern, as well as working to prevent it (Lane, 1997; Ryan et al., 1987; Way and Spieker, 1997; Ryan and Blum, 1993). It is possible to identify foreseeable stressors across the lifespan, and consciously plan for long-term relapse prevention. Such strategies can address life events known to be stressful to most human beings (global), as well as those that may be very personal and unique to the individual. For example, times of transition or loss are likely to be stressful for most people; whereas, the infancy of one's own child or the death of a grandparent might be uniquely stressful for a person who was abused or neglected as an infant or whose primary attachment was to the grandparent. One's ability to anticipate and prepare for both common and unique foreseeable stress is the basis for good relapse prevention work in treatment.

It is also possible (and entirely normal) to think through one's plans for the day and the immediate future in order to anticipate and plan for possible risks or stressors, and make informed choices about such circumstances. Table 4 depicts examples of both global and circumstantial risk factors thought to be particularly relevant to

fuelling or supporting the dysfunctional cycle associated with abusive behaviours.

By identifying risk factors specifically relevant to the likelihood of person's getting into the dysfunctional/abusive cycle, interventions to avoid, decrease, desensitise, replace or manage those risks becomes possible. Some risks are associated with emotionally charged issues or memories, which may benefit from psychotherapy to make conscious, desensitise, and integrate old emotional triggers. Some risks are associated with cognitive beliefs or perceptions, which can benefit from conscious rethinking and cognitive restructuring. Some are related to true vulnerabilities resulting from either external circumstances or internal deficits that cause a sense of helplessness and can benefit from changes in the ecological pond or the development of increased skills and competency. Clinicians treating abusive clients will recognise the relationship of the dynamic risk factors to elements which manifest specifically in the abusive cycle (Ryan et al., 1987; Lane, 1997; Way and Spieker, 1997; Ryan et al., 1999) and which many offence specific treatment interventions address. These dynamic risk factors are also congruent with many of the dynamic factors identified by Prentky et al. (2000) Gilgun (1998) and Hanson (2000).

Implications for prevention

Recognition of different types of risk factors provides numerous and diverse opportunities for preventive interventions. The static risks can only be prevented before they occur. For example, preventive interventions to optimise the condition at birth can be found in good prenatal care and it may become possible to minimise the risks of some genetic or heritable characteristics and disabilities. Helping children arrive in the world in the best possible condition should be the first step in every public health effort.

The family of origin is a powerful factor from the moment of birth and immediately contributes to the risks and assets that the child will carry with them throughout life. Assuring that every child is born into the best possible family of origin is another relevant prevention goal. By identifying risk factors for new parents, both universal and targeted interventions have been demonstrated to optimise the functioning of the family of origin. Such diverse interventions as family planning, parenting education, maternity/paternity leave, the WIC programmes and food stamps, and home visitation for new parents all aim to improve the conditions for families and children. Olds et al. (1998) have provided powerful evidence that targeting at-risk mums with the services of a nurse home visitor during the first two years of life can not only reduce immediate risks for the child and improve the mother's life course, but also have long lasting effects on the successful functioning of the child across the span of childhood and adolescence.

Enriching a child's early life experience and protecting the infant, toddler, and child from neglectful, aversive, and traumatic experiences is the responsibility of both the family and the community (Kempe and Helfer, 1980; Krugman and Davidson, 1991). Paediatric, child protection, child welfare, child care, developmental and childhood education professionals all commit themselves to various aspects of enrichment and protection, and represent the community's interest in the child. Policy makers, legislators, and adult services all affect the ecological pond and many consider or disregard the impact of their actions on children, to the benefit or detriment of individual children and the community. Risks can be moderated and assets enhanced in every area of the child's growth and experience. History can be changed only prospectively, as it is created and experienced, but can never be relived later despite the most rigorous corrective interventions. Therefore, the static factors relevant to the child's risk of becoming abusive to themselves, others, or

property are best addressed preventively, within public health models which can reasonably be expected to extend benefits to all children, and to target selected risk factors to provide additional services to those most in need.

The factors which have been described here as stable may be unchangeable, although some may be prevented through the previously described interventions. However, the effects of stable factors on the daily functioning and overall success of individuals can be moderated or exacerbated by both internal and external factors. For example, Whitaker (1990) and Gilgun (1996, 1998) have suggested that the effects of risks (relevant to a child continuing to engage in sexually abusive behaviour) may be moderated by increasing assets so that the balance is tipped in a positive direction. The same concept can be applicable in a more global sense to prevention efforts. Wherever we are able to moderate the effects of stable risk factors by increasing the functional developmental, contextual, and ecological assets we can decrease the likelihood of dysfunction.

Just as the brain grows in 'use dependent' ways, the child's development and experiences are also shaped in 'use dependent' ways. When developmental or experiential risks require the child to operate in a constant defensive mode in order to cope with those risks, the dysfunctional pattern is likely to become deeply ingrained. For example, if a child's difficult temperament traits subject them to chronic conflicts and negative feedback, increasing understanding, acceptance, and strategies to moderate these effects may tip the balance. Some interventions may aim to change the way the trait is manifest by the child, others may seek to change the expectations and reactions of others. Discovery of the assets that offset the effect of the risks is the key. Similarly, intellectual, learning or developmental disabilities can be moderated by special educational interventions and remedial interventions, some of which directly change the functioning of the individual, and others which change the expectations and responses of others.

The constant interaction of the individual and the ecological pond is clear. The role of attachment and bonding in creating an 'internal model or template for relationships has been explored in relation to many aspects of human functioning (Ainsworth, 1985; Bowlby, 1985; Lindstrom, 1999), including its relationship to differences in the sexual offending of adolescents or adults (Marshall et al., 1993 and 1995; Ward et al., 1995). The sensitivity, responsiveness, and consistency of the caregiver during the first weeks and months of life have been shown to form the capacity for empathy (Landry and Peters, 1992) and communication (Donovan and McIntyre, 1990) as well as the basis for self-image and expectations of others in future relationships. The toddler's ability to achieve the critical development of 'basic trust' is the product of an attachment to a trustworthy caregiver. Prevention of attachment disorders lies in assuring that every child has a dependable and trustworthy caregiver, and minimising disruptions in that relationship. Prevention is likely to be more effective than any subsequent intervention, but when a child has developed a negative internal representation of self and/or others, the effects can only be moderated by new experiences in a long-term, consistent relationship (Blanchard, 1995; Pullen, 1999).

Developments in psychiatry over the past decade have applied both genetic and neurological research to expand our knowledge about the heritability of certain psychiatric disorders. Brain imaging technology promises to increase the accuracy and specificity of early childhood diagnostic procedures (Cavezos, 2000). Foreseeing the risk and screening for earlier identification should enable much earlier interventions to moderate the effects of disorders associated with organic and neurochemical differences in the brain. However, our ability to moderate the effects of inherited, stable conditions in the brain which manifest in disordered coping/functioning will depend on not only the development of accurate diagnostics, preventive pharmacology and therapies for the individual child, but also on education to increase awareness and acceptance and decrease stigmatisation of such abnormalities in the family and community: another public health concern. Normative brain functioning is an asset, whether inborn or achieved by corrective pharmacological maintenance.

Finally, as we have learned that for some victims of trauma, brain functioning is permanently changed, chronic reactivity to some stimuli may be foreseeable and stabilise risk (Van der Kolk, 1987). Obviously, primary prevention lies in protecting children from exposure to traumatic events, but when trauma has created chronic reactivity in the brain it may be a stable factor which increases risk across the life span.

For some, pharmacological treatment may be a necessary condition to enable the individual to participate in psychotherapeutic and cognitive therapies which moderate this reactivity, but for others, pharmacological prescriptions may be indicated as a life long need to moderate these effects.

If we foresee that these 'stable' factors will require life long management strategies to moderate risk, interventions may be a part of secondary prevention for at-risk persons as well as an integral part of tertiary relapse prevention strategies.

The implications for prevention which come from identifying the global and circumstantial dynamic risk factors increase our ability to foresee problems associated with a specific dysfunctional pattern. While we appreciate that the basic pattern represented in Figure 3 is a common human response to stress, we can also foresee the problems which arise when humans rely exclusively on defensive strategies (and especially when they arrive at abusive behaviours as solutions to compensate for overwhelming emotions and negative expectations), in order to regain equilibrium.

Even very young children can be observed using dysfunctional patterns to cope with stressful situations (Figure 4). Caregivers and gatekeepers to services for children can be trained to see the manifestation of avoidant, dysfunctional, and abusive defensive strategies in the way children express themselves and behave. Adults can:

1. Intervene to increase assets in the child and his environment which will provide more functional solutions.
2. Act to interrupt the habituation of dysfunctional coping strategies where they are observed.

For example, anticipatory desensitisation of situations which are emotionally charged, validation of emotional cues, and increasing emotional expressiveness, address the risk of the child becoming overwhelmed by unexpected or unresolved emotional stress. Fostering the development of new skills and orchestrating successful experiences provides a basis for more self-esteem and more hopeful expectations. Decreasing the frequency of avoidant, isolating strategies of children and the fuelling of their anger with projection and misattributions of responsibility decreases the externalising and

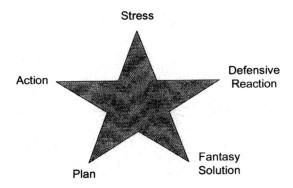

Figure 13.3 Common human adaptive response to stress

Figure 13.4 The high risk cycle associated with dysfunctional coping

control-seeking pattern. A critical intervention which serves as both primary and secondary prevention lies in successful development of skills and positive experiences which increase the child's repertoire of possible 'solutions' or coping skills. Finally, increasing communication, empathy, and accurate attributions of responsibility for self and others may be seen as 'universal goals' to promote non-abusive, empathic interpersonal functioning in general (Bennett, 1979) as well as healthy sexual development specifically (Ryan et al., 1988; Ryan, 2000). Effective verbal communication requires language to support learning and successful interactions. Recognition of cues of distress and a sense of personal responsibility for the effect of one's behaviour decreases one's ability to disregard, minimise, or justify the harm of abusive behaviours.

Successful outcomes

Drawing on the research and study described, it becomes possible to more clearly articulate what might constitute successful outcomes relevant to the prevention of abusive behaviours. Table 5 suggests observable evidence from daily functioning that is thought to be relevant to decreasing the risk of abusive behaviour and increasing the likelihood of healthy, successful functioning. These can be described as the 'dynamic assets' which counter the dynamic risks, previously described.

Consistently defining all abuse is a marker of recognition and vigilance which makes it less likely that individuals might unwittingly engage in, or be victims of, abuse without defining it as such. This awareness increases the recognition of risk and the clear attribution of responsibility relevant to all forms of abuse. Acknowledging the

Table 13.5 Dynamic assets

Evidence of decreased risk	Evidence of increased health
• Consistently defines all abuse (self, others, property) • Acknowledges risk (foresight and safety planning) • Consistently recognises/interrupts cycle (no later than the first thought of an abusive solution) • Demonstrates new coping skills (when stressed) • Demonstrates empathy (sees cues of others and responds) • Accurate attributions of responsibility (takes responsibility for own behaviour, not try to control behaviour of others) • Able to manage frustration and unfavourable events (anger management and self protection) • Rejects abusive thoughts as dissonant (incongruent with self image)	• Pro-social relationship skills (closeness, trust, and trustworthiness) • Positive self image (able to separate, independent, competent) • Able to resolve conflicts and make decisions (assertive, tolerant, forgiving, cooperative; able to negotiate and compromise) • Celebrates good and experiences pleasure (able to relax and play) • Works/struggles to achieve delayed gratification (persistent pursuit of goal, submission to reasonable authority) • Able to think and communicate effectively (rational cognitive processing; adequate verbal skills; able to concentrate) • Prosocial peers • Family and/or community support system • Adaptive sense of purpose and future

risk of abuse occurring in one's daily life supports the continued use of foresight and planning for the safety of self and others across the lifespan. Recognising the cycle and mastery of the skills to interrupt it must be demonstrated consistently, ideally avoiding the pattern, but always interrupting the progression no later than the first thought of an abusive fantasy solution. Parallel to the need to avoid the dysfunctional cycle is the need to demonstrate mastery of alternative coping strategies when coping with stress or experiencing highly charged emotions.

Demonstrating empathy in one's daily interactions is observable as one recognises and responds to the cues of self and others which indicate needs and emotions. The accurate attribution of responsibility for behaviour manifests in taking personal responsibility for one's own behaviour, as well as not accepting or trying to assume control of others or responsibility for things beyond the individual's control. In addition, judging behaviour without judging oneself or others is related to tolerance for abuse in one's life. Ideally, rejecting abusive thoughts as dissonant with one's view of self demonstrates the acquisition of a non-abusive self-image/identity. This is of critical importance (and a great source of hope) for youth who have not yet completed the task of identity formation.

Avoiding the abusive pattern is likely to be most successful and to generalise across the lifespan when one is able to function successfully

in their daily lives. Specifically, one's ability to create psychologically safe, empathic relationships may be one of the most protective factors in decreasing the risk of interpersonal abuse. Pro-social relationship skills, and especially one's ability to establish intimacy, closeness, and trustworthy relationships, demonstrates and supports a belief in the value of such relationships. A positive self-image is reliant on mastery of the developmental skills which enable individuals to be separate and independent, while a sense of personal competency supports personal responsibility. The ability to resolve conflicts and make good decisions is reliant on both assertiveness and tolerance, as well as one's ability to forgive the failures of others, and to negotiate and compromise cooperatively.

It is especially important to counter the deviant reinforcements of abusive behaviours with healthy pleasures. One's ability to relax and play, to celebrate good, and to experience pleasure directly parallels the risk of reliance on deviant or harmful solutions to compensate or feel better in times of stress. Being able to think clearly, process experiences without distortion, and effectively communicate contribute to an internal sense of control.

Anger management and self-protection go hand in hand with one's ability to tolerate frustration, and to make accurate attributions of responsibility in unfavourable circumstances. The willingness to struggle to achieve delayed gratification, to pursue goals without distraction or discouragement, and to be able to pursue one's own goals within the parameters set by reasonable authorities are characteristics of successful pro-social functioning. Finally, an adaptive and realistic sense of purpose, and the ability to foresee and anticipate success in the future are the fuel to drive continued motivation to avoid abusive behaviours.

Conclusions

This paper has reviewed a wide range of research and thought relevant to the development and maintenance of abusive behaviours, and suggests many hypotheses that require additional research to correct and validate our understanding of the balancing roles of risks and assets. 'Offence specific' interventions are widely described in the literature specific to the treatment of those who sexually offend, and research and theories relevant to the sexual aspects of development and sexual abuse have been described elsewhere (Ryan, 1998; Ryan, 2000). For some sexually abusive youths, individualised assessment may reveal other risks and/or deficits that will require specialised risk management strategies. Some 'offence specific' interventions may require balancing the needs and best interests of the individual against those of the community, and some may cause unintended consequences which create new risks (Berliner, 1998; Chaffin and Bonner, 1998; Dishion et al., 1999). However, the outcome measures suggested here are observable in terms of the daily functioning of individuals, and might be considered successful outcomes for all children, even if they have not been considered at-risk or identified because of abusive behaviours.

The primary, secondary or tertiary interventions suggested in this paper as a means to achieve the suggested outcomes need not be intrusive and are not likely to cause iatrogenic harm to any child or the community. A real potential to reduce the risk of children becoming or continuing to be abusive is suggested by these hypotheses, and provides an invitation to action. Research is needed to test these hypotheses and will be most efficiently carried out by implementing these suggestions within prospective studies, providing an immediate possibility of abuse reduction while testing their validity, and further refining our ability to prevent perpetration.

The ideas contained in this paper were first presented at the First National Sexual Violence Prevention Conference in Dallas, Texas, March 2000, sponsored by the Centre for Disease Control; and were subsequently presented at the Positive Outcomes Conference in Manchester, England, July 2000. The author is indebted to many colleagues who have shared in the study of these issues over a span of 15 years, including members of the Kempe Study Group; and the National Adolescent Perpetration Network. This course of study has been supported by the Kempe Centre; the University of Colorado School of Medicine, Department of Paediatrics; and the Kempe Foundation.

References

Ainsworth, M.D.S. (1985) Attachments Across the Lifespan. *Bulletin of New York Academy of Medicine*, 61, 792–812.

Alexander, M. (1999) Sexual Offender Treatment Efficacy Revisited. *Sexual Abuse: Journal of Research and Treatment*, 11: 2, 101–16.

Araji, S. (1997) *Sexually Aggressive Children*. Thousand Oaks, CA: Sage.

Baumbach, J. (2000) *When Making it Simpler isn't so Simple: Adaptations to meet the Treatment Needs of Sexually Abusive Youth with Foetal Alcohol Syndrome*. Presentation at the 15th National Conference of the National Adolescent Perpetration Network; Denver CO.

Becker, J.V., Kaplan, M.S., Tenke, C.E. and Tartaglini, A. (1991) The Incidence of Depressive Symptomatology in Juvenile Sex Offenders with a History of Abuse. *Child Abuse and Neglect*, 15, 531–6.

Bennet, M. (1979) Overcoming the Golden Rule: Sympathy and Empathy. In Nimmo, D. (Ed.) *Communication Yearbook*. 3rd edn. New Brunswick, NJ: Transaction Press.

Berliner, L. (1998) Juvenile Sex Offenders: Should they be Treated Differently? *Journal of Interpersonal Violence*, 13: 5, 645–6.

Blanchard, G. (1995) *The Difficult Connection*. Orwell, VT: Safer Society Press.

Borduin, C.M., Henggeler, S.W., Blaske, D.M. and Stein, R.M. (1990) Multisystemic Treatment of Adolescent Sexual Offenders. *International Journal of Offender Therapy and Comparative Criminology*, 34: 105–13.

Bowlby, J. (1985) Violence in the Family as a Function of the Attachment System. *American Journal of Psychoanalysis*, 44, 9–27.

Bremer, J. (1998) Challenges in the Assessment and Treatment of Sexually Abusive Youth. *Irish Journal of Psychology*, 19: 1, 82–92.

Camino, L. (2000) *Treating Sexually Abused Boys*. San Francisco, CA: Jossey Bass.

Cavazos, E. (2000) *Dual Diagnosis and Medication Options for Sexually Abusive Youth*. Presentation at the 15th National Conference of National Adolescent Perpetration Network, Denver CO.

Chaffin, M. and Bonner, B. (1998) Don't Shoot, We're your Children: Have we Gone too far in our Response to Adolescents and Children with Sexual Behaviour Problems? *Child Maltreatment*, 3: 4, 314–6.

Dailey, L. (1996) *Biomedical Treatments with Sexually Abusive Youth*. Presentation at the Twelfth National Conference of National Adolescent Perpetration Network, Minneapolis, MN.

Dishion, T., McCord, J. and Poulin, F. (1999) When Interventions Harm: Peer Groups and Problem Behaviour. *American Psychologist*, 54: 9, 755–64.

Donovan, D. and McIntyre, D. (1990). *Healing the Hurt Child: A Developmental Contextual Model*. New York: Norton.

Gilgun, J. (1996) Human Development and Adversity in Ecological Perspective. *Families in Society*, 77: 8, 395–402 and 459–76.

Gilgun, J. (1998) CASPARS: Clinical Instruments for Assessing Client Assets and Risks in Mental Health Practice. *Medical Journal of Allina* 7, 1. www.allina.com

Goldson, E., Fitch, M., Wendal, l.T. and Knapp, G. (1978) Child Abuse: Its Relationship to Birthweight, Apgar Score, and Developmental Testing. *American Journal of Disabled Children*, 132, 790–3.

Hanson, K. (2000) *Static 99*. Beaverton, OR: Association for Treatment of Sexual Abusers.

Hunter, J. (1999) *Understanding Juvenile Sexual Offending Behaviour: Emerging Research, Treatment Approaches and Management*. Silver Spring, NY: Centre for Sex Offender Management.

Hunter, J.A. (1996). *Working with Children and Adolescents who Sexually Abuse Children*. Paper presented at the 11th International Congress on Child Abuse and Neglect, Dublin, Ireland.

Hunter, J.A. and Becker, J. (1994) The Role of Deviant Arousal in Juvenile Sexual Offending Etiology, Evaluation and Treatment. *Criminal Justice and Behaviour*, 21, 4.

Karr-Morse, R. and Wiley, M. (1997) *Ghosts from the Nursery: Tracing the Roots of Violence*. New York: Grove Atlantic.

Kavoussi, R., Kaplan, M. and Becker, J. (1988) Psychiatric Diagnoses in Adolescent Sex Offenders, *Journal of Child and Adolescent Psychiatry*, 27, 241–3.

Kempe, C.H. and Helfer, R.E. (1980) *The Battered Child*. 3rd edn. Chicago: University of Chicago Press.

Knopp, F. and Benson, A. (1996) *A Primer on the Complexities of Traumatic Memory*. Brandon, VT: Safer Society Press.

Krugman, R. and Davidson, H. and US Advisory Board on Child Abuse and Neglect (1991) *Creating Caring Communities*. Washington: USDHS.

Landry, S. and Peters, R.D. (1992) Toward Understanding of a Developmental Paradigm for Aggressive Conduct Problems during the Preschool Years. In Peters, R.D., McMahon, R. and Quinsey, V. (Eds.) *Aggression and Violence throughout the Lifespan*. Newbury Park, CA: Sage.

Lane, S. (1997) The Sexual Abuse Cycle. In Ryan, G. and Lane, S. (Eds.) *Juvenile Sexual Offending: Causes, Consequences and Correction*. 2nd edn. San Francisco: Jossey-Bass.

Lindstrom, B. (1998) Attachment, Separation and Abuse Outcomes: Influence of Early Life Experience and Family of Origin. In Ryan et al. *Web of Meaning*. Brandon, VT: Safer Society Press.

Malamuth, N. (1986) Predictors of Naturalistic Sexual Aggression. *Journal of Personality and Social Psychology*, 50, 953–62.

Marshall, W.L., Hudson, S.N. and Hodkinson, S. (1993) The Importance of Attachment Bonds and the Development of Juvenile Sex Offending. In Barbaree, H.E., Marshall, W.L. and Hudson, S.M. (Eds.) *The Juvenile Sex Offender*. New York: Guilford.

Marshall, W.L. and Mazzucco, A. (1995) Self-esteem and Parental Attachments in Child Molesters. *Sexual Abuse: A Journal of Research and Treatment*, 7: 4, 279–86.

National Task Force on Juvenile Sexual Offending (1993) The Revised Report. *Juvenile and Family Court Journal*, 44: 4, 1–120.

Olds, D. et al. (1998) The Promise of Home Visitation: Results of Two Randomised Trials. *Journal of Community Psychology*, 20: 1, 5–21.

Prentky, R., Harris, B., Frizzell, K. and Righthand, S. (2000) An Actuarial Procedure for Assessing Risk with Juvenile Sex Offenders. *Sexual Abuse: Journal of Research and Treatment*, 12: 2, 71–94.

Pullen, C. (1999) The Therapist's Experience of Sexual Abuse Treatment. In Ryan et al. *Web of Meaning*. Brandon, VT: Safer Society Press.

Quinsey, V. (1995) Actuarial Prediction of Sexual Dangerousness. Paper presented at the Fourteenth ATSA Conference, New Orleans, LA.

Quinsey, V., Khanna, A. and Malcolm, B. (1998) A Retrospective Evaluation of the Regional Treatment Centre Sex Offender Treatment Program. *Journal of Interpersonal Violence*, 13: 5, 621–44.

Rasmussen, L., Burton, J. and Christopherson, B. (1992) Precursors to Offending and Trauma Outcome Process in Sexually Reactive Children. *Journal of Child Sexual Abuse*, 1: 1, 33–48.

Rasmussen, L. (2000) *The Trauma Outcome Process: An Integrated Model for Guiding Clinical Practice with Children with Sexually Abusive Behaviour Problems*. (Submitted for publication)

Rich, P. (2000) Stetson School: Juvenile Sexual Offender Risk for Re-offending Assessment. (Unpublished) Barre, MA: Stetson School.

Rind, B., Tromovitch, P. and Bauserman, R. (1998) A Meta-analytic Examination of Assumed Properties of Child Sexual Abuse using College Samples. *American Psychological Bulletin*, 124: 1, 22–53.

Ryan, G. (1989) Victim to Victimizer: Rethinking Victim Treatment. *Journal of Interpersonal Violence*, 4: 3, 325–41.

Ryan, G. (1998) The Relevance of Early Life Experience to the Behaviour of Sexually Abusive Youth. *The Irish Journal of Psychology*, 19: 1, 32–48.

Ryan, G. (1999) The Treatment of Sexually Abusive Youth: The Evolving Consensus. *Journal of Interpersonal Violence*, 14: 4, 422–36.

Ryan, G. (2000) Childhood Sexuality: A Decade of Study. *Child Abuse and Neglect*, 24: 1, 33–61.

Ryan, G. et al. (1998) *The Web of Meaning: A Developmental-contextual Approach in Treatment of Sexual Abuse*. Brandon, VT: Safer Society Press.

Ryan, G. et al. (1988) *Understanding and Responding to the Sexual Behaviour of Children: Trainer's Manual*. Denver, CO: Kempe National Centre, University of Colorado Health Sciences Centre.

Ryan, G. and Blum, J. (1993) Managing Chronic Behaviour Problems. In *Understanding and Responding to the Sexual Behaviour of Children: Trainer's Manual*. Denver, CO: Kempe National Centre, University of Colorado Health Sciences Centre.

Ryan, G., Lane, S., Davis, J. and Issac, C. (1987) Juvenile Sexual Offenders: Development and Correction. *Child Abuse and Neglect*, 3: 3, 385–95.

Scales, P. and Leffert, N. (1998) *Developmental Assets: A Synthesis of the Scientific Research on Adolescent Development*. Minnesota, MN: Search Institute.

Steele, B.F. (1987) Abuse and Neglect in the Earliest Years: Groundwork for Vulnerability. *Zero to Three*, 7: 4, 14–15.

Strayhorn, J.M. (1988) *The Competent Child. An Approach to Psychotherapy and Preventive Mental Health*. New York: Guilford Press.

Taussig, H. (2000) Risk Behaviour in Maltreated Adolescents: A Prospective Investigation of Protective and Vulnerability Factors. Preparing for publication, Denver, CO: Kempe Centre.

Terr, L. (1990b) *Too Scared to Cry: Psychic Trauma in Childhood*. New York: Harper and Row.

Thomas, A. and Chess, S. (1977) *Temperament and Development*. New York: Brunner/Mazel.

Turecki, S. (1985) *The Difficult Child*. New York: Bantam Books.

Van der Kolk, B.A. (Ed.) (1987) *Psychological Trauma*. Washington, DC: American Psychiatric Press.

Ward, T., Hudson, S., Marshall, W. and Siegert, R. (1995) Attachment Style and Intimacy Deficits in Sexual Offenders: A Theoretical Framework. *Sexual Abuse: Journal of Research and Treatment*, 7: 4, 317–35.

Way, I. and Spieker, S. (1997) *The Cycle of Offence*. Notre Dame, IN: Jalice Publishers.

Whitaker, M. (1990) Personal Communication to the National Task Force on Juvenile Sexual Offending regarding competency based treatment models.

Widom, C.S. and Williams, L. (1996) *Cycle of Sexual Abuse. Research Inconclusive about whether Child Victims become Adult Abusers*. Report to House of Representatives, Committee of Judiciary, Subcommittee on Crime. General Accounting Office, Washington DC.

Worling, J. (2000) Adolescent Sexual Reoffense Recidivism: 10 year Follow-up of Specialized Treatment and Implications for Risk Prediction. *Child Abuse and Neglect*, 24, 4.

Yager, J., Knight, L., Arnold, L. and Kempe, R. (1998) The Process of Discovery. In Ryan et al. *The Web of Meaning*. Brandon, VT: Safer Society Press.

Yochelson, S. and Samenow, S. (1977) *The Criminal Personality*. New York; Jason Aronson Publishers.

Chapter 14

Empirically Guided Practice with Young People Who Sexually Abuse: A Risk Factor Approach to Assessment and Evaluation

Lucinda A. Rasmussen and L.C. Miccio-Fonseca

Introduction

This chapter presents the *Multiplex Empirically Guided Inventory of Ecological Aggregates for Assessing Sexually Abusive Children and Adolescents (Ages 19 and Under) – MEGA* (Miccio-Fonseca, 2006b) the first empirically guided tool for assessing risk of sexually abusive behaviour in *all* youth under the age of 19, male or female, child or adolescent, and youths with developmental disabilities. *MEGA* is based on an *Ecological model* asserting that:

1. Multiplex triggering factors (i.e., factors that occur simultaneously) contribute to risk for youth to engage in sexually abusive behaviour.
2. Protective factors serve to mitigate this risk.
3. Improving self-governance increases capacity for self-regulation, leading to reduced risk for sexually abusive behaviour and recidivism.

(Miccio-Fonseca and Rasmussen, 2006a)

MEGA is developmentally sensitive; all of its elements are anchored on empirical research for risk and/or recidivism related to sexually abusive youth, not adults. It is a time sensitive risk assessment tool that can be utilised to evidence improvement in specified areas of functioning that relate to risk for sexually abusive behaviour, as compared to baseline assessment.

Empirically Guided Practice with Young People who Sexually Abuse: A Risk Factor Approach to Assessment and Evaluation

Crime statistics in the United States suggest that many adolescents and children engage in sexually abusive behaviour, although recent reports indicate that the overall number is declining (Finkelhor and Jones, 2004). Data compiled in 12 states between 1991 and 1996 by the National Incident-Based Reporting System (NIBRS) indicated that 23 per cent of sexual assault offenders were under age 18 (Snyder, 2000). The percentage of juvenile offenders varied according to type of offence – in forcible rapes, 17 per cent of the offenders were under age 18, compared with 23 per cent in sexual assaults with an object, 27 per cent in forcible fondling and 36 per cent in forcible sodomy. Only 16 per cent of the reported juvenile offenders were children ages 7 to 11; they comprised only 7 per cent of juvenile offenders in forcible rapes, while they made up greater proportions of the juvenile offenders in forcible fondling (19 per cent), sexual assaults with an object (17 per cent), and forcible sodomies (23 per cent). The single age with the greatest number of offenders (either juvenile or adult) was age 14. Although it is unknown whether these data from the NIBRS and some juvenile courts generalise across all states, it is evident that a considerable number of children and adolescents abuse other children sexually, and that a certain percentage of their offences involve physical force and coercive behaviour.

Despite evidence that some youth are at risk to commit sex offences, the field of treatment of sexually abusive youth lacks a comprehensive empirically guided tool for assessing risk for sexually abusive behaviour and documenting evidence of improvement in *all* youth 19 years and under, both adolescents *and* children (Prescott and Longo, 2005). Three empirically based tools are currently available for assessing sexually abusive youth; however, these tools apply primarily to adjudicated male adolescents and are not designed to assess female youth, children under 12, or youth who are developmentally delayed. The three tools are:

- *Juvenile Sex Offender Assessment Protocol* (*J-SOAP-II*, Prentky, Harris, Frizzell, and Righthand, 2000; Prentky and Righthand, 2003: 2004; Righthand et al., 2005).
- *Estimate of Risk of Adolescent Sexual Offence Recidivism* (*ERASOR, Version 2.0*, Worling and Curwen, 2001; Worling, 2004).

- *Juvenile Sexual Offender Recidivism Risk Assessment Tool-II (J-SORRAT-II,* Epperson, Ralston, Fowers, and DeWitt, 2005).

The *J-SOAP-II* and *ERASOR, Version 2.0* are based on an adult research paradigm, which fails to account for the obvious disparity in developmental challenges and milestones between adults and youth and the more extensive offence histories of adults. Remarkably, these risk assessment tools are not designed to be developmentally sensitive to different ages of youth. Nor are these tools intended to monitor the youth's risk over time to evidence change and improvement.

This chapter reviews literature on definitions and risk assessment of children and adolescents who are engaging in sexually abusive behaviours. It discusses an *Ecological model* that we have formulated, which provides the conceptual framework of a new risk assessment tool, the *Multiplex Empirically Guided Inventory of Ecological Aggregates for Assessing Sexually Abusive Children and Adolescents (Ages 19 and Under) (MEGA)* (Miccio-Fonseca, 2006b). *MEGA's* inclusive *Ecological model* (see Discussion section of this chapter) offers assumptions and premises hypothesising that ecological systems are 'multiplex,' that is, they interact and simultaneously influence the youth in ways that may, or may not be reciprocal (Brofenbrenner, 1989; Miccio-Fonseca and Rasmussen, 2006a, 2006b). These multiplex systems are assessed through the seven 'Ecological Aggregates' of *MEGA.* The term 'Aggregate' refers to 'a group or mass of distinct things gathered into, or considered as a total or whole' (Webster's New World College Dictionary, 2004: 26). The Aggregates of *MEGA* (i.e., *Neuropsychological, Family Lovemap, Anti-social, Sexual Incident, Coercion, Stratagem,* and *Relationship [Predatory Elements])* were taken from similar domains in a previous tool, the *Fonseca Inventory of Sex Offenders' Risk Factors (FISORF-1998)* (Miccio-Fonseca, 1998b, 1999b: [Revised: 2002–5]). Each Aggregate consists of several elements that have been identified in the literature on sexually abusive youth to be empirically associated with risk for sexually abusive behaviour (Miccio-Fonseca and Rasmussen, 2006b). *MEGA* is a versatile tool that can augment data obtained in a comprehensive assessment for sexually abusive youth (including children under 12 and adolescents 12 to 19). The elements within its seven Aggregates are used to:

1. Assess a youth's risk for sexually abusive behaviour.
2. Identify and target in the first interview specific areas of the youth's functioning that are directly related to risk for sexually abusive behaviour and may need to be addressed in the youth's treatment.
3. Monitor the youth over time to evidence changes in those areas of the youth's functioning that were identified as specific areas of concern.

Review of literature

Identifying the range of sexualised behaviours and sexually abusive dynamics in youth

Assessment of children and adolescents who engage in sexualised and sexually abusive behaviours must take into account an immensely heterogeneous group of young people whose sexual behaviours fall along a continuum of concern (i.e., none, low, moderate, high, very high/lethal) (Miccio-Fonseca and Rasmussen, 2005d, 2006a; Rasmussen and Miccio-Fonseca, 2007). At the lowest end of the continuum, are those youth who engage in behaviours that are developmentally expected for their age and stage of development. Others are outside of these 'norms' and manifest sexual behaviours and/or interactions that are beyond their sexual readiness age (Miccio-Fonseca, 1993, 1994/1997). These children are eroticised; they have been prematurely exposed to sexual material beyond their sexual readiness age through:

1. Any medium form (e.g., TV, Internet, still photos, DVD/video recordings of movies, writings, tapes, songs).
2. Observing or participating in actual sexual behaviours.
3. Being sexually abused.

> (Miccio-Fonseca, 1993, 1994/1997;
> Miccio-Fonseca and Rasmussen,
> 2005c, 2005e, 2006a; Rasmussen
> and Miccio-Fonseca, 2007)

Eroticised youth may cope with their eroticisation in various ways. Some youth cope effectively, and their premature exposure to eroticised material does not present problems or concerns in their psychosexual development and/or social functioning (Miccio-Fonseca, 1993, 1994/1997). Another group of youth display sexualised behaviours and/or interactions that may cause problems for themselves or others, interfere with activities of daily functioning (e.g., performing well in school, participating in social activities), and present concerns relative to their psychosexual development (Ryan, 1997a). These youth are not sexually abusive, but nonetheless may need brief intervention to help them redirect their behaviour. For the most part, however, we believe that many eroticised children do not require clinical intervention.

Children in need of intervention are those who manifest sexual behaviour that is harmful to others (Hall, Mathews, and Pearce, 1998, 2002; Johnson, 2000; Ryan, 1997a). These youth manifest *'Sexually Abusive Dynamics'* (Rasmussen and Miccio-Fonseca, 2007), which we define as 'elements of interaction in the relationship between the youth and other persons involved in a sexually abusive incident' (Miccio-Fonseca and Rasmussen, 2006b). *Sexually Abusive Dynamics* are unique to each youth; they are typically evidenced in the sustained behaviour of the youth over time (Burton et al., 1998; Miccio-Fonseca, 1994/1997; Money, 1986, 1988, 1995; Rasmussen, 1999b, 2001) and present a level of concern that can be low, moderate, high, or very high/lethal (Miccio-Fonseca and Rasmussen, 2005d, 2006a; Rasmussen and Miccio-Fonseca, 2007). We based the construct of *Sexually Abusive Dynamics* on comprehensive reviews of the literature on sexually abusive youth that were completed during the construction of *MEGA* (Miccio-Fonseca and Rasmussen, 2006b) and its parent tool, the *FISORF-1998* (Miccio-Fonseca, 1998b, 1999b: [Revised: 2002–5]).

Over the past 25 years, several authors have proposed formulations for defining sexually abusive behaviour in youth. The groundbreaking research of Groth and Loredo (1981) identified several factors clinicians and non-clinical professionals should consider when assessing whether or not a particular youth is sexually abusive: age relationship, social relationship, type of sexual activity being exhibited, use of deception and/or enticement, persistence of the sexual activity, evidence of progression, nature of fantasies that precede or accompany the sexual behaviour, and distinguishing characteristics of the persons targeted by the youth's activities (e.g., mental or physical disability). Later authors (Gil,

1993; Hall et al., 1996; Johnson, 2004) asserted these criteria could be applied to children under 12, but identified additional factors to distinguish children who are sexually abusive from eroticised children or children whose sexual behaviours are developmentally expected:

1. Frequency of the behaviours (and their occurrence in different times and situations).
2. Degree the child's behaviours interfere with normal development.
3. Affect that the child displayed when involved in sexual behaviour.
4. Degree of coercion present in the youth's sexual behaviour.
5. Tendency of child to continue the behaviours despite adult intervention and supervision.

In their seminal text on sexually abusive youth, Ryan and Lane discussed three hallmark factors – inequality, lack of consent, and coercion – that need to be considered when assessing children or adolescents referred for treatment of problematic or sexually abusive behaviour (Ryan, 1997b). Rasmussen and colleagues (Burton et al., 1998; Rasmussen, 1999b, 2001, 2004) combined Ryan's hallmark factors with the early definitional guidelines proposed by Groth and Loredo (1981) to describe four abusive dynamics (i.e. power differential, intimidation, manipulation, and coercion) that they hypothesised were present in the relationships of children under 12 who are sexually abusive. The presence of coercion, in the absence of other dynamics, was considered sufficient to indicate that a child was sexually abusive (Rasmussen, 1999b).

The formulations defining sexually abusive behaviour discussed above (e.g., Burton et al., 1998; Gil, 1993; Hall et al., 1996; Johnson, 2004; Rasmussen, 1999b, 2001, 2002; Ryan, 1997b) are limited in their scope; they are not inclusive and do not apply to *all* sexually abusive youth – children, adolescents, males, females, and youth of different developmental abilities. Moreover, these definitions do not go far enough in specifying the various aspects of coercion (i.e., manipulation, deceit, predatory behaviour, physical force, threats, and/or use of weapons) that young people, particularly violent and aggressive youth, may show when they are sexually abusive. Our construct of *'Sexually Abusive Dynamics'* provides an inclusive and comprehensive definition of sexually abusive behaviour that applies to *all* youth and takes into account aspects of sexually abusive behaviour manifested by the small percentage of youth whose sexual behaviours are violent and predatory (Miccio-Fonseca and Rasmussen, 2005a, 2005b, 2005e; Rasmussen and Miccio-Fonseca, 2007):

- Anti-social behaviour (i.e., behaviours that disregard the rights of others, which may include aggression toward people and animals and sexual abuse of animals [bestiality]).
- Extreme coercion (i.e., using threats of bodily harm, lethal consequences, and/or weapons)
- Predatory elements (i.e., abusing strangers or persons of casual acquaintance).

Risk assessment tools for sexually abusive youth

Two types of risk assessment tools are available in the research literature – actuarial and empirically guided (Prescott, 2004). Actuarial tools give an objective scoring scheme based on a fixed number of risk factors, with a total score that estimates the probability of re-offending over a fixed time period (e.g., five years). The *J-SOAP-II* (Prentky et al., 2000; Prentky and Righthand, 2003, 2004; Righthand et al., 2005) and *J-SORRAT-II* (Epperson et al., 2005) represent two attempts to develop an actuarial tool for sexually abusive adolescents; both tools are currently undergoing validation studies. In contrast, empirically guided tools, such as the *ERASOR, Version 2.0* (Worling and Curwen, 2001; Worling, 2004), identify risk factors repeatedly shown in prior research to be associated with risk and/or recidivism. These tools are reviewed below.

Juvenile Sexual Offender Assessment Protocol (J-SOAP-II)

The *J-SOAP* (Prentky et al., 2000; Prentky and Righthand, 2003, 2004; Righthand et al., 2005) was the first tool designed for assessing risk in sexually abusive youth. The most recent version of this tool, the *J-SOAP-II* (Prentky and Righthand, 2004; Righthand et al., 2005) is a 28-item checklist consisting of four rationally developed scales – two assessing static, historical risk factors (i.e., sexual drive/preoccupation and impulsive, anti-social behaviour) and two assessing dynamic factors that may change over

time (i.e., clinical treatment and community adjustment/stability). Initially 23 items, the *J-SOAP* was developed on a subject sample of 96 male sexually abusive youth (age range = 9 to 20; two thirds adjudicated and one third non-adjudicated); 75 of whom were followed for 12 months. The follow-up psychometric data showed the *J-SOAP* scales had good interrater reliability (average = 0.85) and moderate to high internal consistency (alphas ranging from .68 to .85) (Prentky et al., 2000). Nevertheless, this study's predictive validity can be questioned due to the large 11-year age span (ages 9 to 20) of the 75 youth in the sample; presumably only a few youth represented each specific age, limiting the *J-SOAP*'s ability to generalise to the heterogeneous population of sexually abusive youth and/or estimate recidivism.

Prentky and colleagues subsequently modified the *J-SOAP*, resulting in a revised 26-item version (Prentky and Righthand, 2003; Righthand et al., 2005), which was administered to a subject sample of 134 male sexually abusive youth (ages 7 to 20) referred from the correctional and child welfare systems in a rural state (Maine). Almost a third (29 per cent) had open child welfare cases, although the researchers do not state if these youth were solely dependency cases, or were also adjudicated. The scales of the revised version showed good interrater reliability (average = .86) and moderate to excellent internal consistency (i.e., ranging from .64 to .95) (Righthand et al., 2005). Righthand et al. (2005) completed a factor analysis (exploratory principal components analysis), which showed a four-factor solution essentially mirroring the scales created by the researchers. The revised version of the *J-SOAP* was highly correlated with another tool used to assess juvenile offenders, the *Youth Level of Service/Case Management Inventory* (YLS/CMI, Hoge and Andrews, 1996); however these findings were constrained by missing data since only 39 of the 134 youth in the sample had scores on the *YLS/CMI*. Discriminant analysis using a truncated version of the revised *J-SOAP* (without the community stability scale) found that 89 youth placed in residential facilities scored significantly higher on the scales tested than the 45 youth treated in the community (Righthand et al., 2005).

The *J-SOAP/J-SOAP-II* has been widely used in clinical practice, and has been recommended to practitioners by various state and county protocols (e.g., Colorado Sex Offender

Management Board, 2003; San Diego County Probation Department and the Sex Offender Management Council, 2005). Fanniff and Becker (2006) recently stated that the *J-SOAP-II* is, 'a reliable instrument that can detect differences within populations of juvenile sex offenders' (p. 271), though they did question its ability to predict recidivism. However, it is important to note that published validation research on the *J-SOAP/J-SOAP-II* is limited to the two studies reviewed above that utilised very small samples and reported low base rates of sexual re-offending (Prentky et al., 2000; Righthand et al., 2005). Furthermore, as noted above, the *J-SOAP* incorporates the adult research paradigm; Prentky et al. (2000) utilised adult research when developing the four scales of the *J-SOAP*. This raises questions about the overall validity of the *J-SOAP-II* when applied to sexually abusive youth (Miccio-Fonseca and Rasmussen, 2006a, 2006b; Rasmussen and Miccio-Fonseca, 2007). Clinicians and non-clinical professionals need to seriously consider these limitations of the *J-SOAP-II* before deciding to use it.

Estimate of Risk of Adolescent Sexual Offence Recidivism (ERASOR, Version 2.0)

Adapted from the adult tool, the *Sexual Violence Risk-20* (*SVR-20*, Boer, Hart, Kropp, and Webster, 1997), the *ERASOR, Version 2.0* (Worling and Curwen, 2001; Worling, 2004) is an empirically guided tool that assesses short-term risk (no more than one year follow-up) for male adolescents, ages 12 to 18 who have previously committed a sexual offence. It consists of 25 risk factors covering five categories (i.e., sexual interests, attitudes, and behaviours; historical sexual assaults; psychosocial functioning; family/environmental functioning; and treatment). Initial psychometric data for the *ERASOR, Version 2.0* were based on ratings obtained after 28 masters' or doctoral level professionals with expertise in treating sexually abusive youth were trained on using the tool. Working in pairs, these professionals used the *ERASOR, Version 2.0* to code archival data obtained from comprehensive clinical interviews of a sample of 136 male adolescents (ages 12 to 18) receiving community-based treatment. Interrater reliability was acceptable for the individual risk factors (average interclass correlation coefficient = .60), and excellent for the

overall clinical risk estimate (interclass correlation coefficient = .90). Item–total correlations were also acceptable for most of the risk factors, and the estimate of internal consistency was significant. The researchers found that the overall clinical rating (i.e., low, moderate, high) and the Total score significantly differentiated adolescents who had re-offended after receiving adult sanctions from those who had no history of re-offending (Worling, 2004). Although this research indicates that the *ERASOR, Version 2.0* may have the ability to differentiate youth who have engaged in sexually abusive behaviour prior to their index offence from those who have no prior history, it does not give evidence that the tool can assess recidivism. Establishing the predictive validity of the *ERASOR, Version 2.0* or the *J-SOAP-II* is likely to be difficult due to the low base rate of sexual offending (Fanniff and Becker, 2006).

When compared to the *J-SOAP-II*, the *ERASOR, Version 2.0* is better at assessing change in the youth over time; 16 of its 25 risk factors are dynamic. Nevertheless, it still relies on adult research; the tool's instructional manual cites adult sex offender risk factors and liberally applies them to sexually abusive youth (Worling and Curwen, 2001). There do appear to be linkages to adult sexual offenders in some very distant, general ways (e.g., difficulties with anger, parent/child separation before age 16, negative affect, history of prior reports of sexually abusive behaviours). Development does not cease at the end of adolescence; adults are still unfolding and maturing and are dealing with their own developmental milestones. However, adults are qualitatively different than youth and face considerably different developmental issues, milestones and concerns than those of children and adolescents. More attune to developmental concerns than the *J-SOAP-II* and more encompassing, the *ERASOR, Version 2.0* still inappropriately borrows from the adult paradigm.

Juvenile Sexual Offender Recidivism Risk Assessment Tool-II (J-SORRAT-II)

Developed to address the limitations of the *J-SOAP-II* and *ERASOR, Version 2.0*, the *J-SORRAT-II* (Epperson et al., 2005) is the most empirically robust of existing risk assessment tools. Epperson and colleagues developed this tool by coding archival data of youth whose sex offences were documented by the Utah Juvenile

Justice management information system. In a retrospective recidivism study that previously utilised the Utah Juvenile Justice management information system, Rasmussen (1999a) coded archival data of a sample of 167 male and 3 female sexually abusive youths, aged 7–18 who offended during 1989 and followed these youths over a five year period (1989–94). Event history analysis (Cox Regression) was used to identify predictor variables of recidivism (both sexual and non-sexual). In contrast to Rasmussen's study when developing *J-SORRAT-II*, Epperson and colleagues:

1. Used an exhaustive sample ($N = 636$) consisting of all male sexually abusive adolescents ages 12 to 17 who were adjudicated in Utah in 1990 to 1992 (Epperson, 2006), and
2. Coded and analysed a wider variety of variables. Variables were grouped 'based on conceptual similarity' (Epperson et al., 2005: 5) into 10 'families' of variables (i.e., sex offending history, sex offence characteristics, prior sex offence treatment history, special education history, school discipline history, mental health diagnosis, prior mental health treatment, family instability, and non-sex offence history).

The researchers used hierarchical and simultaneous logistic regression to analyse 10-year follow-up data of the 636 youth, identifying variables in each family that were the 'best marker' variables for sexual recidivism. The *J-SORRAT-II* consists of the 12 best marker variables (from seven families) that emerged from the final hierarchical logistic regression analysis.

The *J-SORRAT-II* (Epperson et al., 2005) has several important strengths that give it promise as an actuarial tool and make it more robust than the *J-SOAP-II* or the *ERASOR, Version 2.0*, including its large representative sample ($N = 636$) and empirically sound statistical methodology. It is also more developmentally sensitive than the *J-SOAP-II* or the *ERASOR, Version 2.0*. For example, Epperson indicated that he and his colleagues elected to eliminate the item 'diagnosis of paraphilia' from the final version of the *J-SORRAT-II* since this item was 'technically inappropriate for adolescents under the age of 16' (D. Epperson, personal communication, June 3, 2005). Nevertheless, like the *J-SOAP-II* and *ERASOR, Version 2.0*, the *J-SORRAT-II* is designed for assessing ad

judicated male adolescents and does not apply to non-adjudicated youth, females, the developmentally delayed, and/or children under the age of 12. It is also limited by its almost exclusive focus on assessing static (historical), rather than dynamic (changeable) factors; all but two of its 12 items, placement in special education and number of education periods with discipline problems, reflect historical factors.

Tools to assess sexual behaviours in children under 12

Although there are no risk assessment tools for assessing risk for sexually abusive behaviour in children under 12 (Prescott and Longo, 2005), there are three descriptive tools clinicians can use to assess children's sexual behaviours – the *Child Sexual Behaviour Inventory* (CSBI, Friedrich, 1997), *Child Sexual Behaviour Checklist* (CSBCL, Johnson, 1994, 2002), and *Clinical Assessment Package of Risks and Strengths* (CASPARS, Gilgun, 1999; Gilgun et al., 1999). The *CSBI* has advantages over the *CSBCL*, as it was developed using a large normative sample (Friedrich, 1997) and can be used to estimate the type and frequency of a child's sexual behaviours as compared against a normative population. Neither the *CSBI* nor the *CSBCL* is purported to be a risk assessment tool; they are therefore not helpful in assessing children's risk for sexually abusive behaviour. The third tool, the *CASPARS* (Gilgun, 1999; Gilgun et al., 1999), consists of a battery of instruments that measures a variety of things about a youth, none of which is specifically for sexually abusive behaviours. One of the *CASPARS* instruments is the Sexuality Scale, which Gilgun (1999) indicated 'is to aid in the identification of patterns that indicate healthy and unhealthy sexual development and expression' (p. 450) and assess youth who are, 'at risk to develop sexual issues of various sorts' (p. 450). These purposes provide a generic description of all types of children with sexual behaviour problems, but are not specific to those children who engage in sexually abusive behaviours, which would indicate that the *CASPARS* is not a risk assessment tool.

Summary of risk assessment tools

We concluded after reviewing the three existing empirically based risk assessment tools (i.e.,

J-SOAP-II, ERASOR, Version 2.0, and *J-SORRAT-II)* that each tool has limitations as far as its ability to provide a comprehensive, developmentally sensitive assessment of sexually abusive youth. Our primary concern is that many of the items of these tools are inappropriately grounded in adult research. Although it is possible to apply some of the adult risk and recidivism data to youth, we contend that tools or measures designed for adults inherently have no substantial validity or reliability when applied to youth. Distinctions must be made for sexually abusive youth according to the developmental milestones of their particular age (i.e., young children under 8, preadolescent children 9 to 11, young adolescents 12 to 14, middle adolescents 15 to 16, and late adolescents 17 to 19) (Miccio-Fonseca and Rasmussen, 2006a). Tools designed for adult sex offenders typically do not:

1. Assess whether they differ in achieving developmental milestones in young adulthood, midlife, or senior years.
2. Take into account the ways children and adolescents are developmentally different than adults.

(Chaffin and Bonner, 1998; Miccio-Fonseca, 2003; Miccio-Fonseca and Rasmussen, 2005c; 2006a)

The risk assessment tools reviewed above take templates drawn from adult research and superimpose the distant similarities indiscriminately on sexually abusive youth, without accounting for the special needs of adolescents (Miccio-Fonseca and Rasmussen, 2006a).

The ecological model and aggregates of MEGA

Unlike the aforementioned risk assessment tools above, the *Multiplex Empirically Guided Inventory of Ecological Aggregates for Assessing Sexually Abusive Children and Adolescents (Ages 19 and Under) (MEGA)* (Miccio-Fonseca, 2006b) is empirically guided by the research that is specifically on youth; *all* of its items are drawn from the research on sexually abusive youth, not adults. *MEGA* is sensitive to the different developmental ages and milestones of sexually abusive youth; for example, its items are applicable to the needs and concerns of younger children and the developmentally delayed, as

well as older adolescents, and females as well as males. It provides a set of seven Aggregates comprised of elements (criteria) that can be used with *all youth under age 19* to:

- Comprehensively define *Sexually Abusive Dynamics* (Rasmussen and Miccio-Fonseca, 2007) in the youth's interaction with other persons involved in a sexual incident.
- Assess the youth's level of risk for sexually abusive behaviour (i.e., low, moderate, high, very high).
- Monitor the youth's progress in specified areas of functioning directly related to risk for sexually abusive behaviour and evidence change and/or improvement.

The conceptual framework of *MEGA* reflects an *Ecological model* that is based on:

- Miccio-Fonseca's research for the parent tool of *MEGA,* the *FISORF-1998,* which identified several aggregates of empirically guided elements associated with risk in sexually abusive youth (Miccio-Fonseca, 1998b, 1999b: [Revised: 2002–5]).
- Rasmussen's conceptual model describing behavioural outcomes of traumatic experiences, the *Trauma Outcome Process Assessment (TOPA)* model (Rasmussen, 1999b, 2001, 2002, 2004, 2006; Rasmussen, Burton, and Christopherson, 1992).

MEGA's *Ecological model* consists of:

1. General assumptions from Ecological Systems Theory (Brofenbrenner, 1989).
2. Four domains (or systems).
3. Three premises.

Ecological systems theory 'posits that individuals constantly engage in transactions with other humans and with other systems in the environment, and that these individuals and systems reciprocally influence each other' (Hepworth et al., 2006: 17). An overarching assumption of an ecological theoretical perspective is that optimal human functioning is associated with positive transactions between individuals and the different systems in their environment. *MEGA*'s *Ecological model* asserts that transactions between individuals become negative when duress is a component of their relationship, resulting in different types of coercion (i.e., threats, force, using weapons) or

Sexually Abusive Dynamics (Rasmussen and Miccio-Fonseca, 2007). Assessing the transactions in a relationship includes evaluating whether *Sexually Abusive Dynamics* are present.

MEGA's Ecological model asserts that the human organism is embedded in various multidimensional, multiplex and interconnected systems, which synergistically influence one another in ways that are idiosyncratic to a particular individual (Miccio-Fonseca and Rasmussen, 2005a, b, d). These systems are classified into four broad ecological domains that represent the individual's:

1. *Psyche/Soma* (i.e., intrapsychic functioning).
2. *Family Lovemap* (i.e., family dynamics and family culture).
3. *Social Fabric* (i.e., immediate social network).
4. *Mezzo and Macro Community and Culture* (connection to the larger community and cultural and political context).
   (Miccio-Fonseca and Rasmussen, 2006a, b)

The first system of *MEGA's Ecological model*, Psyche/Soma includes those variables associated with the individual's own physio-biological and psychological functioning (e.g., the individual's inherited characteristics, constitution of the organism, physio-biological and medical functioning, temperament (Chess and Thomas, 1986), and psychological make-up). A literature review of the empirical research on sexually abusive adolescents and children, completed during the construction of the *FISORF-1998* (the parent tool of *MEGA*), found several physio-biological and neuropsychological variables that are associated with greater risk for sexually abusive behaviour in youth (Miccio-Fonseca, 1998b, 1999b: [Revised: 2002–5]).

Family Lovemap (Miccio-Fonseca, 1994, 2005, 2006a), the second system of *MEGA's Ecological model*, 'is the product of generations; it depicts the individual's overall family history, which is specific to relationships, bonding and intimacy' (Miccio-Fonseca, 2006a: 4). Factors or dynamics that comprise the *Family Lovemap* include:

1. The family's hereditary predispositions and the multitude of ways inheritable characteristics are manifested in various family members.
2. The family's history of romantic bonding, erotic bonding, and reproductive bonding, and the products of such – *the sexualities*. Just as the

individual is unique, each human organism's family system has a history and culture.
(Miccio-Fonseca, 2006a)

The *Family Lovemap* profoundly influences the individual; when *Sexually Abusive Dynamics* (Rasmussen and Miccio-Fonseca, 2007) are present in a family, the *Family Lovemap* is vandalised (Miccio-Fonseca, 2006a; Money, 1986).

The third system is the individual's *Social Fabric*, which consists of the social interconnections and relationships that the individual has with acquaintances, friends, and peer network; extended family members; associates at work and/or school; teachers, mentors, and/or religious or political leaders; and/or professionals who provide needed services. Early experiences in attachment and bonding influence the individual's ability to form and maintain relationships (Davies, 1999). Difficulties in attachment and bonding may reflect a vandalised *Family Lovemap* (Miccio-Fonseca, 2006a) and profoundly influence a youth (Friedrich, 2002; Miccio-Fonseca and Rasmussen, 2006a; Rasmussen, 2001, 2004; Rich, 2003), contributing to subsequent aberrations in the youth's social interactions (e.g., *Sexually Abusive Dynamics*, Rasmussen and Miccio-Fonseca, 2007).

Mezzo and Macro Community and Culture, the fourth system in *MEGA's Ecological model*, consists of the individual's relationship with and connection to the larger social environment, which can be on the mezzo level (i.e., immediate ecological influences), as well as the macro level (i.e., broader social and political context). The immediate connections of the individual's mezzo system consist of those entities with which the individual has direct communication, involvement, and some degree of influence (e.g., school, work, church congregation, clubs, as well as medical, mental health, and social services) (Brofenbrenner, 1989). Research has shown that a supportive environment in the youth's immediate social connections and community is important in reducing risk for sexually abusive behaviour (Gray and Pithers, 1993; Katz, 1997; Rasmussen, 1999, 2004). The research for *MEGA's* parent tool, the *FISORF-1998*, documented several empirically supported variables in the youth's immediate social environment related to risk for sexually abusive behaviour (Miccio-Fonseca, 1998b, 1999b: [Revised: 2002–5]). Macro influences in the fourth system include larger societal institutions that the individual interfaces with; the individual may have limited personal contacts with public institutions (e.g., hospitals, school districts, mental health and/or social service agencies/institutions, law enforcement agencies, courts, etc.), yet still may be greatly influenced by their policies and procedures (Brofenbrenner, 1989). The fourth system of *MEGA's Ecological model* also includes the broader social and political influences of the culture and society in which individual resides or with which they most identify. Cultural groups may view abuse and trauma in ways that are not helpful (e.g., minimising the abuse, viewing normal responses to traumatic experiences as pathological, blaming the victim) (Root, 1992, as cited in Sinacore-Guinn, 1995) which may contribute to a youth developing maladaptive coping strategies (e.g., sexually abusive behaviour) (Rasmussen, 1999b).

There are three premises in *MEGA's Ecological model*. The first premise posits that there are multidimensional, multiplex predisposing and/or triggering factors and/or circumstances that elicit the onset or recurrence of sexually abusive behaviours (Miccio-Fonseca and Rasmussen, 2006a, b, d). The multiplex systems described above (i.e., *Psyche/Soma, Family Lovemap, Social Fabric,* and *Mezzo and Macro Community and Culture*) function simultaneously and, consistent with Ecological Systems Theory (Brofenbrenner, 1989) influence the youth in ways that may or may not be reciprocal. This premise asserts that clinicians need to assess the ways that individual, family, and environmental risk factors interact and create vulnerabilities or resiliencies for a youth (Rasmussen, 1999b, 2001, 2002, 2004).

The seven Ecological Aggregates of *MEGA* (i.e., *Neuropsychological, Family Lovemap, Anti-social, Sexual Incident, Coercion, Stratagem,* and *Relationship (Predatory Elements)*) assess the impact of the simultaneous, multidimensional interactions of the systems described above (i.e., *Psyche/Soma, Family Lovemap, Social Network,* and *Mezzo/Macro Community and Culture*) on the youth's functioning, as directly related to increasing risk for sexually abusive behaviour. Aggregates include items related to the previously mentioned construct of *Sexually Abusive Dynamics* (Rasmussen and Miccio-Fonseca, 2007) (i.e., extreme coercion, threats, use of weapons, predatory behaviour, and physical and sexual abuse of animals) (Miccio-Fonseca, 1998b, 1999b: [Revised: 2002–5]).

(For a description of the empirical research that supports the Seven Aggregates, please refer to Chapter 1 of the *MEGA Manual and Rating Booklet* (Miccio-Fonseca and Rasmussen, 2006b).)

The second premise of *MEGA's Ecological model* postulates that 'Protective Factors' are found in each of the above seven Aggregates (Miccio-Fonseca and Rasmussen, 2005d, 2006a, b; Rasmussen and Miccio-Fonseca, 2007). The protective factors assessed in *MEGA* are taken from the template of the *FISORF-1998* (Miccio-Fonseca, 1998b, 1999b: [Revised: 2002–5]). These protective factors assist or reduce the likelihood of sexually abusive behaviours and contribute to lowering risk and/or recidivism. Previous researchers have highlighted the importance of identifying and assessing protective factors when evaluating sexually abusive youth (Bremer, 2001; Gray and Pithers, 1993; Katz, 1997; Rasmussen, 1999b, 2004). An example of a protective factor is having a positive, supportive relationship with a parent (in contrast to having conflict in the parent/child relationship). Protective factors can mitigate risk, reduce the exposure of the youth to adverse experiences, and contribute to resiliency in the face of difficult or traumatic experiences (Katz, 1997). When providing treatment services, clinicians and other professionals need to identify and harness protective factors on behalf of a youth, creating a 'prevention team' that can help the youth improve his or her degree of self-governance and self-manage his or her behaviour (Gray and Pithers, 1993). This includes identifying sources of environmental support in the *Social Fabric* and *Mezzo and Macro Community and Cultural* connections for the youth and his or her family (e.g., at school, church or other cultural support systems, extended family, friends, neighbours). *MEGA* includes two constellations of elements that assist in assessing the protective factors currently present in the youth's immediate ecological environment – the Dynamical and Protective Factors scales. The Dynamical scale assists in following the youth over time to see evidence of improved stability for the youth and reduced risk for sexually abusive behaviour (Miccio-Fonseca, 2006c). The Protective Factors scale assesses elements that mitigate or assist in reducing risk (i.e., having a support system, getting along with others, being more involved in school and community, being more rule bound); expanding these resources further reduces risk (Miccio-Fonseca, 2006c).

The third premise of *MEGA*'s *Ecological model* asserts that self-governance is related to emotional regulation, and improvement in self-governance:

1. Helps reduce the likelihood of sexually abusive behaviours.
2. Strengthens prevention strategies.
3. Reduces risk and/or recidivism.
(Miccio-Fonseca and Rasmussen, 2005d, 2006a, b)

Friedrich (2002) pointed to emotional dysregulation as an important risk factor contributing to children and adolescents becoming involved in sexually abusive behaviour. In Rasmussen's *TOPA* model, emotional dysregulation is seen as a salient individual risk factor that makes individuals more vulnerable for maladaptive responses to traumatic experiences (Rasmussen, 2001), including developing *Sexually Abusive Dynamics* (Rasmussen and Miccio-Fonseca, 2007). The research for the *FISORF-1998* confirmed that elements related to self-regulation were empirically associated with risk and for sexually abusive behaviour in youth (Miccio-Fonseca, 1998b, 1999b: [Revised: 2002–5]). Providing interventions to increase skills in self-governance will help the youth develop improved emotional regulation, leading to decreased risk for recurrence of sexually abusive behaviour (Miccio-Fonseca and Rasmussen, 2006a, 2006b).

The Construction of MEGA

MEGA is a 76 item tool consisting of six scales (Risk, Static, Principles, Dynamical, Protective Factors and Female) (Miccio-Fonseca, 2006b, 2006c) provides a multidimensional assessment protocol for evaluating all sexually abusive youth, male or female, ages 19 and under. Theoretically grounded on the premises of its *Ecological model*, the six scales of *MEGA*'s multiplex assessment consider multiple systems functioning simultaneously and influencing the youth's behaviour (Miccio-Fonseca and Rasmussen, 2006a, 2006b). *MEGA* is empirically anchored on research on sexually abusive youth; its underpinnings are:

1. The findings of a seven-year study of 323 male and female sexually abusive adolescents and young adults, the majority of whom were

junior high and high school students (Miccio-Fonseca, 1996, 2000; 1)
2. A comprehensive literature review related to risk in sexually abusive youth and risk for sexually abusive behaviour completed during the construction of the *FISORF-1998* (Miccio-Fonseca, 1998b, 1999b: [Revised: 2002–5]).
3. A review of current descriptive studies and empirical research related to risk of sexually abusive behaviour in youth (as well as recidivism), including the empirically based risk assessment tools currently used in clinical practice (e.g., *J-SOAP-II*, *ERASOR*, *Version 2.0* and *J-SORRAT-II*) (Miccio-Fonseca and Rasmussen, 2006b).

The research that guided the construction of *MEGA* and its parent tool, the *FISORF-1998* came out of a large seven-year descriptive study ($N = 656$, 64 per cent males, 36 per cent females, the majority of whom were junior high and high school students). This study compared four groups:

- Offenders who were victims ($n = 179$);
- Offenders only, not victims ($n = 171$);
- Victims only ($n = 129$); and
- Individuals in neither category ($n = 177$)

The Victims only and Individuals in neither category groups were older; their mean age was 31 and 37 respectively. Of the sexually abusive individuals in the study, 72 per cent were under the age of 19 and 53 per cent were under the age of 16; the youngest was eight years old (Miccio-Fonseca, 1996, 2000, 2001). The *Fonseca Inventory of Sex Offenders' Risk Factors (FISORF-1998)* (Miccio-Fonseca, 1998b), one of the paper and pencil tools that developed from this research, is an empirically guided structured clinical inventory designed to assist the professional in assessing important historical (*static factors*) and current information (*dynamic factors*) found to be empirically related to risk and/or recidivism for individuals who are sexually abusive. In contrast to *MEGA*, which focuses strictly on youth, the *FISORF-1998* was applicable to all ages: adults, adolescents, and children. Aspects of the *FISORF-1998* that served as a template for *MEGA* included the format of the tool, the method of scoring the items, and several of its domains (which are mirrored by *MEGA*'s Aggregates).

The studies reviewed during the construction of the *FISORF-1998* included all populations of sexually abusive youth (i.e., males and females, adolescents and children, and youth who were developmentally delayed). Elements identified as statistically significant and associated with risk and/or recidivism, were included in the *FISORF-1998* (Miccio-Fonseca, 1998b, 1999b: [Revised: 2002–5]), and a substantial number of these items were later incorporated into *MEGA*. Additional elements for *MEGA* were selected based on our current review of the literature pertaining to sexually abusive youth, including descriptive and outcome studies on all types of youth – males and females, adolescents and children, and the developmentally delayed (Miccio-Fonseca and Rasmussen, 2006b). We identified and selected for inclusion in *MEGA* only those elements or items in the *FISORF-1998* and in our current review of literature that had been shown repeatedly by the research on sexually abusive youth to be related to risk and/or recidivism. We deliberately avoided using any adult findings and did not select for inclusion in *MEGA* either, items from the *FISORF-1998* that focused on adults, or variables mentioned in the literature that appeared to relate primarily to sexually abusive adults. For example, we excluded diagnosis of personality disorder as an item in *MEGA*. Although psychological reports of sexually abusive youth ages 16 and under often offer diagnostic impressions of personality disorder or sex disorder, we agree with Chaffin and Bonner (1998) that affixing such labels to immature adolescents and children is inappropriate and would likely be damaging to these youth over the long-term.

Once all the empirically guided items for *MEGA* had been selected, we analysed them for conceptual similarity and organised them into 14 Aggregates, some of which reflected the original domains of the *FISORF-1998* (e.g., *Neuropsychological Aggregate, Relationship (Predatory Elements) Aggregate*) (Miccio-Fonseca, 1998a, 1999b [Revised: 2002–5]). Principles of test construction were followed in constructing the 14 Aggregates in a rationally derived manner, drawing upon the empirical literature on sexually abusive youth (Miccio-Fonseca, 2006c). We next compared our items against the items repeatedly found in the existing empirically based risk assessment tools (i.e., *J-SOAP-II, ERASOR, Version 2.0*, and *J-SORRAT-II*), as well as the tools

designed to assess sexual behaviours in children under 12 (i.e., *CSBI, CSBCL*, and *CASPACS*) (see above review). The *J-SORRAT-II* was the most helpful tool in this regard, as Epperson et al. (2005) had generously made available on the public domain the statistical data from its construction. (See Table: 'Selected Variables from the Ten Families and Their Bivariate Relations with Juvenile Sexual Recidivism'; available by contacting Dr Epperson (website at: http://www.psychology.iastate.edu/faculty/epperson). These data were invaluable in providing an empirical 'compass' that guided us in constructing *MEGA*, finalising its scales and establishing its ad hoc scoring scheme (Miccio-Fonseca and Rasmussen, 2006b).

We compared the elements in each of the 14 Aggregates against the variables in Epperson et al.'s (2005) table. We determined if the elements should remain in the Aggregate or be reassigned to a different Aggregate. We deleted elements that were too similar to each other, eliminating redundancy between the different Aggregates and combining some Aggregates to make *MEGA*'s scales more robust. This reduced the overall items in *MEGA* and condensed the number of Aggregates from 14 to seven. The seven Aggregates mirrored the original domains that had been formulated for the *FISORF-1998* (Miccio-Fonseca, 1998b, 1999b: [Revised: 2002–5]), making *MEGA* an evolution of this earlier tool.

Consistent with principles of test construction, *MEGA*'s scoring scheme was formulated through an ad-hoc estimation of risk for each element of *MEGA*, an ad-hoc estimation of risk for each of the seven Aggregates (i.e., *Low, Moderate, High*), and an ad-hoc estimation of overall risk (or total score – *Low, Moderate, High, Very High*) (Miccio-Fonseca, 2006a). The formulation of these estimates involved comparing the elements in *MEGA*'s Aggregates against the selected variables from the construction of the *J-SORRAT-II* that Epperson made available on his website. We assigned 'weights' to items in *MEGA* that were similar to Epperson et al.'s (2005) items. Each of *MEGA*'s items was given a 'weight' that corresponded with the proportion listed for a similar item in Epperson's table that was established through statistical analysis during the construction of the *J-SORRAT-II*. We assigned a 'weight' to the remaining items in *MEGA* by comparing them against those items that we had compared to the items in Epperson's table. When an item was found to be closely related to another item that we had weighted using Epperson's table, we assigned it the same weight, or a lower estimated weight, never higher. We arrived at and made these clinically educated, empirically estimated proportions through:

1. Reviewing the specific empirical research literature on sexually abusive youth.
2. Reviewing and examining the current tools available in the field (*J-SOAP-II ERASOR, Version 2.0* and *J-SORRAT-II*) and their respective manuals.
3. Drawing upon our almost half a century of combined direct clinical and research experience.

A current validation study testing *MEGA* on samples of sexually abusive youth is the first step in evaluating whether the proportions we estimated will hold up statistically. Although at this time *MEGA* offers an ad-hoc educated estimation, we are confident of its ability to be accurate in assessing the risk level of a youth. It is robust and sensitive to the developmental needs of children and adolescents; it is not based on research on adult sex offenders, but reflects state of the art knowledge on sexually abusive youth.

Incorporating *MEGA* into an assessment empirically informs and strengthens the data obtained through clinical interview, clinical judgment, and collateral sources. Predictive accuracy of estimates of risk is increased because the descriptors (the constellation of elements within each Aggregate) are anchored in researched variables that are part of other risk assessment tools specifically designed to assess sexually abusive youth. When applied in a structured clinical interview, the items in *MEGA*'s seven Aggregates provide a comprehensive, holistic, empirically guided assessment of a sexually abusive child or adolescent. *MEGA* is a flexible tool that can be used by either clinicians (e.g., psychologists, psychiatrists, clinical social workers, marriage and family therapists) or non-clinical professionals (e.g., probation or parole officers, child protective services caseworkers, school social workers, mental health counsellors and case managers). Professionals who wish to use *MEGA* should have extensive experience (i.e., a minimum of two years) in working with sexually abusive youth.

MEGA's instructional set includes an extensive empirically guided *Manual and Rating Booklet* (Miccio-Fonseca, 2006c) that provides the user with:

1. Detailed guidelines and specific directions on how *MEGA* is to be administered.
2. A complete discussion of *MEGA*'s seven Aggregates and six scales, with documentation of the empirical research that supports the elements of each Aggregate and their relation to risk for sexually abusive behaviour (Miccio-Fonseca and Rasmussen, 2006b).
3. Specific guidelines for gathering together in a systemised manner the particular elements that assess a particular area of functioning or multiplex dynamics influencing the youth.

To use *MEGA* to assess a sexually abusive youth, the clinician or other non-clinical professional first gathers together and examines all relevant information ethically obtained from collateral sources through appropriate releases of information. This occurs as the professional considers the empirically guided elements in each of the seven Aggregates and, using the guidelines in *MEGA*'s instructional *Manual and Rating Booklet* determines whether the elements within the different Aggregates apply to the youth. Items must be *clearly and undeniably present* in order to be assessed as applying to the youth. Failure to follow the guidelines in the instructional set invalidates the findings of the assessment, and any results or interpretations of the results given by the professional would be seriously questionable. The six scales of the completed *MEGA* assessment furnish an empirically guided estimate of risk for sexually abusive behaviour, based on a composite picture obtained about the youth. *MEGA* looks at the youth's overall functioning of the last six months up to time of interview. This assessment:

1. Evaluates the quality of the transactions between various systems influencing the youth.
2. Identifies the internal and external risk factors that may be associated with a youth's sexually abusive behaviour.
3. Identifies the protective factors/resources in the youth's family system and ecological environment (e.g., extended family, school, job, religious affiliation, health care, mental health/social services, and/or other resources in the community) mitigating against risk. It taps into a variety of domains that consider empirically guided, dynamic risk factors.

The constellation of elements included in the Dynamical scale of *MEGA* establishes the dynamic risk factors on first presentation of the youth; these elements serve as a baseline for comparing the youth's behaviours at different points in time against the first assessment and evaluating whether the youth's risk for sexually abusive behaviour is decreasing. The constellation of elements included in *MEGA's* Protective Factors Scale includes mitigating elements that assist in reducing risk. *MEGA* is time sensitive and ecologically valid; the Dynamical and Protective Factors Scales ensure that the assessment can be compared from first time assessment to successive assessments, that is, assessments are updated as the youth matures and progresses through subsequent developmental stages (Rasmussen and Miccio-Fonseca, 2007). However, we caution that *MEGA* is not a treatment tool; it is specifically designed for assessing and identifying those elements that are directly related to risk for sexually abusive behaviours; these identified elements may in turn speak to treatment needs and services. We encourage professionals to use

MEGA in tandem with other tools that directly relate to assessing the need for treatment, determining the focus of interventions, and making decisions pertaining to supervision and/or placement.

Table 14.1 briefly describes each of the seven Aggregates of *MEGA* and gives examples of some of the elements. We caution clinicians that they must have the complete version of *MEGA* (including the instructional set contained in the *MEGA Manual and Rating Booklet* (Miccio-Fonseca, 2006c)) before proceeding to use it in assessing a youth's risk for sexually abusive behaviour. It is inappropriate to apply only the summary of the seven Aggregates, without the specified parameters for scoring the seven Aggregates and their respective elements contained in the *MEGA Manual and Rating Booklet*. *Proceeding with MEGA assessment without the instructional set would result in an inadequate assessment of the youth's functioning.*

Table 14.1   The Aggregates of *MEGA*

Neuropsychological Aggregate	Assesses elements related to neuropsychological functioning including: lower level of intellectual functioning, history of epilepsy; attention problems/deficits, special education.
Anti-social Aggregate	Assesses the youth's history of law enforcement involvement (nonsexual offences) and other anti-social behaviour (behaviour problems at school, animal abuse) that may bring youth to the attention of authority figures (e.g., parents, preschool or day care workers, teachers, residential staff).
Family Lovemap Aggregate	Assesses several aspects of the youth's family background including: *Family Lovemap* (Miccio-Fonseca, 2005, 2006a) (i.e., family's sexual history and family's familial psycho-sexio-social history); family history of experiencing various types of abuse; youth's individual history of experiencing various types of abuse.
Sexual Incident Aggregate	Assesses the number of incidents of non-consensual, sexual behaviour, and whether the youth's behaviours show progression across time and situations, or into more sophisticated sexual behaviours involving penetration.
Coercion Aggregate	Assesses the degree of coercion that the youth uses in influencing another person to comply with a sexual behaviour including: intimidation or use of force, use of general threats and threats of bodily harm or threats of lethal consequences, and whether the youth has utilised a weapon or weapons for the purposes of procuring compliance in sexual behaviour from another person, and the type of weapon used (e.g., rocks, guns, knives, tire iron, baseball bat, poles and sticks, air gun, hammer, chains, and explosives).
Stratagem Aggregate	Assesses behaviours of the youth that may suggest intent or motivation for engaging in the sexual behaviour including: use of deceit, trickery, and lying; evidence of planning.
Relationship Aggregate (Predatory Elements)	Assesses the relationship that the youth has with the person or persons involved in the sexual behaviour, whether there is an age difference or difference in mental capacity, or difference in physical capacity, and whether the relationship is 'predatory' (i.e., a relationship with a stranger or casual acquaintance that the youth engages in for the primary purpose of carrying out abusive dynamics of manipulation and coercion).

Neuropsychological aggregate

The first Aggregate of *MEGA, Neuropsychological Aggregate*, is based on a major domain in the *FISORF-1998* and is a key to all the other *Aggregates*. This Aggregate focuses on the integral relationship that the brain has with sexual functioning (Miccio-Fonseca, 1998a, 1999b). It is the brain that is 'the responsive organ that reacts to sexual stimuli, initiates a cognitive response, and propels the genitals to function' (Miccio-Fonseca, 1998a: 1). Neuropsychological factors or dynamics comprise an intricate system within the individual that affects day-to-day functioning. The Neuropsychological Aggregate is not diagnostic, but is both instructive and informative. It highlights possible vulnerabilities that may be either directly or indirectly linked to problems or concerns in the youth's *overall* functioning that have been shown in the literature to be empirically related to risk related to sexually abusive youth (e.g., negative affect, impulsivity, difficulty managing anger, aggressive outbursts, attention difficulties, self-regulation and self-monitoring problems, mood disorders including depression, deviant sexual behaviour) (Miccio-Fonseca, 1998b, 1999b: [Revised: 2002–5]). The instructional manuals of the *J-SOAP-II* and *ERASOR, Version 2.0* indicate that variables related to impulsivity and affect regulation need to be identified and addressed when assessing a youth (Prentky et al., 2000; Prentky and Righthand, 2003, 2004; Righthand et al., 2005; Worling and Curwen, 2001); however, these tools give minimal attention to neuropsychological factors.

The seven-year research study from which *MEGA* and its parent tool, the *FISORF-1998* were developed found a constellation of self-reported mental symptoms to be important in differentiating the three groups (i.e., sex offenders, victims, and people who were neither sex offenders nor victims) of a subject sample of 352 male adolescents and adults referred for outpatient treatment (Miccio-Fonseca, 2001). Symptoms assessed included: feeling depressed, feeling shame, easily distracted, feeling lonely, feeling alone, poor judgment, acting impulsively, feeling isolated, difficulty making decisions, inability to plan ahead, withdrawal from others, and decrease in sexual interest. The Sex Offender group ($n = 269$), the majority of whom were high school and junior high students, scored significantly higher ($p = .001$) on self-reported

mental symptoms than either the Victim group ($n = 19$) or the Non-offender/Non-victim group ($n = 64$). The Sex Offender group and Victim group scored the same for mental symptoms of poor concentration and difficulty thinking clearly. The neuropsychological dynamics highlighted in Miccio-Fonseca's study are extremely important to consider when evaluating adolescents and children and assessing their risk for sexually abusive behaviour. Yet despite its integral relationship with human sexuality, research on sexually abusive adults and adolescents has generally overlooked neuropsychological aspects of the individual's functioning and not given credence to their role in contributing to risk and/or recidivism (Miccio-Fonseca, 1993).

Recent authors have pointed out that intervention for sexually abusive youth, 'must take into account their developmental abilities as well as potential developmental lags' (Prescott and Longo, 2005: 8). Some neuropsychological factors (e.g., learning disabilities, auditory processing difficulties, and/or speech difficulties) may interfere with the child or adolescent understanding what is expected from him or her in treatment and/or supervision (Miccio-Fonseca, 1998b, 1999b: [Revised: 2002–5]). Clinicians or non-clinical professionals may view some youth as 'resistant', or 'noncompliant' when it simply may be that these youth do not remember instructions or understand what is expected due to learning disabilities or processing problems. They may be oppositional, defiant and noncompliant as a coping strategy for dealing with the confusion and frustration they may feel in not understanding what adults expect from them (Miccio-Fonseca and Rasmussen, 2006b). When assessing and treating youth with neuropsychological vulnerabilities, clinicians and non-clinical professionals should clearly explain expectations for treatment and supervision, as well as check to make sure that these youth have clearly understood what was said.

Anti-social behaviour elements

The second Aggregate in *MEGA, Anti-social Behaviour Aggregate* refers to behavioural characteristics contributing to a youth's propensity to enact *Sexually Abusive Dynamics* (Rasmussen and Miccio-Fonseca, 2007). Sexually abusive youth display a whole host of anti-social behaviours (Miccio-Fonseca, 1996, 2000) that may include a pervasive pattern of blatant and flagrant disregard of other people (e.g., deceit, manipulation, lack of empathy, being callous and contemptuous of the feelings, rights and sufferings of others). Chronic, longstanding anti-social elements may be seen in sexually abusive older adolescents who have a history of behaviours that violate the rights of others (e.g., cheating, lying, stealing, and disruptive behaviour in the classroom, fighting, and history of school suspensions or expulsions) (Miccio-Fonseca, 1998b, 1999b: [Revised: 2002–5]). Occasionally acute anti-social behaviour may spontaneously emerge following a traumatic event or stress. Sexually abusive youth may direct anti-social behaviour toward either people or animals. Abuse of animals can be either physical or sexual (i.e., bestiality) and is associated with youth who meet diagnostic criteria of conduct disorder (Ascione, 2001). Sexually abusive youth who show evidence of abusing animals should be considered to have higher risk for sexually abusive behaviour, particularly when abuse of animals is combined with other *Sexually Abusive Dynamics* (Rasmussen and Miccio-Fonseca, 2007), which may include anti-social behaviours and/or aspects of extreme coercion (i.e., use of threats of lethal consequences, use of weapons). Youth who make lethal threats or use weapons are rare; they must be considered to be very high risk.

The comprehensive literature review completed during the construction of the *FISORF-1998* found that anti-social behaviour has repeatedly been shown in the empirical literature on sexually abusive youth to be associated with risk and/or recidivism for sexually abusive behaviour in youth under the age of 19 (Miccio-Fonseca, 1998b, 1999b: [Revised: 2002–5]). Adolescents who commit sexual offences are more at risk to commit other non-sexual delinquent offences than to reoffend sexually (Kahn and Chambers, 1991; Milloy, 1994; Rasmussen, 1999a; Schram, Milloy, and Rowe, 1991). In fact, recent reviews of the literature have shown that sexually abusive youth have similar patterns of anti-social behaviour to juvenile offenders who do not commit sex offenders (Righthand and Welch, 2001, 2004). For example, a longititudinal study of 986 10 to 13 year-old boys found no differences between the sexually abusive youth in the sample ($n = 39$) and youth who were violent, but not sexually abusive ($n = 330$) on several variables related to anti-social behaviour (e.g., total delinquency, theft, fraud,

serious delinquency, physical aggression, cruel to people, truancy, suspensions, covert behaviour, lack of guilt, positive attitude to problem behaviour, positive attitude to delinquency, bad friends, peer delinquency) (van Wijk et al., 2005).

The aforementioned risk assessment tools (i.e., *J-SOAP-II, ERASOR, Version 2.0, J-SORRAT-II*) include aspects of anti-social behaviour as salient elements associated with risk and/or recidivism. Righthand et al. (2005) found that youth who were placed in residential facilities had significantly higher scores on the 'impulsive, anti-social behaviour' scale of the *J-SOAP* than youth who were placed in community-based programmes. Waite et al. (2002) found the re-offence rate of youth who received high scores on the impulsive, anti-social behaviour scale of the *J-SOAP* was three times greater than youth who received low scores (9.8 per cent as opposed to 2.9 per cent $N = 253$). Epperson et al. (2005) found a constellation of anti-social variables was statistically predictive of sexual recidivism; several of these variables are among the final 12 risk factors that comprise the *J-SORRAT-II* (e.g., number of adjudications for sex offences, length of sexual offending history based on charged sex offences, use of deception or grooming in any charged sex offence, number of education time periods with discipline problems, number of adjudications for non-sexual offences). In contrast, the authors of the *ERASOR, Version 2.0* (Worling and Curwen, 2001) found mixed findings supporting the inclusion of anti-social variables (e.g., anti-social interpersonal orientation, negative peer associations and influences, interpersonal aggression) as risk factors in their tool. In the manual of the *ERASOR, Version 2.0*, they noted that anti-social behaviour in sexually abusive youth was significantly associated with recidivism of non-sexual offences (Langström, and Grann, 2000; Worling and Curwen, 2000), but was not significantly associated with sexual recidivism. When assessing sexually abusive youth, it is important to identify the specific anti-social behaviours that a youth manifests. When professionals fail to account for differences in anti-social behaviour and/or other *Sexually Abusive Dynamics* (Rasmussen and Miccio-Fonseca, 2007), they may end up viewing and treating all sexually abusive youth the same without differentiating them according to their level of risk.

MEGA's Ecological model asserts that there is a transactional relationship between the youth's anti-social behaviour and his or her family dynamics, as well as with the family's community and cultural context (Miccio-Fonseca and Rasmussen, 2006a, b). We contend that anti-social behaviour generally reflects a historical pattern of behaviour problems that are often traceable to the youth's early development and reflect the youth's functioning at home, school, and the community (Miccio-Fonseca and Rasmussen, 2006a, b). These ecological influences are assessed in more depth in *MEGA* through the *Family Lovemap Aggregate*. A full discussion of the *Family Lovemap Aggregate* is beyond the scope of this chapter; for an in-depth discussion please see a recent article on the *Family Lovemap* in the *ATSA Forum* (Miccio-Fonseca, 2006a).

Coercive elements in relationships – threats, physical force, and use of weapons

Several Aggregates in *MEGA* are focused on assessing *Sexually Abusive Dynamics* (Rasmussen and Miccio-Fonseca, 2007): *Antisocial, Sexual Incident, Coercion, Stratagem,* and *Relationship* (*Predatory Elements*). The above formulations defining sexually abusive behaviour in youth (Burton et al., 1998; Groth and Loredo, 1981; Gil, 1993; Hall et al., 1996; Johnson, 2004; Rasmussen, 1999b, 2001: 2; Ryan, 1997b) considered coercion to be important; yet they provided limited discussion about the aspects of coercion a youth might incorporate, including:

- General threats that elicit fear.
- Threats of bodily harm and/or lethal consequences.
- Physical force.
- Use of weapons (e.g., guns, knives, sticks).
- Combined coercive elements (i.e., using a combination of force, threats, and weapons).

The research that informed the construction of the *FISORF-1998* found that severe aspects of coercion, including threats of bodily harm and use of weapons, were empirically associated with high-risk sexually abusive youth (Miccio-Fonseca, 1998b, 1999b: [Revised: 2002–5]). Research literature related to risk assessment tools also affirms that severe coercion is important to consider when assessing sexually abusive youth, either with adolescents or children. In their manual for the *ERASOR, Version 2.0,* Worling and

Curwen (2001: 15) asserted that sexually abusive adolescents who use threats and/or use of excessive violence and weapons during their offences 'are more likely at greater risk to commit further sexual assaults'. Johnson (2000) described different types of children with sexual behaviour problems and indicated that the most severe type, 'children who molest' may use bribery, trickery, manipulation, or other kinds of emotional and physical coercion to get other children, particularly significantly younger children, to participate in sexual behaviours. In a study of 127 children ages 6 to 12 who were referred to treatment for problematic sexual behaviour, Pithers, Gray, Busconi, and Houchens (1998) found positive correlations between the number of victims that were abused by the children and use of a weapon during an abusive act ($r = .21$, $p \rrbracket .02$). It is evident from this research that at least some children show coercion in their sexually abusive behaviour. Our construct of *Sexually Abusive Dynamics* (Rasmussen and Miccio-Fonseca, 2007) differentiates the various types of coercion, and these are assessed through the Aggregates of *MEGA*.

Predatory behaviour

Predatory behaviour is included in our construct of *Sexually Abusive Dynamics* (Rasmussen and Miccio-Fonseca, 2007), while it is missing in previous definitions of sexually abusive behaviour (Burton et al., 1998; Groth and Loredo, 1981; Gil, 1993; Hall et al., 1996; Johnson, 2004; Rasmussen, 1999, 2001, 2002; Ryan, 1997b). We use the term '*predatory elements*' to describe the relationship dynamics present when a youth establishes a relationship with a stranger or person of casual acquaintance for the primary purpose of carrying out *Sexually Abusive Dynamics* of manipulation and coercion (Rasmussen and Miccio-Fonseca, 2007). When predatory elements are involved, combined with any type of coercion (i.e., threats, force, and/or use of a weapon or weapons), the level of abusiveness in the relationship rises exponentially as does the level of risk for recurrence of sexually abusive behaviour (Miccio-Fonseca and Rasmussen, 2005e, Rasmussen and Miccio-Fonseca, 2007).

Many clinicians, researchers, and non-clinical professionals in the field of sexual abuse resist viewing youth as capable of committing predatory sexual behaviours. However, crime statistics (e.g., Violent Crime Index for 2001) have documented that the age group in youth that commits most of the predatory offences (i.e., offences against strangers or persons of casual acquaintance) is the older adolescent male (Office of Juvenile Justice and Delinquency Prevention (OJJDP), 2005). The above crime data showed that children under 12 committed only a minute percentage (.02 per cent) of violent crimes (i.e., murder, non-negligent manslaughter, forcible rape, robbery, aggravated assault) (OJJDP, 2005). Make no mistake, children who display predatory behaviour or use weapons are anomalies. Nonetheless, definitions of sexually abusive youth, as well as assessment tools, need to be comprehensive enough to incorporate the infrequent, out of the ordinary cases involving violent behaviour and predatory elements; otherwise, risk factors are not adequately assessed.

Intra-familial cases are more commonly seen in clinical practice; these typically involve children and adolescents who sexually abuse a family member rather than strangers or people of casual acquaintance (Miccio-Fonseca, 1996). Similar to findings in adult sex offender research (Hanson and Bussiere, 1998; Hanson and Morton-Bourgon, 2004), research on sexually abusive youth indicates that youth who offend within the family are less dangerous. Studies have shown that youth who sexually abuse strangers were significantly more likely to re-offend sexually (Smith and Monastersky, 1986) and were 'three times more likely to be convicted of a subsequent sexual offence' (Långström and Grann, 2000; as cited in Worling and Curwen, 2001: 17).

Predatory elements are assessed in *MEGA* through the *Relationship (Predatory Elements)* and *Stratagem Aggregates*, which are based on similar domains in the *FISORF-1998* (Miccio-Fonseca, 1998b, 1999b: [Revised: 2002–5]). The *Relationship (Predatory Elements)* Aggregate assesses the relationship the youth has with other people involved in a sexual incident, including whether the other person is known to the youth or is a stranger or casual acquaintance. The *Stratagem Aggregate* assesses:

1. The degree of planning and manipulation (e.g., deceit, lying, trickery) that the youth has engaged in prior to a sexual incident.
2. Intrinsic indicators of the youth's sexual thoughts or planning (e.g., writings, drawings,

Internet postings) (Miccio-Fonseca and Rasmussen, 2006b).

The Risk, Static and Principles scales in *MEGA* work in tandem to identify those idiosyncratic coercive and predatory risk factors that make the youth a very high risk for continued and sustained sexually abusive behaviour.

Considerations for special populations

A unique and important strength of *MEGA* is its applicability to special populations of sexually abusive youth. Considerations for these populations are discussed below.

Female sexually abusive youth

The incidence of sexual offending by girls is estimated to be between two and 11 per cent; available studies are based on small samples (Righthand and Welch, 2004). More females are found in younger samples; studies of sexually abusive children under 12 have documented that about a third of their samples were females (Bonner, Walker, and Berliner, 1999; Pithers et al., 1998). Research has shown that adolescent females are less likely to use force in their sexually abusive behaviour than older adolescent males (ages 16 to 19) (Ray and English, 1995; English and Ray, as cited by Araji, 1997; Righthand and Welch, 2001).

One of the studies from the seven-year research that informed the construction of the *FISORF-1998* and *MEGA* (Miccio-Fonseca, 2000) compared a large subject sample (*N* = 565) consisting of three groups: 1. Relatively young (adolescent and adult) females who had committed sex offences (*n* = 18, average age = 22), 2. Older females who had not committed sex offences (*n* = 215, average age = 34) and 3. Relatively young (adolescent and adult) males who had committed sex offences (*n* = 332, average age = 21). When compared to males who had committed sex offences, the sexually abusive females reported:

1. Significantly more concerns related to their gynaecological histories (e.g., abortions, unwanted pregnancies, history of sexually transmitted diseases/sexual illnesses).
2. Significantly higher number of sexual illnesses and reproductive concerns.

This research affirms that clinicians and non-clinical professionals need to assess female sexually abusive youth for gynaecological health concerns, including sexual illnesses.

MEGA assessment emphasises the need for a comprehensive assessment of all areas of the youth's functioning – including biological and neuropsychological concerns (Miccio-Fonseca and Rasmussen, 2005e, 2006a, 2006b; Rasmussen and Miccio-Fonseca, 2007). *MEGA* is sensitive to gender differences; it includes a constellation of elements (i.e., Female scale) that assess factors particularly relevant to female sexually abusive youth. This scale is used to identify elements that may put females at risk for sexually abusive behaviour, as well as highlight particular concerns that need to be addressed for sexually abusive females in treatment.

Sexually abusive children under 12. The first studies on sexually abusive children under 12 were not published until the late 1980s (Friedrich and Luecke, 1988; Johnson, 1988, 1989). Recent reviews of the descriptive and outcome studies published since that time indicate that the empirical data related to risk of children under 12 for sexually abusive behaviour are limited (Araji, 1997; Burton et al., 1998; Chaffin, Letourneau, and Silovsky, 2002; Friedrich, 2002; Johnson, 2000; Lane, 1997; Miccio-Fonseca, 1998b, 1999b: [Revised: 2002–5]; Rasmussen, 2004). Studies of sexually abusive children under 12 have documented that boys and girls differ in the level of coercion shown in their *Sexually Abusive Dynamics* (Rasmussen and Miccio-Fonseca, 2007). In a study of 271 children under 12, Ray and English (1995) found that the girls ($n = 34$) used less force and violence in their sexually abusive behaviours than the boys ($n = 237$). In a separate study comparing 182 adolescents against 87 preadolescents, adolescents were found to use more aggression, coercion, and sophistication in their sexually abusive behaviours than the preadolescents (English and Ray, as cited in Araji, 1997). These studies point to important differences between adolescents and children who are sexually abusive; young people have different needs and concerns, depending on their age and stage of development.

The *Neuropsychological* and *Family Lovemap Aggregates* in *MEGA* are particularly informative when assessing young children, as these Aggregates pick up on important internal and external risk factors related to early development that may relate to risk for sexually abusive

behaviour. We caution non-clinical professionals and clinicians to be discrete and exercise great caution when applying the *Anti-social, Sexual Incident, Coercion, Stratagem,* and *Relationship (Predatory Elements)* to children (ages 5 to 12). *Very few children have predatory and/or anti-social elements in their sexually abusive behaviour, make threats of bodily harm, use physical force, or use a weapon.* The rare occurrence of predatory and anti-social behaviours in young children was documented by both the literature review completed for the *FISORF-1998* (Miccio-Fonseca, 1998b, 1999b: [Revised: 2002–5]); and the updated literature review we completed while developing *MEGA* (Miccio-Fonseca and Rasmussen, 2005c, 2005e, 2006a, b). Nevertheless, we believe *MEGA* is a useful tool for assessing the small percentage of children under 12 who display predatory elements, anti-social behaviour and/or show extreme coercion in their sexually abusive behaviour. *MEGA* can help professionals and clinicians identify whether these severe *Sexually Abusive Dynamics* (Rasmussen and Miccio-Fonseca, 2007) are present for a particular child.

A third special population, developmentally disabled youth, require an individualised assessment focusing on neuropsychological dynamics (e.g., learning disabilities, cognitive deficits) (Miccio-Fonseca, 1998b, 1999b: [Revised: 2002–5]). Assessments of these youth need to be multidimensional in identifying and assessing the support these youth have in their environment (American Association of Mental Retardation, 2005). Clinicians and non-clinical professionals must take into account the degree of culpability these youth have for their sexually abusive behaviour, as well as their level of control/self-governance they have over their behaviour (Blasingame, 2003). Research on developmentally disabled youth is extremely limited; only one published study (Gilby, Wolf and Goldberg, 1989) has specifically focused on describing the characteristics of these youth. Gilby et al. found that developmentally delayed adolescents were more likely to sexually abuse peers or people they did not know than adolescents with average intelligence. Similarly, Knopp (in a chapter of an edited book by Haaven, Little and Petre-Miller, 1990) stressed the importance of assessing these youth for predatory behaviour and other behavioural problems (i.e., impulsive behaviour, use of force and/or weapons, substance abuse, fire setting, animal abuse, and failed treatments). Several of the

Aggregates in *MEGA* can be used to assess these behaviours (i.e., *Relationship (Predatory Elements), Stratagem, Anti-social Behaviour, and Coercion)*.

Interventions for developmentally delayed youth must be tailored to 'their learning styles' (Righthand and Welch, 2004: 27) and address their special needs (Haaven et al., 1990). Treatment plans for these youth should include goals related to improving self-care and learning life skills (Flora, 2001). Clinicians who work with youth with developmental disabilities will likely find *MEGA* to be a helpful addition to an assessment protocol. The *Neuropsychological Aggregate* is essential to consider when assessing these youth; as it can help identify internal risk factors (e.g., lower level of intellectual functioning, history of epilepsy, attention deficit disorders) contributing to the limitations these youth experience that empirical research indicates are associated with risk for sexually abusive behaviour (Miccio-Fonseca, 1998b, 1999b: [Revised: 2002–5]; Miccio-Fonseca and Rasmussen, 2006a; b). Careful assessment of neuropsychological concerns is critical to reduce risk for sexually abusive behaviour in developmentally delayed youth.

Conclusion

This chapter emphasises the need for empirically guided assessment of sexually abusive youth. It presents a new risk assessment tool, *MEGA* (Miccio-Fonseca, 2006b) that is empirically guided entirely by the research on sexually abusive youth, not adults. *MEGA* is designed to be inclusive, comprehensive, applying to all types of sexually abusive youth under the age of 19 years, irrespective of gender, age, and developmental abilities. It focuses on elements (i.e., neuropsychological dynamics), and *Sexually Abusive Dynamics* (Rasmussen and Miccio-Fonseca, 2007) (i.e., anti-social behaviour, extreme coercion, and relationship (predatory elements)) that have been traditionally overlooked or minimised in previous definitions of sexually abusive behaviour and in risk assessment tools for sexually abusive youth. The seven Aggregates and six scales of *MEGA* will provide clinicians and non-clinical professionals with empirically guided data that identifies specified areas of concern in the youth's functioning related to risk for sexually abusive behaviour. These data can be instructive and informative when combined with results from assessment tools that are intended to identify treatment needs and are used for the purpose of making decisions related to supervision or placement. The estimates provided by *MEGA* related to identifying the youth's risk for sexually abusive behaviour are an important source of data to include when planning treatment for the youth and making decisions related to supervision and placement. In addition to assessing children and adolescents of low and moderate risk, *MEGA* provides criteria/elements for assessing adjudicated sexually abusive youths that are engaged in deviant sexually abusive behaviours (e.g., raping, gang rape, kidnap and sexual assaults, bestiality), where the people that they abuse are peers or adults, and their sexually abusive behaviours incorporate violence and aggression and are beyond child molestation.

Validation research on *MEGA* has recently begun. We invite other researchers who are studying risk and/or recidivism in sexually abusive youth to consider designing studies incorporating *MEGA* as part of the assessment protocol. We are confident *MEGA* will yield a wealth of information at one sitting. *MEGA* is currently in the publication process; please contact us regarding its availability. *We caution professionals and clinicians that they must have the complete version of MEGA (including the instructional set contained in the MEGA Manual and Rating Booklet (Miccio-Fonseca, 2006c)) before proceeding to use it in either defining a sexually abusive youth or assessing risk*. When using *MEGA* in an assessment, clinicians or non-clinical professionals must apply *all* of the seven Aggregates, with their respective elements. It is inappropriate to apply only the summary of the seven Aggregates (without the specified parameters contained in *MEGA*'s instructional *Manual and Rating Booklet)*; doing so would result in an inadequate or invalid assessment of the youth's functioning.

References

American Association of Mental Retardation (2006) *Policies: Definition of Mental Retardation.* Retrieved March 19, from: http:// www.aamr.org/Policies/faq_mental_ retardation.shtml

Araji, S. (1997) *Sexually Aggressive Children: Coming to Understand Them.* Thousand Oaks, CA: Sage.

Ascione, F.R. (2001) Animal Abuse and Youth Violence. *OJJDP Juvenile Justice Bulletin*, 1–15.

Blasingame, G.D. (2003) A Developmental Perspective on Sexual Abuse. *Perspectives: California Coalition on Sexual Offending (CCOSO) Quarterly Newsletter*, 6.

Boer, D.P., Hart, S.D., Kropp, P.R. and Webster, C.D. (1997) *Manual for the Sexual Violence Risk-20.* Burnaby, British Columbia: The Mental Health Law and Policy Institute. Simon Fraser University.

Bonner, B.L., Walker, C.E. and Berliner, L. (1999) *Children with Sexual Behaviour Problems: Assessment and Treatment.* Washington, DC: Administration for Children, Youth, and Families, Department of Human Services.

Bremer, J.F. (2001) *Protective Factors Scale: Determining the Level of Intervention for Youth with Harming Sexual Behaviour.* St. Paul, MN: Project Pathfinder.

Brofenbrenner, U. (1989) Ecological Systems Theory. In Vista, R. (Ed.) *Annals of Child Development: Six Theories of Child Development: Revised Formulations and Current Issues.* Greenwich, CT: JAI Press.

Burton, J. et al. (1998) *Treating Children with Sexually Abusive Behaviour Problems: Guidelines for Child and Parent Intervention.* New York: Haworth Press.

Chaffin, M. and Bonner, B. (1998) 'Don't Shoot, We're Your Children': Have we Gone too far in our Response to Adolescent Sexual Abusers and Children with Sexual Behaviour Problems? *Child Maltreatment*, 3: 4, 314–16.

Chaffin, M., Letourneau, E. and Silovsky, J. (2002) Adults, Adolescents, and Children who Sexually Abuse Children. In Meyers, J.E.B. et al. (Eds.) *The APSAC Handbook on Child Maltreatment.* 2nd edn. Thousand Oaks, CA: Sage.

Chess, S. and Thomas, A. (1986) *Temperament in Clinical Practice.* New York: Guilford.

Colorado Sex Offender Management Board (2003) *Standards and Guidelines for the Evaluation, Assessment, Treatment, and Supervision of Juveniles who Have Committed Sexual Offences.* Denver, CO: Colorado Department of Public Safety, Division of Criminal Justice.

Davies, D. (1999) *Child Development: A Practitioner's Guide.* New York: Guilford Press.

Epperson, D. (2006) *Resolving Public Policy Conflicts Through the Presentation of Accurate Risk Assessment: Development of the J-SORRAT-II as an Illustration.* Keynote address at the Ninth Annual Training Conference of the California Coalition on Sexual Offending, San Mateo, CA.

Epperson, D., Ralston, C.A., Fowers, D. and DeWitt, J. (2005) *The Juvenile Sexual Offence Recidivism Risk Assessment Tool (J-SORRAT-II)* Retrieved June 12, 2005 from: http://www.psychology.iastate.edu/faculty/epperson.

Fanniff, A.M. and Becker, J.V. (2006) Specialized Assessment and Treatment of Adolescent Sex Offenders. *Aggression and Violent Behaviour*, 11, 265–82.

Finkelhor, D. and Jones, L.M. (2004) Explanations for the Decline in Child Sexual Abuse Cases. *Juvenile Justice Bulletin*, Office of Juvenile Justice and Delinquency Prevention (OJJDP) Retrieved March 19, 2006 from: http://www.ojp.usdoj.gov/ojjdp

Flora, R. (2001) *How to Work with Sex Offenders: A Handbook for Criminal Justice, Human Services, and Mental Health Professionals.* New York: Haworth.

Friedrich, W.N. (1997) *Child Sexual Behaviour Inventory: Professional Manual.* Odessa, FL: Psychological Assessment Resources.

Friedrich, W.N. (2002) *Psychological Assessment of Sexually Abused Children and Their Families.* Thousand Oaks, CA: Sage.

Friedrich, W.N. and Luecke, W.J. (1988) Young School-age Sexually Aggressive Children. *Professional Psychology, Research, and Practice*, 19: 2, 155–64.

Gil, E. (1993) Age Appropriate Sex Play versus Problematic Sexual Behaviours. In Gil, E. and Johnson, T.C. (Eds.) *Sexualized Children: Assessment and Treatment of Sexualized Children who Molest.* Walnut Creek, CA: Launch Press.

Gilby, R., Wolf, L. and Goldberg, B. (1989) Mentally Retarded Adolescent Sex Offenders: A Survey and Pilot Study. *Canadian Journal of Psychiatry*, 34, 542–8.

Gilgun, J. (1999) CASPARS: New Tools for Assessing Client Risks and Strengths. *Families in Society*, 80: 5, 450–60.

Gilgun, J., Keskinen, S., Marti, D.J. and Rice, K. (1999) Clinical Applications of the CASPARS Instruments: Boys who Act out Sexually. *Families in Society*, 80: 6, 629–42.

Gray, A.S. and Pithers, W.D. (1993) Relapse Prevention with Sexually Aggressive Adolescents and Children: Expanding Treatment and Supervision. In Barbaree, H., Marshall, W. and Hudson, S. (Eds.) *The Juvenile Sexual Offender.* New York: Guilford Press.

Groth, A.N. and Loredo, C.M. (1981) Juvenile Sex Offenders: Guidelines for Assessment. *International Journal of Offender Comparative Criminology*, 25: 1, 31–9.

Haaven, J., Little, R. and Petre-Miller, D. (1990) *Treating Intellectually Disabled Sex Offenders: A Model Residential Program.* Brandon, VT: Safer Society.

Hall, D., Mathews, F. and Pearce, J. (1998) Factors Associated with Sexual Behaviour Problems in Young Sexually Abused Children. *Child Abuse and Neglect*, 22: 10, 1045–63.

Hall, D., Mathews, F. and Pearce, J. (2002) Sexual Behaviour Problems in Sexually Abused Children: A Preliminary Typology. *Child Abuse and Neglect*, 26, 289–312.

Hall, D., Mathews, F., Pearce, J., Sarlo-McGarvey, N., and Gavin, D. (1996) *The Development of Sexual Behaviour Problems in Children and Youth.* Ontario, Canada: Central Toronto Youth Services.

Hanson, R.K. and Bussiere, M.T. (1998) Predicting Relapse: A Meta-Analysis of Sexual Offender Recidivism Studies. *Journal of Consulting and Clinical Psychology*, 66: 2, 348–62.

Hanson, R.K. and Morton-Bourgon, K. (2004) Predictors of Sexual Recidivism: An Updated Meta-analysis. *Public Works and Government Services Canada.*

Hepworth, D.H. et al. (2006) *Direct Social Work Practice: Theory and Skills.* 7th edn. Pacific Grove, CA: Thomson.

Hoge, R.D. and Andrews, D.A. (1996) *The Youth Level of Service/Case Management Inventory and Manual.* Ottawa, Canada: Carleton University, Department of Psychology.

Johnson, T.C. (1988) Child Perpetrators: Children who Molest Other Children: Preliminary Findings. *Child Abuse and Neglect*, 12, 219–29.

Johnson, T.C. (1989) Female Child Perpetrators: Children who Molest Other Children. *Child Abuse and Neglect*, 13, 571–85.

Johnson, T.C. (1994) *Child Sexual Behaviour Checklist.* Pasadena, CA. Author.

Johnson, T.C. (2000) Sexualized Children and Children who Molest. *SIECUS Report*, 29: 1, 35–9.

Johnson, T.C. (2002) *Child Sexual Behaviour Checklist: Second Revision.* Pasadena, CA: Author.

Johnson, T.C. (2004) *Children who Sexually Abuse.* Unpublished handout distributed at an invited workshop on Assessing Children with Sexual Behaviour Problems given to the staff of the STEPS Program, August 2004. San Diego, CA.

Kahn, T.J. and Chambers, H.J. (1991) Assessing Re-offence Risk with Juvenile Sexual Offenders. *Child Welfare*, 70, 333–45.

Katz, M. (1997) *On Playing a Poor Hand Well: Insights from the Lives of those who have Overcome Childhood Risks and Adversities.* New York: W. W. Norton.

Lane, S. (1997) Special Populations: Children, Females, the Developmentally Disabled and Violent Youth. In Ryan, G. and Lane, S. (Eds.) *Juvenile Sexual Offending: Causes, Consequences, and Correction.* Rev. edn. San Francisco: Jossey-Bass.

Långström, N. and Grann, M. (2000) Risk for Criminal Recidivism among Young Sex Offenders. *Journal of Interpersonal Violence*, 15, 855–71.

Miccio-Fonseca, L.C. (1993) *Eroticised Children: Clinical Considerations.* Invited presentation to the San Diego County Department of Social Services, San Diego, CA.

Miccio-Fonseca, L.C. (1994) *Erotic Development.* The Society for the Scientific Study of Sex Annual Western Region Conference.

Miccio-Fonseca, L.C. (1994/1997) *Personal Sentence Completion Inventory, (PSCI) An Inventory that Explores Erotic Development and Sexual Functioning. A Supplemental Tool for the Clinician in Assessments and Evaluations.* San Diego, CA: Clinic for the Sexualities; Brandon, VT: Safer Society Press.

Miccio-Fonseca, L.C. (1996) Research Report: on Sex Offenders, Victims and their Families. Special Edition, *Journal of Offender Rehabilitation*, 23: 3/4, 71–83.

Miccio-Fonseca, L.C. (1998a) *Assessing Sexual Perversion in Adults, Adolescents and Children.* Invited presentation at the San Diego Conference on Responding to Child Maltreatment, Center for Child Protection and American Professional Society on the Abuse of Children, San Diego, CA.

Miccio-Fonseca, L.C. (1998b) *Fonseca Inventory of Sex Offenders' Risk Factors (FISORF)* San Diego, CA: Author.

Miccio-Fonseca, L.C. (1999a) *Brain, Sex and Sex Offenders.* Invited presentation at the San Diego Conference on Responding to Child Maltreatment, Center for Child Protection and American Professional Society on the Abuse of Children. San Diego, CA.

Miccio-Fonseca, L.C. (1999b: Revised 2002–5) *Fonseca Inventory of Sex Offenders' Risk Factors (FISORF) – Professional Manual.* San Diego, CA: Author.

Miccio-Fonseca, L.C. (2000) Adult and Adolescent Female Sex Offenders: Experiences Compared to Other Females and Male Sex Offenders. Special Edition, *Journal of Psychology and Human Sexuality*, 11, 75–88.

Miccio-Fonseca, L.C. (2001) Somatic and Mental Symptoms of Male Sex Offenders: A Comparison among Offenders, Victims, and Their Families. *Journal of Psychology and Human Sexuality*, 13: 3/4, 103–14.

Miccio-Fonseca, L.C. (2003) Sex, Research and Etcetera. *Perspectives: California Coalition on Sexual Offending (CCOSO) Quarterly Newsletter*, 4.

Miccio-Fonseca, L.C. (2005) *Erotic Development: Sexual Deviancy and Technology*. Invited presentation at the Eighth Annual Training Conference of the California Coalition on Sexual Offending, San Diego, CA.

Miccio-Fonseca, L.C. (2006a) Family Lovemaps: Challenging the Myths Related to Multiple Paraphilias, Denial, and Paraphilic Fugue States. *ATSA Forum, Winter*.

Miccio-Fonseca, L.C. (2006b) *Multiplex Empirically Guided Inventory of Ecological Aggregates for Assessing Sexually Abusive Children and Adolescents (Ages 19 and Under) – MEGA*. San Diego, CA: Author.

Miccio-Fonseca, L.C. (2006c) *Multiplex Empirically Guided Inventory of Ecological Aggregates for Assessing Sexually Abusive Children and Adolescents (Ages 19 and Under) – MEGA: Manual and Rating Booklet*. San Diego, CA: Author.

Miccio-Fonseca, L.C. and Rasmussen, L.A. (2005a) *A Comprehensive Ecologically Valid Protocol for Assessing Sexually Abusive Youth Ages 19 and Under: A Risk Factor Approach to Guiding Interventions and Providing Treatment*. Invited seminar sponsored by the Israeli Association for Child Protection (ELI), Tel Aviv, Israel.

Miccio-Fonseca, L.C. and Rasmussen, L.A. (2005b) *Evaluating Sexually Abusive Youth Ages 19 and Under: A New Paradigm in Defining Abusive Dynamics*. Poster presentation at the Eighth Annual Training Conference of the California Coalition on Sexual Offending, San Diego, CA.

Miccio-Fonseca, L.C. and Rasmussen, L.A. (2005c) Defining Sexually Abusive Behaviour in Youth Ages 19 and Under: New Paradigm and New Tool. *Perspectives: Quarterly Newsletter of the California Coalition on Sexual Offending*.

Miccio-Fonseca, L.C. and Rasmussen, L.A. (2005d) *Implementing a Comprehensive, Ecologically Valid Assessment Protocol: A Paradigm Shift in Identifying and Assessing Sexually Abusive Dynamics in Sexually Offending Youth Ages 19 and Under*. Invited pre-conference workshop at the 10th Annual International Conference on Family Violence, San Diego, CA.

Miccio-Fonseca, L.C. and Rasmussen, L.A. (2005e) *Paradigm Shift in Defining Sexually Abusive Youth: Ages 19 and Under*. Manuscript submitted for publication.

Miccio-Fonseca, L.C. and Rasmussen, L.A. (2006a) *Implementing MEGA, a new tool for assessing risk of concern for sexually abusive behaviour in youth ages 19 and under: An empirically guided paradigm for risk assessment: Revised*. Available from: http://www.ccoso.org.

Miccio-Fonseca, L.C., and Rasmussen, L.A. (2006b) Empirical Support for *MEGA*. In Miccio-Fonseca L.C. *Multiplex Empirically Guided Inventory of Ecological Aggregates for Assessing Sexually Abusive Children and Adolescents (Ages 19 and Under) – MEGA: Professional Manual and Rating Booklet*. San Diego, CA: Author.

Milloy, C.D. (1994) *A Comparative Study of Juvenile Sex Offenders and Non-sex Offenders*. Olympia, WA: Washington State Institute for Public Policy.

Money, J. (1986) *Lovemaps: Clinical Concepts of Sexual/Erotic Health and Pathology, Paraphilia, and Gender Transposition in Childhood, Adolescence, and Maturity*. New York: Irvington, (Paperback Amherst, NY, Prometheus Books 1988).

Money, J., (1988) *Gay, Straight and in Between*. New York: Oxford University Press.

Money, J. (1995) *Gendermaps: Social Constructionism, Feminism, and Sexosophical History*. New York: Continuum.

Office of Juvenile Justice and Delinquency Prevention (2005) *Statistical Briefing Book*. Retrieved February 4, 2005 from: http://ojjdp.ncjrs.org/ojstatbb/crime/qa05301.asp?qaDate=20040801andtext=yes

Pithers, W. D., Gray, A., Busconi, A. and Houchens, P. (1998) Children with Sexual Behaviour Problems: Identification of Five Distinct Child Types and Related Treatment Considerations. *Child Maltreatment*, 3: 4, 384–406.

Prentky, R., Harris, B., Frizzell, K. and Righthand, S. (2000) An Actuarial Procedure for Assessing

Risk with Juvenile Sex Offenders. *Sexual Abuse: A Journal of Research and Treatment*, 12: 2, 72–93.

Prentky, R. and Righthand, S. (2003) *Juvenile Sex Offender Assessment Protocol-II (J-SOAP-II) Manual*. NCJ 202316. Office of Juvenile Justice and Delinquency Prevention, Juvenile Justice Clearinghouse. Retrieved October 7, 2005 from: http://ncjrs.gov.

Prentky, R. and Righthand, S. (2004) *Juvenile Sex Offender Assessment Protocol II (J-SOAP-II: Manual*. Retrieved October 30, 2005 from: http://www.forensicexaminers.com/jsoap.pdf.

Prescott, D.S. (2004) Emerging Strategies for Risk Assessment of Sexually Abusive Youth: Theory, Controversy, and Practice. Special Edition, *Journal of Child Sexual Abuse*, 13: 3/4, 83–105.

Prescott, D.S. and Longo, R.E. (2005) Good People do Bad Things. *Perspectives: California Coalition on Sexual Offending (CCOSO) Quarterly Newsletter, Summer*, 1 and 8–10.

Rasmussen, L.A. (1999a) Factors Related to Recidivism among Juvenile Sexual Offenders. *Sexual Abuse: A Journal of Research and Treatment*, 11: 1, 69–85.

Rasmussen, L.A. (1999b) The Trauma Outcome Process: An Integrated Model for Guiding Clinical Practice with Children with Sexually Abusive Behaviour Problems. *Journal of Child Sexual Abuse*, 8: 4, 3–33.

Rasmussen, L.A. (2001) Integrating Cognitive-Behavioural and Expressive Therapy Interventions: Applying the Trauma Outcome Process in Treating Children with Sexually Abusive Behaviour Problems. *Journal of Child Sexual Abuse*, 10: 4, 1–29.

Rasmussen, L.A. (2002) An Integrated Systemic Approach to Intervention with Children with Sexually Abusive Behaviour Problems. In Calder, M. (Ed.) *Young People who Sexually Abuse: Building the Evidence Base for your Practice*. Lyme Regis: Russell House Publishing.

Rasmussen, L.A. (2004) Differentiating Youth with Sexual Behaviour Problems: Applying a Multidimensional Framework when Assessing and Treating Subtypes. Special Edition, *Journal of Child Sexual Abuse*, 13: 3/4, 57–82. Published simultaneously in: Geffner, R., Franey, K.C., Arnold, T.G. and Falconer, R. (Eds.) *Identifying and Treating Youth Who Sexually Offend: Current Approaches, Techniques, and Research*. Binghamton, NY: Haworth Trauma and Maltreatment Press.

Rasmussen, L.A. (2006) *Assessing Children and Adolescents who Sexually Abuse Using the Trauma Outcome Process Assessment (TOPA) Model*. Invited workshop at the 3rd Annual Assessing and Treating Childhood, Adolescent, and Adult Trauma Conference, Institute on Violence, Abuse, and Trauma, Honolulu, HI.

Rasmussen, L.A. and Miccio-Fonseca, L.C. (2007) Paradigm Shift: Implementing *MEGA*—, A New Tool Proposed to Define and Assess Sexually Abusive Dynamics in Youth Ages 19 and Under. *Journal of Child Sexual Abuse*, 16: 1, 85–106.

Ray, J.A. and English, D.J. (1995) Comparison of Female and Male Children with Sexual Behaviour Problems. *Journal of Youth and Adolescents*, 24: 4, 439–51.

Rich, P. (2003) *Understanding, Assessing, and Rehabilitating Juvenile Sexual Offenders*. Hoboken, NJ: John Wiley.

Righthand, S. et al. (2005) Factor Analysis and Validation of the Juvenile Sex Offender Assessment Protocol (J-SOAP) *Sexual Abuse: A Journal of Research and Treatment*, 17:1, 13–30.

Righthand, S. and Welch, C. (2001) *Juveniles who have Sexually Offended: A Review of Professional Literature*. Washington, DC: Office of Juvenile Justice and Delinquency Prevention.

Righthand, S. and Welch, C. (2004) Characteristics of Youth who Sexually Offend. *Journal of Child Sexual Abuse*, 13: 3/4, 15–32.

Ryan, G. (1997a) Perpetration Prevention: Primary and Secondary. In Ryan, G. and Lane, S. (Eds.) *Juvenile Sexual Offending: Causes, Consequences, and Correction*. Revised edn. San Francisco: Jossey-Bass.

Ryan, G. (1997b) Sexually Abusive Youth: Defining the Population. In Ryan, G. and Lane, S. (Eds.) *Juvenile Sexual Offending: Causes, Consequences, and Correction*. Revised edn. San Francisco: Jossey-Bass.

San Diego County Probation Department and Sex Offender Management Council (2005) *Supervision Standards for Sexually Abusive Youth: Revisions*. San Diego, CA: Author.

Schram, D.D., Milloy, C.D. and Rowe, W.E. (1991) *Juvenile Sex Offenders: A Follow-up Study of Re-offence Behaviour*. Olympia, WA: Washington State Institute for Public Policy.

Sinacore-Guinn, A.L. (1995) The Diagnostic Window: Culture and Gender-Sensitive Diagnosis and Training. *Counselor Education and Supervision*, 35, 18–34.

Smith, W.R. and Monastersky, C. (1986) Assessing Juvenile Sexual Offenders' Risk of

Re-offending. *Criminal Justice and Behaviour*, 13, 115–40.

Snyder, H. (2000) *Sexual Assault of Young Children as Reported to Law Enforcement: Victim, Incident, and Offender Characteristics: A Statistical Report using Data from the National Incidence-Based Reporting System* (NCJ 182990) Washington, DC: US Department of Justice, Office of Justice Programs, National Center for Juvenile Justice.

van Wijk, A. et al. (2005) Violent Juvenile Sex Offenders Compared with Violent Juvenile Non-sex Offenders: Exploratory Findings from the Pittsburgh Youth Study. *Sexual Abuse: A Journal of Research and Treatment*, 17: 3, 333–52.

Webster's New World College Dictionary (2004) 4th edn. Agnes, M. and Guralnik, D.B. (Eds.) Cleveland, OH: Wiley Publishing.

Worling, J.R. (2004) The Estimate of Adolescent Sexual Offence Recidivism (ERASOR): Preliminary Psychometric Data. *Sexual Abuse: A Journal of Research and Treatment*, 16: 3, 235–54.

Worling, J.R. and Curwen, T. (2000) Adolescent Sexual Offender Recidivism: Success of Specialised Treatment and Implications for Risk Prediction. *Child Abuse and Neglect*, 24, 965–82.

Worling, J.R. and Curwen, T. (2001) *The ERASOR: Estimate of Risk of Adolescent Sexual Offence Recidivism (Version 2.0)* Toronto, Ontario, Canada: Sexual Abuse Family Education and Treatment (SAFE-T) Program, Thistletown Regional Center for Children and Adolescents, Ontario Ministry of Community and Social Services.

Chapter 15

The Implications of Attachment Theory in the Treatment of Sexually Abusive Youth*

Phil Rich

Introduction

In order to understand the relevance and implications of attachment theory, as well as its application, it is important, of course, that the reader understand the concepts and principles of attachment theory. However, given necessary limitations on chapter space, I have chosen to not describe attachment theory and instead use the chapter to describe ideas about the relevance of the theory (and attachment itself) in understanding sexually abusive behaviour, and implications for its use in an attachment-informed model of treatment.

At heart, attachment theory is a biologically-based model of human development, in which it is hypothesised that social interactions and self-regulatory behaviours, and an 'internal working model' of the world containing mental representations of self and others, result from early attachment experiences between a child and primary caregivers. Patterns of attachment are formed in the child between 12–18 months of age, and are believed to remain relatively stable, serving as a template for both sense of self and future relationships, throughout life. The early attachment experience is considered by many to be central in the development of social skills and social behaviours at all levels, including the development of metacognition, empathy and intimacy, self-regulation, moral behaviour, and bonded ties to the larger social environment. Built on this very basic understanding, the ideas and perspectives in this chapter will certainly give the reader a clear sense of some of the ideas of attachment theory, as well as the elements of an attachment-based treatment, but will not substitute for a more thorough knowledge of attachment theory itself. As volumes have been

written on the subject, including a volume written by this author (Rich, 2006), I recommend that interested readers explore the subject further.

The interest in attachment theory

It has become common to increasingly attribute attachment difficulties, and even attachment disorders, to the development of and engagement in sexually abusive behaviour. For over a decade, Marshall and colleagues have described attachment and social skills deficits in adult sexual offenders, hypothesising not only a developmental link, but a *causal* pathway, in which it is proposed that attachment difficulties, in some cases, result in sexual offences, which, in turn, create a behaviourally conditioned propensity to further sexually abusive behaviour. The model recognises, of course, that not all children experiencing attachment difficulties develop sexually abusive behaviour, and emphasises the importance and power of other developmental and risk factors that catalyse, compound, or mediate early developmental and attachment experiences. Nevertheless, the model proposes that poor attachment experiences create early developmental vulnerabilities in the child that may emerge in later years. Additionally, these vulnerabilities set into motion a pathway along which further vulnerabilities may develop and which themselves contribute to the child's failure to develop resiliency and also contribute to situations in which the child may be subject to victimisation, thus creating further vulnerabilities.

It is not much of a jump from Marshall's model (described in Marshall and Marshall, 2000) of an attachment pathway to sexually abusive behaviour in adults, to linking attachment difficulties to sexually abusive behaviour in children and adolescents. In fact, if one does not look at the Marshall model with discerning eyes, it is an obvious connection, if only because adult

---

*Nevertheless, given the broad range of treatment services actually provided by treatment programmes, many of which appear psychodynamic, it may be cognitive-behavioural and relapse prevention approaches are reported as predominant because the survey format itself, in design and structure, unintentionally elicits this response.

sexual offenders were children and adolescents before they became adults. As attachment experiences and patterns are considered to develop in infancy and early childhood, remaining relatively stable and active throughout the life span, it is clear that adults with attachment problems must have formerly been adolescents with attachment problems. Further, it is, at face value, obvious that the same mechanisms that link attachment deficits to sexually abusive behaviour in adults must also be in place for juvenile sexual offenders and sexually reactive children. Hence, in trying to understand sexually abusive behaviour in both adolescents and children we have arrived at a place where we have begun to commonly link attachment difficulties to juvenile sexual abuse, as though the link is both self-apparent and obvious.

However, after some 15 years of research, and particularly in the past few years, we find little empirical evidence to link attachment and sexual offending behaviour. As such, although an intuitive and attractive means to understand the development of sexually abusive behaviour, any attribution of attachment difficulties as *causal* is theoretical only. Nevertheless, we face the distinct risk that, with the appeal of and increasing interest in the 'attachment link,' we will uncritically accept another simple and appealing model that has theoretical value only.

The application of attachment theory: a note of caution

In general, one of the problems with the application of attachment theory, or at least ideas derived from attachment theory, is an indiscriminate use of its ideas without a more complete understanding of the theory itself, which is essentially a theory of both child development and object relations. It is not that attachment theory is not a useful way to understand the development of sexually coercive and aggressive behaviour, but its use in sex offender work has stretched the boundaries of attachment theory, both simplifying and sometimes misunderstanding and misapplying its concepts and principles. It is as if we have found something that looks promising and have taken those parts of the theory that we like and disregarded, or failed to study, the entire theory, failing to understand the parts within the context of the larger theory.

An attachment model is not without merit, neither is it unjustifiable to hypothesise an attachment link to the development of and engagement in sexually abusive behaviour. To the contrary, a model of etiology, assessment, and treatment that is informed by an understanding of attachment experiences, patterns of attachment, and childhood and adolescent development is of great value. Through such an attachment-informed model we find new eyes with which to see the children and adolescents (and adults) we treat, and new ears by which to hear and understand their stories and the development of their behaviour. An attachment-informed framework can guide assessment and treatment, including the direction of treatment and the development of a treatment model that recognises phases of attachment, even in adolescent and adult clients. Such a perspective can change the way we think about the behaviour of our clients, and allow us insights into the influences and pressures on children that contribute to *all* of their attitudes, relationships, and behaviours, including those that are sexually abusive in nature.

However, attachment theory is not without its own weaknesses, often failing to remain internally consistent or coherent. Here, we note Karen's (1994: 437) conclusion that attachment theory leaves 'huge unanswered questions' and Bolen's (2000) admonishment that attachment theory has many problems to resolve in both theory and proof. To this end, Lewis (1997: 162) writes that attachment theory 'tries to explain too much and, in doing so, explains little' and Greenberg (1999: 472) has warned against seeing attachment theory as the 'Holy Grail of psychopathology'. It is important to apply the same warning to the use of attachment theory in our attempt to understand the etiology of sexually abusive behaviour. That is, it is unlikely that attachment theory is a white horse coming in from the horizon, bringing answers to all the questions we seek.

Furthermore, because attachment theory was, in origin, predominately a theory of early object relationships and child development, Rutter (1997: 25) has noted 'the problem in the wish of many adult attachment theorists to extend attachment concepts to sexual relationships and to parents' relationships with their young children'. This problem is of particular importance as we review and discuss ideas of theorists who postulate that early attachment experiences and patterns are significantly connected to the development of sexually abusive behaviour. Following Rutter's criticism, we must raise the possibility that a similar process is occurring within the field of sex offender specific research or, to paraphrase Rutter, the wish of many sexual offender theorists to extend attachment concepts to sexually coercive and abusive relationships and to adult sexual molestation of children. We risk not only blending concepts, but also weak, ambiguous, and biased research designs that *prove*, rather than *test*, theoretically attractive hypotheses, and hence yield data that, despite the appearance of empirical 'fact,' are more speculative than certain. Here, we must bear in mind Lamb's (1987) warning that the design and methodology of attachment research may actually bias results in a manner that supports the attachment hypotheses.

A change in direction

Attachment theory is an object relations theory (Bowlby, 1988; Holmes, 2001) as well as a theory of child development. Applying a child development model to a criminological model of sexually abusive behaviour in itself represents a change in orientation. However, adopting an object relations theory is a radical departure from the psychoeducational and cognitive-behavioural approach that has been applied to sex offender specific treatment, as object relations theory is psychoanalytic in origin, and is and essentially remains a psychodynamic model. This is noteworthy, and should not go unrecognised, given the apparent disdain and disregard directed towards the application of a psychodynamic model in the treatment of sexual offenders, and the continued clear preference for cognitive-behavioural and psychoeducational treatment.

For instance, a nationwide study of outpatient and residential programmes treating adult and juvenile sexual offenders in the United States (McGrath, Cumming, and Burchard, 2003) found that cognitive-behavioural, psychoeducational, and relapse prevention planning models continue to predominate treatment by far. In fact, in the treatment of sexual offenders, cognitive-behavioural therapy receives the most support as the treatment of choice, and psychodynamic treatment has been repeatedly considered less effective, or not effective at all. The Association

for the Treatment of Sexual Abusers (2005: 19) writes that cognitive-behavioural approaches appear the most effective in treating adult sexual offenders, and 'insight-oriented treatment programs are less likely to be effective in reducing sexual re-offending and do not constitute primary interventions of the treatment of men who sexually offend'. ATSA (2001: 18) wrote that 'abstract treatment programs are much less likely to be effective in reducing rates of offending, and some may even increase the risk of re-offending'. Many others in the field have also asserted the superiority of cognitive-behavioural treatment, or report that it is the most commonly used and accepted treatment practice, and Cooke and Philip (2001), for example, not only report the treatment of choice as cognitive-behavioural, but unequivocally state that psychodynamic models have no impact on reducing recidivism.*

Our new embrace of attachment theory, then, marks a shift in perspective away from a dedicated cognitive-behavioural/relapse prevention approach. Here, we move towards an approach that recognises not just the part played by social and psychodynamic development, but the active role played by early influences and psychodynamic factors *throughout* life. A shift in thinking, then, ushers in a new age in our understanding of sexually abusive behaviour, and perhaps of greater importance, in our thinking *about* sexually abusive behaviour and its roots and mechanisms.

Nevertheless, the application of attachment theory is not to be taken lightly, or its 'correctness' simply assumed, because it has potential risks as well as benefits. The risks involve uncritical and widespread acceptance of unproven, inconsistent, and sometimes vague and misunderstood ideas about attachment; the introduction of new 'certainties' and misapplied diagnoses; and the over-simplification of complex and interactive emotional and cognitive processes that contribute to adult and juvenile sexual aggression.† On the other hand, the benefits include the introduction of a theory that recognises the complexity, richness, and diversity

---

*In fact, there is little to no evidence that a cognitive-behavioural/relapse prevention approach works either, as recently described by Marques et al. (2005).

† For instance, Reactive Attachment Disorder of Infancy or Early Childhood (RAD) is often misdiagnosed in older children, and even adolescents and adults, given both its focus on children of age four and younger, and the extreme behavioural disturbance that is the hallmark of RAD.

of human psychology, going far beyond a simple model of criminal thinking, deviant sexual arousal, thinking errors, and relapse prevention plans. An attachment approach allows us to recognise the significance of early development and experience; the critical nature of relationships and social connection, and the central role played by psychodynamic processes in tying together emotion, cognition, behaviour, and relationships; and the ecological interactivity of multiple systems, risk factors, and protective elements that combine to form individualised pathways, some of which lead to sexually abusive behaviour.

This new era will expand treatment (and already has) beyond a simple, one-size-fits-all model to holistic approaches that blend together and integrate cognitive-behavioural, psychoeducational, and psychodynamic models into a pan-theoretical model of assessment and treatment that is formulation-driven. Described by Drake and Ward (2003) formulation-based approaches require an understanding of the psychological problems and vulnerabilities of individual clients, rather than 'manualised' assessment that offers cookbook approaches for understanding behaviour. Despite the prevailing perspective that adult sexual offenders share common dysfunctions and can thus be treated through prescribed, manualised treatment, Drake and Ward argue that, although it is reasonable to assume that most adult sexual offenders have dysfunctions involving intimacy, sexual behaviour, and emotional regulation, individualised case formulation is likely to improve understanding and lead to a more precise and finely tuned treatment.

Attachment theory helps us to understand both normal (i.e., expected) and pathological personal and social development in general, as well as the path taken by each individual. If we understand it, attachment theory offers us the opportunity to apply an attachment lens precisely for the purposes of individualised formulation. It allows us to understand the specific course of development for *each* individual, rather than simply casting the attachment deficit net upon all sexual offenders, juvenile or adult, as if they are all the same or all tread the same developmental pathways. An attachment-informed treatment framework can reveal the stories and patterns that influence, shape, and even direct behaviour and relationships in clients, and allow us the opportunity to not only more fully recognise and understand behaviour but design treatment

programmes that themselves are attachment informed.

Empirical links between attachment and sexually abusive behaviour

Of special concern, of course, is whether attachment difficulties are in some way related to the onset of sexually abusive behaviour, or are instead a general risk factor for antisocial behaviour but not specifically related to sexual offences.

However, regardless of increasing truisms that imply or assert that the development of pathology in sexual offenders is linked to under-developed attachment in children, there is little evidence that the existence of attachment deficits has any *direct* connection to the onset of sexually abusive behaviour in children or adolescents, and hence adults. Despite the attractiveness of the position and its appearance as having explanatory power, the idea that poor attachment experiences serve as a developmental pathway to juvenile sexual offending remains specious at this time. This is not to say that attachment difficulties do *not* play a role, whether major or minor, but merely that we must put such ideas into a context informed by a broad understanding of attachment, sexually abusive behaviour, and evidence that links the two, rather than interesting and intuitively attractive theory alone.

Evidence of attachment deficits and a link to juvenile sexual offending is drawn largely from investigations into the attachment status of adult sexual offenders, but even in this domain such evidence is both limited and questionable. A critical review of the research with adult sexual offenders suggests that, despite the use of empirical research designs, there is a *confirmatory bias*. That is, research seems to be used to confirm *a priori* theory almost uncritically, rather than discover, test, or evaluate it. In fact, it is not uncommon to read in much of the present research, that, although the data do not *yet* support the theory, there is nevertheless good reason to believe that attachment deficits *are* key, and it is simply a matter of time, better research design, and improved measurement processes until evidence supporting theoretical assumptions *is* discovered. For instance, despite the many limitations reported in most studies acknowledged by Mulloy and Marshall (1999: 106) they write that they continue to be sure that 'despite the problems ... there appears to be no doubt that attachment styles are an important area of dysfunction in sexual offenders'. Similarly, Smallbone and Dadds (2000: 13) write that 'notwithstanding these limitations, these results indicate that childhood attachment may play some role in the development of coercive sexual behaviour'. It is as though we have decided that the attachment deficit link *is* there and we will find it, if not now then soon.

It may be true that difficulties and disruptions in the experience of early attachment and the development of satisfactory and nourishing social relationships contribute significantly to the onset of coercive and abusive sexual behaviours in some men, and this idea has both obvious face validity and intuitive appeal. But, so far, this is just an attractive theory that seeks to answer disturbing and complex questions for which we have few other answers. In fact, there is very limited support that the attachment classifications of adult sexual offenders differ significantly from that of non-sexual criminal offenders or non-offenders (i.e., the general population). Accordingly, research has so far engaged largely in a theoretical assumption that attachment deficits *do* exist and that they *are* significantly linked to the development of sexually abusive behaviour (in men, at least) despite failing to find strong or consistent proof for this attractive idea.

Even across similar studies, researchers have failed to demonstrate any consistent or predictable outcomes that support attachment deficit or related hypotheses, although tend to focus on almost any data that even minimally support the already assumed presence of attachment deficits. In most cases, other data from the same research could just as easily suggest that differences in attachment deficits are no more apparent in sexual offenders than non-sexual criminal offenders, or even the general public. Even when researchers do provide some evidence for their hypotheses in this area, a more critical look at the data shows flaws and weaknesses.

In fact, despite attractive ideas and some compelling data, at best there is partial and inconsistent evidence to support attachment as a primary cause of sexual coercion. In addition, a critical review of attachment-based research suggests that it is inconsistent, weak in instrumentation, and difficult to replicate across studies. It is also not clear that such studies always have a firm grasp on the ideas of

attachment theory, or how to apply them. Further, the conclusions of many research studies seems to fit the data to theory, rather than either confirming or repudiating theory or developing a grounded theory that allows theory to emerge from the data. Although researchers are frank and honest in describing the weaknesses and unexpected outcomes of studies designed to find evidence for an *a priori* theory of attachment-driven sexual coercion, almost every study of attachment in sexual offenders optimistically concludes partial support for the theory, sometimes with little justification. However, as we have not been able to find a significant distinction between the attachment experiences and classifications of sexual offenders and non-sexual criminal offenders, it is prudent to be cautious in accepting research conclusions that are often not heavily supported by the data.

Aside from limitations in adult sexual offender research, attachment research in adolescent sexual offenders is even more rare than the relatively sparse research into attachment in adult sexual offenders, and is just getting underway at this point. See Rich (2006) for a detailed review of the research into correlations and links between attachment and sexual offending, including studies of adult sexual offenders conducted over the past 15 years, and more recent (and more limited) work with juvenile sexual offenders.

Attachment as risk, not cause

In fact, with such little work undertaken or completed with respect to adolescents, we are not yet in a position to say whether the research will support an attachment-driven theory in the development of juvenile sexual offending. Nevertheless, there is no compelling reason to believe it will, if we discount our very active desire to support this attractive theory. This is especially pertinent in light of the lack of strong evidence found in similar adult studies, and compounded by the limited instrumentation we have available for recognising and measuring attachment in older children and adolescents. Accordingly, at this time, although attachment and social deficits seem apparent in juvenile sexual offenders, as they do in adult sexual offenders, they appear more as a *general* risk factor than a *cause* of sexually abusive behaviour.

There is little more we can say at this time about the relationship between attachment and juvenile sexual offending, other than recognising that suboptimal attachment experience is likely to serve as a predisposing factor and link to the onset of *many* troubled and troubling behaviours in juvenile sexual offenders, including serving as an important factor in the development of sexually abusive behaviour. However, attachment deficits are unlikely to be the *cause* of sexual aggression.

Nevertheless, despite our ability or inability to prove attachment as a cause of sexually abusive behaviour, it seems an obvious and important target for assessment and treatment in juvenile sexual offenders. Indeed, as Smallbone (2005) has written, there is substantial indirect evidence (and some limited direct evidence) to support the idea that attachment-related vulnerabilities are significant predisposing factors in the development of sexually abusive behaviour for some adults and adolescents. In the treatment of sexual offenders, then, we must be alert to, take into account, and be able to recognise attachment difficulties and deficits, building treatment settings that create social connections, restore relationships, and improve social skills. Assessment and treatment of attachment should be a central part of any treatment programme for sexually abusive youth, in some ways serving as the *heart* of the treatment. That is, the role of attachment difficulties, even if not *the* factor, must be recognised as a contributing factor, not just in the etiology of sexually abusive behaviour but in current functioning.

Lack of evidence in itself, of course, does not always mean that our ideas are incorrect or our treatment methods meaningless. Lack of proof sometimes simply means we are unable to prove something, even though it may have actual existence. This leads us to recognise that attachment, although perhaps not linked *directly* to sexually abusive behaviour, nevertheless seems to play a powerful role in the establishment of social relationships, the ability to adequately understand and respond to self and others, and the capacity for self-regulation and self-fulfilment. Accordingly, attachment is a legitimate target, both in the assessment of sexually abusive behaviour and in its treatment. That is, regardless of whether attachment difficulties are specific to the development of sexually abusive behaviour, or more likely a risk factor for more general or otherwise troubled behaviour, it is nevertheless legitimate to apply attachment theory to our work with sexually reactive children and juvenile sexual offenders.

The attachment-informed perspective

Rather than practicing a prescribed attachment therapy, based on a specified model or set of techniques, most clinicians recognising and addressing attachment difficulties use an attachment-informed framework by which psychodynamic and cognitive interventions can be applied with attachment as a target of treatment. A framework of attachment-informed therapy is most often integrated into broader psychodynamic therapies, and is perhaps simply therapy seen through an attachment lens and guided by an attachment framework.

For the therapist focusing on building attachment and a more secure internal working model,* interaction and behaviours are understood through an attachment lens. Behaviours are re-framed and seen as attachment-seeking rather than attention seeking, and healthy, non-pathological behaviours are recognised as possible only in light of a sense of emotional security.†

Exploration behaviours, by which the individual is able to effectively engage in and control the social environment, are activated only when attachment seeking behaviours are deactivated through a sense of comfort, assurance, and safety. Secure attachment, then, is the result of and embodies a sense of comfort and trust in others, whereas insecure attachment‡ results from anxiety and doubt about the capacities of others to provide safety and assurance. Eventually, these experiences of security or insecurity become aspects of personality, in which the individual experiences confidence or doubt in not only others, but self.

Through an attachment-informed framework, we seek causes and explanations for current

---

* The internal working model is considered a mentalised map of the world, containing representations and assumptions about self and others, and resulting cognitive schema and scripts that direct interactions, relationships, and behaviours, almost automatically. The internal working model may be considered the source from which thinking errors are produced.

† From an attachment theory perspective, security is derived from earlier experiences that result in a sense of trust in the responsiveness of primary caregivers and a sense of emotional safety. This results in an internalised 'secure base' from which the individual is able to feel a sense of comfort and explore and engage in the larger social environment.

‡ Although considered suboptimal, insecure attachment is considered adaptive to the environment in which the child was raised, and is viewed as neither maladaptive nor pathological.

behaviour, at both a psychodynamic and cognitive level, an understanding of the transactions and interactions between the internal mentalised world and the external physical world, and recognise social relationships as the outcome of this interaction, driven by emotional and cognitive processes. In our work with clinical populations, the application of attachment theory thus becomes a psychology of social, emotional, and cognitive deficits.

In applying an attachment perspective, we must ask how children experience and internalise representations of their parents, not simply as their parents but as representatives of all adults and authority, and how they come to see themselves reflected through the eyes and behaviours of their parents. How do these children experience attunement and also learn to be attuned to others, learn to be regulated by others and to eventually regulate themselves, and identify with not just family goals and values but eventually social values and norms as well? In aspiring to social values and norms, such as social belonging, social relatedness, social attractiveness, and sexuality, how do these children experience their ability to actually achieve such goals? Have their particular attachment experiences provided them with the capacity to be patient, tolerate frustration, and feel personally and socially successful, or does socially unacceptable (i.e., socially deviant) behaviour represent their best course of action for adhering to social norms and acquiring socially desirable goals?

An attachment-informed framework thus provides a lens through which to see, interpret, evaluate, and make sense of human behaviour that may otherwise make little sense to us. This is of special importance as we work with sexually reactive children and juvenile sexual offenders whose sexual behaviours are often closely tied in with a range of other antisocial and socially deficient behaviours, and who are often emotionally very troubled, and not infrequently psychiatrically and functionally disturbed. Although we seek simple explanations for their sexually abusive behaviours, there often are no clear or obvious answers and we also recognise that these behaviours and relationships cannot be separated from their other behaviours and relationships, which are often just as, if not more, troubled.

The attachment lens, then, provides a way of seeing things otherwise invisible, or a view of behaviour and motivation that, when viewed from another perspective, may look quite different. For instance, callous and unemotional behaviour may be revealed as an avoidant and dismissive attachment stance that is adaptive and defensive in origin, rather than having antisocial or psychopathic roots. Similarly, anxiety may reflect a deeply rooted lack of personal competence whose origins lie in the failure to develop a sense of self-efficacy and a resulting need to be taken care of and protected by others, and dependence on others and a need for reassurance may indicate failure to develop a sense of self-agency. Oppositional behaviours may reflect an unwillingness to trust or yield to authority because of uncertainty about adults, the outcome of inadequate parenting or disruptions or instabilities in early attachment relationships, and impulsive or frustration-driven behaviours may indicate an incapacity for self-regulation. Erratic behaviours that are inexplicable and out of touch with the current situation, such as intermittent explosive disorder or sudden and unexplained mood or behavioural changes, may be the expression of patterns of disorganised attachment.* Troubling and troubled behaviours, then, including those that are sexually abusive of others, may appear and be understood differently when viewed through an attachment lens. Each of these may be seen as failures of the early parent-child relationship and the product of attachment deficits.

An attachment-informed framework can offer another view of behaviour that may otherwise challenge explanation, and add insight and additional perspectives to what we already know. We are thus capable of recognising emotional triggers and behavioural patterns that might otherwise remain unrecognised, and define treatment interventions that match an attachment-informed formulation of the case. This framework can provide a roadmap for treatment

---

*Both secure and insecure patterns of attachment are considered to have organised strategic value. That is, they eventually become adaptations to the environment in which the child was reared, and result in behaviours that are designed and organised to ensure proximity and reduce anxiety. However, the disorganised pattern of attachment, described by Main and Solomon (1986) is considered to be an unusual and particularly troubled form of attachment in which attachment behaviours do not appear to have any organised strategic value, and result in unusual and odd behaviours that fail to meet attachment goals. Further, only disorganised attachment is considered linked to the development of psychopathology.

that recognises the importance and critical quality of the treatment relationship and the treatment environment in bringing about change in the attachment-troubled client, helping us to understand and define the relationship between clinician and client, as well as the actual modes, techniques, and interventions of treatment.

Attachment-informed treatment

For the most part, attachment-informed treatment represents a set of ideas and practices, offering a lens through which client difficulties may be seen and a framework and perspective that individual clinicians may bring to bear in their practices. This fits in well with a model of eclectic or integrated therapy in which the clinician is able to easily and freely switch gears in terms of both technique and even perceptual frameworks, as required by a pantheoretical model of treatment.

A main emphasis of attachment-informed therapy is to understand insecure attachment and obstructions to secure attachment, and assess whether any of these obstacles can be removed, perhaps through individual, family, or group therapy, or even through medication. A second emphasis is to revive and re-engage social behaviour that may have become detached. A third is to help the individual re-organise attachment systems, and a fourth is to eliminate ambiguity and incoherence from attachment narratives, or the expression of internal working models. Another is, of course, to improve self-esteem, as we discuss the development of the secure personality, through increased self-agency and self-efficacy.

Not surprisingly, as attachment theory is essentially a psychodynamic and interactional model, the *therapeutic relationship* comes squarely back into the foreground in attachment-informed therapy. Although cognitive-behavioural work is important in sex offender specific programmes, and will remain central to any sex offender specific treatment programme, rather than teaching or discussing concepts of attachment in a cognitive-behavioural or psychoeducational mode, the therapist uses interactional techniques imparted through the therapeutic alliance. It is through this relationship, as well as other techniques and practices of treatment, that a treatment environment and relationship is established that can help re-build attachment. Ultimately, the emphasis in an

attachment-informed therapy is on the development of an understanding, supportive, and caring relationship, marked by attunement between the therapist and the client.

Although cognitive distortions play a significant role, they are not a central target in attachment-informed treatment. Hudson and Ward (2000) suggest, for instance, that sexual offending might occur impulsively, whereas cognitive distortions and the suppression of empathy may follow, sustaining the ability to re-offend rather than serving as a cause of sexual abuse. On one level in treatment, we *must* target cognitive distortions in order to prevent further abuse. But on another level, it is insecure attachment and attachment deficits that are central to treatment, the wellspring from which cognitive distortions spring. Consequently, in an attachment-informed therapy, rather than technique or content (as in cognitive-behavioural therapy or dialectical behaviour therapy, for instance), the relationship between the clinician and client is primary, as is the treatment environment in which the relationship develops and treatment unfolds.

For the therapist focusing on building attachment, along with a more secure internal working model, narrative coherence, and a stable sense of self, interactions and behaviours are viewed and understood through an attachment lens. Healthy and non-pathological behaviours are recognised as possible only when the client feels secure. Hence, the exploration behaviours we wish to stimulate in our clients are activated only when attachment behaviours,* sparked by insecurity, anxiety, and fear, are deactivated. Behavioural episodes that otherwise appear irrational are recognised and understood as emotional, and even neurobiological, episodes fuelled by poorly processed and unintegrated perceptions in the client, and the development of a 'secure base' injected into the internal working model is paramount.

Seen through this attachment lens, the development of a 'secure base' introjected into

---

*Attachment behaviours do not signify healthy attachment, but instead signal a need for assurance and safety, and are signs that the individual is, at that moment at least, feeling insecure and anxious. Behaviours that suggest secure attachment are not the same as 'attachment behaviours'. Understanding this distinction, it is the *absence* of attachment behaviours, and engagement in exploratory and other social activities, that suggest secure attachment.

the internal working model of the juvenile sexual offender is paramount. Simply put, built on an attachment framework, the goals of treatment include developing in our clients:

- A sense of security (a 'secure base') from which to explore and grow.
- Confidence (security) in and connection to important figures who are accurately and consistently responsive, and thus trustworthy.
- A secure and coherent sense of self, including the experience of self-agency and self-efficacy.
- A balance in the use of affective and cognitive problem solving strategies.* Affective, or emotionally driven, behavioural strategies are often associated with insecure ambivalent attachment, whereas insecure avoidant attachment is often linked to the use of unemotional cognitive strategies.
- The use of cooperative and non-coercive strategies to get needs met in social interactions with others.
- The capacity to tolerate frustration and disappointment, and the capacity for self-regulation.
- The capacity for perspective taking and the unlocking of empathy for others.
- Increased moral understanding, reasoning, and decision making.
- The experience of connection and relatedness to other people.

These goals are already embodied in integrated treatment models that focus on recognising and treating the child or adolescent as a 'whole' person rather than a 'sexual offender.' However, in an attachment-informed model, the desired outcomes are considered, in part, to be attachment-dependent, based upon earlier experiences that have limited the capacity of the youth to engage in healthy and satisfying social relationships.

Providing attachment-informed treatment

The goal of treatment, then, is the rehabilitation of the *current* internal working model, providing for

the juvenile the capacity for self-regulation and a sense of self-efficacy and security that will serve as the basis for all current and future experiences of self and others, and hence current and future relationships and behaviours. From an attachment perspective, we recognise that in treatment:

- There is a need for empathic attunement to the client.
- The client must see his or her value in the minds of other people.
- The client must experience important others as capable and competent.
- Seemingly irrational behaviours can be understood as variants of insecure or disorganised attachment strategies, triggered under specific conditions.
- Change requires giving up prior adaptive strategies.
- Change comes slowly.
- Healthy, or secure, attachment requires a secure base.
- The development of a secure base results from life experience.

Slade (1999) writes that an attachment-informed approach informs, rather than defines, clinical thinking, providing a way for the clinician to think about early patterns of emotional regulation and behaviour, helping them to better understand the developmental experience and behaviours of their clients. She writes that attending to the manner in which attachment themes and organisation are consciously and unconsciously expressed changes how therapists observe their clients and make sense of their cases, recognising that the ability of the client to work with his or her therapist is profoundly shaped by the client's level of attachment security. In a similar vein, Marrone (1998) writes that attachment-informed therapists engage in treatment in much the same way as other psychotherapists, but the incorporation of attachment theory into their framework is likely to influence their therapeutic technique and style. He describes the attachment-oriented therapist as able to recognise the client as a whole person with both pathological and healthy attributes, and through the therapeutic relationship allowing the client to freely explore and develop a sense of autonomy and personal values.

In order to accomplish these tasks, a central task for the therapist is to become a source of security for the client, or a secure base (Bowlby,

---

* Affective, or emotionally driven, behavioural strategies are often associated with insecure ambivalent attachment, whereas insecure avoidant attachment is often linked to the use of unemotional cognitive strategies.

1988; Brisch, 1999) demanding 'great sensitivity and empathy as the therapist adjusts to or feels his way into the patient's . . . attachment needs' (Brisch, 1999: 78). This aspect of therapeutic empathy is central to the therapeutic relationship, described by Rogers (1980) as essential to the facilitative treatment environment through which individuals are able to recognise and modify their attitudes, behaviours, and self-concepts. Bowlby (1980) points out that unless a therapist can enable the client to feel secure, therapy cannot begin, a point echoed by Marrone (1998) who describes sensitivity and responsiveness in the clinician as an essential condition for viable therapy.

Bowlby writes that the therapist's role is 'analogous to that of a mother who provides her child with a secure base from which to explore the world. The therapist strives to be reliable, attentive, and sympathetically responsive to his patient's explorations and, so far as he can, to see and feel the world through his patient's eyes, namely to be empathic' (1980: 140).

The therapeutic relationship

Parish and Eagle (2003) write that therapeutic relationship clearly has many qualities of an attachment relationship. In their study, Parish and Eagle found that therapy clients admired and sought proximity to their therapists, found their therapists emotionally available, evoked mental representations of their therapists in the therapist's absence, and experienced their therapists as a secure base helping them to feel confident outside of therapy. Clients formed strong emotional connections towards their therapists and regarded them as unique and irreplaceable. Amini et al. (1996: 232) write that therapy works *because* it is an attachment relationship 'capable of regulating neurophysiology and altering underlying neural structure'.

Mallinckrodt, Gantt, and Coble (1995) consider attachment theory as a useful way to understand the process of psychotherapy. They write that the therapist gains access to the client's internal working model when the client demonstrates attachment patterns in the therapeutic relationship, thus illuminating and making visible working models which may then become conscious and subject to change. Amini et al. (1996: 213) thus propose that the therapeutic relationship works as a 'directed attachment relationship whose purpose is the revision of the

implicit emotional memory of (earlier) attachment'. We can identify 14 aspects of the therapeutic relationship, specifically from the perspective of the therapist's role in the relationship:

1. The therapist is experienced by the client as a dependable, consistent, and responsive emotional support who is reliably available.
2. The therapist facilitates a therapeutic relationship in which the client can develop security in the therapeutic relationship, form a bond with the therapist, and freely engage in self-expression.
3. The therapist encourages both self-dependency and help-seeking in the client.
4. The therapist provides a secure base through which the client can experience a sense of being recognised and connected, and from which the client may safely engage in psychological exploration, recognising, expressing, and working through problems.
5. The therapist uses attachment-related interactions in the therapeutic relationship as a means to understand the client and the client's attachment patterns and strategies, using these to shape and guide treatment interventions most appropriate for each client.
6. The therapist becomes attuned to the client's emotional and attachment-related states, remaining aware of the need for emotional connection, described by Fosha (2003: 229) as 'bottom-up processing' from an experiential perspective rather than 'the top-down approach of most cognitive and insight-oriented therapies'.
7. The therapist helps the client to recognise and explore attachment relationships and strategies for maintaining connections.
8. The therapist helps the client recognise that current relationships, experiences, ideas, and attitudes are related to, and in many cases the result of, prior experiences, including on-going attachment relationships.
9. The therapist challenges and stretches the client, remaining in the proximal learning zone* but creating opportunities for new learning.

---

*The proximal learning zone refers to developmental learning processes that are in the process of maturation, in which learning capacities are ready to be enacted but are still embryonic. New learning occurs in a manner that stretches clients just beyond their current level learning, within the 'proximal' learning zone.

10. The therapist creates and recognises boundaries, and maintains an appropriate level of closeness that fits the needs and capacities, and the particular attachment style and needs, of each individual client.
11. The therapist remains aware of counter-transference issues, or those feelings that arise in the therapist as a result of the therapeutic relationship, using these to better understand the client and the therapeutic relationship, guide treatment interventions, and maintain appropriate treatment boundaries.
12. The therapist maintains freedom of movement in the relationship, maintaining permeable boundaries, but able to move in and out of engagement with the client as needed.
13. The therapist helps the client develop the capacity to experience and tolerate difficulty, uncertainty, and doubt.
14. The therapist sensitively dissolves the therapeutic bond when appropriate, so that it will serve as a model for handling separations in life.

The attachment-based treatment milieu

If we blend or provide an attachment-informed model of individual treatment into a larger treatment environment that recognises attachment needs and difficulties, and fosters social connection and the development of attached relationships, we create an *attachment-informed treatment environment*. Here, treatment occurs in a caring and supportive manner, through an attachment-friendly environment in which relationships are genuine, respectful, and supportive while at the same time being structured and challenging, and in which the message that comes through is one of care, concern, understanding, and attunement. In this environment, individuals are experienced and treated as individuals, rather than sexual offenders who all share the same backgrounds and behaviours, and in which, despite commonalities, the needs of clients are based on an assessment and interpretation of their individual needs.

This treatment environment results from the interactions that occur between individuals involved in the treatment process, both clients and staff, and includes words, relationships, emotions, and, of course, behaviours. For treatment to be successful, such a climate must foster and support its goals and methods, and indeed in residential treatment the treatment environment is *part* of the treatment method, and may be referred to as a 'facilitative climate.' The treatment environment is the first line of treatment, and must be recognised as such. In this milieu, although clients must be held responsible for their own behavioural choices, we must remember that behavioural difficulties are often the result of poorly regulated interactions with others. That is, although behaviours are generated by the client, the behaviours originate in an interaction with another person. In the therapeutic milieu, then, we recognise treatment growth *and* setbacks as the product, at least in part, of the environment.

Attachment interventions are more than just those interventions and techniques used solely by the individual therapist to build an attached relationship with and instill a sense of attachment in the client. Instead, attachment is built through interventions and experiences that permeate the child's environment and operate on an underlying biological model that resides in the central nervous system. Attachment building occurs in the environment and through the interactions between the caregiver and the client.

Empathy in the attachment-based treatment environment

Carl Rogers (1980: 151) writes that empathy dissolves alienation. Those who experience empathy for others are enabled to feel like 'part of the human race' and feel valued, cared for, and accepted when others demonstrate empathy for them. These are the very qualities that we wish to instil, develop, or unlock in the treatment of juvenile sexual offenders, and are the same qualities that juvenile sexual offenders must experience from others in their environment. Through the warmth, concern, support, caring, safety and structure provided by the empathic therapist and treatment staff, children and adolescents in treatment are seen and *feel* seen. In turn, they are enabled to see, not only themselves, but other people as well, beginning first with the other person in the attachment relationship – in this case, the therapist or treatment staff. Thus, kids who have often felt uncared for, unloved unsupported, misunderstood, and disconnected may, through treatment and the treatment environment, reclaim their humanity and begin to feel a sense of connection to others.

Rogers (1980: 150) tells us that an empathic way of being, central to the treatment relationship and the treatment milieu, can be learned from empathic persons, and that 'perhaps the most important statement of all is that the ability to be accurately empathic is something that can be developed by training'. However, although there are numerous approaches to teaching empathy, 'the first step to teaching clients empathy is first to recognise, understand, and model empathy' (Fernandez and Serran, 2002: 131). Accordingly, we recognise that being the *subject* of empathy is the first step in the development of the capacity to *be* empathic. In fact, it is generally believed that the capacity of treatment staff to recognise and empathically respond to distress in the client influences the development of empathy (Anderson and Dodgson, 2002). In *teaching* empathy, then, it is the therapist and treatment staff who must *demonstrate* empathy, described by Fernandez and Serran as integral to the therapeutic relationship.

Steps and phases in attachment-related treatment

An attachment-informed treatment model must first focus on the steps by which attachment security is established and internalised. In this respect, attachment treatment recognises sequential phases that focus on particular aspects of attachment formation, and recognises the goal of each phase as the accomplishment of tasks associated with the phase. An attachment-informed model thus recognises the building blocks of attachment that signal the development, deepening, and internalisation of attachment structures, patterns, and strategies.

Phase one. Containment and stabilisation

The first step involves the containment of emotional and behavioural episodes triggered by insecurity and reactivity to the environment, driven by the attachment behavioural system. Attachment behaviours reflect insecurity and are sparked by anxiety, are characterised by

proximity seeking and behaviours designed to get the attention of an attachment figure, are antithetical to exploratory behaviours, and signal a lack of secure base. Active attachment elements that are a focus during this treatment phase include establishing a sense of safety in the child and ensuring his or her proximity to reliable and responsive attachment figures. A focus, then, is on the deactivation of attachment behaviour, and increasing the child's capacity for self-regulation. Therefore, phase one focuses on the stabilisation and containment of emotion, anxiety, and often destructive behaviour, as well as the development of the secure base from which the child can explore emotions, thoughts, and behaviours, and engage in new relationships and activities.

Phase two. Engagement and exploration

This step focuses on and leads to the building and expansion of the behaviours, social skills, and relationships developed during the first phase of treatment. Although connections and relationships form with treatment staff and peers during the first phase, the emphasis and main focus of that phase is on stabilising behaviours and creating emotional containment and self-regulation. That first phase represents a primary building block in the formation of secure attachment and the experience of felt security that paves the way for further development. Thus, although engagement and exploration are present in phase one, acting on the secure base and engaging in healthy and secure exploration becomes possible only after the child has stabilised and anxiety-driven behaviours are contained. The child experiences security and a sense of safety, exhibiting less insecurity and fewer attachment behaviours, thus signaling a movement in attachment building to this second phase.

Phase three. Connection and partnership

During this phase, attached treatment relationships and social connections are more fully formed, in which the child feels an attachment bond and is more clearly involved in a partnership with treatment staff. Building on a more established sense of security in self and others, this attachment step expands on the work started in phase two, continuing to develop self confidence (self-efficacy and self-agency) metacognition (awareness and understanding of self and others) and self-regulation. However, in phase three, in older children and particularly in adolescents, attachment work focuses on the exploration of personal and social values and the development of perspective-taking, moral decision making, empathy, and social belonging.

Phase four. Security and social relatedness

In terms of attachment-building, as the child comes close to and enters this phase, he or she is likely to be close to discharge from treatment, where the gains of the stage will be most relevant post-discharge and for the rest of his or her life. Here, the goals are to fully cement and ensure the internalisation of self-confidence, recognition of others, and social connection. Phase four represents an on-going embodiment of representations of self and others, reflected and demonstrated in a combination of self-agency, self-efficacy, prosocial behaviours, and healthy and socially appropriate relationships.

These four phases, or steps in attachment-related treatment, describe a developmental progression in which attachment representations and patterns and beliefs about self and others are shaped, re-shaped, and internalised in a rehabilitated internal working model.

Phase-related treatment activities and elements

Treatment interventions related to specific phases reinforce the formation and internalisation of attachment rather than serving as activities or interventions used to directly address trauma or attachment issues. Although most treatment activities are common to all phases, simply developing and expanding over time in treatment, some activities are clearly more related to certain phases than others:

- Phase one (containment and stabilisation) interventions will focus on and involve reassuring and calming activities that include staff responsiveness, availability, and proximity in a manner appropriate to the age of the client, that establish a sense of safety and structure, aiming for the development of self-regulation.
- Activities and interventions most relevant to the second phase (engagement and exploration) will increasingly include those intended to foster responsibility-taking, aimed at building a sense of self-agency and self-efficacy, and establishing the groundwork for metacognition, at least with respect to self-reflectivity.
- During the third phase (connection and partnership), interventions will be aimed at building treatment relationships in which clients are actively working *with* the therapists and other treatment staff, enhancing and capitalising upon the strengths that the client brings to treatment (extra-therapeutic treatment factors), as well as a sense of hope and expectancy, and the therapeutic relationship itself.
- Phase four (security and social relatedness) activities will most focus on fully internalising gains in attachment and social connection, understanding self and others, and preparing the client for attached relationships in the post-treatment world.

No matter how provided, a number of specific treatment components will be incorporated into an attachment-based model. They may be provided through psychodynamic, cognitive-behavioural, psychoeducational, or experience-based treatment, and one way or another must also be present, modelled, and experienced both in the therapeutic relationship and, in residential treatment, the therapeutic milieu. Of special importance, treatment interventions and activities must be sensitive to the cognitive and emotional needs of each individual client, as well as age appropriate and, perhaps more to the point, age relevant from a developmental perspective. In addition, no matter how well constructed and delivered, given the pre-conscious aspect of the attachment experience, consideration should be given to the need for wordless, brain-based learning. Brain-based learning is essentially a teaching approach designed to directly tap into the natural learning capacity of the brain, recognising that learning is complex and operates along multiple and simultaneous paths (Jensen, 2000).

All treatment components are wrapped and delivered within a treatment environment that is attuned to and responsive to clients, and in which clients are recognised and understood. In this environment, opportunities are available for taking responsibility, realising potential, and experiencing success, and thus building self-agency and self-efficacy. Although there are many elements to be transmitted to and nurtured in the client engaged in attachment-based treatment, several stand out as essential, including the development of empathy, metacognition, morality, and self-regulation:

- *Empathy training and development* includes a focus on the cognitive components of empathy such as the capacity to recognise and identify emotions in others and perspective taking, and affective components that include exploring and identifying with the distress of the other person.
- *Metacognitive skill development* is related to empathy development in its emphasis on recognising the emotional and cognitive states of self and others, but also involves the ability to *think* about thoughts and feelings and recognise how one's own mind and the mind of others works.
- *Moral decision making and behaviour* is also related to empathy and perspective taking, involving value clarification and exploration of personal and social values, the attachment of values to behavioural decisions, the consequences of behaviour and its impact on others, and acceptance of personal responsibility.
- *Self-regulation* training provides clients with a means to manage and release stress, including 'mindless' methods which include techniques of guided imagery, yoga, and recreation, and expressive therapies that are wordless in their effects, and may also employ cognitive-behavioural strategies for problem recognition and solution, cognitive restructuring, environmental monitoring, distress tolerance, and relaxation.

Beyond these treatment components, however, which are related specifically to the attachment goal, treatment for juvenile sexual offenders is, of course, sex offender specific. This includes cognitive-behavioural, psychoeducational, and psychodynamic treatment specifically directed towards sexually abusive behaviour, as well as treatment that recognises and addresses important collateral issues such as trauma resolution, anger management, self-expression, and psychiatric co-morbidity.

Conclusion: re-constructing attachment

Attachment deficits and insecure attachment may be a necessary condition for the development of sexually abusive behaviour in many children and adolescents, but it is certainly not a sufficient condition. In fact, insecure attachment and related attachment difficulty is just one element in a complex pathway that, for some, leads to sexual aggression. We see how attachment, to some degree, sets the pace for and shapes the pathway along which we develop, but although we can see certain trajectories developing, even early in life, we recognise that forces other than attachment act upon the pathway to re-shape, re-direct, or solidify it. Although we understand that insecure attachment itself is neither maladaptive nor pathological, as we move along often self-reinforcing developmental pathways, the combination of insecure attachment and other risk factors generates, in some cases, pathological thinking, behaviour, and relationships.

Nevertheless, although attachment is not *the* thing that leads to sexually abusive behaviour, if understood and applied carefully, attachment theory offers a powerful and useful way to understand current functioning and behaviour in light of social connectedness and internalised representations of self and others. That is, although attachment difficulties are not the direct cause of sexually abusive behaviour, attachment theory is nonetheless capable of providing an important explanatory link in understanding the etiology of sexual aggression. Similarly, attachment-based treatment is not likely to solve or cure the problem. However, it does offer a powerful means for understanding prior behaviours and development, as well as helping to instill a sense of self, others, and values that may go a long way towards preventing future sexually abusive behaviour, as well as other antisocial and self-destructive behaviours.

Attachment theory and attachment-informed treatment is not a technique. Instead, it is a tool that can help us to recognise *how* connections are made, how they are damaged, and how they took shape in each individual with whom we work. An attachment-informed framework can help us to better see and understand our clients, and help us recognise how to re-form or re-activate that sense of being understood and thus become more attached to others. Attachment theory can teach us how to build our treatment programmes, so that behind technique lies connection. It is through the driving force of relationships and *feeling* connected to others that we are most likely to bring about change and stand the best chance of eliminating sexually abusive behaviour and improving the lives of the children and adolescents with whom we work.

References

Amini, F. et al. (1996) Affect, Attachment, Memory: Contribution Toward Psychobiologic Integration. *Psychiatry*, 59, 213–39.

Anderson, D. and Dodgson, P.G. (2002) Empathy Deficits, Self-Esteem, and Cognitive Distortions in Sexual Offenders. In Fernandez, Y. (Ed.) *In Their Shoes*. Oklahoma City, OK: Wood 'N' Barnes.

Association for the Treatment of Sexual Abusers (2001) *Practice Standards and Guidelines for Members of The Association for The Treatment of Sexual Abusers*. Beaverton, OR: Author.

Association for The Treatment of Sexual Abusers (2005) *Practice Standards and Guidelines for Members of the Association for the Treatment of Sexual Abusers*. Beaverton, OR: Author.

Bolen, R.M. (2000) *Validity of Attachment Theory*. Trauma, Violence and Abuse, Vol. I, 2: 128–53.

Bowlby, J. (1980) *Attachment and Loss, Vol. 3. Loss: Sadness and Depression*. New York: Basic Books.

Bowlby, J. (1988) *A Secure Base: Clinical Applications of Attachment Theory*. London: Routledge.

Brisch, K.H. (1999) *Treating Attachment Disorders: From Theory to Therapy*. New York: Guilford.

Cooke, D.J. and Philip, L. (2001) To Treat or Not to Treat? An Empirical Perspective. In Hollin. C.R. (Ed.) *Handbook of Offender Assessment and Treatment*. Chicester: John Wiley.

Drake, C.R. and Ward, T. (2003) Practical and Theoretical Roles for the Formulation Based Treatment of Sexual Offenders. *International Journal of Forensic Psychology*, 1, 71–84.

Fernandez, Y.M. and Serran, G. (2002) Empathy Training for Therapists and Clients. In Fernandez, Y. (Ed.) *In Their Shoes*. Oklahoma City, OK: Wood 'N' Barnes.

Fosha, D. (2003) Dyadic Regulation and Experiential Work With Emotion and Relatedness in Trama and Disorganised Attachment. In Solomon, M.F. and Siegel, D.J. (Eds.) *Healing Trauma: Attachment, Mind, Body, and Brain*. New York: Norton.

Greenberg, M.T. (1999) Attachment and Psychopathology in Childhood. In Cassidy, J.

and Shaver, P.R. (Eds.) *Handbook of Attachment: Theory, Research, and Clinical Application*. New York: Guilford.

Holmes, J. (2001) *The Search for The Secure Base: Attachment Theory and Psychotherapy*. Hove: Brunner-Routledge.

Hudson, S.M. and Ward, T. (2000) Interpersonal Competency in Sex Offenders. *Behaviour Modification*, 24, 494–527.

Jensen, E. (2000) *Brain-Based Learning*. San Diego, CA: The Brain Store.

Karen, R. (1994) *Becoming Attached: First Relationships and How They Shape Our Capacity to Love*. New York: Oxford University Press.

Lamb, M.E. (1987) Predictive Implications of Individual Differences in Attachment. *Journal of Consulting and Clinical Psychology*, 55, 817–24.

Lewis, M. (1997) *Altering Fate: Why The Past Does Not Predict The Future*. New York: Guilford.

Main, M. and Solomon, J. (1986) Discovery of A New, Insecure-Disorganised/Disoriented Attachment Pattern. In Brazelton, T.B. and Yogman, M.W. (Eds.) *Affective Development in Infancy*. Norwood, NJ: Ablex Publishing.

Mallinckrodt, B., Gantt, D.L. and Coble, H.M. (1995) Attachment Patterns in The Psychotherapy Relationship: Development of The Client Attachment to Therapist Scale. *Journal of Counseling Psychology*, 42, 307–17.

Marques, J.K., Wiederanders, M., Day, D.D., Nelson, C. and Van Ommeren, A. (2005) Effects of A Relapse Prevention Program on Sexual Recidivism: Final Results From California's Sex Offender Treatment and Evaluation Project. *Sexual Abuse: A Journal of Research and Treatment*, 17, 79–107.

Marrone, M. (1998) *Attachment and Interaction*. London: Jessica Kingsley.

Marshall, W.L. and Marshall, L.E. (2000) The Origins of Sexual Offending. *Trauma, Violence, and Abuse*, 1, 250–63.

Marshall, W.L., Serran, G.A. and Cortoni, F.A. (2000) Childhood Attachments, Sexual Abuse, and Their Relationship to Adult Coping in Child Molesters. *Sexual Abuse: A Journal of Research and Treatment*, 12, 17–26

McGrath, R.J., Cumming, G.F. and Burchard, B.L. (2003) *Current Practices and Trends in Sexual Abuser Management: The Safer Society 2002 Nationwide Survey*. Brandon, VT: Safer Society Press.

Mulloy, R. and Marshall, W.L. (1999) Social Functioning. In Marshall, W.L., Anderson, D. and Fernandez, Y. (Eds.) *Cognitive-Behavioural*

Treatment of Sexual Offenders. Chichester: John Wiley.

Parish, M. and Eagle, M.N. (2003) Attachment to The Therapist. *Psychoanalytic Psychology,* 20, 271–86.

Rich, P. (2006) *Attachment and Sexual Offending: Understanding and Applying Attachment Theory to The Treatment of Juvenile Sexual Offenders.* Chichester: John Wiley.

Rogers, C.R. (1980) *A Way of Being.* Boston, MA: Houghton Mifflin.

Rutter, M. (1997) Clinical Implications of Attachment Concepts Retrospect and Prospect. In Atkinson, L.K. and Zucker, J. (Eds.) *Attachment and Psychopathology.* New York: Guilford.

Slade, A. (1999) Attachment Theory and Research. Implications for The Theory and Practice of Individual Psychotherapy With Adults. In Cassidy, J. and Shaver, P.R. (Eds.) *Handbook of Attachment: Theory, Research, and Clinical Application.* New York: Guilford.

Smallbone, S.W. (2005) Attachment Insecurity as a Predisposing and Precipitating Factor for Young People Who Sexually Abuse. In Calder, M.C. (Ed.) *Children and Young People Who Sexually Abuse: New Theory, Research and Practice Developments.* Lyme Regis: Russell House Publishing.

Smallbone, S.W. and Dadds, M. (2000) Attachment and Coercive Sexual Behaviour. *Sexual Abuse: A Journal of Research* and *Treatment,* 12, 3–15.

NOTE
Portions of the material in this chapter have been reproduced from Rich, P. (2006) *Attachment and Sexual Offending: Understanding and Applying Attachment Theory to the Treatment of Juvenile Sexual Offenders,* with permission of the publishers, John Wiley and Sons.

Chapter 16

Assessment Issues with Young People Who Engage in Sexually Abusive Behaviours Through the New Technologies

Ethel Quayle

Introduction

In 2005 meetings were held throughout the world to inform the global study commissioned by the United Nations on violence against children. One topic that attracted little attention was whether cyberspace and the new technologies should be considered as a separate category, or should simply be thought of as another location in which harm might be done to children that would be subsumed under all other categories, such as the family, institutions, the community and the workplace. Indeed, it might also have been argued that such violence against children, even if it does exist, was largely confined to the western countries where computer and Internet saturation was high. For practitioners and researchers working in this area this raised difficult challenges. What is different about the new technologies? Why are they important media to consider in relation to young people? This is also the starting point for this chapter, because what sparse research has been done in this area would suggest that the new technologies are different in many ways and that the largest consumers and, indeed creators, of the new technologies are young people. It might follow from this that some of the sexually abusive behaviours evidenced in relation to the new technologies are practiced by children and young people in a context that normalises such practices.

The abundance of publications concerning young people who engage in sexually abusive behaviours is evidence of a general concern about this population (Concepcion, 2004). This concern in part relates to the belief that many sexually aggressive practices emerge during adolescence and that without intervention, children and young people who engage in such behaviours will grow into adults who offend against others. Such research also sits alongside other work which suggests that only a very small number of young people who engage in sexually abusive behaviours ever go on to offend as adults (Righthand and Welch, 2001). For practitioners,

tensions exist about the need to protect other, vulnerable children, and the possibility of over-evaluating risk to the detriment of the young people themselves. Hackett (2004: 51) has suggested that, 'In an area of practice which remains controversial and contested, and which often presents professionals with a high degree of anxiety, good assessments can help ensure that young people are treated equitably, that the nature and meaning of their sexual behaviours are understood, that their specific needs are highlighted and that risks are quantified and strategies to manage such risks are identified'.

In the context of the new technologies it is not even clear what it is that we are concerned about. What constitutes sexually abusive practices in these media? Are we concerned that children will continue to engage in such practices or that this will develop into other sexually abusive behaviours that involve physical off-line contact with a child? In relation to sexually abusive behaviours all together, authors such as French (2005) have argued that there are difficulties in providing adequate definitions of sexually abusive behaviour by young people, which are compounded by the absence of literature regarding 'normal sexual development' and confusion about what is appropriate at different ages. However, most definitions acknowledge that abusive behaviour involves force or coercion of another child and the severity of the behaviour increases with greater disparity between the ages of the children involved. These definitions will pose some difficulties for us in relation to the new technologies.

Araji (2004: 4) raised the question as to what are the factors that can be used to determine when the sexual behaviour of children, 'cross the line from normative to non-normative or criminal behaviours', again raising the important issue that youths should not be labelled 'deviants' if their behaviours are normative. This author posed a series of questions that parents, clinicians and other professionals can use as a general guide for determining whether sexual behaviours are problematic and these include:

- Whether the behaviour puts the individual at risk of physical harm, disease or exploitation.
- Does it interfere with the person's overall development, learning, social or family relationships?
- Does it interfere as above in relation to others?
- Does it violate a rule or a law?
- Does it cause the person to feel confused, embarrassed, guilty or negative about themselves?
- Does it cause the above in relation to others?
- Is the behaviour abusive because of lack of consent, inequality, coercion or force?
- Is it dysfunctional in relation to the development of healthy relationships?
- Is it destructive to the family, peer groups, school, community or society?

These are useful questions for us to keep in mind in relation to the new technologies and we will come back to many of the issues they raise. One central aspect of these questions relates to the importance of considering the problematic behaviour within a developmental framework (Medoff, 2004). Prentky and Righthand (2003: 1) have suggested that, 'Unlike adults, adolescents are still very much 'in flux.' No aspect of their development, including their cognitive development, is fixed or stable. In addition, their life circumstances often are very unstable. In a very real sense, we are trying to assess the risk of 'moving targets'.

A further challenge for this chapter relates to the lack of empirical data. Hackett (2004) has emphasised that information gained as part of an assessment needs to be evaluated in order to generate hypotheses about an individual case and how best to proceed. The context for this part of the assessment should be a wider frame of reference, grounded in research evidence about the nature and progression of the problem in other cases. Such evidential material is lacking in the context of the new technologies, and we therefore run the risk that our frame of reference is based on limited clinical experience or on the limited data with adult offenders, or on a more substantial body of research that predates the development of the Internet. It is with this in mind that the chapter will attempt to examine what constitutes a 'normal framework' for how young people use the new technologies, what

little empirical evidence there is about abusive practices and what issues these may raise for the assessment of abusive practices. This is not to ignore the considerable body of evidence as to what constitutes effective assessment (Becker, 1990; Hackett, 2004; Print et al., 2001; French, 2005; Araji, 2004; O'Reilly and Carr, 2004; Knight, 2004; Will, 1999; Calder, 2001) but rather to look at additional issues which may be important to consider when the young person's abusive behaviour relates to the new technologies.

Young people and the new technologies

When conducting an assessment of young people and the new technologies, it is important to consider what in fact most young people do. The literature in this area has been written within the last few years and reflects the rapidly changing nature of the Internet. No doubt that by the time the current book has been published this will have changed yet again. In 2003, DeBell and Chapman reported computer and Internet use by 28,002 children and adolescents between the ages of 5–17 in the United States during 2001. They found that 90 per cent of their sample used computers and 59 per cent used the Internet, with such use starting at an early age (twenty-five percent of five year olds) and increasing over the age groups. While there were no gender differences in overall computer or Internet use, girls were more likely to use e-mail, and boys use them for games, shopping and finding information about news, weather or sports, with home the most common location for Internet access. Another study examined Internet usage among Australian children (NetRatings Australia, 2005) and found that most of the 502 children in their sample had accessed the Internet within the last three years. Boys and younger children were more likely to access the Internet for entertainment (games, websites, music) while girls and older children were likely to use it as a communication resource.

In the UK, Madell and Muncer (2004) have suggested that Internet use appears to have plateaued, with about 42 per cent of homes having access. However, they noted that there is evidence that a disproportionate number of non-users appeared to be over the age of 50, and that the young are most likely to go online eventually. In a collaborative study between

Ireland, Denmark, Sweden, Iceland and Norway (SAFT, 2003) it was found that 80 per cent of Irish children had access to the Internet at home, although only 12 per cent said that they used it everyday, compared to 46 per cent of children in Sweden. A further UK study by Livingstone and Bober (2005) of 1,511 children and young people aged 9–19 indicated that school access to the Internet was almost universal (92 per cent) with 75 per cent having access at home. Within this study, 71 per cent of children had their own computer, 38 per cent a mobile phone, 17 per cent a digital TV and 8 per cent a games console, all with Internet access.

Such studies suggest widespread use of the Internet by young people, and it is now hard to imagine a world where it does not exist as an educational and information resource, a facilitator of communication and a source of inexpensive entertainment accessed from the apparent safety of home, school or the library. However, the Internet is also a provider of information and materials that many of us would see as problematic. Kanuga and Rosenfeld (2004: 120) suggested that the World Wide Web makes it easier for an adolescent to stumble across sites with 'nefarious intention, such as sex-seeking chat rooms and pornographic websites, while searching for answers about sexual health'. If we refer back to Araji's (2004) guidelines for harmful or problematic behaviours, one area of concern was whether such behaviours may place the person at risk by having a negative effect on overall development, learning, social or family relationships, or whether it causes feelings of confusion, embarrassment, guilt or negativity about themselves. This will be the first area that we will give consideration to, as accidental and intentional exposure to sexualised materials occurs frequently to many young people. As yet we do not know whether this may be a source of continuing harm to themselves or to others.

Accidental and intentional exposure to sexualised materials

It would be naïve to assume that pornographic or sexualised materials did not exist prior to the Internet. However, in answering the question posed at the beginning of this chapter about what makes the new technologies different, the Internet has brought with it a proliferation of sexualised material. On the Internet it is possible to find material to suit all interests and proclivities (Taylor and Quayle, 2003), either through purposeful or accidental exposure. The accessibility, interactivity and anonymity of the Internet, however, are the very factors that increase the likelihood of exposure to violent or sexual material. In the SAFT (2003) study, almost one in five children had been invited to a face-to-face meeting with a stranger, and 34 per cent had viewed a violent website, either accidentally or on purpose. Other authors have highlighted the accidental exposure of young people to unwanted sexual material on the Internet (Mitchell et al., 2003; Finkelhor et al., 2000: 334) but have also acknowledged the fact that existing research examining the effects of exposure to unwanted sexual material had been, 'almost entirely based on college students and other adults. None of it concerns children, certainly not younger than aged 14. Moreover, the existing social research is all about voluntary and anticipated exposure. No research on children or adults exists about the impact of exposure that is unwanted or unexpected'.

In their national sample of 1,501 US Internet using youth, Mitchell et al. (2003: 342) indicated that one in four of children who regularly used the Internet encountered unwanted sexual pictures in the year prior to data collection. Seventy-three per cent of such exposures occurred while the youth were searching or surfing the Internet, and the majority happened while at home. These authors also discussed the ways in which Internet protocols maintained such exposure, 'Explicit sex sites are also sometimes programmed to make them difficult to exit, referred to as 'mouse-trapping'. In fact, in some sites the exit buttons take a viewer into other sexually explicit sites. Indeed, in 26 per cent of the surfing incidents, youth reported they were brought to another sex site when they tried to exit the site they were in. This happened in one third of the distressing incidents'. The majority of children who were exposed to material regarded such exposure as not particularly distressing. However, the authors emphasised that such exposure, particularly unwanted exposure, may affect attitudes about sex, the Internet, and young people's sense of safety and community. Greenfield (2004) similarly discussed how on peer-to-peer file sharing programmes, banner advertisements provided a source of inadvertent exposure to sexuality, which were viewed as soon as one entered the programme, and which could not be controlled by the user. Livingstone and Bober's (2005) study also indicated high levels of exposure to online pornography, with 57 per cent of young people having come into contact with it. Most of this material was viewed unintentionally, through a pop-up advert, when searching for something else or through junk mail. Again, 54 per cent of these children claimed not to have been upset by it, but a significant minority did not like it.

Cameron et al. (in press) used a web-based focus group methodology to examine 40 young people's exposure to sexually oriented websites (SOWs) and sexually explicit web sites (SEWs). Within this sample, there was a sub-group of boys who described intentional exposure to SEWs, citing curiosity and arousal as reasons for visiting these websites. As with Mitchell et al.'s (2003: 4) study, the majority of participants suggested that exposure to SEWs had no negative impact on them. The authors concluded, 'A notable finding was the perception of exposure to SEW on oneself. Results show that the participants perceived no impact on themselves. This perception may be problematic because previous research had documented negative effects of exposure to sexually explicit content.It may be that adolescents are developmentally unable to judge how this content affects them or that there are other individual characteristics (e.g. liberal attitudes, attitudes toward censorship) that may affect their perceptions'.

Potential problems related to exposure

How then can we conceptualise the problems in relation to adolescents, sexual material and the new technologies? Such problems may include:

- An adverse impact on current or future sexual and emotional development.
- Exposure to online deviant sexual material may act as a catalyst to engage in a sexually problematic way with another child or children.
- Finding material on the Internet leaves the young person open to sexual exploitation by others, either adults or children.
- Victimisation which may occur to other young people through accessing images of child abuse (also referred to as 'child pornography') through the new technologies, or through

making sexual solicitations to others (Taylor and Quayle, 2005).
- Sexually abusive behaviours that may be construed as 'self-victimising' or 'self-harming'.

A largely unknown factor relates to the nature of harm through exposure, and how it might manifest itself. Kanuga and Rosenfeld (2004: 120) have argued that, 'While there is little documentation of the influence of unrestrained access to pornography on adolescents, there is, at minimum, concern that this may have a negative influence on the psychosocial developmental process which takes place during puberty.While it might not be possible to precisely define what constitutes normal sexual behaviour, there should be concern for young people with a relatively narrow perspective who are exposed to frequent images of behaviours such as sodomy, group sex, sadomasochistic practices, and bestiality'. In a similar vein, in a review of the literature related to inadvertent exposure to pornography, Greenfield (2004a) concluded that the evidence indicates that pornography and related sexual media can influence sexual violence, sexual attitudes, moral values and sexual activity for children and youth. In a further study of teen chatrooms in which Greenfield (2004b: 757) was a participant-observer, she concluded that, '. . . we cannot speak of the Internet as simply doing something to teens; teens are also constructing the Internet . . .' She summarised the likely developmental effects of online sexual activity as:

- Disinhibition related to sexuality, aggression and race relations.
- Early sexual priming.
- Models for racism, negative attitudes towards women and homophobia.

However, what we do not know in this area far exceeds what we do know, and while such research alerts us to the possible dangers of unrestrained access to violent or coercive sexual materials, it does not help us quantify who is at risk or what factors might increase either vulnerability or resilience.

To date, there is little written about the elective use of pornography by young people who sexually abuse (Epps and Fisher, 2004). Alexy (2003) re-examined a data set of 160 sexually reactive children and adolescents and compared the characteristics of those who used pornography and those who did not. The study indicated several significant positive associations between pornography use and psychiatric symptoms, non-sexual criminal, antisocial and delinquent behaviours, and sexually aggressive behaviours. However, the data used came from the 1990s and pre-dated the use of the Internet to access pornographies. Kaufman et al. (1998) have suggested that being interested in pornography represents a normative, developmental experience for a large number of adolescents and a significant source of information about sexuality. However, Malamuth (1993) emphasised the importance of the content of the material, in that if the portrayal of sex was intertwined with violence, hatred, coercion and humiliation of women, then the individual could have the experience of being aroused to such material, with the result that those who already have a sense of being attracted to sexual aggression are most likely to be influenced by such material. Malamuth (2000) further contended that associations between pornography consumption and aggressiveness toward women could be explained by a circular relationship between high coercive tendencies and an interest in certain content in pornography, whereby aggressive men are drawn to the images in pornography that reinforce and therefore increase the likelihood of their control, impersonal and hostile association to sexuality. What may be of particular importance in relationship to this is the emphasis placed by Malamuth on the fact that pornographic stimuli are part of a larger corpus of media images, and that the role of media stimuli cannot be appreciated in isolation from other variables. Browne and Hamilton-Giachritsis (2005: 78) have also acknowledged the methodological problems with media research, including the difficulty of control for people exposed to media sources containing violent imagery at only one time, making it, '. . . difficult to establish causal links between one media influence and changes in attitude and behaviour'.

Establishing the degree of influence that pornography and related sexual media can have on sexual violence, sexual attitudes, moral values and sexual activity of children and young people is complex. Studies such as that of Emerick and Dutton (1993) had suggested that with high-risk adolescents, 80 per cent acknowledged the use of pornography for stimulation, and the number of female child victims was said to have increased progressively with the severity of the

pornography used as a stimulus for masturbation. Similarly, studies by Zolondek et al. (2001) and Ford and Linney (1995) found an elevated use of pornographic materials amongst young people engaged in sexually abusive behaviour. However, other research (O'Reilly et al., 1998) showed no differences in pornography use (magazines, films and sex lines) between youths who engaged in sexually abusive behaviour and those who did not.

Recent research by Burton and Meezan (2005) have suggested that pornography may be a medium for learning sexually abusive behaviour, where orgasm reinforces cognitive rehearsals of sexual behaviours or aggression generated from memories of sexual victimisation. Masturbatory fantasies, which are stimulated by pornography, then lead to cognitive distortions about sex, possible sexual partners, or potential partners for sexually aggressive behaviours.

Sexually problematic behaviours and the new technologies

To date, there is very little published research that helps us understand what it is that young people do (as opposed to what they may be exposed to), that constitutes sexually problematic behaviour in relation to the new technologies. In this section, we are going to consider three classes of behaviours, none of which are unique to children and young people, but which might help in our understanding of the problems. These are:

- Soliciting, or sexually harassing behaviours.
- Downloading, trading and production of child abuse images (the legal definition of which would be child pornography).
- Self-victimising behaviours.

The first of these, soliciting activities, was examined in a study by Finkelhor et al. (2000) through the analysis of telephone interview data from a large sample (1,501) of young Internet users about their experiences online. Their findings indicated that one in five children who regularly used the Internet experienced a sexual solicitation or approach over the year examined by the study. One in 33 received an aggressive sexual solicitation, which included being asked to meet offline, telephone calls or things sent through the post. One in four had unwanted exposure to sexual images, and one in 17 were threatened or harassed. Approximately one quarter of the children who reported these incidents were distressed by them. The data from Finkelhor et al.'s (2000) survey indicated that juveniles made up 48 per cent of the overall, and 48 per cent of the aggressive solicitations against youth (27 per cent were of an unknown age). These authors concluded that not all of the sexual solicitors on the Internet fit the media stereotype of an older, male predator. Many were young and some were women. A number of the sexual solicitations appeared to be propositions for 'cybersex', and in almost half of the incidents the young person did not tell anyone about the episode.

The second group of sexually abusive practices by adults and young people, involving abusive images of children, were described in an important research report examining cases investigated by the Department of Internal Affairs Censorship Compliance Unit (CCU) in New Zealand. The results of this study were subsequently updated later that year by Wilson and Andrews (2004) using the same methodology, and including an additional 79 offenders. Their results indicated that of the 184 people in the study, only one was female, and 89 per cent were classified as New Zealand Europeans. The largest single group of offenders, which remained the same as in Carr's (2004: 2) study, 'continues to be aged between 15 and 19 years. Those under 20 years at the time of detection comprise a quarter (24.3 per cent) of all offenders'. The largest occupational group was students (32.4 per cent), followed by those whose career was in information technology (19.5 per cent). The majority of the offenders were found to be in possession of child sex abuse material, with images of bestiality and material containing the use of urine and excrement being the second and third most commonly found sorts of objectionable material. These two New Zealand reports provided the first systematic analysis of seized materials. They caused considerable concern because they identified a high number of young people engaged in the collection of illegal images and this was substantiated in the second data set. The results were somewhat different from those reported by Wolak et al. (2005) in the US in a study called N-JOV (National Juvenile Online Victimisation Study) where only three per cent were younger than 18.

While Carr's (2004) study does not systematically analyse the nature of the activities

relating to the use of abuse images, they seemed to be largely the same as those reported in other adult samples (Quayle, 2004) and included downloading, trading and producing illegal images. Carr's (2004) data analysis of the New Zealand sample revealed other interesting findings about the young people in the study. The collection of material portraying the exploitation of children, young people or both, for sexual purposes was common across all of the age and occupation categories, but those individuals identified as school students were much more likely to trade or possess images of teenagers or older children than any other group of individuals. They were also most likely to select material showing children and young people with others of their age. Indeed, even when they chose images pertaining to other categories of the Censorship Act, school students tended to select materials portraying youth aged under 17 years. The author concluded that, 'As such, it appears that their interest was within the realms of 'age appropriateness''.

However, it should be noted that all of the school students were found to trade or possess images of children and young people engaged in explicit sexual activity, including images of children aged between two and seven years, giving cause for concern about their activities. Also of concern was that school children were also proportionately more likely to trade or possess images of children and young people that suggested or implied incest. Nonetheless, Carr (2004) felt that the data did provide clues as to the motivation for initially accessing this material and that it offered support for, 'the concept of a sexually curious group of adolescents'. In contrast to the results of school students, those individuals who were identified as tertiary students aged under 25 years and non-students aged under 25 were found to demonstrate a much greater range of image preferences and were identified as being proportionately more likely to collect images portraying babies as the subject of sexual exploitation. In addition, 60 per cent of those aged under 25 spent less than 10 hours per week using the Internet. The research did not provide any evidence that these individuals were involved in the commission of physical sexual offences against children, but the author expressed concern about the nature of the images in the light of research suggesting offence behaviour beginning in adolescence.

The results of the New Zealand study also indicated that offenders identified as secondary school students were more likely than the others to collect large numbers of images that were well indexed. They were also more frequently associated with the collection of images of older children and teenagers, portrayed with other children, and were much less likely to collect images of adult rape or the torture of adults or children. Carr (2004) concluded that what is worrying was that their Internet based exploration had led them to subject matter involving largely deviant activities at a time when they were most likely to be influenced by the message it conveys.

The third category of sexually abusive practices relates to what might be called self-victimising activities through both the Internet and mobile phone technology. The evidence would suggest that mobile phone ownership may be higher among children aged 11–16 than among adults, with 76 per cent of children having their own phone (Child-Wise Monitor, 2002). Madell and Muncer (2004) surveyed 1,340 secondary school children from the Teesside area of the UK. Of these 86 per cent owned a mobile phone (89.7 per cent of females and 82.3 per cent of males). In this study, mobile phone use was restricted to voice calls and text, but there is evidence that increasingly mobile phones can also act as other forms of communication. As already noted, Livingstone and Bober (2005) however, have argued this is now diversifying, and in their study 38 per cent of the young people had a mobile phone, 17 per cent a digital television and 8 per cent a games console, all with access to the Internet. For many young people, the mobile phone is both a vital means of communication and a way of relating to, and participating in, an extended social world.

However, there are emerging concerns that such participation may involve abusive practices that target other individuals or are self-victimising. As yet, no published accounts of such activities have emerged outside of anecdotal or clinical case material, but it is an area that is worthy of consideration. In March 2005, two girls, in separate incidents, took indecent photographs of themselves in their homes without realising how widely they could be circulated on the Internet (TES Cymru, 2005). The first case involved a 14-year-old girl who took naked pictures of herself using a digital camera, which she downloaded on to her computer and sent via an instant messaging service. The second case involved a 13-year-old girl who sent photographs

of herself in underwear, with handcuffs and a whip, via a web cam to an Internet site. This set of photographs were widely accessed by other pupils and led to a fight in the school grounds. The child's parents were very distressed by the event as they thought she was using the computer to do her homework. Both of the girls described their actions as either a dare, or fun. In a similar incident, the *Daily Herald* (2005) reported that police and social services were called in after six Suffolk schoolgirls took topless photographs of each other and posted them on the Internet. The 15-year-olds posted the pictures on a website they had set up and one of the girls was arrested on suspicion of taking indecent photographs of a child.

A further report (BBC News, 2005) involved both mobile phones and the Internet. It related to an adolescent boy in India who recorded a sexual act between himself and a sixteen-year-old schoolgirl on his mobile phone. The pictures were then circulated across India and abroad. The clip, which lasted 2 minutes 37 seconds was copied onto video CDs and sold. Subsequently the head of an auction Website was arrested after the sale of CDs appeared on the Internet showing the sexual activity between the two students. The person who had attempted to sell the clip on the auction site was himself a student.

Assessment

As already stated, there is little to help inform our assessment of young people who engage in sexually abusive behaviours through the new technologies. Indeed, it may be argued that existing assessment frameworks are sufficient. For example, Print et al. (2001) describe their AIM model as providing a conceptual framework for the initial assessment of young people which is based on four key domains:

- Offence specific factors, such as the young person's offending history, the nature of the offence behaviours and any previous offence history.
- Developmental issues, including any experiences of abuse or trauma, the quality of earlier life experiences and wider behavioural issues.
- Family, including functioning within the family, their attitudes and beliefs, sexual boundaries and parental competence.

- Environment, including opportunities for further offending and the degree of community support.

All of these would clearly have relevance to young people engaging in abusive behaviours through the use of the Internet. In addition, it has also been emphasised that when evaluating the sexual behaviours of adolescents, it is critical to avoid dichotomous thinking, and instead view them on a continuum from healthy to problematic (Longo et al., 2002). These authors have also emphasised that it is important to assess the function that the sexual behaviour serves for the particular young person, stressing that an important indicator of sexual health for teenagers is the degree to which the sexual behaviour is in the service of developmentally appropriate sexual needs as opposed to primarily non-sexual needs. Examples may include exploring personal identity through sexuality, where surfing the web, participating in chat rooms and engaging in Internet sex may be ways of trying on multiple identities to see which fit. Greenfield (2004b: 759) gave an interesting example of this in relation to teen chat rooms that were controlled or moderated (and therefore assumed to be 'safer' than others). These sites still made frequent references to sex, but all in code. 'The codification of the allusions to sexuality made them not only aware about sex, according to Turkle, but also about ingroup-outgroup issues, which . . . is how teenagers use any medium . . . Coded sexuality is all about the co-construction of cultural norms that are utilised in this online community'.

Equally, the function of sexual engagement with the Internet many relate to managing negative feelings. Longo et al. (2002) have argued that sexual behaviour and pleasure is a powerful way to feel better in the moment, and that this may result in the compulsive use of pornography and masturbation. The literature pertaining to the relationship between affect, emotions and sex offending has been recently reviewed by Howells et al. (2004: 180). They have suggested that; 'An emerging issue in the field of sex offender theory and treatment is whether emotional and other affective states in perpetrators are functionally important, particularly as antecedents, for offences. In rehabilitation terms, are affective states criminogenic needs?' Within this review, it was noted that there are problems with definition, in that negative affect is used to describe emotions, moods and feelings, and they

questioned whether states such as boredom or excitement might be genuinely construed as moods. These authors provided substantial empirical support for the relationship between affect and offending in relation to studies on anger and sexual arousal, offence pathways studies, and sexual fantasy studies, and concluded that the most convincing evidence for the role of affect as a causal factor in sex offending comes from the offence-process or offence chain studies. In this context, earlier work by Hudson et al. (1999) had described positive and negative affect routes to sexual offending. While the context of much of this research is with adult offenders, the function of activity for the individual lies within a broader behavioural context (Quayle et al., 2006) and is worth further consideration in relation to young people and sexually abusive behaviours.

Earlier work by Marshall and Marshall (2000) (again in the context of adult offenders) looked at affective states and coping behaviour. These authors proposed that when in a state of negative affect, sex offenders are more likely to use sexual behaviours as a means of coping than are non-offenders. Sex becomes a way of resolving non-sexual problems which Howells et al. (2004) have suggested is reinforced and learned precisely because it is effective in reducing a state of negative affect. Linked to this is the idea that some states of emotional arousal, such as anger, anxiety and loneliness, may produce situational suppression of empathic responses and affect subsequent decision making processes.

A further assessment area that has received attention (although not in relation to the new technologies) relates to pornography use. Knight (2004) compared 452 adult offenders to 227 juvenile offenders on selected rationally constructed scales and on 32 scales derived factor analytically from eight of the domains assessed by the MASA (Multidimensional Assessment of Sex and Aggression). One of the derived scales included Pornography Exposure. Juveniles acknowledged being exposed to more pornography in their family homes, but the adult offenders used conventional heterosexual pornography considerably more than adolescents. Adults were also exposed to violent pornography more frequently then juveniles, but there were no differences in terms of exposure to homosexual or child pornography. Knight concluded from this '. . . that some family members might be providing the juvenile offenders with sexual materials that they might encounter more difficulty in obtaining elsewhere'. With the arrival of the Internet, there is a proliferation of sexual material that is freely available and easy to access, which renders this assumption questionable at best. Similarly Prentky and Righthand (2003: 15) in the development of J-SOAP-II (Juvenile Sex Offender Assessment Protocol-II) included a scale on sexual drive and preoccupation which they described as; 'This item measures "hypersexuality" (i.e. the strength of the sexual drive and preoccupation). This is a behaviourally anchored item that focuses on evidence of an excessive amount of sexual activity (exceeding what might be considered normative for youths of that age) or excessive preoccupation with sexual urges or gratifying sexual needs. Evidence includes, but is not limited to, paraphilias (exposing, peeping, cross-dressing, fetishes, etc.) compulsive masturbation; chronic and compulsive use of pornography; frequent highly sexualised language and gestures; and indiscriminate sexual activity with different partners out of the context of any relationship'. Again, this is a useful reference point in terms of assessment, but in the context of the new technologies, we have as yet little understanding about the purposive use of sexually related materials on the Internet by young people, particularly those that relate to extreme sexual practices.

Quayle and Taylor (2002) in the context of adult offenders, attempted to produce guidelines for practitioners that would help form the basis of an assessment, and which would ensure some level of consistency from case to case. The usefulness for such a framework remains to be evaluated. In the context of children and young people, we are still at the stage of exploring what issues may be relevant in relation to abusive practices and the new technologies. It is also acknowledged that young people are not always forthcoming in the information that they are prepared to give (Lambie, 2005) and that it would make sense to collate information from a variety of sources, including where possible a technical forensic report provided by the police.

It is with this in mind that the following guidelines for assessment have been suggested.

The offence behaviours

A description of the sexually abusive behaviours, which would include the following:

- What did the young person do?
  - Where did it take place?
  - When did it take place?
  - Were others involved, either online or offline?
  - How often?
  - Over what period of time?
  - What immediately preceded the abusive behaviours?
  - What terminated these abusive behaviours?
- What was the function of the activity for the individual? What needs was it meeting and did these change over time?
  - Sexual (and in what way)?
  - Social?
  - Emotional avoidance?
  - As part of other collecting or obsessive compulsive behaviours?
  - Risk taking?
- What was the context for the individual?
  - What were the number of hours spent on-line in any one week?
  - How much of this time was engaged in problematic activity?
  - Has there been a reduction in other preferred activities?
  - How much time is spent thinking about their latest Internet experience (chat or image) or planning the next?
- What have the consequences been for the individual?
  - Change in social relationships?
  - Change in family relationships?
- What level of knowledge does the individual possess about the new technologies?
  - How would they (or others) describe themselves in relation to this?
  - What kinds of Internet media would the person have used, and what for? (e.g. Web sites, chatrooms, email, instant messaging, peer to peer).
- Were these activities part of other sexually abusive practices?
  - Engaging in cyber sex?
  - Sexual harassment or bullying?
- Has the young person been sexually victimised?
- Has any victimisation included the use of photography?

Where the sexually abusive behaviours included images

1. Downloading images

- How many images were accessed and from where?
- Were the images predominantly of one gender?
- Did any one category of images exceed the others in terms of quantity?
- What activities were included in the images?
- How were images saved and organised?
- How much time was spent offline looking at the images?
- How often did masturbation take place in relation to the images?
- What fantasies were associated with the images, and did this change over time?
- Have any fantasies been acted out with real children (which may or may not be of an explicitly sexual nature)?

2. Trading images
   - Have images been exchanged with others (how has this been done, what volume and what purpose did this serve)?
   - Over what period of time?
   - With whom?
   - Has there been any contact in real life with people (adults or children) met on-line?

3. Producing images
   - Have images been created through scanning, use of software, use of a digital camera?
   - Were any images of children within the young person's family or social network?
   - Were any images taken of themselves?

Social and family context

- How do respective members of the young person's family view the nature of the abusive activities?
- What level of awareness was there about Internet use?
- What level of supervision was given with regard to Internet use?
- What level of Internet use is there by other members of the family?
- Do other members of the family engage in legal (or illegal) online sexual activities?
- What level of pornography use is there by family members?
- What level of social isolation is present in the young person?
- How much social activity takes place online?
- Has there been self-representation as other individuals (either same or other sex or age)?

- Does the young person have a nickname(s), and what does it mean/signify to them (why did they choose it)?
- Has the person gone on to meet off-line people who have been met through the new technologies?
- Does the young person engage in the abusive behaviours with others known to him/her (e.g. school)?
- Have any of the abusive practices taken place outside of home, and if so where?

Conclusion

Over the last few years, young people are increasingly engaged with the new technologies, and are likely to continue to do so. Such engagement positions them not as passive consumers, but as social actors who are part of the creation of these new media. The Internet has been a largely unregulated environment, and as such has provided a context for the proliferation of sexual materials which bring with them access, availability and a perceived level of anonymity which has never been seen before. We do not know what the impact of both accidental and purposive exposure might be for young people, both in terms of their own development or the possible impact that this might have on their actions towards other young people. This touches upon several of the points raised by Araji's (2004) list of useful questions. Of concern is that access to such material 'moves the goalposts', both for adults and young people, in terms of what is socially acceptable, and normalises sexual practices that until recently would (and remain so for many people) have been seen as extreme or abusive. The anonymity of the Internet also gives access to an unlimited number of communities, many of which are created by young people, with whom it is possible to share ideas, fantasies and products.

It is also the case that the perceived anonymity of the Internet not only facilitates access to both legal and illegal sexual material, but allows for sexual harassment and bullying. Each new technical progression, for example the advent of inexpensive digital cameras, has brought with it the possibility of abusive activity, either through the production of sexualised images of others, for example, or of the young people themselves. And all this at a time when sexual curiosity and risk taking is at their highest. For most adults reading this book, such unrestrained access to a highly sexualised social world lies beyond the range of our own adolescent experiences. However, the reality is that many adults engage in online sexual activities which are both legal and illegal (Cooper and Griffin-Shelley, 2002), and which challenges some of our traditional notions of what constitutes 'normal' engagement or preoccupation.

It is with this in mind that the chapter has tried to situate assessment in the context of how young people use the new technologies and how they might function in their lives. Thinking about function might help us work fairly with young people, and also enable us to formulate their problems in ways that increases the likelihood of a working hypothesis that enables us to proceed, evaluate and monitor progress. It also allows us to think about behaviours as being topographically similar, but which may function in different ways. What this chapter has not been able to do is to give any easy answers about risk. We do not know whether a young person who has largely downloaded images of male children is more problematic than someone who has downloaded images of female children (although assessments such as J-SOAP-II might give reason to believe this). We equally do not know whether volume of material is important, particularly as many young people may have obtained illegal images through peer-to-peer or other file sharing networks. We know that to some extent a collection of images relates to sexual fantasies, but we do not know whether a young person who has collected highly abusive or degrading images is any more at risk of committing further offences than someone who has collected images that do not depict specific sexual activities. It is also the case that where trading takes place, people often keep images not because they are of sexual interest, but because they may be useful currency to secure other images (Quayle et al., 2000).

Any assessment needs to take account of the fact that the media are a dominant and influential activity of childhood and adolescence and an increasingly important force in our culture (Horner, 2004). As has been suggested by Greenfield (2004b) young people are active media consumers who choose, interpret and apply the media in a variety of ways, and the media as accessed through the new technologies are increasingly interactive and multisensory. At present, the largely unregulated content of the Internet provides not only a vehicle for offending

behaviour but an interactive cyberspace which is both challenging and reflecting societal values. It is important not to exaggerate the potential problems of the new technologies, in that the Internet cannot be seen to cause sexually abusive behaviours in young people. It may be, however, that violent content and the ease with which it is engaged with on the Internet, may be one factor that for some children influences the occurrence of problematic behaviour, both in the present and in the future.

References

Alexy, E.M. (2003) *Pornography in the Lives of Sexually Reactive Children and Adolescents.* Unpublished doctoral thesis. University of Pennsylvania.

Araji, S.K. (2004) Preadolescents and Adolescents: Evaluating Normative and Non-Normative Sexual Behaviours and Development. In O'Reilly, G., Marshall, W.L., Carr, A. and Beckett, R.C. (Eds.) *The Handbook of Clinical Intervention With Young People Who Sexually Abuse.* Hove: Psychology Press.

BBC News (24/04/2005) Available online from: http:newsvole.bbc.co.uk/mpapps/pagetools/print/news.bbc.co.uk

Becker, J.V. (1990) Treating Adolescent Sex Offenders. *Professional Psychology: Research and Practice,* 21: 5, 362–5.

Browne, K.D. and Hamilton-Giachritsis, C. (2005) The Influence of Violent Media on Children and Adolescents: A Public Health Approach. *Lancet,* 365: 702–10.

Burton, D.L. and Meezan, W. (2005) Revisiting Recent Research on Social Learning Theory as an Etiological Proposition for Sexually Abusive Male Adolescents. In Calder, M. (2005) (Ed.) *Children and Young People Who Sexually Abuse. New Theory, Research and Practice Developments.* Lyme Regis: Russell House Publishing.

Calder, M.C. (2001) *Juveniles and Children Who Sexually Abuse: Frameworks for Assessment.* 2nd edn. Lyme Regis: Russell House Publishing.

Cameron, K.A., Salazar, L.F., Bernhardt, J.M. Burgess-Whitman, N., Wingwood, G.M. and DiClemente, R.J. (2005) Adolescents' Experience With Sex on the Web: Results From Online Focus Groups. *Journal of Adolescence,* 28: 4, 535–40.

Carr, A. (2004) *Internet Traders of Child Pornography and Other Censorship Offenders in*

New Zealand. Available online at: http://
www.dia.govt.nz?pubforms.nsf/URL/
entirereport.pdf/$file/entirereport.pdf
Child-Wise Monitor (2002) Available online at:
http://www.ecpat.org/media-releases.html.
Concepcion, J.I. (2004) Understanding
Preadolescent Sexual Offenders: Can These
Children Be Rehabilitated to Stem the Tide of
Adult Predatory Behaviors? *Florida Bar Journal.*
LXXVIII: 7; July/August.
Cooper, A. and Griffin-Shelley, E. (2002) The
Internet: The Next Sexual Revolution. In
Cooper, A. (Ed.) *Sex and the Internet. A Guidebook
for Clinicians.* New York: Brunner Routledge.
Daily Herald (2005) Available online at: http://
www.newutah.com/print.php?sid=53417. 24
April.
Daily Mail Thursday 21 April 2005 page 24.
Available online at: http://
www.communitycare.co.uk/AccessSite/
articles/
article.asp?liSectionID=4andliarticleID=49007
DeBell, M. and Chapman, C. (2003) *Computer and
Internet use by Children and Adolescents in 2001.*
Washington, DC: US Department of Education,
National Center for Education Statistics.
Emerick, R.L. and Dutton, W.A. (1993) The Effect
of Polygraphy on the Self-Report of Adolescent
Sexual Offenders: Implications for Risk
Assessment. *Annals of Sex Research,* 6: 83–103.
Epps, K. and Fisher, D. (2004) A Review of the
Research Literature on Young People Who
Sexually Abuse. In O'Reilly, G., Marshall, W.L.,
Carr, A. and Beckett, R. (Eds.) *The Handbook of
Clinical Intervention with Young People who
Sexually Abuse.* Sussex: Routledge.
Finkelhor, D., Mitchell, K.J. and Wolak, J. (2000)
*Online Victimisation: A Report of the Nation's
Youth.* Washington: National Center for
Missing and Exploited Children.
Ford, M.E. and Linney, J.A. (1995) Comparative
Analysis of Juvenile Sexual Offenders, Violent
Nonsexual Offenders and Status Offenders.
Journal of Interpersonal Violence, 10: 56–70.
French, C. (2005) Assessment and Treatment
Strategies for Children With Sexually Abusive
Behaviours: A Review of Cognitive,
Developmental and Outcome Considerations.
In Calder, M. (Ed.) *Children and Young People
who Sexually Abuse. New Theory, Research and
practice Developments.* Lyme Regis: Russell
House Publishing.
Greenfield, P.M. (2004a) Developmental
Considerations for Determining Appropriate

Internet Use Guidelines for Children and
Adolescents. *Applied Developmental Psychology,*
25: 751–62.
Greenfield, P.M. (2004b) Inadvertent Exposure to
Pornography on the Internet: Implications of
Peer-to-peer File Sharing Networks for Child
Development and Families. *Applied
Developmental Psychology,* 25: 741–50.
Hackett, S. (2004) *What Works for Children and
Young People with Harmful Sexual Behaviours?*
Nottingham: Barnardo's.
Horner, G. (2004) Sexual Behaviour in Children:
Normal or Not? *Journal of Paediatric Health Care,*
18: 57–64.
Howells, K., Day, A. and Wright, S. (2004) Affect,
Emotions and Sex Offending. *Psychology, Crime
and Law,* 10: 2, 179–95.
Hudson, S.M., Ward, T. and McCormack, J.C.
(1999) Offense Pathways in Sexual Offenders.
Journal of Interpersonal Violence. 14, 779–98.
Kanuga, M. and Rosenfeld, W.D. (2004)
Adolescent Sexuality and the Internet: The
Good, the Bad and the URL. *Journal of Pediatric
Adolescent Gynecology,* 17: 117–24.
Kaufman, K.L. et al. (1998) Factors Influencing
Sexual Offenders Modus Operandi: An
Examination of Victim-Offender Relatedness
and Age. *Child Maltreatment,* 3: 349–61.
Knight, R.A. (2004) Comparisons Between
Juvenile and Adult Sexual Offenders on the
Multidimensional Assessment of Sex and
Aggression. In O'Reilly, G. Marshall, W.L.
Carr, A. and Beckett, R.C. (Eds.) *The
Handbook of Clinical Intervention With Young
People Who Sexually Abuse.* Hove: Psychology
Press.
Lambie, I. (2005) You Can Get an Adolescent to
Grunt But You Can't Make Them Talk:
Interviewing Strategies With Young People
Who Sexually Abuse. In Calder, M. (Ed.)
*Children and Young People who Sexually Abuse.
New Theory, Research and practice Developments.*
Lyme Regis: Russell House Publishing.
Livingstone, S. and Bober, M. (2005) *UK Children
Go Online.* Available from: http://
www.children-go-online.net.
Longo, R.E., Brown, S.M. and Orcutt, D.P. (2002)
Effects of Internet Sexuality on Children and
Adolescents. In Cooper, A. (Ed.) *Sex and the
Internet. A Guidebook for Clinicians.* New York:
Brunner Routledge.
Madell, D. and Muncer, S. (2004) Back From the
Beach But Hanging on the Telephone? English
Adolescents' Attitudes and Experiences of

Mobile Phones and the Internet. *CyberPsychology and Behavior*, 7: 3, 359–67.

Malamuth, N.M. (1993) Pornography's Impact on Male Adolescents. *Adolescent Medicine*, 4: 563–76.

Malamuth, N.M. (2000) Pornography and Sexual Aggression: Are These Reliable Effects and can we Understand Them? *Annual Review of Sex Research*, 11: 26–91.

Marshall, W.L. and Marshall, L.E. (2000) The Origins of Sexual Offending. *Trauma, Violence and Abuse*, 1, 250–63.

Medoff, D. (2004) Sexual Offenders: Developmental Considerations in the Forensic Assessment of Adolescent Victim Selection, Intervention and Offender Recidivism Rates. *Forensic Examiner*, 13: 4–6.

Mitchell, K.J., Finkelhor, D. and Wolak, J. (2003) The Exposure of Youth to Unwanted Sexual Material on the Internet. A National Survey of Risk, Impact and Prevention. *Youth and Society*, 34: 3, 330–50.

Net Ratings Australia (2005) Kidsonline@home. *Internet Use in Australian Homes*. Available online at: http://www.netalert.net.au?02010-kidsonline@home-Internet-use-in-Australia-homes-April–2005.pdf.

O'Reilly, G. and Carr. (2004) The Clinical Assessment of Young People With Sexually Abusive Behaviour. In O'Reilly, G. Marshall, W.L. Carr, A. and Beckett, R.C. (Eds.) *The Handbook of Clinical Intervention With Young People Who Sexually Abuse*. Hove: Psychology Press.

O' Reilly, G. et al. (1998) A Descriptive Study of Adolescent Sexual Offenders in an Irish Community-Based Treatment Programme. *Irish Journal of Psychology*, 19: 1, 152–67.

Prentky, R. and Righthand, S. (2003) *Juvenile Sex Offender Assessment Protocol-II (J-SOAP-II)*. US: Office of Juvenile Justice and Delinquency Prevention.

Print, B., Morrison, T. and Henniker, J. (2001) An Inter-Agency Assessment Framework for Young People Who Sexually Abuse: Principles, Processes and Practicalities. In Calder, M. (Ed.) *Juveniles and Children Who Sexually Abuse; Frameworks for Assessment*. 2nd edn. Lyme Regis: Russell House Publishing.

Quayle, E., Vaughan, M. and Taylor, M. (2006) Sex Offenders, Internet Child Abuse Images and Emotional Avoidance: The Importance of Values. *Aggression and Violent Behavior*, 11: 1, 1–11.

Quayle, E (2004) The Impact of Viewing on Offending Behaviour. In Calder, M.C. (Ed.) *Sexual Abuse and the Internet: Tackling the New Frontier*. Lyme Regis: Russell House Publishing.

Quayle, E. and Taylor, M. (2002) Paedophiles, Pornography and the Internet: Assessment Issues. *British Journal of Social Work*, 32, 863–75.

Quayle, E., Holland, G., Linehan, C. and Taylor, M. (2000) The Internet and Offending Behaviour: A Case Study. *Journal of Sexual Aggression*, 6: 1/2, 78–96.

Righthand, S. and Welch, C. (2001) *Juveniles Who Have Sexually Offended: A Review of the Professional Literature*. Washington: Office of Juvenile Justice and Delinquency Prevention.

SAFT (2003) *Children's Study: Investigating Online Behaviour*. Available at: http://www.ncte.ie/InternetSafety/Publications/d1736.PDF.

Taylor, M. and Quayle, E. (2005) Abusive Images of Children. In Cooper, S., Giardino, A., Vieth, V. and Kellogg, N. (Eds.) *Medical, Legal and Social Science Aspects of Child Sexual Exploitation*. Saint Louis: GW Medical Publishing.

Taylor, M. and Quayle, E. (2003) *Child Pornography: An Internet Crime*. Brighton: Routledge.

TES Cymru (2005) *Web Picture Dangers: Warning as Schoolgirls Post Indecent Photos on Internet 'for a bit of fun'*. 9 March.

Will, D. (1999) Assessment Issues. In Erooga, M. and Masson, H. (Eds.) *Children and Young People who Sexually Abuse*. Oxford: Routledge.

Wilson, D. and Andrews, C. (2004) *Internet Traders of Child Pornography and Other Censorship Offenders in New Zealand: Updated Statistics*. Available online from: http://www.dia.govt.nz/puforms.nsf/URL/profilingupdate.pdf/$file/profilingupdate.pdf.

Wolak, J., Finkelhor, D. and Mitchell, K.J. (2005) *Child-Pornography Possessors Arrested in Internet-Related Crimes: Findings from the National Juvenile Online Victimisation Study*. Washington: National Center for Missing and Exploited Children.

Zolondek, S., Abel, G., Northey, W. and Jordan, A. (2001) The Self-Reported Behaviors of Juvenile Sex Offenders. *Journal of Interpersonal Violence*, 16: 1, 73–85.

Chapter 17

Restorative Justice: Can it Work with Young People Who Sexually Abuse?

Julie Henniker and Vince Mercer

Introduction

This chapter draws on the ongoing work of the authors undertaken in an inter-agency project working with children and young people who sexually harm in Greater Manchester. The project known as the AIM (Assessment Intervention and Moving on) project was established in 2000 to co-ordinate a collaboration between key agencies and 10 local authorities across a population in excess of 2.5 million people in developing policies, procedures, multi-disciplinary assessment models, training and a range of intervention services to meet the diverse needs of this group of children, young people and their families.

From the outset the AIM project was keen to focus on the developmental aspect of this area of work and 'test out' new ideas and approaches. It was this underlying philosophy that brought together the authors who are from different fields of knowledge; the world of children and young people who sexually abuse and the world of restorative justice 'RJ' that incorporates both the criminal and welfare approach to resolution. For most practitioners the combination of adolescent sexual abuse and 'RJ' may be an unfamiliar concept; yet in the UK and many other criminal justice systems 'RJ' is perhaps the most profound and innovative approach to the way we think about and do work with young offenders and their victims, indeed criminologists see 'RJ' as being 'one of the most significant developments in criminal justice and criminological practice over the past two decades' Crawford and Newburn, 2003.

The results of the work in Greater Manchester to date are drawn together in this chapter which explores the practicalities, problems and possibilities of applying a restorative approach to situations where a child or young person has sexually harmed. The work is ongoing and continually informed by practice and as such we pose this question to the reader:

Can restorative approaches evolve to effectively balance the needs and rights of the victim, the abuser, their families and the community effectively and without bias, in cases of sexual harm?

What is restorative justice?

Restorative justice is borne out of a critique of 'conventional justice' and an appeal to the notion of a more person centred approach which sees 'conflict' as being an interaction between individuals rather than between the state and individuals. It is a process that brings individuals together and gives them a voice; to address, seek to resolve and prevent repetition of the harm caused via reparation and rehabilitation. To paraphrase Crawford and Newborn (2003) 'RJ' seeks to hold 'offenders' accountable in a meaningful way and respond appropriately to victims, whilst not relying wholly on punishment as a response to the harm done.

Thus, the 'RJ' movement has established an oppositional stance to the current and conventional method of 'doing' criminal justice; by tapping into a broad consensus of dissatisfaction with contemporary systems and their perceived lack of effectiveness. This would mirror a number of frustrations with the criminal justice system in respect of young people who sexually harm and their potentially damaging labelling such as inclusion on the sex offenders register, which has long term and wide ranging implications for their life chances.

There is an irony that whilst 'RJ' is seen as a relatively recent arrival in the criminal justice world, Professor John Braithwaite (1998) one of the leading theoretical exponents in the field suggests that, 'restorative approaches were the norm in pre-industrial societies and in fact restorative justice has been the dominant model of criminal justice throughout human history for all the worlds' people'. Many commentators support this approach by highlighting the importance of the way that the Maori and native

American peoples addressed harm done to their communities and how these models evolved into contemporary approaches such as Family Groups Meetings 'FGCs'. Others such as Daly and Blagg have suggested this is a simplistic and overly romantic re-interpretation of pre-industrial practice which may be guilty of re-colonising native/pre-industrial justice practices as being restoratively focused whilst at the same time ignoring the punitive reality (Daly, 2000; Blagg, 1997).

Offering the reader a clear definition of 'RJ' as a base line to continue this chapter is not as straight forward as it might seem since there is such a wide range of restorative practices and many more which claim this mantle. Our approach will be to offer a number of widely regarded definitions and then attempt to distil the essential characteristics of 'RJ' contained within them.

Restorative Justice has been described as involving victims, offenders and others who have been affected, in resolving how to deal with the aftermath of an offence. It seeks to help victims regain a feeling of safety and to help offenders make things right. It seeks to make offenders accountable and to reconcile victims and offenders. It aims to strengthen communities in order to prevent further offences.

Marshall (1999) offers:

Restorative Justice is a process whereby parties with a stake in a specific offence resolve how to deal with the aftermath of the offence and its implications for the future.

Sharpe (1998) offers five key principles to distinguish a restorative approach, these are:

- Inviting full participation and consensus.
- Seeking to heal what is broken.
- Seeking full and direct accountability.
- Seeking to reunite what has been divided.
- Seeking to strengthen the community in order to prevent further harm.

More specifically, we suggest that the key features/factors of 'RJ' include and can be defined as:

- A focus on the victim and a recognition of their needs/interests.
- A broader consideration beyond the victim, to recognise that others have been affected or harmed.

- The need to hold the offender accountable in a meaningful way.
- The potential for areas of mutual concern/interest to be examined.
- An emphasis upon the value of participation, communication and dialogue.
- A recognition of the need to repair/restore disrupted relationships.
- A focus to the future.

Significantly, these 'RJ' features/factors 'fit' comfortably with current features/factors emerging from research and the ethos of work with children and young people who sexually abuse:

- A holistic approach – that has an offence specific domain but also considers developmental, family and environmental factors (Gilgun, 1999).
- Recognition of the importance of child/young person/families strengths/resilience and their capacity to develop and reflect on a coherent story about what happened and what is happening to them (DoH, 2000b).
- Affirmation of the parents role in any process following the sexual harm incident that recognises their need to process the emotional crisis surrounding them, particularly in cases of sibling abuse (Morrison and Wilkinson, 2002).
- An approach that aims to help a child/young person back on to a healthy sexual development pathway and believes that treatment/intervention is effective.
- The presence of healthy family and community relationships are positively significant (Gilgun, 1990).
- Overall a belief that young people can change their abusive behaviour and that work with them should focus on their healthy sexual development in the future.

Four primary models of restorative practice

In England and Wales following the Crime and Disorder Act (1998) 'RJ' as a 'face to face' approach became evident in a number of operational models within the criminal justice system. The most widely adopted approach was 'Restorative Conferencing' 'RC' which was a scripted model, derived from original Family Group Conferencing practice often police led and usually delivered as part of the newly introduced Final Warning scheme. In practice 'RC' has had a greater impact in England and Wales than the Family Group Conferencing 'FGC' model. It was intended that those affected by the offence attend the conference but often in practice it focused on the victim/offender and a small number of supporters/family. Despite some initial concerns around poor implementation expressed in the interim evaluation, the final evaluation indicated satisfaction with the process and it forms the basis of restorative interventions delivered by the newly established Northern Ireland Youth Conferencing Service.

The longest standing 'face to face' model is that of Victim Offender Mediation 'VOM', a widely accepted practice that originated in Ontario in the mid 1970s and became readily used in England and Wales from the late 1970s.

Intensive preparation is usual in 'VOM' cases; it is usually incident specific and may or may not generate an agreement; it operates along free based humanistic dialogue driven lines, without the use of a script which puts greater emphasis on the skills and abilities of the mediator who acts as a facilitator of the communication. The mediator has no authority to enforce either a decision or a settlement. This reflects the position of the mediator as being neither a caseworker nor therapist but as an impartial third party. Participants may choose to communicate without meeting, through a 'shuttle' or indirect process. In practice 'VOM' has not had the same impact as other 'RJ' models due to its limited application and the sometimes hesitant use of external voluntary agencies as it is not structurally linked with a particular Criminal Justice process such as diversion or a sentence such as a Referral Order.

The 'RJ' model which is most common in New Zealand is the Family Group Conferencing model 'FGC'; its key features are:

- Engagement with the wider family of the 'offender' to maximise them as a potential source of support/resource.
- In restorative 'FGCs' the inclusion of a victim/offender dialogue which both offers a restorative potential and enables the victim's perspective/concerns to be fed directly into the planning process.
- The attendance of appropriate professionals to report to the 'FGC' their concerns/issues and at the same time to offer services/resources to address these concerns.

- The use of 'Family Private Planning Time' when participants, excluding the professionals, adjourn, having heard the perspective/concerns of the victim and professionals create a 'Family Action Plan' to address them.

As such an 'FGC' is both a restorative and planning process combined and one which we would favour as a key model for use with children and young people who sexually abuse.

The final model is the Referral Order 'RO', introduced as part of a consolidating piece of legislation following the Crime and Disorder Act. Again derived from 'FGC' practice, the 'RO' responds to first time guilty pleas in the Youth Court, and young people may be sentenced to a 3/6/9/12 month 'RO' and subsequently appearing before a community based referral order panel where they are given the opportunity to meet with the victims or at least hear how people have been affected by the offence before an intervention plan is agreed. In essence the frame of the order is drawn by the court, proportionate to the estimated seriousness of the offence but the restorative element and content of the order is delivered and determined by attendance at the community panel.

Following the Crime and Disorder Act 1998, the Youth Justice Board approach to RJ was one of 'let a thousand flowers bloom.' However, practice experience was limited and as a consequence a range of models developed, some face to face as described above and some more marginal but focused upon delivery of victim awareness or reparation schemes. Because of the lack of an operational definition at this stage and significant difficulties around data protection there was considerable pressure on the Youth Offending Teams to achieve outcomes determined by performance management targets and consequently the emphasis shifted away from face to face meetings and towards the easier to deliver models such as reparation. However, as practitioners gained experience and confidence increasingly the 'RJ' community began to test out application of the model on the more serious and persistent offenders, leading to Hudson (2002) asking the question, 'What is at issue for the future of 'RJ' is this; is it to be justice-at-the-margins or will 'RJ' become mainstream justice?

In reality the introduction of the 'RO' partly answered the question. For the first time here was a high volume statutory intervention, based around the notion of a face to face meeting which in design at least was explicitly restorative. This order currently accounts for a significant proportion of the volume of all YOT statutory work. In addition Referral Orders were beginning to net offences which initially the 'RJ' community approached with extreme caution or judged them inappropriate; the adolescent sex offender.

These are the four primary 'face to face' models of 'RJ'; there are other approaches which claim the title 'RJ' but for the purpose of this chapter these are the primary models which offer an opportunity for consideration of facilitated contact between victim and offender.

Why apply 'RJ' to sexually abusive behaviour?

The simple answer is that in many cases it would be inappropriate to do so. 'RJ' has not traditionally worked in the field of sexual abuse for reasons outlined previously and even today, in the UK with the exception of the 'RO' and the Conferencing Service in Northern Ireland most restorative practice will avoid sexually harmful behaviour. However, we believe that to ignore the possibility of this approach passes up some exceptionally powerful opportunities and possibilities.

Looking at the South Australian conferencing experience in these situations it is clear that the majority of victims they work with are known to the abuser; either in an inter-family or step family relationship as sister, brother, cousin or as close friends. Indeed they consider that the nature of an existing or potential ongoing relationship is one of the most positive indicators for a restorative process. Our Greater Manchester experience recognises that one powerful driver for a potential restorative approach is a past and therefore potential future relationship between the young abuser and the victim. Hence much of our initial work is focusing on cases of sibling/wider family sexual abuse. So, in an example of intrafamilial/extended family abuse, an existing social relationship between the protagonists and their parents/siblings/social networks within the community is altered but the need/likelihood of potential future contact remains a significant factor for all concerned. The need to regulate future contact which leaves the victim safe and holds the offender accountable in a meaningful way within the social context of

where the abuse took place; the family, the school, youth group or community. Moreover, the alternative to 'relationship repair' or as we would prefer 'relationship negotiation' is the painful fracture of what may have previously been a positive coherent family unity.

A further compelling reason to consider the application of an 'RJ' approach in cases of sexual offending is highlighted by the criminal justice system, which defines the extent and nature of the offending behaviour in terms of what can be proved most easily. The description of the behaviour is highly codified and stylised to enable problem free processes, the consequences of which are observed by Lacy (1998) that real experiences are silenced. 'RJ' allows the possibility to view the behaviour through the real experience of the participants; the narrative is their narrative, not reframed by the constraints of the criminal justice system. Hudson (2002) notes 'In 'RJ' proceedings the abuser cannot ignore her, as is possible in the conventional court; her story will not be retracted through legal language but will be told in her words, using forms of speech with which she always speaks to him, so he cannot claim not to understand. She will be the centre of her story.'

In a real sense those affected by the behaviour will be present; the family, friends, and carers of both victim and abuser. This is a more genuine 'audience of accountability' than any court process could construct, yet achieved in a way which commits to re-integration, condemning the behaviour and not the individual.

Advantages and disadvantages of application

In exploring the application of an 'RJ' process to a sexual abuse situation we were particularly mindful of the need to offer a parallel process around addressing the victims needs as well as focusing on the abuser and both their families. This led us to consider the potential advantages and disadvantages for all concerned and they are summarised below, drawn from Daly and Curtis-Fawley, 2004.

Victims

The potential difficulties in the application of 'RJ' for victims of sexual abuse are:

- **Victim safety** – as an informal process as opposed to a more formal criminal justice process 'RJ' applied in inappropriate cases may put victims at risk of continued abuse; it may permit power imbalances to go unchecked and reinforce abusive behaviour.
- **Manipulation of the process by the offender** – offenders may use the informal 'RJ' process to diminish or transfer their own guilt, trivialise the abuse or shift blame to the victim.
- **Pressure on victims** – some victims may not be able to effectively advocate on their own behalf and this may be particularly true if the victim is a child or young person. A process such as 'RJ' which is based upon group consensus building has the potential to minimise or overshadow a victim's interests. As a result a victim may be pressurised to accept certain outcomes, such as an apology, even if they feel it is inappropriate or insincere.
- **Mixed loyalties** – friends and family may 'support' victims but may also have divided loyalties especially in cases of sibling and intra-familial abuse.

With regard to potential benefits for victims:

- **Victim voice and participation** – victims have the opportunity to voice their story in their own words and for their story to be heard. They can be empowered by 'confronting/facing' their abuser.
- **Part of the recovery process** – increases their sense of safety and their needs have been identified and addressed. Assists them in gaining a sense of closure on the events and promotes a return to 'normality'. The recently published Smith Institute study, *Restorative Justice: the Evidence*, suggested that in some serious crimes RJ had a significant impact on reducing Post Traumatic Stress Symptoms (PTSS) (Sherman and Strang, 2007).
- **Victim validation and offender responsibility** – the victims account of what happened can be validated by participants of the 'RJ' process followed by an acknowledgment that they were not to blame. Offenders are required to take responsibility for their behaviour.
- **Communication and flexible environment** – the process can be tailored to the child or adolescent victim's needs and capacities because it is a flexible and less formal system. It may be less threatening and more able to respond to the individual needs of victims than the formal criminal justice system.

- **Relationship repair (this is a possible goal)** – the process can address the abuse between those who want to continue the relationship. It can create opportunities for the relationship to continue/be repaired/be reconstructed differently if this is what the victim truly wants. (Adapted from Daly and Curtis-Fawley, 2004)

On balance 'RJ' may have much to offer victims. Its main problems are ensuring safety for victims, overcoming the potential for power imbalances in a face to face encounter and the appearance of too lenient processes and penalties.
Daly and Curtis-Fawley, 2004

Finally, we should acknowledge that certain sex offender projects in the USA have adopted a related approach. This practice by and large originates from a therapeutic intervention base with an offender perspective. Many of these models frequently see dialogue between victim/offender as being primarily around advancing the 'treatment' of the offender by confronting distorted thinking and raising empathy/awareness levels.

The 'victim clarification' model described by Rich (2003) very much revolves around the victims issues being brought into the therapeutic context to assist the offender in their rehabilitation, by holding them directly accountable, raising their levels of understanding and appreciation of the consequences of their behaviour and perhaps offering a conduit for remorse. Rich uses the term Victim Clarification meaning that 'the offender' has clarified in his mind:

- That there is a victim.
- Who was the victim.
- That there is likely to be more than one victim in every offence (e.g. the direct victim of the offence, the victim's family, the offender's family and the community at large).

Within the therapeutic context of his work Rich sees the victim clarification process as a prerequisite for any desired family re-unification. Indeed he goes further to suggest 'This should be a goal for all clinicians in their family work, unless contraindicated or disallowed by specific circumstances'.

It is very much constructed within a clinical paradigm. '. . . as victim clarification is considered a clinical intervention, it requires that a clinician facilitate the process and run face-to-face sessions rather than other treatment staff, *including those trained in other forms of offender victim mediation*' (Rich: 351).

In these circumstances this cannot be seen as a purely restorative process. Despite identifying the 'Addressing and resolving issues for the victim' (Rich: 348) as a primary purpose, the location of the activity firmly within a clinical paradigm and intervention process for the offender means that the victims interests and needs cannot be explicitly central to the process; the focus of the intervention remains the offender. Moreover, it would appear that in many cases the emphasis is upon clinical decision making involving the therapists of both the victim and offender who in most cases facilitate the process. The issue of the need for the independence and neutrality of the mediator is not considered and instead the process becomes 'in many ways . . . Simply a variation of family therapy' (Rich: 366).

Returning back to our experience in Greater Manchester, we concluded that the potential difficulties in the application of 'RJ' for children and young people who sexually abuse are:

Abusers

- **Public shame and embarrassment** – for children and young people for whom sexual issues are a difficult subject in the light of their emotional immaturity and emerging sexuality.
- **Accepting victim 'blame'** – shouldering responsibility for their behaviour can be a difficult and challenging concept, for which the child and young person will need help and support.
- **Having the offence discussed outside the confines of a formal/legal process** – will raise issues of information sharing and confidentiality about the behaviour which will be shared with a wider and more meaningful audience.

With regard to the potential benefit for young abusers:

- **The 'RJ' preparatory process offers a reflective opportunity** – for the abuser to consider the consequences and impact of their behaviour in the widest sense both for themselves and for others.
- **An opportunity to express remorse** – in a way which may or may not lead to some form of

reconciliation and reconstruction of a relationship if the victim chooses.
- **Relieves the victim of possible guilt and self blame** – with the abuser publicly 'owning' their abusive behaviour.
- **Begins a rehabilitation process** – which seeks to hold the abuser accountable and facilitates a 'moving on' process.
- **Can establish a supportive network** – both physically and emotionally that will support the child or young person through a treatment programme.

We concluded that the potential problems in the application of 'RJ' for family members where sexual abuse has taken place are:

- **Potential to scapegoat** – re-enact family patterns of poor communication and damaged relationships. Highlight existing family splits and divided loyalties.

With regard to the potential benefits for families:

- **The opportunity to highlight the broader picture that says 'others' have been harmed by the behaviour** – the family can explain how they have been affected by the behaviour and the resulting position which they find themselves in. This is particularly important for those parents who will be 'wearing two hats', that of parent of both abuser and victim.
- **Highlight their essential role** – values their participation in the decision making process and in recognition that family is a major component in the process not an optional extra. Sibling abuse research identifies that the parental role in responding to both these children is highly significant in terms of outcome, Jones and Ramchandani (1999) Gilgun et al. (2000).
- **Enables and potentially restores communication** – in order to repair disrupted relationships and clarify the 'family narrative' about what has happened.
- **Identification of the family as a treatment support mechanism** – to the young people; victim, abuser and non abused siblings. Focus on living environment is as important as individual treatment.
- **Recognition and identification of resilience factors or assets** – that are available in the young person and significantly their family which are likely to prove significant in

reducing risk. Equipping parents to offer supervision and emotional care is very important.

Thus, having established for ourselves the principle that 'RJ' and sexual abuse could be compatible, we identified potential barriers for organisations as being:

- Anxiety of professionals on individual/ organisational and inter agency level. Indeed, Banks (2000) in his study of specialist workers noted how 'their anxiety' to ensure young people took responsibility for their sexually abusive behaviour was reflected in the ways in which workers dominated sessions, talking ten times as much as the young person talked.
- Could lead to over reliance on rules and procedures: inward survival focus.
- Too ambitious.
- Resource intense – multiple and complex – funding uncertainties, competing and conflicting priorities in agencies.
- Requires high levels of multi disciplinary working.
- Trained staff – ability of agencies to recruit and maintain committed and motivated staff.
- Shift from a risk led to needs led approach.

It is our experience that advantages of applying an 'RJ' approach in cases of sexual abuse generally outweigh the disadvantages. Each case should be considered on its own merits and we strongly feel that progression of the process should be dependent on 'RJ' specific assessment models.

Restorative justice applied to sexual abuse cases; the Greater Manchester experience

The initial case which triggered our involvement, was one where a YOT manager had dismissed the use of a restorative conference for a final warning case concerning an indecent assault. The management position was that 'RJ' doesn't 'do sex offending'. Yet the parents and adults in the case felt the need to address the consequences of the offence for themselves both individually and collectively. Put quite simply, the parents knocked on each others doors in the small cul-de-sac where they all lived and said 'we need to talk'. In practice they facilitated their own

meeting and in a true restorative sense this was a positive and voluntary move on their part. However, we as professionals were left with the feeling that we had abandoned our responsibilities to offer a restorative service and that this abandonment was borne out of professional fear and conservatism. So, instead of accepting the notion that 'RJ' doesn't 'do sex offending', we asked ourselves the more useful question 'what would we need to have in place to offer an 'RJ' service safely and effectively in cases of sexual abuse'? At that point in 2002, we concluded that we needed the following:

- An initial assessment framework to identify risks, concerns and strengths of the abuser. At this point we already had within Greater Manchester the AIM initial assessment model integrated into the child protection procedures of the 10 local authorities with a significant number of practitioners trained in its application. First box ticked.
- A reasoned commitment to extending practice in this area. Second box ticked in respect of the authors and number of Greater Manchester practitioners.
- A 'RJ' assessment practice model sensitive to the complex needs/interests of all potential participants in the 'RJ' process that could be informed by the AIM initial assessment and layered on top of that assessment. Work to be done . . .

Within the RJ field, assessment raises particular issues. The first being, that 'RJ' is a universal service where the primary focus for decision making lies with the key participants. In this sense it marks a shift in power from the professional to the individual and therefore as assessment is a professional task it is also a means by which professional control is established, continued and strengthened and therefore has no place in a restorative intervention.

The contra position is that which recognises the need to offer services which are respectful of the principle 'do no harm' in a general sense. In this context 'RJ' is not seen as a universal panacea and when working within a serious, complex and statutory legislative framework some critical decisions have to be made around applicability and suitability of a 'RJ' approach. Moreover, as 'RJ' practitioners have a duty to offer safe practice, assessment in these cases is seen as crucial. Indeed, 'in areas which are deemed to be sensitive and complex, such as sex offending the need for informed practice decision making is even more acute' (Pressener and Lowencamp, 1999).

Moreover this position reflects the section of the Home Office Best Practice guidance (2004) which has a section relating to sensitive and complex cases. This recognises that in this area restorative skills are required at a higher level and that practitioners must be able to 'apply a more thorough initial and ongoing risk assessment than would be required for less complex cases, including a formal written risk assessment, and *ensuring that any relevant specialist risk assessment tool is applied*'.

We then looked to progress our work, mapping existing models nationally and internationally. In the UK we found virtually no practice, but had more success sourcing overseas. Daly (2004) notes that 'at present there are only two jurisdictions in the world, South Australia and New Zealand, which routinely use 'RJ' in youth sexual assault cases. In New Zealand conferences are used in court diversion and for pre-sentencing advice'.

However, the greatest volume of practice seems to have occurred in the State of South Australia. Between 1994 and 1998 the South Australian Conferencing service which offers FGCs as a diversionary process to prosecution delivered a total of 92 FGCs on adolescent sex offending. They have a number of pre-conditions to undertake the work:

- A guilty plea by the offender.
- Support and counselling for the victim.

In addition they observed the following factors around the cases:

- In the majority of cases there was a prior relationship between victim and offender, often in an inter-family or step-family relationship.
- Very few were cases involving multiple victims.
- Most victims were younger than the offender.
- Many victims were ashamed or embarrassed by focus on the offence and may show related distressing behaviours which generates more anger and hostility towards the offender by the parents of the victim.
- Most of the offenders had no previous offending history.
- The multiple roles occupied by adults in the conference, e.g. parent/grandparent of both victim and offender causes complexity but

offers the opportunity to articulate this conflict and avoid being forced to reject one child to protect another.
- The FGC is often the first time the family have been able to discuss what has happened and consider its impact.
- Conferences need to be mindful of the positive elements of the offender and without reducing responsibility for his actions allow a balanced picture of the offender to be drawn.
- Engagement in a 'counselling' or intervention package for the offender often assists the participation of the offender in the process. Indeed Daly notes 'The timing of the conference may be determined, in part, by how far the offender is along the therapeutic process. Unlike conferences for other offences, those for sexual assault have a heightened degree of symbolism that mark a stage in an ongoing therapeutic process' (Daly, 2002).

Reflecting on conferencing they note 'Conferences tend to be more intense for participants (than other offences) because the effects of the offence have been usually more severe for the victim and his/her family; and the disclosure of the offence usually has consequences for the offending youth and his family prior to the conference. The indications for us are that family conferences are useful in dealing with sexual offences where there is a past, and potentially future relationship between the young offender and the victim and that the process does achieve resolution for the victim and appropriate outcomes for the offender' (Doig and Wallace, 1999).

Research in the USA indicates that for most adolescent sex offenders the victim is not a stranger. Indeed Ryan and her colleagues study (1996) found that only 6 per cent of victims were strangers and a significant number were blood relatives of the offender (38.3 per cent).

It appeared to us from the beginning of our work that the most appropriate restorative model/vehicle for us to develop in cases of sexual abuse was that of Family Group Conferencing 'FGC', which crucially invited involvement of the wider family and saw that involvement as being instrumental to the offender being able to make a full and sincere admission of responsibility to the audience who needed to hear it most, including the victim of the offence and their family. We also acknowledged at that early stage, that we should not preclude a role for victim/offender mediation or the value of indirect meetings if that suited the needs/interests of the participants.

In recognition that disclosure of such an offence often has devastating effects on the family, uninvolved family members may find themselves invited to or expected to take sides, to condemn the behaviour in a way that drives a fault line across family cohesion. Similarly, family members may find themselves in conflicting and seemingly irreconcilable positions as mother/father, brother/sister and uncle/aunt to both the victim and offender. As such, they may be faced with the impossible choice of rejecting one child in order to affirm love and compassion for another child.

Our experience has been that those previously close families who had shared long-term significant family and social time suddenly feel they have to cross the road if they encounter those previously close members of the family. The whole experience renders them unable to explain in a meaningful way to children through to grandparents the behaviour, rift and pain that has blown extended families apart. In addition, we were keen to explore the development of an assessment framework as being an aide to effective practice, identifying significant issues which warranted further attention in the preparation process. Consequently the additional 'RJ' assessment model was created to be an additional layer on the existing initial AIM model.

The AIM initial assessment – the first stage

The AIM initial assessment models have four variations; children under 10 years, adolescents, adolescents with a learning disability and the families and carers of these children and young people. It draws on available literature and research to provide a structured approach to the gathering and analysis of information about a young person, their problematic behaviour, their family and their environment.

The models are intended as a framework that will assist practitioners in gathering and organising relevant information in order to make an initial assessment and recommendations about needs and concerns. For some young people and their families an initial assessment will be only the first stage in dealing with the young person's sexually harmful behaviour. There may be a need for a more comprehensive assessment together with longer term therapeutic interventions.

The models are not intended to be used as a checklist that provides automatic answers but as a tool that provides a framework for structured decision making at a multi-agency meeting.

The RJ assessment process – the second stage

The 'RJ' assessment model developed by the authors can be applied following the completion of the AIM initial assessment for young people who sexually abuse.

We are careful not to suggest that FGCs or indeed any other 'RJ' intervention will offer a panacea in all cases, but in many cases from our experience, there is the opportunity to address the abuse and make the situation safe for those affected. This restorative process must be assessment led to give an indication of its appropriateness and relevance. That is the purpose of our 'RJ' assessment model which provides a format of assessment for key participants, together with practice guidance on undertaking the assessment for professionals.

Following a referral from the AIM strategy meeting, a coordinator, who is independent of any agency, will contact all the parties to be involved to explain the process and gain their commitment to be involved. The independence of the coordinator is crucial as the previous experience of the family(s) with the statutory agencies may affect their willingness to participate and how they perceive the actual meeting. Additionally, it is crucial that neither party, the abuser nor the victim sees the coordinator as favouring or responsible for promoting the interests and views of the other.

FGCs will only take place after all the necessary preparation has been undertaken with all the participants, including the professionals. The FGC's success or otherwise is often largely dependent on the quality of the preparation and the meeting itself is seen as the finale to a lot of preparatory work. For this reason FGCs rarely offer a 'quick fix'. We estimate that an average of around 36 hours is spent in preparation for the meeting.

Preparatory work with the victim will focus upon identifying their needs and interests and how these can be best represented at the meeting. Victims interests are paramount if the FGC is to be truly restorative, however the meeting will need to acknowledge that in addition to the 'index' victim, many others are affected by the abuse.

Preparation with the abuser will need to examine how the young person might avoid being intimidated by what could be a large group and a very challenging experience. It will focus upon the expression of remorse and the need to construct a plan which both addresses the abuse and re-integrates the abuser back into a supportive network to prevent a re-occurrence of the behaviour.

Preparation with all other participants is to ensure that they all understand the reason they have been invited; to meet the needs of the victim and address the abuse. Participants need to be aware that the meeting is intended to be constructive and future focused. It is not a forum to attack and marginalise. A 'bottom line' is often established in the plans which need to reflect the crucial concerns of the statutory agencies.

Preparation with the professionals should focus upon their specific role in the meeting. This is limited to expressing what concerns might be and providing information to the meeting as to what services and resources are available to facilitate the plan. In that sense professionals do not control the meeting and this is a crucial factor in the empowering philosophy, which underpins all FGC practice.

The coordinator has primary responsibility to ensure the safe and just application of the process but no overall responsibility for the implementation of the plan. In some circumstances a review FGC may be called to monitor the plan.

The meeting will normally take place at a neutral and independent venue, at a time agreed by the participants. The meeting falls into four main stages:

- Information sharing; the facts of the offence are established, victims have the opportunity to explain how they have been affected and the 'offender' has the opportunity to make an initial response.
- Professionals say what concerns/resources they have and outline their 'bottom line' with regards to a plan.
- Private family planning time; the family alone have the opportunity to talk and devise a plan of action to address the concerns raised in parts one and two of the 'FGC'.

- Agreeing the plan; all participants re-convene and consider the plan, services are agreed, the plan is 'reality checked' and review arrangements considered.

The following case study illustrates the process and issues encountered in the application of the models.

Case study

Background

Referral January 2005 – Steven, aged 14 years committed an indecent assault on Jessica aged 12, the best friend of his sister. As a result he was made subject to a 12 month Referral order.

An initial AIM assessment was completed by February and placed Steven in the low concern/medium – high strengths category but noted that Steven had mild learning disabilities and that his parents experience a level of difficulty/inconsistency in setting and enforcing boundaries. This was further exacerbated by the fact that his care was shared by his parents Lyn and Jim, who had lived apart since his early childhood.

In March the coordinator visited Steven and his parents to explore the potential for an FGC and Stevens's attitude to the offence and its consequences. It was clear that Steven was a quiet and shy individual who was overwhelmed by events. Whilst Jim remained in the background throughout the interview, Lyn was more vocal and felt strongly that Jessica bore some responsibility for the offence and she clearly felt judged that her actions on the day of the offence in not contacting Jessica's mother required justification. Time was given for them to think about their involvement in the restorative process.

Subsequent visits built a rapport and sense of trust with Steven which enabled him to talk in his own words about what had happened. It became clear that he was placed in the impossible position of accepting responsibility for the offence with the support of his father but having to reconcile this with his mother's view which placed far more responsibility on Jessica and was defensive in approach.

A referral panel meeting was set for early April and Steven and his father attended; neither the victim nor her mother attended but Susan a victim contact worker employed by the YOT attended and gave a brief account of the victim's views. As part of the contract it was agreed that Steven would continue with the FGC process on a voluntary basis.

Jessica

First contact made in March with Jessica and her mother, Kate; Jessica appeared to have recovered from the initial trauma of the abuse, she wanted to put it behind her and 'get on with her life'. For her the greatest repercussion had been in respect of her friendship with Paula, Stevens's younger sister. This relationship had continued but was under tremendous stress.

Two weeks later during a follow up visit both Jessica and her mother expressed an interest in taking the process further. It was agreed that Jessica's father, who was estranged from Kate would not participate. A further two visits addressed issues outlined by the RJ Assessment framework. The final stages of preparation focused on a jointly agreed set of ground rules in respect of how the meeting would run.

Steven

At the Referral Order Panel the option of a FGC was discussed and seen as beneficial.

At this stage it was important to involve Lyn since she was the major 'opinion former' within the family. Lyn's volatility and unwillingness to move from her fixed interpretations of the assault made this element of the process very difficult. She would speak on behalf of Steven and close down any opportunity for him to express his own views. She constantly characterised her communication within the FGC with Kate as being volatile and confrontational. We agreed with her a strategy for managing her temper and monitoring her own emotions. At the time she felt she may 'lose it' she would make a coded statement to the meeting facilitator which would instigate a break to be called and Jim to respond to her concerns outside of the meeting.

Professionals

Preparation took place with the Referral Order Coordinator and two follow up meetings were held with the YOT caseworker. Steven had been out of education for over two years and this offence further complicated and reduced his opportunities to return to education. It was agreed that the meeting should invite the education worker to participate, this was presented to Jessica and Kate and resulted in a week's delay of the meeting, which they agreed to.

The meeting

The venue was the local victim support office and participants included; Jessica (victim of the offence), Kate (victims mother), Steven (offender), Jim (Steven's father), Dave (YOT education worker), Chris (Steven's mentor).

- Steven was able to hear and respond to the questions raised by Jessica and Kate. These related to the potential for continuing Jessica's and Paula's friendship. Steven was able to give a sincere and direct assurance of Jessica's safety to her and her mother.
- Steven was able to express an apology for his behaviour.
- Jessica and Kate were able to hear the efforts made by Steven to address the behaviour and the support given by his father to achieve this.
- Plans were made for Steven to return to school and his education worker was able to answer questions from Steven.
- Jim was able to describe the impact of the offence on him and his family, the rows caused between him and Lyn and the shame he felt about Steven's behaviour.
- Jim quietly, but powerfully said that the meeting had been a lot to do with Steven but that he wanted to hear what had been done to assist and support Jessica. Kate thanked him for his concern.
- Both families were able to see the impact of the offence for all concerned and the commonality of that experience and the need to prepare a joint plan to prevent re-occurrence and resolve future friendships and contact issues.
- An action plan was created with regard to Steven with his full cooperation.
- The question of Jessica's ongoing contact with Paula was considered and it was agreed how it could be continued in a way which offered safety to Jessica.
- Lynn withdrew from the process, but had her view represented by a statement read by the facilitator.

This early case represents the benefits of the approach but also highlights some of the difficulties such as adult agendas having the potential to overwhelm or subvert the process. Since then we have continued to develop the practice. Around 50 per cent of all referrals have led to a meeting being held. Reasons for not progressing include victims declining involvement or assessment indicating inappropriateness. Some cases have worked alongside the formal criminal justice processes such as the case study; others have been completed well beyond formal sentencing, at a time when the offender has completed an intervention programme.

Issues of timing are critical and particular to each situation and it is difficult to give a generalised ruling that fits all cases.

Lessons learnt on the Greater Manchester journey

We have been cautiously encouraged by developments in Greater Manchester so far and our experience usefully indicates a number of lessons/considerations in applying a restorative model to cases of sexual abuse.

Timing is crucial as it might be that the criminal justice system via a referral order sees an ideal opportunity early in the process but the victim or the family may not be ready to engage in the process. Whilst many decisions need to be made shortly after disclosure and the planning element of the FGC might facilitate family engagement in this, the raw feelings and shock after the event can make effective dialogue difficult to achieve. Invitations to support have consolidated into condemnation and the only conceivable reaction is one of exile for the abuser.

It is important to allow sufficient time to undertake what is often a time consuming and complex process. The time spent in sensitive preparation more than pays dividends in terms of effective meetings.

The abusers attitude to the abuse and its aftermath is central and critical to the process; there is great danger in attempting to use the meeting to force issues of remorse, accountability and shame on behalf of the abuser. The cost to be paid here is potential re-victimisation of the victim. However, hearing and others hearing, a genuine admission of responsibility and expression of remorse is a very powerful

vindication and affirmation for the victim. Again this might have influence upon the timing issue since the abuser's initial attitudes may well be altered by engagement in an intervention programme.

Consideration needs to be given to issues of power, authority, gender and parental roles. This is true of most conflict resolution processes but clearly it is more acute and complex with a case of a sexual nature. Issues of what constitutes acceptable behaviour may not be commonly shared by participants. Equally a well-facilitated conference will enable a discussion and articulation of these differences leading to a challenge of oppressive beliefs and behaviour. Mediator neutrality does not equate to maintenance of power imbalance and oppression.

Access of specialist services for victims needs to be identified. A parallel planning process around addressing the victim's needs as well as the needs of the abuser should be in place; this can be achieved by the development of an assessment model in respect of victims to ascertain their level of resilience and need. 'Each victim reacts in a very individual way to their experience' (Doig and Wallace, 1999). In addition, the relatively young age of the victim presents significant challenges around engagement and representation.

One of the significant inhibiters on the development of restorative approaches may well be the fragmented approach of victim services for children who have been abused. It is our experience that some victims receive prompt and appropriate services but many do not.

Consider and include the impact upon siblings. Increasingly work with sexual offenders attempts to locate effective practice in the social ecology of the offender, recognising the value and importance of family work in consolidating resilience. In a recent survey of practitioners in the field (Hackett, 2004) there was a strong consensus on the need to work with parents and families in seeking to manage sexually abusive behaviour, with 85 per cent of the whole sample 'agreeing that interventions need to be focused on the young person's living environment as much as individual treatment'.

Be sensitive to the use of language. Endeavour to use the participants language as much as possible and not resort to the 'protection' offered by professional speak which is excluding and unhelpful. Language can be problematic when describing sexual behaviour, and is important when assigning meaning and value as well as motive in respect of the behaviour.

Fundamentally, the assessment process should endeavour to identify positive and resilience factors as well as risk. Over emphasis upon risk and deficit dysfunction often skews professionals to conservatism and denial of potential and prevents a more balanced view of a given situation.

Conclusion and where to from here . . .

In this chapter we have focused on the potential for restorative approaches to adolescent sexual abuse. As our experience accumulates we are also realising the benefits of related practices and models and gaining some confidence in adapting the process to the particular needs of the family or situation. Thus, if victims are not willing or yet able to participate there is often real benefit in 'welfare' FGC to facilitate a family discussion on the impact of what has happened and the effect it has had on others within the abuser's family. The planning focus may well be the monitoring strategy for the young person.

One such case example is a 15-year-old boy who sexually assaulted his five-year-old cousin. The FGC considered issues around his return to the family after serving a period in custody. It also enabled the family members to articulate the conflict and confusion they have acutely felt in trying to come to terms with what has happened and their fears and hopes for the future.

Ultimately we would hope to facilitate conferences which had a planning focus upon the needs and interests of the victim; this would be a truly balanced restorative approach. However, to achieve this self evidently requires the reality of specific and comprehensive services to young victims of sexual abuse.

There is hope for this in the UK with the establishment of Sexual Assault Referral Centres and the moves they are making towards meeting the needs of young victims. We are working in partnership with our local 'SARC' to assist in creating a service more appropriate to the needs of younger victims and recognising the implications that follow from the reality that the young abuser may well be in the same immediate or extended family.

In other cases the particular need to make a

plan is not so acute. Instead, the focus shifts to the emphasis upon dialogue and communication. It would be wrong to describe these meetings as FGC's as the private planning element may be absent. Instead, we see them as facilitated restorative meetings.

What we know from evaluations of the FGC's we have run around sexually harmful behaviour is that overwhelmingly what participant's value the most highly is the opportunity to have dialogue around the harm and consequences of the abuse.

Family members tell us that they have not had the opportunity to simply just sit, talk and listen in an environment that doesn't invite blame, labelling, anger and further hurt. They wanted an emotionally safe space in which to talk about the conflict they have to manage, the pain of seeing the family pulled apart, the shame and danger of wider community knowledge, the practical consequences of re-structured family rules and the sometimes resented and resisted intrusion of professional 'help'.

In effect, what we are offering is a facilitated dialogue which is only part of a process of the re-narration of that family identity. They draw upon the reservoirs of family strength and resource to consider what can be done to enable them to move forward. This metaphor of journey and progress features so often in their reflections. Not a return to 'normality' as the events have been so momentous that this can never happen, but an inclusion of the learning and understanding and a re-assertion that despite what has happened this is a strong and 'viable' family which can both condemn and support as appropriate. There is, then, a desire to restore positive pathways.

The anthropologist Gay Becker, in her book *Disrupted Lives* (1999) tells us 'We see how people organise stories of disruption into linear accounts of chaos that gradually return to order'. And how very often narrative is the primary form for the mediation of this disruption. Becker goes on to observe '. . . through stories people organise, display and work through their experiences. Narrative can be a potent force in mediating disruption . . . narratives are performative, and thus empowering. They represent action, and thus agency.' Family members place great value on this agency and often contrast it with the powerlessness they felt in the face of the initial disclosure and the subsequent response from associated concerned professionals. The metaphor of recovery of strength and inclusion of the experience is regularly expressed by family members: 'We are stronger after this'; 'We have had to pull together'; 'It blew us apart, but now in many ways we are closer together'.

The preparation to enable the FGM to take place may be seen as assistance to this process, opening up safe channels of communication and encouraging reflection. On some occasions the 'formality' of the FGM represents the culmination of this process.

As facilitators we have a sense that, in reality, though it may mark some sense of 'milestone on the journey', what we have done in that process is create safe spaces, give permission (or even expectation) to talk and listen, and this process continues for the family well beyond the final facilitated event.

In addition to the FGC's that we have run, we see the need for facilitation of dialogue and conversation on a macro scale, between the two professional populations of restorative practitioners and those working in the sexually harmful youth field. Towards this end in June 2006, together with the UK's Restorative Justice Consortium, we organised a national conference to consider the application of restorative processes in the SHB field. This drew practitioners from the two areas into a conversation, which was informed by examples of practice from both the UK and with young adults in Denmark.

Locally, we have been keen to train and equip Referral Order panel members with sufficient skills and knowledge to feel confident in using this process with cases of sexually harmful behaviour and enable Youth Offender Teams Victim Contact staff to make sensitive contact with a group whom the criminal justice system have continued to ignore.

We are taking this work forward cautiously but with conviction and confidence. The potential is to combine the traditionally opposed victim and abuser perspectives to increase the effectiveness of addressing the offence. The progress of restorative approaches within the Criminal Justice system echoes advances in addressing adolescent sexual abuse. Moreover, the particular profile of the adolescent sexual abuser offers unique possibilities for restorative approaches. That it also offers particular challenges and difficulties goes without saying; however this should not deflect us or deter us from considered and thoughtful progress. To do otherwise is to allow professional fear and prejudice to overcome the need to face the future.

References

Becker, G. (1999) *Disrupted Lives: How People Create Meaning in a Chaotic World.* University of California Press.

Blagg, H. (1997) A Just Measure of Shame. *British Journal of Criminology*, 37: 4, 481–501.

Braithwaite, J. (1998) Restorative Justice. In Tony, M. (Ed.) *Handbook of Crime and Punishment.* Oxford University Press.

Crawford, A. and Newburn, T. (2003) *Youth Offending and Restorative Justice.* Willan Publishing.

Daly, K. (2002) *Restorative Justice: The Real Story.* Paper presented at Scottish Criminology Conference, Edinburgh, Sept 2000.

Daly, K. (2004) Sexual Assault and Restorative Justice. In Strang, H. and Braithwaite, J. (Eds.) *Restorative Justice and Family Violence.* Cambridge University Press.

Daly, K. and Curtis-Fawley, S. (2004) Restorative Justice and Sexual Assault. In Heimer, K. and Kruttschnitt, C. (Eds.) *Gender and Crime: Patterns of Victimization and Offending.* New York: New York University Press.

Doig, M. and Wallace, B. (1999) *Family Conference Team,* Paper presented to Restoration for Victims of Crime Conference, Australian Institute of Criminology, Sept 1999.

Gilgun, J. F. (1990) Factors Mediating the Effects of Childhood Mistreatment. In Hunter, M. (Ed.) *The Sexually Abused Male: Prevalence, Impact and Treatment.* Lexington, MA: Lexington Books.

Gilgun, J. F. (1999) CASPARS: New Tools for Assessing Client Risks and Strengths. *Families in Society*, 80, 450–9.

Gilgun, J. F. (1999) CASPARS: Clinical Assessment Instruments that Measure Strengths and Risks in Children and Families. In Calder, M. C. (Ed.) *Working with Young People who Sexually Abuse: New Pieces of the Jigsaw Puzzle.* Lyme Regis: Russell House Publishing.

Gilgun, J. F. (2000) Clinical Applications of the CASPARS Instruments; Boys who act out sexually. *Families in Society*, 80, 629–41.

Hackett, S. (2004) *What Works for Children and Young People With Sexually Harmful Behaviours?* Basingstoke: Barnardo's.

Heimer, K. and Kruttschnitt, C. (Eds.) (2005) *Gender and Crime; Patterns of Victimization and*

Offending. New York: New York University Press.

Hudson, B. (2002) Restorative Justice and Gendered Violence. *British Journal of Criminology*, 42: 3.

Jones, D. and Ramchandani, P. (1999) *Child Sexual Abuse: Informing Practice from Research*. Oxford: Ratcliffe Press.

Lacy, N. (1998) Unspeakable Subjects, Imposible Rights; Sexuality, Intregrity and Criminal Law. *Canadian Journal of Law and Jurisprudence*, 11: 1, 47–68.

Marshall, T. (1999) *Restorative Justice, An Overview*. London: Home Office.

Pressener, L. and Lowencamp, C.T. (1999) Restorative Justice and Offender Screening. *Journal of Criminal Justice*. 27: 4, 333–43.

Rich, P. (2003) *Understanding, Assessing and Rehabilitating Juvenile Sex Offenders*. NY: John Wiley and Sons.

Ryan, G. et al. (1996) Trends in a National Survey of Sexually Abusive Youths. *Journal of the American Academy of Child and Adolescent Psychiatry*. 33:17–25.

Sharpe, S. (1998) *Restorative Justice*. Alberta, Edmonton Victim Offender Mediation Society.

Sherman, L.W. and Strang, H. (2007) *Restorative Justice: The Evidence*. Esmee Fairburn Foundation/Smith Institute Report.

Chapter 18

Treating Juveniles Who Commit Sex Offences: Historical Approaches, Contemporary Practices and Future Directions

Kurt Bumby and Thomas Talbot

Introduction

Unless the recommendations in this paper are followed, the balance of research on juvenile sexual aggression will likely shift from psychology to criminology. The groundswell of support that launched so many JSO programs will eventually die out for wont of data on effectiveness.

(Weinrott, 1996: 88)

A full decade has passed since Weinrott proffered this cautionary statement about juvenile sex offender treatment which, at the time, was founded on tenuous empirical footings at best. Prompted then by largely unquestioned assumptions about commonly employed interventions with these youth, this warning remains a reasonable concern today in some ways. Indeed, despite the paucity of a compelling research-based endorsement of prevailing approaches to juvenile sex offender treatment, the number of specialised programmes has continued to increase substantially. In the United States alone, well over 900 treatment programmes are currently available for juvenile sex offenders, nearly twice the number of programmes in existence in 1996 (McGrath, Cumming and Burchard, 2003).

Although rigorous treatment outcome research has not advanced at an adequate pace to fully justify this proliferation of juvenile sex offence-specific programming, there has been an expansion of important research and professional literature involving this special population of youthful offenders that can be useful for informing intervention strategies. The aim of this chapter is to highlight some of this literature within the context of contemporary approaches, with an eye toward the future of promising practices for the treatment of juvenile sex offenders. Before providing an analysis of where the field currently stands, we will first review the shadows from which offence-specific treatment for juveniles has emerged.

The beginnings

The unofficial birth of juvenile sex offender treatment can be traced conservatively to the early to middle part of the twentieth century, during which time interventions for these youth were relatively scarce, largely uninformed, and widely varied. Among the approaches to treatment were short-term psychiatric services, traditional psychoanalysis, juvenile court-referred counselling, and a range of individual and family interventions through child guidance clinics (Atcheson and Williams, 1954; Doshay, 1943; Karpman, 1954; Maclay, 1960; Markey, 1950). Notwithstanding these variations, it is of interest to note that in its infancy, some of the underlying tenets of juvenile sex offender treatment appeared to foreshadow modern-day considerations and approaches to intervention for these youth.

For example, early researchers and practitioners hypothesised that a range of etiological considerations and multiple developmental pathways were associated with juvenile sex offending, and suggested that treatment should be multifaceted and designed to address these multiple determinants (Arieff and Rotman, 1942; Doshay, 1943; Karpman, 1954; Markey, 1950; Richmond, 1933; Waggoner and Boyd, 1941). Moreover, through preliminary research, the diversity of juvenile sex offenders became evident: some youth were determined to be psychosexually disturbed and in need of specialised treatment, others were considered to be predisposed to *non*-sexual behaviour problems and thus warranting more delinquency-focused legal interventions, and still other youth were deemed to have no intervention needs, either because their sexual behaviours were believed to be transitory in nature or within the realm of normal adolescent development (Arieff and Rotman, 1942; Atcheson and Williams, 1954; Doshay, 1943; Gardner, 1950; Karpman, 1954; Markey, 1950; Richmond, 1931; Waggoner and Boyd, 1941). In addition, during these early years, various scholars recognised the importance of considering adolescent development when designing interventions for youthful sex offenders and alluded to the need for approaches to treatment that differed from adult programming (Doshay, 1943; Gardner, 1950; Maclay, 1960). Finally, initial research revealed a noteworthy feature that has since been replicated – that juveniles who commit sex offences do not inevitably commit further sex crimes as adults; rather, if these youth recidivate, the crimes are more likely to be non-sexual in nature (Doshay, 1943).

Although professional writings of the times suggested a modicum of interest in the treatment of juvenile sex offenders, these youth were largely overlooked in the scientific community and society in general in the many years that followed. This neglect was, in part, a function of the belief that deviant or problematic sexual behaviours were a phase out of which these youth would grow. Ironically, it was this inattention to juvenile-perpetrated sex offences that would become a phase out of which the *field* would grow.

The formative years

The social sciences literature was nearly silent on the topic for roughly two decades, after which time juvenile sex offender treatment entered a more prominent stage of development and appeared as an area of growing import among researchers and practitioners (see e.g., Groth, 1977, 1979; Knopp, 1982; Lewis, Shankok and Pincus, 1978; Wakeling, 1979). The burgeoning interest in the treatment of juvenile sex offenders can be principally attributed to the discovery that, for many adult sex offenders, the onset of their offending behaviours occurred during adolescence (see e.g., Abel, Mittleman and Becker, 1985; Groth, 1979; Groth, Longo and McFadin, 1982; Longo, 1982; Longo and Groth, 1983). An accompanying assumption was that the prevention of additional sex crimes was in part contingent upon the provision of specialised intervention for youthful sex offenders.

Because a widely accepted model of offence-specific treatment had already emerged with adult sex offenders internationally – namely cognitive-behavioural and relapse prevention interventions carried out in a peer-group modality – it was presumed that such interventions were generalisable to juveniles.

Perhaps understandably, practitioners readily adopted these adult-oriented treatment models with youthful offenders, and juvenile sex offender treatment became inextricably linked to, and largely dependent on practices within, the adult sex offender treatment field. As such, when formalised sex offence-specific treatment programmes for juveniles emerged in the late 1970s and early 1980s, it became difficult to discern significant differences between adult and juvenile programming, with the exception of the inclusion of family systems interventions for juvenile sex offenders (see e.g., Knopp, 1982, 1985).

To illustrate, commonly referenced targets of intervention for juvenile sex offenders included identifying a cycle or pattern of offending behaviours, interrupting this abusive cycle, developing victim empathy, managing deviant sexual arousal, identifying and modifying cognitive distortions that support offending behaviour, and developing relapse prevention plans (see e.g., Knopp, 1982, 1985). And although some juvenile sex offender treatment pioneers recognised the need for developmentally responsive interventions, the absence of a body of empirical research to inform treatment practices remained a barrier to the design, implementation, and evaluation of specialised services for these youth.

The growth period

During the latter part of the twentieth century, juvenile sex offender treatment evolved into a cottage industry. The number of identified programmes for youthful sex offenders expanded exponentially in North America, from less than two dozen specialised treatment programmes in 1982 to roughly 800 such programmes ten years later (see Freeman-Longo et al., 1995; Knopp, 1985; National Adolescent Perpetrator Network, 1988, 1993). Emerging data on the incidence and prevalence of sexual victimisation, indicating that juveniles were responsible for a significant proportion of these offences, served as one catalyst for the marked expansion of these programmes (see e.g., Barbaree and Marshall, 2006; Ryan, 1997; and Zimring, 2004 for reviews).

This surge in specialised programming for juvenile sex offenders also coincided with a dramatic shift within the broader juvenile justice field. Sparked by a 'juvenile crime wave' within

North America during the mid-1980s and early 1990s, sweeping reforms were implemented in the United States and Canada, reflecting an emerging desire to 'treat juveniles like adults' as a means of enhancing public safety (see e.g., Fagan and Zimring, 2000; Howell, 2003; Torbet and Szymanski, 1998). Without question, crimes such as sex offences were among those targeted as many of the juvenile crime reforms were enacted (see e.g., Heinz and Ryan, 1997; Letourneau, 2006; Zimring, 2004).

The intense focus on crime prevention with youthful offenders in general prompted an exploration of 'what works' to rehabilitate juvenile sex offenders specifically. Ironically, at a time when some scholars questioned the efficacy of sex offence-specific treatment for adults, many professionals championed the promise of such treatment for youth, further contributing to the flourishing of specialised programming for juvenile sex offenders. These programmes, however, continued to be plagued by a lack of empirically-supported direction and, in many ways, continued to parallel treatment interventions originally designed for adult sex offenders.

In partial response to this challenge in the United States, the National Adolescent Perpetrator Network (NAPN) established the Task Force on Juvenile Sex Offending to review the relevant literature and provide consensus-driven guidance to the field (NAPN, 1988, 1993). The Final Report, heralded as the 'current "state of the art" as it is understood by experts, researchers, and practitioners' (NAPN, 1993, p. 6), drew widespread attention to the importance of individualised and developmentally sensitive treatment for juvenile sex offenders, emphasised the need to ensure a continuum of services, highlighted the importance of family interventions, and argued for a more holistic view of these youth (NAPN, 1993).

This era also gave rise to the first major texts on treatment for juvenile sex offenders (see e.g., Barbaree, Marshall and Hudson, 1993; Ryan and Lane, 1991) providing resources that had been sorely lacking for years. Written by a small group of internationally renowned researchers and practitioners, these seminal works began to articulate more explicitly some of the unique developmental considerations and etiological factors warranting consideration when developing effective interventions for juvenile sex offenders. In so doing, they began to shape the field by challenging the blind application of adult treatment models to juvenile programming, emphasising that 'it is clear that the juvenile sex offender is not simply a smaller or younger adult sex offender, and he should not be treated as such' (Barbaree et al., 1993: xiv).

Taken together, these guidebooks and an ever-growing body of research and practice literature set the stage for a more tailored approach to – and informed consistency across – juvenile sex offender treatment programming. Moreover, these resources advocated for better integrated, coordinated, and multidisciplinary responses to juvenile sex offenders that extended beyond the sole reliance on treatment interventions, through the suggested development of multidisciplinary partnerships that included specialised treatment providers, supervision agents, juvenile court personnel, child welfare and family services representatives, and victim therapists and advocates (see e.g., American Academy of Child and Adolescent Psychiatry, 1999; Barbaree and Cortoni, 1993; Becker and Kaplan, 1993; NAPN, 1993; Ryan and Lane, 1991).

By this point in time, the foundation of contemporary juvenile sex offender treatment had become firmly established. Specialised programmes were beginning to address issues that were particularly germane to adolescents, such as dating and relationship skills, sex education, positive and healthy sexuality, and values clarification. Additionally, the importance of involving and intervening with caregivers and other sources of support had gained prominence in the treatment literature and was becoming common practice in programmes for youthful sex offenders (see e.g., Ryan and Lane, 1997). And to a lesser extent, treatment programmes began to incorporate multimodal approaches such as experiential, expressive, and art therapies into the cadre of adjunctive interventions, thus offering the potential to be more responsive to the varying developmental needs of these youth (Freeman-Longo et al., 1995).

However, while emphasising a number of adolescent-oriented treatment needs and strategies, many of the proposed models of intervention for sexually abusive youth continued to mirror in many ways the original 'adult-like' models of treatment (see e.g., Barbaree et al., 1993; NAPN, 1993) – and it was not long before these approaches began to draw sharp criticism.

Concerns about labeling these youth emerged, apprehension around a primary focus on peer-group interventions arose, and uncertainty about the lack of demonstrated efficacy of specialised, offence-specific treatment approaches surfaced (see e.g., Chaffin and Bonner, 1998; Ryan, 1997b; Weinrott, 1996). Consequently, the juvenile sex offender treatment field, much like adolescents in general, began to experience growing pains as it began to mature, struggle with its identity, and strive for separation and individuation apart from the adult sex offender field.

The maturation phase

The turn of the century has been marked by a period of slowed growth relative to the number of specialised programmes for juvenile sex offenders, while giving rise to more sophisticated research about sexually abusive youth – research that has the potential to inform treatment practices in significant ways. Most noteworthy are the attempts to provide empirical support for juvenile sex offender typologies, identify research-supported pathways and developmental trajectories for youth, confirm risk factors and validate risk assessment strategies specifically for youthful sex offenders, and conduct more rigorous evaluations of the efficacy of specialised treatment programmes (see e.g., Hunter, Figueredo, Malamuth and Becker, 2003; Hunter, Gilbertson, Vedros and Morton, 2004; Knight and Sims-Knight, 2003; Prentky, Harris, Frizzell and Righthand, 2000; Reitzel and Carbonell, 2006; Seto and Lalumiere, 2006; Smallbone, 2006; Worling and Curwen, 2001). Put simply, the underlying movement to become more evidence-based has become increasingly apparent within the field of juvenile sex offender management.

In addition, professional organisations around the globe have assumed a clear leadership role in advancing the cause of ensuring more informed approaches to juvenile sex offender treatment. For example, in the United Kingdom, the National Organisation for the Treatment of Abusers (NOTA) issued a position paper on the management of youth who have engaged in sex offending behaviours, emphasising the differences between adults and juveniles and the need for individualised, flexible, and integrated system responses (NOTA, 2005). Similarly, the

Association for the Treatment of Sexual Abusers (ATSA), an international organisation that had traditionally focused on adult sex offender management, also produced a position statement regarding juveniles who commit sex offences and outlined the importance of measured clinical and legal responses to these youth (ATSA, 2000). Along a similar vein, the American Academy of Child and Adolescent Psychiatry (AACAP), the Center for Sex Offender Management (CSOM), and the National Center on the Sexual Behaviour of Youth (NCSBY) – to name a few – have all argued for the importance of developmentally responsive approaches to treatment for youth who have engaged in sex offending behaviours (AACAP, 1999; CSOM, 1999; NCBSY, 2003).

Moreover, the rapidly increasing body of contemporary academic and clinical literature within the juvenile sex offender management arena reflects the need to reconsider, revise, and expand the range of treatment interventions and other strategies for these youth. These writings emphasise the importance of addressing the multiple determinants of delinquent and other problem behaviour during adolescence and advocate for more integrated and holistic approaches to treatment for juveniles who have committed sex offences (Barbaree and Marshall, 2006; Borduin and Schaeffer, 2002; Hunter et al., 2004; Hunter and Longo, 2004; O'Reilly, Marshall, Carr and Beckett, 2004; Rich, 2003; Worling, 2004). Following a series of false starts, it appears that the time has come to move officially beyond the adult-oriented approaches to treating juveniles who have committed sex offences.

At the same time, however, when examining current practice patterns in juvenile sex offender treatment programmes, some interesting findings emerge. Mirroring the theories, frameworks, and key principles underlying adult sex offender treatment, the vast majority of contemporary programmes for juveniles continue to employ long-term, peer-group interventions in treatment programmes that are based on the traditional cognitive-behavioural and relapse prevention models (see e.g., Becker and Hicks, 2003; Chaffin, Letourneau and Silovsky, 2002; Hunter and Longo, 2004; McGrath et al., 2003; Worling, 2004). In addition, most specialised treatment programmes for youth report primary targets of intervention that are nearly identical to those within adult sex offender treatment programmes and, when placed side by side for comparison, the core components and approaches used in juvenile and adult sex offender programmes remain nearly indistinguishable in many ways (see e.g., McGrath et al., 2003). And although social-ecological and multi-systemic approaches have been touted as especially promising models of intervention for juveniles who have committed sex offences (Borduin, Henggeler, Blaske and Stein, 1990; Borduin and Shaeffer, 2002; Hunter et al., 2004), only a relatively small percentage of programmes report employing a multisystemic framework as a primary theory to drive programming efforts (McGrath et al., 2003). Furthermore, although the majority of juvenile sex offender treatment programmes report using family interventions as part of an overall approach to intervention, a closer inspection reveals that family sessions are only provided on the average of once per month (McGrath et al., 2003).

At this point, the perplexed reader may be tempted to pose the question: 'Then what has *genuinely* changed with respect to treating juvenile sex offenders?' – and such a query could be met with the pessimistic response 'not much.' Despite the advances in research that have led to an increased understanding of juvenile sex offenders and the important differences between juvenile and adult sex offenders, and the mounting evidence highlighting the need to modify treatment programmes accordingly, the possibility exists that the field has not yet 'caught up' with the emerging professional lore. We offer, however, a more optimistic perspective about the current state of juvenile sex offender treatment.

With respect to the polls of professional practice patterns from which the more dismal conclusion might be drawn, we submit that it is quite difficult in broad quantitative surveys to fully capture some of the specific qualitative shifts (e.g. the use of developmentally sensitive language, consideration of process-related variables, more integrated service delivery, increased focus on family, peer, and school factors) that have been highlighted in contemporary literature and have begun to occur in the delivery of juvenile sex offender treatment. Thus, the apparent similarities in programmes for adults and juveniles who commit sex offences may actually be an artefact of measurement challenges, rather than a widespread failure to modify treatment practices for youthful offenders.

Notwithstanding the seemingly minimal changes in surveyed programmes and their

practices, it can also be reasonably argued that many of the typical targets of intervention within juvenile sex offender treatment programmes are not, by any means, without merit. Indeed, given the type and nature of the behaviours to be addressed and some of the risk factors and intervention needs that are common to both juvenile and adult sex offenders, it is perhaps illogical to expect that treatment programmes for juveniles and adults must be mutually exclusive in theoretical approach or content. Moreover, one cannot dismiss the treatment outcome research which, although quite limited, provides some evidence of the efficacy of the more 'traditional' cognitive-behavioural programmes for youthful sex offenders; significantly lower rates of sexual and non-sexual recidivism have been revealed for treated versus untreated juvenile sex offenders (see e.g., McGovern, Poey and Otis, 2004; Reitzel and Carbonell, 2006).

Contemporary challenges and controversies

Certainly, the need for further refinement of juvenile sex offender treatment and the importance of additional rigorous treatment outcome research are clear. For example, it has yet to have been determined which treatment modalities or approaches yield the most promising outcomes overall, or if different types of interventions are more effective with different types of youth (see e.g., Chaffin et al., 2002; Hunter and Longo, 2004; Langton and Barbaree, 2006; Marshall and Fernandez, 2004; O'Reilly and Carr, 2006). The issue of desistance also warrants examination, as it is increasingly clear that juveniles who commit sex offences are not destined to continue perpetrating into adulthood and, indeed, some juvenile sex offenders desist without formal intervention (Nisbet, Wilson and Smallbone, 2004; O'Reilly and Carr, 2006; Smallbone, 2006; Worling and Langstrom, 2006). In addition, treatment interventions have not been sufficiently tailored to address special populations, including juvenile female sex offenders (see e.g., Bumby and Bumby, 2004; Hunter, Becker and Lexier, 2006; Mathews, Hunter and Vuz, 1997), individuals who suffer from significant mental health difficulties or cognitive impairments (see e.g., Haaven and Coleman, 2000; Lane and Lobanov-Rostovsky, 1997; O'Callaghan, 1999, 2004), or juveniles whose cultural differences may warrant different approaches to intervention (see e.g., Bullens and Van Wijk, 2004; Burton, Smith-Darden and Frankel, 2006; Longo, 2003; Thomas, 2004). Beyond the differential treatment implications for these and other special populations, it is commonly recognised that juveniles who commit sex offences are a heterogeneous group with varied levels of risk and needs. As such, 'one-size-fits-all' approaches to intervention are neither appropriate nor likely to be effective. Yet to date, questions still remain about the extent to which programmes have risen to the challenge of genuinely individualising treatment to meet both the common and unique needs of juveniles and their families.

Furthermore, a number of controversial areas of practice exist within the juvenile sex offender field, with accompanying implications for the effective treatment of these youth. Perhaps most noteworthy are the continued emphasis on peer-group interventions with juveniles, an over-reliance on residential and institutional placements, the increasing use of the polygraph in treatment programmes, pharmacological medications as adjunctive interventions, and the growing tendency to apply legislation and other management policies to juveniles who have committed sex offences in the same manner as adult sex offenders.

Peer-group interventions

Although individual and family therapies are commonly reported components of juvenile sex offender treatment, the group modality remains favoured in many programmes (Longo, 2003; McGrath et al., 2003; Worling, 2004). This has become a source of heightened concern and controversy, in light of the research indicating potential for iatrogenic outcomes when delinquent peers are treated together in a group setting (see e.g., Arnold and Hughes, 1999; Chamberlain and Reid, 1998; Dishion and Andrews, 1995; Dishion, McCord and Poulin, 1999). More specifically, researchers warn that through 'deviancy training,' or the peer reinforcement of antisocial or delinquent attitudes and values, the anticipated positive effects of intervention may be potentially mitigated or undermined in some circumstances (Arnold and Hughes, 1999; Chamberlain and Reid, 1998; Dishion et al., 1999).

It is also recognised, however, that the group modality can maximise limited treatment resources, and can provide important opportunities to teach, model, and practice prosocial skills and relationships with peers (AACAP, 1999; Jones, 2003; Rich, 2003; Rose, 1998; Worling, 2004). In addition, there is a considerable body of literature to support peer group interventions within the child and adolescent mental health and juvenile justice arena (see e.g., Lipsey and Wilson, 1998; Rose, 1998). Moreover, the vast majority of research demonstrating a significant treatment effect for juvenile sex offenders has been conducted on programmes using a peer-group modality as the primary strategy (see e.g., Alexander, 1999; Aos, Phipps, Barnoski and Lieb, 2001; Worling and Curwen, 2000). For these and other reasons, groups remain a common modality of treatment with youth. However, the research findings exposing the potential deleterious impact of group-based interventions with delinquent youth have justifiably given pause to experts and practitioners in the field of juvenile sex offender treatment. Further research on the risks and benefits of peer-group intervention with these youth is clearly necessary, particularly juvenile sex offenders in residential or institutional placements.

Over-reliance on residential and institutional placements

Interestingly, while the majority of treatment programmes for juvenile sex offenders in the United States are community-based, nearly half of all youthful sex offenders are actually placed in a residential or institutional setting for treatment (McGrath et al., 2003). This is not particularly surprising, in light of the out-of-home placement trends for youth in the juvenile justice system overall. To be sure, the number of youth – including juvenile sex offenders – placed in residential or institutional custody has increased markedly during the past two decades (see e.g., Bengis et al., 1999; Howell, 2003; Sickmund, 2002, 2004). The over-reliance on residential or institutional placements for juvenile sex offenders occurs for a host of speculative reasons – including myths about the appropriateness of community placement for juveniles who commit sex offences, understandable concerns about victim protection and public safety, a lack of confidence in available community-based treatment services, and limited capacity for specialised interventions in some communities.

Of great concern is that no evidence suggests that this often costly practice results in substantial reductions in recidivism for youthful offenders (Chaffin et al., 2002; Howell, 2003; Lipsey and Wilson, 1998). On the contrary, research suggests that interventions provided in a youth's natural environment are more likely to result in better outcomes (see e.g., Aos et al., 2001; Elliot, 1998; Henggeler et al., 1998; Kashani et al., 1999; Lipsey and Wilson, 1998; Tarolla et al., 2002). And with length of stays for juvenile sex offenders averaging over 16 months (McGrath et al., 2003), significant concerns are raised about the significant financial costs associated with extended placement, the potential for increased delinquency, interference with normal social development, and prolonged detachment from positive, prosocial supports and productive involvement within the family and community (Chaffin et al., 2002; Gies, 2003; Hunter et al., 2004). As such, a critical challenge within the juvenile sex offender treatment field centres around the successful transition and re-entry of these youth into their homes, schools, and communities following placement in residential or institutional settings (AACAP, 1999; Bengis, 1997; Bengis et al., 1999; Glover and Bumby, 2002; Greer, 1997).

Unfortunately, re-entry and aftercare have been long neglected within the juvenile justice system, with a lack of attention to the range of barriers that hamper reintegration efforts, including limited release planning, an erroneous belief that treatment must begin and end within the confines of a residential or institutional programme, incongruous polices and practices across relevant agencies, lack of coordinated service delivery and continuity of care, negative community sentiment, inadequate periods of post-release supervision in the community, and limited community supports (Altschuler and Armstrong, 1994; Altschuler, Armstrong and MacKenzie, 1999; Bumby, Talbot and Carter, in press; Gies, 2003; Glover and Bumby, 2002; Greer, 1997). On the bright side, surveys of both residential and community-based programmes for juvenile sex offenders indicate that the vast majority make dedicated efforts to educate family members about being part of a support system, and roughly one third of programmes also educate other members in the community (McGrath et al., 2003). Nonetheless, given the overall absence of a comprehensive re-entry strategy for youthful sex offenders, this will remain an area warranting additional attention in the field.

Pharmacological interventions

Among the more controversial areas of practice with juvenile sex offenders is the viability of pharmacological approaches to treatment. Such interventions, primarily the use of hormonal agents, antiandrogens, and selective serotonin reuptake inhibitors (SSRIs), are an arguably critical adjunct to traditional cognitive behavioural treatment with adult sex offenders whose deviant sexual fantasies, urges, or behaviours have proven particularly challenging to manage (see e.g., Bradford and Fedoroff, 2006; Glaser, 2003; Grubin, 2000). And because of the potential additive value under prescribed circumstances, some pharmacological interventions may be appropriate when included as part of a broader treatment regimen for certain juveniles who have committed sex offences – namely older, more impulsive youth, and those who evidence symptoms of paraphilic disorders (Bradford and Fedoroff, 2006; Hunter and Lexier, 1998; Rich, 2003; Sheerin, 2004; Worling, 2004).

Antiandrogens and hormonal agents are commonly referenced in the *adult* sex offender treatment literature because of their demonstrated efficacy on reducing sexual drives, urges, and behaviours (see e.g., Berlin, 2000; Glaser, 2003; Grubin, 2000). For adolescents, however, a lack of research – coupled with concerns about the potential impact on developmental and hormonal issues – has led experts to recommend against their use (AACAP, 1999; Bradford and Fedoroff, 2006; Hunter and Lexier, 1998). Consistent with the associated controversies, only a very small percentage of programmes for youthful sex offenders – less than 10 percent – report using antiandrogens and hormonal agents (McGrath et al., 2003).

The SSRIs, on the other hand, are considered an appropriate first line medication with both adult and juvenile sex offenders, particularly those who have comorbid mood, anxiety, or impulse-control disorders, because of their demonstrated efficacy for ameliorating symptoms of these disorders and the additional benefits derived from the common sexual side effects, such as reduced sexual drives and urges (AACAP, 1999; Bradford and Fedoroff, 2006; Sheerin, 2004). Indeed, a relatively large percentage of juvenile sex offender treatment programmes utilise SSRIs as a means of addressing deviant sexual arousal, fantasies, and urges (McGrath et al., 2003). Despite the promise of SSRIs, the Food and Drug Administration, the federal oversight agency in the United States that is responsible for regulating medications, recently warned about their use with adolescents because of the increased potential for increased self-harm and aggression toward others (FDA, 2004).

It is important to note that even within the field of *adult* sex offender treatment, the use of pharmacological interventions is not without controversy; questions exist regarding the potential range of side effects, the provision of informed consent with often involuntary clients, and the failure to use these agents as part of a more comprehensive and integrated treatment strategy (Glaser, 2003). In addition, some experts argue that neither the positive benefits nor the negative side effects of hormonal agents are understood fully (Glaser, 2003; Sheerin, 2004). Moreover, none of the classes of pharmacological agents has been sanctioned for use in the treatment of sexual deviance by the respective regulatory bodies in the United States, Canada, United Kingdom, or most other Western countries (Bradford and Fedoroff, 2006). Further research is clearly needed. In the meantime, careful risks-benefits analyses must be conducted before using pharmacological agents with juveniles, and close monitoring by qualified and experienced medical professionals is required in the event that such medications are deemed necessary (Bradford and Fedoroff, 2006; CSOM, 1999; Hunter and Lexier, 1998; Rich, 2003).

The polygraph in treatment

Originally popularised in adult sex offender treatment programmes, the use of the polygraph as a 'treatment tool' in programmes serving juvenile sex offenders has increased dramatically over the past few years. To illustrate, in North America alone, recent data indicates that 44 per-cent of community-based programmes and 30 percent of residential programmes use the polygraph to augment assessment and treatment strategies for youthful sex offenders, primarily as a means of facilitating the disclosure of sexual histories and monitoring treatment compliance; this reflects a nearly two- to three-fold increase over a five year period of time (McGrath et al., 2003).

Rudimentary examinations of polygraphy for sex offender management purposes reveal an increase in offence-related disclosures when this technology is employed, and proponents cite these findings as evidence of its utility and value (Ahlmeyer et al., 2000; Hindman and Peters, 2001). Critics counter with the absence of well-controlled research demonstrating the reliability or validity of the polygraph with adolescents (Becker and Harris, 2004; Hunter and Lexier, 1998). Nor is there any empirical evidence indicating that cumulative disclosures elicited through polygraphy have a deterrent effect on juvenile-perpetrated sex offences, promote within-treatment changes, or enhance treatment outcomes with juvenile sex offenders. Ongoing debates and opposing viewpoints about the ethics, value, and appropriateness of the polygraph have served to widen the professional chasm that exists around the use of this technology in juvenile sex offender treatment.

'Treat youth like adults' legislation

It is of interest to note that Weinrott's (1996) seminal review and critique also warned that, in the absence of a more systematic and empirically-grounded approach to juvenile sex offender treatment, policymakers would likely demand more punishment-driven and corrections-focused efforts and eliminate support for rehabilitative efforts. The very real potential for such a shift within the field of juvenile sex offender treatment has been foreshadowed by the movement toward punitive legislation and other management policies in the adult sex offender field. And, as anticipated, juvenile sex offenders have indeed become the subject of increased scrutiny from policymakers in recent years, with many of the legal mandates once reserved for adult sex offenders subsequently applied to juveniles in a burgeoning 'get tough' movement (Becker and Hicks, 2003; Caldwell, 2002; Letourneau, 2006; Letourneau and Miner, 2005; Trivits and Reuppucci, 2002; Zimring, 2004).

For example, when originally enacted, sex offender registration and notification requirements were applicable only to adult sex offenders in most states, yet most states now subject juveniles to these laws and policies (Caldwell, 2002; CSOM, 1999b; Garfinkle, 2003; Letourneau, 2006; Letourneau and Miner, 2005; Matson and Lieb, 1996; Trivits and Reppucci,

2002; Zimring, 2004). Similarly, while civil commitment and other sexually violent predator statutes generally did not apply to juvenile sex offenders, an increasing number of states require or allow for juveniles to be considered for indefinite commitment (Caldwell, 2002; Letourneau, 2006; Shaw, Heesacker and Delgado-Romero, 2001). And at the present time, lifetime supervision, electronic monitoring, and other punitive management approaches are pending in states and at the federal level (Letourneau, 2006; Schwartz, 2003; Zimring, 2004). Many of these adult-like policies and practices, which tend to be implemented at the expense of effective treatment interventions, have a significant potential to be unintentionally counter-therapeutic when applied to juveniles who have committed sex offences (Garfinkle, 2003; Howell, 2003; Shaw et al., 2001; Trivits and Reppucci, 2002; Zimring, 2004).

Promising practices and future directions: treatment and beyond

Lest the reader assume falsely that the current state of juvenile sex offender treatment is grim, we will close this chapter – with great enthusiasm – by highlighting some of the more noteworthy contemporary advances in the treatment and management of juveniles who commit sex offences. Building upon the theories and work of researchers and practitioners around the world, these approaches appear to be among the strategies that hold promise for shaping the future of the field.

Multisystemic therapy

It has become increasingly recognised that juveniles who commit sex offences are not 'specialists' and that these youth are more prone to commit crimes of a non-sexual nature than additional sex offences (Caldwell, 2002; Nisbet et al., 2004; Seto and Lalumiere, 2006; Smallbone, 2006). Consequently, researchers and practitioners have begun to consider more routinely the multiple correlates of sex offending and other delinquent behaviour among youth when designing interventions, to ensure that these treatment strategies can be maximally effective over time. Social-ecological approaches, namely multisystemic therapy (MST), recognise

the critical interactive nature of elements that extend beyond the youth alone – including the family, peer, school, and community systems (see e.g., Henggeler et al., 1998).

Well-controlled empirical examinations of MST have demonstrated the efficacy of this approach with more serious and chronic delinquents, revealing lower recidivism rates and increased family functioning, school performance, and involvement with prosocial peers (see e.g., Henggeler et al., 1998). Moreover, MST has been applied to the treatment of juvenile sex offenders, with very encouraging results from strong experimental designs (Borduin et al., 1990; Borduin and Shaeffer, 2002). In contrast to youth who were randomly assigned to individual therapy and 'traditional' cognitive-behavioural interventions, juvenile sex offenders who received MST interventions recidivated at significantly lower rates, both sexually and non-sexually, and demonstrated significant improvements across measures of school performance, behavioural adjustment, family functioning, and peer relationships (Borduin et al., 1990; Borduin and Shaeffer, 2002). As such, this social-ecological approach to intervention is undoubtedly an area of great promise with juveniles who commit sex offences.

Approach goals and the 'good lives' model

Consistent with the more holistic, social-ecological, and multiple systems approaches to juvenile sex offender treatment which emphasise the importance of promoting the overall wellness and success of these youth, experts have begun to question the primarily deficits-driven risk management strategies used in most traditional models of treatment (see e.g., Hunter and Longo, 2004; Marshall et al., 2005; Thakker, Ward and Tidmarsh, 2006). More specifically, concerns have arisen around the traditional relapse prevention approaches which, because of the tendency to exert external pressures to avoid and eliminate negative attributes and behaviours, tend to define individuals as 'incurable' sex offenders and may inadvertently foster hopelessness and a negative sense of identity (Hunter and Longo, 2004; Marshall et al., 2005; Thakker et al., 2006; Ward and Mann, 2004; Ward and Stewart, 2003). The deleterious implications of such an approach are particularly salient for youth, who are participating in treatment during a critical developmental period when the sense of self is still evolving.

As such, promising reconceptualisations of treatment philosophies and strategies are geared toward encouraging youth and their families to work toward improving quality of life through the attainment of meaningful life goals, or approach goals, rather than concentrating on risk management strategies as the exclusive means to an end (see e.g., Hunter and Longo, 2004; Thakker et al., 2006). While promoting healthy self-concept and intrinsic motivation, treatment is designed to assist youth within identifying a range of positive needs and desires – both basic and higher order. Furthermore, youth are encouraged to explore the various means of meeting these needs in order to lead 'good lives,' including the effective management of potential obstacles, risk factors, or behaviours that may have previously interfered with or have the potential to impede positive goal attainment (see e.g., Thakker et al., 2006). These approaches are especially promising for youthful sex offenders as they are centred around promoting success, rather than being driven by an implicit expectancy for potential failure. Furthermore, such a positive, approach-oriented philosophy of treatment has promising implications for the community supervision of youth who commit sex offences.

Treatment-supportive approaches to supervision

Congruent with a more success-driven framework for juvenile sex offender treatment, approach goals have become an emerging area of promise within supervision strategies as well. To illustrate, the roles and responsibilities of community supervision agents have been expanded deliberately in some jurisdictions to complement and support rehabilitative efforts (see e.g., Bumby et al., in press; Cumming and McGrath, 2000, 2005; Hunter et al., 2003). Indeed, as researchers have revealed that exclusive reliance on punishment and intensive surveillance of youthful offenders is not effective in reducing recidivism (see e.g., Aos et al., 2001; Lipsey and Wilson, 1998), it has been argued that community supervision strategies should reflect the importance of case management functions

such as identifying rehabilitative needs, brokering services, communicating routinely with treatment providers, and establishing community support networks (see e.g., Bumby et al., in press; Cumming and McGrath, 2000, 2005; Hunter et al., 2004). The recognition that outcomes are enhanced with this more balanced and rehabilitative-oriented approach to supervision is especially critical at this juncture, given the proliferation of more punitive legislation and widespread implementation of technology such as electronic monitoring within the sex offender management field (Pratt, 2000; Winick and LaFond, 2003; Zimring, 2004).

Therefore, in addition to outlining restrictions and prohibitions through the implementation of specialised supervision conditions and avoidance strategies, success-oriented approaches to the supervision and overall management of sex offenders emphasise the attainment of positive goals – including success in school, in treatment, with peers, and at home – and incorporate the use of incentives and rewards as a means of facilitating positive changes (see e.g., Bumby et al., in press; Cumming and McGrath, 2000, 2005). In addition, restorative justice principles have been considered within the context of juvenile sex offender supervision in an attempt to ensure that the voices of victims and communities are heard (Koss, Bachar and Hopkins, 2006). Although the effects of rehabilitation-focused or success-oriented supervision models with youthful sex offenders have yet to be examined empirically, there exists some evidence to suggest that such approaches hold promise (see e.g., Aos et al., 2001).

Interagency collaboration as an underlying philosophy

As highlighted in the NAPN Task Force Report and other key resources decades ago, effective juvenile sex offender management must reach beyond the boundaries of specialised, offence-specific treatment; a comprehensive, integrated, multi-agency strategy is warranted (see e.g., Barbaree et al., 1993; NAPN, 1993; Ryan and Lane, 1991, 1997). Historically, such an approach had not been operationalised, although more recently, a variety of factors – including budgetary constraints and reduced resources, the high level of public scrutiny associated with these cases, and the recognition that these juveniles possess diverse and specialised needs – have provided a necessary catalyst for policy makers and practitioners from various agencies and disciplines to work more closely, efficiently, and effectively around juvenile sex offender management. Reflecting the now relatively common assertion that 'no single entity can do this work successfully alone,' interagency teams have been established both at the policy and case management level to identify common goals around juvenile sex offender management, develop coordinated strategies, and share critical resources (Calder, 1999; Jones, 2003; McGarvey and Peyton, 1999; Morrison, 2004). These multidisciplinary teams include treatment providers, juvenile and family court judges and other court personnel, juvenile probation or parole officers, mental health agency personnel, school officials, social services and child welfare agencies, juvenile correctional staff, family therapists, and victim services providers.

In some locales, these stakeholders have developed specialised cross-training initiatives with the goals of enhancing substantive knowledge about these youth and effective management strategies, building capacity for appropriate interventions, and promoting sustainable partnerships. Additionally, treatment providers and supervision agents working with youthful sex offenders in many jurisdictions now take more active steps to routinely exchange critical information as a means of improving treatment and management practices. Among the associated benefits of these and other iterations of multi-agency collaborative approaches are reduced fragmentation and unnecessary duplication of services, decreased likelihood of either offenders or victims 'falling through the cracks,' and increased consistency, efficiency, and effectiveness in the system's responses to juvenile sex offenders, victims, and families. Indeed, multidisciplinary collaboration is increasingly becoming an area of promise within the juvenile sex offender management field (CSOM, 1999; Hunter et al., 2003; Koss et al., 2006; Morrison, 2004).

Concluding comments

While this chapter has presented a less than radiant review of the evolution of the field of juvenile sex offender treatment and the current state of affairs, there is room for much optimism. Weinrott's words – as outlined in the opening of this chapter – may not have been well received or heard loudly at the time, but there is mounting evidence that professionals in the field have since taken heed. Indeed, there appears to be a growing recognition of the need to critically assess and re-examine current practices and use research to inform not only treatment approaches, but also policy-level responses regarding juveniles who commit sex offences.

We are enlightened by the increased efforts to identify distinguishing characteristics between juveniles and adults who perpetrate sexually, to explore the similarities and differences between youthful sex offenders and other delinquent youth, and to recognise the heterogeneity within the juvenile sex offender population itself. This clearly necessitates the need to abandon template programmes that are assumed to be equally appropriate for all youth in favour of more informed and assessment-driven intervention strategies tailored to meet the unique needs and circumstances of each juvenile and family.

In addition, we are encouraged by the current trends that reflect more integrated, collaborative, and holistic approaches for juveniles and their families. We also take great comfort in the growing tendency to draw upon effective strategies from the juvenile justice field overall, rather than transfusing approaches from the adult field. This is particularly important, given that these youth appear more similar to other juvenile delinquents and different from adult sex offenders (see e.g., Letourneau and Miner, 2005; Miranda and Corcoran, 2000; Smallbone, 2006). Yet we acknowledge that some of the aforementioned practices remain *merely promising* in nature, and that only through additional research will the value and impact of these approaches be demonstrated.

Finally, we recognise that the phrase 'contemporary approaches' is not static terminology. As such, it is our hope and belief that when the next chapter on contemporary approaches is published, the field will have continued to advance sufficiently to render this review as simply one chapter in the history books of the evolving practices of juvenile sex offender management.

References

Abel, G.G., Mittleman, M.S. and Becker, J.V. (1985) Sex Offenders: Results of Assessment and

Recommendations for Treatment. In Ben-Aron, M.H., Hucker, J.S. and. Webster, C.D. (Eds.) *Clinical Criminology: The Assessment and Treatment of Criminal Behaviour.* Toronto: M and M Graphic.

Ahlmeyer, S., Heil, P., McKee, B. and English, K. (2000) The Impact of Polygraphy on Admissions of Victims and Offences in Adult Sexual Offenders. *Sexual Abuse: A Journal of Research and Treatment,* 12, 123–38.

Alexander, M. (1999) Sex Offender Treatment Efficacy Revisited. *Sexual Abuse: A Journal of Research and Treatment,* 11, 101–16.

Altschuler, D.M. and Armstrong, T.L. (1994) *Intensive Aftercare for High Risk Juveniles: A Community Care Model.* Washington, DC: Department of Justice, Office of Juvenile Justice and Delinquency Prevention.

Altschuler, D.M., Armstrong, T.L. and Mackenzie, D.L. (1999) *Reintegration, Supervised Release and Intensive Aftercare.* Washington, DC: Department of Justice, Office of Juvenile Justice and Delinquency Prevention.

American Academy of Child and Adolescent Psychiatry (1999) Practice Parameters for the Assessment and Treatment of Children and Adolescents Who Are Sexually Abusive of Others. *Journal of The American Academy of Child and Adolescent Psychiatry,* 38, 55–76.

Aos, S., Phipps, P., Barnoski, R. and Lieb, R. (2001) *The Comparative Costs and Benefits of Programs to Reduce Crime.* Olympia, WA: Washington State Institute for Public Policy.

Arieff, A.J. and Rotman, D.B. (1942) One Hundred Cases of Indecent Exposure. *Journal of Nervous and Mental Disorders,* 96, 523–9.

Arnold, M. and Hughes, J.N. (1999) First Do No Harm: Adverse Effects of Grouping Deviant Youth for Skills Training. *Journal of School Psychology,* 37, 99–115.

Association for The Treatment of Sexual Abusers (2000) *The Effective Legal Management of Juvenile Sexual Offenders.* Beaverton, OR: Author.

Atcheson, J.D. and Williams, D.C. (1954) A Study of Juvenile Sex Offenders. *American Journal of Psychiatry,* 111, 366–70.

Barbaree, H.E. and Cortoni, F.A. (1993) Treatment of The Juvenile Sex Offender Within The Criminal Justice and Mental Health Systems. In Barbaree, H.E., Marshall, W.L. and Hudson, S.M. (Eds.) *The Juvenile Sex Offender.* New York: Guilford.

Barbaree, H.E. and Marshall, W.L. (2006) *The Juvenile Sex Offender.* 2nd edn. New York: Guilford.

Barbaree, H.E., Marshall, W.L. and Hudson, S.M. (1993) *The Juvenile Sex Offender.* New York: Guilford.

Becker, J.V. and Harris, C. (2004) The Psychophysiological Assessment of Juvenile Offenders. In O'Reilly, G. Marshall, W.L. Carr, A. and Beckett, R.C. (Eds.) *The Handbook of Clinical Intervention With Young People Who Sexually Abuse.* New York: Brunner-Routledge.

Becker, J.V. and Hicks, S.J. (2003) Juvenile Sexual Offenders: Characteristics, Interventions, and Policy Issues. In Prentky, R. Janus, E.S. and Seto, M.C. (Eds.) *Sexually Coercive Behaviour: Understanding and Management.* New York: New York Academy of Sciences.

Becker, J.V. and Kaplan, M.S. (1993) Cognitive Behavioural Treatment of The Juvenile Sex Offender. In Barbaree, H.E. Marshall, W.L. and Hudson, S.M. (Eds.) *The Juvenile Sex Offender.* New York: Guilford.

Bengis, S. (1997) Comprehensive Service Delivery With A Continuum of Care. In Ryan, G.D. and Lane S.L. (Eds.) *Juvenile Sexual Offending: Causes, Consequences, and Correction.* San Francisco: Jossey-Bass.

Bengis, S. et al. (1999) *Standards of Care for Youth in Sex Offence-Specific Residential Programs.* National Offence-Specific Residential Standards Task Force; Holyoke, MA: NEARI Press.

Berlin, F.S. (2000) The Etiology and Treatment of Sexual Offending. In Fishbein, D.H. (Ed.) *The Science, Treatment, and Prevention of Antisocial Behaviours: Application to The Criminal Justice System.* Kingston, NJ: Civic Research Institute.

Borduin, C.M., Henggeler, S.W., Blaske, D.M. and Stein, R.J. (1990) Multisystemic Treatment of Adolescent Sex Offenders. *International Journal of Offender Therapy and Comparative Criminology,* 34, 105–13.

Borduin, C.M. and Schaeffer, C.M. (2002) Multisystemic Treatment of Juvenile Sex Offenders: A Progress Report. *Journal of Psychology and Human Sexuality,* 13, 25–42.

Bradford, J.M. and Fedoroff, P. (2006) Pharmacological Treatment of The Juvenile Sex Offender. In Barbaree, H.E. and Marshall, W.L. (Eds.) *The Juvenile Sex Offender. Second Edition.* New York: Guilford.

Bullens, R. and Van Wijk, A. (2004) European Perspectives on Juveniles Who Sexually Abuse. In O'Reilly, G. Marshall, W.L. Carr, A. and Beckett, R.C. (Eds.) *The Handbook of Clinical Intervention With Young People Who Sexually Abuse.* New York: Brunner-Routledge.

Bumby, N.H. and Bumby, K.M. (2004) Bridging The Gender Gap: Addressing Juvenile Females Who Commit Sexual Offences. In O'Reilly, G. Marshall, W.L. Carr, A. and Beckett, R.C. (Eds.) *The Handbook of Clinical Intervention With Young People Who Sexually Abuse.* New York, NY: Brunner-Routledge.

Bumby, K.M., Talbot, T.B. and Carter, M.M. (in press) Sex Offender Reentry: Facilitating Public Safety Through Successful Transition and Community Reintegration. *Criminal Justice and Behavior.*

Burton, D.L., Smith-Darden, J. and Frankel, S.J. (2006) Research on Adolescent Sexual Abuser Treatment Programs. In Barbaree, H.E. and Marshall, W.L. (Eds.) *The Juvenile Sex Offender.* 2nd edn. New York: Guilford.

Calder, M.C. (1999) *Working With Young People Who Sexually Abuse: New Pieces of The Jigsaw Puzzle.* Lyme Regis: Russell House Publishing.

Caldwell, M.F. (2002) What We Do Not Know About Juvenile Sexual Reoffence Risk. *Child Maltreatment,* 7, 291–302.

Center for Sex Offender Management (1999) *Understanding Juvenile Sexual Offending Behaviour: Emerging Research, Treatment Approaches, and Management Practices.* Silver Spring, MD: CSOM.

Chaffin, M. and Bonner, B. (1998) Don't Shoot, We're Your Children: Have We Gone Too Far in Our Response to Adolescent Sexual Abusers and Children With Sexual Behaviour Problems? *Child Maltreatment,* 3, 314–6.

Chaffin, M., Letourneau, E. and Silovsky, J.F. (2002) Adults, Adolescents, and Children Who Sexually Abuse Children: A Developmental Perspective. In Myers, J.E. and Berliner, L. (Eds.) *The APSAC Handbook on Child Maltreatment.* 2nd Edn. Thousand Oaks, CA: Sage.

Chamberlain, P. and Reid, J.B. (1998) Comparison of Two Community Alternatives to Incarceration for Chronic Juvenile Offenders. *Journal of Consulting and Clinical Psychology,* 66, 624–33.

Cumming, G.F. and McGrath, R.J. (2000) External Supervision: How Can it Increase the Effectiveness of Relapse Prevention? in Laws, D.R. Hudson, S.M. and Ward, T. (Eds.) *Remaking Relapse Prevention With Sex Offenders: A Sourcebook.* Thousand Oaks, CA: Sage.

Cumming, G. and McGrath, R.J. (2005) *Supervision of The Sex Offender: Community Management, Risk Assessment, and Treatment.* Brandon, VT: Safer Society Press.

Dishion, T.J. and Andrews, D.W. (1995) Preventing Escalation in Problem Behaviours with High-risk Young Adolescents: Immediate and one year outcomes. *Journal of Consulting and Clinical Psychology,* 63, 538–48.

Dishion, T.J., McCord, J. and Poulin, F. (1999) When Interventions Harm: Peer Groups and Problem Behaviour. *American Psychologist,* 54, 755–64.

Doshay, L.J. (1943) *The Boy Sex Offender and His Later Career.* New York: Grune and Stratton.

Elliott, D.S. (1998) *Blueprints for Violence Prevention.* Boulder, CO: University of Colorado, Center for The Study and Prevention of Violence.

Fagan, J. and Zimring, F.E. (2000) *The Changing Borders of Juvenile Justice: Transfer of Adolescents to The Criminal Court.* Chicago: University of Chicago Press.

Food and Drug Administration (2004) *Public Health Advisory.* United States Department of Health and Human Services, Center for Drug Evaluation and Research.

Freeman-Longo, R., Bird, S., Stevenson, W.F. and Fiske, J. (1995) *1994 Nationwide Survey of Treatment Programs and Models.* Brandon, VT: Safer Society.

Gardner, G.E. (1950) The Community and The Aggressive Child. *Mental Hygiene,* 34, 44–63.

Garfinkle, E. (2003) Coming of Age in America: The Misapplication of Sex-Offender Registries and Community-Notification Laws to Juveniles. *California Law Review,* 91, 163–208.

Gies, S. (2003) *Aftercare Services.* Juvenile Justice Practices Series. Washington, DC: US Department of Justice, Office of Justice Programs, Office of Juvenile Justice and Delinquency Prevention.

Glaser, W. (2003) Integrating Pharmacological Treatments. In Ward, T. Laws, D.R. and Hudson, S.M. (Eds.) *Sexual Deviance: Issues and Controversies.* Thousand Oaks, CA: Sage.

Glover, K. and Bumby, K.M. (2002) Re-Entry at The Point of Entry. In *Juvenile Justice Today: Essays on Programs and Policies.* Lanham, MD: American Correctional Association.

Greer, W.C. (1997) Aftercare: Community Integration Following Institutional Treatment. In Ryan, G. and Lane, S. (Eds.) *Juvenile Sexual Offending: Causes, Consequences, and Correction.* San Francisco: Jossey-Bass.

Groth, A.N. (1977) The Adolescent Sexual Offender and His Prey. *Journal of Offender Therapy and Comparative Criminology,* 21, 249–54.

Groth, A.N. (1979) *Men Who Rape: The Psychology of The Offender.* New York: Plenum.

Groth, A.N., Longo, R.E. and McFadin, J.B. (1982) Undetected Recidivism Among Rapists and Child Molesters. *Crime and Delinquency, 128,* 450–8.

Grubin, D. (2000) Complementing Relapse Prevention With Medical Intervention. In Laws, D.R. Hudson, S.M. and Ward, T. (Eds.) *Remaking Relapse Prevention With Sex Offenders: A Sourcebook.* Thousand Oaks, CA: Sage.

Haaven, J.L. and Coleman, E.M. (2000) Treatment of The Deveopmentally Disabled Sex Offender. In Laws, D.R., Hudson, S.M. and Ward, T. (Eds.) *Remaking Relapse Prevention With Sex Offenders: A Sourcebook.* Thousand Oaks, CA: Sage.

Hanson, R.K. et al. (2002) First Report of The Collaborative Outcome Data Project on The Effectiveness of Psychological Treatment for Sex Offenders. *Sexual Abuse: A Journal of Research and Treatment, 14,* 169–94.

Heinz, J. and Ryan, G. (1997) The Legal System's Response to Juvenile Sexual Offenders. In Ryan, G. and Lane, S. (Eds.) *Juvenile Sexual Offending: Causes, Consequences, and Correction.* San Francisco: Jossey-Bass.

Henggeler, S.W. et al. (1998) *Multisystemic Treatment of Antisocial Behaviour in Children and Adolescents.* New York: Guilford.

Hindman, J. and Peters, J.M. (2001) Polygraph Testing Leads to Better Understanding Adult and Juvenile Sex Offenders. *Federal Probation, 65,* 8–15.

Howell, J.C. (2003) *Preventing and Reducing Juvenile Delinquency: A Comprehensive Framework.* Thousand Oaks, CA: Sage.

Hunter, J.A., Becker, J.V. and Lexier, L.J. (2006) The Female Juvenile Sex Offender. In Barbaree, H.E. and Marshall, W.L. (Eds.) *The Juvenile Sex Offender. Second Edition.* New York: Guilford.

Hunter, J.A. et al. (2003) Juvenile Sex Offenders: Toward The Development of A Typology. *Sexual Abuse: A Journal of Research and Treatment, 15,* 27–48.

Hunter, J.A. et al. (2004) Strengthening Community-Based Programming for Juvenile Sex Offenders: Key Concepts and Paradigm Shifts. *Child Maltreatment, 9,* 177–89.

Hunter, J.A. and Lexier, L.J. (1998) Ethical and Legal Issues in The Assessment and Treatment of Juvenile Sex Offenders. *Child Maltreatment, 3,* 339–48.

Hunter, J. and Longo, R.E. (2004) Relapse Prevention With Juvenile Sexual Abusers: A

Holistic and Integrated Approach. In O'Reilly, G. et al. (Eds.) *The Handbook of Clinical Intervention With Young People Who Sexually Abuse.* New York: Brunner-Routledge.

Jones, R. (2003) Research and Practice With Adolescent Sexual Offenders: Dilemmas and Directions. In Ward, T. Laws, D.R. and Hudson, S.M. (Eds.) *Sexual Deviance: Issues and Controversies.* Thousand Oaks, CA: Sage.

Karpman, B. (1954) *The Sexual Offender and His Offences: Etiology, Pathology, Psychodynamics, and Treatment.* New York: The Julian Press.

Kashani, J.H. et al. (1999) Youth Violence: Psychosocial Risk Factors, Treatment, Prevention, and Recommendations. *Journal of Emotional and Behavioural Disorders, 7,* 200–10.

Knight, R.A. and Sims-Knight, J.E. (2003) The Developmental Antecedents of Sexual Coercion Against Women: Testing Alternative Hypotheses With Structural Equation Modeling. In Prentky, R. Janus, E.S. and Seto, M.C. (Eds.) *Sexually Coercive Behaviour: Understanding and Management.* New York: New York Academy of Sciences.

Knopp, F.H. (1982) *Remedial Intervention in Adolescent Sex Offences: Nine Program Descriptions.* Orwell, VT: Safer Society Press.

Knopp, F.H. (1985) *The Youthful Sex Offender: The Rationale and Goals of Early Intervention and Treatment.* Orwell, VT: Safer Society Press.

Koss, M.P., Bachar, K. and Hopkins, C.Q. (2006) Disposition and Treatment of Juvenile Sex Offenders From The Perspective of Restorative Justice. In Barbaree, H.E. and Marshall, W.L. (Eds.) *The Juvenile Sex Offender. Second Edition.* New York: Guilford.

Lane, S. and Lobanov-Rostovsky, C. (1997) Special Populations: Children, Females, and The Developmentally Disabled, and Violent Youth. In Ryan, G. and Lane, S. (Eds.) *Juvenile Sexual Offending: Causes, Consequences, and Correction.* San Francisco: Jossey-Bass.

Langton, C.M. and Barbaree, H.E. (2006) Conceptual Issues in Treatment Evaluation Research With Juvenile Sexual Offenders. In Barbaree, H.E. and Marshall, W.L. (Eds.) *The Juvenile Sex Offender. Second Edition.* New York: Guilford.

Letourneau, E.J. (2006) Legal Consequences of Juvenile Sex Offending in The United States. In Barbaree, H.E. and Marshall, W.L. (Eds.) *The Juvenile Sex Offender. 2nd edn.* New York: Guilford.

Letourneau, E.J. and Miner, M.H. (2005) Juvenile Sex Offenders: A Case Against The Legal and

Clinical Status Quo. *Sexual Abuse: A Journal of Research and Treatment,* 17, 293–312.

Lewis, D.O., Shankok, S.S. and Pincus, J.H. (1979) Juvenile Male Sexual Assaulters. *American Journal of Psychiatry,* 136, 1194–6.

Lipsey, M.W. and Wilson, D.B. (1998) Effective Intervention for Serious Juvenile Offenders: A Synthesis of Research. In Loeber, R. and Farrington, D.P. (Eds.) *Serious and Violent Juvenile Offenders: Risk Factors and Successful Interventions.* Thousand Oaks, CA: Sage.

Longo, R.E. (1982) Sexual Learning and Experience Among Adolescent Sexual Offenders. *International Journal of Offender Therapy and Comparative Criminology,* 26, 235–241.

Longo, R.E. (2003) Emerging Issues, Policy Changes, and The Future of Treating Children With Sexual Behaviour Problems. In Prentky, R. Janus, E.S. and Seto, M.C. (Eds.) *Sexually Coercive Behaviour: Understanding and Management.* New York: New York Academy of Sciences.

Longo, R.E. and Groth, A.N. (1983) Juvenile Sexual Offences in The Histories of Adult Rapists and Child Molesters. *International Journal of Offender Therapy and Comparative Criminology,* 27, 150–5.

Maclay, D.T. (1960) Boys Who Commit Sexual Misdemeanors. *British Medical Journal,* 51, 186–90.

Markey, O.B. (1950) A Study of Aggressive Sex Misbehaviour in Adolescents Brought to Juvenile Court. *American Journal of Orthopsychiatry,* 20, 719–31.

Marshall, W.L. and Fernandez, Y.M. (2004) Treatment Outcome With Juvenile Sexual Offenders. In O'Reilly, G. Marshall, W.L. Carr, A. and Beckett, R.C. (Eds.) *The Handbook of Clinical Intervention With Young People Who Sexually Abuse.* New York: Brunner-Routledge.

Marshall, W.L. et al. (2005) Working Positively With Sexual Offenders: Maximising The Effectiveness of Treatment. *Journal of Interpersonal Violence,* 20, 1096–114.

Mathews, R., Hunter, J.A. and Vuz, J. (1997) Juvenile Female Sexual Offenders: Clinical Characteristics and Treatment Issues. *Sexual Abuse: A Journal of Research and Treatment,* 9, 187–99.

Matson, S. and Lieb, R. (1997) *Megan's Law: A Review of State and Federal Legislation.* Olympia, WA: Washington State Institute for Public Policy.

McGarvey, J. and Peyton, L. (1999) A Framework for A Multi-Agency Approach to Working With Young Abusers: A Management Perspective. In Calder M. (Ed.) *Working With Young People Who Sexually Abuse: New Pieces of The Jigsaw Puzzle.* Lyme Regis: Russell House Publishing.

McGrath, R.J., Cumming, G.F. and Burchard, B.L. (2003) *Current Practices and Trends in Sexual Abuser Management: The Safer Society 2002 Nationwide Survey.* Brandon, VT: Safer Society.

Miranda, A.O. and Corcoran, C.L. (2000) Comparison of Perpetration Characteristics Between Male Juvenile and Adult Sexual Offenders: Preliminary Results. *Sexual Abuse: A Journal of Research and Treatment,* 12, 179–88.

Morrison, T. (2004) Preparing Services and Staff to Work With Young People Who Sexually Abuse: Context, Mandate, Pitfalls, and Frameworks. In O'Reilly, G. et al. (Eds.) *The Handbook of Clinical Intervention With Young People Who Sexually Abuse.* New York: Brunner-Routledge.

National Adolescent Perpetrator Network (NAPN) (1988) Preliminary Report From The National Task Force on Juvenile Sexual Offending. *Juvenile and Family Court Journal,* 39, 1–67.

National Adolescent Perpetrator Network (NAPN) (1993) The Revised Report From The National Task Force on Juvenile Sexual Offending. *Juvenile and Family Court Journal,* 44, 1–120.

National Center on Sexual Behaviour of Youth (2003) *Fact Sheet: What Research Shows About Adolescent Sex Offenders.* Center on Child Abuse and Neglect: University of Oklahoma Health Science.

National Organization for The Treatment of Abusers. (2005) Work With Young People Who Have Committed Sexual Offences. Retrieved December 14, From Http:// Www.Nota.Co.Uk/Notadol.Html.

Nisbet, I.A., Wilson, P.H. and Smallbone, S.W. (2004) A Prospective Longitudinal Study of Sexual Recidivism Among Adolescent Sex Offenders. *Sexual Abuse: A Journal of Research and Treatment,* 16, 223–34.

O'Callaghan, D. (1999) Young Abusers With Learning Disabilities: Towards Better Understanding and Positive Interventions. In Calder, M. (Ed.) *Working With Young People Who Sexually Abuse: New Pieces of The Jigsaw Puzzle.* Lyme Regis: Russell House Publishing.

O'Callaghan, D. (2004) Adolescents With Intellectual Disabilities Who Sexually Harm: Intervention Design and Implementation. In O'Reilly, G. et al. (Eds.) *The Handbook of Clinical Intervention With Young People Who Sexually Abuse.* New York: Brunner-Routledge.

O'Reilly, G. and Carr, A. (2006) Assessment and Treatment of Criminogenic Needs. In Barbaree, H.E. and Marshall, W.L. (Eds.) *The Juvenile Sex Offender.* 2nd edn. New York: Guilford.

O'Reilly, G. et al. (2004) *The Handbook of Clinical Intervention With Young People Who Sexually Abuse.* New York: Brunner-Routledge.

Pratt, J. (2000) Sex Crimes and The New Punitiveness. *Behavioural Sciences and The Law,* 18, 135–51.

Prentky, R. et al. (2000) an Actuarial Procedure for Assessing Risk in Juvenile Sexual Offenders. *Sexual Abuse: A Journal of Research and Treatment,* 12, 71–93.

Reitzel, L.R. and Carbonell, J.L. (2006) The Effectiveness of Sex Offender Treatment for Juveniles as Measured by Recidivism: A Meta-analysis. *Sexual Abuse: A Journal of Research and Treatment.*

Rich, P. (2003) *Understanding, Assessing, and Rehabilitating Juvenile Sexual Offenders.* Hoboken, NJ: John Wiley and Sons.

Richmond, W. (1933) *The Adolescent Boy.* New York: Farrar and Rinehart.

Righthand, S. and Welch, C. (2001) *Juveniles Who Have Sexually Offended: A Review of The Professional Literature.* Washington, DC: Office of Juvenile Justice and Delinquency Prevention.

Rose, S.D. (1998) *Group Therapy With Troubled Youth: A Cognitive Behavioural Interactive Approach.* Thousand Oaks, CA: Sage.

Ryan, G. (1997a) Incidence and Prevalence of Sexual Offences Committed by Juveniles. In Ryan, G. and Lane, S. (Eds.) *Juvenile Sexual Offending.* San Francisco: Jossey-Bass.

Ryan, G. (1997b) The Evolving Response to Juvenile Sexual Offences. In Ryan, G. and Lane, S. (Eds.) *Juvenile Sexual Offending: Causes, Consequences, and Correction.* San Francisco: Jossey-Bass.

Ryan, G.D. and Lane, S.L. (1991) *Juvenile Sexual Offending.* Lexington, MA: Lexington Books.

Ryan, G. and Lane, S. (1997) *Juvenile Sexual Offending: Causes, Consequences, and Correction.* San Francisco: Jossey-Bass.

Schwartz, B.K. (2003) Overview of Rehabilitative Efforts in Understanding and Managing Sexually Coercive Behaviours. In Prentky, R.

Janus, E.S. and Seto, M.C. (Eds.) *Sexually Coercive Behaviour: Understanding and Management.* New York: New York Academy of Sciences.

Seto, M.C. and Lalumiere, M.L. (2006) Conduct Problems and Juvenile Sexual Offending. In Barbaree, H.E. and Marshall, W.L. (Eds.) *The Juvenile Sex Offender.* 2nd edn. New York: Guilford.

Shaw, T., Heesacker, A.K. and Delgado-Romero, E.A. (2001) Implications of Sexually Violent Predator Laws for Youthful Offenders. In Schlank, A. (Ed.) *The Sexual Predator: Legal Issues, Clinical Issues, Special Populations.* Kingston, NJ: Civic Research Institute.

Sheerin, D. (2004) Psychiatric Disorder and Adolescent Sexual Offending. In O'Reilly, G. et al. (Eds.) *The Handbook of Clinical Intervention With Young People Who Sexually Abuse.* New York: Brunner-Routledge.

Sickmund, M. (2002) *Juvenile Offenders in Residential Placement: 1997–1999.* Washington, DC: US Department of Justice, Office of Juvenile Justice and Delinquency Prevention.

Sickmund, M. (2004) *Juveniles in Corrections.* Bulletin. Washington, DC: US Department of Justice, Office of Juvenile Justice and Delinquency Prevention.

Smallbone, S.W. (2006) Social and Psychological Factors in The Development and Delinquency of Sexual Deviance. In Barbaree, H.E. and Marshall, W.L. (Eds.) *The Juvenile Sex Offender.* 2nd edn. New York: Guilford.

Tarolla, S.M. et al. (2002) Understanding and Treating Juvenile Offenders: A Review of Current Knowledge and Future Directions. *Aggression and Violent Behaviour,* 7, 125–43.

Thakker, J., Ward, T. and Tidmarsh, P. (2006) A Reevaluation of Relapse Prevention With Adolescents Who Sexually Offend: A Good Lives Model. In Barbaree, H.E. and Marshall, W.L. (Eds.) *The Juvenile Sex Offender.* 2nd edn. New York: Guilford.

Thomas, J. (2004) Family Intervention With Young People With Sexually Abusive Behaviour. In O'Reilly, G. et al. (Eds.) *The Handbook of Clinical Intervention With Young People Who Sexually Abuse.* New York: Brunner-Routledge.

Torbet, P. and Szymanski, L. (1998) *State Legislative Responses to Violent Juvenile Crime: 1996–7 Update.* Washington, DC: US Department of Justice, Office of Juvenile Justice and Delinquency Prevention.

Trivits, L.C. and Reppucci, N.D. (2002) Application of Megan's Law to Juveniles. *American Psychologist*, 57, 690–704.

Waggoner, R.W. and Boyd, D.A. (1941) Juvenile Aberrant Sexual Behaviour. *American Journal of Orthopsychiatry*, 11, 275–92.

Wakeling, A. (1979) A General Psychiatric Approach to Sexual Deviation. In I. Rosen (Ed.) *Sexual Deviation*. Oxford: Oxford University Press.

Walker, D.F., McGovern, S.K., Poey, E.L. and Otis, K.E. (2004) Treatment Effectiveness for Male Adolescent Sexual Offenders: A Meta-analysis and Review. In Geffner, R., Crumpton Franey, K., Geffner Arnold, T. and Falconer, R. (Eds.) *Identifying and Treating Youth Who Sexually Offend: Current Approaches, Techniques and Research* (pp. 281–93). Binghamton, NY: Haworth Press.

Ward, T. and Mann, R. (2004) Good Lives and The Rehabilitation of Sex Offenders: A Positive Approach to Treatment. In Linley, A. and Stephen, J. (Eds.) *Positive Practice in Psychology*. Chichester: Wiley.

Ward, T. and Stewart, C.A. (2003) Good Lives and The Rehabilitation of Sexual Offenders. In Ward, T. Laws, D.R. and Hudson, S.M. (Eds.) *Sexual Deviance: Issues and Controversies*. Thousand Oaks, CA: Sage.

Weinrott, M. (1996) *Juvenile Sexual Aggression: A Critical Review*. Boulder, CO: University of Colorado, Institute for Behavioural Sciences, Center for The Study and Prevention of Violence.

Winick, B.J. and Lafond, J.Q. (2003) *Protecting Society From Sexually Dangerous Offenders: Law, Justice, and Therapy*. Washington, DC: American Psychological Association.

Worling, J.R. (2004) Essentials of A Good Intervention Programme for Sexually Abusive Juveniles: Offence Related Treatment Tasks. In O'Reilly, G. et al. (Eds.) *The Handbook of Clinical Intervention With Young People Who Sexually Abuse*. New York: Brunner-Routledge.

Worling, J.R. and Curwen, T. (2000) Adolescent Sexual Offender Recidivism: Success of Specialised Treatment and Implications for Risk Prediction. *Child Abuse and Neglect*, 24, 965–82.

Worling, J.R. and Curwen, T. (2001) *The ERASOR: Estimate of Risk of Adolescent Sexual Offence Recidivism*. Toronto: SAFE-T Program.

Worling, J.R. and Langstrom, N. (2006) Risk of Sexual Recidivism in Adolescents Who Offend Sexually: Correlates and Assessment. In Barbaree, H.E. and Marshall, W.L. (Eds.) *The Juvenile Sex Offender. Second Edition*. New York: Guilford.

Zimring, F.E. (2004) an *American Travesty: Legal Responses to Adolescent Sexual Offending*. Chicago: University of Chicago Press.

Chapter 19

An Overview of Social Responsibility Therapy for Preteen Children with Sexual Behaviour Problems

James Yokley, Jennifer LaCortiglia, and Brigette Bulanda

Introduction

Population description

Preteen children referred for sexually abusive behaviour along with other abuse behaviour problems are often too young for incarceration. Their age and size set adults up to minimise and normalise their behaviour using terms such as 'curiosity' and 'exploration' in place of 'imposition' and 'abuse'. This may cause the need for treatment to be minimised due to the assumption that 'they will grow out of it'. It has been pointed out that 'there has been an over-identification of children who engage in problematic sexual behaviours as children who are molesting' (Johnson, 2002). However, children engaging in age-inappropriate sexual behaviour still require intervention and redirection, regardless of the reasons for their behaviour.

In addition, preteen sexual behaviour can involve elements of the same spectrum of actions that teenage sexual abusers use to isolate and get cooperation from their victims (e.g., bribery, games, coercion, threats and physical force). They can be involved in similar sexually abusive behaviours ranging in severity from voyeurism to rape where prior to the age when erection occurs, penetration may occur with objects. A theory-driven cluster analysis of 127 children (ages 6–12) with sexual behaviour problems revealed five types of children with sexual behaviour problems: Sexually Aggressive, Non-symptomatic, Highly Traumatised, Rule Breaker and Abuse Reactive (Pithers et al., 1998). Significant differences were found among these five sexual behaviour problem types on a large number of variables. Change scores on sexualised behaviours revealed that, 'At least for the highly traumatised children, modified relapse prevention resulted in significantly greater reduction in sexual behaviours relative to the expressive therapy after 16 weeks of a 32-week treatment regimen' (Pithers et al., 1998: 399). Thus, in addition to making an important

contribution to the classification of children who sexually aggress, Pithers et al. (1998) offers evidence for treatment efficacy in this young age group.

However, at this young age, sexual behaviour patterns have not been solidified. Thus the differences between groups of preteens referred for sexual behaviour problems are on non-sexual variables, not sexual behaviour patterns. Miranda and Davis (2002: 5) point out that the differences in the five clusters of preteens with sexual behaviour problems found by Pithers et al. (1998) 'originated from maltreatment histories; objective scores on parent, teacher, and self-report measurements; psychiatric diagnoses; and numerous indices of aggression. The findings suggest that the sexual behaviours of children who sexually aggress are minimally relevant in what differentiates among them. Rather, most of the relevant and statistically significant factors are extrasexual'.

Some age group differences have been observed. In comparison to older children (ages 10–12) younger children (ages 6–9) with sexual behaviour problems were abused (sexually and physically) at an earlier age and more likely to have witnessed violence between parents. In addition, younger children exhibited sexual behaviour problems at an earlier age, at a higher annual rate and with a higher percentage of hands-on sexual behaviours (Gray et al., 1997). They have the same history of often (but not always) being a past victim of child neglect and abuse as their older counterparts. Study data from treatment programme intakes on 127 children (ages 6–12) with sexual behaviour problems revealed that this population had been abused both sexually and physically by more than two different perpetrators, one-third of whom were less than 18 years old (Gray et al., 1999). Most importantly, they travel the same path of increasing behaviour frequency across time making early intervention critical.

As is the case with all conduct-disordered children, parental and family problems are apparent. A study of 72 children (6–12 years old) with sexual behaviour problems clearly demonstrated an array of parental and familial distress characteristics (Gray et al., 1997). High levels of distress in the children and their caregivers were evident across a number of psychometric and historical variables (Gray et al., 1999).

Children with sexual behaviour problems do not have the specific, entrenched sexual abuse behaviour pattern (e.g., specific age, sex and type of sexual behaviour) that adult paedophiles exhibit. They also have not settled on a specific type of abusive behaviour to use in externalising (acting out) their feelings. Thus, various combinations of multiple forms of abusive behaviour are quite common in youth sex abusers. Children who sexually abuse frequently have histories of other types of abuse and criminal activity. Sex abuser research indicates that 41 to 86 per cent have histories of other types of abuse and criminal activity (Awad, Saunders and Levene, 1984; Amir, 1971; Becker et al. 1986; Fehrenbach et al. 1986; Shoor, Speed and Bartelt, 1966; Van Ness, 1984; Yokley, 1996). Demographic data from Forensic Foster Care (i.e., therapeutic foster care using SRT) for youth sex offenders has revealed that the average number of different types of abuse exhibited was 4.5 and 59 per cent exhibited problems at admission with five types of abuse (Yokley and Boettner, 2002). In summary, when children are referred for abuse behaviour problems, the referral type of abuse is not usually the only type of abuse and many abusers are multiple abusers.

A last point about age has to do with developmental level. Since human beings basically have three ages, their chronological age, their mental age and their social-emotional age, candidates for preteen Social Responsibility Therapy (SRT) includes some 13 and 14-year-olds whose mental and social-emotional age are in the preteen range. Conversely, it may be that some high functioning, higher risk 12 year-olds may need to receive SRT with teenagers or receive some of the treatment approaches typically applied to the teenage multiple abuser population. For a description of these techniques, see Yokley, in press.

The need for preteen treatment

Child delinquents, compared to juveniles who start offending at a later age, tend to have longer delinquent careers (Loeber and Farrington, 2000).

Two-thirds of the boys who come to the attention of the juvenile court have already had behaviour problems for at least five years but less than half received any help from mental health professionals or school personnel. Nearly half of the boys who eventually become chronic serious offenders exhibited the onset of their serious delinquent behaviour by age 12 (Stouthamer-Loeber and Loeber, 2002) and onset prior to age 13 increases the risk of later serious, violent and chronic offending by a factor of two to three (Loeber and Farrington, 2000).

The need for preteen treatment is especially pronounced in the area of sexually abusive behaviour where child abuse has reached epidemic proportions. For example, a national survey of adults found that 27 per cent of the women and 16 per cent of the men have reported being sexually abused during their lifetime (Finkelhor, 1990). Almost 40 per cent of all child sexual abuse is performed by youth less than 20 years old, with six to 12-year-old children being the source of 13–18 per cent of all substantiated child sexual abuse (Pithers and Gray, 1998). Arrests of children under 12 have increased 125 per cent for sex offences (excluding rape) and 190 per cent for forcible rape between 1980 and 1995 (Butts and Snyder, 1997).

Research on preteen children (i.e., ages 6–12) with sexual behaviour problems reveals that each child abuser has an average of 2.1 sexual abuse victims (Gray et al., 1997). This number rises to a mean of 6.8 sexually abusive acts for adolescents (Abel et al., 1987) and a mean of 75 different victims has been reported for adult sex abusers (Abel et al., 1987). The fact that the median number of adult sex abuser victims was far less (Abel et al. 1987), indicates that a few perpetrators have many victims and the vast majority do not. These data reveal the critical need to intervene with the preteen age group before an ingrained behaviour pattern has been developed and to identify the sub-group at risk for becoming 'habitual' repeat offenders.

Overview of preteen Social Responsibility Therapy (SRT)

Overall goal of preteen Social Responsibility Therapy

Preteen SRT is an innovative new cognitive-behavioural treatment designed to help develop social responsibility in children whose multiple forms of abusive behaviour impacts the future quality of living in our society. This treatment approach was developed on children from multiple cultural backgrounds who were removed from the home and referred for Forensic Foster Care treatment of sexually abusive behaviour along with other forms of abuse requiring treatment.

Important advantages of targeting multiple forms of abusive behaviour include: the fact that exhibiting multiple forms of abuse is common (Andrews and Duncan, 1997; Jessor and Jessor, 1977); multiple abuse treatment avoids the harmful effects of prematurely labelling a child as a specific type of abuser before they have developed a specific well-entrenched abuse behaviour pattern (Yokley and Boettner, 2002) and multiple abuse treatment enhances relapse prevention, since one type of abuse can trigger another, for example, substance abuse can set the occasion for sexual and physical abuse including homicide (Lightfoot and Barbaree, 1993; Carden, 1994; Fendrich et al., 1995).

Preteen SRT was not designed with the intent to replace abuse-specific treatment programmes with multiple abuse treatment programmes. This is not practical because the community (human services and the courts) always has a target abuse behaviour (i.e., identified problem) that has created a danger to self or others and requires immediate intervention. Preteen SRT simply acknowledges that the referral type of abuse is not usually the only type of abuse and provides an abuse treatment approach with the goal of improving community safety by developing a level of socially responsible behaviour control that can contain multiple forms of abusive behaviour.

The overall prosocial goal of preteen SRT involves addressing the multiple forms of abuse that tear at the moral fabric of democratic society by teaching and reinforcing the prosocial multicultural values and behaviours needed to strengthen a society of diverse traditions by improving its ability to function together, respect individual differences and embrace similarities.

What is preteen Social Responsibility Therapy?

Preteen SRT is a skills-based treatment aimed at achieving developmental mastery of the multicultural prosocial values, beliefs and behaviours needed for a socially responsible lifestyle free of behaviours that are abusive to self or others. In preteen SRT, abuse is the primary symptom of an underlying pathological social-emotional immaturity and associated lack of social responsibility. 'Most children who molest are immature. This means they are not able to 'reason out' what they are doing; want things 'now' and cannot tolerate feeling frustrated' (Gil, 1987).

A very basic summary is that preteen SRT teaches multicultural prosocial values (i.e., honesty, trust, loyalty, concern and responsibility which includes self-control) as competing factors against multiple forms of abuse (i.e., sexual abuse, physical abuse, property abuse, substance abuse and trust abuse). The multicultural prosocial values taught in preteen SRT are subsumed by multicultural human requirement theory. Specifically, honesty and trust are encompassed by the 'Maturity' domain, Loyalty and Concern are encompassed by the 'Prosocial' domain and Responsibility is encompassed by the 'Restrictive Conformity' domain of the universal, multicultural human requirement domains put forth by Schwartz and Bilsky (1987).

Preteen SRT teaches boundary establishment taking the therapeutic community discouragement of sexual relationships between residents who are viewed as 'brothers' and 'sisters' to the next level in a treatment family environment where sexual relationships are viewed as 'foster family incest' and are thus considered a sex offence relapse. The phase system of responsibilities and privileges utilised in outpatient preteen SRT is similar to the highly structured hierarchy of job functions and privileges found in residential therapeutic communities.

Who is on the Social Responsibility Therapy treatment team?

'It takes a village to raise a child' is the SRT approach to intervention. Thus, the treatment team consists of three basic support groups who, when combined, are able to monitor the child's behaviour at home, in the treatment setting and in the community. These groups consist of primary caretakers (e.g. birth parents, kinship parents, foster parents, adoptive parents or residential setting staff trained in managing child forensic issues including abusive behaviour that can or has resulted in legal problems), intervention staff (e.g., social workers, counsellors, psychologists or psychiatrists) and community supervision staff (e.g., teachers, probation officers, mentors, case managers or human services caseworkers).

The multicultural intervention approach of preteen Social Responsibility Therapy

Teaching multicultural prosocial values as competing factors against multiple forms of abusive behaviour is an important aspect of preteen SRT. The theory that certain human values have universal content and structure, are basic and multicultural (Schwartz and Bilsky, 1987) has been tested in a study of values in Australia, Finland, Hong Kong, Spain and the United States. The results revealed that with an exception in Hong Kong, the motivational dynamics underlying people's value priorities are similar across the cultures studied (Schwartz and Bilsky, 1990).

Preteen SRT focuses on developing the positive multicultural prosocial values and behaviours that made our society a global model for socially responsible democracy. By teaching multicultural prosocial values (i.e. honesty, trust, loyalty, concern and responsibility) and behaviours (i.e. self-control and the work ethic) preteen SRT: respects cultural diversity; develops the individual social maturity needed to succeed in a democratic society and addresses the call that has been made for multicultural applications of cognitive-behavioural therapy (Hays, 1995). Since preteen SRT develops positive values and prosocial behaviours as competing factors against antisocial values and behaviour, it can be viewed as a criminal subculture antidote. The focus on the positive multicultural values of honesty, trust, loyalty, concern and responsibility makes preteen SRT ideal for parenting children who have prosocial values deficits associated with conduct problems.

The utility of the multicultural therapeutic community social learning approach of preteen SRT involving social learning experiences implemented by rational authority and supported by socially responsible peer role models in a functional family setting has been demonstrated throughout the world with multicultural research spanning back almost 20 years (Biase and

Sullivan, 1986). With respect to one type of abuse behaviour (i.e., substance abuse), the social learning approach used in preteen SRT has been referred to as 'The predominant residential modality for treating addictions from Chile to China' (Waters et al., 2002). Multicultural research on Therapeutic Community treatment procedures has been implemented to improve treatment retention of both African Americans and Native Americans in the United States (DeLeon et al., 1993; Fisher, Lankford and Galea, 1996).

The best practice treatment approach of preteen Social Responsibility Therapy

Preteen SRT utilises best practice social learning and operant conditioning methods to address multiple forms of abusive behaviour. Social learning in a Therapeutic Community environment is a best practice behaviour management procedure for preteen children with abuse behaviour problems. Since children with social-emotional immaturity and associated abuse behaviour problems are not good vicarious learners and learn best by experience, Therapeutic Community learning experiences employ experiential treatment approaches that frequently require action on the part of the client. These experiential procedures use engrossment (exaggeration) of a point to illustrate it and over-correction by setting the self-control bar higher in treatment than is required to remain out of court custody in the community. This training approach is expressed in the slogan; 'You have to go to the opposite extreme to meet the median'.

The Therapeutic Community social learning approach fosters social-emotional maturity and empathy. Therapeutic Community Learning Experiences get the abuser in touch with the feelings of others, provide role reversal experiences and develop emotional expression responding which satisfies the three-component model of empathy (Feshbach and Feshbach, 1982) which has been found to facilitate prosocial behaviour and reduce aggressive behaviour (Eisenberg and Miller, 1987; Miller and Eisenberg, 1988).

The Therapeutic Community social learning emphasis on 'Right Living' is a best practice treatment for conduct disordered children with abusive behaviour because it specifically focuses on important values. The preteen SRT focus on developing honesty, trust, loyalty, concern and responsibility can be viewed as a behaviourally specific version of the Therapeutic Community focus on 'Right Living' and developing a positive lifestyle. Put another way, 'Right Living' in SRT means meeting operationally defined behaviour-specific social responsibility indicators of honesty, trust, loyalty, concern and responsibility.

Operant conditioning with a Token Economy point-level system is another best practice behaviour change procedure for preteen children with abuse behaviour problems. The Token Economy point-level system best meets the abuse-reactive child's treatment needs for rigid structure, parenting consistency and objective discipline. The Token Economy system addresses parenting practices known to result in abuse reactive conduct problem behaviour, i.e. increasing structure, involvement, supervision, discipline consistency and reinforcement while decreasing emotion-based discipline (Brand, Crous and Hanekom, 1990; Goldstein and Heaven, 2000; Jang and Smith, 1997). The Token Economy system provides a very high level of structure where all target behaviours and consequences are clearly defined and learning is improved through repetition. This learning environment meets the support needs of both insecure victims and immature abusers who need rigid structure.

The Token Economy point-level system extends beyond the home into the school and community. It involves change agents in all settings where the child must learn adaptive prosocial functioning for consistent, contingent, supportive intervention. This intervention across settings helps regain control over free time and peer relations. School is monitored through a behaviour point card that is brought home each day, 'an adult who is aware of their problem' supervises community activities and peer activities are with approved associates (positive, age appropriate peers met and approved by a supervising adult).

Conduct disordered, maltreated children tend to get preoccupied with injustices. This preoccupation can trigger resentful reactions that divert the emphasis away from the treatment and blocks the development of prosocial skills. Thus, in best practice socially responsible parenting, objective discipline based on behaviour and choices replaces subjective discipline based on parent emotion. 'You get what you earn' not what someone feels like you deserve. This is important in order to counteract the dysfunctional family environment where punishment occurred when adults were angry, not when the child misbehaved. A 'matter of fact' point system helps stop emotion-based discipline that triggers resentful reactions.

Best practice social learning and operant conditioning methods are combined in preteen SRT. Present research tends to indicate that Token Economy operant conditioning and Therapeutic Community social learning are equally effective behaviour change methods. For example, a comparison study with conduct-disordered adolescents (age 14–18) receiving treatment in a Therapeutic Community and a modified token economy were compared ($n = 288$) on multiple measures at three points in the treatment process. The results revealed that despite an overall trend toward improvement in both groups, there was little difference between the rates of progress over time (Mann-Feder, 1996).

From a clinical standpoint, it is important to combine an effective method of decreasing negative, antisocial behaviour, such as the Token Economy approach, with an effective method of developing positive, prosocial behaviour, such as the Therapeutic Community approach, for maximum client benefit. While neither of these approaches appear to have a stronger impact than the other, another reason to combine these methods has to do with targeting social interaction. While very effective at modifying target behaviours, the Token Economy does not appear to impact social interaction. Specifically, while token reinforcement control is clearly demonstrated with behaviour compliance in delinquent boys, social interaction behaviour shows fluctuations, which appear unrelated to reinforcement contingencies (Holt, Hobbs and Hankins, 1976). Since abusive conduct behaviour involves social interactions and social interactions appear independent of external token rewarded behaviour, a method to target social interactions is needed. The Therapeutic Community approach targets social interaction and focuses on teaching prosocial values and skills.

In order to provide education and the social development of positive, prosocial behaviour as an alternative to existing negative antisocial behaviour in children with abusive behaviour, two basic things must occur. An effective intervention to modify negative, antisocial behaviour must be implemented at the same time that an effective intervention to develop positive, prosocial behaviour is implemented. Thus, Therapeutic Community social methods need to be combined with the Token Economy operant conditioning approach in best practice treatment protocols.

The clinical and theoretical support for combining the Token Economy and Therapeutic Community has research support as well. For example, one study revealed that including a token economy in a therapeutic community model as an alternative to incarceration for adolescent multiple offenders revealed a recidivism rate of 15 per cent compared to the state training school rate of 50–80 per cent at two-year follow-up (Martin and Rash, 1978). In another study, conduct disordered, substance-abusing children (aged 9–16 years) receiving residential therapeutic community treatment, which included a token economy system, revealed 92 per cent substance-free behaviour at three to five years post-treatment (Lowenstein, 1991).

Developing social responsibility skills: Re-parenting with preteen Social Responsibility Therapy

The purpose of parenting is to assure success in the world by teaching social responsibility skills. In a socially responsible society, which honours diversity and protects the rights of all citizens, a least common denominator of positive multicultural values includes honesty, trust, loyalty, concern and responsibility. These positive multicultural values cannot be implemented without self-control. Reasons why these social responsibility skills were not learned by abusive children include: (1) no teachers (absent parents); (2) unskilled teachers (parents lacked these skills themselves, involved criminal or addict lifestyle); (3) impaired teachers (parent psychopathology required all their energy to maintain self, parents present but not able to teach, e.g. depressed) or (4) refusal to learn (parents taught social responsibility but child authority problem resulted in rejecting their teaching).

Punishment by the justice system for abusive behaviour is not sufficient to stop abusive behaviour. Punishing irresponsible behaviour without rewarding responsible behaviour is asking our children to figure out what is wrong with them and then correct it themselves. In SRT,

what is considered wrong with them is pathological social-emotional immaturity manifest by a deficit in honesty, trust, loyalty, concern, responsibility, self-awareness, self-efficacy and self-control. Thus, regardless of the reason that these social responsibility skills were not acquired, it is everyone's responsibility to re-parent abusive children, to help them develop these skills and learn to accept the social responsibilities that were either not acquired or were rejected in the past.

Parental practices and characteristics are the best predictors of later conduct problems and abusive delinquent, behaviour (Baldry and Farrington, 2000; Farrington et al., 2001; Farrington and Loeber, 2000; Sirpal, 2002). SRT in the family setting involves socially responsible parenting by the primary caretaker staff (e.g. birth parents, kinship parents, foster parents, adoptive parents or residential setting staff). The main goal of socially responsible parenting is social-emotional maturity development, which involves teaching the prosocial multicultural values of honesty, trust, loyalty, concern, responsibility as competing factors to antisocial abusive behaviour.

Abuse-reactive children need to be re-parented through the phases of social responsibility development that they missed as a result of their past dysfunctional, abusive or neglectful family life. Socially responsible parents and intervention staff need to implement a supportive Structured Discovery through these phases by being a good teacher of the SRT multicultural prosocial values using effective supervision, instruction tenacity, confrontation with concern, responsible assertiveness and rational responding to provocation. Neglected, parentalised children who have had to take on the responsibilities of absent parents or abused children who have had to deal with the problems of abusive parents never moved through the normal developmental stages where parents were absolute authorities as preschoolers (compliance training – learning to listen), life teachers during grade school, coaches during high school (initiative training – learning by trying and doing) and finally mentor friends when they became adults (responsibility training – learning by positive role modelling). Many were just thrown into the role of friends with parents who needed them too much or enemies with parents who did not want them. The SRT responsibility-privilege system re-parents these children beginning by providing them with a high level of authority and phasing that out as they respond to the consistency, structure and behaviour-based empowerment of the social responsibility development programme.

The present responsibility development-based treatment teaches prosocial alternatives to antisocial abusive behaviours as a primary method to develop socially healthy, positive living habits in abuse-reactive conduct problem children. Since many of these children have a complete lack of socially responsible behaviour control, socially healthy development begins with a focus on behaviour compliance during Phase One while responsibility completion and emotion management skills are being taught. The healthy development focus is expanded to include responsibility completion on Phase Two while emotion management skills continue to be taught. On Phase Three, the healthy development focus is expanded again to include development of behaviour compliance, responsibility completion and emotional control. A summary of the preteen social responsibility skills development in the phases of SRT is provided in Table 19.1 below.

Abuse-reactive conduct problem children have problems forming attachments; it wouldn't be as easy for them to abuse if they could attach. This directly interferes with primary caretaker bonding and the intervention staff therapeutic alliance, which is usually the basis for developing cooperation in the home. With these children, 'the goal of bonding needs to be replaced with the goal of responding'.

Bonding can be replaced with responding through the use of a Token Economy because although these children cannot attach enough to work for people, they can work for points. Put another way, although initially they do not trust enough to work for others, they can still work for themselves. Doing the right thing for the wrong reason is still a first step in the right direction. Later as responsibility and social maturity develops, this will open an emotional attachment opportunity. At first, the reason for the child to be responsible will be to get trust in order to get what they want. Later the reason to be responsible will be to maintain the trust of valued relationships or 'attachment'.

Preteen SRT addresses immature acting out by developing security through structure (i.e., 'Immature people need rigid structure') and self-control through over-correction (i.e. 'You have to go to the opposite extreme to meet the median'). In addition, preteen SRT addresses transfer of training by creating a treatment environment similar to the community environment in order to maximise positive community adjustment (i.e. 'Make the inside of the house like the outside world'). These three basic guidelines for social maturity development are greatly aided by peer support of social responsibilities to 'Think the right thing, Say the right thing and Do the right thing' using ongoing written and verbal feedback.

Preteen SRT intervention procedures and techniques are not dependent on a particular delivery method and can be applied to group, family or individual session format depending on the clinician's preferences, training, experience and method that they are most effective in

Table 19.1   Phases of preteen social responsibility development

Phase	Behaviour compliance	Responsibility completion	Emotional control
Phase 1 One social maturity skill is developed	**Focus on:** (1) **Development** of behaviour compliance through reinforced practice	**Teaching** proper completion of basic responsibilities	**Teaching** basic emotion reaction prevention methods
Phase 2 Two social maturity skills are developed	**Focus on:** (1) **Development** of behaviour compliance through reinforced practice (2) **Development** of responsibility completion through reinforced practice		**Teaching** basic emotion reaction prevention methods
Phase 3 Three social maturity skills are developed	**Focus on:** (1) **Development** of behaviour compliance though reinforced practice (2) **Development** of responsibility completion through reinforced practice (3) **Development** of emotional control through reinforced practice		

utilising. In general, the behaviour change feedback in individual therapy comes from the individual, in family therapy it comes from the family and in group therapy it comes from the group. In preteen SRT, the environment is structured to help those in treatment discover things about themselves from their entire social setting. This Structured Discovery environment captures individual feedback, family feedback, group feedback and community feedback (i.e. school or job site) to provide social responsibility development data.

Structured discovery in preteen Social Responsibility Therapy

Preteen SRT uses a Structured Discovery approach, which provides a high-structured therapeutic behaviour feedback framework within which an individual discovers their thoughts, feelings, and motivations to act out irresponsibly. The preteen SRT Structured Discovery approach is more than just a set of psychoeducational lectures and involves interacting with others to experience the negative habitual responses presented through a structured feedback system in order to implement reinforced practice of prosocial alternatives. Put simply, 'If you always do what you've always done, you'll always get what you always got'. In other words, you need to do differently in order to discover that your different behaviour produces a different outcome and Structured Discovery provides the experiential human feedback and interaction needed for individuals to discover that critical life learning experience.

The first important piece of the structural framework in the SRT Structured Discovery approach for preteens is a clearly defined set of social responsibilities. The biggest social responsibility bestowed on humans is mobilising self-control to follow rules developed to protect the rights of others. Development of social

responsibility rule compliance can't occur if there are no responsibility rules to comply with so a structured set of SRT guidelines are provided. A second important piece of the structural framework in the preteen SRT Structured Discovery approach for preteens is a behaviour feedback system to reinforce socially responsible behaviour and extinguish socially irresponsible behaviour. As mentioned earlier, the preteen SRT programme utilises elements of the Token Economy approach to help preteens decrease their own irresponsible, antisocial behaviour and develop responsible, prosocial behaviour by targeting key social responsibilities to be developed and to provide the high level of structure needed by preteens with abuse behaviour problems.

The structural framework of the Structured Discovery used with preteen children is a set of social responsibilities (rules and responsibilities) motivated by an operant conditioning-based token economy and a behaviour management slip feedback system supported by the Therapeutic Community philosophy encouraging peer feedback to expedite and reinforce behaviour change (Table 2).

The discovery methods in SRT Structured Discovery involve Awareness Training (e.g. basic social responsibilities),Tolerance Training (e.g. tangible reinforcement of social responsibilities) and Responsibility Training (e.g. peer support of social responsibilities).

The 'ART' of preteen Social Responsibility Therapy

The structure portion of Structured Discovery for preteens involves basic social responsibilities, tangible reinforcement of those responsibilities and peer support of those responsibilities. Since children with social-emotional immaturity and associated abuse behaviour problems are not good vicarious learners and learn best by experience, treatment learning experiences must

Table 19.2 The Social Responsibility Therapy Structured Discovery approach for preteens with abusive behaviour

Structured procedures	Discovery methods
Basic social responsibilities	Awareness training
Tangible reinforcement of social responsibilities	Responsibility training
Peer support of social responsibilities	Tolerance training

be experiential in nature in order to promote their 'learning by doing' needs. Thus, preteen SRT includes many exercises designed to develop the child's social-emotional awareness, social responsibility and frustration tolerance.

A socially responsible preteen is aware, responsible and tolerant. The Structured Discovery methods in preteen SRT involve the ART of Awareness Training, Responsibility Training and Tolerance Training.

Awareness Training – makes you aware of the feelings and motivations that create the urge to act out. Just like you can't change a feeling that you're not aware of, you also can't change a behaviour pattern unless you're aware of it. Awareness Training in preteen SRT is based on the premise that in order to improve you must first become aware of what needs to be changed. Awareness of what needs to be changed is the first step towards change. Self-awareness is not automatic and must be developed. Awareness begins with learning to use feedback from others to develop awareness of self. Awareness Training makes you aware of the feelings and motivations that you have the urge to act out. 'Learning how to learn' involves getting to the point where you can accept that 'Other people see you better than you see yourself' and use the feedback of others to learn about yourself and what you need to change. Awareness is trained in three basic areas: Awareness of our self; Awareness of others and Awareness of our past.

Since it is important for abusive children to gain some understanding of how they developed their abusive behaviour, a developmentally appropriate explanation of the Abuse Development Triad (Yokley, 1996) which covers how abusive behaviour was acquired, maintained and generalised is needed. Depending on their developmental level, with preteens, this is sometimes explained as: Steps that lead to Trouble; the Trouble Cycle and the Troubled Child. Since the number of abuse victims for this population is relatively small (i.e. an average of two victims) compared to adolescents and adults, the emphasis is on how the behaviour was acquired and how it spread into several problem areas. The behaviour maintenance cycle is covered but emphasised only on cases with a pattern of continually repeating a behaviour that is sexually abusive, physically abusive, abusive to others' property or to self (e.g. substance abuse).

An Awareness Training exercise example is the handprint history. This exercise helps children become aware of the history of abuse they perpetrated and endured (i.e. physical and/or sexual) as well as identifying the feelings of everyone involved in those abusive situations. The children begin by making several handprints on paper plates which are colour coded to represent the different feelings that they disclosed when discussing their histories of abusive behaviour (red) and being abused (blue). The children are then asked to detail one abusive situation per picture that depicts who, what, when, where, how and why they perpetrated the abuse along with how they felt after being abused. For example, 'My second handprint is a red one. I got it at age six when I touched my little sisters private parts. She was four. I did this to my sister because I wanted to do to her what my step-dad did to me'.

Responsibility Training – involves using awareness to act responsibly by doing what you need to do to help self and others. Responsible actions are based on awareness and tolerance of behaviour feedback. Initially, the preteen SRT programme provides behaviour feedback with a Token Economy point system, which is later thinned out to a behaviour feedback slip system. Responsibility training occurs during SRT group, family and individual sessions through support for and reinforcement of responsible actions.

Human beings were built to react to environmental stimuli with self-protective defences. All humans react to things; the key is to react responsibly. Responsible reaction involves being aware of your feelings, what you want to do (i.e. irresponsible urges) and what you need to do (i.e. responsibility knowledge). In addition to on the spot reactions to situations, humans plan deliberate actions to address problems and meet needs. Responsible actions are rational actions. Rational actions are thought-out actions unbiased by emotions (i.e. actions based on social responsibility, not actions that are justified by feelings). Therefore, responsible actions often need to be delayed until alternatives have been considered and the best action is selected based on the expected impact to self and others. The preteen key to responsible action is 'Think the responsible thing, say the responsible thing and do the responsible thing'.

A Responsibility Training exercise example involves teaching preteens to consistently use their responsibility scales. Often children overestimate the cost of doing the responsible thing and underestimate the cost of failing to do so (Adapted from common rationalisations-Josephson Institute of Ethics). When looking at 'what I want to do' (i.e. the irresponsible thing) and 'what I should do or need to do' (i.e. the responsible thing), a big help in deciding to do the responsible thing is to ask yourself how necessary, important or bad would it be to do the responsible thing or not to do the irresponsible thing? This is done using one of three scales to help the child see reality and avoid emotion-based decisions by thinking through feelings. Older children are usually capable of learning and using the survival and success scales for the right situation, but younger children may have to be taught to use a single 'Bad' Scale for all reality testing. The Bad Scale (termed 'Awful Scale' by Bernard and Wolfe, 1993) evaluates how bad doing the responsible thing or failing to do it would be on a scale of zero (not bad at all) to 10 (so bad that it can stop your heart and breathing). For example, how bad would it be if I didn't hit or touch this person? Would it stop my heart and breathing?

Tolerance Training – targets the 'Problem of Immediate Gratification – PIG' (Marlatt, 1989) involving the lack of tenacity, self-control and ability to delay gratification that results in abusive acting out. Tolerance Training involves the development of enough frustration tolerance and emotional control to do what you need to do to help self and others consistently and under stress. Abusive children do what they want to do, when they want to do it for the reason they want to do it. They have no tolerance for frustration of their needs or urges and must have 'my way right away'. Tolerance training involves developing the ability to delay gratification of needs in order to be able to cope with the four abusive urges to touch, hit, take or lie. Tolerance Training teaches children tolerance of frustration, tenacity, delay of gratification and the self-efficacy needed to 'stop feeding the PIG' and suppress the urge to act out.

A Frustration Tolerance Training example would be implementing a chain of command and procedure system where children must submit a request to the appropriate person for what they want and then wait for it in order to teach the child to delay gratification by 'making the inside of the house like the outside world'. For instance, if the child is looking to participate in an activity, they are required to get permission from their parent first before asking the Social Responsibility Therapy staff. If the child attempts to ask the

therapist first, they are immediately redirected back to their parent. This teaches the child that in the real world, you can't get what you want, when you want it, you must follow the appropriate procedure and wait to get what you want.

Discharge planning

With automobiles, there is no sense in repairing damage if you are not working on a solution to prevent another collision. Fixing fenders without sending drunk drivers for treatment before giving them their license back sets the community up for a vicious cycle of destructive behaviour. Likewise, getting a preteen abuser to the point where they are able to control their behaviour within the confines of a supportive, structured Forensic Foster Care environment and then transferring them to an unsupportive, unstructured parent care environment also sets the community up for a vicious cycle of destructive behaviour. Ideally, the primary caretakers in the aftercare plan are motivated to be involved in treatment from the beginning, including training. In less ideal cases, Human Services reunification plans need to mandate parent training for abusive children in SRT methods used to manage abusive behaviour prior to actual family reunification. In problem cases, failure to follow reunification plans involving the completion of parent training in abuse behaviour management will require a reunification plan change to a caretaker willing to complete that training. This is needed to provide the support and structure necessary to maintain healthy behaviour after completion of preteen SRT Forensic Foster Care treatment.

Discharge planning in preteen SRT begins at admission of the child. Ideally, the aftercare parent (birth parent, relative, foster parent or adoptive parent) should be receiving parallel treatment and training during the course of the child's preteen SRT placement. This is important because of the research which shows that in order to maximise the efficacy of treatment for their children, parents of children with sexual behaviour problems must be centrally involved and receive services coordinated with those of their child (Pithers et. al., 1998b).

Family reunification readiness involves a case review meeting where it is determined if the child's social responsibility, openness to family about abuse behaviour, acceptance of aftercare supervision contract and commitment to avoid negative peers is high while relapse risk is low.

The last assignment to complete in preteen SRT is the Commitment Letter which reviews the past abuse behaviour along with what was learned about how to avoid further abuse behaviour (i.e. social responsibility skills/behaviours) and a commitment to maintain socially responsible behaviour control by continuing to practice those social responsibility skills/behaviours.

Often times, treatment providers of children moving on to the next level of care become concerned about their ability to adapt and succeed especially in 'sleeper' cases where it seems that social responsibility has been developing at a snails pace. Since 'people grow up when they have to', a well supervised discharge plan can sometimes force 'sleeper' cases to wake up, rise to the challenge and use the treatment tools that providers have heard them repeat but not seen them put into practice.

Summary and conclusion

In summary, preteen SRT addresses multiple forms of abuse that create a danger to self and others, violate our basic human rights and tear the moral fabric of our society, i.e. sexual abuse, physical abuse, property abuse, substance abuse and trust abuse. The cost in human suffering and tax dollars associated with any one of these abuse behaviour problems is enormous but, when combined, a state of social emergency is created.

Preteen SRT is a responsible behaviour development approach for individuals who exhibit multiple forms of abusive behaviour. Preteen SRT addresses abuse with research-informed techniques and best practice procedures. This is accomplished with a Structured Discovery approach that teaches prosocial alternatives to antisocial abusive behaviour and promotes successful community adjustment by developing multicultural family values.

Preteen SRT gradually exposes children to more and more socially healthy development tasks in a cumulative manner beginning with behaviour compliance moving on to include responsibility completion and finally adding emotional reaction control. The main focus of preteen SRT is on preteens learning to evaluate

whether the action being considered is helpful or harmful to self or others. If it is helpful to self and others it is socially responsible and needs to be implemented. If it is harmful to self and others it is socially irresponsible and needs to be blocked.

Preteen SRT has a multicultural pro-social values focus which: respects cultural diversity; develops the individual social maturity children need to succeed in a democratic society; addresses the call for multicultural applications to cognitive-behavioural therapy (Hays, 1995) and parenting skills programmes; makes it easily adaptable to diverse family settings and multi-denominational faith-based treatment initiatives. This is critical to the maintenance of democratic society where social responsibility is a purpose in life. The social learning experiences utilised in preteen SRT addresses the special needs of the abuser population and has been demonstrated throughout the world with almost 20 years of multicultural Therapeutic Community research support.

A final point that needs to be underscored is that SRT has strong social validity, i.e. social significance of treatment goals, social appropriateness of procedures and social importance of the effects (Wolf, 1978). The SRT goals of developing honesty, trust, loyalty, concern, and responsibility are necessary for stopping abusive behaviour and starting healthy relationships.

The increasing lack of social responsibility and associated multiple forms of abusive behaviour consistently described in the news media tears at the moral fabric of our society and threatens the civil rights, safety and security of our citizens. Continued media commentary about the increase in crime, erosion of family values and glorification of the criminal subculture have made it clear that a preteen Social Responsibility Therapy capable of addressing multiple forms of abuse needs to begin now if we intend to maintain a society which is equipped to guarantee our basic human rights.

This chapter has been condensed and reprinted from *Social Responsibility Therapy for Preteen Children: A Multicultural Treatment Manual for Parents, Therapists and Program Administrators.* (2004) with copyright permission from the author. Available from James Yokley, Ph.D. www.forensicare.org.

References

Abel, G.G. et al. (1987) Self-reported Sex Crimes of Nonincarcerated Paraphiliacs. *Journal of Interpersonal Violence.* 2, 3–25.

Amir, M. (1971) *Patterns of Forcible Rape*, Chicago: University of Chicago Press.

Andrew, J.M. (1981) Delinquency: Correlating Variables. *Journal of Clinical Child Psychology.* 10: 2, 136–40.

Andrews, J. and Duncan, S. (1997) Examining the Reciprocal Relation between Academic Motivation and Substance Use: Effects of Family Relationships. Self-esteem and General Deviance. *Journal of Behavioural Medicine,* 20: 6, 523–49.

Awad, G., Saunders, E. and Levene, J. (1984) A Clinical Study of Male Adolescent Sexual Offenders. *International Journal of Offender Therapy and Comparative Criminology.* 28, 105–15.

Baldry, A.C. and Farrington, D.P. (2000) Bullies and Delinquents: Personal Characteristics and Parental Styles. *Journal of Community and Applied Social Psychology.* 10: 1, 17–31.

Becker, J. et al. (1986) Characteristics of Adolescent Incest Perpetrators: Preliminary Findings. *Journal of Family Violence.* 1, 85–97.

Bernard, M. and Wolfe, J. (1993) *The RET Resource Book for Practitioners: Innovative RET Techniques for Practitioners With Reproducible Client Self-Help Articles and Handouts.* New York: Institute for Rational-Emotive Therapy.

Biase, D. and Sullivan, A. (1986) Emerging Cross-Cultural Therapeutic Community Research. *Journal of Psychoactive Drugs.* 18: 3, 199–201.

Brand, H.J., Crous, B.H. and Hanekom, J.D. (1990) Perceived Parental Inconsistency as a Factor in the Emotional Development of Behaviour-Disordered Children. *Psychological Reports.* 66: 2, 620–2.

Butts, J.A. and Snyder, H.N. (1997) The Youngest Delinquents: Offenders Under Age. *Juvenile Justice Bulletin,* 1–11.

Carden, A. (1994) Wife Abuse and the Wife Abuser: Review and Recommendations. *The Counseling Psychologist.* 22: 4, 539–82.

DeLeon, G. et al. (1993) Is the Therapeutic Community Culturally Relevant? Findings on Race/Ethnic Differences in Retention in Treatment. *Journal of Psychoactive Drugs.* 25: 1, 77–86.

Eisenberg, J.G. et al. (1975) Differences in the Behaviour of Welfare and Non-Welfare Children in Relation to Parental Characteristics. *Journal of Community Psychology.* 3: 4, 311–40.

Eisenberg, N. and Miller, P.A. (1987) The Relation of Empathy to Prosocial and Related Behaviours. *Psychological Bulletin.* 101: 91–119.

Farrington, D.P. and Loeber, R. (2000) Epidemiology of Juvenile Violence. *Child and Adolescent Psychiatric Clinics of North America,* 9: 4, 733–48

Farrington, D.P. et al. (2001) The Concentration of Offenders in Families, and Family Criminality in the Prediction of Boys' Delinquency. *Journal of Adolescence.* 24: 5, 579–96.

Fehrenbach, P. et al. (1986) Adolescent Sexual Offenders: Offender and Offense Characteristics. *American Journal of Orthopsychiatry.* 56, 225–33.

Fendrich, M. et al. (1995) Substance Involvement Among Juvenile Murderers: Comparisons With Older Offenders Based on Interviews With Prison Inmates. *International Journal of the Addictions.* 30: 1, 1363–82.

Feshbach, N. and Feshbach, S. (1982) Empathy Training and the Regulation of Aggression: Potentialities and Limitations. *Academic Psychology Bulletin.* 4, 399–413.

Finkelhor, D. (1990) Early and Long-Term Effects of Child Sexual Abuse: An Update. *Professional Psychology: Research and Practice.* 21: 5, 325–30.

Fisher, D., Lankford, B. and Galea, R. (1996) Therapeutic Community Retention Among Alaska Natives: Akeela House. *Journal of Substance Abuse Treatment.* 13: 3, 265–71.

Frick, P.J. et al. (1992) Familial Risk Factors to Oppositional Defiant Disorder and Conduct Disorder: Parental Psychopathology and Maternal Parenting. *Journal of Consulting and Clinical Psychology.* 60: 1, 49–55.

Gallup, G.H., Jr., Moor, D.W. and Schussel, R. (1997) *Disciplining Children in America.* Princeton, NJ: The Gallup Organisation.

Gil, E. (1987) *Children Who Molest: A Guide for Parents of Young Sex Offenders.* Walnut Creek, CA: Launch Press.

Goldstein, M. and Heaven, P.C.L. (2000) Perceptions of the Family, Delinquency, and Emotional Adjustment Among Youth. *Personality and Individual Differences.* 29: 6, 1169–78.

Gray, A. et al. (1997) Children With Sexual Behaviour Problems and Their Caregivers: Demographics, Functioning, and Clinical Patterns. *Sexual Abuse: Journal of Research and Treatment.* 9: 4, 267–90.

Gray, A. et al. (1999) Developmental and Etiological Characteristics of Children With Sexual Behaviour Problems: Treatment Implications. *Child Abuse and Neglect.* 23: 6, 601–21.

Gray-Ray, P. and Ray, M.C. (1990) Juvenile Delinquency in the Black Community. *Youth and Society.* 22: 1, 67–84.

Haapasalo, J. and Tremblay, R.E. (1994) Physically Aggressive Boys From Ages 6 To 12: Family Background, Parenting Behaviour, and Prediction of Delinquency. *Journal of Consulting and Clinical Psychology.* 62: 5, 1044–52.

Hays, P. (1995) Multicultural Applications of Cognitive-Behavioural Therapy. *Professional Psychology: Research and Practice.* 26: 3, 309–15.

Herrenkohl, T.I. et al. (2001) Early Adolescent Predictors of Youth Violence as Mediators of Childhood Risks. *Journal of Early Adolescence.* 21: 4, 447–69.

Holt, M.M., Hobbs, T.R. and Hankins, R. (1976) The Effects of Token Reinforcement on Delinquents' Classroom Behaviour. *Psychology in the Schools.* 13: 3, 341–7

Jang, S.J. and Smith, C.A. (1997) A Test of Reciprocal Causal Relationships Among Parental Supervision, Affective Ties, and Delinquency. *Journal of Research in Crime and Delinquency.* 34: 3, 307–36.

Jessor, R. and Jessor, S.L. (1977) The social-psychological framework. In Jessor, R. and Jessor, S.L. (Eds.) *Problem Behaviour and Psychosocial Development: A Longitudinal Study of Youth.* New York: Academic Press.

Johnson, B.D., Dunlap, E. and Maher, L. (1998) Nurturing for Careers in Drug Use and Crime: Conduct Norms for Children and Juveniles in Crack-Using Households. *Substance Use and Misuse.* 33: 7, 1511–46.

Johnson, T. (2002) Some Considerations About Sexual Abuse and Children With Sexual Behaviour Problems. *Journal of Trauma and Dissociation.* 3: 4, 83–105.

Kandel, D.B. (1990) Parenting Styles, Drug Use, and Children's Adjustment in Families of Young Adults. *Journal of Marriage and the Family.* 52: 1, 183–96.

Koznar, J. (1976) Family Rearing in Relationship to Dissocial Behaviour and Its Prevention. *Psychologia a Patopsychologia Dietata.* 11: 1, 45–52.

Lahey, B.B. et al. (1995) Four-year Longitudinal Study of Conduct Disorder in Boys: Patterns and Predictors of Persistence. *Journal of Abnormal Psychology.* 104: 1, 83–93.

Laybourn, A. (1986) Traditional Strict Working Class Parenting: An Undervalued System. *British Journal of Social Work.* 16: 6, 625–44.

Lightfoot, L. and Barbaree, H. (1993) The Relationship Between Substance Use and Abuse and Sexual Offending in Adolescents. In Barbaree, Marshall and Hudson (Eds.) *The Juvenile Sex Offender.* New York: The Guilford Press.

Loeber, R. and Dishion, T. (1983) Early Predictors of Male Delinquency: A Review. *Psychological Bulletin.* 94: 1, 68–99.

Loeber, R. and Farrington, D.P. (2000) Young Children Who Commit Crime: Epidemiology, Developmental Origins, Risk Factors, Early Interventions, and Policy Implications. *Development and Psychopathology.* 12: 4, 737–62

Lowenstein, L.F. (1991) The Relationship of Psychiatric Disorder and Conduct Disorders With Substance Abuse. *Journal of Psychoactive Drugs.* 23: 3, 283–7.

Mak, A.S. (1994) Parental Neglect and Overprotection as Risk Factors in Delinquency. *Australian Journal of Psychology.* 46: 2, 107–11.

Mak, A.S. (1996) Adolescent Delinquency and Perceptions of Parental Care and Protection: A Case Control Study. *Journal of Family Studies.* 2: 1, 29–39.

Mann-Feder, V. (1996) Adolescents in Therapeutic Communities. *Adolescence.* 31: 121, 17–28.

Marlatt, G.A. (1989) Feeding the Pig: The Problem of Immediate Gratification. In Laws, R. (Ed.) *Relapse Prevention With Sex Offenders.* New York: Gilford Press.

Martin, C.V. and Rash, J.D. (1978) The Therapeutic Community in an Open Ward Psychiatric Hospital as Alternative for Incarceration for Juvenile Offenders. *Corrective and Social Psychiatry and Journal of Behaviour Technology, Methods and Therapy.* 24: 2, 51–5.

Miller, P.A. and Eisenberg, N. (1988) The Relation of Empathy to Aggressive and Externalising Antisocial Behaviour. *American Association.* 103: 3, 324–44.

Miranda, A. and Davis, K. (2002) Sexually Abusive Children: Etiological and Treatment Considerations. In Schwartz, B. (Ed.) *The Sex Offender.* Kingston, NJ: Civic Research Institute.

Patterson, G.R. and Yoerger, K. (1995) Two Different Models for Adolescent Physical Trauma and for Early Arrest. *Criminal Behaviour and Mental Health.* 5: 4, 411–23.

Pithers, W.D. and Gray, A. (1998) The Other Half of the Story: Children With Sexual Behaviour

Problems. *Psychology, Public Policy, and Law.* 4: 1–2, 200–17.

Pithers, W.D. et al. (1998) Children With Sexual Behaviour Problems: Identification of Five Distinct Child Types and Related Treatment Considerations. *Child Maltreatment: Journal of the American Professional Society on the Abuse of Children.* 3: 4, 384–406.

Pithers, W.D. et al. (1998b) Caregivers of Children With Sexual Behaviour Problems: Psychological and Familial Functioning. *Child Abuse and Neglect.* 22: 2, 129–41.

Robins, L.N., West, P.A. and Herjanic, B.L. (1975) Arrests and Delinquency in Two Generations: A Study of Black Urban Families and Their Children. *Journal of Child Psychology and Psychiatry and Allied Disciplines.* 16: 2, 125–40.

Schwartz, S. and Bilsky, W. (1990) Toward a Theory of the Universal Content and Structure of Values: Extensions and Cross-Cultural Replications, *Journal of Personality and Social Psychology.* 58: 5, 878–91.

Schwartz, S.H. and Bilsky, W. (1987) Toward a Psychological Structure of Human Values. *Journal of Personality and Social Psychology.* 53, 550–62.

Shoor, M., Speed, M. and Bartelt, C. (1966) Syndrome of the Adolescent Child Molester. *American Journal of Psychiatry.* 122, 783–9.

Sirpal, S.K. (2002) Familial Criminality, Familial Drug Use, and Gang Membership: Youth Criminality, Drug Use, and Gang Membership-What are the Connections? *Journal of Gang Research.* 9: 2, 11–22.

Smith, S.M. and Hanson, R. (1975) Interpersonal Relationships and Childrearing Practices in 214 Parents of Battered Children. *British Journal of Psychiatry.* 127: 513–25.

Stenmark, D.E. et al. (1974) Substance Use Among Juvenile Offenders: Relationships to Parental Substance Use and Demographic Characteristics. *Addictive Diseases: An International Journal.* 1: 1, 43–54.

Stouthamer-Loeber, M. and Loeber, R. (2002) Lost Opportunities for Intervention: Undetected Markers for the Development of Serious Juvenile Delinquency. *Criminal Behaviour and Mental Health.* 12: 1, 69–82.

Van Ness, S. (1984) Rape as Instrumental Violence: A Study of Youth Offenders. *Journal of Offender Counseling, Services and Rehabilitation,* 9, 161–70.

Viemeroe, V. (1996) Factors in Childhood That Predict Later Criminal Behaviour. *Aggressive Behaviour.* 22: 2, 87–97.

Walker-Barnes, C.J. and Mason, C.A. (2001) Ethnic Differences in the Effect of Parenting on Gang Involvement and Gang Delinquency: A Longitudinal, Hierarchical Linear Modeling Perspective. *Child Development.* 72: 6, 1814–31.

Waters, J. et al. (2002) The Story of CURA, a Hispanic/Latino Drug Therapeutic Community. *Journal of Ethnicity in Substance Abuse.* 1: 1, 113–34.

Wolf, M.M. (1978) Social Validity: The Case for Subjective Measurement. *Journal of Applied Behaviour Analysis,* 11: 203–14.

Yokley, J. (1996) *The Development of Abuse in Youth Sex Offenders: A Conceptual Model with Treatment Implications.* The 12th Annual Conference of the National Adolescent Perpetrator Network, Minneapolis, Minnesota.

Yokley, J. (in press) *Social Responsibility Therapy for Adolescents: A Multicultural Treatment for Harmful Behavior.* Trepper, T. (Ed.) Binghampton, NY: Haworth Press.

Yokley, J. and Boettner, S. (2002) Forensic Foster Care for Young People Who Sexually Abuse: Lessons from Treatment. In Calder, M. (Ed.) *Young People Who Sexually Abuse: Building the Evidence Base For Your Practice.* Lyme Regis: Russell House Publishing.

Chapter 20

Integrated Group Work for High Risk Adolescents with Diverse Needs

Rachel Edwards, Julian Dunn and Arnon Bentovim

Background

SWAAY is a residential therapeutic provision for young males age 11–15 years at referral, who are at high risk of sexual recidivism and also present with diverse needs. At inception in 1989 the organisation consisted of just one foster home and in the following 15 years has grown to six residential homes of an average of four young people. Although based in the Thames Valley referrals are taken from all over the UK and Ireland (Figure 20.1).

Maximum capacity is 22 residential placements; however, SWAAY continues to work with young people after a move to independence. SWAAY also has a growing assessment service.

The client group

SWAAY has worked with 105 individual young people at the time of writing, some of whom are currently still in placement. The ethnic mix (Figure 20.2) includes at least 14 per cent non white British. A high percentage of the SWAAY client group have some level of learning disability (Figure 20.3) which has to be accounted for in the treatment approach. The group have also been

Figure 20.1 Catchment area of SWAAY clients

Ethnicity

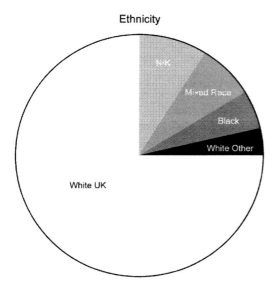

Figure 20.2   Ethnicity of SWAAY group

Learning Disability

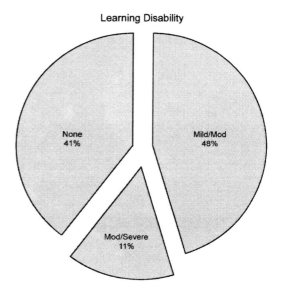

Figure 20.3   Learning disability of SWAAY group

subjected to a high level of trauma over the course of their lives, which in many cases has been multiple (Table 20.1).

Eighty eight per cent of the sample experienced five or more of the significant stressful experiences and 20 per cent experienced as many as nine or more. In the cross-sectional and longitudinal research at Great Ormond Street (GOS) (Skuse et al.) what differentiated a group of sexually abused boys who went on to abuse sexually was the number of additional abusive experiences they were exposed to. The most revealing difference was that the level of emotional abuse and rejection was only 57 per

cent in this community sample compared with potentially over 90 per cent of the SWAAY sample. Figure 20.4 illustrates the co-morbidity of diagnoses across the group, with Conduct and Emotional Disorders and Paraphilias relatively common. Attention Deficit Hyperactivity Disorder, Eating Disorders, Post Traumatic Stress Disorder as well as other disorders are less common, however, significantly impact on an individual's treatment plan.

When comparing offender type within the SWAAY population with a community based sample (Figure 20.5) it is possible to identify a more severe offending pattern in the SWAAY

Table 20.1   Significant stressful experiences of SWAAY group

Significant stressful experience	% yes	% suspected	% no	% not known
Exposed to known sex offender	37	8	44	11
Sexually maltreated	57	21	17	5
Witnessed sexual violence within the family	14	21	32	31
Witnessed pornography or sexual activity	54	15	16	14
Witnessed physical violence within the family	59	10	16	15
Physically abused	69	9	16	7
Neglect of care/exposure to danger	73	10	13	4
Emotional abuse/rejection/scapegoating in family	82	10	6	3
Social rejection in peer group	64	19	12	5
Bullied in peer group	64	15	15	6
Frequent moves	46	2	52	0
Other significant stressful experiences	49	3	47	2

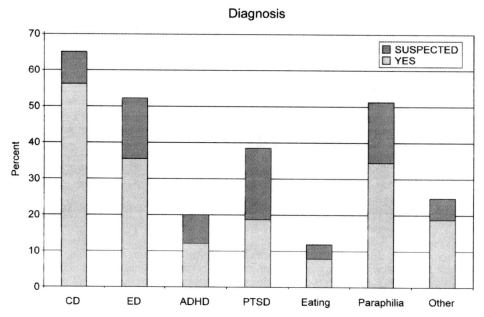

Figure 20.4   ICD 9 Diagnoses of SWAAY group

group with more individuals showing a cross over regarding age of victims (i.e. falling within the indiscriminate group). This may partly be a result of the actual number of victims per individual, in that the community sample were mostly limited to the one victim (73 per cent) in comparison to 27 per cent of the SWAAY sample. Of those individual's who admitted to more than one victim the mean number for the community sample was 3.3 compared with 4.3 in the SWAAY sample. Sixty one per cent of the SWAAY group committed some type of penetrative abuse (oral, anal, vaginal, or a combination) and another 15 per cent were suspected to have used penetration in their offences. In terms of cross over, 54 per cent of the SWAAY sample had abused male and female victims and 47 per cent had abused both within and outside the family. The SWAAY

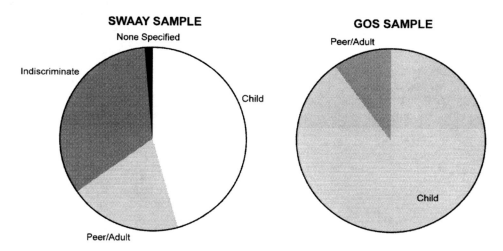

Figure 20.5   Offender type

group, therefore, cause significant concern in the community and hence require an intensive programme of work within the relative safety of a residential placement.

The philosophy

SWAAY is based on the philosophy that two preconditions must exist in order for sexual abuse to be perpetrated. These are:

1. A negative imbalance of power between the victim and abuser.
2. Secrecy.

The axiom on which SWAAY bases its work is thus the opposite of these:

1. Equality of communication of which:
2. Openness is the necessary condition.

Therefore: 'open' means 'equal' means 'same rights'.

The integrated approach

The general consensus through research is that a multi-modal treatment approach is preferred with adolescents who have a variety of developmental needs that must be addressed concurrently, and as a part of, their sex offence specific treatment (Cellini, 1995). Multi-modal methodology involves the use of several different treatment interventions simultaneously whilst having due regard for the triage approach to working with young people i.e. responding first and foremost to those needs which are most evident. Serious antisocial behaviour (Borduin, 1999) in adolescents is multi-determined, therefore, and requires a flexible approach in order to address these multiple determinants. SWAAY is a multi-component treatment facility which seeks to maximise the range of resources and services available to young people, while allowing for the highest level of continuity and coordination amongst these services. It is, therefore, a fully integrated approach to working with youth who have sexually abused (Figure 20.6).

The young person is considered at SWAAY to be central to his individualised treatment and care plan. It is thus necessary to have a structured process which is comprehensive and regularly reviewed. A Needs Assessment and Treatment planning (NAT) meeting takes place at three months into a young person's placement. By this point the young person will have settled in and will have a better idea about his own needs and goals, therefore, completes a personal assessment which is central to the meeting and resulting plan for the next nine month period. Representatives

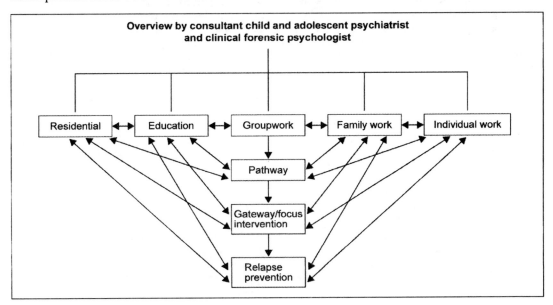

Figure 20.6 The integrative approach

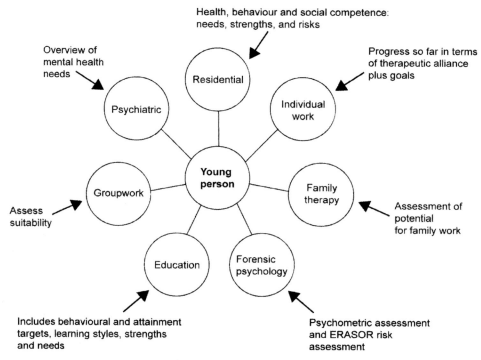

Health, behaviour and social competence:
needs, strengths, and risks

Overview of
mental health
needs

Progress so far in terms
of therapeutic alliance
plus goals

Residential

Psychiatric

Individual
work

Young
person

Groupwork

Family
therapy

Assess
suitability

Assessment of
potential
for family work

Education

Forensic
psychology

Includes behavioural and attainment
targets, learning styles, strengths
and needs

Psychometric assessment
and ERASOR risk
assessment

Figure 20.7   Needs Assessment and Treatment Planning meeting

from all aspects of the multi-component treatment programme (Figure 20.7) focus on strengths, needs, risks, strategies, future plans and targets. The resultant document covers all aspects of the young person's treatment plan.

The young person's Personal Assessment focuses on what they believe are their main strengths, concerns, and goals for the future. Their view on relationships within and outside the organisation is commented upon as well as any requests and feedback on their experiences in SWAAY so far. Development of items considered in the Residential section were guided by the Salford Needs Assessment (Kroll et al., 1999) and the Framework for the Assessment of Children in Need and their Families (DoH et al., 2000). The 14 health items include immunisations, dental care, eye sight, general health, sleep patterns, diet, and personal hygiene. The five social items focus on relationships with peers and adults as well as cultural and leisure needs. The behavioural section contains 10 items covering issues such as damage to property, interpersonal aggression and oppositional behaviour, self harm, ability to stick to agreements, respect for personal space, and commitment to stay on supervision.

Strengths and risks are also examined, and recently this has extended to a full ERASOR (Worling and Curwen, 2001) risk assessment protocol. The education section makes reference to specific learning needs indicated through the Consultant Educational and Clinical Psychologists report, as well as links to specific goals identified – Individual Education Plans (IEPs). A summary of the full psychometric assessment undertaken includes measures of personality, offence related attitudes and behaviour, as well as mental health measures. Each specific therapeutic component comments on the development of the therapeutic alliance, work achieved to date and goals for the next nine months. Key areas of integration are highlighted at the end of each document. In order to illustrate this process consider the case example of KM (Table 20.2) and the summary of his NAT document, which is an illustration of some of the key issues in each section rather than a fully comprehensive plan. This individualised plan indicates specific interventions and time frames appropriate to KM's needs and thus is only one example of a possible plan.

Case summary KM

KM, a white male, was referred at 15 years of age. He sexually abused his younger half sister at home and later on contact visits, as well as a seven year old girl in the neighbourhood. KM experienced significant neglect and abuse at the hands of his mother and her partners whilst growing up, including witnessing violent and sexual behaviour. KM was often left to take responsibility for the care of his siblings and thus had little opportunity to experience childhood. He was bullied at school, experienced frequent moves, and hence tended to be socially isolated. In fact he experienced all 12 of the significant stressful experiences in Table 20.1, with the 'other' being the death of a significant foster mother. Although generally overly compliant KM had difficulties managing his anger and a history of behavioural problems which included fire setting and stealing. An above average IQ and high level of expressed motivation for a placement represented significant strengths.

The key to our success is likely to be in the milieu in which the young people engage in specific therapeutic work. The generalised context of close supervision and emotional support provided by a therapeutic community allows for necessary re-parenting and the development of healthy attachments, which supports the more specific therapeutic programmes. The consistency of approach achieved through good communication between the various components enables continual monitoring and reinforcement of the learning gained from Individual and Group work programmes.

Specific programmes of work developed within SWAAY based on available research and substantial clinical experience consist of:

- The Pathway social and emotional competency group work programme.
- The Gateway offence-specific group work programme.
- The Focused Intervention adapted offence-specific programme.
- The Relapse Prevention/Moving on group work programme.

Group work programmes are undertaken in conjunction with individual (CBT based) therapeutic work, family therapy work and psychoanalytic psychotherapy where possible and appropriate.

The Group Work Programmes

'Since sexual offending is a social behaviour problem and sex offenders typically suffer pervasive deficits and distortions in the realm of social relations, it makes sense that group treatment would be a highly beneficial modality' (Sawyer, 2000). It can also be a less threatening environment than one to one therapy where the intensity of the situation can be disabling for some young people rather than enabling. Group work provides a context where young people can work alongside their peers who have similar issues. The knowledge that every other group member is there to work on sexually abusive behaviour removes the stigma to some extent as well as the 'collusiveness' which the individual context of one-to-one work can recreate. For some young people the group context is the only one in which they can engage fully. Porter (1986) in working with sexually abused young boys made the point that one-to-one discussions of sexuality with an adult who keeps the material a 'secret' may have an implicit expectation regarding sexual favours, despite clearly defined boundaries.

The Pathway Programme

Within 3–4 months of a young person arriving at SWAAY a place is offered in the Pathway social and emotional competency Group Work Programme. This inclusive programme aims to engage young people of all abilities, ages, degrees of sexually problematic behaviour, and all types of behavioural issues. The group provides for functions such as building attachments, managing emotional issues, and gaining a sense of self confidence in relationships. In addition it can provide a useful insight into an individual's ability to function in groups and assists in both the timing and decisions around the type of moves onto other group work programmes. As a joint endeavour between the therapy and education teams at SWAAY the Pathway programme forms a vital part of the education syllabus. Developed to use the National Curriculum Assessment framework for Personal Health and Social Education (PHSE) it has been

Table 20.2   First Needs Assessment and Treatment Plan for KM at 3 months

	Identified issue	Response
Health	Removal of brace overdue from last placement.	Appointment made, brace removed, teeth needed cleaning, electric toothbrush to be bought, appointment with hygienist to be made.
	Often wakes up in night, wanders round room, after experiencing flashbacks.	To work through victimisation workbook in Individual Work (I/W) in order to start putting significant stressful experiences in past.
	Often snacks on junk food and avoids eating a healthy diet.	Encouraged to eat more at meal times, also to write a list of food he likes to enable staff to better support a more varied and interesting diet.
Social	Difficulty forming and sustaining friendships, due to isolating himself in room or being overly harsh and aggressive when challenging others.	(a) Staff to recognise the level of difficult behaviour presented by other residents currently and allow KM some space at times at home as pattern not the same in education or groupwork (G/W). (b) Improving the tone of his challenges to be included as one of his weekly behavioural goals.
	Staff changes in the house, KM's social worker and team manager leaving within a short space of time, has meant attachments to adults have been difficult to assess. Request to join local football team.	Encouraged to talk about feelings (in therapy and in meetings) about his belief that everybody leaves him. To be reminded at these times that people are not leaving because of him. Agreed in principal during the next 9 months. KM to make enquiries.
Behaviour	Breaks own belongings when stressed and angry.	(a) Encouraged by staff to come out of room to talk through grievances and recognise his part. (b) More strategies in dealing with difficult feelings to be learnt in I/W and G/W.
	Can be aggressive and hostile in tone of voice and eye contact with peers and staff.	Challenged at time and encouraged to talk about feelings behind actions, which he tends to deny at time, but will return to issue at later date.
	Urinates in bedroom on floor and in cups belonging to house.	(a) Attempts to talk about this have been hit with resistance so far although he will eventually clean it up. (b) KM feels there is a problem with holding urine until he reaches bathroom: a Dr's appointment to be made. (c) Joint Psychiatrist and I/W appointment to made to explore psychological reasons behind behaviour. (d) Issue to be explored in Psychoanalytic Psychotherapy.
Strengths	• Well mannered and socially skilled in the community. • Very bright with IQ of 125. • Good at sport and well coordinated.	
Risks	KM's frustration level has the potential of reaching a state where he is so enraged, that physically and sexually aggressive behaviour become a substantial risk. Tendency to draw some targeting his way, through intense competitiveness. Can be impulsive in a high and aroused state e.g will get drawn into sexual conversations in large peer group.	

Table 20.2 *Continued*

	Identified issue	Response
Education Short-term attainment targets	Continue ICT skills in order to build more confidence and self esteem. Reduce 'bad loser' behaviour in sport. Reduce distractibility.	Provide more courses in ICT and allow access to suitable equipment. Reward and praise positive characteristics and identify when he gets it wrong. Special Education Needs Coordinator (SENCO) to work with KM on short term module on CD-Rom called structured word attack.
Education Long-term goals	Achieve GCSEs at top grades (As and Bs) to enable him to go onto college and study what he chooses.	KM was put back a year as he had missed a year of school previously due to frequent moves and the extra time would allow him to achieve his potential academically as well as focus on his therapeutic work.
Psychological Psychometric results	Personality strengths: • Open about general thoughts and feelings. • Good self esteem and no more emotionally lonely than the average adolescent. • No problems with assertiveness. • Perspective-taking skills and ability to express empathic concerns for others are good. Personality concerns: • Considerable difficulty coping with angry thoughts and feelings, as well as with managing behaviour when angry. Very hostile attitude and experiences anger as long lasting and intense. • Generally impulsive, as well as impulsive when angry, and reacts in an indirect and direct way to these angry feelings. Offence-specific strengths: • Normally open about sexual drives and interests. • Could assess the likely impact of sexual abuse on a boy in vignette scenario. • Doesn't report being sexually obsessed. • Does not significantly externalise blame for his abusive actions. • Sexual knowledge is very good. Offence-specific concerns: • Considerably distorted perception regarding the impact the abuse had on both his victims. • Holds globalised distortions about children and their sexuality. • Justifies sexually abusive behaviour. • Feels sexually unattractive and emotionally congruent with children. • Low motivation for change indicated by Multiphasic Sex Inventory (MSI) measure.	
I/W	Completed so far: • Built therapeutic alliance and drawn up contract. • Started structured assessment (personal history). Plan: • Complete structured assessment and explore issues as they arise. • To start to work through victimisation workbook. • To explore sense of grievance and develop more effective strategies to cope with angry feelings, through the use of a diary or log.	
G/W	Completed so far: • Started Pathway group and displayed a high level of commitment and motivation as well as ability to understand new concepts. Plan: • To complete the remaining modules of the Pathway programme, in order to benefit from developing peer relationships and new techniques for dealing with difficult feelings. • To move directly onto the Gateway group.	

Table 20.2 *Continued*

	Identified issue	Response
Psychoanalytic Psychotherapy		Completed so far: • Assessment meeting revealed a genuine interest in working in this way again, having undertaken a year of this type of therapy previously. • KM identified the anger as well as love for his mother being an issue as well as feeling out of control with his angry feelings. Plan: • Build therapeutic alliance. • Start to explore origins of anger and sexuality. • Explore feelings of being cheated by family, particularly mother and start to come to terms with ambivalence towards her and other adults.
Psychiatric		Completed so far: • Assessment revealed considerable propensity for aggressive thoughts and cognitive distortions, although no requirement for medication. Plan: • Monitor potential for depressive feelings as therapeutic work progresses. • Support victimisation work which will encourage him to face past experiences of neglect, frequent moves, and other traumas. • Explore whether urinating issue is triggered by memories and experiences being released at night.
Family work		Completed so far: • KM is motivated for therapeutic work and has identified his first step father and mother as being people he would like to work with. • KM's social worker has been informed and is trying to contact both individuals to see if they would be interested. Plan: • If contact is established with mother then regular family sessions and visits will take place. • Visit arranged for half sisters, who have been adopted, but stopped currently with abused sibling.
Integrated issues		• Maintain balance between education and therapy. • Monitor learning across contexts, not allowing him to fade into background. • To support KM to start to make the progress in all his issues in order to lead an abuse free and happy life. • To support KM with those things he has identified as his most important goals currently: changing behaviour, developing family contact, coping with reduced freedom, and continuing with his football.

recognised by a Local Education Authority inspectorate as an innovative alternative to a more standard PHSE curriculum. External accreditation has been agreed through the ASDAN system; a skill based accredited award scheme which can be accessed from a very basic level up to degree level. Other skill based tasks completed in Residential and Education contexts can also be accredited through the Award Scheme Development and Accreditation Network (ASDAN) system. It is, therefore, the ultimate in rewarding the integrated approach. In essence by using this framework the importance of all aspects of the SWAAY therapeutic programme, particularly putting new social and behavioural

skills into practice across all aspects of a young person's life, is monitored and progress evidenced.

Social skills training is seen to be vital in order to reduce the risk of further sexual offending (Worling, 2004). A meta-analysis conducted by Lipsey and Wilson (1998) of 200 programmes for serious juvenile offenders found those providing social skills and behavioural change interventions to provide the most significant treatment effects. Prentky and Knight (1993) and Prentky et al. (2000) found adolescent abusers to have poor social competency and those who recidivate to be less socially competent with a history of antisocial behaviour. Boyd et al. (2000) suggested that adolescent sexual abusers feel particularly isolated and estranged, have interpersonal difficulties and few friends. The group of young people at SWAAY often have a history of antisocial behaviour and interpersonal problems in addition to their history of sexually abusive behaviour and attitudes. It is therefore vital to address a wider aspect of problematic behaviour which considers further criminogenic needs in addition to the index offence. Crick and Dodge (1994) found that children with aggressive behaviour more often make errors interpreting intent in ambiguous social situations and selectively attend to more hostile cues, indicating a need for the emotional intelligence component of this programme. In addition, Loeber et al. (1998) found social skills deficits to be associated with an increased risk of more general interpersonal aggression in juveniles, thus supporting the view that addressing these needs early on is likely to reduce further offending in general not just specific to sexual offences.

The structure of the content of the programme is based on the SWAAY philosophy and consists of three modules: Rights and Responsibilities; Equality; and Openness. Each module consists of four sessions; therefore, one rotation of the programme consists of 12 weeks. At this point it is assessed whether an individual should progress to the Gateway group/Focused Intervention group, or whether they should complete another rotation of the Pathway group. There are three rotations of the programme in total with the same learning objectives and assessing the same key skills. The content, however, varies to enable those who are in need of further social and emotional skills training to undertake additional work in this area through extra rotations without repetition. The differentiated content of each session allows options to adapt the material to the needs of particular group members if functioning at a very low cognitive level or are behaviourally extremely difficult to manage. The learning objectives and key skills for the entire Equality module as well as an associated session plan developed from the overall aims are as follows:

Equality

Learning objectives

- To have the ability to recognise and accept diversity of culture/race/ability/sexual orientation without prejudice.

- To have started to develop respect for themselves and others regardless of age/ability/beliefs.

Key skills assessed

- Refraining from discrimination.
- Allowing others to express their opinions without talking over them/turn-taking.
- Showing an interest about other people's beliefs.
- Showing an understanding that although other people think in different ways they deserve respect.
- Showing confidence that their views and opinions are as important as everybody else's.
- Demonstrating/expressing knowledge as to what constitutes bullying behaviour.
- Refraining from bullying behaviour.
- Demonstrating skills in how to challenge bullying, supporting themselves and others.
- Demonstrating/expressing knowledge as to what constitutes prejudice and stereotyping.
- Ability to recognise personal strengths.

Equality 'B': Session 1

By the end of this session group members will:

1. Have begun to gain an understanding of self-esteem.
2. Have an appreciation of their own and others strengths.
3. Have a better understanding of the importance of communication skills: turn-taking, talking and listening to each other.
4. Have begun to gain an understanding of how 'core beliefs' are formed.

The group consists of two to eight young people, has two facilitators, one observer, as well as a designated support role to assist and manage any group members who are having difficulties and need time out. The approach is psycho educational primarily, however, uses both Cognitive Behavioural principals and a basic grounding in the role of beliefs and attitudes as a pre-cursor to the other group programmes. A multi-media approach is used to try and encourage interest and engagement. Board games, roleplays, art work, videos, and other creative ideas form the basis of the content of the

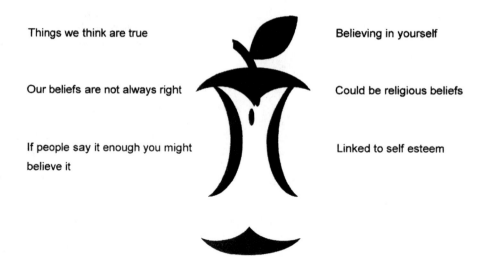

Things we think are true

Our beliefs are not always right

If people say it enough you might believe it

Believing in yourself

Could be religious beliefs

Linked to self esteem

Figure 20.8   Pathway exercise on core beliefs

sessions. Through the variety of ways the material is presented the variety of preferred learning styles of group members can also be accommodated. For example learning objective 3 in the equality session above is covered through a 'circle time' activity, where each group member in turn is asked to share some of their own feelings and past experiences, through responding to questions such as 'when in the past have you felt proud?' and 'tell us about an activity you have really enjoyed'. Core beliefs are introduced pictorially with a brainstorm, see Figure 20.8, which is an example of one done by a particular group. Homework (Figure 20.9)

I may not have got straight As in my exams but I did my best.

I may not have got straight As in my exams but I did my best.

I may not have got straight As in my exams but I did my best.

Figure 20.9   Pathway exercise 'Seeds that will help you grow' (adapted from Pincus, 1990)

involves identifying a core belief which would help that individual feel confident and thus maintain good self esteem. This belief would then be written on an actual flower pot, a sunflower seed planted and group members instructed to nurture that belief by watering the seed regularly until it grows.

Other exercises used to assist group members in achieving the learning objectives in the above session on equality include a short DVD on communication skills for young citizens called 'Joe's story' which includes on-screen questions.

The most important thing I learnt was getting used to working in groups as at that time I would have preferred to work individually or not do it at all, but now I prefer working in the group probably because you get other people's opinions and help who are in the same situation. It also helped me to start to come to terms with the seriousness of what I had done I was on the Pathway to the main offence-specific programme and was thinking I wouldn't be doing this if I didn't need to.

The most memorable parts were . . . The activities we did lightened what was daunting . . . the Crystal Maze was really fun and really cool, also decorating a shoe box as our feelings box . . . I still had that box when I moved onto another house you know and was still using it a bit. Standing in a circle saying our names in a specific way which everybody then had to copy highlighted that I was in a group, part of it and not alone in the work I needed to do. Getting my certificate at the end and finishing gave me the confidence that I've achieved the first step and that the next step is not such a dark place . . . Pathway showed me I could do it!

Comments by KM

The Gateway programme

The Gateway offence-specific programme (Table 20.3) is modular and takes around 18 months to complete. Each element is 4–5 weeks in duration and occasional one off relapse prevention sessions take place in between elements in order for each group member to have the opportunity to discuss and prepare their individualised Relapse Prevention plan, named by the young people as their 'Gateway to Success'. The group takes a rolling format which allows new members to be introduced every four weeks wherever necessary, although not beginning with either of the Victim Empathy modules. The advantage of this approach is that more experienced group members can support the newer members as well as provide role models which are motivating for

those just starting out on what seems like a programme that lasts a life time. The main themes are repeated in a variety of ways, thus helping to consolidate and further integrate this learning. One of the main theories underpinning the Gateway programme is Rational Emotive Behaviour Therapy (REBT), which is one of a number of cognitive behavioural therapies. The focus is on identifying and challenging maladaptive belief systems. The principles are that there are three aspects of human functioning:

- thoughts
- feelings
- behaviour

And that it is not events that make us feel good or bad but our perception of these events, which subsequently influence our behaviour. This model developed in the early 1990s from the combination of Ellis' Rational-Emotive Therapy and Beck's Cognitive Therapy (see Froggatt, 2005) focuses on an ABC approach where:

A = Activating event

B = Beliefs (about the event) which are either *Rational* or *Irrational*

C = Consequences (determined by our beliefs) *Feelings* and *Behaviour*

Ellis states that healthy consequences are determined by rational beliefs and unhealthy consequences are driven by irrational beliefs. Unrealistic, unattainable demands that we place on ourselves, others, and the world as a whole are irrational and constitute dysfunctional thinking. This is because when examined logically, rationally, and empirically it is virtually impossible to meet every demand and trying to do so will only lead to frustration which if we perceive we cannot tolerate, will generate dysfunctional feelings and behaviours. Group facilitators assist group members to identify their own dysfunctional thoughts and irrational belief systems, which in some cases are likely to have been engrained over many years. Group members are encouraged with the assistance of their peers to start to challenge them in a more rational way. This process of 'Disputation' and 'Evaluation' as referred to by Ellis, allow group members to adopt more adaptive rational beliefs about the activating event and, therefore, bring about a more healthy consequence in the future when faced with a similar situation. The skill of cognitively proving or disproving beliefs based on wider consideration can also be transferred to

Table 20.3   Gateway programme

Prog. No.	Module	Element	Brief Rationale
1	Sex and relationships	Sex education (1)	Confusion regarding sexuality is common in families of sexual offenders, thus there is a lot of aberrant learning to re-address (Driskill and Decampo, 1993). Even in the non-abusive adolescent population by the age of 15 years, some youths still lacked the knowledge necessary in order to prevent pregnancy (Winn, Roker and Coleman, 1995).
2	Decision making	Linked decisions (SIDS)	Ryan and Lane (1997) state that 'all behaviour is preceded by some contemplation and decision to engage in the behaviour, although the processes may become so rapid for more habitual behaviours that the youth is not even aware of the thought.'
3	Rights and responsibilities	Denial	Numerous studies have indicated that when adolescent sex offenders begin treatment they are in some state of denial. It has been demonstrated that those offenders who deny their offence are not motivated to learn self-management skills because they do not consider themselves to have a problem (O'Donohue and Letourneau, 1993).
4	Victim focus	Victim empathy (1) (understanding victims)	Research suggests that adult sexual offenders have a tendency to lack empathy for their own victims, as well as for other victims of sexual abuse (Beech et al., 1999). It is generally thought that increasing empathy for victims increases an adolescent's motivation to engage in treatment (Ryan and Lane, 1997).
5	Sex and relationships	Sex education (2)	Research has shown that some adult sex offenders lack adequate knowledge of sexual skills to deal appropriately with their adult partners (Abel et al. 1984). Knopp (1982) also found that sex offenders generally lack knowledge about positive and consensual sexuality.
6	Decision making	Pre-conditions	Beech et al. (2003) suggest that sex offenders are often reluctant to discuss their own thoughts and feelings with regard to their offending and the behaviour that they have presented. It is therefore proposed that by providing a framework, such as Finkelhor's (1984) preconditions, to understand the process of offending, then the offender may be more able to discuss the thoughts and feelings that they had prior to their offence(s).
7	Rights and responsibilities	Anger	Anger has been shown to be one of the many factors which cause young people to sexually abuse. This anger, in many cases, emanates from the externalisation of the trauma that the group member has suffered in their past. (Bentovim, 1995).
8	Sex and Relationships	Sexual aggression	Many adolescent sex offenders have experienced violent parenting styles and insecure attachments. These create low self-esteem, emotional loneliness and strong feelings of resentment and hostility in puberty (Bowlby, 1972). This, in turn, is suggested to affect the acquisition of inhibitory controls over sex and aggression (Davis and Leitenberg, 1987).

Table 20.3 *Continued*

Prog. No.	Module	Element	Brief Rationale
9	Decision making	Problem solving (2) (instant gratification, thinking skills, survival issues)	Researchers have identified that adolescent sex offenders have difficulties with impulse control and judgement (Virginia Commission on Youth, 2003). It has also been suggested that sex offenders exhibit a high prevalence of thought processes, which allow them to neutralise their feelings of guilt and shame.
10	Rights and responsibilities	Passive and active outlook (ownership of sexually offending behaviour)	Cognitive behavioural literature indicates that adolescent sex offenders are treatable if they can accept responsibility for their offence by understanding the sequence of events thoughts and feelings (Steene and Monette, 1989).
11	Victim focus	Victim empathy (2) (process of objectification and shut down)	Ryan (1998) suggests that in order for the young person to 'revive their dormant sensitivity' and to prevent themselves from ignoring the emotions of others, they need to become conscious of their own cues so that they can then apply this to others.
12	Sex and relationships	Relationship's	Award et al. (1984) highlights that one of the difficulties that adolescent sex offenders face is that they generally have a lack of role models for intimacy due to high levels of neglect when growing up.
13	Decision making	Problem solving (1)	Research has identified that sexual offenders and those who have been raised in an abusive environment, have impairments in certain important developmental functions, such as problem solving and impulse control (Gordon and Porporino, 1990; and Winn, 1994).
14	Rights and responsibilities	Assertiveness	In the relevant literature (e.g. Ennis et al. 1993) the importance of teaching adolescent sexual abusers assertiveness skills, is highlighted, as it provides the young people the skills so that they are able to identify and pursue appropriate relationships in order to meet their needs.

new and original situations. A positive evaluation is likely to lead to the skill being repeated and thus eventually integrated into the young person's behavioural pattern more permanently:

> ... people like ... Were all really respected and it was like I'd been chosen out of loads of people to go into that group and be really responsible ... I'd been the one selected to go in ... I wanted to take this opportunity to learn from the older young people and gain from their experience, but it was also nice to go into it with people I'd know in Pathway as I felt more secure knowing them already.

> Group work is like a football league with Focused Intervention being like West Bromwich and Gateway being like Arsenal... they both play football in the premier league but not up to the same standard! ... people then look up to you, its like coming through the ranks and feeling like you are part of the best.
>
> KM

> I found Finkelhor in my first module incredibly helpful because it immediately sets it out ... in Gateway we talk about realising what can happen before it happens ... it helped me define where I could stop it and helps me keep it in my mind ... you can also relate it to anything not just sexual abuse ... if you want to fight someone for example.

> 'Passive and Active I found really helpful too, not directly as a module but one I found easier to use outside of Gateway, it helped me question my own behaviour at times such as aggressive behaviour and is something I've kept in mind.

> Anger was another one that helped me in general.
>
> KM

Techniques employed by the group facilitators are motivational interviewing, high focus exercises, multi media presentation, role play etc. The skill of the facilitators is fundamental in how effective the programme is as it determines how well the material is delivered. A team of facilitators is used which rotate bringing in new facilitators in a way which is similar to the group members, allowing for personal growth through experience and modelling skills off more experienced workers. The observer role which is also rotated from the team of facilitators is a vital component of the programme, allowing for constructive feedback to be given to facilitators regarding their performance in a particular session as well as a more objective view of the group dynamics. This style of working provides a more collaborative message from the team of workers, as group members can experience several different adults including importantly both male and female workers, adhering to the same non abusive or prejudice belief system.

> *Something else that was brilliant was at the end of every module was the 'hot seat' and you knew that you were building up to it at the end of each month having to put your trust in the other people because you can. There are not a lot of people our age that would listen to you talk about this sort of thing.*
>
> KM

The content of each session follows a similar format each week, with burning issues and homework first on the agenda before the main content of the session and a 'feelings' round at the end. Aims and learning objectives are identified for each session and each group member is scored on whether he manages to reach these as well as on process skills, such as demonstrating empathic concern and how they challenge and accept challenge from others. Brief summaries of the session content and any specific concerns are faxed across to the residential and education teams. Any concerns remaining at the end of the module will be indicated in the modular report for the individual worker to explore further in their sessions. Other processes such as negotiated time out and group agreements are all part of the contract each new group member has to sign before they join the programme.

> *All was really really helpful and some of it kind of fun, making me feel confident and good about myself some of the time ... thinking I'm making a difference here to myself and for me specifically who has had lots of previous therapy before SWAAY I felt I am actually achieving with these people what no therapist has ever been able to achieve with me before ... and I'm helping everybody else at the same time as helping myself ... if other people weren't helping me I wouldn't be able to do it on my own, you are not in it alone, it's not just for you, but for everybody.*
>
> KM

The following element of the Sex and Relationships module has been selected as an illustration of the diversity of presentation of ideas, of some of the techniques and processes, of integration with the subject matter from other modules, and of how specific exercises can be used outside the group work setting or this specific programme. One area where this element is atypical is that it does not follow a gradual development from a general concept, to a link made between the concept and general offending, then to sexual offending, and finally to group members own sexual offending.

Session 1

Learning objectives

By the end of this session group members will:

1. Be able to understand the definitions of the 3 Cs ('consent', 'compliance', and 'coercion').
2. Be able to recognise and understand the difference between consenting and non-consenting sexual behaviour.
3. Be able to acknowledge the types of coercive behaviour used in their sexually abusive behaviour towards their victims.

Session plan

- 'Burning issues': Feelings round at the beginning of every session is the opportunity for group members to share current issues and specifically difficulties which may encroach on the session.
- Exploration of definitions of the terms 'consent', 'compliance', and 'coercion'.
- Role play: Cards given out to each pair of group members have an everyday situation to be acted out using one of the 3 C's. It is the task of the rest of the group to identify which 'C' is being used. The idea of the exercise is to clarify the meaning of the terms.
- Consenting and non-consenting pictures: Line drawings of people involved in sexual acts from the 'Sex and 3R' pack (McCarthy and Thompson, 1998) are distributed within the group and group members have to decide (a) what is going on in the picture; (b) whether they believe its consenting or not; (c) give a reason for their answer. This is a task they can

complete individually before discussing answers in the group.

- High focus exercise: Each individual sits in turn in a specific chair for a short defined period of time, usually 5 minutes. Their task for this session is to say to the group which of the 3 C's were part of their own sexually aggressive behaviour, specifically focusing on the things they said or did which either encouraged compliance on the part of their victim or coerced them.
- Feelings round: Follows every high focus exercise and is conducted to check out how individuals are feeling, to ensure the importance of the work they have achieved is highlighted and to ensure as far as possible that negative emotions are not acted out outside the group context.
- Relaxation: One of a selection of exercises can be used at the end of a session such as this in order to reduce levels of stress.
- Home work (a vital part of the Gateway programme): Venn diagram in which group members have to decide what people should/should not do in relation to their sexual behaviour, and therefore, start to explore their own beliefs about issues such as 'be monogamous', 'use pornography', and 'be in love'.

Session 2

Learning objectives

By the end of this session group members will:

1. Be aware of the contribution of pornography to sexual offending.
2. Be able to identify the sort of beliefs that underpin sexually aggressive behaviour.
3. Be able to dispute and evaluate those distorted beliefs.

Session plan

Before embarking on this session facilitators must be clear on their own belief systems about pornography and be in line with those of their co-facilitator so as to give a consistent message rather than a contradictory one. The most important messages are that violent pornography and that which involves people who cannot consent is abusive, and that pornography is often involved in the pattern of sexually abusive behaviour.

- Burning issues.
- Discussion of previous week's homework.
- Definitions of pornography: Group members brainstorm and decide on a definition, which is subsequently compared to the following 'that which is graphic and sexually explicit and subordinates women'.
- Common beliefs about pornography: 'Bubbles' with common beliefs about pornography are distributed throughout the group and each member is given a blank 'bubble' on which to write one of their own honest beliefs about pornography. These 'belief bubbles' are then discussed and stuck on the wall.
- Role play: A debate is organised between 'the researchers' who are given facts and figures about the harm caused by pornography and the 'publishers' of pornographic magazines. Group members are instructed to argue for or against pornography from the side to which they are assigned and not necessarily from their own beliefs.
- Is all pornography harmful?: The idea of different types of pornography is presented and group members asked to consider whether they believe all three are harmful a) sexually explicit and violent, b) sexually explicit and non-violent but subordinating and dehumanising, c) sexually explicit material which is non-violent and non-subordinating, which is based on mutuality and equality (called erotica). After a discussion the relevant research is presented indicating that the third type is the only one which so far no negative impact has been proven.
- Homework: (a) 'Challenging exploitation': a worksheet from the Lions/Tacade Skills for Life pack (1994), and (b) Figure 20.10: an exercise devised to combine the issue of pornography and Finkelhor's Pre-conditions.

Group members are asked to consider how pornography could contribute to the breaking down of each barrier and allows someone closer to sexually offending.

Motivation	Internal Barriers	External Barriers	Victim Resistance
How may pornography motivate someone to sexually offend?	How may pornography break down internal barriers by normalising something?	How may pornography help create a world which is more accepting of sexual aggression?	Why may pornography be involved in overcoming the resistance of the victim?

Figure 20.10 Breaking down barriers

Session 3

Learning objectives

By the end of this session group members will:

1. Understand the legal terminology relating to sexual offending.
2. Be able to identify under which legal category their sexually aggressive behaviour falls.
3. Be able to identify the emotional states which were triggers to their sexual offending.
4. Have started to apply the knowledge they have gained to specific situations in order to minimise their risk of re-offending.

Session plan

- Burning issues.
- Discussion of previous week's homework.
- Legal terms for sexual offences: Brainstorm official terms and brief description of all illegal

sexual acts. A handout is provided and any discrepancies discussed.

- High focus (the legal context): Each group member is asked to say the legal terms for their offences even if not actually charged with the act, and to briefly say why they would constitute such an offence.
- Emotional Triggers: Using individual icebergs diagrams representing the offence and behaviour as only the tip above the surface and the thoughts and feelings the vast area hidden under the surface, group members are asked to identify the emotional triggers to their own offences.
- Offence cycle: A previously drawn up typical adult offence cycle is presented to the group and they are invited to consider how relevant the theory is to their offending patterns and whether some of the issues and ideas covered in the 'Sexual Aggression' element of the programme would fit. In Fig. 20.11 the italics represents one previous group's ideas, which include the possibility of appropriate sexual

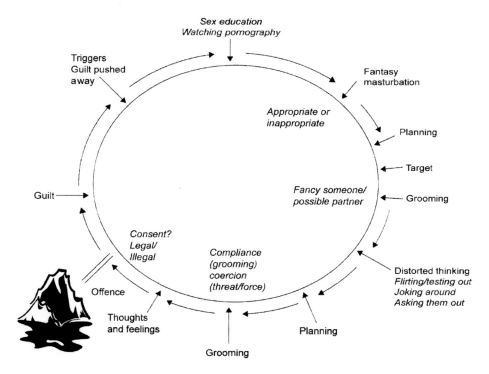

Figure 20.11 A group's development of a typical offence cycle

behaviour forming a similar cycle, but with distinctly different trajectories.
- Homework: (a) Work sheet focusing on identifying legal/illegal sexual behaviour from vignettes and (b) Identification of a situation in the coming week when a trigger feeling or thought is experienced and then describing how they dealt with it (the outcome could be positive or negative but is unlikely to involve sexually abusive behaviour within this time scale and context).

Yes that cycle fits both of my offences actually'.
                                                    KM

Session 4

Learning objectives

By the end of this session group members will:

1. Understand and accept the link between mis-cueing and sexually aggressive behaviour.
2. Be able to identify the types of beliefs that underpin sexually aggressive behaviour.

3. Be able to demonstrate skills in disputing and evaluating distorted beliefs.
4. Be able to accurately identify both verbal and non-verbal cues in interpersonal situations.

Session plan

- Burning issues.
- Discussion of part b) of previous week's homework (collect in part a).
- Introduction to verbal and non-verbal mis-cueing and its potential link to sexually aggressive behaviour. Group members understanding of the concept of beliefs should be checked out at this point.
- Roleplay 'Brian': One of the facilitators reads out a story about a character called Brian who has mis-read his wife's cues due to holding faulty beliefs and ended up raping her. After the vignette has been read any beliefs the group feel Brian has to act in the way he did are noted. Group members are asked to volunteer to play Brian's mate down the pub listening to him justify what he has just done. More beliefs which become apparent should be noted at this stage. It is then the task of a new

mate to try and make Brian understand what he has done is wrong by challenging some of his statements and beliefs in another role play.

- ABC: The Activator, Belief, Consequence (the sexually abusive act) concept is used with examples given of situations using the A and C categories and group members asked to make suggestions regarding possible beliefs. D and E: Dispute and Evaluate are then introduced where group members are asked to challenge the faulty beliefs and thus modify the behaviour.
- DVD 'Don't get me wrong': A specially designed resource 'Don't get me wrong' (available to purchase from SWAAY alongside relevant training) is then used to reveal group members tendencies to mis-cue and promote discussion which may reveal faulty beliefs and provide opportunity to challenge these beliefs.
- Homework: (a) Worksheet 'What is harassment' from the Lions/Tacade Skills for Life pack (1994), and (b) Design a poster to represent the issue of consent using the following acronym REAL: Respect, Equality, Agreement, and Legal. Other scenes from the DVD can be used in Individual work sessions.

Before I came to SWAAY when I used to go out I didn't think about anything I'm now thinking in advance, backing myself up in my mind so that I know what I am going to do if something goes wrong, not just in terms of sexual abuse, but if I think someone is going to start on me or was following me.

KM

The Focused Intervention Programme

This is an adapted version of the Gateway programme, in that it allows an opportunity to access vital offence-specific work in some sort of group format at a pace and level members can cope with. Individuals with particular difficulties managing their behaviour in larger groups, those with moderate learning disabilities, those with lower levels of motivation, and those whose sexually abusive behaviour is more part of a general disorder, with no specific victim identified, would all be candidates for this type of approach. A pair working design allows careful selection of the most suitable combination of individuals and two group facilitators in a pair provides more focused support. Sessions are limited to a more manageable hour and a half with a short break and group agreements are similar to the Gateway group. To date this project

has proved a great success with the original two pairs remaining engaged in weekly programmes, and one pair successfully integrating into the Gateway programme despite prior scepticism due to them both having shown a strong resistance to taking responsibility for their sexually abusive behaviour in individual work sessions. It appears that this medium was less threatening than individual work for those particular young people. Further pairings are planned as well as an experimental group of three. Spencer, below, is a typical candidate for this type of programme.

Case Summary Spencer

Spencer had been in SWAAY several years without having completed any direct work focused on his sexually offending behaviour, which involved the indecent assault of two peer aged females at his school. He had struggled to engage in Individual work and only after the third attempt managed to successfully complete the Pathway programme. The Focused Intervention programme seemed to offer the only alternative to address these vital needs before he was due to move out into the community.

Spencer had a statement of Special Educational Needs due to his severe emotional, social and behavioural difficulties and to his general developmental delay when he was a child. It was suggested that Spencer benefits most from working independently in quiet classrooms, where he can have individual attention.

Spencer had been assessed by educational psychologists as being in 'low-average' range of ability and as being a 'visual print learner', therefore, not responding well to auditory based learning. Spencer fell within the range diagnostic of hyperactivity and of attention deficit/hyperactivity disorder (ADHD) and thus presented with difficulties in maintaining his level of concentration, particularly when asked to divide his attention between two tasks. He was also a restless young person. The most effective ways suggested in which to work with him were: to teach material in chunks followed by brief breaks, as this helps maintain his level of concentration; to elicit eye contact with Spencer in order to gain his full attention when imparting information to him; and for spoken instructions to be reinforced by written materials when possible.

Specific needs can be met more easily in the FIP primarily due to the context and dynamics of the group. Language can be simplified and examples made more relevant to the experiences of the individuals in a smaller group. Personalising the material more easily than in a larger group, a shorter session time, and less waiting time between exercises specifically the high focus type meets the needs of those individuals with concentration difficulties. With a smaller group it is also easier to adapt on the spur of the moment if necessary and constantly check out understanding on a more individual basis. Facilitators are more able to give individual attention and eye contact which is essential with individuals such as Spencer particularly when one group member starts to loose focus. Spencer being a visual print learner is assisted through the constant recording and revision of flip chart work which is attached to the walls as it is completed to constantly refer to and remind. One of the most significant achievements is that group members have felt proud of themselves as they are aware that they are undertaking 'the same' work as the Gateway group.

The Relapse Prevention/Moving on Group

Following the Gateway offence-specific or Focused Intervention programmes, a period of consolidation and maintenance is vital to future success. This is the purpose of the Relapse Prevention/Moving on group for which members are required to have succeeded in gaining a certain level of independence. From having 24 hour supervision at the beginning of their placement individuals will have progressed to 'full discretion' (i.e. they are not required to be supervised with their peers within SWAAY establishments or to be supervised by staff in the local community). Some will be attending local colleges of further education, some living independently, some in transition, but all will have the opportunity to put their relapse prevention skills and strategies into practice in the 'real world'. Learning to avoid where possible, and safely manage risky thoughts, feelings, and situations, by putting positive strategies into practice is focused upon. Motivating individuals towards achieving life goals and praising their successes is also an essential component in line with the 'Good Lives'

approach (Ward and Mann, 2004). Many of SWAAY's graduates choose to settle in the local area at least for a period of time before moving on, as generally moving back to live with their families is not an option despite the inclusion of family therapy in the integrated programme which often succeeds in strengthening more positive family ties. Moving on to independent living from care is a mine field for any young person, but for these individuals who have been high risk with diverse needs this period of transition requires excellent management in order to negate the potential increase in risk at this time. The focus of sessions, therefore, has to include discussion around practical problems being experienced. Although from time to time specific sessions are planned on issues such as drug and alcohol education, predominantly the group consists of an open format and the same issues continually re-emerge: forming and maintaining friendships; relationship difficulties; money management; appropriate offence disclosure; accessing benefits; finding work; interview skills; finding accommodation; and so on. Stress and loneliness are two of the well known acute dynamic risk factors to sexual recidivism in both adolescents (Gray and Pithers, 1993) and in adults (Hanson and Harris, 2000), therefore, a supportive group where individuals know they can come on a weekly basis to discuss difficulties, access support, and get advice is a vital means of emotional management. Occasionally social activities are organised for particular purposes, such as swimming at public baths as a risk management exercise.

It's different, not like modules you just come and say what you want. It's a bit like the work I do in Psychoanalytic Psychotherapy but in a group. You just say what you need to say and get help.

It integrates therapy and home at the same time. In both places you are egged on to get jobs.

Again I'm with the older and more experienced people. It shows I've achieved and overcome a lot of things and have the ability to overcome anything else. Other people now come to me for help and opinions, respect me and look up to me.

KM

On role models

*. . . if people want to be like me they want to be **like me** and not look up to a person who is trying to pretend they are this responsible person they are not . . . that's not a role model.*

On the future

... I am hoping the group will be able to give me more advice as to how to move on with the support of the social services ... I want to make it clear to social services that I shouldn't have to chase them up on things that should be happening ... they are there for me and now I know how to take my power and complain if it doesn't happen.

Programme evaluation

SWAAY as an organisation have always promoted the importance of research and it has always been integrated into the programme. The ASAP (Adolescent Sexual Abuser Project) was set up in 1996, headed up by Richard Beckett and co funded through SWAAY and the NHS, and aimed to explore the use of psychometric assessment with adolescents who have sexually abused. Following the successful 'what works' approach within the adult field and the successful use of the psychometric pack to measure deviancy, treatment change, and supplement the risk assessment process which had previously been based on actuarial measures based on static factors only (Beech et al., 2002); the aim was to determine if a similar process of evaluation would be successful with adolescents. The project set about firstly adapting measures, then establishing normal distributions based on non-abusing adolescents and non-abusing delinquents as well as running them consistently on a pre mid and post treatment abuser sample. The recidivism part of the study is still outstanding; however, despite the lack of data to use this process as a pure method of risk assessment, it is a useful measure of treatment progress. As many of the psychometric questionnaires are concerned with measuring personality features e.g impulsivity, as well as attitudes supportive of sexual offending e.g. victim blaming, identified by the research as being associated with future re-offence risk (Lipsey and Derzon (1998) and Kahn and Chambers (1991)) they are legitimate targets for treatment change. For a more in depth discussion of these psychometric measures see Beckett (1999). The Briere Trauma Symptom checklist (1996) is also included as a measure of mental health problems associated with trauma, as the aim is to heal the effects of victimisation

experiences as well as change distorted attitudes and beliefs about offence related behaviour.

At SWAAY we have a unique way of utilising the psychometric results, where clinical and behavioural observations as well as the individual's comments are included in the report. Through this method we are acknowledging that self report measures are only one way of examining progress made by individuals during the course of treatment and general day to day behaviour, and fulfilling potential in education are equally important. Overall the process adds another opportunity to disclose past abuses, it provides further guidance for setting therapeutic goals, and is generally motivating as it highlights areas of strength as well as areas of concern, the latter of which generally decreases over the course of treatment. Beckett and Gerhold (2001) found that early data gathered during the Adolescent Sexual Abuser Project suggested SWAAY clients presented with more difficulties than the average adolescent who had sexually abused i.e. poorer self esteem, higher levels of emotional loneliness, higher levels of cognitive distortions and poorer victim empathy, but after 18 months of treatment more significant improvements had been made in all areas except emotional loneliness.

Application of in house research by Edwards et al. (2005) has since positively impacted on the SWAAY programmes drop out rate and, therefore, potentially on recidivism levels. Edwards et al. (2005) found that those who dropped out of treatment had a greater chance of re-offending sexually (none of those who completed the programme available at the time re-offending sexually), as well as statistically being more likely to commit general and violent offences. Follow up questionnaires to last known professional contacts, although the response rate was poor, indicated that the overall success of those who stayed in treatment was much higher in terms of further education and employment, housing, and relationships.

In addition to the empirical basis for success of the SWAAY approach, individual cases indicate positive growth and development of specific individuals (see Table 20.4) which considers the case of KM at 22 months into his placement. Whilst there are still persistent issues progress is evident and the process of transition to independence has been initiated.

Table 20.4   KM Second Review of Needs Assessment and Treatment Plan at 22 months

	Identified issue	Response
Health	When feeling low is likely to snack on junk foods.	(a) Staff continue to encourage him to eat properly and allow him to negotiate to eat with the group rather than independently when he is feeling low. (b) KM needs to take responsibility to talk about his feelings when he needs to.
	When feeling low he does not take care of his appearance.	(a) Staff continue to let him know, encourage him both to care for himself and express his feelings.
	Has sports induced asthma and uses an inhaler for this when necessary.	Staff encourage him to make and attend check ups at the asthma clinic.
Social	KM despite his friendly personality is still concerned about his ability to make friends in the future and still at times challenges his peers in a way that appears aggressive.	(a) Staff to encourage KM to apply for further independence such as a part time job so that he can begin to build social networks outside of SWAAY. (b) Encouraged to concentrate on his own progress rather than pursue unnecessary challenges towards others.
	Extreme competitiveness and being a perfectionist often results in angry and aggressive responses during team games.	(a) Asking KM to take time away to calm down usually makes him more annoyed in the short term, so often alternative activities which are not team based are encouraged. (b) Point out when KM is being too harsh on himself and continue to praise his achievements.
	Tendency to make many observations and analyse them in minute detail until he becomes over loaded and forms opinions based on misperceptions of other's behaviour.	Reminded to remain open with regards to his thoughts, observations and feelings and to take a step back when he begins to go into too much depth in his analysis.
Behaviour	Although much more able to express anger appropriately still occasionally swears, punches or throws things. Tendency to misread what people say, causing feelings of hurt, defensiveness, and argumentative behaviour. He can be reluctant to listen to the opinions of others during these times saying they are not listening to him and confuses aggression for assertion, but will return to issue at later date.	Encouraged to be more assertive with his feelings using his own words rather than getting people to 'guess' what the issues are. (a) Staff to be clear they will not enter into an argument and will discuss it when he has calmed down, which helps him to accept challenge more readily and realistically. (b) Roleplays to be undertaken in I/W to help him identify the differences between aggression and assertion. (c) To have a weekly behavioural goal on this issue.
	Has been targeting female staff in an emotionally demanding manner, although this has reduced recently. One trigger has been identified as going on camp.	(a) Staff to maintain clear boundaries. (b) KM to continue to be open with his thoughts and feelings and to treat people equally. (c) Explore in I/W the link between this behaviour and going on camp.
Strengths	• He generally takes pride in his appearance asking for regular hair cuts and smart clothes. This extends to physical health, enjoying regular exercise. • He is charismatic and pleasant company, enjoying being the centre of attention without putting others down. • He can relate well to people and in particular has a way of helping others without being patronising. He is an excellent communicator.	

Table 20.4   *Continued*

	Identified issue	Response
Risks	• KM has reduced his potential risk of sexually re-offending to moderate on the ERASOR risk assessment protocol, however, misreading and misinterpreting others (both current issues) and consequently indulging in risky thoughts such as 'nobody cares' is a substantial risk issue. • Being very competitive and a perfectionist, results in anger and aggression specific risk triggers for KM in terms of sexually and physically abusive behaviour. This also results in pushing people away so that they no longer wish to play sport with him. • The desire to 'fit in' and make friends may put him at risk of getting involved in illegal or dangerous activities out in the community which would be out of character.	
Education S.T. attainment targets	To complete all GCSE coursework	(a) Providing encouragement and motivation through the reward system b) Monitoring progress and keeping him informed as to what is required.
	To gain GCSE qualifications in 5 subjects to the best of his ability.	Giving encouragement and advice, providing opportunities for revision and giving feedback from mock exams.
	To obtain a suitable college placement.	Assist in the decision making process (including arranging Connexions appointments) regarding choosing a suitable course and making a proper and timely application.
Education L.T. goals	Begin college next term, study for a National Diploma then eventually go on to university.	To continue to work with KM both residentially and therapeutically once he has left SWAAY school and attending a local sixth form college.
Psychological (Psychometrics 2nd assessment completed 7 months prior to NAT meeting)	Personality strengths: • Reasonably open about general thoughts and feelings. • Improved self esteem, perspective-taking and general empathic skills. • No longer indicating significant anger related problems and impulsivity score now falls within average range. No problems still with assertiveness. Personality concerns: • Now indicating more emotional loneliness than average for his age. • May have an unrealistic view in his ability to exercise control over life events as now indicating an internal locus of control. Offence-specific strengths: • No longer holds globalised distortions about children and their sexuality nor does he over-identify with children. Continues to be normally open about sexual drives and interests. • Could now assess the likely impact of sexual abuse on all his own victims accurately as well as the boy in the vignette. • Now appears to accept full accountability for his sexually abusive behaviour, being more open in relation to the fantasy and grooming element and less likely to justify his behaviour. Offence-specific concerns: • His sexual knowledge has not increased since his initial assessment, therefore, no longer falls within the average range for his age. • He continues to have a slight tendency to blame others and situations for troubles in his life. • MSI still indicating he may not be motivated for treatment.	
I/W	Completed so far: • Completed structured assessment and explored related issues. • Started work on victimisation workbook. • Substantial work on exploring sense of grievance and anger management strategies. • Completed individual part of Gateway to Success Relapse Prevention plan. Plan: • To finish victimisation workbook. • To continue to look at current issues identified as his emotionally demanding targeting of female members of staff and roleplays around anger and aggression. • To work on transition issues into greater independence and the community.	

Table 20.4 *Continued*

	Identified issue	Response

G/W

Completed so far:
- Successfully completed Pathway programme.
- Completed the majority of the Gateway programme, showing considerable insight about others behaviour and the concepts explored.

Plan:
- To complete the remaining modules of the Gateway programme, developing further his ability to apply the material to himself and his behaviour outside of the group.
- To move directly onto the Relapse Prevention group.

Psychoanalytic Psychotherapy

Completed so far:
- Working through feelings of anger and frustration, making links with sadness he feels as a result of his early experiences, significantly the abuse and neglect he suffered at the hands of his mother and her partners.
- The therapeutic alliance has continued to develop so that he has been able to capture and share traumatic incidents from his past.
- Begun to explore and discuss his fears, specifically his distress and emotional loneliness, resulting in more ability to take personal responsibility for his behaviour.
- Explored the macho element to his belief system, which believes women need protecting, and thus his justification of his position as identification with the aggressor.

Plan:
- Assist him to transfer from dependent absorption in the mother and towards identification with an emotionally absent father.
- To continue to work on the understanding of his feelings, particularly shame and humiliation. With the goal of recounting the trauma story, integrating it into the present in a more open and real way.

Psychiatric

Completed so far:
- Explored issue of urinating and now no longer an issue.
- Continued to monitor mental health, exploring some of the depressive symptoms he has recently been showing. Specifically the negative thinking cycle which leads him to behave in a rejecting way.

Plan:
- Monitor general mood and whether anti-depressant medication would be beneficial at any stage.

Family work

Completed so far:
- Sessions have taken place with KM and his mother and he now has regular contact.
- KM has some contact with his half siblings who are adopted and re-introduction work with his half sister victim has been completed.
- Further information revealed that contact with his grandfather would not be appropriate. The social worker has informed step grandfather and step father of the reasons KM is here. No contact made with father as yet.

Plan:
- Maintain contact with family members.
- Continue family therapy with mother where possible as there are still issues to resolve.
- See whether step father will agree to a session.

Integrated issues

Continue to assist further integration of learning across contexts, especially with increased independence in the community setting.
- To continue to support KM to progress further in all his main issues, particularly dealing with past sadness and loss, and current grievance and frustration, in order for him to achieve an abuse free and happy life.
- To support KM in the transition period, helping him to maintain as many strong family relationships as is possible and retaining a link to the organisation to be able to access support such as the Relapse Prevention group.

Conclusions

The series of group programmes described in this chapter: the Pathway programme which focuses on social and emotional competency; the Gateway programme which focuses on offence-specific issues; and the Relapse Prevention moving on programme which focuses on maintenance and moving on skills, have developed in response to the perceived requirements of a group of young people with complex and diverse needs. Variations include the Focused Intervention Programme for young people who cannot participate as a result of their particular complexity of needs. It is of course right that a therapeutic residential provision such as SWAAY should be used for young people with more severe offending patterns and diversity of complex needs. It is therefore vital that once in the residential context these young people should be able to access the modality of treatment tailored to their specific needs. As is described in this chapter, one way in which this is achieved at SWAAY is through initial and ongoing assessment during the individual's period of placement (through the use of the Needs, Assessment and Treatment process). This seeks to maximise each young person's potential and reduce the risk of recidivism whilst adequately preparing them for the future. The capacity to integrate the groupwork programmes into the daily lives of the young people offers the opportunity for further assessment and is a core component of this multi modal approach. Research into the area of adolescent sexual offending continues to develop and inform our practice. It is important however not to forget that, as in the case of KM's experiences cited in this chapter, we need to listen to the young person's experiences and to be able to respond to their concerns and successes as this is likely to enhance their ability to benefit from the formal programmes of work and the wider experiences of their placement at SWAAY.

The groupwork programme is the core of this multi-modal approach in a residential context, fostering their maturation, linked with individual, family, and educational work. It is difficult to be clear which are the key components of the programme which results in change and a good outcome. Group work is likely to foster attachments, help regulate emotional life through sharing painful topics and receiving support, enhance the sense of self through positive

feedback processes, and enhance understanding of themselves and others. The approaches described here also have application to community contexts to support non-residential programmes.

References

Abel, G.G., Becker, J.V. and Cunningham-Rathner, J. (1984) Complications, Consent and Cognitions in Sex Between Children and Adults. *International Journal of Law and Psychiatry.* 7, 89–103.

Award, G., Saunders, E. and Levene, J. (1984) A Clinical Study of Male Adolescent Sex Offenders. *International Journal of Offender Therapy and Comparative Criminology.* 28: 2.

Beckett, R. (1999) Evaluation of Adolescent Abusers. In Erooga, M. and Masson, H. (Eds.) *Children and Young People Who Sexually Abuse Others.*

Beckett, R. and Gerhold, C. (2001) Unpublished manuscript.

Beech, A., Friendship, C., Erikson, M. and Hanson, K. (2002) The Relationship Between Static and Dynamic Risk Factors and Reconviction in a Sample of UK Child Abusers. *Sexual Abuse: A Journal of Research and Treatment.* 14, 155–67.

Beech, A.R., Fisher, D. and Beckett, R.C. (1999) *An Evaluation of the Prison Sex Offender Treatment Programme.* UK Home Office Occasional Report.

Beech, A.R., Fisher, D. and Thornton, D. (2003) Risk Assessment of Sex Offenders. *Professional Psychology Research and Practise.* 34: 4, 1–12.

Bentovim, A. (1995) *Trauma-organised Systems.* London: Karnac.

Borduin, C.M (1999) Multisystemic Treatment of Criminality and Violence in Adolescents. *Journal of the American Academy of Child and Adolescent Psychiatry.* 38: 3, 242–9.

Bowlby, J. (1972) *Attachment and Loss Volume 1: Attachment.* Middlesex: Penguin.

Boyd, N.J., Hagan, M. and Cho, M.E. (2000) Characteristics of Adolescent Sex Offenders: A Review of the Research. *Aggression and Violent Behaviour.* 5: 2, 137–46.

Briere, J. (1996) *Trauma Symptom Checklist for Children: Professional Manual.* Florida: Psychological Assessment Resources.

Cellini, H.R. (1995) Assessment and Treatment of the Adolescent Sexual Offender. In Schwartz,

B.K. and Cellini, H.R. (Eds.) *The Sex Offender: Vol 1, Corrections, Treatment and Legal Practice.* Kingston, NJ: Civic Research Institute.

Crick, N. R. and Dodge, K. A (1994) A Review and Reformulation of Social Information-Processing Mechanisms in Children's Social Adjustment. *Psychological Bulletin.* 115, 74–101.

Davis, G.E. and Leitenberg, H. (1987) Adolescent Sex Offenders. *Psychological Bulletin.* 101: 3, 17–427.

Department of Health, Department of Education and Home Office (2000) *Framework for the Assessment of Children in Need and their Families.* London: DoH.

Driskill, P. and Delcampo, R.L. (1993) Sex Education in the 1990s: A Systems Perspective on Family Sexuality. *Journal of Sex Education and Therapy.* 18: 3, 175–85.

Edwards, R. et al. (2005) Predicting Dropout From a Residential Programme for Adolescent Sexual Abusers Using Pre-Treatment Variables and Implications for Recidivism. *Journal of Sexual Aggression.* 11: 2, 139–55.

Ennis, J., Williams, B. and Kendrick, A. (1993) *Practice Issues in Work with Perpetrators of Child Sexual Abuse.* Downloaded from the Worldwide Web on 06/10/04 from: http://homepages.strath.ac.uk/zns01101/prep.htm

Finkelhor, D. (1984) *Child Sexual Abuse: New Theory and Research.* New York: Free Press.

Froggatt, W. Brief Introduction to Rational Emotive Behaviour Therapy. http://www.rational.org.nz/prof/docs/intro-rebt.htm.

Gordon, A. and Porporino, F.J. (1990) *Managing the Treatment of Sex Offenders: A Canadian Perspective.* No B-05 Research and Statistics Branch Correctional Service of Canada. Downloaded from the Worldwide Web on: 4th May 2005 from: http://www.csc-scc.gc.ca/text/rsrch/briefs/b5/b05e_e.shtml

Gray, A.S. and Pithers, W.D. (1993) Relapse Prevention With Sexually Aggressive Adolescents and Children: Expanding Treatment Supervision. In Barbaree, H.E.et al. (Eds.) *The Juvenile Sex Offender.* New York: Guildford Press.

Hanson, R.K. and Harris, A.J.R. (2000) *The Sex Offender Needs Assessment Rating (SONAR): A Method for Measuring Change in Risk Levels.* Ottawa: Department of the Solicitor General of Canada.

Kahn, T.J. and Chambers, H.J. (1991) Assessing Reoffence Risk With Juvenile Sexual Offender Treatment. *Crime and Delinquency.* 39, 543–53.

Knopp, F.H. (1982) *Remedial Intervention in Adolescent Sex Offenses: Nine Program Descriptions.* Orwell, VT: Safer Society.

Kroll, L. et al. (1999) *The Salford Needs Assessment Schedule for Adolescents (SNASA).* NHS Trust.

Lipsey, M.W. and Derzon, J.H. (1998) Predictors of Violent or Serious Delinquency in Adolescents and Early Adulthood: A Synthesis of Longitudinal Research. In Loeber, R. and Farrington, D.P. (Eds.) *Serious and Violent Juvenile Offenders: Risk Factors and Successful Interventions.* London: Sage.

Lipsey, M.W. and Wilson, D.B. (1998) Effective Intervention for Serious Juvenile Offenders: A Synthesis of Research. In Loeber, R. and Farrington, D.P. (Eds.) *Serious and Violent Juvenile Offenders: Risk Factors and Successful Intervention.* Thousand Oaks, CA: Sage.

Loeber, R. and Farrington, D.P. (Eds.) (1998) *Serious and Violent Juvenile Offenders: Risk Factors and Successful Interventions.* Thousand Oaks, CA: Sage.

Marshall, W.L., Anderson, D. and Fernandez, Y.M. (1999) *Cognitive Behavioural Treatment of Sexual Offenders.* London: Wiley.

McCarthy, M. and Thompson, D. (1998) *Sex and the 3R's: Rights, Responsibilities, and Risk.* Pavilion.

O'Donohue, W. and Letourneau, E. (1993) A Brief Group Treatment for the Modification of Denial in Child Sexual Abusers: Outcome and Follow-up. *Child Abuse and Neglect.* 17, 299–304.

Pierce, L. and Pierce, R (1987) as cited in Adolscent Sex Offenders, National Clearinghouse on Family Violence Publication, Public Health Agency of Canada. Downloaded from the Worldwide Web on 22nd March 2005 from: www.phac-aspc,gc.ca/ncfv-cnivf/familyviolence/html/nfntsxadolinfractions_e.html

Pincus, D. (1990) *Feeling Good About Yourself: Strategies to Guide Young People Toward More Positive Personal Feelings.* Good Apple.

Porter, E. (1986) Treating the Young Male Victim of Sexual Abuse. In Friedrich, W.N. (1995) *Psychotherapy With Sexually Abused Boys: An Integrated Approach.* Thousand Oaks: Sage.

Prentky, R., Harris, B., Frizzell and Righthand, S. (2000) An Actuarial Procedure for Assessing Risk With Juvenile Sex Offenders. *Sexual Abuse: a Journal of Research and Treatment.* 12: 2, 71–93.

Prentky, R.A. and Knight, R.A. (1993) Age of Onset of Sexual Assault: Criminal and Life History Correlates. In Hall, G.C.N., Hirschman,

R., Graham, J.R. and Zaragoza, M.S. (Eds.) *Sexual Aggression: Issues in Etiology, Assessment, and Treatment.* Washington DC: Taylor and Francis.

Ryan, G. (1998) The Relevance of Early Life Experience to the Behaviour of Sexually Abusive Youth. *The Irish Journal of Psychology.* 19: 1, 32–48.

Ryan, G. and Lane, S. (1997) Integrated Theory and Mind. In Ryan, G. and Lane, S. (Eds.) *Juvenile Sexual Offending: Causes, Consequences and Correction.* New York: Jossey-Bass.

Sawyer, S. (2000) Some Thoughts About Why We Believe Group Therapy is the Preferred Modality for Treating Sex Offenders. *The ATSA Forum.* 12, 11–2.

Skuse, D.H. et al. (1999) *A Prospective Study of the Onset of Sexually Abusive Behaviour in Males Who Were Sexually Abused in Early Childhood.* Interim Report to the DoH.

Steen and Monette (1989) as cited in Ennis, J., Williams, B. and Kendrick, A. (1993) *Practice Issues in Work with Perpetrators of Child Sexual Abuse.* Downloaded on 06/10/04 from: http://homepages.strath.ac.uk/zns01101/prep.htm

Virginia Commission on Youth (2003) Maladaptive Behaviours, Sexual Offending. Downloaded on 26th Oct 2004 from: http://www.coy.state.va.us/Modalities/sexoffend.htm

Ward, T. and Mann, R.E. (2004) Good Lives and the Rehabilitation of Sex Offenders: A Positive Approach to Treatment. In Linley, A. and Joseph, S. (Eds.) *Positive Psychology in Practice.* John Wiley.

Winn, U. (1994) *Treatment for Abused and Neglected Children: Infancy to Age 18 User Manual Series.* US Department of Health and Human Services. Downloaded on 4th May 2005 from: www.nccanch.acf.hhs.gov/pubs/usermanuals/treatment/treatmenc.cfm

Winn, S., Roker, D. and Coleman, J. (1995) Knowledge about Puberty and Sexual Development in 11–16 year olds: Implications for Health and Sex Education in Schools. *Educational Studies*, 21, No. 2.

Worling, J.R and Curwen, T. (2001) *The 'ERASOR': Estimate of Risk of Adolescent Sexual Offender Recidivism, Version 2.0.* unpublished manuscript. SAFE-T Program, Thistledown Regional Centre, Toronto.

Worling, J.R. (2004) The Estimate of Adolescent Sexual Offence Recidivism (ERASOR): Preliminary Psychometric Data. *Sexual Abuse: A Journal of Research and Treatment.* 16: 3, 23–54.

Tel:
Fax: 0125
e-mail: help@